IARIA Congress 2024

The 2024 IARIA Annual Congress on Frontiers in Science, Technology, Services, and Applications

June 30 - July 4, 2024

Porto, Portugal

IARIA Congress 2024 Editors

Timothy T. Pham, Jet Propulsion Laboratory - California Institute of Technology, USA

Ejike Nwokoro, HealthNet, UK

Printed from e-media with permission by:

Curran Associates, Inc.
57 Morehouse Lane
Red Hook, NY 12571

Some format issues inherent in the e-media version may also appear in this print version.

International Academy, Research, and Industry Association (IARIA)
412 Derby Way
Wilmington, DE 19810

Phone: (408) 893-6407
Fax: (408) 527-6351

petre@iaria.org

Additional copies of this publication are available from:

Curran Associates, Inc.
57 Morehouse Lane
Red Hook, NY 12571 USA
Phone: 845-758-0400
Fax: 845-758-2633
Email: curran@proceedings.com
Web: www.proceedings.com

Table of Contents

IARIA Congress 2024

Forward

The 2024 IARIA Annual Congress on Frontiers in Science, Technology, Services, and Applications (IARIA Congress 2024), held between June 30th and July 4th, 2024, continued a series of international events keeping pace with the achievements and challenges our society is facing in science, technologies, services, and applications.

The annual event was a multidomain assembly of scientists, specialists, and decision makers from all economical, educational, and governmental entities, on Social Systems, Software, Data Science Analytics, Communications, Technology, and Networked Services. Apart from classical topics, the congress targeted frontier achievements on Knowledge Science, Data Science, Artificial Intelligence / Machine Learning (AI/ML)-based systems, Self-managing systems, Human-centric technologies, Advanced robotics, Virtual Worlds, Mobility, Sensing, Energy, Electric Vehicles, Green Energy, etc.

The IARIA Congress had a special scientific format where outstanding former IARIA scientists delivered dedicated speeches (Keynote speeches, Tutorial lectures) along with peer-reviewed contributions on the themes of achievements and challenges in science, technologies, services, and applications.

We take here the opportunity to warmly thank all the members of the IARIA Congress 2024 technical program committee, as well as all the reviewers. The creation of such a high-quality conference program would not have been possible without their involvement. We also kindly thank all the authors who dedicated much of their time and effort to contribute to IARIA Congress 2024. We truly believe that, thanks to all these efforts, the final conference program consisted of top-quality contributions. We also thank the members of the IARIA Congress 2024 organizing committee for their help in handling the logistics of this event.

We hope that IARIA Congress 2024 was a successful international forum for the exchange of ideas and results between academia and industry and for the promotion of progress in our society. We also hope that Porto provided a pleasant environment during the conference and everyone saved some time to enjoy the historic charm of the city.

IARIA Congress 2024 Chairs

IARIA Congress 2024 Steering Committee

Carlos Becker Westphall, Federal University of Santa Catarina, Brazil
Luigi Lavazza, Università dell'Insubria – Varese, Italy
Timothy T. Pham, Jet Propulsion Laboratory - California Institute of Technology, USA
Arcady Zhukov, University of Basque Country (UPV/EHU), San Sebastian / Ikerbasque, Basque Foundation for Science, Bilbao, Spain
Lasse Berntzen, University of South-Eastern Norway, Norway
Yasushi Kambayashi, Sanyo-Onoda City University, Japan
Gerhard Hube, Technical University of Applied Sciences Würzburg-Schweinfurt, Germany

IARIA Congress 2024 Publicity Chairs

Sandra Viciano Tudela, Universitat Politecnica de Valencia, Spain
Lorena Parra Boronat, Universitat Politecnica de Valencia, Spain
Jose Miguel Jimenez, Universitat Politecnica de Valencia, Spain

IARIA Congress 2024

Committee

IARIA Congress 2024 Steering Committee

Carlos Becker Westphall, Federal University of Santa Catarina, Brazil
Luigi Lavazza, Università dell'Insubria – Varese, Italy
Timothy T. Pham, Jet Propulsion Laboratory - California Institute of Technology, USA
Arcady Zhukov, University of Basque Country (UPV/EHU), San Sebastian / Ikerbasque, Basque Foundation for Science, Bilbao, Spain
Lasse Berntzen, University of South-Eastern Norway, Norway
Yasushi Kambayashi, Sanyo-Onoda City University, Japan
Gerhard Hube, Technical University of Applied Sciences Würzburg-Schweinfurt, Germany

IARIA Congress 2024 Publicity Chairs

Sandra Viciano Tudela, Universitat Politecnica de Valencia, Spain
Lorena Parra Boronat, Universitat Politecnica de Valencia, Spain
Jose Miguel Jimenez, Universitat Politecnica de Valencia, Spain

IARIA Congress 2024 Technical Program Committee

Tamer Abdou, Ryerson University, Canada
Nitin Agarwal, COSMOS Research Center | University of Arkansas at Little Rock, USA
Abiola Akinnubi, Infinity Ward (Activision Publishing) Woodland Hill / COSMOS Research Center Little Rock, Arkansas, USA
Sedat Akleylek, Ondokuz Mayis University, Samsun, Turkey
Murat Akpinar, ASELSAN A.Ş., Ankara, Turkey
Raid Rafi Omar Al-Nima, Northern Technical University, Iraq
Alaa Alghazo, Hashemite University, Jordan
Hesham Ali, University of Nebraska Omaha , USA
Ali T. Alouani, Tennessee Technological University, USA
Mohammad Alsulami, University of Connecticut, USA
Slimane Bah, Mohammadia Engineering School - University Mohammed V in Rabat, Morocco
Lasse Berntzen, University of South-Eastern Norway, Norway
Ayush Bhargava, Meta, USA
Sandjai Bhulai, Vrije Universiteit Amsterdam, Netherlands
John Blake, University of Aizu, Japan
Oleksandr Blazhko, National University «Odessa Polytechnic», Ukraine
Natalia Bogach, Peter the Great St. Petersburg Polytechnic University, Russia

Filipe Lautert, UTFPR, Brazil
Luigi Lavazza, Università dell'Insubria, Varese, Italy
Vitaly Levashenko, University of Zilina, Slovakia
Hongda Li, Palo Alto Networks Inc., USA
Wenjuan Li, Hong Kong Polytechnic University, China
Xing Liu, Kwantlen Polytechnic University, Canada
Rakesh Matam, Indian Institute of Information Technology Guwahati, India
Weizhi Meng, Technical University of Denmark, Denmark
Ioannis Moscholios, University of Peloponnese, Greece
Ejike Nwokoro, HealthNet Homecare, UK
Shashi Raj Pandey, Aalborg University, Denmark
Lorena Parra, Universitat Politècnica de València, Spain
Timothy Pham, Jet Propulsion Laboratory, USA
Krzysztof Pietroszek, American University, Washington, USA
Ivan Pires, Universidade de Trás-os-Montes e Alto Douro, Portugal
Chinthaka Premachandra, Shibaura Institute of Technology, Japan
Evgeny Pyshkin, University of Aizu, Japan
Ahmad Qawasmeh, The Hashemite University, Jordan
Md Muzakkir Quamar, King Fahd university of Petroleum and Minerals (KFUPM) / Interdisciplinary centre for smart mobility and logistics (IRC-SML), KSA
Catarina I. Reis, ciTechCare | School of Technology and Management | Polytechnic of Leiria, Portugal
Huamin Ren, Kristiania University College, Norway
Christophe Roche, University Savoie Mont-Blanc, France
Gunter Saake, Otto-von-Guericke-University Magdeburg, Germany
Zsolt Saffer, Institute of Statistics and Mathematical Methods in Economics - Vienna University of Technology, Austria
Sergei Sawitzki, FH Wedel (University of Applied Sciences), Germany
Hans-Werner Sehring, NORDAKADEMIE - University of Applied Sciences, Elmshorn, Germany
Ivana Semanjski, Universiteit Gent, Belgium
Davide Senatori, Università degli Studi di Genova, Italy
Shouqian Shi, Google, USA
Hemraj Singh, NIT Warangal, India
Miloudia Slaoui, Mohammed V University (UM5) in Rabat, Morocco
Michael Spranger, Hochschule Mittweida | University of Applied Sciences, Germany
Grażyna Suchacka, Institute of Informatics / University of Opole, Poland
Weiwei Zhu Stone, University of Maryland Eastern Shore, USA
Christos Troussas, University of West Attica, Greece
G. Vadivu, SRM Institute of Science & Technology, Kattankulathur, India
Jos van Rooyen, Huis voor software kwaliteit, The Netherlands
Eric MSP Veith, OFFIS e.V. - Institut für Informatik, Oldenburg, Germany
Tim vor der Brück, Fernfachhochschule *Schweiz* (*FFHS*), Switzerland
Zhijie Xu, University of Huddersfield, UK

Nanmiao Wu, Center for Computation and Technology of Louisiana State University, USA
Zhengxun Wu, Independent researcher, USA
Bo Yang, The University of Tokyo, Japan
Linda Yang, University of Portsmouth, UK
Maram Bani Younes, Philadelphia University, Jordan
Elena Zaitseva, University of Zilina, Slovakia
Jorge Zavaleta, CNPq, Rio de Janeiro, Brazil
Xingyu Zhou, Dow Inc., USA
Arkady Zhukov, University of Basque Country - UPV/EHU | IKERBASQUE - Basque Foundation for Science, Spain

Copyright Information

Using Artificial Intelligence for Object Localization in Autonomous Vehicles

Xiaobo Liu-Henke
Research Group for Control Engineering and Vehicle Mechatronics
Ostfalia University of Applied Sciences
Wolfenbüttel, Germany
e-mail: x.liu-henke@ostfalia.de

Sven Jacobitz
Research Group for Control Engineering and Vehicle Mechatronics
Ostfalia University of Applied Sciences
Wolfenbüttel, Germany
e-mail: sve.jacobitz@ostfalia.de

Marian Göllner
Research Group for Control Engineering and Vehicle Mechatronics
Ostfalia University of Applied Sciences
Wolfenbüttel, Germany
e-mail: mar.goellner@ostfalia.de

Taihao Li
Research Group for Control Engineering and Vehicle Mechatronics
Ostfalia University of Applied Sciences
Wolfenbüttel, Germany
e-mail: ta.li@ostfalia.de

Abstract— **The fast development of autonomous vehicles requires advanced technologies for precise object localization, which play a key role for the safety and efficiency of these systems. In this work, we present a novel Artificial Intelligence (AI) based algorithm for object detection and localization, specifically developed for use in autonomous vehicles. By integrating modern machine-learning methods and an innovative architecture, we were able to significantly increase the accuracy and processing speed of object localization. The algorithm was validated using a holistic model-based methodology with Model-in-the-Loop (MiL), Software-in-the-Loop (SiL), and Hardware-in-the-Loop (HiL) simulations, demonstrating its robustness and reliability. The results show that the approach pursued improves detection accuracy and minimizes response times, making it ideal for real-time application in interconnected cyber-physical traffic systems. This paper discusses both the theoretical foundations and the measurement results of the presented localization method, and underlines the potential of AI for the further development of autonomous mobility.**

Keywords—autonomous vehicles; artificial intelligence; object localization; machine learning; validation of AI algorithms; real-time systems.

I. INTRODUCTION

The revolution in the field of mobility, particularly through the introduction of Autonomous Vehicles (AVs), is on the cusp of significant technological breakthroughs. At the heart of this transformation are modern control engineering techniques extended with Artificial Intelligence (AI), which plays a key role in the development and optimization of autonomous vehicle systems. A critical aspect for the functionality and safety of these vehicles is the ability to precisely localize surrounding objects, such as other road users, pedestrians, or traffic signs. AI based technologies are becoming increasingly important in the area of object localization.

This article focuses on the methodological development of an innovative object detection and localization algorithm based on AI and designed specifically for use in autonomous vehicles. A central challenge here is the complex machine learning for each new object type to be localized. However, this effort can be significantly reduced by using a new type of architecture. The developed AI approach is able to process and interpret complex environmental information in order to ensure precise object localization. This combines extensive knowledge from various successful research projects, such as the Lower Saxony Future Mobility Lab.

The aim of this paper is to discuss the theoretical and practical aspects of AI-assisted object localization and to contribute to the further development of intelligent autonomous vehicles. By combining theoretical research and practical experiments, the aim is to gain a deeper understanding of the potential of AI in the domain of autonomous vehicles and to provide a solid starting point for future innovations.

The structure of this article is as follows: Section II is devoted to the discussion of the current state of knowledge, including aspects of object detection and localization. Section III deals with the model-based development methodology for interconnected cyber-physical systems. In Section IV, the concept of an innovative intelligent function for object localization is developed. This begins with the definition of requirements and evaluation metrics, followed by a discussion of the architecture and the concepts of self-localization and object detection. Finally, the machine learning method used is explained. Section V briefly summarizes the results of the various investigations to assess the new object localization. The article ends in Section VI with a summary and an outlook.

II. STATE OF KNOWLEDGE

The following section discusses the state of knowledge on localization and object detection methods.

A. Localization methods

Localization plays a central role in the navigation of AVs. Numerous methods have already been proposed and implemented. Effective navigation and safe driving are based on precise self-localization, which requires a real-time sampling rate at the millisecond level and accuracy down to the centimeter [1]. This self-localization forms the basis for accurate position estimation of other detected objects.

Recently, sensor technologies for vehicle localization have developed significantly [2]. A sensor data fusion of Global Navigation Satellite Systems (GNSS), Light Detection and Ranging (LiDAR) systems and cameras contributes to highly effective localization. In addition, the movement of the vehicle can be tracked and estimated through the use of Inertial Measurement Units (IMU) and odometry. This approach to active localization offers both flexibility and increased precision.

Furthermore, localization techniques can be roughly divided into map-based and non-map-based methods. Map-based positioning, which uses common map-matching algorithms, integrates LiDAR [3], camera [4] and wireless communication [5]. It proves to be more accurate and more suitable for determining the position of a vehicle in a global coordinate system. In contrast, non-map-based localization, usually realized by Simultaneous Localization and Mapping (SLAM), provides accurate mapping of the environment independent of existing maps, especially for indoor applications. A detailed investigation of existing map-based localization algorithms and their most important mechanisms is given in [6].

B. Object detection approaches

Numerous approaches have been developed in object detection research, which can be roughly divided into traditional methods and modern techniques based on machine learning [7].

Early techniques, such as edge detection and segmentation use simple features to detect object boundaries and similar visual features in images. These approaches are fast and less computationally intensive, but often offer lower accuracy and robustness in complex or variably lit scenarios [8].

The introduction of deep learning, in particular Convolutional Neural Networks (CNNs), has revolutionized object detection. Architectures, such as R-CNN, YOLO and SSD achieve a high level of accuracy by learning from large amounts of data automatically [9]. These functions are able to recognize objects nearly in real time, making them ideal for applications in AV. Current research focuses on improving accuracy under different conditions and reducing false alarms to further optimize the technologies [10].

In summary, it can be said that, despite the numerous research efforts, there is currently no seamless object detection and localization approach with sufficient accuracy and real-time capability for use in autonomous vehicles.

III. METHODOLOGY

A structured, systematic approach is required to develop AI-based functions for complex cyber-physical systems. The complexity of autonomous vehicles in particular poses a special challenge due to the high degree of internal and external networking and the growing number of intelligent and powerful hardware and software components. For this reason, the holistic, verification-oriented, model-based design methodology based on Rapid Control Prototyping (RCP) with Model-in-the-Loop (MiL), Software-in-the-Loop (SiL) and Hardware-in-the-Loop (HiL) simulations has been established [11].

The core of the methodology is the iterative mechatronic development cycle according to [11] as shown in Figure 1. Starting with the requirements and specifications, the system is first modeled and analyzed. The function is initially designed and optimized offline using a data management system. Once a sufficient level of functionality has been achieved, the function is transformed into C code via automatic code generation and tested and further optimized using SiL. The function is then automatically implemented on real-time hardware and further optimized and tested under real-time conditions using HiL simulations.

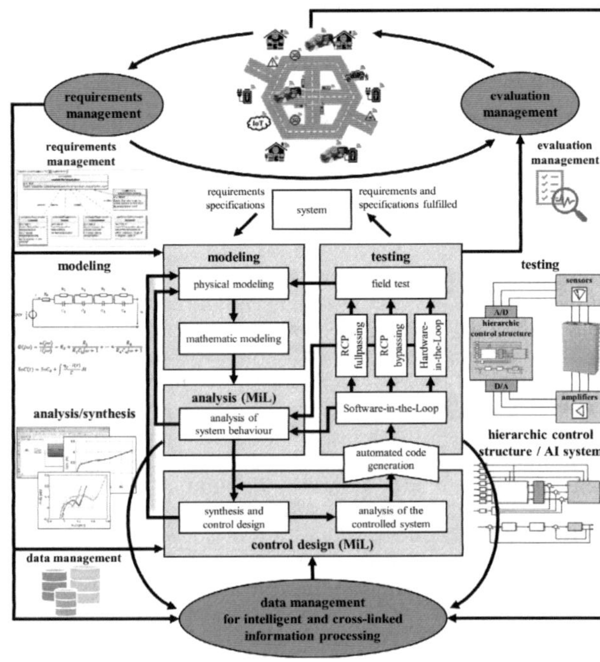

Figure 1. Mechatronic development cycle according to [11].

By using this structured, seamless model-based development process, AI-based functions can be developed in a focused and efficient manner.

IV. CONCEPT OF THE INTELLIGENT OBJECT LOCALIZATION

As shown in section II, there is currently no seamless real-time-capable function for object localization. The following section therefore deals with the detailed conception of the AI-based object localization algorithm for AV. Based on the requirements specified, evaluation metrics are established for the machine learning methods that will be used later. The central aspect is the architecture of the new function. Finally, the approaches of the specific localization algorithms and the machine learning used are discussed.

A. Requirements and evaluation metrics

In the development of an AI function for object localization for AV, specific requirements manifest themselves that affect both the precision and reliability of localization as well as the integration capability and scalability of the AI systems. Firstly, the AI function must be highly accurate in order to reliably determine the position and movement of surrounding objects even under varying and potentially challenging environmental conditions. Secondly, the dynamic nature of the traffic environment requires a high reaction speed and real-time capability to support time-critical decisions. Third, the AI localization function must demonstrate robust performance against sensor data inconsistencies and failures, which implies advanced error handling and tolerance. Finally, the architecture of the AI function must be modular and flexible to allow easy integration into different vehicle platforms and to adapt to future technological developments. Compliance with these requirements is crucial to ensure the safety and effectiveness of autonomous vehicles in complex and unpredictable environments and to ensure their acceptance and trustworthiness by end users.

Given these diverse and demanding requirements, it is clear that a precise and comprehensive evaluation of AI functions is essential. This need leads to the development and application of specific metrics that are able to measure and validate the effectiveness and reliability of AI-driven localization systems in detail. Key metrics include localization accuracy, which is usually measured as the mean square error between the estimated and actual positions of objects. In addition, robustness to sensory interference and environmental variability is critical, assessing the consistency of localization results under different operating conditions.

The response time of the AI function, defined as the time between data acquisition and the provision of localization information, is also critical, especially in dynamic traffic environments where quick decisions are required. Finally, the ability to integrate into existing vehicle systems plays a role in the evaluation, taking into account compatibility and the impact of the AI function on system resources. The careful selection and application of these evaluation metrics enables a sound assessment of AI object localization capabilities and supports the continuous optimization of these essential systems in autonomous vehicles.

In particular, the metrics Average Precision (AP) and mean Average Precision (mAP) are used to evaluate the performance of the developed algorithms for object detection and localization. The AP measures the quality of an AI model in terms of its ability to correctly detect and localize objects within a predefined class (e.g., cars, trucks, etc.). It is determined by integrating the precision-recall curve $p(r)$ according to equation (1). This curve represents the relationship between the accuracy of recognition (precision) and the proportion of correctly identified positive cases (recall). A higher AP value indicates better performance in relation to the class under consideration.

The mAP value, calculated according to equation (2), aggregates the AP values across N predefined detection classes and thus provides a comprehensive measure of the overall performance of the detection and localization system. The mAP value is particularly meaningful for applications where multiple object classes need to be detected simultaneously. This metric shows the average performance of the system across all classes, which enables a holistic evaluation of the algorithms.

$$AP = \int_0^1 p(r)\, dr \quad (1)$$

$$mAP = \frac{1}{N}\sum_{i=1}^{N} AP_i \quad (2)$$

B. Architecture of the novel AI function

The architecture of the new AI function is characterized by its modularity and flexibility, which enable efficient integration and processing of various sensor data. It implements a multi-layered modularized approach with data collection and sensor data fusion, self-localization of the vehicle, object detection and external localization (see Figure 2).

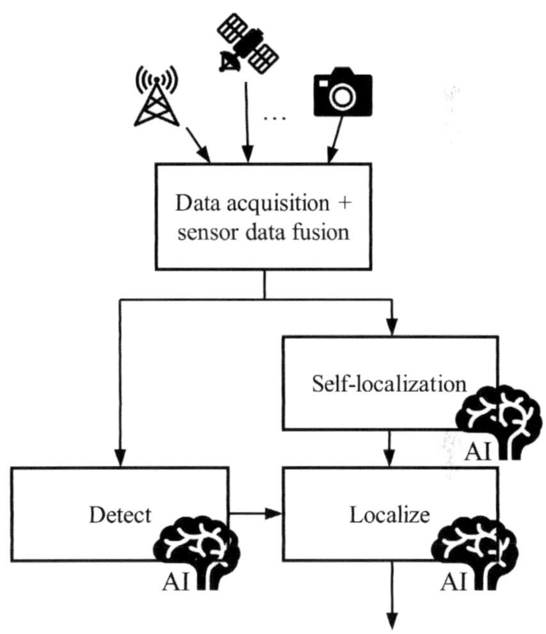

Figure 2. Architecture of the new AI based localization function.

This ensures high cohesion within the modules and low coupling between them. Core of the architecture is the use of advanced machine learning and AI algorithms, which enable precise and robust localization information to be extracted from the raw, multimodal sensor data. This architecture underlines the potential of a systematic and modular approach to the development of complex solutions for autonomous vehicles and provides a solid basis for further research and development in this dynamic field.

C. Sensor data fusion for self-localization

Figure 3 shows the concept of self-localization according to [12]. The interface to the inputs and outputs of the function is defined. The LiDAR and IMU mounted on the vehicle can be used for self-localization. The LiDAR scans the environment and transfers the data to the localization function block in the form of a point map.

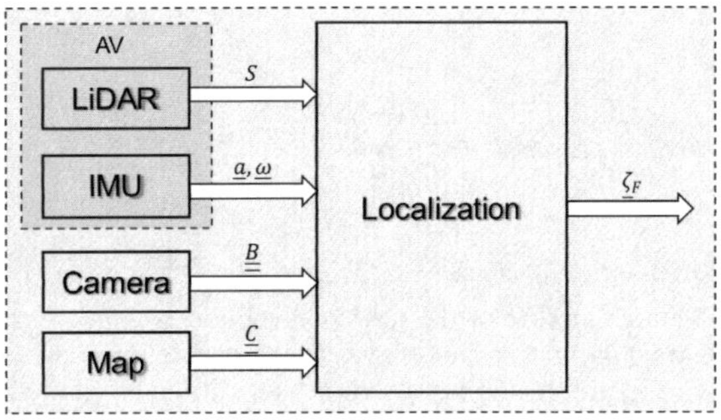

Figure 3. Concept of the self-localization function according to [12].

The IMU can be used to detect the movement of the AV in order to implement the local localization function. The localization function module also receives information from the map, camera and LiDAR. By comparing the map information with the measurement information from the built-in sensors, the AV can then be localized (global localization). Finally, the function module also receives image information from an external reference camera, a sensor in the traffic environment. The camera is permanently installed in the application scene and records the position of the vehicle for validation and correction. For this purpose, each vehicle in the laboratory setup is clearly identified by two infrared LEDs. The position transmitted by the camera is regarded as the reference position of the vehicle. In addition to validation, this reference position can be transmitted to the AV in order to eliminate self-localization errors.

D. Object detection and localization

The innovative AI-based object detection and localization is based on the use of neural networks. The core of the approach lies in the integration of CNNs, which have been specially trained to recognize relevant objects from a variety of sensor inputs, such as camera images and radar or LiDAR data. These networks are able to extract and learn complex features from the input data, enabling precise object detection even under difficult environmental conditions, such as poor lighting conditions or rapid changes in the field of view.

The object detection concept also relies on a robust parallel data processing architecture as shown in Figure 4, which enables efficient handling and analysis of large volumes of data. This is based on smart tagging using an existing, pretrained neural network (e.g., YOLO) and a specialized detection network. The results of both networks are merged and provide robust object detection. A box surrounding the object marks the detected areas.

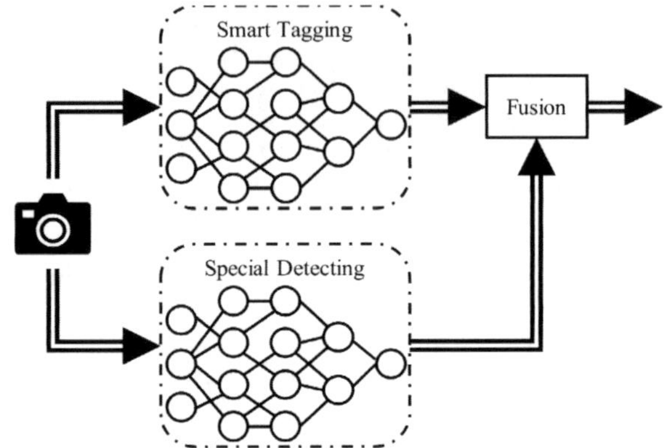

Figure 4. Concept of parallel detection.

Localization is based on the transformation of the received fused detected data into a bird's eye view. Using geometric transformation, the object coordinates can be determined relative to the vehicle's own position.

E. Machine Learning Method

The neural network used is specially developed and trained for detection and positioning in 3D environments. The training process of this network includes the generation of a suitable training data set that maps the object features to be detected with sufficient accuracy. It is particularly important to ensure that the training data covers the entire possible event space of the use case in order to guarantee a high degree of generalizability and reliability in real application scenarios. The data sets are either recorded under realistic conditions or generated by an image-realistic simulation and include a wide range of scenarios and object positions in order to effectively prepare the network for detection and precise localization.

During training, various criteria based on the metrics presented in Section IV.A are used in a loss function to optimize the accuracy of object localization, using machine-learning methods. Figure 5 illustrates an example of the progression of a loss function during the learning process. The calculated loss value is plotted against the number of training steps performed. A downward trend can be seen. However, due to the special learning procedure for finding a global minimum, fluctuations are included. The training process is terminated when a termination criterion is met, such as falling below a limit value or reaching a maximum number of steps.

Finally, the trained network is validated through tests under real conditions in order to confirm the performance and reliability of the localization algorithm.

V. Results of the Object Localization

For initial tests, the designed function for object detection and localization was trained to recognize a special laboratory vehicle using about 2000 data records. These data sets are generated automatically with the help of CAD software. Subsequently, the function was tested in detail using MiL simulations. These were used for the initial validation of the algorithms. Particular attention was paid to the accuracy of object positioning to ensure that the algorithm accurately detects the environment and reliably localizes objects.

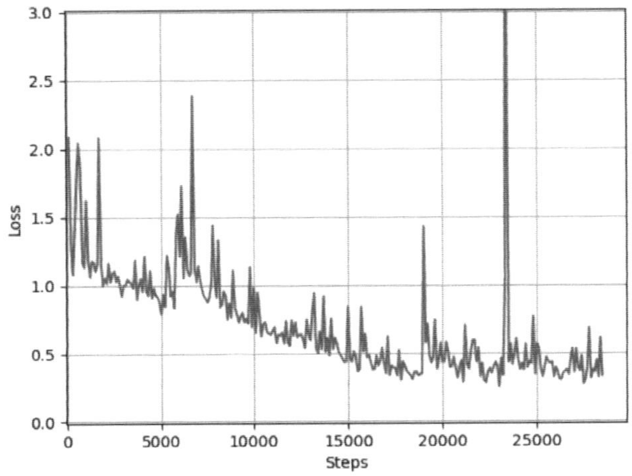

Figure 5. Sample loss history during training.

In the subsequent SiL and HiL phases, the interaction between real test vehicles and the algorithms was examined under realistic conditions. The SiL tests focused on refining the algorithms by simulating different traffic scenarios and object interactions, enabling a comprehensive evaluation of the algorithm performance under different conditions. The HiL tests extended these investigations by incorporating real hardware to test the algorithms under real-time conditions. These tests showed that the developed algorithms are robust to different environmental conditions and capable of precise localization in dynamic scenarios.

For basic optimization, validation and performance analysis, the test setup shown schematically in Figure 6, is first used in the laboratory. A laser-based reference sensor is utilized to verify the results of the algorithm. A camera captures a defined image section. Vehicles are positioned at different angles and orientations to the camera in a referenced grid.

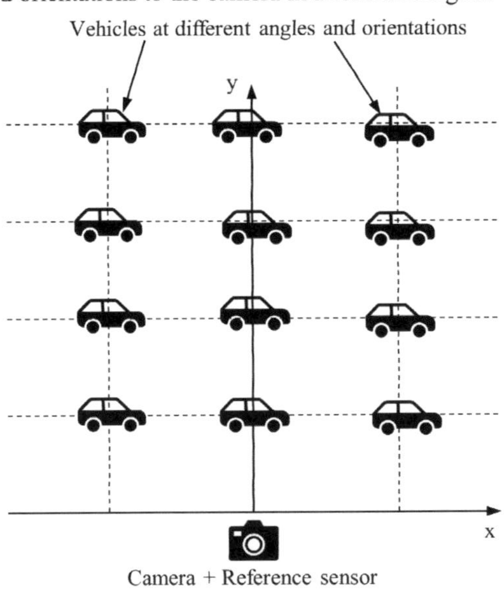

Figure 6. Schematic test setup for the first verification of AI-based object localization.

Figure 7 illustrates an example of the result of a localization in a laboratory environment. The detection and localization of an autonomous vehicle can be seen, outlined in red. The analysis of the test results revealed a high efficiency and accuracy of the developed object detection and localization algorithms. By applying specific metrics, such as mAP and evaluating the required computing power, the performance of the algorithms could be quantitatively assessed. The results confirm that the algorithms not only have a high detection rate, but also perform localization with good accuracy.

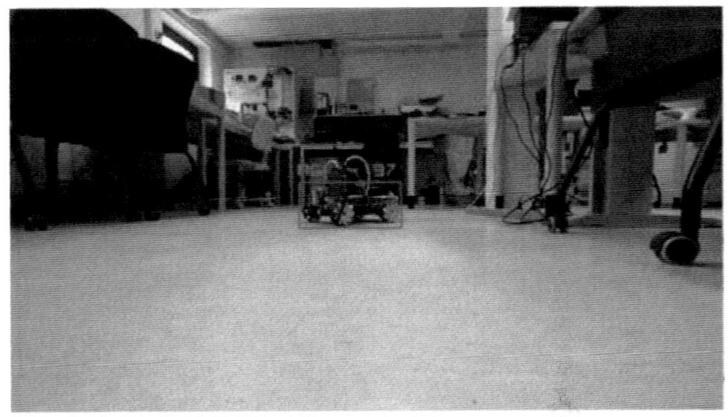

Figure 7. Exemplary localization result in a laboratory environment.

The computation time required by the function is a critical factor in the performance of the developed object detection function, especially in applications that require fast response times, such as autonomous vehicles. The efficiency of the algorithm has therefore been intensively optimized to minimize the latency between data acquisition and decision making. By using optimized neural network architectures and advanced hardware acceleration techniques, the processing time has been significantly reduced. This makes it possible to process even complex scenes with multiple objects to be localized. The versatile tests under various operating conditions have shown that object detection and localization is performed within less than ten milliseconds. A Raspberry Pi 4 single-board computer with hardware acceleration was used for this purpose.

VI. CONCLUSION AND FUTURE WORK

This publication presents a novel AI-based algorithm for object localization in autonomous vehicles. By developing a new architecture and using modern machine learning techniques, the authors were able to significantly increase the accuracy and efficiency of object recognition. Various optimizations and tests, including MiL, SiL and HiL simulations, confirmed the effectiveness of the approach, making the algorithm a solid basis for practical application in the navigation of autonomous vehicles.

The research results provide a promising basis for future developments in AI-assisted object localization. It is expected that further optimizations, especially in terms of reducing false alarms and increasing algorithm efficiency, will improve the applicability in real traffic situations. In addition, the integration of further sensor technologies and an increased focus on interdisciplinary research could further increase the accuracy and robustness of localization systems in order to make autonomous vehicles safer and more reliable.

ACKNOWLEDGMENT

Funded by the Lower Saxony Ministry of Science and Culture under grant number ZN4172 in the Lower Saxony Advance of the Volkswagen Foundation and supervised by the Center for Digital Innovations (ZDIN).

ZDIN Zentrum für digitale Innovationen Niedersachsen

VolkswagenStiftung

Niedersächsisches Ministerium für Wissenschaft und Kultur

REFERENCES

[1] Y. Lu, H. Ma, E. Smart, and H. Yu, "Real-Time Performance-Focused Localization Techniques for Autonomous Vehicle: A Review," *IEEE Trans. Intell. Transport. Syst.*, vol. 23, no. 7, pp. 6082–6100, 2022, doi: 10.1109/tits.2021.3077800.

[2] S. Campbell, N. O'Mahony, et al., "Where am I? Localization techniques for Mobile Robots A Review," in *2020 6th International Conference on Mechatronics and Robotics Engineering (ICMRE)*, Barcelona, Spain, 2020, pp. 43–47. doi: 10.1109/ICMRE49073.2020.9065135.

[3] X. Zhang, Z. Li, and Y. Wang, "Global Localization based on Road-centric 3D Point Cloud Descriptor in Urban Environments," in *2022 6th CAA International Conference on Vehicular Control and Intelligence (CVCI)*, Nanjing, China, 2022, pp. 1–6. doi: 10.1109/CVCI56766.2022.9965007.

[4] H.-Y. Lin and C.-H. He, "Mobile Robot Self-Localization Using Omnidirectional Vision with Feature Matching from Real and Virtual Spaces," *Applied Sciences*, vol. 11, no. 8: 3360, 2021, doi: 10.3390/app11083360.

[5] Y. Yan, I. Bajaj, R. Rabiee, and W. P. Tay, "A Tightly Coupled Integration Approach for Cooperative Positioning Enhancement in DSRC Vehicular Networks," *IEEE Trans. Intell. Transport. Syst.*, vol. 23, no. 12, pp. 23278–23294, 2022, doi: 10.1109/TITS.2022.3208257.

[6] L. Li, M. Yang, B. Wang, and C. Wang, "An overview on sensor map based localization for automated driving," in *2017 Joint Urban Remote Sensing Event (JURSE)*, Dubai, United Arab Emirates, 2017, pp. 1–4. doi: 10.1109/JURSE.2017.7924575.

[7] S. Kaur, A. L. Yadav, and A. Joshi, "Real Time Object Detection," in *2022 International Conference on Cyber Resilience (ICCR)*, Dubai, United Arab Emirates, 2022, pp. 1–5. doi: 10.1109/ICCR56254.2022.9995738.

[8] J. Parekh, P. Turakhia, H. Bhinderwala, and S. N. Dhage, "A Survey of Image Enhancement and Object Detection Methods," in *Advances in Intelligent Systems and Computing, Advances in Computer, Communication and Computational Sciences*, S. K. Bhatia, S. Tiwari, S. Ruidan, M. C. Trivedi, and K. K. Mishra, Eds., Singapore: Springer Singapore, 2021, pp. 1035–1047. doi: 10.1007/978-981-15-4409-5_91.

[9] J. S. Murthy, et al., "ObjectDetect: A Real-Time Object Detection Framework for Advanced Driver Assistant Systems Using YOLOv5," *Wireless Communications and Mobile Computing*, vol. 2022, pp. 1–10, 2022, doi: 10.1155/2022/9444360.

[10] C. Gupta, N. S. Gill, P. Gulia, and J. M. Chatterjee, "A novel finetuned YOLOv6 transfer learning model for real-time object detection," *J Real-Time Image Proc*, vol. 20, no. 3, pp. 1–19, 2023, doi: 10.1007/s11554-023-01299-3.

[11] X. Liu-Henke, et al., "A Holistic Methodology for Model-based Design of Mechatronic Systems in Digitized and Connected System Environments," in *Proceedings of the 16th International Conference on Software Technologies*, Online conference 2021, pp. 215–223. doi: 10.5220/0010566702150223.

[12] X. Liu-Henke, T. Li, M. Göllner, S. Jacobitz: "Self-Localization with internal an external sensors in the Labortery test field". In *Proceedings of the 3rd International Conference on Computers and Automation (CompAuto 2023)*, Paris, France, 07.12. - 09.12.2023, pp. 1–6.

Complementing the Impact and Economic Potential of Patient Support Programs through Artificial Intelligence (AI) Augmentation

Daniela Zanni
Department of Health Outcomes
HealthNet Homecare UK Ltd.
Swadlincote, Derbyshire, UK
Email: daniela.zanni@healthnethomecare.co.uk

Joshua Hinton
School of Psychological and Behavioural Sciences
London School of Economics (LSE)
London, UK
Email: j.d.hinton@lse.ac.uk

Ejike Nwokoro
Department of Patient Insights & Data Strategy
HealthNet Homecare UK Ltd.
Swadlincote, Derbyshire, UK
Email: ejike.nwokoro@healthnethomecare.co.uk

Abstract - **Patient adherence to medication has been a long-sought health outcome measure, with the demonstrable benefits of reduced disease-related complications, improved quality of life, and reduced mortality. However, when not adequately supported, chronic disease patients often experience a downward trend in their adherence over time. Patient Support Programs are designed to address this issue by keeping patients engaged throughout their chronic disease management journey and supporting them in developing increasing accountability for their own health and wellbeing. Although these Patient Support Programs have been shown to be a viable tool in supporting treatment retention and adherence, there remains sparse evidence relating to quantifiable economic benefit, both from a pharmaceutical revenue and a health system cost-saving perspective. To this end, this study sought to explore the impact of Patient Support Programs on treatment retention as well as the medicine revenue implication of any observed impact of these programs. We found that adoption of Patient Support Programs reduces patient drop-off from treatment (1.1% drop off compared to 2.8% when patients are not enrolled in the program). Additionally, the observed impact translates to economic benefits, in terms of medicine revenue, of between £2,156,561 and £4,714,787, over a 6-month period. Furthermore, our analysis suggests that complementing these Patient Support Programs with prior prediction of patient risk of poor adherence (through machine learning) can result in the generation of additional medicine revenue of almost £500,000 over a 6-month period. We opine that this enhancement is made possible through early deployment of the programs, as well as their deployment in a manner that is guided by a better understanding of individual patient risk of poor adherence.**

Keywords-Patient Support Program; medication adherence, artificial intelligence; predictive analysis.

I. INTRODUCTION

Patient Support Programs are increasingly popular in the healthcare sector. For most pharmaceutical companies, these Patient Support Programs are intended as wraparound services for new medicines, with a view to supporting patients with treatment compliance. In general, initiatives that support improved access and adherence to medicines are expected to help drive better patient outcomes and positive experience with treatments.

Needless to say, adherence to treatments for chronic diseases is of public health relevance - it is estimated that there would be 18 million people in the UK living with a chronic physical illness by 2025 [1] and it is widely cited that up to 50% of medications are not taken as prescribed [2], with these rates possibly varying considerably across different conditions [3].

Crucially, it has been argued by other authors that AI can support early deployment of Patient Support Programs, thus making them more effective [4], as well as enhance the potential of Patient Support Programs to improve medication adherence [5].

The rest of the paper is structured as follows. In Section 2, we establish the objectives of this paper. In Section 3, we assess the methodology used to achieve the objectives of the study. In Section 4, we discuss the results in greater detail, and in Section 5, we conclude by highlighting the implications of our findings, as well as indicating areas of future research.

II. OBJECTIVES

This study had three overarching objectives:

- To examine the efficacy of Patient Support Programs in mitigating patient drop-off from treatment (as an indicator of non-adherence)
- To understand the medicine revenue implications of reduced drop-off rates
- To explore the potential of AI augmentation in enhancing the impact and economic potential of Patient Support Programs, etc.

III. METHODOLOGY

A. Study dataset and patient categories

The study population data pertains to patients diagnosed with chronic diseases and who are receiving one of three possible service levels from a Clinical Homecare company (n=97,795) between January 2016 and March 2024. The three possible service levels were: (1) Level 1 Service - entails a direct-to-patient delivery of prescribed medication at a frequency dictated by their prescription (2) Level 2 Service - entails Level 1 service plus a nurse-led training of a patient to correctly self-administer their medication independently (3) Level 3 Service – entails Levels 1 and 2 services plus a Patient Support Program designed to facilitate sustained medication adherence.

Only services that had 100 or more patients were included in the analysis. The period covered was for patients enrolled in one of the above three services between May 2016 and March 2024.

B. Inclusion criteria for Treatment drop-off categorisation

Patient drop-off from treatment was analyzed across all three service levels. In the context of this study, "drop-off" is defined as patients who are no longer receiving their medication either due to: their unwillingness to engage with the service, a no-response to engagement attempts from the service provider and where patients have requested the service to be put on hold. In these three instances, the patients is considered as no longer taking their medication as prescribed and thus classed as non-adherent.

C. Analysis approach for Medicine revenue impact

The study extrapolated maintenance posology for all medicines prescribed to the patients whose data were part of the study and calculated the applicable dose per week. Then, the NHS England indicative price was collected for each medicine, with cost per unit subsequently calculated. Following this, cost per dose was identified for each medicine, both on a weekly and a 6-monthly basis. Finally, bearing in mind the treatment drop-off across all three service levels, potential additional medicine revenue (over 6 months) was calculated for scenarios where level 1 and Level 2 service patients are instead enrolled in a Level 3 service.

D. Analysis approach for Impact of AI augmentation

AdherePredict [6][7] (an AI platform designed to predict which patients are most likely to drop off their prescribed medicine and therefore enabling the early and targeted deployment of impactful Patient Support Programs) estimates that one of the benefits of an early deployment of a Patient Support Program that is based on predictive insight includes better patient engagement and reduced drop-off from treatment.

This Machine Learning model, which utilizes a Convolutional Neural Network, identifies the patients most at risk of non-adherence. In this context, non-adherence is defined by using the metric known as Proportion of Days Covered (PDC) of 100% for the period covered by the patient's prescription. Therefore, a patient is deemed non-adherent if they do not have any medication at any point within the period the period that they are supposed to, based on their prescription. Accurately predicting the patients most at risk of non-adherence allows a more purposeful, and early, deployment of Patient Support Programs, in a manner that is better tailored to each individual patient risk. Research has shown that such early and proactive deployment of patient support initiatives makes them more impactful [8] [9].

We calculated the additional medicine revenue implication, over 6 months, of an assumed 0.2% less drop-off in targeted Patient Support Programs that are complemented by AI-based predictive insight.

IV. RESULTS

A. Treatment drop-off rate across Service Levels

Fewer patients drop off from treatment when they are on Patient Support Programs, i.e., Level 3 service (1.1%), compared to those that are on Level 2 service (2.1%) or Level 1 service (2.8%).

B. Medicine revenue implications of drop-off across Service Levels

The medicine revenue analysis shows that if the Level 1 and Level 2 service patients were instead enrolled into a Level 3 service, and as a result are subject to a similar drop-off rate as the current Level 3 service patients, then this translates to an additional drug revenue, over 6 months, of £2,156,561 compared to Level 1 service, £2,558,226 compared to Level 2 service, and £4,714,787 compared to both Level 1 and 2 services together.

C. Additional Medicine revenue from AI-augmented Patient Support Programs

Assuming a further decrease of 0.2% in the Patient Support Program drop off rate due to targeted and early deployment driven by predictive insight, the medicine revenue analysis showed an additional medicine revenue, over 6 months, of £5,206,399 compared to £4,714,787 for a Patient Support Program not complemented by such AI-based prediction.

V. CONCLUSION

Investing in Patient Support Programs and AI integration potentially not only improves medication adherence but also produces significant financial benefits. Further research is required to understand how such benefits may vary across different therapy areas and within primary, secondary and homecare settings.

REFERENCES

[1] C. Abraham, M. Conner, F. Jones, and D. O'Connor, "Health Psychology," Topics in Applied Psychology (2nd ed.), Routledge, doi: 10.4324/9781315776453, April 2016.

[2] E. Sabaté, "Adherence to long-term therapies: Evidence for action," World Health Organization, 2003.

[3] B. Vrijens et al., "A new taxonomy for describing and defining adherence to medications," British Journal of Clinical Pharmacology, vol. 73 no. 5, pp. 691–705, doi: 10.1111/j.1365-2125.2012.04167, 2012.

[4] V. Koesmahargyo et al., "Accuracy of machine learning-based prediction of medication adherence in clinical research," Psychiatry Research,, vol. 294, no. 113558; ISSN0165-1781. doi: 10.1016/j.psychres.2020.113558, December 2020

[5] A. Bohlmann, J. Mostafa, and M. Kumar, "Machine Learning and Medication Adherence: Scoping Review," JMIRx Med, vol. 2, no. 4, p. 26993. doi: 10.2196/26993, November 2021.

[6] B. Malin, T. Kalganova, E. Nwokoro, and J. Hinton, "Medication Adherence Prediction for Homecare Patients, Using Medication Delivery Data," HEALTHINFO 2023, The Eighth International Conference on Informatics and Assistive Technologies for Health-Care, Medical Suppot and Wellbeing, IARIA 2023, pp. 30-38.

[7] HealthNet Homecare UK Ltd. "How HealthNet are driving patient safety and positive experience through cost-effective Clinical Homecare," HealthNet Homecare, 2023.

[8] T. Patel, "Medication nonadherence: Time for a proactive approach by pharmacists," Canadian Pharmacists Journal, SAGE Publications Ltd, vol. 154, no. 5,, pp. 292–296, doi: 10.1177/17151635211034216. September 2021.

[9] A. G. G. Stuurman-Bieze, E. G. Hiddink, J. F. M. van Boven, and S. Vegter, "Proactive pharmaceutical care interventions decrease patients' nonadherence to osteoporosis medication," Osteoporosis International, vol. 25, no. 6, pp. 1807–1812, 2014, doi: 10.1007/s00198-014-2659-8.

Physician Awareness of Cybersecurity risks and the Barriers to Implementation of Cybersecurity Measures in a Private Healthcare Setting

Njideka Nto
Mediclinic
Dubai, UAE
email: Njide@doctors.org

Ejike Nwokoro
HealthNet Homecare
Derbyshire, United Kingdom
email: Ejike.nwokoro@healthnethomecare.co.uk

Abstract— **The healthcare industry has witnessed significant advancement in recent years, with technological innovations and the application of digital health solutions that broaden access, playing a key role. This has led to a dramatic rise in the volume of patient and healthcare data available within the healthcare ecosystem and, along with this, greater attention and concerns around data security and the need to prevent data breaches. Needless to say, proactive cybersecurity measures are essential to mitigate risks, ensure resilience, and uphold the highest standards of patient care and trust. However, despite the widely accepted notion that robust cybersecurity measures are essential to fortify the resilience of medical infrastructure and mitigate the risk of service interruptions, there remains sparse evidence as to the state of cybersecurity behavior of health care workers and medical private practices. In view of this, this study seeks to explore health professionals' attitudes to, and awareness of, cybersecurity considerations in a private healthcare setting, with a view to clarifying implementation barriers for routine cybersecurity measures. This survey-based cross-sectional study will adopt a thematic analysis approach that is aimed at identifying any patterns in clinicians' perception/awareness of the threat to cybersecurity with respect to medical records and patient data, as well as bottlenecks that prevent the implementation of cybersecurity measures in practice. This study, which will commence in Q2 2024 within a large ambulatory care center, will add to the body of knowledge that will support the removal of barriers to the practical implementation of routine cybersecurity practices, particularly in a private healthcare setting.**

Keywords- cybersecurity; physician awareness; healthcare; personal health information; health data breach.

I. INTRODUCTION

The positive impact of technological advancements in healthcare is evident as it has played a crucial role in improvements in the efficiency of patient care, as well as in medical research. Furthermore, there has been an escalation in digital health solutions, interconnected medical devices and telehealth provisions, all of which are designed to reduce fragmentation in patient care, whilst supporting positive patient experiences and better clinical outcomes.

The resulting exponential growth of healthcare data, from all the advancements, presents both opportunities and threats. On the one hand, big data analytics hold immense potential for accelerating medical research, improving patient care, and generating value for healthcare organizations [1]. However, on the other hand, such data-driven evolution in healthcare requires a high-level assurance of data integrity and confidentiality. The proliferation of health data and the increasing interconnectedness of health systems, as well as their integration into networked environments renders them vulnerable to hacking and exploitation. It will come as no surprise therefore, that healthcare systems face various risks, including data breaches, theft, and damage.

The relevance of such risks cannot be overstated as patient confidentiality stands as a cornerstone of ethical medical practice. Electronic Health Records (EHRs) store a wealth of sensitive information, including medical history, diagnoses, treatments, and personal identifiers.

The structure of this paper is as follows: Section II describes the significant role of cybersecurity in healthcare, whilst Section III outlines the part that human error plays in cybersecurity breaches within healthcare and thus providing a rationale for the stated objectives of this study. Section IV details the objectives of this study, and Section V describes the proposed methodology through which the study objectives will be achieved. In Section VI, there is a detailed description of the data source for this study, as well as the steps that will be taken to ensure that quality is maintained throughout the data collection process. Finally, Section VII concludes with an explanation of the added value that findings of this study intend to bring to the field of cybersecurity in healthcare, as well as highlighting any potential limitations of the study or areas of future research.

II. CYBERSECURITY AND HEALTHCARE

The imperative to protect patient privacy, safeguard medical infrastructure, secure connected devices, and preserve data integrity underscores the critical role of cybersecurity in healthcare delivery. A breach in cybersecurity not only compromises patient privacy, but also exposes individuals to identity theft, financial fraud, and reputational damage.

Experts in the field of internet security have argued that Personal Health Information (PHI) is often considered more valuable on the illegal market than credit card credentials or regular Personally Identifiable Information (PII), hence the higher incentive for cyber criminals to target medical databases [2].

As technology continues to evolve, and healthcare systems become increasingly interconnected, proactive cybersecurity measures are essential to mitigate risks, ensure resilience, and uphold the highest standards of patient care and trust.

III. ROLE OF HUMAN FACTOR IN CYBERSECURITY BREACHES

Factors that lead to breaches in the healthcare sector can take different forms, including, but not limited to, hacking, purposeful or accidental disclosure of data, system failures and lost equipment. According to the US Department of Health and Human Services (HHS) Office for Civil Rights (OCR), over the past five years, there has been a 256% increase in large breaches reported to OCR involving hacking and a 264% increase in ransomware [3]. Interestingly, other authors have argued that most breaches in cybersecurity have been attributed to human error [4]. Similarly, according to another data security survey, human error was the most common cause of data breaches, ahead of other factors like theft, malware, hacking and misuse of data [5].

IV. PROPOSED STUDY OBJECTIVES

Notably, research elsewhere has shown that despite the well-documented cyber threats to patients' PHI, sparse evidence exists about the state of cybersecurity behavior of health care workers and medical private practices [6]. In view of this, this study seeks to explore health professionals' attitudes to, and awareness of, cybersecurity considerations in a private healthcare setting.

Subject to obtaining the relevant Institutional Review Board (IRB) approvals, the objective of this study, which will commence in Q2 2024, is to:

- Assess medical professionals' perception of the threat to cybersecurity with respect to medical records and patient data
- Assess medical professionals' perspectives of the common cybersecurity practices
- Assess medical professionals' experience of challenges/barriers in implementing cybersecurity measures
- Assess the awareness of medical professionals, in a large private hospital, of cybersecurity measures and applicable regulations

V. PROPOSED METHODOLOGY AND ANALYTICAL PROTOCOL

To fulfil the stated objectives, a survey-based cross-sectional study will be implemented to assess medical professionals' perception/awareness of the threat to cybersecurity with respect to medical records and patient data.

This study will adopt a thematic analysis approach with a view to identifying any patterns in participants' responses. This approach will entail a review of the frequency of response types under each survey category. A thematic analysis approach has been chosen for this study because it has been recognized as a credible research method for identifying, analyzing, organizing, describing, and reporting themes found within a data set [7]. In terms of choice of thematic analysis protocol, this study will adopt Braun & Clarke's six-phase framework for doing a thematic analysis [8] comprising: step 1- becoming familiar with the data; step 2- generating initial codes; step 3- searching for themes; step 4- reviewing the identified themes; step 5- defining the themes; step 6- write up of the interpretation. This framework is recognized as one of the most delineated methods of conducting a thematic analysis [9].

The results will categorize the respondents using demographic and screener questions, including clinical specialty, years of experience, as well as experience with EHRs, or with health technology in general.

Subsequently, the participants' anonymized responses with respect to the level of cybersecurity awareness, implementation of cybersecurity measures and experience of practical challenges with real world implementation of cybersecurity practices will be measured and reported.

No identifiable patient information will be collected as part of this study and there will be no direct patient contact or implementation of any clinical intervention as part of this study. Furthermore, responses by study participants will be anonymized and identities of study participants would not be revealed.

VI. DATA SOURCE AND QUALITY ASSURANCE

All licensed physicians contracted to large ambulatory care center in the United Arab Emirates will be invited to participate in the survey. Participation will be completely voluntary; no compensation will be offered to participants and complete anonymity of responses and participants will be maintained.

The survey questionnaire will be developed on Microsoft Forms and sent by email to all participants. The questionnaire would describe the background and rationale for the study, with participants given the opportunity to consent.

The survey themes and questionnaire contents will be supplemented and informed by relevant published literature search (including of published cybersecurity guidelines and regulations), as well as with qualitative discussions at Senior Leadership (SLT) and departmental meetings. This is with a view to validating understanding, applicable assumptions and to confirm the chosen themes and response categorizations for the study.

To assure good data quality during the data collection process, the study will:

- Implement a pretesting of the survey questionnaire and the channel of data collection (Microsoft Forms) before administering them. This is to ensure the tools are working as expected and that they adequately cover the research objectives
- Ensure that the survey duration does not exceed 10 minutes to avoid respondent fatigue
- Implement routine data collection checks to ensure that the data being collected is of the intended quality
- Ensure secured storage of the study data in encrypted and password-protected files

- Ensure that anonymity of responses and study participants is fully maintained and protected

VII. CONCLUSION

In an era where technological advancements have revolutionized healthcare delivery, cybersecurity is an indispensable safeguard for the sanctity of patient data and the integrity of medical systems. We believe that the insight that will be generated in this study will add to the body of knowledge that will support the removal of barriers to the practical implementation of cybersecurity practices and measures, particularly in a private healthcare setting. As the primary target audience for the study are clinicians working in a private healthcare setting, we recognize that an area of further research could include other stakeholders, e.g., Information Technology (IT) professionals within healthcare, who also play a critical role in healthcare cybersecurity.

REFERENCES

[1] R. Pastorino et al., "Benefits and challenges of Big Data in healthcare: an overview of the European initiatives," Eur J Public Health, Oct 2019, vol. 29 (Supplement_3), pp. 23-27, doi: 10.1093/eurpub/ckz168.

[2] MS-ISAC, "Data Breaches: In the Healthcare Sector," Center for Internet Security, New York: Insights and Blogs, 2016, https://www.cisecurity.org/insights/blog/data-breaches-in-the-healthcare-sector.

[3] HHS, "Cyberattack on Change Healthcare," US Department of Health and Human Services, Washington: Press Release, 2024.

[4] K. Hore et al., "Cybersecurity and critical care staff: A mixed methods study," Int J Med Inform, 2024 May, vol. 185, p. 105412, doi: 10.1016/j.ijmedinf.2024.105412.

[5] A. Seh et al., "Healthcare data breaches: Insights and implications in Healthcare," Multidisciplinary Digital Publishing Institute, 2020, vol. 8, p. 133.

[6] J. Dykstra, R. Mathur, and A. Spoor, "Cybersecurity in Medical Private Practice: Results of a Survey in Audiology," IEEE 6th International Conference on Collaboration and Internet Computing (CIC), 2020, pp. 153–181, doi: 10.1109/CIC50333.2020.00029.

[7] L. Nowell, J. Norris, D. White, and N. Moules, "Thematic Analysis: Striving to Meet the Trustworthiness Criteria," International Journal of Qualitative Methods, 2017 Oct, vol 16, p. 1, doi:10.1177/1609406917733847.

[8] M. Maguire, and B. Delahunt, "Doing a Thematic Analysis: A Practical, Step-by-Step Guide for Learning and Teaching Scholars," All Ireland Journal of Higher Education, 2017 Oct, vol 9, p. 3.

[9] D. Byrne, "A worked example of Braun and Clarke's approach to reflexive thematic analysis," Qual Quant, 2021 June, vol 56, pp. 1391–1412, doi: 10.1007/s11135-021-01182-y.

Patient-Provider Communication Technologies, Patient Preferences and Medication Adherence: An In-depth Analysis

Ben Malin
Dept. Electronic and Electrical Engineering
Brunel University London
London, United Kingdom
e-mail: ben.malin@brunel.ac.uk

Joshua Hinton
Patient Insights and Data Strategy Unit
HealthNet Homecare
London, United Kingdom
email: joshua.hinton@healthnethomecare.co.uk

Ejike Nwokoro
Patient Insights and Data Strategy Unit
HealthNet Homecare
London, United Kingdom
email: ejike.nwokoro@healthnethomecare.co.uk

Tatiana Kalganova
Dept. Electronic and Electrical Engineering
Brunel University London
London, United Kingdom
email: tatiana.kalganova@brunel.ac.uk

Abstract— **Communications between a patient and their health service provider are essential in ensuring sustained engagement and achievement of optimal clinical outcomes. To generate valuable insight on how to optimize interactions with patients, and to preserve both adherence and patient satisfaction, this study analyses different patient-provider communication modalities, user preferences, and medication adherence across a range of covariates. To evaluate how patient-provider communications relate with these covariates, and to adherence, we identify which Channel of Communication (CoC) is used by the patient to confirm every medication delivery. This is used to display preference as well as how successful each CoC is. In this study, we define adherence as the Percentage of Days Covered (PDC) by medication stock. Three CoCs are covered in this study: phone calls, email, and portal (a web platform), all of which enable the user to confirm medication deliveries, enabling them to have the required medication stock, in alignment with their doctor's prescription. Through this analysis, we find that each CoC has a significant influence on medication adherence, with portal users having relatively better adherence for any given month (PDC reduction of 6.7-6.8% for phone users, compared to portal users). Additionally, the use of the portal increases by 4.7% month on month, whilst phone call use decreases by 4.6%. We opine that the impact seen in portal usage is due to patients growing in familiarity with digital health solutions, as well as the benefit attained via digital health means. Furthermore, this study shows that patients who are consistent with their preferred CoC attain greater adherence than those with inconsistent CoCs. In any given month, patients who continue to use a CoC that was an initially stated preference typically have a PDC 6.1-6.3% greater than their counterparts with inconsistent CoC preferences. The insights gained around the temporal nature of patient behavior and communication preferences will allow for their health service providers to better support their patients, with dynamic and tailored interventions. Such tailored services are consequently better positioned to improve adherence, patient outcomes and satisfaction.**

Keywords- medication adherence; healthcare; homecare; communication; engagement; digital health.

I. INTRODUCTION

Efficient and reliable patient-provider communication has been shown to positively influence adherence [1]. Whilst tailored communication has been acknowledged by many as having a major influence on medication adherence and overall health outcomes [2], the channel through which such tailored communication is made available to the patient is equally crucial. With the escalation in the variety of communication tools available today, including web portals, apps, automated text and email messaging, phone calls and many more, healthcare providers have an arsenal of communication channels at their disposal to effectively communicate with their patients. Furthermore, patient-centered communication is believed to drive engagement, trust, and improvement in health outcomes [3]. Such patient-centered communication encompasses patient preferences, amongst other factors, with respect to how healthcare is delivered. It is crucial therefore to have a deeper understanding of patterns in patient behavior and preferences with a view to ensuring that relevant communication is delivered in a format, and through a channel, that benefits engagement and drives persistent medication adherence. To this end, this study seeks to analyse the communication patterns for chronic disease patients who have their medicines (which they self-administer) delivered to them. The reasoning behind this is to identify the communication channel's impact on medication adherence behaviors, as well as how communication channel preferences can evolve over the length of a patient's time on service/treatment. Insight from these analyses would support the optimization of interventions that are designed to ensure patient engagement in their care and ultimately improve medication adherence over a sustained period. To this end, the Research Questions (RQ) and hypotheses for this study include:

RQ1: Does the Channel of Communication (CoC) used influence patient adherence?

Hypotheses:

H_0 Channel of communication does not affect adherence.

H_1 Channel of communication affects adherence.

RQ2 How dynamic are patient communication preferences?

Hypotheses:

H_0 Patient communication preferences are static over time.

H_1 Patient communication preferences are dynamic and change throughout time on service.

RQ3 Does inconsistency in communication preference influence patient adherence?

Hypotheses:

H_0 Inconsistency in communication preference does not affect adherence.

H_1 Inconsistency in communication preference affects adherence.

The structure of this paper is as follows: Section II outlines the importance of this study, whilst Section III provides a review into other studies with comparable objectives. Section IV details the data that is utilized within this study, leading into Section V where each RQ is evaluated and discussed. Finally, Section VI concludes our findings and provides suggestions for future work.

II. Background

The World Health Organisation (WHO) suggests that adherence is affected by healthcare system or provider-patient relationship, amongst other factors [4]. Many studies have focused on the quality of physician communication and patient adherence, finding a strong positive relationship between the two [5]. Intuitively, provider communication and patient adherence are inextricably linked. The healthcare provider is the patient's initial contact point at diagnosis, the executor of any changes to treatment regimen, and the support should any difficulties arise with the condition or therapy. Resultantly, ensuring that the patient-provider relationship is strong is a primary goal of communication and is fundamental in active patient engagement [6].

Providing flexibility in the way that a patient accesses support is crucial in ensuring their long-term engagement, not least because it accommodates patient choice and changing preferences. Interestingly, despite a common belief that face-to-face interactions are superior to digital communication forms for patient outcomes, other studies have pointed out the paucity of data to support this view [7]. Notably, technological developments have resulted in a fundamental shift in health service delivery approaches, with the increasing popularity of digital forms of communication. For instance, 68% of the UK now advocate for the use of digital health technology within the NHS [8], with £2 billion in funding recently allocated to support the transition to electronic patient records within the NHS [9]. Aside from the increased convenience and accessibility made possible through digital communication options, some studies have demonstrated that technological advancements, like AI-driven SMS communication of tailored messages are associated with higher medication adherence rates [10].

Health Literacy and Adherence

If patients are not self-motivated to learn, it is very likely that their healthcare provider will be the source of any accrued knowledge around their condition. The complexities inherent to patient adherence necessitate some formal modelling to segment and understand the processes at play. Whilst impossible to focus on all factors (both internal and external to the patient) that influence non-adherence, streamlining the communication and decision-making phases of the patient's health journey (Figure 1) can potentially enhance health literacy and, ultimately, their likelihood to adhere to their prescribed medication [11]. Health literacy is the patient's ability to obtain, process, communicate and understand basic health information and services [12].

The Dunn-Conard health literacy instructional model is founded on the grounds that the monitoring and control of chronic health conditions is complex and requires a high level of patient involvement [13][14]. Whilst bolstering all the factors listed in Figure 1 would be the most beneficial for patient outcomes, this study primarily focuses on assessing the impact of patient-provider communications on adherence. To understand the behavioral mechanisms behind patient-provider communication, Table I assesses the relationship through a COM-B model, which postulates that performing a behavior is linked to capability, opportunity, and motivation [15].

Whilst communication regarding the delivery of medication may not seem complex, it is multi-faceted in its behavioral components. Several factors can deter patients from ordering their medication on time. For example, patients may not have the capability to communicate with their homecare provider. Usually, these patients would be assisted by a carer, or through bespoke facilitation by a Clinical Homecare provider. However, in some circumstances, this may not be the case. Equally, patients may have limited access to the technological mediums required to place an order for their medication. Many Clinical Homecare

Figure 1. Dunn-Conard Health Literacy Model

TABLE I. COM-B MODEL OF COMMUNICATION BEHAVIOR

	Capability	**Opportunity**	**Motivation**
Definition	*The individual's physical and psychological capacity to engage in the behavior.*	*All factors lying outside the individual that make performance of the behavior possible or prompt it.*	*All brain processes that energize and direct behavior.*
Behaviors	Understanding the communication methods available to them.	Access to channels of communication.	Self-efficacy and willingness to engage with the provider.
	Psychological capability to communicate i.e. disabilities and mental health considered.	Severity of condition/regimen complexity	Condition-specific factors i.e. immediacy of side-effects, tangibility of medication efficacy.
	Common language of communication.		Cues for action from the homecare provider.

Note. All statements in italics are definitions taken from Michie et al. (2011) [15]. General model applied in Jackson et al. (2014) [17]

providers in the UK are transitioning to digital communication channels. Some patients may not have access to an internet-capable device, although this is a very small subset of the UK, where 97.8% use the internet, up from 56.5% in 2002 [16]. Lastly, patients must also be motivated to order their medication, whereby their motivation to do so may be impacted by a number of factors. For example, if non-adherence to medication has no immediate side-effects, adherence to medication has immediate side effects, or a patient is not provided sufficient cues from their Clinical Homecare provider, they may be less motivated to order and take their medication [17]. Ultimately, it is essential to understand why patients may have less than 100% adherence to provide solutions. This study does not granulate communication into the factors listed in Table I but does assess the overall impact of communication channel choice on non-adherence to medication in patients with chronic conditions. The granular take on communication in Table 1 should be explored further in future research.

III. RELATED WORK

Studies elsewhere have found that poor adherence to medication is linked to negative clinical outcomes and increased utilization of healthcare resources, and it is estimated that poor medication adherence costs NHS England approximately £1bn annually [28][29]. However, measuring adherence, particularly in a chronic disease setting, is often challenging given that approaches such as clinician observation of medicine intake or biological testing for presence of the therapy, are neither economically nor logistically sustainable. Approaches to measuring adherence can largely be grouped into subjective, indirect, and direct categories, as shown in Table II.

This study measures adherence using pharmacy records, and more specifically, the Proportion of Days Covered (PDC). Simply put, this is the percentage of days within a time period that a patient has access to the medication that they are prescribed.

PDC data is obtained from a UK-based Clinical Homecare organisation, focusing on patients who self-administer subcutaneous injections across respiratory, rheumatology, dermatology, and gastroenterology therapy areas. This form of adherence was chosen due to its conservatism, which other pharmacy-based metrics like medication possession ratio (MPR) fail to exercise. The PDC metric has been advocated for by various bodies (e.g., the Pharmacy Quality Alliance (PQA)) as the preferred quality indicator for estimating adherence to therapies for chronic diseases [30].

The literature is sparse on communication modality and its effect on adherence, however, a 2021 study found that agency with regards to digital reminder modality had a positive effect on patient adherence in asthma patients [31]. Studies in

TABLE II. METHODS OF MEASURING MEDICATION ADHERENCE

Measurement Category	**Types of measurement**	**Author/ year**
Subjective	Self-reported questionnaires Homecare providers perception of adherence	Gupta et al., 2016 [18] Nguyen et al., 2014 [19] Alili et al., 2016 [20]
Indirect	Pharmacy records Pill counting Electronic monitoring devices	Gupta et al., 2016 [18] Denicolò et al., 2021 [21] Mackridge & Marriott, 2007 [22] Lam & Fresco, 2015 [23] Paterson et al., 2017 [24]
Direct	Direct observed therapy Digital pills Chemical adherence testing	Lane et al., 2019 [25] Gupta et al., 2016 [18] Denicolò et al., 2021 [21] Pitt, 2009 [26] Patel et al., 2010 [27]

adjacent domains looked at the preference in communication modality and physical activity in patients with musculoskeletal disorders and adherence in HIV, finding a preference for printed materials and text messaging respectively [32][33].

To our knowledge, this study appears to be the first of its kind to assess the impact of communication channel on patient adherence across several chronic diseases and medication types, in a Clinical Homecare setting, using a larger patient cohort than other studies in adjacent domains.

IV. METHODOLOGY

The data used within this study is comprised of patients who are enrolled in a UK-based Clinical Homecare service. All data has been pseudonymized and processed in compliance with General Data Protection Regulation. All data processing is conducted using Python and the Pandas library, all statistical analysis is conducted using STATA 18.1.

A. Study Data

The data used within this study focuses on specific medications which cover a range of conditions (gastrointestinal, respiratory, dermatological, rheumatoid, and ophthalmic indications). This representative sample contains 30,102 patients, with all patient-provider communications logged from their initialization on the service, beginning in 2018, until January 2024. This timestamped data contains the CoC, which can be phone calls, direct email communication and the use of an online portal (which can be accessed directly by the patient or be encouraged through email/text one-time links). All these CoCs can be used to confirm a medication delivery, which is what will be measured in this study to establish the patient's preference.

A patient's stated CoC preference is collected when they join the service. Patient revealed preferences will be identified by establishing the CoC that was used to confirm every patient's medication delivery. It is worth noting that in the absence of any delivery confirmation, when one would be expected, the Clinical Homecare provider will telephone the patient to confirm the delivery.

Demographic data is also collected in addition to the communication and delivery data, specifically, age, gender, diagnosis, location and whether the patient is on a patient support program.

B. Data cleaning and processing

Prior to data processing, redundant communication data is removed, such as logged questionnaire activity.

We primarily wish to identify how consistent a patient's initial preference for a CoC is with the communication behavior they exhibit over their time on service. To capture and analyse this behavior, whenever a patient receives medication stock, the CoC that led to this delivery is recorded. Through identification of which CoCs have been used to confirm an upcoming medication delivery, we can analyse its relationship with both adherence and initial stated preferences.

The data is processed monthly, for the statistical analysis, to ensure a high-level of granularity. The timepoint when a patient has their first communication with their Clinical Homecare provider, marks the beginning of their Length Of Service (LOS). After this period, the CoC used by the patient to confirm each medication delivery is considered as a successful CoC.

Panel data is configured by establishing a timeline for each patient, where their monthly communication behavior is recorded. In addition to this, other variables such as whether this CoC matches stated preference, total medication deliveries, and the percentage of successful deliveries that used a stated preference are created. It is worth noting that not every month has a delivery, with most deliveries having a frequency of 8 weeks or longer. The months without delivery data are left null and omitted from our models. This monthly data is also pooled to produce one data point per patient, for every patient's full time on service (up until the current date). This produces cross-sectional data, from which alternative research questions can be answered.

To answer the research questions, PDC values were calculated at each month and across the whole service duration to establish how changing preferences influence monthly adherence, as well as their overall relationship. To calculate PDC, the timestamp of a medication delivery and the number of days' worth of medication the delivery contains is recorded. This provides a patient timeline, which displays the quantity of medication that each patient should have at any given date, further details of this technique have been provided in a previous study [34]. The data allows for the stockpiling of medication (when a patient receives an additional delivery before their current medication stock has depleted, these stock values are added together), as this is common behavior for chronic disease patients [35][36]. Finally, a variable to describe each patient's approximate level of economic deprivation is created using UK-based Index of Multiple Deprivation (IMD) data [37]. This variable is inputted as a percentile.

C. Dataset outline

To better understand the data utilized in this study, this section covers the demographics and descriptive statistics of the patients within the sample. Table III displays the number of deliveries that have resulted from each CoC, as well as the number of patients that state an initial preference for each CoC.

The summary statistics on dichotomous demographics and disease-specific variables are presented in Table IV. Patient receives Enhanced Services (PES) stipulates whether the patient receives additional nurse visits to support treatment compliance.

The summary statistics for the continuous demographic variables are presented in Table V, where all patients have data for each variable.

TABLE III. COMMUNICATIONS OUTLINE

CoC	Initial Preference	Total Successful Uses
Portal	24,976	125,065
Calls	3,597	178,974
Emails	8,171	1,067

V. RESULTS AND DISCUSSION

This section will cover each of the research questions and hypotheses outlined in the Introduction and discuss the statistical methodologies that have been used to answer these questions. In addition, analysis and discussion of these results is provided.

RQ1: DOES CHANNEL OF COMMUNICATION USED INFLUENCE PATIENT ADHERENCE?

- H_0 Channel of communication does not affect adherence.
- H_1 Channel of communication affects adherence.

A. Results

It is important to understand how CoC affects adherence within the sample. For example, as many healthcare service providers transition to digital-first communication strategies to aid with optimization, labor-force allocation, and costs, it is important to know if patient outcomes are affected. Whilst the Clinical Homecare provider that is the subject of this study have kept traditional communication methods available to their patients, the default option for arranging deliveries is now through the patient portal, which is the reference category for the analysis shown in Table VI. Panel 1 uses a random effects panel regression to establish the effect of CoC on adherence, each month. Panel 2 uses an identical model, with additional demographic and diagnosis covariates to confirm the relationship observed in Panel 1.

In Panel 1, the coefficient for calls is $\beta = -0.0667$, with a standard error of 0.00116, and the coefficient for emails is $\beta = 0.0924$, with a standard error of 0.000660. Both effects are highly significant at the $p < 0.01$ level. In Panel 2, the effect sizes increase to $\beta = -0.0680$ for calls, and $\beta = 0.110$, with standard errors of 0.00127 and 0.00242 respectively. Both effect sizes are significant at the $p < 0.01$ level. This is indicative that people who use calls to arrange their medication are predicted to have lower adherence, whilst patients that use emails to arrange their medication are predicted to have higher adherence and are robust to the inclusion of demographic and diagnosis covariates.

TABLE IV. PATIENT DEMOGRAPHIC AND DIAGNOSES DESCRIPTIVE STATISTICS

Category	Variable	Frequency
Gender	Male	13,034
	Female	12,846
PES	Yes	10,055
	No	20,047
Disease	Atopic Dermatitis	12,776
	Hidradenitis Suppurativa	472
	Juvenile Arthiritis	225
	Psoriasis	3,268
	Crohn's Disease	2,928
	Eosinophilic Eosophagitis	10
	IBD (Inflammatory Bowel Disease)	48
	Ulcerative Colitis	950
	Uveitis	225
	Severe Asthma	3,647
	Axial Spondyloarthritis	1,518
	Rheumatoid Arthritis	3,181

TABLE V. CONTINUOUS DEMOGRAPHIC VARIABLES DESCRIPTIVE STATISTICS

Variable	Frequency	Median	Standard Deviation
Age	30,097	47	17.856
IMD	30,097	46	24.031
LOS	30,097	20	18.457

TABLE VI. PANEL DATA MODEL: CoC AND ADHERENCE - DIRECT EFFECTS (PANEL SAMPLE)

Variable	Panel 1		Panel 2	
	Coefficient	Std. Error	Coefficient	Std. Error
CoC: Call	-0.0667***	0.00116	-0.0680***	0.00127
CoC: Email	0.0924***	0.000660	0.110***	0.00242
Gender			-0.00345**	0.00167
Age			0.000667***	0.0000501
IMD			0.0000305	0.0000342
PES			0.00371**	0.00170
Hidradenitis Suppurativa			-0.0146**	0.00712
Juvenile Arthritis			-0.0179	0.0146
Psoriasis			-0.0145***	0.00307
Crohn's Disease			-0.00468	0.00337
Eosinophilic Esophagitis			0.0134	0.0218
IBD			0.0434**	0.0174
Ulcerative Colitis			0.0227***	0.00493
Uveitis			-0.0113	0.0115
Severe Asthma			0.0396***	0.00219
Axial Spondylarthritis			-0.00766*	0.00450
Rheumatoid Arthritis			-0.0167***	0.00334
Chi^2	40415.250		33920.440	
$p > chi2$	0.000		0.000	
# Observations	285,621		230,687	
# Patients	28,311		23,820	

Note: Panel regression models with random effects and robust standard errors. Outcome variable: Monthly PDC (100% days covered=1, 0% days covered=0). Panel 1 regresses monthly communication type (Portal=omitted category) and Panel 2 includes covariates age (in years), gender (Female=omitted category), IMD (Index of Multiple Deprivation in percentiles), PES (tailored interventions (with homecare provider interactions at pre-determined intervals) designed to improve treatment adherence/compliance), and diagnosis (Atopic Dermatitis=omitted category) (*** p<0.01, **p<0.05, *p<0.1).

B. Discussion

Whether a given CoC was an initial preference or not, the CoC that is used, has significant influence on a patient's behavior. This is evidenced by the coefficients displayed in Table VI, which shows that at any given month, patients who utilize calls to confirm their deliveries have a PDC 6.67% - 6.80% (range dependent on predictive model) lower than portal users. Whilst patients that confirm deliveries via email have a PDC 9.24%-11.0% greater than those using portal. These findings are indicative of the crucial role of patient engagement, as the use of portal and email requires more patient engagement than receiving a phone call, showing a level of commitment to their treatment which is directly correlated with increased adherence (i.e., PDC). Whilst these objective findings are useful for a Clinical Homecare provider looking to drive better patient engagement, understanding the motive for that communication preference is vital.

Patients using call, for example, may be calling because of a missed delivery, looking for an immediate resolution. On occasion, this missed delivery could result in a lower PDC. Likewise, the Clinical Homecare provider within this study prioritizes communicating with patients via phone call when a patient is at risk of being overdue for their medication, due to the immediacy offered in resolving the situation.

The relationship between email usage and PDC in this study may also have been influenced by the relative infrequency of emails compared to communications using the portal, or call. 41.04% of communications were through the portal, 58.60% through calls, and 0.37% through email. Further analysis shows that the maximum number of communications any patient has through email is 1, indicating that email is unlikely to be a consistent CoC for a patient, and used sporadically for specific events only.

RQ2: HOW DYNAMIC ARE PATIENT COMMUNICATION PREFERENCES?

- H_0 Patient communication preferences are static over time.
- H_1 Patient communication preferences are dynamic and change throughout time on service.

C. Results

Understanding how patient behavior evolves over time is vital in establishing effective healthcare provisions. To model changing patient communication behaviors, we ran mixed-effects logistic regression analysis on revealed communication preferences over time. This model was chosen as it is preferential for modelling binary outcomes as a linear combination of the constituent factors. The results are displayed in Table VII.

The use of portal communication increases significantly as the length of time on service increases (Odds Ratio (OR) = 1.047, 95% Confidence Interval (CI) [1.047, 1.048], $p <$ 0.0001), the use of calls decreases significantly as LOS increases (OR = 0.954, 95% CI [0.954, 0.955], $p <$ 0.0001), and the use of emails decreases significantly as LOS increases (OR = 0.533, 95% CI [0.513, 0.B554]).

D. Discussion

For each additional month a patient is on service, their likelihood of using portal to confirm their deliveries increases by 4.7%. Likewise, their likelihood of medication delivery confirmation via calls decreases by 4.6% and with email by 46.7%. The increased use of successful portal delivery confirmations as LOS increases is a positive finding, highlighting an increased willingness to engage in digital health over time. Additionally, this CoC requires a higher level of proactivity from the patient than phone calls, as the patient is required to actively log on to a service to confirm their delivery, rather than passively receive a phone call. The increasing use of the portal is therefore indicative of increasing patient engagement as length of time on service increases. Some potential reasons for this could be increased habituation to the service, although further data analysis would be required to substantiate this. The decrease in confirmed deliveries via calls, as LOS increases, is also a reassuring finding as it showcases a willingness from patients to pivot to more active treatment management channels. Additionally, within our sample, calls are prioritized by the Clinical Homecare provider when a medication delivery is at risk of being overdue because it requires the least effort from the patient to confirm their delivery. The decreasing frequency in the use of calls to confirm medication delivery as LOS increases could also be an indication of habituation to service or the establishment of effective equilibrium between the patient and the provider.

Finally, the use of emails as a means of medication delivery confirmation suffers a large reduction as LOS increases. In this sample, no patients have ever been shown to utilize email more than once in successfully confirming their medication delivery, over their entire service-duration. These

TABLE VII. MIXED-EFFECTS LOGISTIC REGRESSION – PATIENT COMMUNICATION PREFERENCES OVER TIME

Communication Type	**Odds ratio⁺ (Std. error)**	**Z-value**	**Chi^2 ($p > chi2$)**
Portal	1.047*** (0.000326)	148.60	22082.50 (0.000)
Call	0.954*** (0.000236)	-188.52	35538.97 (0.000)
Email	0.533*** (0.0106)	-31.70	1004.76 (0.000)

Note. Three mixed-effects logistic regression models were run to ascertain these results. Communication type is recorded every month, with a maximum of one communication type per month. This communication type corresponds to the generation of a successful delivery. (*** p<0.01, **p<0.05, *p<0.1).⁺ (OR) observations suggest that emails are used by some patients to confirm deliveries at the beginning of their service due to uncertainty or unfamiliarity with the other CoCs, or in specific situations which require the provision of more information to the service provider. On some occasions, it could also result from a patient being referred to the service from a center which did not provide the patient's contact number, but this is infrequent. Emails are not used by patients consistently, which should be considered by healthcare providers with several channels of communication available.

RQ3: DOES INCONSISTENCY IN PATIENT COMMUNICATION PREFERENCE INFLUENCE ADHERENCE?

- H_0 Inconsistency in communication preference does not affect adherence.
- H_1 Inconsistency in communication preference affects adherence.

To answer RQ3, both pooled and panel analysis is required. The reasoning behind both approaches is to assess how patient adherence is predicted to change over the duration of their time on service, and in any given month.

E. Pooled Analysis Results

Initially, we performed pooled analysis using aggregated adherence data, in the same manner as previous analysis. To establish whether patients' stated preference at the beginning of their Clinical Homecare service are consistent with their revealed communication behavior through the course of their time on the service, we compare all patient's stated preferences with their modal CoC and introduced it as a binary variable. For 53.1% of the patients in the sample, there was a match between their stated and revealed preferences. The results of the Linear Probability Model (LPM) assessing the effect of preference consistency on PDC are displayed in Table VIII.

In LPM 1, the coefficient for consistent preferences is $\beta = 0.0118$, with a standard error of 0.00220. This effect is highly significant at the $p < 0.01$ level. In LPM 2, the effect size increases to $\beta = 0.0202$, with a standard error of 0.00237, which is also significant at the $p < 0.01$ level. This is indicative that people who have consistent preferences are more likely to adhere to their medication – these findings are even more robust with the inclusion of demographic and diagnosis covariates.

F. Pooled Analysis Discussion

Consistency in the CoC preference results in a 1.2% to 2.0% higher PDC across the service-life of a patient. Simply put, if a patient's modal CoC is the same as their stated communication preference at the onset of the service, their adherence will be 1.2% to 2.0% greater than patients with inconsistent preferences. Whilst the findings of overall consistent preferences are useful, it is vital to have a sense of how inconsistent these preferences can be. To ascertain this, we generated a categorical variable which captured how often the patient's Stated preferences matched their Revealed (SR Percentage), using monthly data. The results of the LPM are detailed in Table IX.

TABLE VIII. LPM: PREFERENCE CONSISTENCY AND ADHERENCE - DIRECT EFFECTS

Variable	LPM 1		LPM 2	
	Coefficient	**Std. Error**	**Coefficient**	**Std. Error**
Consistent Preferences	0.0118***	0.00220	0.0202***	0.00237
Gender			0.00496**	0.00235
Age			0.000218**	0.0000731
IMD			0.0000916*	0.0000477
PES			-0.00350	0.00248
Hidradenitis Suppurativa			-0.0640***	0.0119
Juvenile Arthritis			-0.0453***	0.0170
Psoriasis			0.000268	0.00383
Crohn's Disease			-0.0192***	0.00486
Eosionophilic Eosophagitis			0.0249	0.0479
IBD			0.0404	0.0253
Ulcerative Colitis			0.0119	0.00732
Uveitis			-0.0164	0.0139
Severe Asthma			0.0631***	0.00315
Axial Spondyloarthritis			-0.0120**	0.00595
Rheumatoid Arthritis			-0.0206***	0.00458
F-stat	28.72		55.60	
$p > F$	0.0000		0.0000	
# Observations	29,499		24,730	

Note: Linear probability regression models. Outcome variable: PDC (100% days covered=1, 0% days covered=0). LPM 1 regresses only preference consistency (consistent=1, inconsistent=0) and LPM 2 includes covariates age (in years), gender (Female=omitted category), IMD (index of multiple deprivation in percentiles), PES (tailored interventions (with homecare provider interactions at pre-determined intervals) designed to improve treatment adherence/compliance), and diagnosis (Atopic Dermatitis=omitted category) (*** p<0.01, **p<0.05, *p<0.1).

In LPM 3, the coefficient for the proportion of communications which match the stated preference is $\beta = -0.0235$, with a standard error of 0.00669 and high significance at the $p < 0.01$ level. However, post the inclusion of demographic and diagnosis covariates in LPM 4, the finding loses significance as the coefficient decreases to $\beta = -0.00487$ with a standard error of 0.00723. The variation within LPM 3 caused by the consistency percentage can be attributed to demographic and condition-specific variation. This finding is reassuring, as it demonstrated that preference consistency, with respect to which CoC is used by the patient, has a positive effect on PDC, which is not affected by the degree of this consistency. The takeaway is that patients may use non-preferred communication methods for a host of reasons, and if their modal communication method matches their stated preferred, adherence is not affected.

TABLE IX. LPM: PREFERENCE CONSISTENCY % AND ADHERENCE - DIRECT EFFECTS

Variable	LPM 3		LPM 4	
	Coefficient	Std. Error	Coefficient	Std. Error
Consistent Preferences	0.0233***	0.00381	0.0225***	0.00399
SR Percentage	-0.0235***	0.00669	-0.00487	0.00723
Gender			0.00498**	0.00235
Age			0.000214***	0.0000736
IMD			0.0000913*	0.0000477
PES			-0.00361	0.00249
Hidradenitis Suppurativa			-0.0640***	0.0119
Juvenile Arthritis			-0.0455***	0.0170
Psoriasis			0.000293	0.00383
Crohn's Disease			-0.0192***	0.00486
Eosionophilic Eosophagitis			0.0246	0.0483
IBD			0.0402	0.0253
Ulcerative Colitis			0.0119	0.00731
Uveitis			-0.0164	0.0139
Severe Asthma			0.0632***	0.00317
Axial Spondyloarthritis			-0.0119**	0.00595
Rheumatoid Arthritis			-0.0205**	0.00458
F-stat	22.12		52.29	
$p > F$	0.0000		0.0000	
# Observations	29,499		24,730	

Note: Linear probability regression models. Outcome variable: PDC (100% days covered=1, 0% days covered=0). LPM 3 regresses preference consistency (consistent=1, inconsistent=0) and preference percentage (modal CoC and total communications are equal=1, modal CoC and total communications are unequal=0) and LPM 4 includes covariates age (in years), gender (Female=omitted category), IMD (index of multiple deprivation in percentiles), PES (tailored interventions (with homecare provider interactions at pre-determined intervals) designed to improve treatment adherence/compliance), and diagnosis (Atopic Dermatitis=omitted category) (*** p<0.01, **p<0.05, *p<0.1).

G. Panel Analysis Results

Whilst the pooled analysis helps to reveal overall trends within our patient population, month-by-month data gives greater granularity about patient adherence behaviors and its drivers, as well as tangible effects which could be expected in a shorter, more defined timespan.

It is important for us to validate the use of a random effects model over a fixed effects model for our panel analysis. Many of the independent variables utilized in this study are time-invariant. As a result, the use of a fixed effects model is inappropriate. Fixed effect modelling establishes how much of the variation in independent variables stems from a time-only relationship. In essence, how much the independent variables change because of time. In this scenario, where the independent variables do not change over time, this leads to an almost-entirely omitted panel regression model. However, this is not enough to validate the use of a random effects model. By running the Breusch and Pagan Lagrangian multiplier test (BPLM), we can ascertain that random effects are present in our model, assuring that panel regression with random effects is a superior model to pooled Ordinary Least Squares (OLS) regression for our sample. The results of the BPLM are shown in Table X.

The BPLM evidences a significant presence of random effects in the model, which means the variation in adherence across patients is significant and should be accounted for in the regression model.

The panel data model with random effects estimates the effect of preference consistency on monthly adherence and is detailed in Table XI.

In Panel 3, the coefficient for consistent preferences is $\beta = 0.0611$, with a standard error of 0.00118. This effect is highly significant at the $p < 0.01$ level. In Panel 4, the effect size increases to $\beta = 0.0632$, with a standard error of 0.00130, which is also significant at the $p < 0.01$ level.

Thus, the results of this analysis are indicative that people who have consistent preferences are more likely to adhere to their medication in any given month and is robust to the inclusion of demographic and diagnosis covariates.

H. Panel Analysis Discussion

Our panel analysis has shown that dynamic communication preferences have a statistically significant effect on adherence. When a patient uses a CoC that was their initial preference, in any given month, their PDC is predicted to be 6.1% to 6.3% greater than those displaying inconsistent preferences in that month. Thus, a patient who is inconsistent in their choice of CoC is likely to have a lower PDC than those who are consistent. These findings are positive, as it allows Clinical Homecare providers to utilize knowledge of a patient's consistency (or lack of it) with respect to their CoC preference over time, to tailor support that is provided to the patient in order to foster better adherence.

TABLE X. BREUSCH AND PAGAN LAGRANGIAN MULTIPLIER TEST (BPLM): VALIDATING A RANDOM EFFECTS MODEL

	Variance	Standard Deviation
PDC this month	0.104	0.322
e	0.0725	0.269
u	0.0243	0.156
Test: Var(u) = 0		
Chi^2		770,000
$p > chi2$		0.0000

Note. The BPLM test for the presence of random effects. e represents the idiosyncratic error term, the part of the error term which varies between patients and over time. u represents the random effects, the part of the error term that varies between patients but is constant over time for each patient.

TABLE XI. PANEL DATA MODEL: PREFERENCE CONSISTENCY AND ADHERENCE - DIRECT EFFECTS (PANEL SAMPLE)

Variable	Panel 3		Panel 4	
	Coefficient	**Std. Error**	**Coefficient**	**Std. Error**
Consistent Preferences	0.0611***	0.00118	0.0632***	0.00130
Gender			-0.00335**	0.00168
Age			0.000636***	0.0000505
IMD			0.0000356	0.0000344
PES			0.00296*	0.00179
Hidradenitis Suppurativa			-0.0155**	0.00716
Juvenile Arthritis			-0.0455	0.0170
Psoriasis			-0.0150***	0.00309
Crohn's Disease			-0.00816**	0.00341
Eosionophilic Eosophagitis			0.0147	0.0128
IBD			0.0431**	0.0184
Ulcerative Colitis			0.0199***	0.00495
Uveitis			-0.0126	0.0116
Severe Asthma			0.0404***	0.00222
Axial Spondyloarthritis			-0.00834*	0.00452
Rheumatoid Arthritis			-0.0202***	0.00338
Chi^2	2688.50		3286.03	
$p > chi2$	0.0000		0.0000	
# Observations	285,621		230,687	
# Patients	28,311		23,820	

Note: Panel regression models with random effects. Outcome variable: Monthly PDC (100% days covered=1, 0% days covered=0). Panel 3 regresses monthly preference consistency (consistent=1, inconsistent=0) and Panel 4 includes covariates age (in years), gender (Female=omitted category), IMD (Index of Multiple Deprivation in percentiles), PES (tailored interventions (with homecare provider interactions at pre-determined intervals) designed to improve treatment adherence/compliance), and diagnosis (Atopic Dermatitis=omitted category) (*** p<0.01, **p<0.05, *p<0.1)..

VI. CONCLUSION

Across the studied research questions many valuable insights have been uncovered, which can be used by Health service providers to maximize a patient's engagement with their diagnosis management and thus improve adherence. It was found that patients who exhibit consistent CoCs for their medication delivery confirmations have a 1.2%-2.0% higher PDC than patients exhibiting relatively more inconsistency with their CoC use. This insight can be used to provide additional support or communication with patients who are observed to have such inconsistencies. Furthermore, this insight also facilitates a more efficient and informed use of resources in a bid to drive better patient engagement.

It was observed that patients gravitate towards the use of a web portal as their service-duration increases, with a 4.7% increase month on month. Whilst the use of phone calls exhibits a reduction of 4.6% month on month. This is a finding that validates the use of digital forms of communication in healthcare and is also indicative of increasing levels of engagement from patients over time (as the use of a web portal requires more initiative from the patient to confirm a delivery than receiving a phone call does). Additionally, it was shown that users who confirm their medication deliveries via portal have a PDC 6.67%-6.80% greater than those that use phone calls for such delivery confirmation – providing further support for the validity of digital healthcare and its benefit for users.

Through these observations, we aim to improve patient satisfaction and adherence through greater understanding of when they are at increased risk of not engaging with their treatment/communication with their health service provider. These insights can have utility in optimizing resource management to patients most in need and improving treatment outcomes.

However, the research conducted is not exhaustive and there are other areas that can be the focus of future research. For instance, it is likely that there is a relationship between demographic and diagnosis-specific data with adherence, and a further understanding of this would provide additional benefit to the insights uncovered in this work. Likewise, the behaviors that are exhibited through patient stockpiling of medication, and the dynamics between this and other patient behaviors, such as adherence and communications, could uncover further utility.

ACKNOWLEDGMENTS

This work was conducted as part of a project funded by HealthNet Homecare UK LTD.

REFERENCES

[1] L. R. Martin, S. L. Williams, K. B. Haskard, and M. R. DiMatteo, "The challenge of patient adherence," *Ther Clin Risk Manag*, vol. 1, no. 3, pp. 189–199, Sep. 2005, doi: 10.2147/tcrm.s12160382.

[2] A. M. Dulmen, "The value of tailored communication for person-centred outcomes," *J Eval Clin Pract*, vol. 17, pp. 381–383, Nov. 2010, doi: 10.1111/j.1365-2753.2010.01586.x.

[3] N. Ratanawongsa *et al.*, "Communication and medication refill adherence: the Diabetes Study of Northern California," *JAMA Intern Med*, vol. 173, no. 3, pp. 210–218, Jan. 2013, doi: 10.1001/JAMAINTERNMED.2013.1216.

[4] E. Sabaté and WHO., *Adherence to long-term therapies : evidence for action*. World Health Organization, 2003.

[5] K. B. Haskard Zolnierek and M. R. DiMatteo, "Physician Communication and Patient Adherence to Treatment: A Meta-Analysis," *Med Care*, vol. 47, no. 8, 2009, [Online]. Available: https://journals.lww.com/lww-medicalcare/fulltext/2009/08000/physician_communication_and_patient_adherence_to.2.aspx (accessed: June 6, 2024)

[6] L. P. Fumagalli, G. Radaelli, E. Lettieri, P. Bertele', and C. Masella, "Patient Empowerment and its neighbours: Clarifying the boundaries and their mutual relationships,"

Health Policy (New York), vol. 119, no. 3, pp. 384–394, 2015, doi: https://doi.org/10.1016/j.healthpol.2014.10.017.
[7] T. Mirzaei and N. Kashian, "Revisiting Effective Communication Between Patients and Physicians: Cross-Sectional Questionnaire Study Comparing Text-Based Electronic Versus Face-to-Face Communication," *J Med Internet Res*, vol. 22, no. 5, May 2020, doi: 10.2196/16965. [Online]. Available: https://www.jmir.org/2020/5/e16965 (accessed June 6, 2024)
[8] L. Ashall-Payne and ORCHA, "ORCHA (2023)," 2023. [Online]. Available: https://info.orchahealth.com/digital-health-attitudes-behaviour-2023-report (accessed June 6, 2024)
[9] Department of Health & Social Care, "A plan for digital health and social care," 2022. [Online]. Available: https://www.gov.uk/government/publications/a-plan-for-digital-health-and-social-care/a-plan-for-digital-health-and-social-care (accessed June 6, 2024)
[10] A. Babel, R. Taneja, F. Mondello Malvestiti, A. Monaco, and S. Donde, "Artificial Intelligence Solutions to Increase Medication Adherence in Patients With Non-communicable Diseases," *Front Digit Health*, vol. 3, p. 669869, Jun. 2021, doi: 10.3389/FDGTH.2021.669869.
[11] P. M. Ho, C. L. Bryson, and J. S. Rumsfeld, "Medication Adherence," *Circulation*, vol. 119, no. 23, pp. 3028–3035, Jun. 2009, doi: 10.1161/CIRCULATIONAHA.108.768986.
[12] D. W. Baker, "The meaning and the measure of health literacy," *J Gen Intern Med*, vol. 21, no. 8, pp. 878–883, 2006, doi: 10.1111/j.1525-1497.2006.00540.x.
[13] P. Dunn and S. Conard, "Improving health literacy in patients with chronic conditions: A call to action," *Int J Cardiol*, vol. 273, pp. 249–251, 2018, doi: https://doi.org/10.1016/j.ijcard.2018.08.090.
[14] S. C. Smith *et al.*, "AHA/ACCF Secondary Prevention and Risk Reduction Therapy for Patients With Coronary and Other Atherosclerotic Vascular Disease: 2011 Update," *Circulation*, vol. 124, no. 22, pp. 2458–2473, Nov. 2011, doi: 10.1161/CIR.0b013e318235eb4d.
[15] S. Michie, M. M. van Stralen, and R. West, "The behaviour change wheel: A new method for characterising and designing behaviour change interventions," *Implementation Science*, vol. 6, no. 1, p. 42, 2011, doi: 10.1186/1748-5908-6-42.
[16] DataReportal, We Are Social, and Meltwater, "Share of individuals using the internet in the United Kingdom (UK) from 2002 to 2024," 2024. Accessed: May 20, 2024. [Online]. Available: https://www.statista.com/statistics/1124328/internet-penetration-uk/ (accessed June 6, 2024)
[17] C. Jackson, L. Eliasson, N. Barber, and J. Weinman, "Applying COM-B to medication adherence," *The European Health Psychologist*, vol. 16, no. 1, pp. 7–17, 2014.
[18] P. Gupta, P. Patel, R. Horne, H. Buchanan, B. Williams, and M. Tomaszewski, "How to Screen for Non-Adherence to Antihypertensive Therapy," *Curr Hypertens Rep*, vol. 18, no. 12, p. 89, 2016, doi: 10.1007/s11906-016-0697-7.
[19] T.-M.-U. Nguyen, A. La Caze, and N. Cottrell, "What are validated self-report adherence scales really measuring?: a systematic review," *Br J Clin Pharmacol*, vol. 77, no. 3, pp. 427–445, Mar. 2014, doi: https://doi.org/10.1111/bcp.12194.
[20] M. El Alili, B. Vrijens, J. Demonceau, S. M. Evers, and M. Hiligsmann, "A scoping review of studies comparing the medication event monitoring system (MEMS) with alternative methods for measuring medication adherence," *Br J Clin Pharmacol*, vol. 82, no. 1, pp. 268–279, Jul. 2016, doi: https://doi.org/10.1111/bcp.12942.
[21] S. Denicolò, P. Perco, S. Thöni, and G. Mayer, "Non-adherence to antidiabetic and cardiovascular drugs in type 2 diabetes mellitus and its association with renal and cardiovascular outcomes: A narrative review," *J Diabetes Complications*, vol. 35, no. 7, p. 107931, 2021, doi: https://doi.org/10.1016/j.jdiacomp.2021.107931.
[22] A. J. Mackridge and J. F. Marriott, "Returned medicines: waste or a wasted opportunity?," *J Public Health (Bangkok)*, vol. 29, no. 3, pp. 258–262, Sep. 2007, doi: 10.1093/pubmed/fdm037.
[23] W. Y. Lam and P. Fresco, "Medication Adherence Measures: An Overview," *Biomed Res Int*, vol. 2015, p. 217047, 2015, doi: 10.1155/2015/217047.
[24] M. Paterson, M. Kinnear, C. Bond, and B. McKinstry, "A systematic review of electronic multi-compartment medication devices with reminder systems for improving adherence to self-administered medications," *International Journal of Pharmacy Practice*, vol. 25, no. 3, pp. 185–194, Jun. 2017, doi: 10.1111/ijpp.12242.
[25] D. Lane, P. Patel, K. Khunti, and P. Gupta, "Objective measures of non-adherence in cardiometabolic diseases: A review focused on urine biochemical screening," *Patient Preference and Adherence*, vol. 13. Dove Medical Press Ltd., pp. 537–547, 2019. doi: 10.2147/PPA.S162215.
[26] J. J. Pitt, "Principles and Applications of Liquid Chromatography-Mass Spectrometry in Clinical Biochemistry," *Clin Biochem Rev*, vol. 30, no. 1, p. 19, Feb. 2009, Accessed: May 25, 2024. [Online]. Available: /pmc/articles/PMC2643089/ (accessed June 6, 2024)
[27] K. N. Patel, J. K. Patel, M. P. Patel, G. C. Rajput, and H. A. Patel, "Introduction to hyphenated techniques and their applications in pharmacy," *Pharm Methods*, vol. 1, no. 1, pp. 2–13, 2010, doi: https://doi.org/10.1016/S2229-4708(10)11002-4.
[28] A. P. Kengne *et al.*, "Impact of poor medication adherence on clinical outcomes and health resource utilization in patients with hypertension and/or dyslipidemia: systematic review," *Expert Rev Pharmacoecon Outcomes Res*, vol. 24, no. 1, pp. 143–154, 2024, doi: 10.1080/14737167.2023.2266135.
[29] P. Trueman and D. Taylor, "Evaluation of the Scale, Causes and Costs of Waste Medicines," University of London School of Pharmacy, 2010. ISBN: 9780902936201
[30] D. Prieto-Merino *et al.*, "Estimating proportion of days covered (PDC) using real-world online medicine suppliers' datasets," *J Pharm Policy Pract*, vol. 14, no. 1, Dec. 2021, pp.1-14, doi: 10.1186/s40545-021-00385-w.
[31] P. J. Cvietusa *et al.*, "Digital Communication Technology: Does Offering a Choice of Modality Improve Medication Adherence and Outcomes in a Persistent Asthma Population?," *Perm J*, vol. 25, pp. 20–189, 2020, doi: 10.7812/TPP/20.189.
[32] L. Zallman, A. Bearse, C. West, D. Bor, and D. McCormick, "Patient preferences and access to text messaging for health care reminders in a safety-net setting," *Inform Health Soc Care*, vol. 42, no. 1, pp. 32–42, Jan. 2017, doi: 10.3109/17538157.2015.1113177.
[33] S. M. McPhail, M. Schippers, C. A. Maher, and A. L.

Marshall, "Patient Preferences for Receiving Remote Communication Support for Lifestyle Physical Activity Behaviour Change: The Perspective of Patients with Musculoskeletal Disorders from Three Hospital Services," *Biomed Res Int*, vol. 2015, 2015, doi: 10.1155/2015/390352.

[34] B. Malin, T. Kalganova, E. Nwokoro, and J. Hinton, *Medication Adherence Prediction for Homecare Patients, Using Medication Delivery Data*. IARIA, 2023. Accessed: Jan. 12, 2024. [Online]. Available: https://www.thinkmind.org/index.php?view=article&articleid=healthinfo_2023_1_60_80027 (accessed June 6, 2024)

[35] S. Al Zoubi, L. Gharaibeh, H. M. Jaber, and Z. Al-Zoubi, "Household Drug Stockpiling and Panic Buying of Drugs During the COVID-19 Pandemic: A Study From Jordan," *Front Pharmacol*, vol. 12, Dec. 2021, doi: 10.3389/fphar.2021.813405.

[36] I. Arnet, M. J. Kooij, M. Messerli, K. E. Hersberger, E. R. Heerdink, and M. Bouvy, "Proposal of Standardization to Assess Adherence With Medication Records: Methodology Matters," *Annals of Pharmacotherapy*, vol. 50, no. 5, pp. 360–368, Feb. 2016, doi: 10.1177/1060028016634106.

[37] MHCLG, OCSI, NISRA, and Scottish Government, "Index of Multiple Deprivation," 2015. doi: 10.20390/enginddepriv2015.

Fostering Trust and Quantifying Value of AI and ML

Dalmo Cirne
Machine Learning for Financials
Workday
Boulder, Colorado, USA
email: dalmo.cirne@workday.com

Veena Calambur
Responsible AI
Workday
Princeton, New Jersey, USA
veena.calambur@workday.com

***Abstract*—Artificial Intelligence (AI) and Machine Learning (ML) providers have a responsibility to develop valid and reliable systems. Much has been discussed about trusting AI and ML inferences (the process of running live data through a trained AI model to make a prediction or solve a task), but little has been done to define what that means. Those in the space of ML-based products are familiar with topics such as transparency, explainability, safety, bias, and so forth. Yet, there are no frameworks to quantify and measure those. Producing ever more trustworthy machine learning inferences is a path to increase the value of products (i.e., increased trust in the results) and to engage in conversations with users to gather feedback to improve products. In this paper, we begin by examining the dynamic of trust between a provider (Trustor) and users (Trustees). Trustors are required to be trusting and trustworthy, whereas trustees need not be trusting nor trustworthy. The challenge for trustors is to provide results that are good enough to make a trustee increase their level of trust above a minimum threshold for: 1- doing business together; 2- continuation of service. We conclude by defining and proposing a framework, and a set of viable metrics, to be used for computing a *trust score* and objectively understand how trustworthy a machine learning system can claim to be, plus their behavior over time.**

Keywords-artificial intelligence, machine learning, trust, game theory.

I. INTRODUCTION

Much has been said about responsible Artificial Intelligence (AI), but the majority of those conversations are high-level and focused on defining principles—which are important for defining direction—but are rarely coupled with the actual operation of ML-based systems.

Measuring the increase or decrease of trust in this technology is a gap that needs to be addressed, and that is the main proposal of this paper: a quantitative framework to be used in computing the trustworthiness of AI and ML systems. Here, trust is defined as the willingness to interact with an AI/ML system while being aware that a model inference [1] is fallible.

The framework, however, is not without its challenges. There are several other elements to be considered in an AI/ML-powered system in order for it to gain the trust of its users. Good inferences are one of them, but so is data privacy, mitigating bias, measuring qualitative aspects, tracking the trust level over time, model training automation, and so on.

The paradigm explored in this paper assumes that trust is built by the trustor's initial act, signaling that the actor is trustworthy. More specifically, the trustor's act would be to invest in building a product and offer it to customers with the promise that it will generate value to them; more value than what is paid in return for the service. The trustor decides how much to invest, and the trustee decides whether to reciprocate and give continuity to the business relationship.

Note that the trustee does not have to be held to similar standards for trustworthiness as the trustor. The objective is to make the customers trusting—above a minimum threshold T—as to engage in the *Trust Games* [2]. These games are extensions built on top of the *Game Theory* [3]. Furthermore, trust has a temporal element to it. Once established, there are no guarantees that there will be a continuation. Therefore, this is an extensive form of interaction where both actors collaborate and observe each other, reacting to historical actions from one another.

A global study, conducted by the services and consulting firm KPMG, and named "Trust in Artificial Intelligence [4]," has found that there is a wariness sentiment in large sections of the workforce in general. The people surveyed in the study expressed concern about trusting those systems, from financials to human capital management products. The framework proposed in this paper will help address such sentiment by quantifying and measuring trust in AI and ML. The results can then be shared with the workforce or the population as a whole to help them better understand how ML-based solutions function and in turn, develop a positive sentiment towards adopting such products.

The rest of the paper is structured as follows. In Section II, we examine the dynamic of trust between a provider (Trustor) and users (Trustees). In Section III, we propose a quantification of trust over many iterations between trustor and trustee. In Section IV, we define a minimum trust threshold. In Section V, we present simulations of the quantification of trust. In Section VI, we present the categories for measuring trust. In Section VII, we demonstrate how the trust score can be practically implemented. In Section VIII, we define a region of fair trading between trustor and trustee. Section IX concludes our work.

II. TRUST GAMES

The motion of a *trust game* is developed around two actors: a trustor and a trustee. The trustor has a service of value V to offer to a trustee. The value in question is *quality machine learning inferences*. ML is implemented as a software service, and by its nature, software can be replicated to any number n of customers without physical constraints. Thus, V can be offered independently and concurrently to all customers.

It could be the case that the value V of inferences may be only partially absorbed by a trustee. The limited, portioned consumption could be due to a variety of reasons, including, but not limited to: eligibility or capacity to use all the features (i.e., satisfies all requirements), service subscription tiers, users have yet to be trained.

In order to represent the range of scenarios where the trustor may transfer the entirety of value V or a smaller portion of it, we introduce a multiplier p, where $\{p \in \mathbb{R} \mid 0 \leq p \leq 1\}$. Therefore, the initial remittance sent by trustor u is:

$$R_u = pV \tag{1}$$

Depending on the quality of the trustor's results, trustees' perception of value may be magnified or reduced by a factor K, where $\{K \in \mathbb{R}\}$. For $K > 1$, it means that the trustor improved the efficiency of operations for the trustee (they do better than operating on their own). For $K = 1$, the trustee is operating at the same efficiency, and for $K < 1$ (negative values are also possible) the trustee is less efficient than before they started using the service. The initial perceived gain received by trustee v is:

$$\begin{aligned} G_v &= KR_u \\ &= KpV \end{aligned} \tag{2}$$

A trustee is free to reciprocate or not. During a trial period, they may choose to decline further service. Even if under contract, they may choose to skip renewal. On the other hand, assuming that the value received from ML inferences improved their efficiency, the incentive is to continue to engage. In either case, a trustee will give back a portion q of the gain received, where $\{q \in \mathbb{R} \mid 0 \leq q < 1\}$. The value sent back may take the form of monetary payment for the service, interviews, usability feedback, labeling of transactions, or a combination of those. The repayment B expected by trustor u is therefore:

$$\begin{aligned} B_u &= qG_v \\ &= qKpV \end{aligned} \tag{3}$$

There could be a consideration to introduce a magnification factor on the repayment from trustee v. That, however, is not necessary in the scope of this paper since trustees do not need to be trustworthy; the trustor u is not evaluating whether to trust them or not.

Fig. 1 represents the flow of the initial step in this trust game. The blue line segment represents the range of possible values delivered to trustees by the trustor, the large blue circle is the magnification factor applied to the value delivered, and the orange line segment represents the range of possible values reciprocated to the trustor by a trustee.

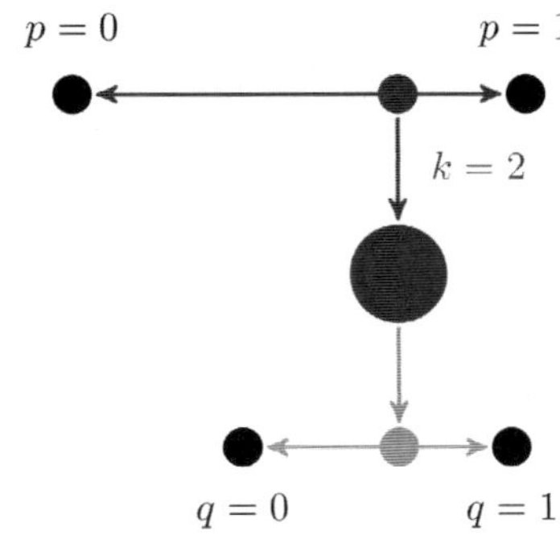

Figure 1. Trust Game payoffs.

Regarding the magnification factor, when $K > 1$, the value received back by trustor u is positive and enables the necessary conditions for an extensive form of the trust game (long-term engagement). It becomes a strong indicator that trustee v trustiness towards trustor u is equal or above the minimum threshold T, where $\{T \in \mathbb{R} \mid 0 \leq T \leq 1\}$.

When $0 \leq K < 1$, the service is causing the trustee some form of disruption (in the sense that efficiency has dropped below the level prior to using the service). This would be acceptable during the development phase of a product where the trustee takes part in a beta test program. In such a situation, the trustee sees a benefit in participating, assuming future value in adopting the service and the ability to harvest the benefits early on.

The worst-case scenario happens when $K < 0$. This could lead to rapid erosion of trustor u trustworthiness, customer churn, and other negative outcomes.

III. Quantifying Trust

The aim of this trust game is to create the circumstances necessary for repeated interactions between trustor and trustee.

After the initial remittance R_u, given by (1), there may be a residual value r on the trustor's side that a trustee did not take advantage of. For instance, maybe not all product features are being used, inference happens in batches and data is yet to be sent through the pipeline, or some other reason. That residual value is what is left from V:

$$\begin{aligned} r_u &= V - R_u \\ &= V - pV \\ &= (1-p)V \end{aligned} \tag{4}$$

The accumulated value A for trustor u upon completing the first cycle is the residual value r_u (4) plus the repayment B_u (3) received from the trustee:

$$\begin{aligned} A_u^{\text{1st cycle}} &= r_u^1 + B_u^1 \\ &= (1-p_1)V + q_1 K_1 p_1 V \\ &= V(1 - p_1 + q_1 K_1 p_1) \end{aligned} \tag{5}$$

On the trustee's side, they will have received a value of G_v (2) and given back a portion q of it. The net gain N for trustee v at the end of the first cycle is:

$$N_v^{\text{1st cycle}} = G_v^1 - q_1 G_v^1 = (1 - q_1) K_1 p_1 V \quad (6)$$

Generalizing the gains for trustor and trustee for n cycles of the trust game, we have equations for trustor:

$$A_u = V \left(1 - \sum_{i=1}^{n} p_i + \sum_{i=1}^{n} (q_i) \sum_{i=1}^{n} (K_i) \sum_{i=1}^{n} (p_i) \right) \quad (7)$$

and trustee:

$$N_v = V \left(1 - \sum_{i=1}^{n} q_i \right) \sum_{i=1}^{n} (K_i) \sum_{i=1}^{n} (p_i) \quad (8)$$

The objective is to maximize the payoff to the trustee and trustor—possibly skewed towards the trustee. As such, trust has to be repaid [5] (i.e., $q > 0$). The trustor benefits from economies of scale by the aggregate of payoffs from all trustees.

IV. Threshold

For a trustor to increase its trustworthiness (W_u) in the eyes of a trustee, the gains delivered by the service must be higher than if the trustee was operating on their own. Such condition is satisfied by the following system of inequalities:

$$W_u \subseteq \begin{cases} pV \geq T \\ K \geq 1 \end{cases} \quad (9)$$

That happens when the value of the remittance R_u is equal or greater than the threshold T (the value sent is at a minimum equal to the perceived value received), and the magnification factor K is greater or equal to one.

Being a system of inequalities, it is also possible to have a lower remittance ($pV < T$) and increase trustworthiness, as long as the magnification factor is large enough ($K \gg 1$) to make up for the shortfall. Although plausible, this would be uncommon.

V. Simulations

The following is a set of four simulations testing scenarios from fostering to eroding trust as a result of the quality of machine learning inference.

All the simulations begin from the same exact starting point, where it is assumed that the potential value of a product being offered to customers is of one million points (1,000,000). The starting number is an arbitrary value and could have been any positive number. We want to observe the shape of the curve formed from plotting interaction cycle after interaction cycle.

The hypothesis is that a trustee would increase their trustiness level towards the trustor by providing good machine learning inferences. Conversely, less than good enough results would have the opposite effect (i.e., erode trust).

Notice that throughout all four simulations, all parameters are kept the same, varying only the magnification factor K.

A. Simulation 1: Machine Learning Inferences Add Value

For this simulation, we will go step-by-step in the first interaction. For subsequent simulations, only the final graph plots will be shown. Irrespective of the simulation, they all can be reproduced using the source code [6] that accompanies this paper.

Assume that in the first cycle iteration, the trustor begins with V = 1,000,000 points and is able to send a remittance of 65% ($R_u = 0.65\times$1,000,000) of inference value to a trustee. The magnification factor perceived by the trustee is $K = 2$, thus, the gain becomes 1,300,000 ($G_v = 2\times$650,000) points.

The trustee sends a portion ($q = 0.14$) of the value back by interacting with the user interface, providing a feedback label, and paying for the service. The rebate received by the trustor is 182,000 ($B_u = 0.14\times$1,300,000) points.

Adding the rebate to the residual value ($r_u = 0.35\times$1,000,000), the trustor's accumulated gain equals 532,000 (A_u = 350,000 + 182,000) points, and the trustee's gain would be 1,118,000 ($N_v = 0.86\times$ 1,300,000) points.

First, the trustee's perception was that they received more value than what the trustor had to offer due to the magnification factor (win). Second, the trustor received a rebate in various formats—accruing value that was not there before (win). And third, after the aggregate across all trustees, the trustor will have accumulated more than the initial value offered (win).

In Fig. 2, we can see the shape of the curve showing the accumulated gains for both trustor and trustee for the four cycles of the simulation.

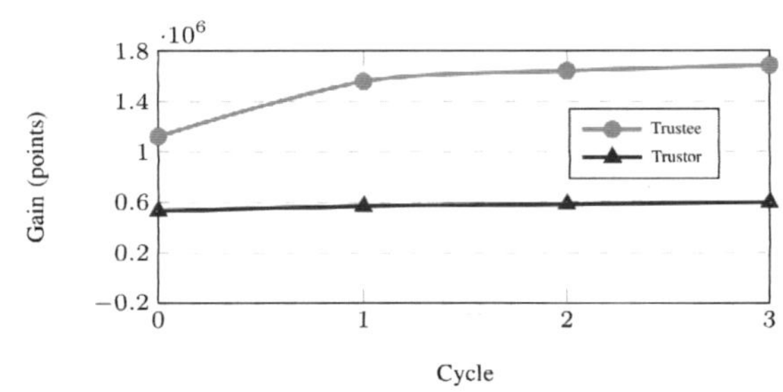

Figure 2. Accumulated gains ($K > 1$).

B. Simulation 2: Machine Learning Inferences Are Neutral

For the second simulation, a neutral magnification factor ($K = 1$) is being simulated. The value sent by the trustor and the value received by the trustee are perceived equally. The curve with the accumulated gains can be seen in Fig. 3. The trustee marginally sees an increase in the received value, whereas the trustor sees a small decline.

This scenario could be acceptable depending on the scale of the service and number of trustees, since the trustor's final gain is the aggregate from all trustees.

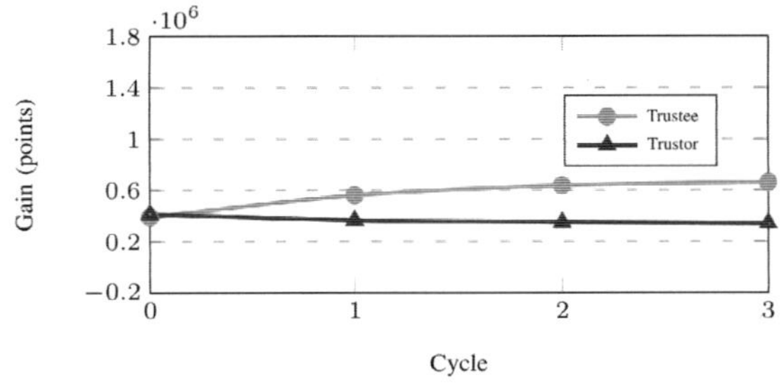

Figure 3. Accumulated Gains ($K = 1$).

C. Simulation 3: Machine Learning Inferences Are Causing Inefficiencies

The third simulation, Fig. 4, shows a scenario where inefficiencies are being brought upon the trustee ($0 \leq K < 1$). Their gains are at best negligible, and at the same time there is a significant drop in the trustor's gains.

This situation would be plausible and acceptable only during the development phase of a product, where a trustee would have accepted to be an early adopter of the service.

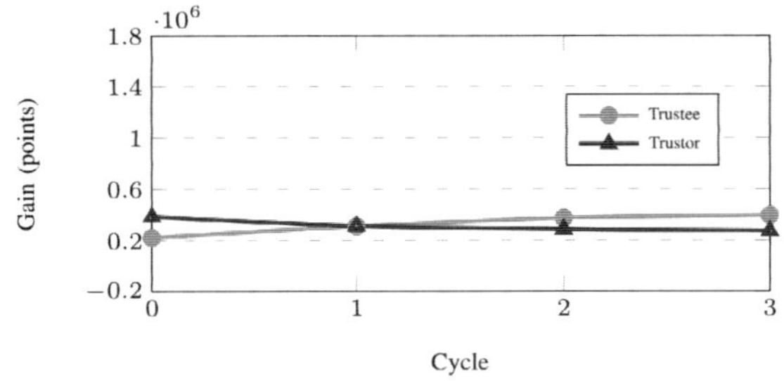

Figure 4. Accumulated Gains ($0 \leq K < 1$).

D. Simulation 4: Machine Learning Inferences Are Rapidly Eroding Trust

The last simulation shows the worst-case scenario where machine learning inferences erode the trustor's trustworthiness ($K < 0$), reducing the trustee's ability to trust. Fig. 5 shows how, in this scenario, there are negative gains (loss) for trustors and trustees. They are both worse off with the service, compared to operating without it.

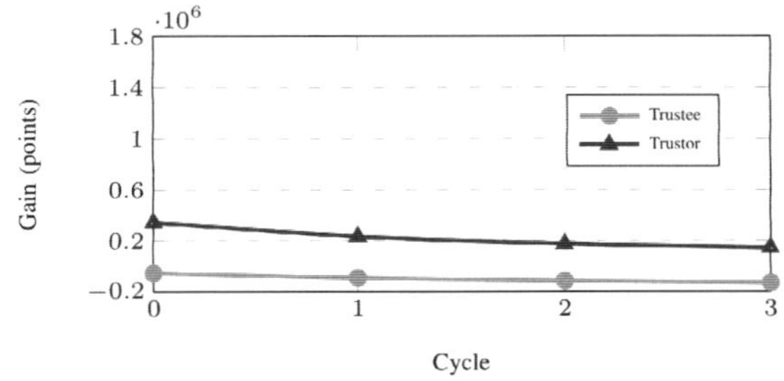

Figure 5. Accumulated Gains ($K < 0$).

VI. MEASURING AI AND ML RISK

One of the intended outcomes of quantifying trust is to define the metrics of risk. Then, it can be measured and monitored.

The National Institute of Standards and Technology (NIST) has published a study called "Artificial Intelligence Risk Management Framework (AI RMF)" [7]. There, they claim that there is a finite set of traits that approximate to a good definition for a system to be trustworthy. We aim to extend the concepts to implement quantitative metrics and create a viable framework to monitor trustworthiness. NIST identifies seven broad categories. They are (The color-coded categories will be useful later in this paper when understanding an example of the framework implementation):

1) Reliability and Validity
2) Safety
3) Security and Resilience
4) Accountability and Transparency
5) Explainability and Interpretability
6) Privacy
7) Bias Management

For each of those categories, this paper proposes metrics that can be measured and used to compute a *trust score*.

A. Reliability and Validity

A system is reliable when it does its job as intended, with minimal disruption of service [8], and when the results produced can be confirmed through objective evidence that the requirements were met [9]. The following are proposed metrics for reliability and validity:

- Uninterrupted uptime.
- Number of crashes.
- True Positives, True Negatives, False Positives, False Negatives.
- Latency between inquiry and returning results.
- Additionally, depending on the specific use case, the adoption of specific metrics (Accuracy, F1 [10], BLEU [11], SuperGLUE [12], HELM [13]) is encouraged.

B. Safety

The state of the data, the system, the people, and the subject of inferences are not at a meaningful risk, that extends beyond physical safety. Those are metrics to represent that:

- System design is represented in a diagram and is peer-reviewed, where appropriate.
- Data handling is done via a well-defined process with clear controls that align with existing regulations and oversight.
- A report that details to customers which data fields are used in training models.
- Access to the data is done with the consent of customers and is system-wide enforced by access roles.
- Once a model architecture is defined, models are trained using automation that does not require the intervention or participation of personnel.

C. Security and Resilience

Everyday operations have the ability to withstand adverse events or unexpected changes in the use or functioning of the environment.

- Systems and people have explicit credentials to run and/or access the data.
- Isolation of data and systems from unauthorized agents.
- Implementation of multiple scopes of granted access/runtime, with each agent being assigned the minimum necessary level to perform a task.

D. *Accountability and Transparency*

Accountability and transparency of operations are necessary conditions for being trustworthy and increasing trust.

- Report the data used in model training back to customers. The system must have a report, accessible by customers, that shows what data was used to train models.

E. *Explainable and Interpretable*

Explainability: the representation of the mechanisms underlying AI systems' operations [7].

Interpretability: the meaning of AI systems' outputs in the context of their designed functional purposes [7].

- Identification of the principal component of inference results.
- Displaying similar records can explain an inference by analogy.
- The ratio between the number of explanations given over the total number of explainable records would be the key metric.

F. *Privacy*

The norms and practices that help safeguard human autonomy, identity, and dignity. Freedom from intrusion, limiting observation, obtaining consent prior to disclosing or using Personally Identifiable Information (PII).

- Definition and implementation of Legal, Privacy, and Responsibility frameworks.
- Transforming raw data into embeddings.
- De-identification and aggregation.
- Privacy awareness and training of the people involved.

G. *Bias Management*

Establish reasonable and viable frameworks for error prevention, then optimization of execution for error correction.

- Number of reported and confirmed use cases.
- Subsequently, it can be offset by releasing new model versions that address those issues.

VII. IMPLEMENTATION

Each of the metrics discussed in the "MEASURING AI AND ML RISK" section become numeric entries in a vector M, and associated with it, there is a stochastic vector S containing weights representing how important each of the traits are in contributing to the creation of value and trustworthiness.

The dot product between M and S produces the *Trust Score* W (10) which is our metric to signify value and trust.

$$W = M \cdot S^{\mathrm{T}} \tag{10}$$

The following is a simulated example of numeric scores attributed to items in each of the 7 categories. The names next to the entries of vector M describe each item, as previously proposed, and the colors represent the categories.

The entries in vector M related to True Positives (TP), True Negatives (TN), False Positives (FP), and False Negatives (FN) share Number of Inferences as common denominator. It is important to clarify that this is the total number of inferences where it is possible to categorize them as [TP, TN, FP, FN]. In many cases, the categorization of an inference is unknowable.

Note that the stochastic vector S contains negative entries. Those are to penalize the corresponding metric in vector M and reduce the trust score. For example, the higher the number of crashes, the lower the score.

$$M = \begin{array}{r} \text{Uptime} \\ \text{Number of Crashes} \\ \text{True Positives/Number of Inferences} \\ \text{True Negatives/Number of Inferences} \\ \text{False Positives/Number of Inferences} \\ \text{False Negatives/Number of Inferences} \\ \text{System Design} \\ \text{Data Handling Processes} \\ \text{Data Points Report} \\ \text{Data Access Consent} \\ \text{Touchless Model Training} \\ \text{Access Control} \\ \text{Tiered Access} \\ \text{Data Isolation} \\ \text{Data Usage Report} \\ \text{Inference Explanation} \\ \text{Present Similar Records} \\ \text{Number of Explanation/Total Inferences} \\ \text{Legal and Privacy Frameworks} \\ \text{De-identification of Data} \\ \text{Privacy Training} \\ \text{Number of Confirmed Bias Issues} \\ \text{Number of Deployed Bias Fixes} \end{array} \begin{bmatrix} 99.99\% \\ 3 \\ 60.00\% \\ 34.29\% \\ 4.29\% \\ 1.43\% \\ 1 \\ 1 \\ 1 \\ 1 \\ 1 \\ 1 \\ 1 \\ 1 \\ 1 \\ 40.00\% \\ 20.00\% \\ 10.00\% \\ 1 \\ 0 \\ 1 \\ 2 \\ 1 \end{bmatrix} \tag{11}$$

$$S = \begin{bmatrix} 0.14 \\ -0.14 \\ 0.24 \\ 0.24 \\ -0.10 \\ -0.10 \\ 0.01 \\ 0.02 \\ 0.02 \\ 0.01 \\ 0.04 \\ 0.06 \\ 0.07 \\ 0.06 \\ 0.05 \\ 0.05 \\ 0.05 \\ 0.05 \\ 0.06 \\ 0.05 \\ 0.02 \\ -0.06 \\ 0.06 \end{bmatrix} \tag{12}$$

Metrics of a qualitative nature are expressed numerically in vector M as 0 or 1, representing their absence or presence. For instance, in the "Accountability and Transparency" section, we mention implementing a report that shows what data was used in training models. Either the report is available, or it is not. Although there may be degrees of completion of adoption in an organization, we are focused on the customer's perspective, that either the item is in place or it is not.

If possible, it will be good to keep the trust score within the [–1, 1] range, where –1 is the worst possible score, and 1 is the best score. We can use (13) to apply this range constraint to the result of the *trust score* computation.

$$W = min(1, max(W, -1)) \quad (13)$$

In the case of the example provided in (11) and (12), the trust score would be:

$$W = 0.635557$$

A. *Temporality*

The trust score W is expected to display fluctuations over time. Since systems could experience an occasional malfunction, a model performance degradation, or an unanticipated incident, however, those fluctuations are presumed to be narrow and gentle, rather than wide and abrupt like a roller coaster.

It is plausible to imagine that after a few cycles of significant fluctuations in the *trust score*, a customer would disengage and discontinue usage of the product.

VIII. FAIR TRADING

Fairness is an intrinsic concept associated with trust. Assuming that the trustor is providing value to a trustee, and in return the trustee is returning something of value to the trustor, the next step is to find that region of equilibrium where both parties accept the exchange as fair trade.

In addition, the region must be defined in such a way that it scales up or down proportionally to the exchange of value. For instance, imagine that a trustor went from providing one service, to providing two or three services; the trustor will expect to charge the trustee more. This section shows how this region of equilibrium is computed in such way that it remains a fair trade for both parties.

From (5) and (6), we know that the accumulated value A_u by the trustor is the product's residual value left, plus the repayment value sent by trustees. The net gain N_v by trustees is the received magnified value, minus the repayment.

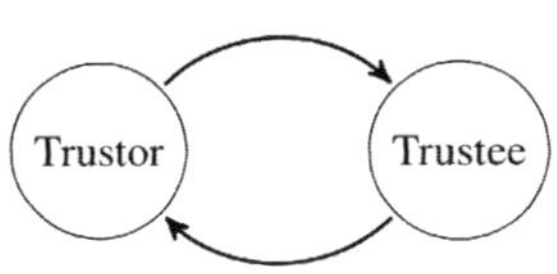

$$A' = (1 - p)A + qN \quad (14)$$

$$N' = KpA - qN \quad (15)$$

From the previous paragraph, we see that (14) and (15) express how the next state of accumulation A' and net gain N' are computed. Expressing them in matrix format gives us (16).

$$\begin{pmatrix} A' \\ N' \end{pmatrix} = \begin{pmatrix} 1-p & q \\ Kp & -q \end{pmatrix} \begin{pmatrix} A \\ N \end{pmatrix} \quad (16)$$

We want to find that region of values that would make the trade between trustor and trustee to be considered fair.

From Linear Algebra, we know that the eigenvectors [14] of a matrix will give us the space that could scale—but otherwise would remain unchanged—irrespective of the linear transformation applied to it (assuming that the eigenvectors are linearly independent and have no imaginary i component).

Given that the conditions are satisfied, the linear transformation would be the addition or subtraction of services and the proportional increase or decrease of charges and feedback interactions, in other words, scaling up, down, or neutral.

The eigenvector associated with the largest, positive eigenvalue of the matrix shown in (16) can be interpreted as the region where both parties should consider transactions between them as fair trade, thus contributing to preventing the erosion of trust.

Let us build an example. Assume that the percentage of remitted value p, the repayment portion q, and magnification factor K have the following values:

$$p = 0.85, \; q = 0.14, \; K = 2$$

Substituting these values in the matrix from (16) leads us to:

$$\begin{pmatrix} A' \\ N' \end{pmatrix} = \begin{pmatrix} 0.15 & 0.14 \\ 1.7 & -0.14 \end{pmatrix} \begin{pmatrix} A \\ N \end{pmatrix} \quad (17)$$

One condition that needs to be satisfied is that the vectors—derived from the matrix in (17)—are linearly independent, so they can span the space being considered. Otherwise, they would only represent a sub-space and not necessarily produce the fair trade region we aim for.

As you can see in Fig. 6, the vectors are linearly independent and also satisfy the other conditions to compute the eigenvectors to determine the fair trade region between trustor and trustee.

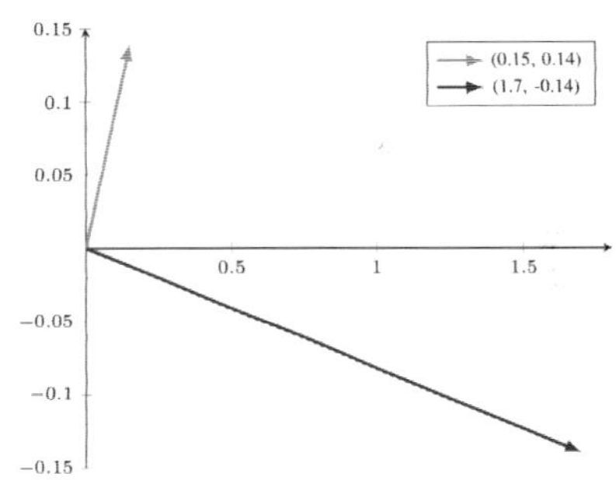

Figure 6. Linearly independent vectors.

The next step is to compute its eigenvalues and eigenvectors, then find the line defined by the eigenvector associated with the largest eigenvalue.

$$\lambda_1^{\downarrow} = 0.513945 \quad (18)$$

$$\lambda_2 = -0.503945 \quad (19)$$

$$E_{\lambda_1} = \begin{pmatrix} 0.384674 \\ 1 \end{pmatrix} \quad (20)$$

$$E_{\lambda_2} = \begin{pmatrix} -0.214085 \\ 1 \end{pmatrix} \quad (21)$$

The largest eigenvalue is $\lambda_1^{\downarrow}$, thus our eigenvector of interest is E_{λ_1}. In order to find the line defined by E_{λ_1} coordinates, we just need to compute its slope, since the eigenvector starts at the origin (0, 0).

$$y = mx + b \tag{22}$$

$$m = \frac{1 - 0}{0.384674 - 0} = 2.599604 \tag{23}$$

$$b = 0 \tag{24}$$

$$y = 2.599604\,x \tag{25}$$

Fig. 7 shows the eigenvector E_{λ_1} in red and the line derived by it, and defined by (25), in blue. The line characterizes the fair trade region since any point on it carries the maximum accumulated value A and net gains N, for the trustor and trustee, respectively.

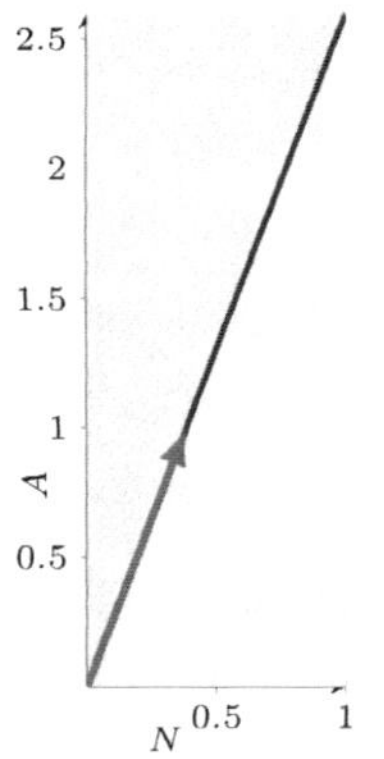

Figure 7. Fair trade region.

The colored areas above and below the line represent the regions where either the trustor would accumulate more value (orange) or the trustee would retain more gains (green).

IX. Conclusion

This paper takes a step forward in contributing to the conversation about trust in ML-based systems. It presented a realistic and viable framework to compute a trust score and demonstrated that good machine learning inference results satisfy a valid criterion to increase a trustor's trustworthiness, allowing for trustees to be more trusting.

A strong motivation exists to provide inferences only when a minimum confidence level has been cleared. It would be preferable to not produce a result than to provide a low-confidence one. When nothing is provided, a customer can still operate at their nominal level of productivity.

We established the items of interest for measuring, defined a system to compute and weigh each contribution, and identified the region of fair trade where win-win relationships between trustor and trustee can take place and scale up or down.

Trust has a temporal nature to it; its behavior is not linear, but instead it is expected to oscillate with gentle fluctuations. Trust and value add are not only earned, but also require maintenance over time.

Lastly, we demonstrated that it is possible to establish a region of fair trading where both trustors and trustees perceive fairness in the exchange of value.

References

[1] K. Martineau, "What is AI inferencing?" 2023. [Online]. Available: https://research.ibm.com/blog/AI-inference-explained (Last accessed: 2024-05-14)

[2] J. Berg, J. Dickhaut, and K. McCabe, "Trust, reciprocity, and social history," *Games and Economic Behavior*, vol. 10, no. 1, pp. 122–142, 1995. [Online]. Available: https://www.sciencedirect.com/science/article/pii/S0899825685710275 (Last accessed: 2024-05-14)

[3] J. von Neumann and O. Morgenstern, *Theory of Games and Economic Behavior*. Princeton University Press, 1944.

[4] N. Gillespie, S. Lockey, C. Curtis, J. Pool, and A. Ali, "Trust in artificial intelligence: A global study," KPMG - The University of Queensland, Tech. Rep., 2023. [Online]. Available: https://doi.org/10.14264/00d3c94 (Last accessed: 2024-05-14)

[5] D. Kreps, "Corporate culture and economic theory," *Perspectives on Positive Political Economy*, pp. 90–142, 1990.

[6] D. Cirne. (2023, 09) Simulations source code. [Online]. Available: https://gist.github.com/dcirne/8c74a2d8d5adaf59f9366a5212d41f22 (Last accessed: 2024-05-14)

[7] NIST, "Artificial intelligence risk management framework (ai rmf 1.0)," Tech. Rep., 01 2023. [Online]. Available: https://nvlpubs.nist.gov/nistpubs/ai/NIST.AI.100-1.pdf (Last accessed: 2024-05-14)

[8] "Trustworthiness — vocabulary," International Organization for Standardization, Geneva, Switzerland, Technical Specification ISO/IEC TS 5723:2022(en), 2022.

[9] "Quality standard," International Organization for Standardization, Geneva, Switzerland, Technical Specification ISO/IEC TS 9001:2015(en), 2015.

[10] Z. C. Lipton, C. Elkan, and B. Narayanaswamy, "Thresholding classifiers to maximize F1 score," 2014. [Online]. Available: https://arxiv.org/pdf/1402.1892.pdf (Last accessed: 2024-05-14)

[11] K. Papineni, S. Roukos, T. Ward, and W. Zhu "BLEU: a Method for Automatic Evaluation of Machine Translation." IBM, 2022. [Online]. Available: https://aclanthology.org/P02-1040/ (Last accessed: 2024-06-17)

[12] A. Wang et al, "SuperGLUE: A Stickier Benchmark for General-Purpose Language Understanding Systems", 2019. [Online]. Available: https://w4ngatang.github.io/static/papers/superglue.pdf (Last accessed: 2024-06-17)

[13] P. Liang et al, "Holistic evaluation of language models," 2022. [Online]. Available: https://arxiv.org/pdf/2211.09110.pdf (Last accessed: 2024-05-14)

[14] G. Strang, *Linear Algebra and Its Applications*, 4th ed. Cengage Learning, 2006.

[15] E. Parliament and C. of the European Union, "Regulation (EU) 2023/656 of the European Parliament and of the council of 14 June 2023 laying down harmonised rules on artificial intelligence and amending certain union legislative acts (artificial intelligence act)," pp. 1–231, 2023. [Online]. Available: https://eur-lex.europa.eu/legal-content/EN/TXT/?uri=CELEX:32023R0656 (Last accessed: 2024-05-14)

[16] C. Alós-Ferrer and F. Farolfi, "Trust games and beyond," *Frontiers in Neuroscience*, vol. 13, 09 2019. [Online]. Available: https://doi.org/10.3389/fnins.2019.00887 (Last accessed: 2024-05-14)

Phytopathogenic Status Induced by Xylella Fastidiosa in Olive Groves in Southern Italy Revealed by Visibility Graph Analysis of MODIS Satellite Evapotranspiration Time Series

Luciano Telesca and Rosa Lasaponara
Institute of Methodologies for Environmental Analysis
National Research Council
Tito, Italy
email: luciano.telesca@cnr.it; rosa.lasaponara@cnr.it

***Abstract*—The Visibility Graph (VG) has emerged as a widely used statistical method for characterizing the dynamical properties of time series. This method transforms time series into networks, wherein nodes represent the series values connected by their reciprocal "visibility." Recently, the VG has found applications in the statistical investigation of time series across various research fields. In this study, we leverage the VG to analyze the topological properties of Moderate Resolution Imaging Spectroradiometer (MODIS) satellite evapotranspiration time series in areas covered by olive groves in southern Italy, aiming to detect the presence of *Xylella Fastidiosa*—a highly destructive phytobacterium known for inducing olive quick decline syndrome in olive trees. Our findings suggest that employing the VG enables a very efficient discrimination between infected and healthy sites. This suggests the potential utility of this network analysis method as an operational tool for early diagnosis of plant deterioration caused by *Xylella fastidiosa*.**

Index Terms*—Visibility graph; network analysis; MODIS; evapotranspiration; Xylella Fastidiosa.

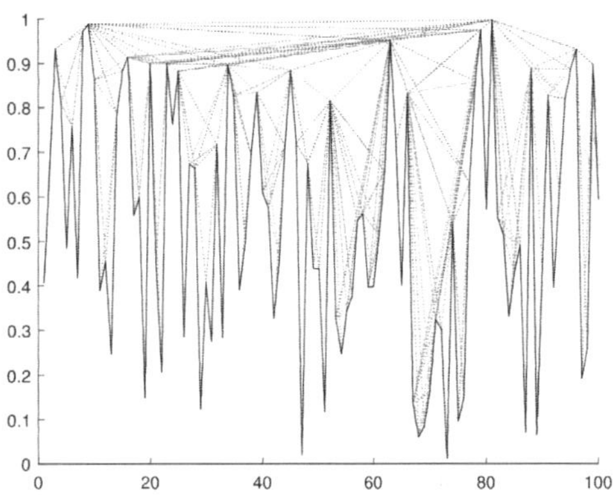

Fig. 1: Representations of the VG for a random signal.

I. Introduction

Invasive pests and alien plant bacteria emerge as significant global threats, capable of triggering severe plant diseases with profound consequences for both natural ecosystems and agricultural productivity. One such example is *Xylella Fastidiosa*, recognized as one of the most dangerous plant bacteria worldwide. This pathogen induces devastating diseases, particularly affecting grapes, citrus fruits, and olive trees. In the European Union, focusing solely on the impact on olive trees, estimates suggest that *Xylella Fastidiosa* can potentially cause an annual production loss of 5.5 billion euros, impacting 70% of the EU production value of mature olive trees. Hence, the timely detection of plant diseases induced by this bacterium become imperative for implementing measures to mitigate their impact [1].

In 2013, the presence of *Xylella Fastidiosa* was first identified in southeastern Italy [2]. Subsequently, it rapidly spred out to various other European countries, giving rise to a critical phytosanitary emergency [3].

Visual inspection stands as the predominant method of contrasting *Xylella Fastidiosa* due to its simplicity and cost-effectiveness; but its precision strongly depends on the subjective evaluation of disease severity.

Recently, Remote Sensing (RS) approaches have been given significant attention, particularly in the monitoring of vegetation dynamics, including those induced by plant diseases [4]. Various RS applications in phytopathology have concentrated on devising methodologies based on multi-temporal and multi-spectral satellite data for monitoring changes in land cover. Statistical approaches, such as principal component analysis [5] and curve-fitting methods [6], are well-established for detecting alterations in vegetation across the land surface.

The potential use of MODIS evapotranspiration (ET) satellite data for monitoring pest and parasite attacks at both landscape and field scales has been investigated in [7], [8], where the effectiveness of MODIS ET and other vegetation indices in assessing the deterioration of pine tree vegetation caused by the parasite *Toumeyella Parvicornis* was evidenced.

Furthermore, the application of multifractal detrended fluctuation analysis and the informational method of Fisher-Shannon on MODIS ET time series indicated the suitability of this satellite-derived data as a reliable indicator for assessing the pathogenic impact caused by *Xylella Fastidiosa* in olive trees [9]–[11].

In this paper, we apply the VG method to discern the presence of diseases induced by *Xylella Fastidiosa.* The VG method is used to characterize the topological properties of a signal and, in our context, is employed to analyze the temporal dynamics of MODIS ET satellite data of olive groves affected by *Xylella Fastidiosa.*

In Section II the applied methods of time series analysis will be described and in Section III the investigatred dataset will be presented. Section IV will show the obtained results that will be discussed in Section V.

II. METHODS

A. The visibility graph

The VG [12] converts a time series into a graph or network. It was applied in several research fields, like economics [13]–[15], weather forecasting [16], [17], medicine [18], oceanography [19], etc. The nodes of the graph are the values of the series and the links between them satisfies the following geometrical visbility rule:

$$y_c < y_b + (y_a - y_b)\frac{t_b - t_c}{t_b - t_a}, \tag{1}$$

where $t_a < t_c < t_b$. In practice, two values $y_a(t_a)$ and $y_b(t_b)$ are visible to each other if any other value $y_c(t_c)$ fulfils the condition from 1 (Figure 1 shows the application of the VG to a random signal). The adiancency matrix associated to VG is given by

$$A_{pq} = \begin{cases} 1 & \text{if nodes p and q are linked} \\ 0 & \text{if nodes p and q are not linked} \end{cases} \tag{2}$$

The visibility graph associated with a time series is characterized by the following properties: 1) connectivity: every node is connected to at least its closest neighbors on both the left and right sides; 2) undirectionality: the links between nodes do not have a defined direction; 3) invariance under affine transformations: the visibility graph remains unchanged when the time series data undergoes rescaling along both horizontal and vertical axes, as well as horizontal and vertical translations.

The connectivity degree $k_i = \sum_j A_{ij}$ is the number of links departing from a node i. Generally, the higher values of the signal are characterized by the larger connectivity degree, because they behave as hubs of the graph "attracting" more links than those converging to the lower ones.

The degree distribution $P(k)$ is an important quantity that explains some of the structure of the time series. For instance, it is well known that $P(k)$ behaves as an exponential or power-law function of the degree k for random or fractal time series, respectively [12]; while for a periodic series it is formed by a finite number of non-null values, with this number depending on the period [21].

B. The ROC analysis

Receiver Operating Characteristics (ROC) analysis is utilized to evaluate the performance of classifiers. In binary classification scenarios, instances are classified as either "positive" or "negative," and a classifier assigns these instances to predicted classes [20].

When assessing a classifier with respect to an instance, four potential outcomes can occur. The categorization of the instance is as follows: True Positive (TP) if it is positive and correctly classified as positive, False Negative (FN) if it is positive but incorrectly classified as negative, True Negative (TN) if it is negative and correctly classified as negative, False Positive (FP) if it is negative but erroneously classified as positive [20]. We can define the following ratios, the *True Positive rate* (TPr) and the *False Positive rate* (FPr)

$$TPr = \frac{Number \quad of \quad TP}{Total \quad positives}, \tag{3}$$

$$FPr = \frac{Number \quad of \quad FP}{Total \quad negatives}. \tag{4}$$

A ROC curve is a graphical representation with TPr plotted on the y-axis and FPr on the x-axis. The construction of the ROC curve proceeds as follows. Defining the two classes of instances as C_1 and C_2, all the values of the chosen parameter are arranged in ascending order. A threshold T is selected within the range of values, from the minimum to the maximum. Supposing that the mean of C_1 is larger than that of C_2, then, a TP is a value of C_1 that is above T, while a FP is a value that is below T. Thus, for each value of the threshold T within the range of minimum to maximum, the TPr and FPr can be calculated, yielding one point on the ROC curve. By varying the threshold value across the entire range and repeating this process, a curve can be traced through ROC space, known as the ROC curve. In ROC space, the point (0, 1) signifies perfect classification, and one point is considered superior to another if it lies to the northwest of the first point. The diagonal line, represented by the equation y = x, corresponds to random classification, while an effective classifier is depicted by a point located in the upper region of the ROC space.

Each point on the ROC curve corresponds to a tradeoff between TPr and FPr associated with a specific threshold. Typically, to optimize this tradeoff, the point on the ROC curve closest to (0, 1) is chosen, and the corresponding threshold is utilized for classification. Also, the Area Under the ROC Curve (AUC) is frequently employed to quantify the classifier's performance.

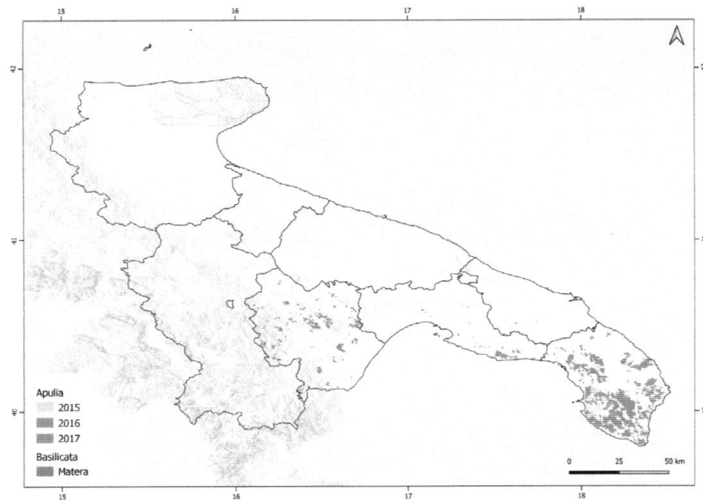

Fig. 2: Investigated area with Matera (unnifected) and X2015, X2016 and X2017 (infected) sites.

III. Data and study area

The primary visible indication of an infection caused by *Xylella Fastidiosa* in olive trees manifests as the desiccation of branches [22]. We analysed the MODIS ET data that possess the capability to monitor the water status of plants, enabling the detection of symptoms associated with this disease. The data exhibit a spatial resolution of 500m and an 8-day sampling rate. They are readily accessible online [23] and are also present in the Google Earth Engine (GEE) cloud database.

The ET is calculated summing up soil evaporation (E_s), canopy evaporation (E_c), and canopy transpiration (T_c):

$$ET = Es + Ec + Tc \tag{5}$$

$$\begin{aligned} E_s = f_w \frac{\Delta A_S + \frac{(1-f_c)\rho_a C_P (e_S - e_a)}{r_a^s}}{\Delta + \gamma \frac{r_S^S}{r_a^S}} \\ + RH^{\frac{(e_S - e_a)}{\beta_{sm}}} (1 - f_W) \frac{\Delta A_S + \frac{(1-f_c)\rho_a C_P (e_S - e_a)}{r_a^s}}{\Delta + \gamma \frac{r_S^S}{r_a^S}} \end{aligned} \tag{6}$$

$$E_c = f_w \frac{\Delta A_S + \frac{f_c \rho_a C_P (e_S - e_a)}{r_a^{wc}}}{\Delta + \gamma \frac{r_S^{wc}}{r_a^S}} \tag{7}$$

$$T_c = (1 - f_w) \frac{\Delta A_C + \frac{f_c \rho_a C_P (e_S - e_a)}{r_a^t}}{\Delta + \gamma (1 + \frac{r_S^t}{r_a^S})}. \tag{8}$$

where f_c is the canopy cover, f_w is the pixel wet surface fraction, *RH* is the relative humidity, Δ is the gradient of the saturation vapor pressure–temperature, A_s and A_c are the available energy to the soil and canopy, respectively, γ is the psychrometric constant, β_{sm} is a parameter related to the soil moisture constraint, r_s^s and r_a^s are the surface and aerodynamic resistance for the soil surface, r_s^{wc} and r_a^{wc} are the surface and aerodynamic resistance for the wet canopy evaporation and r_s^t and r_a^t are the surface and aerodynamic resistance for the canopy transpiration [24].

TABLE I: NUMBER OF PIXELS BEFORE AND AFTER THE GAP FILLING (in bold)

Matera	X2015	X2016	X2017
417	312	446	451
331	**219**	**334**	**371**

In this study, we investigated three datasets consisting of pixels extracted from olive groves affected by *Xylella fastidiosa*: one dataset corresponding to locations where the infection was identified in 2015 (X2015), another in 2016 (X2016), and the third in 2017 (X2017). As reference, we also analyzed a dataset of pixels from unaffected olive groves situated in the Matera area. This reference area shares comparable climatic and topographic conditions with the infected one. The investigated areas are shown in Figure 2. The ET datasets spans from 2010 to 2022, and each pixel's time series has a length of 575 samples, with missing data percentage less than 25%.

IV. Results

The VG can operate only with complete datasets, and therefore, we firstly addressed data gaps in each pixel time series. This was accomplished by replacing the gap with the average of values measured on the corresponding day from other years. In cases where the gap occurred on the same day across all years, the entire pixel was excluded from the analysis. Therefore, after excluding pixels where at least one gap persisted despite the gap-filling procedure, the number of analysed pixels for each dataset is shown in Table I. Figure 3 illustrates an example of gap-filling for a pixel time series.

We applied the VG (code available at [25]) and calculated the degree distribution for the time series of each pixel, as

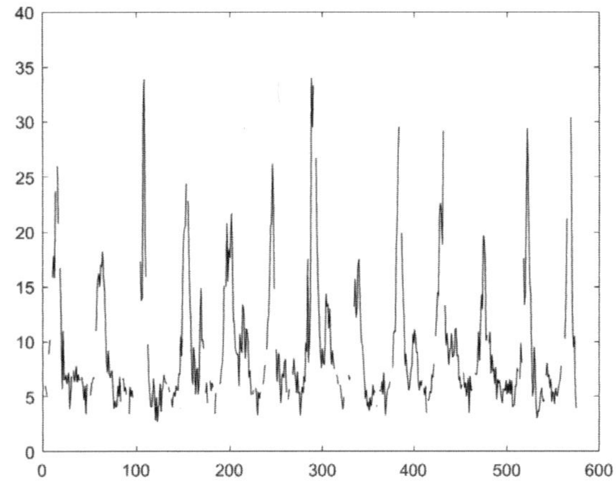

(a)

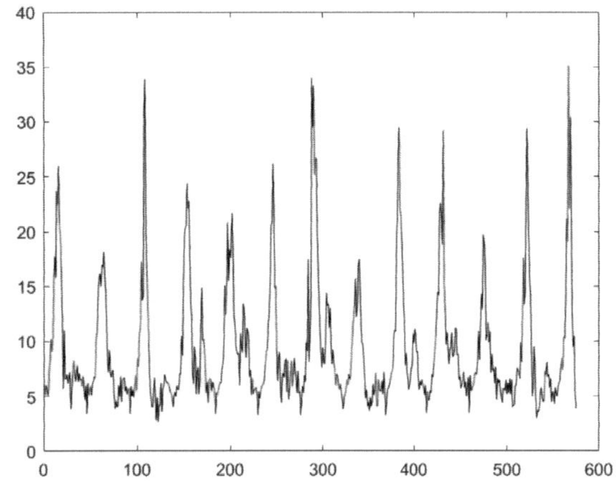

(b)

Fig. 3: A pixel time series before (a) and after (b) the gap-filling.

depicted in Figure 4, for every dataset, and also shown their respective averages.

To evaluate the classification performance of degree distribution $P(k)$, we employed the ROC curve that represents the relationship between the TPr (the fraction of infected pixels correctly classified as infected) and the FPr (the fraction of uninfected pixels incorrectly classified as infected). By fixing a specific value for the degree distribution k, we performed the ROC analysis for each k value, comparing each infected pixel dataset (X2015, X2016, and X2017) with each uninfected pixel dataset (Matera); this involved calculating the AUC_k, TPr_k, FPr_k, and the threshold T_k for each specific k value.

As an example, Figure 5 presents the ROC curve for the degree distribution value at $k = 10$ for X2015 and Matera datasets. The AUC of 0.75 indicates rather good classification performance between infected pixels in the X2015 dataset and uninfected pixels in the Matera dataset. The optimal threshold, identified at 0.0357, corresponds to TPR of 0.72 and a FPR of 0.30.

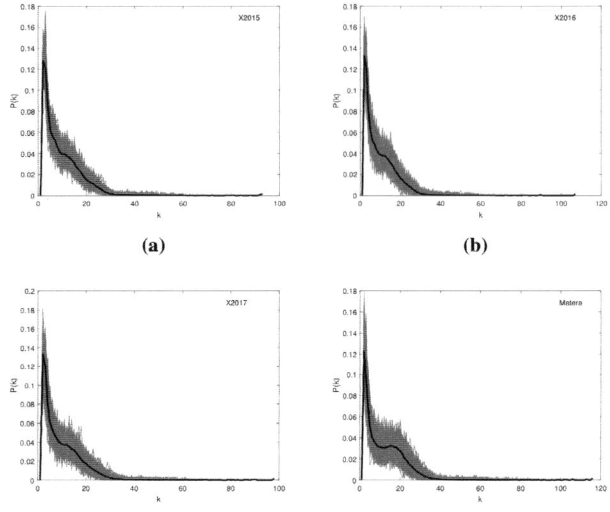

(a) (b) (c) (d)

Fig. 4: Degree distributions (red) and their average (black) of the X2015 (a), X2016 (b), X2017 (c) and Matera (d) ET datasets.

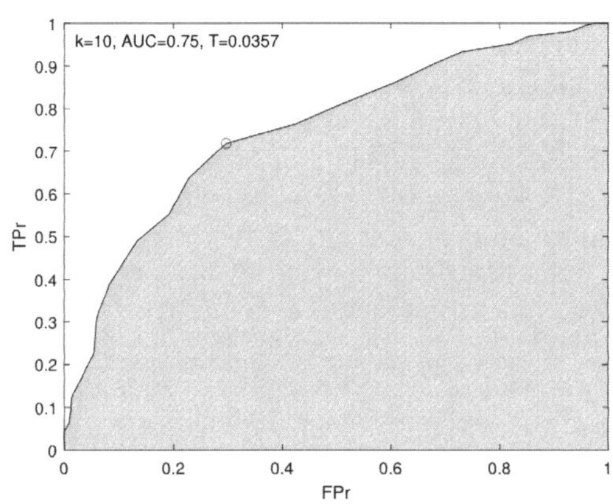

Fig. 5: ROC curve analysis for the degree distribution of the X2015 and Matera datasets at k=10. The AUC is 0.75, with a corresponding threshold of 0.0357, where the TPR is 0.72 and the FPR is 0.30.

TABLE II: RESULTS OF THE ROC ANALYSIS CORRESPONDING TO THE MAXIMUM OF AUC

datasets	ROC parameters				
	k	**AUC**	**TPr**	**FPr**	**T**
X2015-Matera	21	0.90	0.84	0.20	0.02
X2016-Matera	20	0.88	0.87	0.25	0.02
X2017-Matera	21	0.86	0.84	0.25	0.02

The results of the ROC analysis across various values of the degree k for the datasets X2015 and Matera are displayed in Figure 6. The AUC is generally used to quantify the classification performance. Thus we can select the optimal value of k as corresponding to the maximum AUC. In the

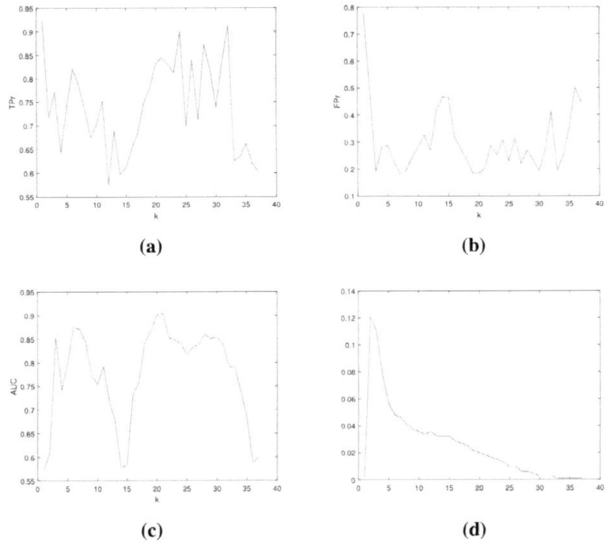

Fig. 6: ROC analysis for the degree distribution of X2015 and Matera datasets: a) TPr, b9 FPr, c) AUC and d) threshold.

specific case, the optimal value of k is determined to be 20, resulting in the following ROC parameters: AUC=0.90, TPr=0.83, FPr=0.18 and threshold T=0.02. A summary of the results obtained applying the ROC analysis to all the datsets are provided inTable II. The optimal value of k for which the AUC is maximized fluctuates between 20 and 21, resulting in AUC values ranging from 0.86 to 0.90, indicative of a highly effective classification performance. The TPr spans from 0.84 to 0.87, while the FPr varies between 0.20 and 0.25. The threshold T remains relatively constant at approximately 0.2.

Since the VG converts the time series into a network, we evaluated the classification performance of some network parameters that are used as network topology metrics. In particular, we analysed the average (μ_k) [26] and the Shannon Entropy (SE) of the connectivity degree [27] defined as:

$$\mathrm{SE} = -\sum_{j=1}^{N_k} P_j(k) \ln P_j(k). \tag{9}$$

Tables III and IV present the outcomes of the ROC analysis conducted on these two parameters. Both parameters exhibit excellent classification performance, with the AUC ranging between 0.93 and 0.97. Additionally, the TPr varies from 0.86 to 0.94, and the FPr ranges from 0.06 to 0.15.

Moreover, focusing on the datasets of infected sites, we observe a slight increase in the averages of both μ_k and SE from 2015 to 2017 (Figure 7).

V. Conclusions

The main factors controlling the evapotranspiration process are influenced by the climate, soil, and vegetation characteristics. In environments where plants inhabit the same ecosystems and encounter similar environmental circumstances, as the cases examined here, differences mainly arise from the varied

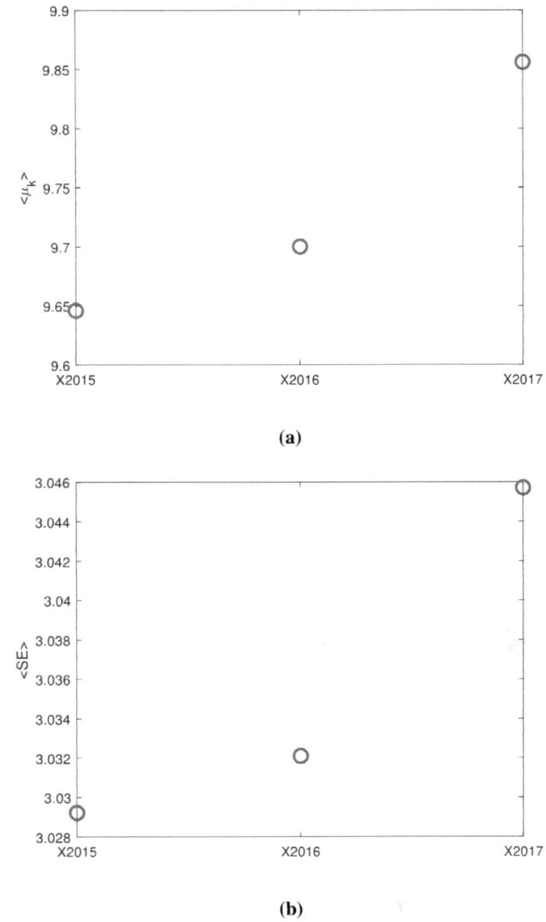

Fig. 7: Averages of a) μ_k and b) Shannon Entropy of the connectivity degree for the infected datasets.

TABLE III: RESULTS OF THE ROC ANALYSIS OF μ_k

datasets	ROC parameters			
	AUC	TPr	FPr	T
X2015-Matera	0.97	0.94	0.07	10.32
X2016-Matera	0.97	0.93	0.08	10.35
X2017-Matera	0.94	0.90	0.15	10.47

TABLE IV: RESULTS OF THE ROC ANALYSIS OF SHANNON ENTROPY

datasets	ROC parameters			
	AUC	TPr	FPr	T
X2015-Matera	0.96	0.92	0.11	3.08
X2016-Matera	0.96	0.88	0.06	3.11
X2017-Matera	0.93	0.86	0.11	3.12

vegetation conditions caused by the presence of *Xylella Fastidiosa* that, since its first detection in Apulia (southern Italy), has affected around 4 million olive trees in the affected region [28]. The presence of this bacterium has led to significant economic losses, particularly in terms of olive trees and oil production, with ongoing repercussions on the economy of the area. Additionally, it has resulted in changing the landscape of the affected area, where olive trees hold deep cultural significance and are a key component of the thriving tourism sector.

The characterization of the impact of *Xylella Fastidiosa* on olive groves is crucial in combating its spread. MODIS ET data appears to offer a valuable tool for achieving this goal, as they enable a differentiation of infected olive orchard areas from those that are uninfected.

Given that one of the main effects of this infection is the fast desiccation of the plant, the utilization of ET seems very suited in effectively characterizing and assessing the impact of this bacterium on plants, since it functions as an indirect indicator of the reduction in water content within plants.

The application of the Visibility Graph to pixels covering both unifected and infected olive groves in southern Italy has suggested to employ classifiers that showed their potential in discriminating between the two classes of pixels, namely the degree distribution, the mean and the Shannon Entropy of the connectivity degree.

It is intriguing to note the rising trend in the average mean connectivity degree and Shannon entropy over time. The datasets for X2015, X2016, and X2017 correspond to sites where the infection was initially identified in 2015, 2016, and 2017, respectively. Therefore, the observed trend in Figure 7 indicates a temporal pattern, implying that the later the plants were infected by the bacterium, the greater the average values of these two network parameters tend to be.

While the results obtained from applying the VG method to MODIS ET time series are still in a preliminary stage, the findings of this study hold significant promise in contributing to the development of operational tools for monitoring vegetation status.

ACKNOWLEDGMENT

This study was supported by the project "Coelum Spies of Climate change and tools for mitigating the effects: EO and AI based methodological approach for Urban Park Management", funded by the National Research Council of Italy.

REFERENCES

[1] https://joint-research-centre.ec.europa.eu/jrc-news-and-updates/monitoring-impacts-xylella-fastidiosa-2019-11-12_en, [retrieved June, 2024]

[2] M. Saponari, D. Boscia, F. Nigro, and G. P. Martelli, "Identification of DNA sequences related to Xylella fastidiosa in oleander, almond and olive trees exhibiting leaf scorch symptoms in Apulia (Southern Italy)," Journal of Plant Pathology, vol. 95, pp. 659–668, 2013.

[3] M. Jeger et al., "Scientific opinion on the updated pest categorisation of Xylella fastidiosa," EFSA Journal, vol. 16, 5357, 2018.

[4] T. Blumensath and M. E. Davies, "Iterative hard thresholding for compressed sensing," Applied and computational harmonic analysis, vol. 27, pp. 265–274, 2009.

[5] J. M. Bioucas-Dias, and M. A. Figueiredo, "A new twist: Two-step iterative shrinkage/thresholding algorithms for image restoration," IEEE Transactions on Image processing, vol. 16, pp. 2992–3004, 2007.

[6] G. Chen, and D. Needell, "Compressed sensing and dictionary learning," Finite Frame Theory: A Complete Introduction to Overcompleteness, vol. 73, pp. 201-241, 2016.

[7] L. Telesca et al., " Exploring Long-Term Anomalies in the Vegetation Cover of Peri-Urban Parks Using the Fisher-Shannon Method," Entropy, vol. 24, 1784, 2022.

[8] L. Telesca et al., "Urban and Peri-Urban Vegetation Monitoring Using Satellite MODIS NDVI Time Series, Singular Spectrum Analysis, and Fisher–Shannon Statistical Method," Sustainability, vol. 15, 11039, 2023.

[9] L. Telesca, N. Abate, F. Faridani, M. Lovallo, and R. Lasaponara, "Revealing Traits of Phytopathogenic Status Induced by Xylella Fastidiosa in Olive Trees by Analyzing Multifractal and Informational Patterns of MODIS Satellite Evapotranspiration Data," Physica A, vol. 629, 129163, 2023.

[10] L. Telesca, N. Abate, F. Faridani, M. Lovallo, and R. Lasaponara, "Discerning Xylella fastidiosa-Infected Olive Orchards in the Time Series of MODIS Terra Satellite Evapotranspiration Data by Using the Fisher–Shannon Analysis and the Multifractal Detrended Fluctuation Analysis," Fractal and Fractional, vol. 7, 466, 2023.

[11] L. Telesca, N. Abate, M. Lovallo, and R. Lasaponara, "Investigating the Impact of Xylella Fastidiosa on Olive Trees by the Analysis of MODIS Terra Satellite Evapotranspiration Time Series by Using the Fisher Information Measure and the Shannon Entropy: A Case Study in Southern Italy," Remote Sensing, vol. 16, 1242, 2024

[12] L. Lacasa, B. Luque, F. Ballesteros, J. Luque, and J. C. Nuno, "From time series to complex networks: The visibility graph," Proceedings of the National Academy of Sciences, vol. 105, pp. 4972–4975, 2008.

[13] R. Zhang, B. Ashuri, Y. Shyr, and Y. Deng, "Forecasting construction cost index based on visibility graph: A network approach," Physica A, vol. 493, pp. 239-252, 2018.

[14] Y. Long, "Visibility graph network analysis of gold price time series," Physica A, vol. 392, pp. 3374–3384, 2013.

[15] N. Wang, D. Li, and Q. Wang, "Visibility graph analysis on quarterly macroeconomic series of China based on complex network theory," Physica A, vol. 391, pp. 6543–6555, 2012.

[16] W. Jiang, B. Wei, J. Zhan, C. Xie, and D. Zhou, "A visibility graph power averaging aggregation operator: A methodology based on network analysis," Computers & Industrial Engineering, vol. 101, pp. 260–268, 2016.

[17] S. Chen, Y. Hu, S. Mahadevan, and Y. Deng, "A visibility graph averaging aggregation operator," Physica A, vol. 403, pp. 1–12, 2014.

[18] M. Yu, A. Hillebrand, A. A. Gouw, and C. J. Stam, "Horizontal visibility graph transfer entropy (HVG-TE): A novel metric to characterize directed connectivity in large-scale brain networks," NeuroImage, vol. 156, pp. 249-264, 2017.

[19] L. Telesca, M. Lovallo, and J. O. Pierini, "Visibility graph approach to the analysis of ocean tidal records," Chaos, Solitons & Fractals, vol. 45, pp. 1087–1091, 2012.

[20] T. Fawcett, "An introduction to ROC analysis," Pattern Recognition Letters, vol. 27, pp. 861-874, 2006.

[21] B. Luque, L. Lacasa, F. Ballesteros, and J. Luque, J., "Horizontal visibility graphs: Exact results for random time series," Physical Review E, vol. 80, 046103, 2009.

[22] M. Saponari, A. Giampetruzzi, G. Loconsole, D. Boscia, and P. Saldarelli, "Xylella fastidiosa in Olive in Apulia: Where We Stand," Phytopathology, vol. 109, pp. 175–186, 2019.

[23] https://lpdaac.usgs.gov, [retrieved June, 2024].

[24] L. Laipelt, R. H. B. Kayser, A. S. Fleischmann, A. Ruhoff, W. Bastiaanssen, T. A. Erickson, and F. Melton, "Long-term monitoring of evapotranspiration using the SEBAL algorithm and Google Earth Engine cloud computing ISPRS," Journal of Photogrammetry and Remote Sensing, vol. 178, pp. 81–96, 2021.

[25] https://www.mathworks.com/matlabcentral/fileexchange/70432-fast-natural-visibility-graph-nvg-for-matlab, [retrieved June, 2024]

[26] G. Bounova, and O. de Weck, "Overview of metrics and their correlation patterns for multiple-metric topology analysis on heterogeneous graph ensembles," Physical Review E, vol. 85, 016117, 2012.

[27] B. A. Gonçalves, L. Carpi, O. A. Rosso, and M. G. Ravetti, "Time series characterization via horizontal visibility graph and Information Theory", Physica A, vol. 464, pp. 93–102, 2016.

[28] K. Schneider, W. van der Werf, M. Cendoya, M. Mourits, J. A. Navas-Cortés, A. Vicent, and A. Oude Lansink, "Impact of *Xylella fastidiosa* subspecies *pauca* in European olives,", Proceedings of the National Academy of Sciences of the United States of America, vol. 117, pp. 9250–9259, 2020.

Alienation in Work

A Comparative Quantative Analysis of On-Site vs. Home Office Environments

Niklas Groffner
Faculty of Computer Science and Business Information Systems
University of Applied Sciences Würzburg-Schweinfurt
Würzburg, Germany
e-mail: niklas.groffner@study.thws.de

***Abstract*—This study delves into the dynamics of work alienation in contrasting environments: traditional on-site workplaces and remote home offices. Anchored in Karl Marx's theory of alienation, this research investigates whether remote working exacerbates or introduces new forms of alienation. It reveals a complex relationship between work setting and alienation, notably finding a decrease in self-alienation among home office employees. This suggests that remote working can mitigate certain alienation aspects, challenging traditional views on Marx's concept in modern work contexts.**

Keywords: Work Alienation; Remote Work; Marxian Theory; Self-Alienation; Digital Work Environments; Employee Well-being.

I. INTRODUCTION

Marx's concept of work alienation [1] provides insight into modern work environments, including home offices. Marx's exploration of alienation in capitalist societies reveals a deep-seated estrangement of workers from their labor, colleagues, and human potential, a theme expanded upon by Lavalette and Ferguson, and Healy and Wilkowska [2][3]. This paper assesses alienation in both home office and traditional work settings, utilizing a questionnaire for deeper insights. The paper also addresses how home office work may alter the experience of alienation. While autonomy in home offices might lessen some alienation aspects, new forms of estrangement, such as isolation and blurred work-life boundaries, may arise. This research delves into these differences, grounding the discussion in Marx's theories and supplementing it by contemporary studies and case analyses. The paper is structured as follows: Section II reviews relevant literature on alienation, providing a theoretical foundation. Section III describes the methodology, including hypothesis formation, data collection, and analytical techniques. Section IV presents the results, highlighting key findings related to work alienation in different settings. Section V discusses these findings in relation to existing research and theoretical perspectives. Section VI concludes the paper by summarizing the main insights and suggesting directions for future research.

II. LITERATURE REVIEW

Marx's theory of work alienation, influenced by Hegel and Feuerbach, remains relevant today, particularly in capitalist systems and the Information and Communication Technology (ICT) industry. His materialistic, historical, and social theory, focusing on the wage worker's alienation from the labor process, is still applicable in modern work scenarios, as evidenced by Giray and Healy [4][5]. Karl Marx's concept of alienation, outlined in his "Economic and Philosophic Manuscripts of 1844," refers to workers becoming estranged from the products of their labor, the labor process, their fellow workers, and their own human potential [1]. This paper's research and analysis are based on Marx's definition of alienation as outlined in his seminal work. The concept of 'disalienation', especially in worker-owned organizations, is discussed as a countermeasure, emphasizing participatory approaches for fostering belonging and control in the workplace [6].

The COVID-19 pandemic's shift to home office settings has further nuanced the understanding of work alienation. Studies like Mehta examine the impact of remote work on alienation, considering factors such as isolation and job insecurity [7]. This shift highlights the need to reassess Marx's theory in the context of remote work, considering both its potential to reduce alienation and the emergence of new forms of estrangement. Moreover, the relevance of Marx's theory in the digital age is affirmed, with Healy emphasizing its applicability in understanding the experiences of ICT professionals [4].

III. METHODOLOGY

A. Hypothesis Formation

This study hypothesizes greater work alienation in home office employees, informed by literature. Mehta's findings on increased alienation due to isolation and loss of task identity in home office work [7], Bočková and Lajčin's link between home office challenges like social isolation and increased alienation [8], and Vinokurov and Kozhina's suggestion that workplace changes influence alienation based on personal and work-related characteristics [9] support this hypothesis. The hypothesis acknowledges potential for both reduced and increased alienation in home office settings compared to on-site work.

B. Methodological Framework

This study employed a quantitative research design to assess work alienation among employees at a privately-owned, large-sized enterprise in Bavaria, Germany. The primary data collection tool was an anonymized online questionnaire, developed by Nair and Vohra, to measure various aspects of work alienation [10]. The questionnaire was used in its original form, with no modifications. Additionally, relevant demographic data such as age, gender, and department were collected. Participants included 95 employees from IT, Manufacturing Control, and Digital Business departments, diverse in age and length of employment. Due to the non-normal distribution of the data, the Mann-Whitney U test was employed for analysis. This non-parametric test compared work alienation levels between two groups: those working more than 75% from home, and those working 25% or less. A secondary analysis compared groups working more than 50% and 50% or less from home. This aimed to understand how remote work impacts feelings of alienation.

IV. RESULTS

The analysis of the data reveals that the p values in Table I show no significant differences in work alienation for most survey items between employees working more than 75% and 50% home office work. However, a significant difference was found for "I feel alienated from myself or as if I am not my true self at work." Employees with more than 75% home office time reported lower self-alienation compared to those with 25% or less. Further analysis revealed a wider range of responses within the group that spent less time in home offices. As illustrated by the error bars in Figure 1, this difference is clearly visible. In summary, while most aspects of work alienation showed no significant differences across different home office arrangements, a disparity was observed in self-alienation. Employees with a higher proportion of home office work reported feeling less alienated from their true selves at work, suggesting a nuanced relationship between work setting and the experience of alienation.

V. DISCUSSION

The study's findings, indicating nuanced experiences of alienation among home office and on-site workers, align with Marx's theory of work alienation. According to Ollman, Marx's perspective on alienation in capitalist systems underscores a disconnection from the labor process, where the worker does not affirm himself, but denies himself, feeling unhappy and not developing freely his physical and mental energy, thus not realizing his own human potential [11]. The reduced sense of self-alienation among employees with more home office work suggests a potential mitigation of alienation in these settings, possibly due to increased autonomy and flexibility.

Contrasting with some existing literature, this study found no significant increase in overall work alienation among home office workers. This contrasts with studies like Mehta, which highlighted the negative impact of isolation and loss of task identity in work-from-home settings [7]. However, it is important to note that, as evident in the error bars on the right side of Figure 1, the division of the second analysis did not exhibit a significant change in self-alienation levels.

TABLE I. RESULTS MANN-WHITNEY-U-TEST

Results Mann-Whitney-U-test		
Item	***>75% & <= 25% Split p Value***	***>50% & <= 50% Split p Value***
I do not take joy in my work.	0.158	0.837
Turning my attention to my work tasks is an unpleasant, boring experience.	0.818	0.253
Work is more of a burdensome duty or a burden to me.	0.684	0.683
I feel alienated from myself or as if I am not myself.	0.025	0.121
I often wish I were doing something else.	0.066	0.402
Over time, I have developed a disillusioning view of my work.	0.482	0.601
I do not feel like exerting myself at work.	0.127	0.477
I do not feel connected to the events at work.	0.094	0.772

Additionally, most of the questionnaire items did not show statistically significant differences. This observation underscores the subtleties in the alienation process, suggesting that the impact of home office environments might vary based on individual differences. Studies like Bergefurt et al. and Xiao et al. have explored the impact of home office workspace characteristics on mental health, indicating the complexity of factors influencing work alienation in remote settings [12][13]. Recognizing the potential for reduced self-alienation in home office environments suggests a need for policies that support flexible work arrangements, considering individual differences in experiences of alienation [9]. Employers should also focus on creating home office conditions that are conducive to mental well-being, as workspace characteristics can impact employees' mental health [13].

VI. CONCLUSION

This study explored nuanced alienation among remote workers, finding decreased self-alienation likely due to increased autonomy and flexibility. The study's limitations include a small, homogeneous sample, highlighting the need for future research with a larger, more diverse participant base to better understand work alienation. Further investigation into factors reducing self-alienation in remote work is needed.

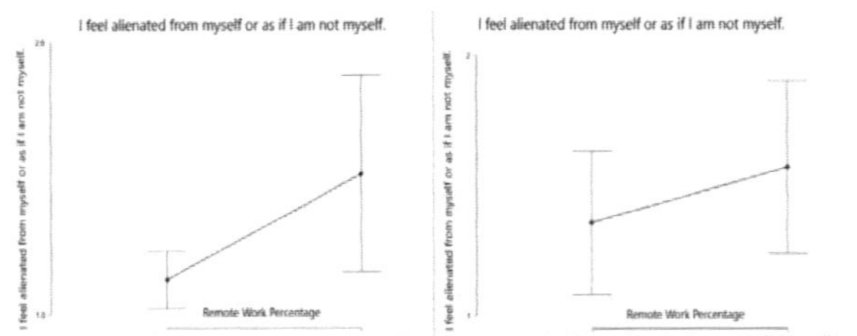

Figure 1. Item for self-alienation

ACKNOWLEDGMENT

This work was supervised by Prof. Dr. Karsten Huffstadt and Prof. Dr. habil. Nicholas Müller from the Faculty of Computer Science and Business Information Systems, University of Applied Sciences Würzburg-Schweinfurt.

REFERENCES

[1] K. Marx, "Economic and Philosophic Manuscripts of 1844." [Online]. Available: https://www.marxists.org/archive/marx/works/1844/manuscripts/labour.htm. [retrieved: May 2024].

[2] M. Lavalette and I. Ferguson, “Marx: alienation, commodity fetishism and the world of contemporary social work,” Crit. Radic. Soc. Work, vol. 6, no. 2, pp. 197–213, Aug. 2018, doi: 10.1332/204986018X15321002618490.

[3] M. Healy and I. Wilkowska, “Marx, Alienation and the Denial of Dignity of Work,” in Dignity and the Organization, M. Kostera and M. Pirson, Eds., in Humanism in Business Series. London: Palgrave Macmillan UK, 2017, pp. 99–124, doi: 10.1057/978-1-137-55562-5_6.

[4] G. Giray, “The foundations of Marx’s theory of alienation: Marx’s critique of his predecessors and alienated labour,” Dokuz Eylül Üniversitesi Sos. Bilim. Enstitüsü Derg., vol. 24, no. 4, Art. no. 4, Dec. 2022, doi: 10.16953/deusosbil.1182181.

[5] D. Harvey, “Universal alienation,” TripleC Commun. Capital. Crit. Open Access J. Glob. Sustain. Inf. Soc., vol. 16, no. 2, pp. 424–439, May 2018, doi: 10.31269/triplec.v16i2.1026.

[6] J. Kociatkiewicz, M. Kostera, and M. Parker, “The possibility of disalienated work: Being at home in alternative organizations,” Human Relations, vol. 74, no. 4, pp. 555–576, 2021. [retrieved: May 20, 2024]. Available: https://journals.sagepub.com/doi/full/10.1177/0018726720916762.

[7] P. Mehta, “Work alienation as a mediator between work from home-related isolation, loss of task identity and job insecurity amid the COVID-19 pandemic,” Int. J. Workplace Health Manag., vol. 15, no. 3, pp. 287–306, Jan. 2022, doi: 10.1108/IJWHM-03-2021-0070. [retrieved: May 2024].

[8] G. J. Submitter, K. Bočková, and D. Lajčin, “Home office and its influence on employee motivation,” Rochester, NY, Jun. 30, 2021. Available: https://papers.ssrn.com/abstract=3873942. [retrieved: May 2024]

[9] L. V. Vinokurov and A. A. Kozhina, “The contribution of individual psychological features to the determination of the phenomenon of work alienation,” Behav. Sci., vol. 10, no. 1, Art. no. 1, Jan. 2020, doi: 10.3390/bs10010034.

[10] N. Nair and N. Vohra, “Developing a new measure of work alienation,” J. Workplace Rights, vol. 14, pp. 293–309, Jan. 2009, doi: 10.2190/WR.14.3.c.

[11] B. Ollman, “Alienation: Man’s relation to his productive activity,” in Alienation: Marx’s Conception of Man in Capitalist Society, Cambridge University Press, 1977, pp. 136–140, doi: 10.1017/CBO9780511611902.022.

[12] L. Bergefurt, M. Weijs-Perrée, R. Appel-Meulenbroek, and C. Maris, “Analyzing the effect of distractions of working from home on mental health of office workers during the COVID-19 pandemic,” Proc. 3rd Int. Electron. Conf. Environ. Res. Public Health—Public Health Issues Context COVID-19 Pandemic, 2021, doi: 10.3390/ECERPH-3-09075.

[13] Y. Xiao, B. Becerik-Gerber, G. M. Lucas, and S. C. Roll, “Impacts of working from home during COVID-19 pandemic on physical and mental well-being of office workstation users,” J. Occup. Environ. Med., vol. 63, pp. 181–190, 2020, doi: 10.1097/JOM.0000000000002097.

Robust Power Prediction of Wind Turbine using Error Detection, Clustering-Based Imputation and Physics-Informed Learning

Swayam Mittal, Vishwaas Narasinh, Nikhil Kulkarni,
Remish Leonard Minz, Nilanjan Chakravortty, Prateek Mital
Research & Development Hitachi India Ltd. Bangalore, India
Email:{swayam.mittal, vishwaas.narasinh, nikhil.kulkarni, remish.minz,
nilanjan.chakravortty, prateek.mital}
@hitachi.co.in

***Abstract*—In this paper, we present a robust power prediction model for wind turbines. Our model leverages error detection in the sensor data, clustering-based imputation of filtered erroneous or missing data, and a Physics-Informed Neural Network (PINN). We introduce data preprocessing steps, including the detection and filtering of erroneous data and clustering-based data imputation. We demonstrate that these preprocessing steps, along with the PINN framework, improve power prediction accuracy in the presence of erroneous sensor data.**

Keywords-wind farm, anomaly detection, power prediction, machine learning, clustering, physics-informed learning.

I. INTRODUCTION

Wind energy has carved a significant niche in today's renewable energy spectrum, offering a sustainable solution to the burgeoning global energy demands. With the increasing deployment of wind turbines, the volume of operational data they generate has surged, highlighting the necessity for advanced analytical techniques [1]. Safeguarding the integrity and precision of this data becomes imperative, particularly in the face of missing or erroneous readings [2]. While traditional solutions have earned recognition, they sometimes fall short of encapsulating the intricate dynamics of wind turbines [4]. Modern advancements lean towards sophisticated models, like auto-encoders, boasting improved accuracy [5]. However, an evident gap persists in ensuring these models align both with data-driven insights and inherent physical principles.

Power prediction of wind turbines faces challenges due to errors in the collected data. It is important to identify the erroneous data using anomaly detection methods to ensure power prediction accuracy. Further, once the detected erroneous data are filtered out, imputation of the filtered data and inherently missing data is required. Imputation may require advanced techniques to address the non-linear nature of the association between the longitudinal data. A particularly promising direction in addressing data imputation is the application of Gaussian Mixture Models (GMM). GMMs have demonstrated advantages in capturing complex data distributions, making them apt for handling the diverse nature of wind turbine data. This paper presents a novel pipeline, which includes error detection and filtering using the anomaly detection methods, clustering-based data imputation and physics-informed learning where we combine data-driven methods with physics-based predictions to address existing gaps.

The motivation for this work stems from the critical need to enhance the reliability and accuracy of power predictions in wind farms. As wind energy becomes a more significant component of the global energy mix, the ability to predict power output accurately under various operational conditions is essential for grid stability and efficient energy management. Traditional methods often fail to adequately address the complexities introduced by erroneous and missing data in wind turbine operations. Our approach aims to bridge this gap by integrating advanced data processing techniques with physics-informed models, thus providing a more robust and accurate power prediction framework.

The remainder of this paper is organized as follows: In Section II, we review related work in the fields of wind turbine data analysis and predictive modeling, emphasizing the significance of integrating data-driven approaches with physical models. In Section III, we detail the data collection process and the characteristics of the dataset used in this study. Section IV discusses our methodology for handling outliers and abnormalities in Supervisory Control and Data Acquisition (SCADA) data. Section V presents the methodologies used for anomaly detection and data imputation, followed by Section VI, where we present the description of our power output modeling approach. In Section VII, we evaluate the performance of our proposed models against various benchmarks and imputation techniques. Section VIII discusses the results of our experiments. Finally, Section IX concludes the paper with a summary of our findings and suggestions for future research.

II. RELATED WORK

Research in wind turbine data analysis and prediction has been a burgeoning field over the past few years, with numerous methodologies developed to navigate the complexities posed by the vast datasets generated by wind turbines.

Errors in the sensor data pose major challenges in wind turbine power prediction. Various anomaly detection techniques are used for the detection of these erroneous data. [8] proposed an anomaly detection method based on a convolutional recurrent autoencoder, showcasing the potential for leveraging deep learning models in this domain.

When the detected erroneous data are filtered from the dataset, they leave gaps in the dataset, making it all the more challenging to construct a correct power prediction model. Data imputation techniques are used to address this issue. [4] delved into traditional data imputation methods. Despite their widespread use, these methods have been found lacking imputation of data with non-linear associations, especially when applied to complex longitudinal data intrinsic to wind turbine operations. The oft-used strategy of substituting missing values with mean or median, as discussed by [2], can occasionally oversimplify the intricate interrelations inherent in turbine datasets.

More advanced techniques like auto-encoders for imputation in wind turbine sensor data have been explored by [5]. While their approach represents one of the latest advancements in data imputation techniques for wind turbines, however, there can be a large number of undetected erroneous data. In this situation, the correctness of the prediction model is questionable when we rely only on the data-driven approach. A promising avenue in addressing this shortcoming is the signals from the physics of the system in consideration. We leverage the use of Physics-Informed Neural Networks (PINNs). [9] presented a study on PINNs for power systems, emphasizing their capacity to integrate physical laws. Further building on this concept, [10] applied PINNs for non-linear system identification in power system dynamics, underlining the potential of combining data-driven models with physical insights.

Our study builds upon these foundational research endeavors. We aim to amalgamate data-driven insights with physics-informed models [7], ensuring that predictions are not only precise but also grounded in real-world operational frameworks.

Recent studies have also explored the use of hybrid models combining machine learning with physical modeling. For instance, [11] proposed a hybrid model integrating a deep neural network with a physical wind model, showing improved accuracy in wind power prediction. Similarly, [12] introduced an ensemble learning approach that combines multiple machine learning models to enhance prediction robustness.

In comparison, our approach integrates Gaussian Mixture Models for imputation and Physics-Informed Neural Networks to ensure that the predictions are not only accurate but also physically plausible. Unlike [11] and [12], which focus primarily on the data-driven aspects, our method emphasizes the integration of physical principles to handle erroneous and missing data more effectively.

Despite the advances in these techniques, several limitations persist in the state-of-the-art methods. Traditional anomaly detection and imputation methods often fail to account for the complex, non-linear relationships in wind turbine data, leading to suboptimal power prediction accuracy. Advanced methods such as auto-encoders improve upon these issues but still suffer from undetected anomalies and reliance on purely data-driven approaches, which may not fully capture the physical dynamics of wind turbines. The integration of physics-informed models, while promising, also presents challenges in terms of model complexity and computational requirements. Our work seeks to address these limitations by providing a comprehensive framework that combines robust data preprocessing, advanced imputation techniques, and physics-informed neural networks to enhance power prediction accuracy and reliability.

III. Data Collection Overview

The wind farm under consideration is an onshore wind farm, built in 2017–2018 and has been operating since 2019. For this investigation, the turbine data was collected between November 1st, 2022 and July 15th, 2023. There are 16 wind turbines with a total of 32MW power generation capacity. The wind farm had access to a collection of 1966 SCADA tags that contained information from various turbine components, including the rotor, brake, pitch control, main shaft, gearbox, generator, yaw system, nacelle, electrical systems, hydraulic systems, etc. Our focus is on two wind turbines. The data samples from the sensors (SCADA parameters) are averaged across a 10-minute timeframe and are recorded at a frequency of roughly 2.00 min. We filtered the data for the wind turbine operational phase, focused on the core aspects of the wind turbine which are power generation, rotor, and pitch, and removed outlier records with very low wind speed (< 3 m/s) and very high wind speed (> 10.5 m/s), or records with no production (0 kWh).

The wind speed classification mentioned above is based on the manufacturer's specifications. However, it is essential to note that specific wind turbine models might have slightly different operational parameters.

IV. Handling Outliers and Abnormality in SCADA Data

A. Outliers Observed

Outliers in SCADA data can greatly influence the performance and accuracy of wind turbine predictive models. In this study, several types of outliers were observed:

- **Non-operating Phase Outliers:** During wind turbine maintenance, the value of the active power is zero even though the wind speed lies between the cut-in and cut-out speeds. These data points were identified as part of the non-operating phase and were systematically removed to avoid misinterpretation.
- **Power Curve Deviation Outliers:** Some data points, although not zero, were observed to deviate significantly from their expected values on the power curve. Probable causes for such deviations include wind curtailment, accumulation of dirt or bugs on the turbine blades, pitch malfunctions, among other operational issues.

B. Methodology for Handling Outliers

The approach adopted to address the identified outliers involved the following steps:

1) **Initial Identification:** A visual examination was first conducted on plots of wind speed versus wind power. This helped in identifying data points that significantly deviated from the expected behavior.
2) **Interval-based Detection:** Following the initial identification, we employed the interval-based detection method as described by [8]. This method allows for the removal of obvious outliers based on set intervals or thresholds in the plot of wind speed and wind power. Specifically, data points that fall outside of expected performance intervals were flagged.
3) **Power Curve Validation:** Given the inherent relationship between wind speed and turbine output power, we used the power curve as a benchmark. Any data points that strayed significantly from the power curve were considered outliers. This step was particularly useful for identifying the Power Curve Deviation Outliers.

However, given the specific nature of wind turbine data, we decided to rely more on domain knowledge for this study. Once outliers were identified through the above methodologies, they were systematically removed from the dataset. Following the removal of these outliers, the refined wind data were employed to train the power curve models. It is worth noting that a meticulous outlier removal process ensures the developed models' robustness and accuracy in predicting wind turbine performance based on SCADA data.

V. METHODOLOGY

The overall methodology of our study is depicted in Figure 1. This flow diagram outlines the primary steps involved in the data processing and analysis phases.

The flow diagram above provides a visual summary of our approach, including the key steps and processes involved.

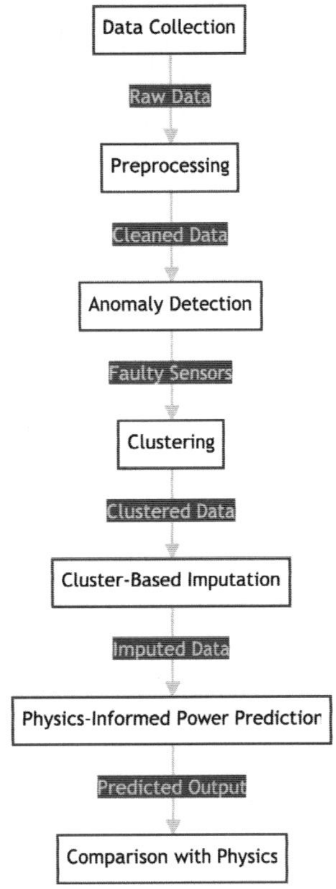

Figure 1. Flow diagram.

A. Outlier Handling

For handling outliers detected during non-operational or maintenance phases, we visually inspected for wind speed versus power plots. Leveraging the domain expertise, we identified and eliminated these outliers, enhancing the data quality for subsequent model training. Detailed data collection processes are discussed in the Data Collection Overview.

B. Feature Selection

Our study utilizes SCADA data obtained from a real-world wind farm situated in Gujarat, India. Spanning a specific timeframe, this dataset offers insights into various turbine components, painting a comprehensive picture of the turbine operations.

Initial feature selection was guided by a combination of domain knowledge, data availability, and feature importance scores. Starting with a broad set of SCADA tags, domain expertise helped shortlist a preliminary set of 80 features. Additionally, essential parameters like wind speed, rotor speed, and pitch angles were mandated by the physics loss function.

To further refine our features list, a Random Forest model was trained using 3-fold cross-validation, and the results yielded the feature importance as demonstrated in Figure 2. From these, the top 10 features were selected for anomaly detection. The figure illustrates the top 5 features with the highest significance. The remaining features, while essential, have lesser importance values and are not prominently displayed in the graph.

The significance of each feature used in our models is illustrated in Figure 2.

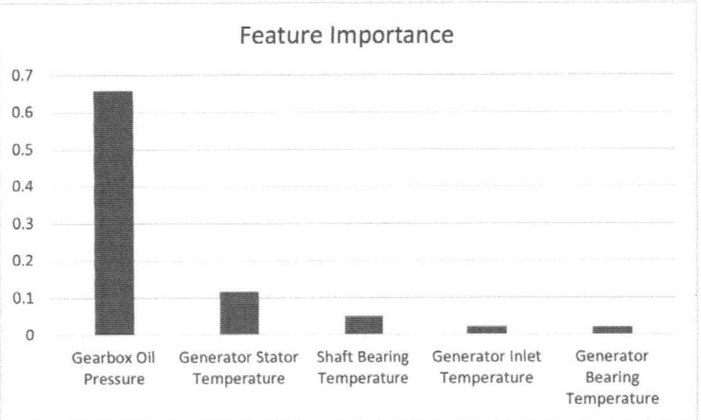

Figure 2. Feature Importances obtained from Random Forest model.

The final set of top 10 features includes:

- Gearbox Oil Pressure
- Generator Stator Temperature
- Shaft Bearing Temperature
- Generator Inlet Temperature
- Generator Bearing Temperature
- Pitch Angle
- Wind Speed
- Rotor Speed
- Nacelle Direction
- Yaw

C. Anomaly Detection

We attempt to identify faulty sensors for anomaly detection using auto-encoders. Consequently, the inputs and the outputs of the auto-encoder are the same. The architecture of the auto-encoder is shown in Figure 3. The input features include the features discussed above.

An auto-encoder is a type of artificial neural network that can learn efficient representations of input data with no need for labels. It consists of two parts: an encoder that compresses the input into a latent-space representation, and a decoder that reconstructs the input from this representation. The goal is to minimize the difference between the input and the reconstructed output.

In Figure 3, the auto-encoder architecture is detailed as follows:

- **Input Layer (input_1):** This layer accepts the input data with shape (None, 3, 11), where 'None' represents the batch size, 3 represents the sequence length, and 11 represents the number of features.
- **Conv1D Layer (conv1d):** This layer applies 1D convolution to the input data, reducing the feature dimension from 11 to 4.
- **Dropout Layer (dropout):** This layer randomly sets a fraction of input units to 0 to prevent overfitting.
- **Conv1D Layer (conv1d_1):** Another convolutional layer that further reduces the feature dimension to 1.
- **Conv1DTranspose Layer (conv1d_transpose):** This transposed convolutional layer starts the decoding process, increasing the feature dimension back to 4.
- **Dropout Layer (dropout_1):** Another dropout layer to prevent overfitting during the decoding process.
- **Conv1DTranspose Layer (conv1d_transpose_1):** The final transposed convolutional layer reconstructs the output to match the original input shape of (None, 3, 11).

We train the model in 3-fold cross-validation for 10 epochs using Mean Absolute Error (MAE) loss between the target and the prediction. The distribution of the training loss is shown in Figure 5. We set the threshold at the 90th percentile which corresponds to a value of 0.15. This decision is based on empirical observations to capture the most significant anomalies while reducing the likelihood of false positives. Consequently, any loss greater than the defined threshold is considered to be an anomaly.

For testing, we randomly select a couple of features, change their value to $\mu_i \pm 2\sigma_i$, and keep the other features at their mean value. i represents the selected features. The output of the anomaly detection model with this anomalous input is subtracted from the mean of the output of the training data to get the loss due to the anomaly. This is shown in Figure 6, where the peaks corresponding to the anomalous features have a higher loss and have crossed the threshold defined above.

However, we only focus on the cases where either one of the sensors that correspond to wind speed, rotor speed, or pitch angle is at fault. This is because the empirical relation to the expected power output and the physics loss functions require these features to be present.

The notation $\mu \pm 2\sigma$ is conventionally used to describe data lying within two standard deviations (σ) from the mean (μ). In a Gaussian distribution, roughly 95.4% of data falls within this range. Before applying this principle to identify outliers, we verified that our features adhere to a Gaussian distribution, with various statistical methods. This validation ensures the appropriateness of the $\mu \pm 2\sigma$ rule in our context.

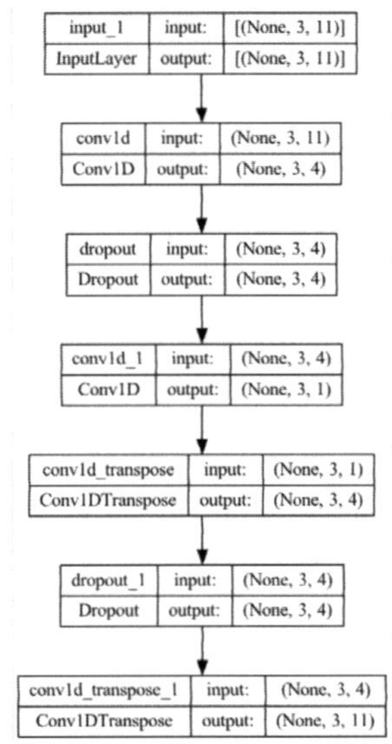

Figure 3. Auto Encoder architecture.

D. Outlier Detection using Standard Deviation

In the process of data pre-processing, it is crucial to identify and handle outliers that can influence the outcomes of the analysis. One effective method employed in this study involves the use of standard deviation.

Given a dataset, the mean (μ) represents the average value, while the standard deviation (σ) provides a measure of the data's spread or dispersion. In a normally distributed dataset, approximately 68.2% of the data lies within $\mu \pm \sigma$, and about 95.4% lies within $\mu \pm 2\sigma$. Data points that fall outside of $\mu \pm 2\sigma$ can be considered as potential outliers, as they deviate significantly from the mean.

In our analysis, data points falling outside the range of $\mu \pm 2\sigma$ were further investigated to determine their validity and were treated or removed accordingly.

E. Clustering

GMMs are chosen to cluster turbines based on multiple features due to their capacity to model complex data distributions. The features selected for clustering are the ones previously mentioned, except for wind speed, rotor speed, and pitch angles. To determine the optimal number of clusters for the GMM, we employ the elbow method, visually represented in Figure 4.

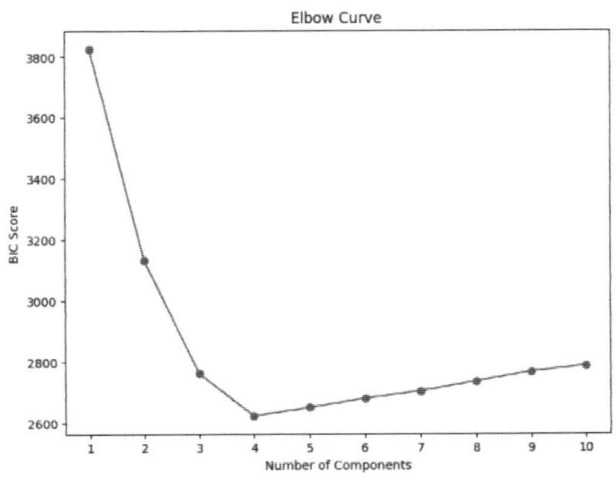

Figure 4. Optimal number of k clusters using the elbow method.

Recognizing the importance of data quality, we introduce a clustering-based imputation methodology. GMMs, with their probabilistic framework, offer an advantage over deterministic clustering methods like K-means. Using the GMM, we cluster wind turbines based on operational and spatial parameters, allowing for effective imputation of missing values. The clustering phase involves grouping wind turbines, guided by important features derived from the Random Forest model. By training the GMM on these scaled features, we ensure uniform scaling and compatibility.

During the validation phase, the test dataset is meticulously constructed with Gaussian distribution to encompass wind turbine feature values that replicate diverse operational scenarios. Here, faulty sensor readings are replaced with the mean values of their corresponding clusters. The findings are compelling, as we observed a close match between the imputed values and the actual expected values across various test scenarios, substantiating the imputation mechanism's accuracy.

Although GMMs come with their assumptions, especially about cluster shapes, and can be sensitive to initialization, we chose to use GMMs because of their strengths and the specific characteristics of our dataset.

The distribution of training loss across various thresholds, which is critical for setting our anomaly detection parameters, is presented in Figure 5.

Figure 6 shows the results of our anomaly detection process, highlighting how our model responds to different types of sensor errors.

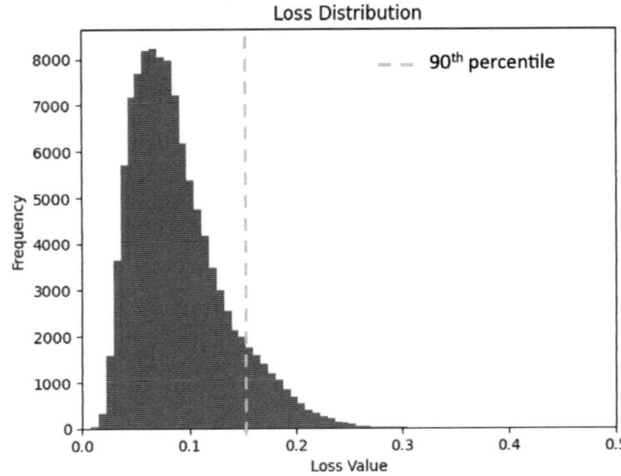

Figure 5. Loss distribution and threshold showing how losses are distributed across different thresholds.

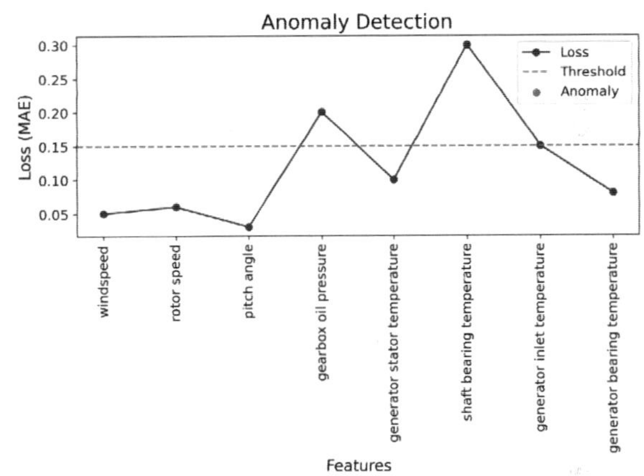

Figure 6. Anomaly detection results.

VI. Power Output Modelling

Our power prediction model, built atop this preprocessed data, comprises multiple layers of fully connected neural networks. The model's architecture, training configurations, and hyperparameters are detailed in this section.

With the imputed values for the faulty sensor data, we model the power output of the wind turbine using the features mentioned above. The model consists of 4 layers of fully connected neural networks with Rectified Linear Unit (ReLU) activation units and dropouts between each layer.

During the training phase, we maintain the actual values for all features, i.e., it is trained with non-faulty sensors in 3-fold cross-validation for 30 epochs, which is approximately the number of steps during which the validation loss stabilizes. During the validation and testing phase, features other than wind speed and rotor speed are fed to the clustering algorithm, which clusters the instances into a cluster. The faulty sensor value is replaced by taking the mean of the actual sensor values from the training data for the selected cluster. We select the best model based on the validation loss.

A. Physics-Informed Loss

The crux of our approach lies in integrating a physics-based loss function. We derive this loss from the energy conservation laws governing wind turbines, ensuring our model's predictions are both data-driven and physically informed. Although the model with traditional MAE loss function converges, there is often a need to include physical laws in the system. We incorporate physics into our model via loss functions. The physical laws are derived using energy conservation laws at different stages of the turbine, as shown in Figure 7.

The stages of power loss throughout the wind turbine system are highlighted in Figure 7. This diagram assists in understanding the energy flow and losses at various stages.

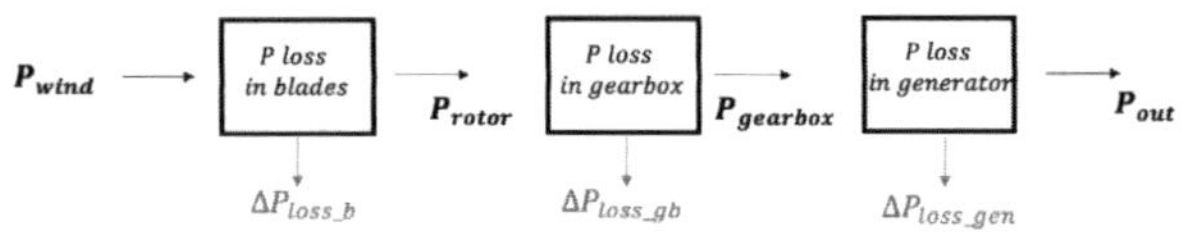

Figure 7. Power Loss at various stages.

The power in the wind is given by [6], where A is the area swept by the blades, v is the wind velocity, ρ is the air density.

$$P_{wind} = \frac{1}{2}\rho A v^3 \tag{1}$$

There are various methods to model the power coefficient, which is a function of the tip speed ratio of the rotor blade, β and the pitch angle, λ, thus $C_p(\lambda, \beta)$. Reyes et at. present a review in [6], stating there are three major approaches to model C_p, namely, the polynomial model, the sinusoidal model and the exponential model. The names indicate how the general function is used to model C_p from either the tip speed ratio λ or both the tip speed ratio λ and the pitch angle β. We use a generic formulation of the widely adopted exponential model from [6] rewritten in equation (2) and (3). The typical values of the coefficients used in both of these equations are described in table 7 and table 8 in [6]. In our implementation, we use the most widely used exponential model's coefficient values, as described in [13].

$$C_p = c_0(c_1\lambda_i^{-1} + c_2\beta + c_3\beta^{c_4} + c_5)e^{c_6\lambda_i^{-1}} + c_7\lambda \tag{2}$$

$$\frac{1}{\lambda_i} = \frac{1}{\lambda + d_0\beta + d_1} - \frac{d_2}{1+\beta^3} \tag{3}$$

The power loss at the blades is given by equation (4). The power loss at the gearbox is given by equation (5). η_{gb} represents the efficiency coefficient of the turbine gearbox. Similarly, the loss at the turbine generator is given by equation (6), where η_{gen} represents the turbine generator's efficiency coefficient. These efficiency values are evaluated using an iterative method, as described in [14].

$$\Delta P_{loss\_b} = (1 - C_p)P_{wind} \tag{4}$$

$$\Delta P_{loss\_gb} = (1 - \eta_{gb})P_{rotor} \tag{5}$$

$$\Delta P_{loss\_gen} = (1 - \eta_{gen})P_{gearbox} \tag{6}$$

The power output accounted for the above losses is given in equation (7). Simplifying equation (7) expressed the power output in terms of the power coefficient, the gearbox efficiency coefficient and the generator efficiency coefficient, presented in equation (8).

$$P_{out} = P_{wind} - (\Delta P_{loss\_b} + \Delta P_{loss\_gb} + \Delta P_{loss\_gen}) \tag{7}$$

$$P_{out} = C_p\eta_{gb}\eta_{gen}P_{wind} \tag{8}$$

The physics loss is given by the difference between the predicted output power of the wind turbine and the actual power produced by the wind turbine for a stipulated period. This is expressed in equation (9), where P_{out} denotes the predicted output power of the wind turbine and P_{actual} denotes the actual power produced by the turbine.

$$Loss_{physics} = P_{out} - P_{actual} \tag{9}$$

TABLE I
COMPARISON OF IMPUTATION ACCURACY USING MEAN ABSOLUTE ERROR (MAE) FOR GMM, K-MEANS, AUTOENCODER, AND SIMPLE AVERAGE METHODS

Method	MAE (Imputation Accuracy)
GMM	9.21
Autoencoder	12.62
KMeans	15.86
Simple Average	32.69

Table I summarizes the efficacy of different imputation methods using the Mean Absolute Error (MAE) metric. The GMM-based method shows the lowest MAE, indicating better imputation accuracy compared to the K-means, Autoencoder, and Simple Average methods.

Figure 8 illustrates the validation of introduced anomalies. The outcomes help verify the sensitivity of our anomaly detection system.

VII. EVALUATION

The evaluation of our proposed methodology focuses on two primary goals: 1) Assessing the accuracy of the power prediction model and 2) Validating the robustness of the model against faulty sensor data and imputation techniques.

A. Evaluation Methodology

To achieve these goals, we conducted a comprehensive set of experiments involving the following steps:

1) **Data Preprocessing:** This step includes outlier detection and handling, feature selection, and anomaly detection, as described in the Methodology section.

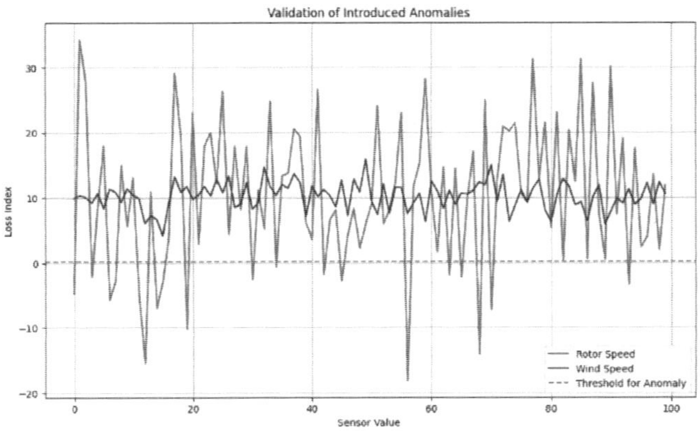

Figure 8. Validation of Introduced Anomalies.

2) **Imputation Techniques Comparison:** We evaluated various imputation techniques, including Gaussian Mixture Models (GMM), Autoencoder-based imputation, K-means clustering, and Simple Average imputation. The effectiveness of these techniques was assessed using the Mean Absolute Error (MAE) metric.
3) **Model Training and Validation:** The power prediction model was trained using the preprocessed and imputed data. We used a 3-fold cross-validation approach to ensure the robustness of the model. The model architecture included multiple layers of fully connected neural networks with ReLU activations and dropout regularization.
4) **Physics-Informed Neural Networks (PINN):** We integrated a physics-based loss function into the neural network to align the predictions with physical laws governing wind turbines. The impact of this integration was evaluated by comparing the performance of models with and without the physics loss.
5) **Benchmarking Against State-of-the-Art:** We benchmarked our model against traditional power prediction models and recent advancements such as autoencoder-based methods.
6) **Ablation Study:** To further understand the contribution of each feature, we conducted an ablation study where each feature was adjusted from its mean value and the prediction accuracy was observed with and without the physics model.

B. Main Goals

The main goals of our evaluation are as follows:

- **Accuracy of Power Prediction:** Determine the accuracy of our power prediction model by comparing predicted power outputs with actual values, using metrics such as Mean Absolute Error (MAE) and the coefficient of determination (R^2).
- **Robustness of Imputation Techniques:** Validate the effectiveness of the GMM-based imputation technique compared to other methods, especially in handling non-linear associations in the data.
- **Impact of Physics-Informed Learning:** Evaluate the contribution of physics-informed neural networks in improving the prediction accuracy and ensuring that the model's predictions adhere to physical principles.
- **Comparative Analysis:** Benchmark the proposed methodology against state-of-the-art approaches to highlight the improvements and advantages of our integrated approach.
- **Feature Contribution:** Through the ablation study, assess the significance of individual features on the model's performance and demonstrate the necessity of combining domain-specific features with data-driven techniques.

The results from these evaluations are discussed in the subsequent section.

VIII. RESULTS

To ensure a comprehensive benchmark, we compared the results of GMM-based clustering with methods [4] that use K-means clustering and also evaluated the two-stage deep autoencoder-based method, as proposed by [5]. Their approach primarily utilizes a deep autoencoder to recover the underlying structure of the data and then imputes the missing value. The proposed method using GMM shows a lower Mean Absolute Error (MAE), as shown in Table I. Our GMM-based clustering not only demonstrates a significant improvement over traditional K-means clustering but also outperforms the recent deep autoencoder-based method in terms of MAE.

For Anomalous sensor value detection, we benchmark the performance by changing the sensor value to various variations, as shown in Figure 8. We see that the induced variations in sensor values result in a loss well above the threshold for most variations of values.

Figure 9 displays the validation loss of our power prediction models over epochs, comparing models with and without the incorporation of physics-informed loss. This graphical representation helps in understanding the impact of physics-based modeling on the convergence and performance of the predictive models.

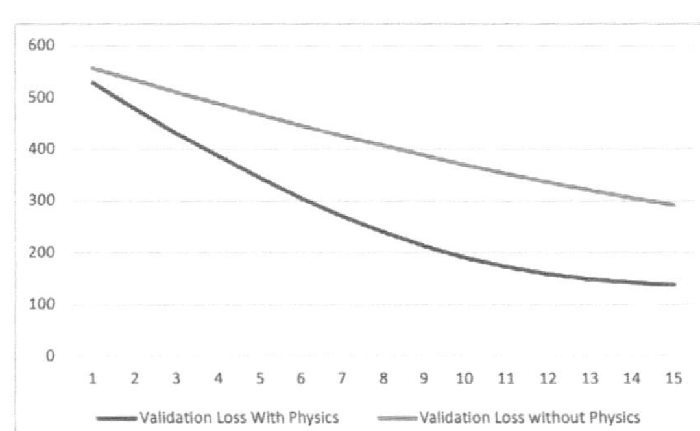

Figure 9. Validation Loss with and without physics loss. The X-axis represents the number of epochs, and the Y-axis represents the validation loss.

We benchmark the performance of our proposed methodology against traditional power prediction models. Both qualitative and quantitative analyses emphasize the advantages of our physics-informed approach. We obtain the results for the power prediction model with and without physics loss. We use the coefficient of determination R^2 as our metric to evaluate the performance of our model. The R^2 with physics loss seems to perform better, as shown in Table II.

We further investigate the convergence of the model with and without physics loss. We train the model in 5-fold cross-validation and aggregate the results and validation loss. We see that the model converges quicker with physics loss, as shown in Figure 9. Our imputation methodology significantly enhances the reliability of predictions. Furthermore, the integration of the physics-informed loss ensures our predictions are not just accurate but also adhere to the physical laws of wind turbine operations.

TABLE II
R^2 OF THE POWER PREDICTION MODEL WITH AND WITHOUT PHYSICS LOSS

Faulty sensor	Without Physics Loss	With Physics Loss
Wind Speed	0.67	0.77
Rotor Speed	0.51	0.58
None	0.77	0.79

TABLE III
ABLATION STUDY SHOWING THE ACCURACY (ACC) OF PREDICTIONS FOR DIFFERENT DEVIATIONS OF EACH FEATURE WITH AND WITHOUT THE PHYSICS (PHY) MODEL

Feature	Deviation	Acc w/o Phy	Acc w/ Phy
Gearbox Oil Pressure	+/- 1%	93.2%	94.1%
Gen. Starter Temp.	+/- 0.7%	92.5%	93.8%
Shaft Bearing Temp.	+/- 0.6%	93.0%	93.5%
Gen. Inlet Temp.	+/- 0.7%	92.8%	93.7%
Gen. Bearing Temp.	+/- 0.6%	93.1%	93.9%
Pitch Angle	+/- 0.5%	92.4%	93.3%
Wind Speed	+/- 2%	91.9%	93.0%
Rotor Speed	+/- 1%	93.2%	94.2%
Nacelle Direction	+/- 0.8%	92.6%	93.6%
Yaw	+/- 0.5%	92.3%	93.2%

To further evaluate our model's robustness to changes in input features, we performed an ablation study. In this study, we adjusted each feature from its mean value and examined the model's prediction accuracy, both with and without the use of the physics model. The findings are outlined in Table III. The table shows that using the physics model consistently improves prediction accuracy across all features. This underscores the importance of combining real-world physical knowledge with data-driven modeling. Features like 'Wind Speed' and 'Pitch Angle', which significantly influences turbine performance, benefits notably from the physics model. This supports the idea of using a physics-based modeling approach.

This study also indicates that our model can handle variations in data, making it suitable for real-world wind farm scenarios.

IX. CONCLUSION

This paper presents a comprehensive approach to wind turbine power prediction. Ensuring data quality through clustering-based imputation and integrating Physics-Informed Neural Networks for power prediction, we ensure that predictions are both accurate and physically feasible. Our methodology, tested on real-world data, underscores the importance of merging data-driven insights with domain-specific expertise, paving the way for future innovations in wind turbine operations and maintenance.

While our approach advances wind turbine power prediction, future work can optimize clustering for enhanced imputation, integrate real-time data with advanced neural architectures, and expand the method's applicability to other renewables like solar, ensuring data-driven yet physically coherent predictions.

REFERENCES

[1] J. Tautz-Weinert and S. Watson, "Using SCADA data for wind turbine condition monitoring—A review," IET Renew. Power Gener., vol. 10, no. 4, pp. 382–394, Sep. 2017.

[2] R. Razavi-Far and M. Saif, "Imputation of missing data for diagnosing sensor faults in a wind turbine," in Proc. IEEE Int. Conf. Syst., Man, Cybern., Hong Kong, Oct. 2015, pp. 99–104.

[3] B. Zhao, Y. Zhong, A. Ma, and L. Zhang, "A spatial Gaussian mixture model for optical remote sensing image clustering," IEEE J. Sel. Topics Appl. Earth Observ. Remote Sens., vol. 9, no. 12, pp. 5748–5759, Dec. 2016.

[4] M. Morshedizadeh, M. Kordestani, R. Carriveau, D. S.-K. Ting, and M. Saif, "Application of imputation techniques and adaptive neuro-fuzzy inference system to predict wind turbine power production," Energy, vol. 138, pp. 394–404, Nov. 2014.

[5] X. Liu and Z. Zhang, "A two-stage deep autoencoder-based missing data imputation method for wind farm SCADA data," IEEE Sensors, vol. 21, no. 9, pp. 10933-10945, May 2021.

[6] V. Reyes, J. J. Rodriguez, O. Carranzo, and R. Ortega, "Review of mathematical models of both the power coefficient and the torque coefficient in wind turbines," 2015 IEEE 24th International Symposium on Industrial Electronics (ISIE), pp. 1-5.

[7] B. Huang and J. Wang, "Applications of Physics-Informed Neural Networks in Power Systems - A Review," IEEE Transactions on Power Systems, vol. 38, no. 1, pp. 572-588, Jan. 2023.

[8] C. Yin, S. Zhang, J. Wang, and N. N. Xiong, "Anomaly Detection Based on Convolutional Recurrent Autoencoder for IoT Time Series," IEEE Transactions on Systems, Man, and Cybernetics: Systems, vol. 52, no. 1, pp. 112-122, Jan. 2022.

[9] G. S. Misyris, A. Venzke, and S. Chatzivasileiadis, "Physics-Informed Neural Networks for Power Systems," 2020 IEEE Power & Energy Society General Meeting (PESGM), Montreal, QC, Canada, 2020, pp. 1-5.

[10] J. Stiasny, G. S. Misyris, and S. Chatzivasileiadis, "Physics-Informed Neural Networks for Non-linear System Identification for Power System Dynamics," 2021 IEEE Madrid PowerTech, Madrid, Spain, 2021, pp. 1-6.

[11] Z. Ma and G. Mei, "A hybrid attention-based deep learning approach for wind power prediction," Energy Reports, vol. 7, 2021, pp. 1461-1472. doi: https://doi.org/10.1016/j.egyai.2022.100199.

[12] J. Lee, W. Wang, F. Harrou, and Y. Sun, "Wind Power Prediction Using Ensemble Learning-Based Models," IEEE Transactions on Sustainable Energy, vol. 12, no. 2, 2021, pp. 1017-1027. doi: 10.1109/TSTE.2020.3042578.

[13] L. Lu, Z. Xie, X. Zhang, S. Yang and R. Cao, "A dynamic wind turbine simulator of the wind turbine generator system", International Conference on Intelligent System design and engineering application,pp. 967–970. DOI: 10.1109/ISdea.2012.549.

[14] J. Tamura, "Calculation Method of Losses and Efficiency of Wind Generators", Wind Energy Conversion System, pp. 25-51, January 2012.

A Greedy Approach for Controller Placement in Software-Defined Networks for Multiple Controllers

Stavroula Lalou
Department of Digital Systems
University of Piraeus
Piraeus, Greece
slalou@unipi.gr

Georgios Spathoulas
Dept. of Inform. Sec. and Comm. Techn.
NTNU
Gjøvik, Norway
georgios.spathoulas@ntnu.no

Sokratis Katsikas
Dept. of Inform. Sec. and Comm. Techn.
NTNU
Gjøvik, Norway
sokratis.katsikas@ntnu.no

***Abstract*—The Controller Placement Problem (CPP) addresses the strategic positioning of Software Defined Networking (SDN) controllers within a network, crucial for efficient network management. It impacts network performance in latency, reliability, scalability, and resource usage. SDN architecture, separating control and data planes, enhances scalability and programmability compared to traditional architectures. Determining the optimal number and placement of controllers is a key challenge, with network latency being a primary performance factor. This study proposes a heuristic greedy algorithm to minimize end-to-end latency and reduce maximum latency between controllers and switches, aiming to mitigate controller queuing delay. Ultimately, deploying controllers in SDN-wide networks seeks to minimize maximum latency between controllers and switches.**

Keywords-Software Defined Networks, multiple controllers, contoller placement, latency.

I. INTRODUCTION

The rise of Software-Defined Networking (SDN) has been prompted by the escalating demands for new networks and the expansion of Internet coverage. As contemporary requirements surpass the limitations of traditional networks, SDN emerges as a promising paradigm. It addresses these challenges by separating the control and data planes, enabling the programmability of network configuration. The pivotal factor influencing SDN deployment and applications is the strategic placement of controllers. Within the SDN architecture, the use of single or multiple controllers is instrumental in achieving programmable, flexible, and scalable configurations. In the current SDN landscape, the employment of multiple controllers has become imperative. Recent developments have introduced various solutions aimed at enhancing scalability and optimizing controller placement selection. This study delves into the CPP by leveraging objective optimization with proposed algorithms.

Interaction time between the controller and the switch is an important parameter in locating the controllers. The proposed approach is a greedy algorithm for controller placement in a network. The algorithm aims to minimize the total cost of connecting nodes to controllers.

SDN is a network architecture that separates the control plane from the data plane. The control plane is responsible for making decisions and configuring the network, while the data plane is responsible for forwarding network traffic.

Multiple controllers are often used in SDN networks to distribute the control plane workload and improve network scalability. However, in a multi-controller SDN network, additional delays can be introduced due to communication between controllers.

Transmission delay between controllers can cause delays in network decision making, leading to reduced network performance and efficiency. In a multi-controller SDN network, each controller must have up-to-date information about the network topology and state, which is communicated through inter-controller messaging. Excessive transmission delay between controllers and switches can lead to increased packet delay, jitter, and even packet loss, leading to reduced network performance and efficiency.

The study aims to contribute to the understanding of relevant open problems in the realm of controller placement. By utilizing objective optimization algorithms, the research seeks to propose effective solutions that address the challenges associated with placing controllers optimally in SDN environments. As the field of SDN continues to evolve, identifying and addressing these challenges becomes crucial for the advancement and sustainability of programmable and scalable network configurations.

The contributions of this paper are:

- An effective solution that addresses the challenges associated with placing controllers optimally in SDN environments with multiple controllers.
- An implementation with greedy algorithm that finds the location that is closest to the most switches that do not have assigned controllers. The algorithm places a controller in that location, assigns each switch within the controller's coverage to that controller and calculates the latency between each switch and its assigned controller.
- A heuristic greedy algorithm designed to address the Controller Placement Problem. It aims to minimize end-to-end latency and reduce maximum latency between controllers and switches. By proposing a specific algorithmic approach, the study contributes to the practical implementation of controller placement strategies within SDN environments.

The remaining of the paper is structured as follows: In Section II, we briefly review necessary background knowledge on CPP in SDN and CPP approaches. In Section III, we discuss related work. In Section IV, we present our heuristic approach for latency. In Section V, we present the experimental setup that we used for evaluating the performance of the proposal and we discuss the results. Finally, Section VI summarizes our conclusions.

II. Background

A. The Controller Placement Problem (CPP)

The CPP [1] in Software-Defined Networking (SDN) involves strategically deploying controllers within the network, impacting various performance metrics like availability, fault tolerance, and convergence time. SDN, with its separated control and data planes, offers solutions to network challenges, making CPP a critical factor for optimizing network performance. Early research by Heller et al. [1] framed CPP as a facility placement problem, highlighting its complexity. Subsequent studies focused on minimizing propagation delay by determining optimal controller locations and quantities. Techniques like K-center and Multiobjective Optimization Controller Placement (MOCP) [8] address different aspects such as network reliability, load balance, and latency. CPP requires careful planning considering factors like network topology, latency, and controller placement to ensure optimal performance and resilience. Our approach offers a heuristic implementation of CPP, aiming to minimize the number of controllers while addressing latency concerns, ultimately enhancing network responsiveness and robustness in the face of failures.

B. General formulation of CPP

The primary network components for an SDN-enabled network are switches, controllers, and the links that join them. Therefore, the network is often modeled as an undirected graph

$$G = (SEC) \qquad (1)$$

where S represents the set of switches and E is the set of physical links among those switches or controllers, and C be the controllers to be placed in the network. The switches and the controllers are represented as follows: S = s1, s2, s3, ... sn, where n denotes the number of switches in the network, and C = c1, c2, c3, ... ck, where k denotes the number of controllers located in the network. Here, Pi = p1, p2, p3, ... pk is one possible placement of the k controllers. The relationship between switches and controllers is represented by the condition that the set of controllers C is a subset of the set of switches S, denoted by $C \subseteq S$. This indicates that controllers are located within the network's switches. The shortest path between a switch $s \in S$ and a controller $c \in C$ indicates the minimum number of links (or hops) required to reach the controller from the switch [2].

C. Multiple controller placement problem

The challenge of deploying multiple controllers arises from the limitations of a single centralized controller, which struggles to keep pace with the growing demands of expanding networks and applications. Relying on a solitary controller creates a potential single-point bottleneck and failure risk, as it shoulders the entirety of control activities. Consequently, any network failure could severely impact overall network performance. Thus, the adoption of a multi-controller approach emerges as a viable solution for large-scale Software-Defined Networking (SDN), particularly concerning the scalability of the control plane. The inadequacy of deploying a single controller for managing extensive networks, advocating instead for the deployment of multiple controllers. However, effectively placing multiple controllers remains a complex task. To optimize network scalability and minimize latency, particularly in larger networks, leveraging multiple controllers to manage control plane traffic is deemed most effective. Two prevalent architectures for multi-controller setups are flat architecture and hierarchical architecture [20]. Deploying multiple controllers in a large-scale SDN environment aims to reduce latency, distribute controller workload, and optimize various network performance indicators related to controller placement. Consequently, an SDN controller can oversee multiple Network Operating Systems (NOS) [19]. While a single controller suffices for small networks like those in data centers, the adoption of multi-controller deployment is increasingly favored to bolster the scalability and stability of Wide Area Networks (WANs). Dhar et al. [21] underscore the necessity of deploying multiple controllers to maintain scalability and reliability in large SDN setups.

III. Related Work

Latency holds significant importance in Software-Defined Networking (SDN) due to the frequent interaction between switches and controllers. Existing solutions for the CPP typically prioritize minimizing both propagation delay and controller processing delay. Regarding propagation delay, CPP resembles the facility location problem.

Heller et al. [1] were pioneers in CPP research, aiming to minimize worst-case delay while proving its NP-Hard complexity. Since then, numerous researchers have proposed diverse CPP solutions, extending optimization objectives from original switch-controller delay to inter-controller delay, controller capacity, and cost considerations.

Zhu et al. [3] focus on minimizing propagation delay between switches and controllers, formulating CPP as a control plane delay minimization problem and introducing a new algorithm based on clustering and Dijkstra's algorithm. For controllers with limited capacities, Yao et al. [5] define a capacitated CPP and develop an efficient algorithm for optimizing propagation delay.

In another study [6], the authors address controller placement under dynamic network traffic by integrating the controller module placement algorithm with a dynamic flow management algorithm, albeit suitable for small-scale networks only.

Tanha et al. [7] concentrate on CPP within Software Defined Wide Area Network (SDWAN), introducing a clique-based approach from graph theory for polynomial-time solution derivation. In subsequent works [2], [8] CPP is formulated considering switch-to-controller delay, controller-to-controller delay, load balancing, and link utilization rate as objectives.

Wang et al. [9] identify that a critical difficulty in SDN is selecting suitable locations for controllers to reduce the latency between controllers and switches. The CPP described a few of the performance factors that were taken into consideration, including control plane overhead, latency, load imbalance, cost, and connection. They use the controller-to-node latency (propagation, queuing, and processing delay) as a crucial performance parameter.

Mamushiane et al. [10] extended and used a facility location approach known as Partition Around Medoids (PAM) with propagation latency to determine the optimum places to put SDN controllers. They suggested using the Silhouette and Gap Statistics algorithms to decide how many controllers to deploy in a wide-area network.

Rasol et al. [11] assess the Joint Latency and Reliability-aware Controller Placement (LRCP) optimization model. With the help of alternate backup channels, LRCP gives network administrators a variety of options for balancing the reliability and latency trade-offs between controllers and switches. This study suggests the Control Plan Latency (CPL) metric, the sum of average switch-to-controller latency and the average inter-controller latency, in order to evaluate the controller placements offered by LRCP and determine how effective they are in an actual controller deployment.

In each link failure state, Fan et al. [13] further take into account the number of control path reroutings and the worst-case latency between the controller and the switch. To solve the problem, they offer a heuristic approach based on particle swarm optimization. The suggested algorithm's usefulness is demonstrated by the numerical results. Additionally, it demonstrates that in the majority of link failure conditions, the suggested technique may ensure the latency and reliability of the control layer.

Fan et al. [14] present the Resilient Controller Placement (RCP) algorithm. The objective of this approach is to to minimize the average latency between all switches and the appropriate controllers in the event of a single broken link. The latency of each path is made up of the latency of the primary path plus the average of any potential backup paths that might be available in the event of a single link failure.

Chen et al. [14] present that the network is separated into many sub-networks, and the essential performance metric is the latency between the controller and switch.

Liao et al. [17] can be used to determine the latency model in this study or a reliable CPP, Singh et al [22]. suggest a Varna Based Optimization (VBO) to guarantee that it reduces the overall average latency. Their results demonstrate that the proposed VBO algorithm outperforms other effective heuristic algorithms for the Reliability-aware CPP (RCPP), such the Particle Swarm Optimization PSO. PSO and Teachning Learning-Based Optimization (TLBO) and their experimental results show that TLBO performs better than PSO for publicly accessible topologies.

In [18], reducing network latency between controllers and switches is crucial for SDN performance. The study introduces a Controller Node Partitioning Algorithm (CNPA) to minimize end-to-end latency. By partitioning the network and deploying controllers strategically, the aim is to decrease latency between controllers and switches in SDN-enabled wide-area networks.

IV. Our proposal

Our research focuses on latency which is one of the most often used performance indicators. Transmission, propagation, queuing, and processing delay make up the total latency. We evaluate latency between switch to controller latency (also known as controller-node latency) and controller-controller latency.

The proposed algorithm is a greedy algorithm for placing controllers near switches to minimize the latency between controllers and nodes. The algorithm calculates the latency between each controller and its assigned nodes. The latency is calculated as the Euclidean distance between the controller and node, plus the transmission delay. The algorithm assigns each node to the controller with the lowest latency.

The algorithm starts by initializing a costs, where each element costs[i][j] represents the cost of connecting switch i to controller j. The costs are calculated by computing the Euclidean distance between the switch and the controller. The algorithm then initializes an assigned array, where each element assigned[i] is a list of nodes assigned to controller i. The unassigned nodes are stored in a list called unassigned. The algorithm then enters a loop, where it repeatedly selects an unassigned node and assigns it to the closest available controller. The closest controller is determined by finding the controller with the smallest cost to the node's switch. If no controller is available, the node is skipped. The algorithm continues until all nodes have been assigned to a controller. The final result is a list of lists, where each inner list contains the nodes assigned to a specific controller.

A. *Implementation*

We use the controller-node latency and controller-controller (propagation, queuing, and processing delay) as a crucial performance parameter. We have implemented a heuristic approach based on greedy algorithm. The basic idea of this approach is to obtain the minimum number of controllers which minimizes inter nodes distances to obtain acceptable latency from nodes to their assigned controller and also between controllers. Greedy algorithm uses the Euclidean distance between nodes and controllers as the cost function to determine the best immediate solution. In the context of the controller placement problem, the greedy algorithm calculates the Euclidean distance between each unassigned node and each available controller, and assigns the node to the controller with the smallest distance. Then, the distance between switches and controllers is calculated and the nodes are allocated to the closest controller.

If the controller does not have the capacity to handle the node, the algorithm searches for the following nearest controller and carry out the same operation. This process will continue until an controller found and allocate rest of the node to the controller. The greedy solution provide by the algorithm fails when no controller can accommodate the required capacity, that case is considered as the worse case.

A greedy heuristic algorithm is a type of algorithm that makes the locally optimal choice at each stage with the hope of finding a global optimum. It is a simple and fast algorithm. In the context of the CPP in multiple software-defined networking, a greedy heuristic algorithm can be used to find a solution that minimizes the latency between controllers and switches. The algorithm would iteratively place controllers in locations that minimize the maximum distance to any switch, without considering the effect on future decisions. This approach is simple and fast, but it may not always find the optimal solution, and it may lead to higher latency between some controllers and switches. Here are the steps of the proposed approach for the CPP in SDN:

- Initialize a list of available locations for controllers.
- While there are still switches without assigned controllers:
  a. Find the location that is closest to the most switches that do not have assigned controllers.
  b. Place a controller in that location.
  c. Assign each switch within the controller's coverage to that controller.
- Calculate the latency between each switch and its assigned controller.

In our approach, switches is a list of (x, y) coordinates representing the locations of the switches, controllers is a list of (x, y) coordinates representing the locations of the controllers, and nodes is a list of nodes to be assigned to controllers. Each node has a switch attribute indicating which switch it is connected to.

The greedy controller placement function first calculates the Euclidean distance between each switch and controller and stores the distances. It then initializes a list assigned to keep track of which nodes have been assigned to which controllers.

The function then permutes the list of unassigned nodes and assigns each node to the controller with the lowest cost. The function returns the assigned list, which indicates which nodes have been assigned to which controllers.

This algorithm initializes a list of available locations for controllers, and then enters a while loop as long as there are still switches without assigned controllers. In each iteration, it finds the location that is closest to the most switches that do not have assigned controllers, places a controller in that location, and assigns each switch within the controller's coverage to that controller. It also calculates the latency between each switch and its assigned controller.

The algorithm uses a vector of Location structs to represent the available locations for controllers. Each Location struct contains the index of the location, the distance to the nearest unassigned switch, and a vector of unassigned switches that are within the controller's coverage.

The algorithm sorts the locations based on their distance and the number of unassigned switches within their coverage. It then iterates over the sorted locations and assigns a controller to each location that has not been assigned yet.

The algorithm returns a vector of Controller structs, where each Controller struct contains the index of the controller and the number of assigned switches.

The switch distances list represents the distances from each switch to a central location, and the controller coverage variable represents the coverage radius of each controller. The function returns a list of controller locations and a modified switch distances list that contains the latency between each switch and its assigned controller.

The function works by iterative placing controllers in the location that is closest to the most unassigned switches, and then assigning all switches within the controller's coverage to that controller. The function continues to place controllers until all switches have been assigned to a controller.

V. Performance Evaluation

A. *Experimental Setup*

A simulation has been conducted to assess the performance of the proposed scheme. The system on which the simulation was executed was based on a Virtual Machine (VM) with Ubuntu 22.04 OS, 16 GB of memory and OpenFlow Switches. We emulate the performance using Mininet and Ryu controller [22] component-based software defined networking framework.

We evaluated the performance of our system in terms of latency and transmission delay. These factors are crucial in Software-Defined Networking (SDN) due to the frequent communication between switches and controllers. The Controller Placement Problem in SDN often focuses on minimizing both transmission delay and controller processing delay. Transmission delay in CPP is similar to the facility location problem, where the goal is to find the best location to place the controllers to reduce the distance between the switches and the controllers. This is an important factor in ensuring efficient communication and reducing latency in SDN networks.

B. *Results*

We have created a network of 6 controllers and 8 nodes (switches). We calculated the latency between controllers to nodes and between controllers.

Controller- Node latency is the time it takes for a message to travel from a controller to a node in a network. Transmission delay, also known as latency, is the time it takes for a message to be transmitted over the physical link between the controller and the node. Figure 1 depicts the latency between each controller and its assigned nodes. The latency is calculated in seconds. The total transmission latency between controllers to nodes is 10.067 seconds, it is the sum of all the latencies between each controller and its assigned nodes as described in Table I. The transmission delay between controllers is 1.414 seconds and is lower than the controller-controller latencies. The transmission latency as shown in Figure 1 includes the time it takes for the switch to receive the data from the sender, process it, and send it to the receiver.

The latency between two controllers is calculated as the Euclidean distance between the two controllers and the transmission delay because the signal has to travel from one controller to the other, and then back to the first controller. It is depicted in Figure 2. The transmission delay is also counted for the round-trip time. The Euclidean distance between two controllers increases as the controllers are placed further apart, so the latency between two controllers will also increase as they are placed further apart.

The nodes are placed at positions (3, 3), (4, 4), (3, 4), (3, 5), (4, 3), (4, 4), (5, 3), and (5, 4). The Euclidean distance between between Controller 1 and Node 1 is math.sqrt((0 - 3) ** 2 + (5 - 3) ** 2) = 3.61 units, so the latency between Controller 1 and Node 1 is 3.61.

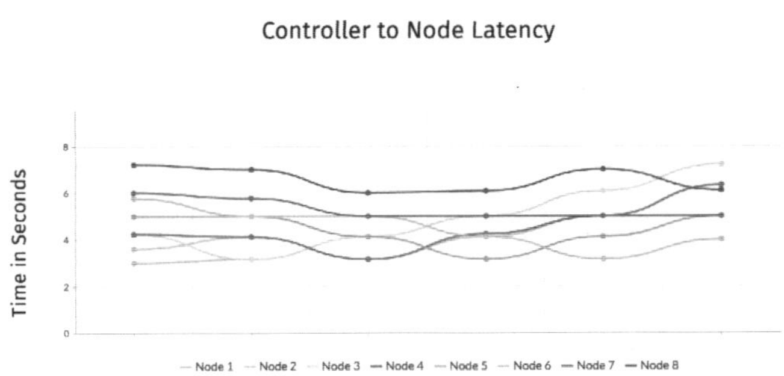

Figure 1. Controllers to Node Latency.

Controllers are placed at positions (0, 5), (10, 5), (20, 5), (30, 5), (40, 5), and (50, 5). The Euclidean distance between two adjacent controllers is 10 units, so the latency between two adjacent controllers is 10 + 2 * transmission delay.

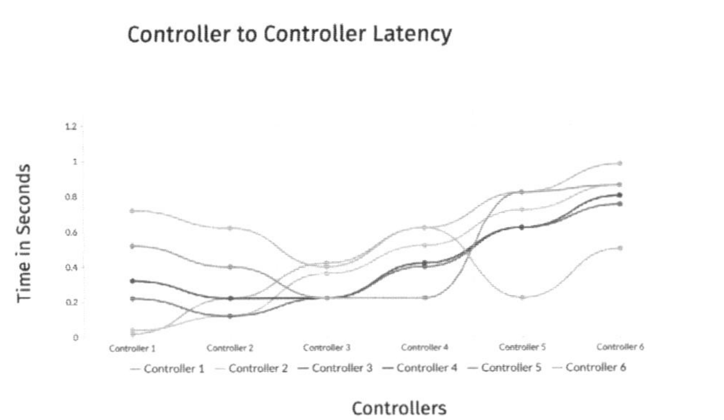

Figure 2. Controller to Controller Latency.

In our implementation, we use a nested loop to iterate over each node and controller, and find the minimum latency between the node and the controller. We then sum up these minimum latencies to get the total transmission delay. The controller with the minimum latency is assigned to the node. Finally, the total transmission delay is calculated by summing up the minimum latencies between each node and its assigned controller.

Table I shows the latency between each controller and the nodes assigned to it. The first controller has a latency of 0.21 seconds for the first node and 0.42 seconds for the second node.

TABLE I
CONTROLLER-NODE TRANSMISSION DELAY IN SECONDS

Controllers	Node 1	Node 2	Node 3	Node 4	Node 5	Node 6	Node 7	Node 8
Controller 1	0.21	0.42	0.44	0.42	0.43	0.44	0.46	0.43
Controller 2	0.48	0.21	0.33	0.33	0.30	0.33	0.36	0.34
Controller 3	0.59	0.43	0.21	0.22	0.22	0.21	0.22	0.22
Controller 4	0.57	0.46	0.32	0.21	0.21	0.22	0.22	0.21
Controller 5	0.53	0.41	0.32	0.33	0.21	0.22	0.22	0.21
Controller 6	0.63	0.48	0.36	0.35	0.34	0.21	0.22	0.21

Table II calculates the average controller latency. The delay is calculated as the sum of the transmission delays. According to the results, in an SDN network with multiple controllers, the latency numbers are low.

TABLE II
AVERAGE TRANSMISSION DELAY PER CONTROLLER

Controllers	Average Transmission Delay per Controller
	Average Latency
Controller 1	0.122 Seconds
Controller 2	0.118 Seconds
Controller 3	0.133 Seconds
Controller 4	0.132 Seconds
Controller 5	0.124 Seconds
Controller 6	0.115 Seconds

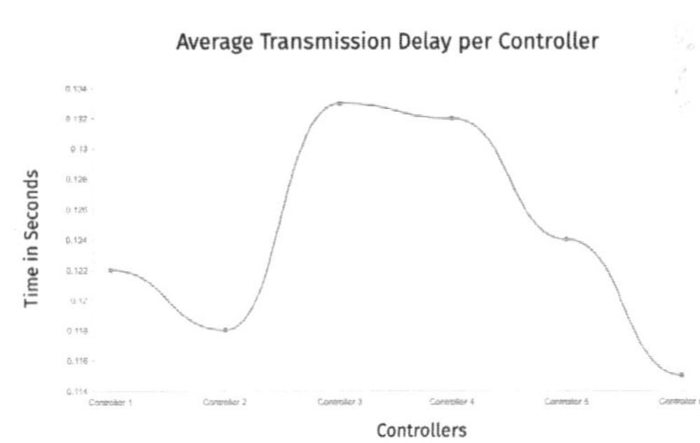

Figure 3. Transmission Delay per Controller.

The latency numbers represent the time it takes for a controller to send a message to another controller. The latency numbers are calculated as the average of the time it takes for the sender to send the message and the time it takes for the receiver to receive the message.

The Controller-Controller latencies show the latency between each pair of controllers. The latencies are relatively small and the switch is able to transmit data quickly between them. The controller-controller latencies represented in Figure 2 are the time it takes for the switch to process the data.

These latencies are lower than the total transmission latencies because the switch only needs to process the data once, not for each controller sending a message to another controller.

Transmission delay per controller is illustrated in Figure 3. The transmission delay per controller is obtaining by dividing the total transmission delay by the number of controllers. The transmission delay per controller is calculated by taking the average of the latencies for each controller, which can be done by summing up the latencies for each controller and dividing by the number of nodes.

The total transmission latency between controllers and nodes is higher than the controller-controller latencies because the switch needs to perform additional processing tasks. It includes the time it takes for the switch to receive the data from the sender, process it, and send it to the receiver.

VI. Conclusion

The idea of CPP in SDN is to adapt the facility location problem concepts to find the best location to place the controllers in the network, in order to reduce the transmission delay and improve the overall performance of the network. This implementation presents a greedy algorithm designed to optimize controller placement within a network, with the aim of minimizing latency between controllers to nodes and controllers to controllers and transmission delay.

Experimental results demonstrate the efficiency of the implementation, achieving near-optimal solutions within the CPP framework. The observed latencies between controllers and nodes, as well as between controllers themselves, remain low, affirming the success of the controller placement strategy. Furthermore, our proposal minimizes transmission delay between controllers, which is critical to ensuring high network performance and efficiency. According to our results, our proposal ensures high network performance, scalability, and efficiency by minimizing transmission delay between controllers and between controllers and switches.

Future work could investigate the impact of different network topologies on controller placement. This could provide insights into the algorithm's performance in different network configurations.

Acknowledgment

This work has been partly supported by the University of Piraeus Research Center.

References

[1] B. Heller, R. Sherwood and N. McKeown, "The controller placement problem", Proc. of the First Workshop on Hot Topics in Software Defined Networks, HotSDN '12, ACM, New York, USA, pp. 7–12, 2012, doi:http://doi.acm.org/10.1145/2342441.2342444.

[2] G. Schütz and J. A. Martins, "A comprehensive approach for optimizing controller placement in Software-Defined Networks", pp. 199, 2020, doi: https://doi.org/10.1016/j.comcom.2020.05.008.

[3] G. Wang, Y. Zhao, J. Huang, Q. Duan, and J. Li, "A K-means-based network partition algorithm for controller placement in software defined network", IEEE International Conference on Communications, Kuala Lumpur, pp. 1–6, 2016.

[4] L. Zhu, R. Chai and Q. Chen, "Control plane delay minimization based SDN controller placement scheme", Proc. 9th International Conference on Wireless Communications and Signal Processing (WCSP), Nanjing, pp. 1–6, 2017.

[5] G. Yao, J. Bi, Y. Li and L. Guo, "On the capacitated controller placement problem in software defined networks", IEEE Commun. Lett. 18, pp. 1339–1342, 2014.

[6] M. T . I. ul Huque, W. Si, G. Jourjon and V. Gramoli, "Large-scale dynamic controller placement", IEEE Trans. Netw. Serv. Manag. 14, pp. 63–76, 2017.

[7] M. Tanha, D. Sajjadi, R. Ruby and J. Pan, "Capacity-aware and delay-guaranteed resilient controller placement for software-defined WANs", IEEE Trans. Netw. Serv. Manag. 15, pp. 991–1005, 2018.

[8] B. Zhang, X. Wang and M. Huang, "Multi-objective optimization controller placement problem in internet-oriented software defined network", Comput. Commun. 123, pp. 24–35, 2018.

[9] G. Wang, Y. Zhao, J. Huang, and Y. Wu, "An effective approach to controller placement in software defined wide area networks," IEEE Trans. Netw. Serv. Manag., pp. 344-355, 2017.

[10] L. Mamushiane, J. Mwangama and A. A. Lysko, "Controller placement optimization for Software Defined Wide Area Networks (SDWAN)", pp. 45-66, 2021.

[11] K. A. Rasol and J. Domingo-Pascual, "Evaluation of joint controller placement for latency and reliability-aware control plane", Eighth International Conference on Software Defined Systems (SDS) IEEE, pp. 1-7, 2021.

[12] E. Borcoci, R. Badea, S. Georgica Obreja, and M. Vochin, "On multi-controller placement optimization in software defined networking-based wans", (ICN 2015), pp. 273, 2015.

[13] Z. Fan et al., "A multi-controller placement strategy based on delay and reliability optimization in SDN". Proc. 28th Wireless and Optical Communications Conference (WOCC), IEEE, 2019.

[14] Y. Fan et al., "Latency-aware reliable controller placements in SDNs", Proc. Communications and Networking: 11th EAI International Conference, (ChinaCom 2016 Chongqing), pp. 152-162, China, September 24–26, 2016.

[15] D. Hock, M. Hartmann, S. Gebert, M. Jarschel, T. Zinner, and P. Tran-Gia, "Pareto-optimal resilient controller placement in sdn-based core networks", Teletraffic Congress (ITC), 25th International IEEE, pp. 1–9, 2013.

[16] W. Chen, C. Chen, X. Jiang and L. Liu, "Multi-controller placement towards SDN based on Louvain heuristic algorithm", IEEE Access, 2018.

[17] J. Liao, H. Sun, J. Wang, Q. Qi, K .Li and T. Li "Density cluster based approach for controller placement problem in large-scale software defined networkings", 2017.

[18] G. Wang, Y. Zhao, J. Huang and Y. Wu, "An effective approach to controller placement in software defined wide area networks", IEEE Trans Netw Serv Manag, pp. 344-355, 2017.

[19] T. Hu, Z. Guo, P. Yi, T. Baker and J. Lan, "Multi-controller based software-defined networking: a survey", IEEE Access, 2018.

[20] M. Dhar, A. Debnath, B. K. Bhattacharyya, M. K. Debbarma and S. Debbarma, "A comprehensive study of different objectives and solutions of controller placement problem in software-defined networks", Trans. Emerg. Telecommun. Technol., pp. 33, 2022.

[21] "Ryu omponent-based software", [Online]. Available from: "https://ryu-sdn.org/", (Retrieved May 2024).

[22] K. Singh, Saurabh, S. Srivastava,"Varna-based Optimization: A New Method for Solving Global Optimization", International Journal of Intelligent Systems and Applications, pp. 1-15, 2018.

Add on Navigation and Control System for Outdoor Autonomous Wheelchairs for Physically and Mentally Challenged People

Ali T. Alouani and Tarek Elfouly
Department of Electrical and Computer Engineering
Tennessee Technological University
Cookeville, USA
aalouani@tntech.edu, telfouly@tntech.edu

Kaydn Brady
Center for Manufacturing Research
Tennessee Technological University
Cookeville, USA
Ktbrady42@tntech.edu

Abstract— **People with serious physical and/or mental disabilities, such as those with spinal cord injury, muscular dystrophy, dementia, etc., cannot benefit from available powered wheelchairs to gain independent mobility. The objective of this paper is to provide a preliminary design platform of an autonomous wheelchair generation capable, in the long run, of helping people with severe disabilities gain independent mobility. A high-level design, design details and development are provided in this paper. The design was extensively tested on the Tennessee Technological campus. Local media outlets presented a demo and interviewed the designers.**

Keywords- Physically challenged people; mentally challenged people; autonomous; deep learning; electric wheelchair; navigation and control.

I. INTRODUCTION

About 2.3 million people become disable each year in the United States [1]. Such accidents may lead to severe disabilities. According to the World Health Organization (WHO), dementia is one of the major causes of disability and dependency among older people globally [2].

Manual wheelchairs were originally invented to help some of the partially physically challenged people. Unfortunately, these devices are not as helpful to those who lack the strength or awareness to physically propel the wheelchair themselves. To solve this problem, electric wheelchairs were invented. A modern electric wheelchair is shown in Figure 1. While the user can just push a joystick with minimal strength to steer the wheelchair, there are still millions of people with severe disabilities that cannot benefit from such wheelchairs [3].

Recent advances in commercial electric wheelchairs have focused on adding alternative user control modules such as navigating based on the gaze or head tilt of the user, hand gesture control, or even voice control which would allow mobility for people of varying disabilities such as paralysis or amputees; however, these devices still fail to cater to so many [4]. This is because each solution still requires the user to have some level of muscular strength and complete awareness of the environment around the wheelchair, the destination he or she is trying to reach, and the path needed to reach the destination.

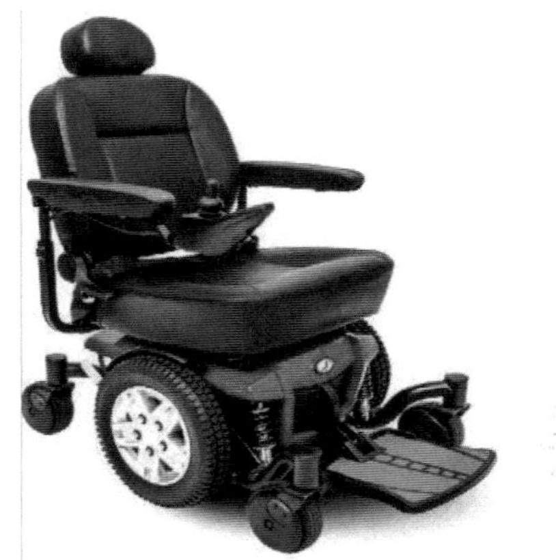

Figure 1. A Modern Electric Wheelchair.

For indoor or outdoor autonomous wheelchairs, the challenging task for a wheelchair is to localize itself in a self-generated map. For indoor navigation, this may be achieved using a Light Detection and Ranging (LiDAR) for Simultaneous Localization And Mapping (SLAM) [5]. Another localization technique uses wireless access points in each room [6].

Four outdoor navigation, autonomous wheelchairs have to navigate wide areas in unknown environments and changing sceneries. In such cases, indoor localization and mapping techniques cannot cope with environment variabilities in wide areas and similarities of features in different geographical locations in the areas to be autonomously navigated. LiDAR range is limited, and its accuracy is reduced with range. Wireless access point solution is too expensive.

For outdoor autonomous wheelchairs, several designs have been proposed. In [7], the authors use a camera to track a yellow line to navigate the wheelchair for people with walking disability. For a fully autonomous wheelchair, this approach is not reliable whenever the line paint becomes old or obstructed. Furthermore, this design does not allow for obstacle detection and avoidance. Finally, this design does not allow for localization of the wheelchair. In [8], the authors use voice command control to navigate the wheelchair. This assumes that the driver has full mental capacity to generate proper control commands and the sense of direction of where to go. In [9], the authors use a web-based mission planning and teleoperation and monitoring for the disabled person and the care giver. This is only an assistive approach as it keeps the care giver in the loop. In [10], deep learning was used to help visually impaired users.

High end Global Positioning System GPS and inertial navigation system were used to provide the autonomous navigation in [11], while landmarks were used for the same purpose in [12]. The location provided by a GPS may not be always reliable, especially whenever interferences, crowded area, and severe weather conditions are present. The use of landmarks is not an economical solution, especially whenever the travel distance is long, and requires maintenance.

The proposed solution takes advantage of already existing maps such as OpenStreetMap [13][14] and uses machine learning to provide a fully autonomous solution for navigation on sidewalks that can be used by a wide segment of people with physical and/or mental disability.

The rest of this paper is organized as follows. In Section II, the high-level conceptual design of the autonomous navigation and control system is presented. Section III contains the hardware and software requirements. Section IV overviews the system operation. Section V contains conclusions and future work.

II. HIGH-LEVEL CONCEPTUAL DESIGN

An important feature of the proposed design is to use already available mapping knowledge in the form of digital maps of the area to be navigated area. In this paper, Open Street Map will be used to provide the digital map the wheelchair will use for navigation from one location to another. Open Street Map is an online collaborative map of the entire world that can be accessed through the open-source Python API OSMNx [13]. From this API, one can gather information, such as building names, street names, sidewalk layouts, construction areas, road layouts, sidewalks, intersections, and much more. In this paper, the focus is on the sidewalk layout and building names/locations of the navigation area. An example of Open Street Map of all the sidewalks of Tennessee Technological University TTU campus is shown in Figure 2. In this map, 1 inch corresponds to 430 ft. Given the Open Street Map of the area where the user lives, he/she can use his/her house/apartment as the origin of a relative coordinate system, then express every point on the original map with respect to the chosen origin to make it a local digital map.

The proposed system has two levels of navigation and control: A high and low levels, Figure 3. The high-level uses the local digital map, acquires information from the onboard sensors and sends a control command to the low-level control. Such commands include obstacle avoidance, move forward, turn left or right, etc. The low-level control translates the commands to control signals applied to the drive motor.

Figure 2. TTU Campus Sidewalks provided by OpenStreetMap.

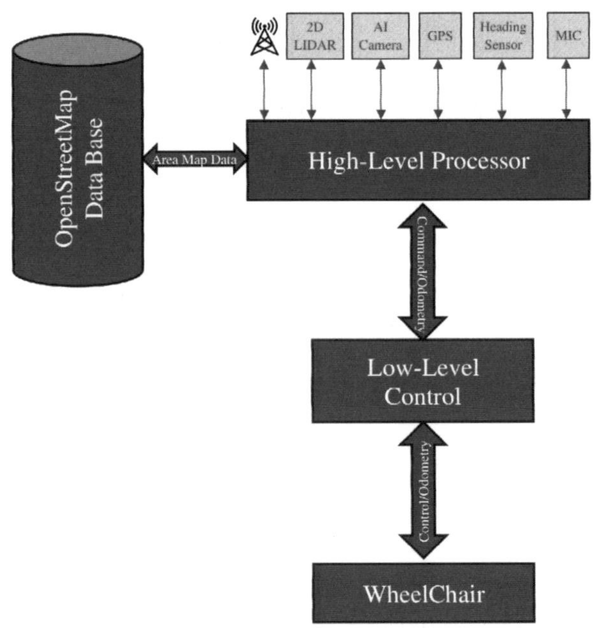

Figure 3. High-Level Conceptual Design of the Navigation and Control System.

III. HARDWARE AND SOFTWARE REQUIREMENTS

In this work, the only requirement from the user is to tell the system the destination location such the name of a building. This can be achieved via a vocal command or by a care giver via wireless communication. The navigation and control system must perform several tasks: host the digital map of the navigation area, execute obstacle avoidance, keep the wheelchair on the sidewalk of the path to be followed, and keep approximate location of the wheelchair until the destination location is reached. For this purpose, the following sensors are needed: 2D LiDAR for obstacle avoidance, a camera for navigation, and odometry to provide approximate traveled distance, a heading sensor, and a GPS to provide an approximate location of the wheelchair, a microphone, and a wireless communication between the wheelchair and the care giver. Note that the GPS is only relied on to obtain an approximate location in navigation area. Furthermore, the objective here is not to follow accurately the desired path but keep the wheelchair approximately in the middle of the sidewalk using the vision-based sensor.

The software design includes several modules. A high-level summary flowchart is provided in Figure 4.

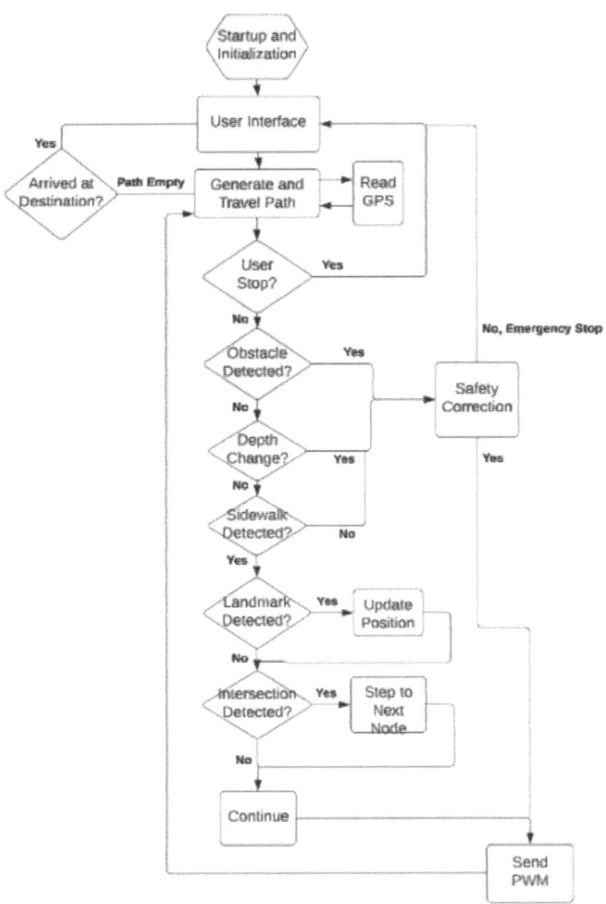

Figure 4. High-Level Software Flowchart.

IV. AUTONMOUS SYSTEM OPERATION

The first task is to use a microphone to tell the wheelchair where its final destination is. It is worth noting that the current location is assumed known such as the front of the house location, where the wheelchair user resides or the name of a building, he/she is at whenever the driver decides to go from one location to another. Then the high-level control system/navigation uses the digital map to determine the shortest path from the chair current location to its final destination. This path consists of a sequence of consecutive segments of the sidewalk. Each segment is characterized by the location of two end nodes and the distance between the two nodes. Given the two nodes, the absolute heading of the line joining the two noes will be determined. The wheelchair has to travel along these segments in the proper order until it reaches its final destination. An example of a generated path going from one building to another is shown in red Figure 5. One major challenge of this control and navigation system is to keep the wheelchair on its intended segment of the sidewalk as it moves toward its destination.

Figure 5. Automatically Generated Shortest Planned Path (in red).

Once a path has been selected, the wheelchair starts with the first segment of the path using the heading of that segment. Using its approximate odometry readings and the known length of the segment, the wheelchair will know that it is about to enter the second segment. At that time, the wheelchair will start turning or continue in the same direction without leaving the sidewalk. Keeping the wheelchair on the sidewalk at all times will use a camera as will be discussed later. The wheelchair keeps track of its position by fusing the information from its odometry and the GPS whenever available, and the heading measurements. Whenever, the wheelchair makes a turn, it will compute the new heading using the two ends of the new segment and uses this new heading as the reference heading and the heading sensor measurements as feedback. Whenever the wheelchair encounters an intersection, it will either go straight, turn left, or turn right, etc. The decision of what to do is based on the planned path and the wheelchair position as it approaches an intersection that is confirmed by the camera sensor. The wheelchair can use its current position on the planned path to predict approximately the next turn and slows down to turn to follow the new heading. If an obstacle appears while traveling, the wheelchair uses the LiDAR information which has enough range to allow the wheelchair to execute the proper maneuver to avoid the obstacle while staying on the sidewalk.

In all cases, the challenge for the wheelchair is to stay on the sidewalk at all times until it reaches its destination. The first solution considered was the use of computer vision-based approach using classical image processing techniques [15]-[19].

Figure 6 shows the performance of lane detection using different edge detection techniques, while Figure 7 shows a sidewalk detection in the presence of grass, where images A and E are raw images of two different scenes.

Figure 6. Lane detection. A raw image, B. using edge detection, and C using Hough line transform.

Because of the variability in the images of the sidewalks due to weather conditions, lighting conditions, crowdedness of the sidewalk, and variability of the scenery, classical image processing techniques did not perform well in keeping the wheelchair on the sidewalk. Since the navigation and control operate in real time and given the variability in the images acquired by the camera, a human-like brain is needed to process images with varying pixel density and still extract the sidewalk from such images in order to keep the wheelchair on the sidewalk.

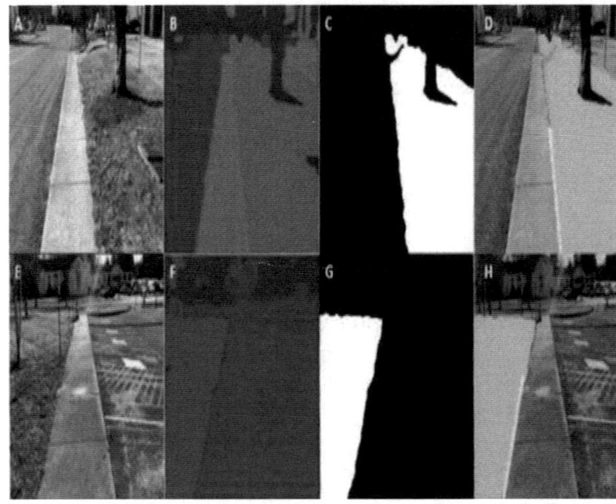

Figure 7. Sidewalk detection in the presence of grass: ((B, F) using the K-Means clustering, (C, G) using color thresholding of the green pixels, and (D, H) using Hough Line.

Artificial Neural Network (ANN) is inspired by the structure and function of neurons in the brain. These networks can take in substantial amounts of data and make inferences based on what it has learned and has previously seen. Much like a brain, the ANN consists of three or more layers of neurons: An Input layer, one or more hidden layers, and an output layer. Each neuron within the neural network has both a weight and threshold. To pass data along to the next neuron this threshold must be surpassed. An example of an artificial neural network is shown in Figure 8, [20].

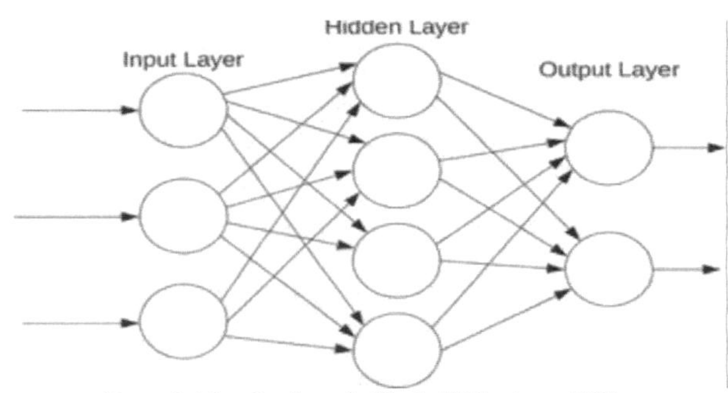

Figure 8. Visualization of a Single hidden layer ANN.

For a complex mapping between the inputs and outputs, more than one hidden layer will be needed. This leads to Deep Neural Networks (DNN) [21]. Because of the increased number of layers, these networks can model complex mapping between inputs and outputs, extract structural knowledge from data, and make inferences from extracted knowledge. Convolutional Neural Networks (CNN) have been extensively used in machine vision [22]. To perform real time semantic segmentation, the bilateral segmentation network (BisNet) and in particular BiseNetV2 architecture is faster than most networks of its type. This is done through the separation of the network into two separate but parallel branches, detail and semantic [22]-[24]. Figure 6 shows the performance of the BiseNetV2 in detecting sidewalks under different scenarios and conditions. In this figure, images in the first column represent the input image of the sidewalk in front of the wheelchair, the second column is the output masks from the BiseNetV2, and the third column is the predictions applied to the input for visualization. This DNN shows its success in detecting the sidewalk in cluttered environments. Figure 9 shows its performance as far as detecting the sidewalk as well as intersections.

Once a final destination is chosen, the system automatically selects the shortest path to travel from its current location to the final destination. The user may choose to change the final destination while traveling. As discussed previously, a path is mostly a collection of consecutive sidewalk segments. In the absence of a curvature, a segment of a sidewalk is a straight line whose length and orientation may be obtained from the OpenSstreetMap. The navigation and control system use its heading sensor as feedback to follow the reference heading provided by the street map for that specific segment.

The camera/control system are responsible for keeping the wheelchair approximately in the middle of the sidewalk at all times. It is worth noting that the wheelchair does not have to follow a very specific path accurately as long as it remains on the sidewalk without oscillations. Figure 9 shows the performance of BiseNetV2 Model in detecting the sidewalk. Its performance allows the wheelchair to stay on the sidewalk for various sceneries and lighting conditions, Figure 10.

In situations where the system detects an intersection of sidewalks where the wheelchair is supposed to go straight, the system uses the heading sensor information to keep the wheelchair moving without executing a turn. Whenever the wheelchair is close to an intersection in which it is supposed to make a turn, it uses the new heading reference, provided by the path planning at that intersection, and uses the heading sensor as feedback to slowly make the turn to align itself with the new segment of the sidewalk of the planned path.

Figure 9. Performance of BiseNetV2 Model.

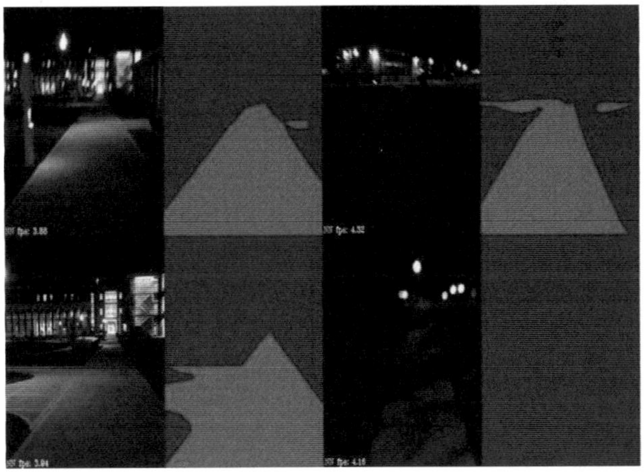

Figure 10. Sidewalk detection at night using BiseNet V2.

V. CONCLUSIONS

In this paper, the design of an autonomous navigation and control system that uses digital maps of a navigation areas of interest was developed and successfully tested on an existing wheelchair that can be manually controlled using joystick. The manual control was totally by passed and the proposed system was added to the wheelchair for autonomous outdoor navigation.

Future work will focus on additional testing in different navigation areas. In addition, more safety features will be added to deal with unforeseen situations such as a pothole in the sidewalk and deal with failure recoveries, while ensuring that the wheelchair to come to a complete stop before it leaves the sidewalks. For people with dementia, a feature that has already been designed, but not tested, consists of pushing a "Home Button" to inform the chair that it is time to go back to the user residence.

REFERENCES

[1] https://www.daveabels.com/blog/what-happens-when-a-car-accident-causes-a-permanent-disability/#:~:text=More%20than%2037%2C000%20people%20die,under%20the%20age%20of%2054. [accessed March 15, 2024]

[2] https://www.who.int/news-room/fact-sheets/detail/dementia [accessed March 15, 2024]

[3] L. Iezzoni, E. McCarthy, R. Davis, and H. Siebens. Mobility difficulties are not only a problem of old age. Journal of general internal medicine, 16, 2001, pp. 235-243.

[4] M. Hossain, M. Khondakar, M. Sarowar, and M. Qureshi "Design and Implementation of an Autonomous Wheelchair.", 4th International Conference on Electrical Information and Communication Technology (EICT), 2019, pp. 1-5.

[5] K. Trejos, L. Rincón, M. Bolaños, J. Fallas, and L. Marín. "2D SLAM algorithms characterization, calibration, and comparison considering pose error, Map accuracy as well as CPU and memory usage." Sensors vol 22, no. 18, 2022, 6903.

[6] B. Kuipers and Y. Byun, (2003). The MIT Intelligent Wheelchair Project: Developing a Voice-Commandable Robotic Wheelchair. IEEE Robotics & Automation Magazine, 10(1), pp. 51-56.

[7] K. Ugur, A. Abdulhafez, and H. Osman. Design and Analysis of a Novel Sidewalk Following Visual Controller for an Autonomous Wheelchair. Advances in Electrical & Computer Engineering, 24(1), 2024.

[8] L. Bouafif and C. Adnen, "A Smart Wheelchair for Autonomous Movements of Disabled People." Technology and Education 2023, 123.

[9] H. Nguyen and A. Göktoğan, "Enabling Autonomous Navigation within Urban Environments for Existing Powered Wheelchairs," 2022 IEEE/ASME International Conference on Advanced Intelligent Mechatronics (AIM), Sapporo, Japan, 2022, pp. 421-426.

[10] M. Elhassan, K. Sirlantzis, and G. Howells. "Indoor/outdoor semantic segmentation using deep learning for visually impaired wheelchair users." *IEEE Access* 9 (2021): 147914-147932.

[11] M. Imamura, R. Tomitaka, Y. Miyazaki, K. Kobayashi, and K. Watanabe, "Outdoor waypoint navigation for an intelligent wheelchair using differential GPS and ins," in SICE 2004 Annual Conference, vol. 3, 2004.

[12] D. Schwesinger et al., A smart wheelchair ecosystem for autonomous navigation in urban environments. Auton Robot 41, 2017, pp. 519–538.

[13] https://wiki.openstreetmap.org/wiki/About_OpenStreetMap [Accessed March 15, 2024]

[14] G. Boeing, "OSMNx: New methods for acquiring, constructing, analyzing, and visualizing complex street networks." Computers, Environment and Urban Systems, 65, 2017, 126-139.

[15] https://analyticsindiamag.com/what-are-the-different-image-thresholding-techniques-and-how-to-implement-them/ [accessed May 12, 2023].

[16] K. Ghazali, R. Xiao, and J. Ma. "Road lane detection using H-maxima and improved Hough transform." IEEE Fourth International Conference on Computational Intelligence, Modelling and Simulation, 2012, pp. 205-208.

[17] Y. Chiu and F. Lin, "Lane detection using color-based segmentation." 2005 IEEE Proceedings. Intelligent Vehicles Symposium, pp. 706-711.

[18] O. Duda and E. Hart, "Use of the Hough transformation to detect lines and curves in pictures." Communications of the ACM, 15(1), 1972, pp 11-15.

[19] Understanding k-means clustering. OpenCV Documentation. [accessed May 14, 2023].

[20] Z. Janikow, "Artificial neural networks methodology." In Soft Computing in Industrial Applications, Springer, Berlin, Heidelberg, 2010, pp. 3-20.

[21] W. Liu, Z. Wang, X. Liu, N. Zeng, Y. Liu, and F. Alsaadi. "A survey of deep neural network architectures and their applications." Neurocomputing 234, 2017, pp. 11-26.

[22] Z. Li, F. Liu, W. Yang, S. Peng, and J. Zhou. "A survey of convolutional neural networks: analysis, applications, and prospects." IEEE transactions on neural networks and learning systems 33, no. 12, 2021 pp. 6999-7019.

[23] C. Yu, J. Wang, C. Peng, C. Gao, G. Yu, and N. Sang. "Bisenet: Bilateral segmentation network for real-time semantic segmentation." In Proceedings of the European conference on computer vision (ECCV), 2018, pp. 325-341.

[24] C. Yu, C. Gao, J. Wang, G. Yu, C. Shen, and N. Sang, "Bisenet v2: Bilateral network with guided aggregation for real-time semantic segmentation." International Journal of Computer Vision, 129, 2021, pp 3051-3068.

A Process-Oriented Decision Support System for Sustainable Urban Development Strategies

Claudia Pedron, Matthias Baldauf, Melanie Rickenmann, Rainer Endl
Eastern Switzerland University of Applied Sciences (OST)
Institute for Information and Process Management (IPM)
Rosenbergstrasse 59, CH-9001 St. Gallen, Switzerland
e-mails: claudia.pedron@ost.ch; matthias.baldauf@ost.ch; rainer.endl@ost.ch; melanie.rickenmann@ost.ch

Abstract—**Political decision-makers play a crucial role in shaping sustainable urban development strategies, yet they often face challenges, such as limited expertise, resources, and access to suitable Information Technology (IT) tools tailored to their needs. In this paper, we introduce a prototype of a decision support system explicitly designed to assist political decision-makers in formulating sustainable urban development strategies, thereby enhancing their capacity in urban planning. Developed collaboratively by urban planners, infrastructure engineers, experts of geoinformation systems and political decision-makers, this tool prioritizes simplicity and intuitiveness. It offers transparent procedures and easy access to expert knowledge, streamlining the decision-making process. By automatically retrieving data from a geographic information system and facilitating calculations, it minimizes time investment. Additionally, it embraces a comprehensive approach that considers diverse stakeholder perspectives. Finally, it enhances adaptability and scalability without requiring advanced IT skills. While the involvement of experts remains vital in crafting sustainable urban development strategies, this tool empowers political decision-makers with a clear understanding of the decision-making-process. Armed with this knowledge, they can engage more effectively with stakeholders, leading to informed, long-term decisions. Looking ahead, the integration of deep learning methods holds potential to further enhance the tool's effectiveness and efficiency.**

Keywords-urban planning; sustainable urban development strategies; digital guide for political decision-makers; decision support system for urban development strategies.

I. INTRODUCTION

Urban systems are growing rapidly all over the world. Forecasts assume that the size of cities will increase dramatically due to the pace of growth. According to a United Nations forecast, more than 66 percent of the world's population will live in urban areas by 2050 [1]. Such rapid urban development poses a challenge for spatial planning and requires integrative approaches to tackle the negative environmental, social and economic impacts of urban development [2]. This is why the concept of sustainable urban development has emerged. In addition to developing compact cities to reduce urban sprawl, other aspects of sustainability, such as environmental quality, social equity, economic viability, life satisfaction, precise urban planning, land use, infrastructure and energy management should be considered [1]. Managing a variety of purposes and striving for many different, often conflicting goals to meet the needs of different stakeholder are required. This poses significant challenges for political decision makers and urban planners. Although they are aware of the goals of sustainable urban development, they often do not know how to achieve these goals [3].

Moreover, the development of compact cities often meets with resistance and triggers public debate. The lack of public acceptance is therefore an important reason for slow pace of urban densification.

Political decision-makers are crucial actors in the development and implementation of sustainable urban development strategies, but they often lack expertise, have limited time, as well as human and financial resources. Furthermore, they do not have suitable IT support tools, as most tools are designed for experts [3].

This article presents a prototype decision support system aimed at assisting political decision-makers throughout the strategic phase of urban development projects. This system facilitates the process, enabling decision-makers to make and advocate for sustainable decisions with confidence, competence, and manageable effort.

This tool was developed in the context of urban planning in Switzerland to provide support for planning authorities in municipalities and cantons. Since the new revision of the Swiss Urban Planning Act, which was passed in 2014, the municipalities and cantons have also played a central role in sustainable urban development in Switzerland. The act requires that future urban development should primarily take place in existing building zones and that cantons and municipalities should be responsible for this. The paradigm shift presents the planning authorities with challenging tasks.

When developing the tool described in this paper, the following research objectives were defined: (1) A digital decision support tool should be realized that implements a transparent and process-oriented approach to accompany political decision-makers step by step in formulating sustainable urban development strategies. This tool should be simple to use, intuitive, not require much effort in collecting, recording and elaborating data. It should enable easy access to the required specialist knowledge, empowering political decision-makers with a clear understanding of the decision-making process. (2) A comprehensive catalog of criteria should be integrated into the tool, allowing the urban development scenarios to be assessed according to the most relevant perspectives and strategic goals. The latest should consider diverse urban contexts, including cities with different urban planning challenges. (3) Rules, i.e., heuristics and calculations for the systematic assessment of urban development scenarios should be modeled transparently, managed centrally and be easy to adapt without specific IT skills, as there are numerous local and cantonal differences in Switzerland. (4) The IT tool should be easy to adapt and scale with little or no IT knowledge if new process steps or thematic aspects are to be considered, as spatial planning is a constantly evolving discipline.

The remainder of this article is structured as follows. Section II discusses the theoretical framework and reviews the international literature with a particular focus on the four research questions. Section III describes the methodological approach used to develop the solution. Section IV explains the technical aspects of the developed solution. Section V critically discusses the results regarding the degree to which the objectives were achieved and points out possible future developments.

II. Related Work

The work described in this paper was inspired by decision support systems in spatial planning. These tools are particularly suited to understand the complex problems of spatial planning in urban areas [3], as they are used to explore weakly structured or unstructured problems characterized by many actors, many options and high uncertainty [4]. They make it possible to create different scenarios in which the objectives of urban development can be adjusted to balance different environmental, social and economic disadvantages and advantages. Furthermore, the analysis of potential positive and negative impacts supports long-term decisions [5], while the consideration of different perspectives promotes stakeholder interest and leadership [6].

The components of a decision support system are (1) a database, which contains georeferenced or non-georeferenced data, (2) a modeling component, which contains various models, such as simulation models, projection and analytical models, and (3) a user interface, which allows the user to easily interact with the system [7]. For solving problems, spatial planners can select the appropriate model, execute it by using the data in the database and use the results coming from the decision support system as a basis for decision-making [7].

The selection of models, suitable data, or the interpretation of results from a decision support system can often pose challenges. Therefore, integrating expert systems presents an interesting solution [8].

Expert systems are computer-based systems that make it possible to access the extensive specialist knowledge of experts in a particular field to solve complex problems and support well-founded decision-making processes. In the context of spatial planning, they can integrate rules, heuristics and experiences of urban planners to help diagnose problems, evaluate options and recommend actions [7][8].

Theories, rules of thumb, estimates and computational methods of experts are included in the knowledge base of the expert systems. The set of rules to manipulate the information of the basic knowledge to generate recommendations is called control system. This is distinct from the basic knowledge so that both systems can be expanded and adapted as required without causing substantial changes to the computer program. The rules in the control system are generally defined in the form of if-then-else statements [7] and their adaptation generally requires programming knowledge.

Given the emphasis on facilitating the creation of sustainable urban development scenarios, integrating expert systems into decision support systems has been explored with keen interest, aiming to ensure easy accessibility to expert knowledge.

Decision support systems have continuously evolved over the years to include more and more advanced technologies. Despite this modernization, however, they still present gaps that result in an obstacle to the use of these tools [3]. These tools are typically very specific, require specialist knowledge to operate, are time-consuming, complex, less intuitive and not scalable [3]. Furthermore, their integration is insufficient [9] to foster a holistic view, a crucial element for sustainable urban development.

In addition, users may struggle to determine which tool is best suited for a given problem [3], as there are many decision support systems for various urban planning problems.

In general, decision support systems focus on the design and evaluation of possible urban solutions, but only a few focus on the decision-making process itself. [10]. According to reference [8], decision-making processes for sustainable urban development require structure and flexible guidance, to support argumentation and communication between stakeholders.

Although there have been attempts to formally model the decision-making processes in spatial planning [11], no relevant work could be found in the literature that systematically implements this approach. Only one paper was found in which a workflow management system was developed on top of a geoinformation system to provide spatial decision support by incorporating environmental data [12].

III. Methodology

For the development of the tool, the Design Science Methodology [13] was employed, which aims to create an artifact to solve a problem and analyze its performance. This methodology consists of three cycles: (1) the relevance cycle, (2) the rigor cycle and (3) the design cycle. The relevance cycle establishes the application context, determines the requirements for the artifact and defines the criteria for its success. In the rigor cycle, existing knowledge and theory is used to influence the design process and expand the knowledge base. In the design cycle, the artifact is designed, evaluated and, if the criteria are met, released into practice.

A. *Rigor cycles*

To develop the tool, experts and user representatives including urban planners, infrastructure engineers, experts of geoinformation systems and political decision-makers were identified. Through workshops and semi-structured interviews, based on a participatory human-centered design approach, functional and non-functional requirements for the tool were developed. These requirements were specified based on test areas with different urban contexts. Evaluation criteria were defined together with the participants. Expert knowledge for the creation and evaluation of urban development scenarios was identified through literature research, as well as workshops and interviews, and then modeled in traditional knowledge representation formats.

B. Relevance cycles

To develop the knowledge base, the approach utilized was based on the results of workshops, expert interviews, and an extensive literature review on decision support systems (see Section II). Additionally, extensive literature reviews were carried out on the following topics to identify useful theories, concepts, and technologies aimed at achieving the research objectives:

- Business process management concepts to design a digital guide that supports users in formulating sustainable urban development strategies.
- WorkFlow Management Systems (WFMS) for the implementation of the digital guide in a simple and flexible way.
- Theories and concepts to building a system of targets and metrics to assess sustainable urban development scenarios.
- Methods for modeling rules using an easy-to-learn language and centralized management of these rules in a user-friendly system.
- Low-code technologies to minimize the time required for programming.

a) Definition and modeling of business processes

For the design of the digital guide, inspiration stemmed from the idea that the process to formulate sustainable urban development strategies can be considered as a business process, consisting of a series of activities to achieve goals [14]. Therefore, business process management methods were employed to first identify the steps involved in formulating urban development strategies, and then to graphically model them, ensuring transparency and clarity [15].

Contrary to a deterministic model, findings from workshops with experts revealed that, while certain steps of the digital guide are essential, others can be optional or less precise. Creating a detailed process model using formal languages, such as Business Process Model and Notation (BPMN), was considered too restrictive, so we modeled the digital guide as a sequence of phases.

The identification of the process steps for strategy development was inspired by the work [11], which describes a metamodel for the spatial planning process. The presented process has a linear execution path over five main steps, organized as an iterative and cyclical process with several feedback transitions. This cyclical pattern facilitates and allows adjustments to the changes and insights arising during the process itself [11].

b) Workflow management systems

Once modeled, processes require effective execution and control, for which technical support is essential. WFMS play a central role in this regard. They have the characteristics of being able to react to changes in processes without program modifications [16], based on parts that can be reused, and are therefore highly adaptable.

Different types of WFMS exist. Form-oriented WFMS have been utilized [17] for implementing each process step of the digital guide. These are mostly used to read and display the content of database tables and are designed to be easily reused and customized, practically without programming knowledge [16].

c) Balanced Scorecard

The Balanced Scorecard (BSC) is a proven method for measuring and evaluating performance and progress in various organizational areas [18]. It offers a holistic, target- and Key Performance Indicator (KPI)-focused, balanced, and strategically oriented approach.

The BSC takes a holistic approach by considering multiple perspectives. It is goal- and KPI-oriented because it combines clear goals with specific performance indicators. It ensures that the assessment provides a balanced and comprehensive view. It is strategy-oriented, as the targets are derived directly from the strategy.

The decision to employ this method in assessing sustainable urban development scenarios was driven by the necessity for a comprehensive, balanced, and strategy-compliant system of targets and key figures. Furthermore, the definition of indicators for evaluating such scenarios was influenced by the findings of the ANANAS research project [19].

d) Modeling of decision rules

The key metrics for evaluating urban development scenarios should be determined using well-defined rules. These rules should not only be transparent and comprehensible for users but also adaptable or expandable if necessary. To achieve this, the rules must be described in a language that is both easily understandable and formal, allowing for straightforward conversion into a machine-interpretable format. The Decision Model and Notation (DMN) meets these requirements. It is a modeling language designed for the formal specification of decision logics and rules [20]. DMN allows for the representation of these logics through easily understandable graphical models. Elements such as decision diagrams and tables are used to formally describe decision rules and logics. Models created in this way can be applied in various contexts to formalize and automate decision-making processes. DMN thus provides a standardized language for communicating and exchanging decision logic [21].

e) Low-code technologies

Low-code technologies were used to develop the digital guide and the system for interpreting the rules created with DMN. This term covers methods and platforms that enable the development of applications with the help of prefabricated software modules without the need for extensive handwritten lines of code [22]. For development, the modules are selected with the help of a visual user interface and configured as required. The corresponding low-code platforms also offer powerful drag-and-drop functionalities, integrated databases and automation tools to speed up the development process. This not only enables faster development, but also means that less software development expertise is required [23].

The use of low-code technologies lent itself to the development of the digital guide because it allowed a prototype to be developed quickly, results from workshops could be visualized quickly, sometimes even 'on the fly', and the time required to develop the complete prototype remained within a manageable framework.

C. Design cycle

In the design cycle, the prototype of the decision support system was developed according to the requirements and evaluated in field tests using the defined test areas. Continuous iterations were carried out to refine and adapt the prototype. This involved optimizing the user interface to enhance user-friendliness, adapting the process steps for formulating sustainable urban development strategies, and refining the system of key figures and associated calculations.

For evaluating the prototype, the users had to assess the following criteria on a scale from 1 (very bad) to 6 (very good): user-friendliness, transparency, time-saving in collecting and analyzing data, accuracy of scenario assessments and easy adaptability and scalability of the tool.

IV. RESULTS

The developed solution comprises the following components:

- A digital guideline that enables the process-oriented recording and assessment of urban development scenarios.
- A system of targets and metrics integrated into the digital guide that enables a holistic, balanced and strategy-conform assessment of the scenarios.
- A separate 'set of rules' that communicates with the digital guide via an interface. It allows the modeling and execution of rules for the calculation of key figures in a formal and simple standard language.
- A geoinformation system that is linked to the digital guide and enables the georeferenced recording of the scenarios on the one hand and the visualization of the calculated key figures (e.g., visualization of land density) on the other.

The combination of the various software components is shown in Figure 1.

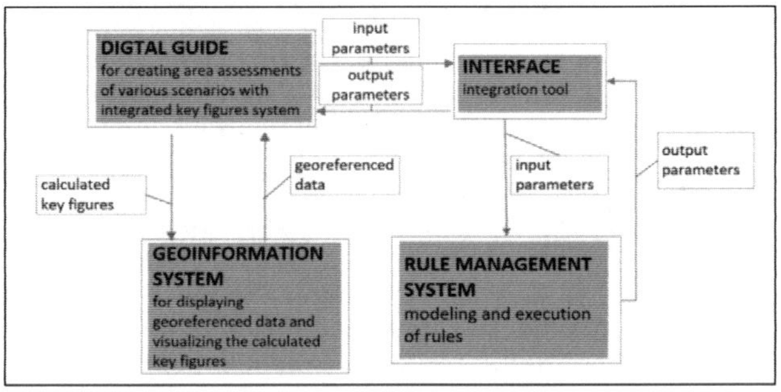

Figure 1. Interaction of the various software components.

A. The digital guide

The prototype was developed as a web-based application, utilizing the Microsoft PowerApps low-code platform [24]. Similar to a digital guide, it leads users through the process, which consists of seven main steps: Step 1: 'Selection of the project-specific development goals'; Step 2: 'Recording the current scenario'; Step 3: 'Evaluation of the current scenario'; Step 4: 'Selecting a scenario'; Step 5: 'Building scenarios'; Step 6: 'Evaluation of scenarios'; Step 7: 'Comparison of scenarios', with further sub-steps as shown in Figure 2. Each process step can be carried out for each of the six defined topic areas: Topic Area 1: 'Settlement'; Topic Area 2: 'Landscape'; Topic Area 3: 'Traffic'; Topic Area 4: 'Supply'; Topic Area 5: 'Building Opportunities'; Topic Area 6: 'Finance', with the respective sub-topic areas of urban development. The process steps in the created prototype are therefore navigated horizontally, while the topic areas are arranged vertically.

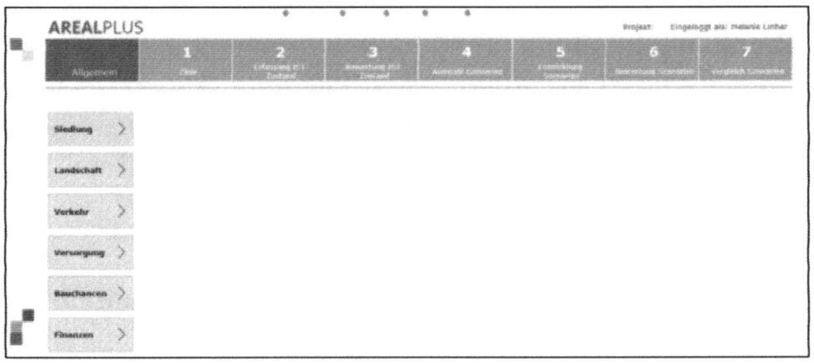

Figure 2. Process flow with the seven main steps and the six topic areas.

Figure 3 shows an example to illustrate the use of the guide, in which step 1, 'Objectives' ('Ziele'), is shown for the topic area 'Settlement' ('Siedlung') and the sub-topic area 'Land and building potential' ('Fläche und Flächenpotential').

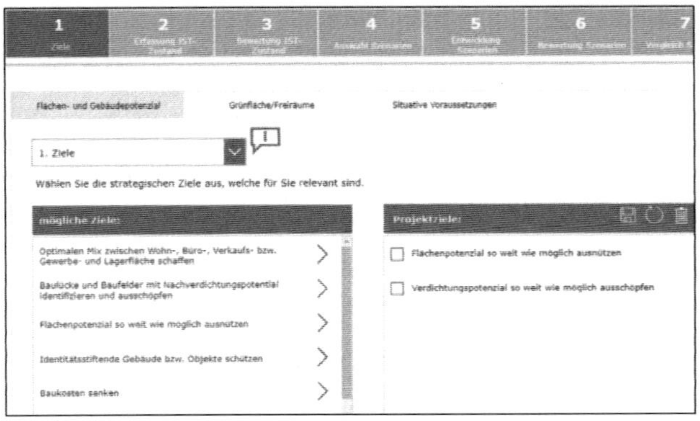

Figure 3. Step 1: Selection of the project-specific development goals.

Specifically, the user selects from a list of possible urban development goals ('mögliche Ziele') on the left-hand side, the specific goals 'utilize space potential as far as possible' ('Flächenpotential so weit wie möglich ausnutzen') and 'utilize densification potential as far as possible' ('Verdichtungspotential so weit wie möglich ausnutzen'). The selected goals for the analyzed test area are listed then on the right-hand side.

In sub-step 2, 'Key Figures' ('Kennzahlen'), which is represented in Figure 4, a list of possible key figures for quantifying the objectives chosen in the previous step is available for selection. In the specific case, the user selects the key figures 'land utilization rate of zone WG3' ('Ausnützungsziffer WG3'), where 'WG3' means 'residential zone with three full stores', 'land density' ('Dichte'), 'degree of land utilization' ('Flächenausnützungsgrad'), and 'degree of land densification' ('Verdichtungsgrad'). After the key figures have been selected, the target, minimum and maximum values should be defined on the right-hand side.

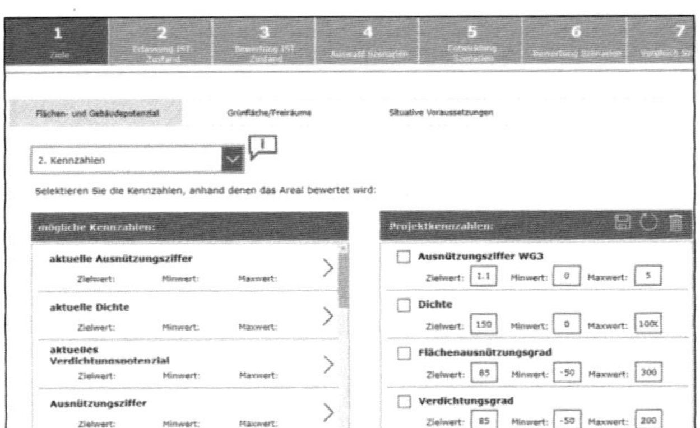

Figure 4. Step 1: Selection of the project-specific key figures.

In step 2, 'Recording the current scenario' ('Erfassung IST-Zustand'), land and building data, if available, should be obtained automatically from the geoinformation system (see Figure 5).

Figure 5. Step 2: Recording the current status (land parcel and buildings attributes).

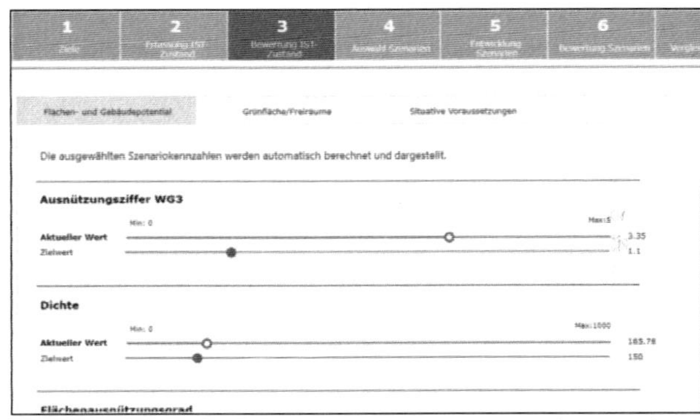

Figure 6. Step 3: Evaluation of the current scenario, with automatic calculation of the key figures 'land utilization rate WG3' and 'land density'.

In step 3, 'Evaluation of the current scenario' ('Bewertung IST-Zustand'), the selected key figures for the current scenario are automatically calculated for the analyzed test area, as illustrated in Figure 6. They are compared with the target value defined in step 1, 'Objective', and sub-step 2, 'Key Figures', allowing for immediate visualization of the effects associated with the created development scenario. This is especially useful when considering the perspectives of the stakeholder involved.

In step 4, 'Selecting a scenario', the user selects the scenario to be considered. The digital forms of step 5, 'Building scenarios' ('Auswahl Szenario'), are similar to those of step 2, 'Recording the current scenario'. Possible scenarios are created directly in the geoinformation system (as explained in sub-section D), and georeferenced information, such as the land area and the green area, is automatically transferred into the digital guide.

In step 6, 'Evaluation of scenarios' ('Bewertung Szenarien'), the key figures selected in step 1, 'Objectives', are automatically determined based on the modified properties of the respective scenario, similar to step 3, 'Evaluation of the current scenario'. In step 7, 'Comparison of scenarios' ('Vergleich Szenarien'), the calculated key figures for each recorded scenario are displayed side by side, as is shown in Figure 7.

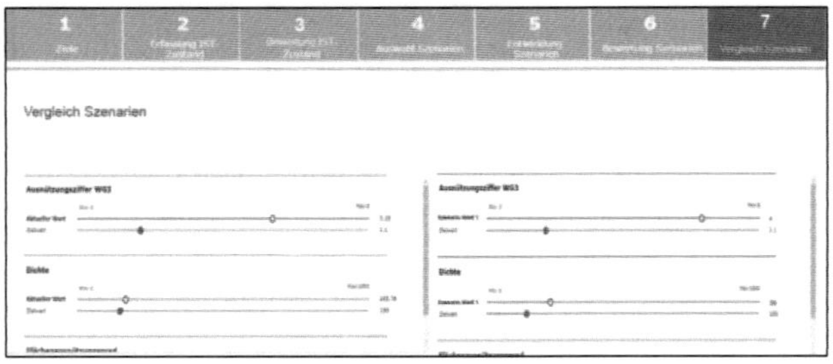

Figure 7. Step 7: Comparison of scenarios.

The digital guide is designed so that the digital forms have the same repetitive structure for each process step and topic area. Basically, three principal functions can be identified in the process of creating a scenario: (1) the recording of geo- or non-georeferenced data for each object related to the analyzed test area (e. g., the recording of the land area for each land parcel of the test area), (2) the calculation of the selected key figures for each object (e.g., the calculation of the land density of each land parcel of the test area), and (3) the calculation of key figures consolidated to the entire analyzed test area (e.g., the land density of the entire test area).

As a prototype version, the digital guide was designed to be as easily adaptable and modular as possible. This means that new topic areas, sub-topic areas, objectives, key figures, and objects, such as buildings and roads, can be easily added with the corresponding information and key figures.

B. *Target and indicator system for the systematic assessment of scenarios*

An important component of the digital guideline is a system of targets and indicators for a holistic and balanced assessment of the generated urban development scenarios. The perspectives of the target and indicator system correspond to the topic areas of the vertical navigation of the digital guide, as shown in Figure 8.

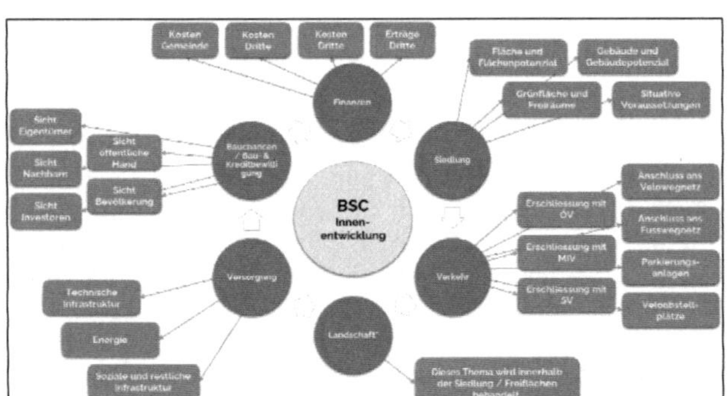

Figure 8. Target system for a holistic and balanced evaluation of scenarios.

The indicators, which correspond to the key figures listed in step 1, 'Objectives', and sub-step 2, 'Key Figures', of the digital guide, are generally quantitative indicators. For example, for the topic area 'Settlement' and the sub-topic area 'Area and Area potential', key figures, such as 'land utilization rate', 'land density', 'degree of land utilization' and 'degree of land densification' are calculated. However, qualitative key figures are also included, such as the assessment of the risk of objection for the topic area 'Building Opportunities' ('Bauchancen') and the sub-topic area 'Interest of Neighbors' ('Sicht Nachbarn'), where a subjective assessment on a scale of 1 to 5 is required.

C. *Rules for evaluating the scenarios*

The key figures for assessing the scenarios according to the selected objectives are calculated automatically within the digital guide. To formalize and simplify the rules for these automatic calculations, the standard language Decision Modeling and Notation (DMN) was utilized. These rules are modeled and executed within a separate low-code application called 'The Universal Process Orchestrator' on the Camunda platform [25], which then communicates with the digital guide via an interface.

Figure 9 illustrates the DMN model for calculating the key figure 'number of inhabitants and employees' (represented by the rectangle 'EW_and_BF').

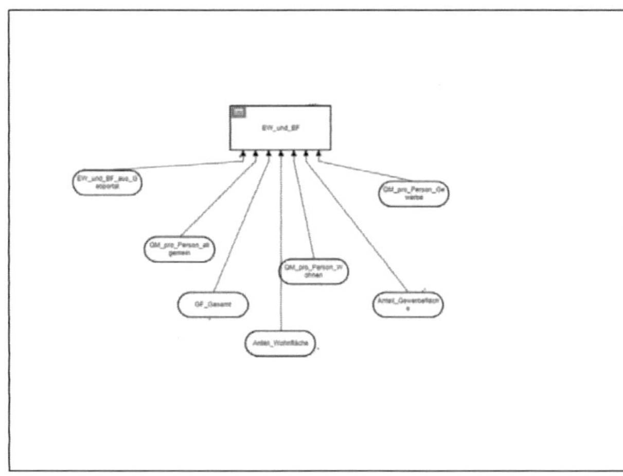

Figure 9. DMN model for the key figure 'Number of inhabitants and employees'.

This key figure depends on various input parameters, which are contained in ovals within the model. The relationships between the input parameters are then defined within a simple decision table.

D. *Geoinformation system for the georeferenced recording of scenarios*

Another important component of the system is the integration of the digital guide with a geoinformation system of GEOINFO [26], enabling the easy and intuitive creation of various urban development scenarios with georeferenced data. Specific aspects for each scenario can be specified using a set of user levels, which are selectable on the left-hand side. For instance, within the 'Settlement' user level, green areas or buildings can be created, while new roads can be recorded within the 'Supply' user level, as depicted in Figure 10.

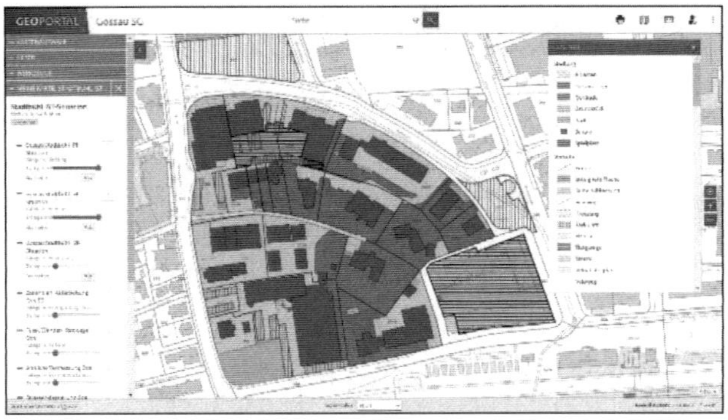

Figure 10. Snap shot of the geoinformation system: user levels 'Settlement' and 'Supply' for the considered test area.

A legend on the right-hand side helps identify which aspect (e.g., streets or green areas) is represented by each color or symbol. The georeferenced data entered in this manner can then be automatically imported into the digital guide for the corresponding topic area and sub-topic area.

Additionally, once key figures (such as 'land density') have been calculated in steps 3 and 6 of the digital guide, they can be displayed in the geoinformation system for each land parcel within the test area under consideration, as illustrated in Figure 11.

Figure 11. Different shades of green represent the land density of each land parcel within the test area under consideration.

V. CONCLUSION AND FUTURE WORK

The primary research question addressed in this paper examines the feasibility of a digital expert decision support system, designed to aid political decision-makers, in formulating and evaluating sustainable urban development scenarios. The objective was to implement a transparent and procedural approach to help the user step by step. Additionally, the tool was intended to be user-friendly, intuitive, and require minimal time for data collection, recording, and analysis.

The objectives associated with the primary research question have been successfully achieved.

The developed tool is user-friendly and intuitive, owing to its process-oriented approach and integration with the geoinformation system interface. This interface facilitates the straightforward creation of georeferenced scenarios and the automatic retrieval of associated georeferenced data. Key figures are also automatically calculated through integration with the rule system, reducing the need for extensive data preparation and analysis. Moreover, the presentation of scenario evaluation results against predefined objectives is clear and intuitive.

The implemented decision support system provides political decision-makers with a tool to comprehend the creation and evaluation of sustainable urban development scenarios in a transparent and systematic manner. This enables them to engage in competent and professional discussions with the involved experts and stakeholders. However, the tool cannot replace the creative process required to generate scenarios. Therefore, the development of sustainable and plausible scenarios still requires the involvement of experts.

The second research question, which related to the integration of a comprehensive catalog of criteria for assessing urban development scenarios according to the most relevant perspectives and strategic goals considering different urban contexts, has also been fully answered. According to project participants, this holistic approach to evaluating urban development scenarios, coupled with real-time visualization of their impacts, will expedite the decision-making process.

The third research question examined how rules, heuristics, and calculations for the assessment of the scenarios can be transparently modeled, centrally managed and executed. This question was fully answered by modeling the calculations using the standard DML language and executing them in a dedicated tool developed specifically for this purpose.

The fourth research question focused on the ease of adaptation and scalability of the IT tool, allowing for the incorporation of additional process steps, thematic aspects, or assessment criteria without requiring extensive IT knowledge. This question was positively addressed through the utilization of low-code technologies, employing both the Camunda software for managing and executing rules and the PowerApps software from Microsoft 365 for the digital guide. Furthermore, significant flexibility was ensured by applying concepts from workflow management software, which rely on reusable forms that can be easily customized.

As a final consideration in relation to the achievement of the project's goals, it is worth mentioning that all the criteria for evaluating the tool prototype, that are listed in section III and subsection C have been met more than satisfactorily by the users.

In summary, the unique value of the prototype tool described in this article lies in its integration of several advanced technologies and methodologies. Unlike existing decision support systems, our prototype offers an intuitive, user-friendly, and time-saving operation, combined with a process-based and transparent approach to the creation and holistic evaluation of urban development scenarios. Furthermore, the specific combination of geoinformation systems with expert systems and low-code platforms is unprecedented, providing a more robust, scalable, and flexible solution.

Drawing from the experiences gained through the development and storage of scenarios, the tool could be further optimized in the future by integrating deep learning methods to provide powerful support in the planning and implementation of sustainable urban developments. Deep learning algorithms are distinguished by their ability to automatically extract relevant features from data [27]. By leveraging these algorithms, along with extensive data analyses and empirical values, the tool could automatically suggest targets and target values for a selected urban area, identify areas with similar characteristics, and generate indications for the development of plausible scenarios. Furthermore, once implemented in reality, scenarios could be subsequently recorded and estimated values could be continually refined, allowing for further optimization.

This combination of traditional estimation methods with the advanced analysis capabilities of deep learning would enable the tool to fully realize its potential. To enhance the tool while maintaining its simplicity and user-friendliness, it is crucial to assess whether integrating deep learning techniques aligns with one of the system's original design objectives: adapting and scaling the tool with little or no IT knowledge.

AKNOWLEDGMENT

The work described in this paper was funded by the Swiss Commission for Technology and Innovation (CTI).

REFERENCES

[1] E. Ahmadian et al., "Sustainable cities: The relationship between urban built forms and density indicators," Cities, vol. 95, p. 102382, 2019, doi:10.1016/j.cities.2019.06.013.

[2] M. Artmann, L. Inostroza, and P. Fan, "Urban sprawl, compact urban development and green cities. How much do we know, how much do we agree," Ecological Indicators, vol. 96, pp. 3-9, 2019, doi:10.1016/j.ecolind.2018.10.059.

[3] M. Schindler, R. Dionisio, and S. Kingham, "Challenges of Spatial Decision-Support Tools in Urban Planning: Lessons from New Zealand's Cities," Journal of Urban Planning and Development, vol. 146, 2020, doi:10.1061/(ASCE)UP.1943-5444.0000575.

[4] D. Rutledge et al., "Development of spatial decision support systems to support long-term, integrated planning," International Congress on Modelling and Simulation (MODSIM 2007), pp. 308-314, 2007.

[5] D. Kim, "Modelling Urban Growth: Towards an Agent Based Microeconomic Approach to Urban Dynamics and Spatial Policy Simulation," (Doctoral dissertation, UCL (University College London)), 2012.

[6] M. R. Dionisio, S. Kingham, K. Banwell, and J. Neville, "Geospatial tools for Community Engagement in the Christchurch Rebuild, New Zealand," Sustainable Cities and Society, vol. 27, pp. 233-243, 2016, doi:10.1016/j.scs.2016.04.007.

[7] L. Ortolano and C.D. Perman, "Applications to Urban Planning: An Overview," in Expert Systems: Applications to Urban Planning, T. J. Kim, L. L. Wiggins, and J. R. Wright, Eds. New York, NY: Springer, 1990.

[8] P. Lombardi and V. Ferretti, "New spatial decision support systems for sustainable urban and regional development," Smart and sustainable urban and regional development, vol. 4, pp. 45-66, 2015.

[9] Z. Kapelan, D. A. Savic, and G.A. Walters, "Decision-support tools for sustainable urban development," Proceedings of the Institution of Civil Engineers - Engineering Sustainability, vol. 158, pp. 135-142, September 2005.

[10] S. Kamps and C. Tannier, "A planning support system for assessing strategies of local urban planning agencies," 6th International Conference of Territorial Intelligence (INTI), October 2008.

[11] M. Maruna and V. Maruna, "Plan development process as a methodology for contemporary urban planning," Journal of Applied Engineering Science, vol. 11, pp. 63-74, 2013.

[12] L. A. Seffino and C. Bauzer Medeiros, J. V. Rocha, and B. Yi, "Woodss — a spatial decision support system based on workflows," Decision Support Systems, vol. 27, pp. 105-123, November 1999, doi:10.1016/S0167-9236(99)00039-1.

[13] A. R. Hevner, S. T. March, J. Park, and S. Ram, "Design Science in Information Systems Research," MIS Quarterly, vol. 28, pp. 75-105, March 2004, doi:10.2307/2514862.

[14] J. Freund and B. Rücker, Praxishandbuch BPMN mit Einführung in DMN/Practical handbook BPMN with introduction to DMN, vol. 6, Carl Hanser Verlag GmbH, 2019.

[15] J. M. Leimeister, Modellierung von Dienstleistungen, Dienstleistungsengineering und -management/Modeling of services, service engineering and management, Springer, Berlin, Heidelberg, p. 189–223, 2012, doi: 10.1007/978-3-642-27983-6_6.

[16] A. Gadatsch, IT-Unterstützung für das Prozessmanagement, Grundkurs Geschäftsprozess-Management/ IT support for process management, basic course in business process management, Springer Vieweg Wiesbaden, 2017, pp. 133-168, doi:10.1007/978-3-658-40298-3_6.

[17] P. Dadam, M. Richert, and S. Rinderle-Ma, "Prozessmanagementsysteme: Nur ein wenig Flexibilität wird nicht reichen/ Process management systems: Just a little flexibility won't be enough," Informatik-Spektrum, vol. 34, pp. 364-376, July 2011, doi:10.1007/s00287-010-0456-0.

[18] R. S. Kaplan, "Conceptual Foundations of the Balanced Scorecard," Handbooks of Management Accounting Research, vol. 3, pp. 1253-1269, 2009, doi:10.1016/S1751-3243(07)03003-9.

[19] M. Hugentobler and D. Wiener, Leitfaden und Checklisten zur nachhaltigen Arealentwicklung: für Städte und Gemeinden/Guidelines and checklists for sustainable site development: for cities and municipalities, Vdf Hochschulverlag AG ETH Zürich, 2016, doi:10.3218/3756-2.

[20] OMG, "OMG Standards Development Organization," April 2023. [Online]. Available: https://www.omg.org/spec/DMN/1.4/PDF. [retrieved May, 2024]

[21] T. Debevoise and J. Taylor, Prozess- und Entscheidungsmodellierung in BPMN/DMN: Eine Kurzanleitung/ Process and decision modeling in BPMN/DMN: A quick guide, Tom Debevoise, 2016.

[22] E. Elshan, P. Ebel, M. Söllner, and J. M. Leimeister, "Leveraging Low Code Development of Smart Personal Assistants: An Integrated DesignApproach with the SPADE

Method," Journal of Management Information Systems, vol. 40, pp. 96-129, 2023, doi:10.1080/07421222.2023.2172776.

[23] D. Hoogsteen and H. Borgman, "Empower the Workforce, Empower the Company? Citizen Development Adoption," 55th Hawaii International Conference on System Sciences, Honolulu, 2022.

[24] Power Apps. [Online]. Available: https://powerapps.microsoft.com/. [retrieved May, 2024]

[25] Camunda. [Online]. Available: https://camunda.com/ [retrieved May, 2024]

[26] Geoinfo. [Online]. Available: https://geoinfo.ch/ [retrieved May, 2024]

[27] I. Goodfellow, Y. Bengio, and A. Courville, Deep Learning, Cambridge, Massachusetts: The MIT Press, 2016.

A Study on Lightweight Sensing Data Verification Scheme for WICN with Blockchain

Shintaro Mori
Department of Electronics Engineering and Computer Science
Fukuoka University
8-19-1 Nanakuma, Jonan-ku, Fukuoka 814-0180, Japan
E-mail: smori@fukuoka-u.ac.jp

***Abstract*—We develop an energy-efficient and reliable wireless information-centric network-based ecosystem for smart-city applications. The proposed scheme utilizes a blockchain-based ledger. Since the conventional mining-based verification method is unsuitable for resource-restricted wireless nodes due to problems with exhaustive computer calculations, our scheme adopts the proof-of-elapsed time consensus method. In this work, we demonstrate the efficiency and feasibility of our scheme through computer simulations.**

Keywords—Wireless information-centric networking; Blockchain; Lightweight data verification scheme

I. INTRODUCTION

Future Wireless Sensor Network (WSN) technologies will provide essential functionalities for smart cities. Sensing data have distinctive features compared to traditional Internet data: namely, they are usually short-lived and require validation. This type of data is costly to collect, store, and deliver due to overwhelming network redundancy. Information-Centric Networking (ICN) [1] is a promising technology poised to replace the conventional Internet architecture in the near future. ICN names each piece of data so that they can identify each other, and the ICN nodes provide an in-network caching for further effective responses. Moreover, the features of ICN can boost location-free data access, i.e., the combination of ICN and a wireless network is suitable, which yields information-centric wireless sensor networks [2] or Wireless ICN (WICN). At the same time, since sensing data have a signature, their originality and integrity can be verified. End-to-end nodes are assured in the current ICN systems, so the proposed scheme relaxes this limitation by using Blockchain (BC). The advantage of BC is that it can provide a distributed, traceable, and immutable ledger without centralized and trusted nodes. However, the data verification process must be performed iteratively for computer calculations, similar to the proof-of-works (PoWs) consensus method. This heavy burden is too much accepted for resource-constrained WICN nodes. The proof-of-stake does not require mining task but is not suitable in an equal peer relationship, resulting in a bias. In light of this background, the proposed scheme utilizes a lightweight consensus method.

The remainder of this paper is organized as follows. Section II describes the proposed scheme. Section III presents numerical results. Finally, Section IV summarizes our findings and concludes the paper.

II. PROPOSED SCHEME

In the proposed scheme, the ICWSN is composed of a group of Sensor Nodes (SNs) and Relay Nodes (RNs), both of which are distributed across the local smart-city area. The proposed scheme overlays the BC on the WICN, and the role of the BC nodes is assigned to the RNs.

As a lightweight verification technique, we utilize the Proof-of-Elapsed-Time (PoET) consensus method. In PoETs, each BC node has a timer, and the first node for which a specified waiting time has elapsed is considered as a winner. Each BC node is classified into one coordinator and several validators, with the coordinator providing a random waiting time to the validators. In contrast to the original PoET method, the proposed scheme rotates the role of the coordinator among the BC nodes. This modification provides fairness and eliminates a single point of failure in the WICN with BC. We assume that the winner node of the k th block ($k = 0$ means the genesis block) is the n-th BC node ($n = 1, 2, \cdots, N$), and the next competition for the $(k+1)$-th block is conducted among the n th node as a coordinator and $(N-1)$ nodes as validators. For the initial process, the validator broadcasts the signed request message, and the coordinator replies with the latest block index and a random waiting time after verifying the message identification.

The validators should wait until the waiting time has passed, and if the n'-th node is first, it obtains a privilege of the block approval as a winner, which is expressed as

$$n' = \underset{i=1,2,\cdots,N;\ i\neq n}{\operatorname{argmin}} \; T_i^{k+1}, \tag{1}$$

where T_i^{k+1} is the waiting time that obtains the i-th validator ($i = 1, 2, \cdots, N$; $i \neq n$). The winner node broadcasts the verified block with an identification and certification of the expired time, and then the other nodes append it to the BC. If two or more validators have won due to the same waiting time, the BC might fork. However, since the proposed scheme will be deployed in a (regional) smart-city area, thus we can ignore such situation because of sufficiently small scale.

In the network diagnosis, if the BC nodes are hijacked by attackers, those nodes will exhibit malicious verification, and the robustness of the BC will collapse. The proposed scheme selects the node that commits the verified block based on equal lottery. In addition, the group of malicious nodes are mutually privileged among them, so to analyze the history of the winner node in the BC, everyone can find them. As for the

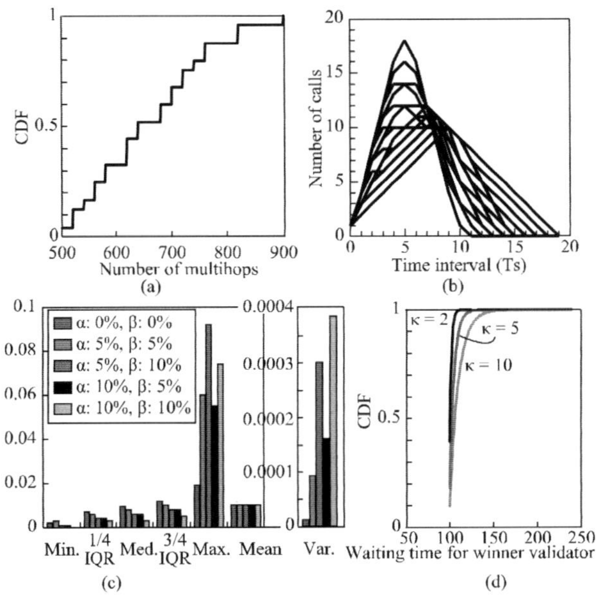

Figure 1. Numerical results

energy consumption of the network, the proposed scheme allows the validators to switch to idle or sleep states while waiting, thereby reducing both the computer resources required and the energy consumption.

III. NUMERICAL RESULTS

In this section, we present fundamental characteristics necessary for our scheme to work effectively and reduce energy consumption. Figure 1(a) shows the number of communications required for the request that the validators acquire a waiting time from the coordinator. The results were obtained through computer simulation implemented using C++. In the simulation, 100 lattice-like BC nodes were placed in a 1-km^2 field with 100-m separations. The results show the number of hops per node based on 10,000 block verifications, where the curve represents a statistical Cumulative Distribution Function (CDF). We found here that the request reached up to 6.60 hops per node and one-way direction on average. At the same time, even if a backhaul network has sufficient capacity, many requests will lead to congestion in the coordinator. For this situation, Figure 1(b) shows the number of call arrivals at the coordinator. The curves show the superimposed results of 100 trials. In the horizontal axis, T_s denotes the average time it takes for data to transmit between BC nodes. The results here show that the calls are centralized around five T_s, since the coordinator begins to accept requests and the coordinator maximally proceeds with 18 calls.

Figure 1(c) shows the distribution of the winner node based on the statistical values (minimum, 1/4 Interquartile Range (IQR), median, 3/4 IQR, maximum, mean, and variance values) related to the malicious node detection. α denotes the proportion of hijacked nodes to overall nodes, and β is the percentage at which the malicious nodes make the waiting time shorter among their member nodes. Note that the member nodes can be more likely to be selected as the next coordinator due to the shorter waiting time based on β. The simulation was performed for 1,000-block verification for combinations of α, and β was set to 0%, 5%, and 10%. In preliminary simulation, we performed the same evaluation for 1,000, 5,000, 10,000, 50,000, and 100,000 blocks, but there were no significant differences. As shown in Figure 1(c), on the basis of the maximum and variance values, the situation where the hijacked nodes are mixed can be detected. Figure 1(d) shows the CDF characteristics for the waiting time of the winner node, i.e., $T_{n'}^{k+1}$ in (1), in the case where $T_{\min}$ = 100 s and κ = 2, 5, and 10. These results are the average values after 1,000,000 trials. The waiting time was distributed based on a uniform distribution $\mathcal{U}(T_{\min}, \kappa N)$, where $T_{\min}$ is the predefined minimum time, N is the number of RNs, and κ is a constant value. As a result, the average verification times were 102 s, 104 s, and 109 s for κ = 2, 5, and 10, respectively.

On the other hand, regarding the comparison between block verification schemes, in general, a block verification scheme has three phases: block proposal, verification, and sharing. The block proposal and sharing phases are mostly the same procedure regardless of the consensus methods used. However, in verification phase, there is a significant difference in terms of whether a mining process is used (in PoWs) or a waiting process (in PoETs). In our previous study [4], we implemented a testbed device and measured the actual energy consumption as follows: 1.63 W (in sleep state), 2.76 W (in idle state), and 3.98 W (in computing state). Supposing the PoW and PoET consensus methods have the same processing time, the energy consumption can be reduced by 30.7% (during the idle waiting) and 59.0% (during the sleep waiting).

IV. CONCLUSIONS

In this paper, we proposed an energy-efficient PoET-based verification scheme. The computer simulations demonstrated the efficiency of the proposed scheme. In future work, we should discuss in-depth protocol design and evaluation.

ACKNOWLEDGEMENT

This work was partly supported by funding from Fukuoka University (Grand No. GW2309).

REFERENCES

[1] H. Asaeda, K. Matsuzono, Y. Hayamizu, H. H. Hlaing, and A. Ooka, "A survey of information-centric networking: The quest for innovation," *IEICE Trans. Commun.*, vol. E107-B, no. 1, pp. 139–153, 2024.

[2] B. S. Kim, C. Zhang, S. Mastorakis, M. K. Afzal, and J. Tapolcai, "Guest editorial special issue on information-centric wireless sensor networking (ICWSN) for IoT," *IEEE Internet of Things J.*, vol. 9, no. 2, pp. 844–845, Jan. 2022.

[3] C. Gündoğan, C. Amsüss, T. C. Schmidt, and M. Wählisch, "Content object security in the Internet of things: Challenges, prospects, and emerging solutions," *IEEE Trans. Network and Serv. Manag.*, vol. 19, no. 1, pp. 538–553, Mar. 2022.

[4] S. Mori, "A preliminary analysis of data collection and retrieval scheme for green information-centric wireless sensor networks," *Proc. ACM SIGCOMM 2022 WS NET4us*, Aug. 2022, pp. 1–6, doi: 10.1145/3538393.3544932.

Audio vs. Visual Approach to Monitor the Critically Endangered Species *Atlapetes blancae*: Developing Deep Learning Models with Limited Data

Julian D. Santamaria P
SISTEMIC, Engineering Faculty
Universidad de Antioquia-UdeA
Cl. 67 No. 53-108
Medellín, Colombia
email: julian.santamaria@udea.edu.co

Jhony H. Giraldo
LTCI, Télécom Paris
Institut Polytechnique de Paris
Palaiseau
Paris, France
email: jhony.giraldo@telecom-paris.fr

Angélica Diaz-Pulido
Alexander Von Humboldt Institute
Neotropical Innovation Corporation
Cl. 28a No. 15-09
Bogotá, Colombia
email: adiaz@humboldt.org.co

Claudia Isaza
SISTEMIC, Engineering Faculty
Universidad de Antioquia-UdeA
67 No. 53-108
Medellín, Colombia
email: victoria.isaza@udea.edu.co

***Abstract*—Using artificial intelligence algorithms for animal passive monitoring is a cost-effective tool. This kind of data analysis permits detailed and efficient tracking of species, as exemplified by the case of the endemic Antioquia brushfinch (*Atlapetes blancae*). *Atlapetes blancae* is from the high-elevation plateau of Santa Rosa de Osos in Antioquia Colombia. These birds are currently listed as critically endangered by the International Union for Conservation of Nature (IUCN). Their population is estimated at approximately 108 individuals. Sound recorders and camera traps are important tools for long-term monitoring as they provide extensive registers of data. However, analyzing this data is a labor-intensive process that requires experts to manually process the extensive amount of information. Additionally, identifying acoustic patterns for the *Atlapetes blancae* species based on artificial intelligent algorithms is problematic due to the lack of labeled data and the complexity of the vocalizations. This study introduces a novel methodology for real-environment audio analysis, addressing the challenge of unlabeled registers using a semi-automatic approach. We leverage the Learning Algorithm for Multivariate Data Analysis (LAMDA) and KiwiNet convolutional network architecture for audio recognition. Additionally, we analyze the videos using Multi-Layer Robust Principal Component Analysis (Multi-layer RPCA) to obtain cropped images from the video, which are then processed using a ResNet-18 architecture for classification. Finally, we compare both models to identify strengths and limitations. With a collection of 7,147 audio recordings and 17,159 videos, only 11 audio and 48 video recordings contain *Atlapetes blancae* presence. Our approach achieves F-measure average scores of 0.823 and 0.562 for audio and video analysis, respectively. Notably, in this case, the audio model is more robust than the video model.**

Keywords*- *Atlapetes blancae identification; Computer vision; Bioacoustics; Passive monitoring.

I. INTRODUCTION

The *Atlapetes blancae* is an endemic bird from the Santa Rosa de Osos high elevation plateau in the Department of Antioquia-Colombia [1]. Currently, it is on the International Union for Conservation of Nature (IUCN) Red List as "critically endangered" [2]. The first *Atlapetes blancae* description was made in 2007 [3]. In this description, it was listed as "possibly extinct" due to deforestation in its locality. However, rediscovery of *Atlapetes blancae* was reported in 2018 [4], supported by photographic evidence confirming its presence. Efforts by organizations such as the Neotropical Innovation Corporation (Neotropical Innovation link) and the Alexander von Humboldt Institute have been crucial in developing conservation strategies for this species. Neotropical Innovation Corporation's latest research reveals that they have estimated a population of only 108 individuals.

Conservation plans require implementing species monitoring to estimate population state variables, such as occupancy. A cost-efficient alternative to studying species is passive monitoring. Audio and video monitoring uses sensors, such as camera traps and sound recorders to make registers over the long term in different geographic locations and throughout the day [5]. Passive Acoustic Monitoring (PAM) offers an alternative method for studying and monitoring wildlife with audio recorders [6], while camera traps serve as the alternative when seeking visual data through images or videos. The ease of data collection is an exceptional advantage since it is a non-invasive technique that does not disrupt the natural behavior of the observed species. Furthermore, a substantial volume of registers are acquired for monitoring with acoustic recorders and camera traps over long periods [7], [8]. Nevertheless, the majority of the registers do not contain the presence of the target species. Therefore, it becomes necessary to have computational tools to assist in the analysis of the obtained video and audio recordings [9], [10]. In recent analyses, supervised artificial intelligence techniques have demonstrated impressive performance in the identification of specific species based on audio data [11], [12] as well as in videos [7], [13]. However, it is worth noting that these methods rely heavily on expert-labeled registers [14], which can be a significant challenge, particularly when dealing with endemic and critically endangered species [8] due to their low probability of occurrence and limited recorded instances.

To address the challenge of spending too much time listening to audio, analyzing spectrograms, and labeling datasets to train models, we propose a semi-automatic methodology. In our approach, we incorporate Guerrero's unsupervised method [15] to uncover potential patterns in relevant vocalizations. The expert's task is simplified to analyzing and confirming the presence of *Atlapetes blancae* within the patterns identified during the unsupervised analysis, instead of manually labeling. To enhance the initial analysis, we recommend using a limited set of species songs as examples, ensuring a more thorough examination of the species' acoustic repertoire. This method enables the identification of distinctive acoustic patterns of the target species, expediting the process. The second part of our methodology employs Arbimon software's pattern-matching algorithm [16] to evaluate the entire dataset. By leveraging the acoustic pattern established in the earlier analysis as a template, this process significantly reduces the need for manual audio analysis and permits experts to automatically label registers. Finally, we employ transfer learning to train our classification model using a pre-trained Convolutional Neural Network (CNN) - KiwiNet [17]. This method is explained in detail in Section III-A.

Recent research has highlighted the capability of CNNs in identifying animal species in camera trap images [18]. Furthermore, adopting segmentation as a preliminary step is an alternative approach that enhances the performance of the model [14]. In our work, we employ Multi-Layer Robust Principal Component Analysis (Multi-layer RPCA) for camera-trap image segmentation [19] to process the videos of our dataset as a preliminary step. Subsequently, we utilize the segmentation images obtained to train a CNN, more specifically a ResNet-18 [20], to classify *Atlapetes blancae* images. This approach is described in Section III-B.

To our knowledge, there is no proposal that leverages unsupervised methods to analyze acoustic patterns from a species with little information and then uses this knowledge to employ a semi-automatic methodology for labeling the recordings. The computational tool developed can be downloaded from [21].

The structure of this article is organized as follows: Section II provides an overview of the related work in the field. Section III outlines the methodology employed in our study. Section IV presents the data base used in our analysis. The results obtained from our analysis are presented in Section V. Finally, conclusions and future work are presented in Section VI.

II. Related Work

A. Audio recognition

In the specific field of *Atlapetes blancae* recognition, Diaz-Vallejo *et al.* [1] used the Raven Pro software (Raven Pro is a software for the visualization, measurement, and acoustic analysis of sound recordings) [22] to estimate occupancy of the *Atlapetes blancae* from audio recordings. However, the annotation process involves manual listening of audio recordings and visualization of audio spectrograms to identify and label different animal vocalizations within them.

For the recognition of other bird species, there are specialized tools available, such as BirNet [23], Merlin Bird ID [24] and KiwiNet [17]. BirNet is a Deep artificial Neural Network (DNN) that uses sound data to identify North American and European bird species. It is trained to recognize 984 bird species, excluding specific species like *Atlapetes blancae*. On the other hand, Merlin Bird ID is a mobile application that incorporates a sound identification feature (Sound ID). It is trained to identify 1,054 species of birds, focusing primarily on birds found in the United States, Canada, Europe, and the Western Palearctic region. Similarly, *Atlapetes blancae* is not included in the species list covered by Merlin Bird ID [24]. Finally, KiwiNet [17] is a CNN specifically trained to identify bird calls, focusing on the Kiwi, a native New Zealand bird species.

In current models for bird species recognition, there is no model that already knows about *Atlapetes blancae*. However, it is possible to enhance the *Atlapetes blancae* sound classification task by utilizing pre-trained representations [8], [25]. Pre-trained CNNs offer starting points for audio-based recognition tasks and can be adaptable for *Atlapetes blancae* with transfer learning. This technique presents a viable solution for mitigating the challenge of limited labeled registers available for training CNNs that normally require a huge amount of data.

Another practical method to handle the problem of *Atlapetes blancae* recognition is clustering. This technique is particularly useful when we are working with unlabeled data because it helps group similar data. This approach provides a different perspective on the dataset and can help us identify interesting connections between data points [15]. The acoustic animal identification method proposed by Guerrero [15] is a clustering-based alternative that can identify sound groups without requiring prior knowledge of the number of different animal sounds. The approach consists of two parts: the first identifies sonotypes and matches them with the cluster that best represents them, while the second attempts to match sounds to specific animals. However, the second part requires a large number of examples of the sounds made by each animal. Unfortunately, we do not have many sound examples of *Atlapetes blancae*, which makes it unsuitable for bioacoustic monitoring and analysis of this bird species.

On the other hand, multispecies sound recognition software is also commonly used for this task. One of the most famous is the Arbimon software [16]. This supervised model is based on Random Forest [26], a technique that combines multiple decision trees to analyze bioacoustic data. Nevertheless, as a supervised model, it requires labeled registers to train a specialized classifier in *Atlapetes blancae*.

B. Image recognition

Research on species image recognition has been limited, especially about bird identification. Even fewer studies have attempted to identify bird species based on images [27], [28].

Generally, birds are treated as a broad category by classifiers [13], [29].

There are several options available for animal image identification, such as Conservation AI [30], Merlin Bird ID [24], MLWIC2 [31], and Wildlife Insights AI model [32]. However, these are supervised models trained on bird datasets that do not include *Atlapetes blancae*. They require a significant number of examples for training as an *Atlapetes blancae* classifier.

Object detection models like MegaDetector [18] and DeepWILD [14] have become crucial for automating wildlife monitoring from camera trap images. While MegaDetector [18] is an image detection model that is capable of detecting images without animals, people, and vehicles in camera-trap images, it requires a significant amount of labeled data and annotated bounding boxes for training examples [33]. Additionally, the model's performance may vary depending on the size of the animal, making it less useful for identifying certain species, such as *Atlapetes blancae*. On the other hand, DeepWILD [14] is used to detect, classify, and count species in camera trap videos with a primary focus on monitoring the wolf's presence.

III. Methodology

This section presents our proposal for recognizing *Atlapetes blancae* in audio recordings and camera-trap videos.

A. Audio analysis proposal

This work proposes a semi-automatic methodology to analyze unlabeled registers, addressing the issue of the unlabeled presence or absence of the *Atlapetes blancae* in audio data. This stage involves identifying vocalization patterns within the complex song of the *Atlapetes blancae*, enabling subsequent labeling of the audio recordings. Following this, a model is trained to recognize the *Atlapetes blancae* in new audio recordings, as illustrated in Figure 1.

1) Preprocessing: In the preprocessing stage, we employ a technique known as acoustic animal identification to extract acoustic data in an unsupervised manner. This technique is based on the research conducted by Guerrero et al. [15], which utilizes segmentation and clustering to extract acoustic data from soundscapes. The segmentation process is based on a modified version of the Acoustic Event Detection (AED) algorithm [34]. The clustering stage utilizes the LAMDA algorithm [35] to make clusters that describe possible sonotypes in the soundscape. The lack of relevant acoustic information of *Atlapetes blancae* makes this technique particularly useful for the purposes of learning about the variable vocal repertory of the endemic species. Using this preprocessing, we identify a representative acoustic pattern for *Atlapetes blancae*.

2) Audios labeling - Pattern Matching: The acoustic representative patterns of *Atlapetes blancae* identified in the last step are used to recognize possible vocalizations in the entire not labeling dataset. We use the pattern-matching tool within the Arbimon software [16]. This tool performs a pattern-matching algorithm by comparing a given pattern with elements in the dataset to identify matching occurrences. The pattern-matching tool provides potential segments in the audio along with their scores. This pattern-matching process does not have high performance when it comes to recognizing the presence of *Atlapetes blancae* in audio recordings. Consequently, we only use this pattern-matching as the previous step in the labeling procedure. A manual validation process is conducted to verify only the segments that match the given audio representative patterns. The labeled audios are subsequently used to create a training and testing set for training a classification model.

3) Supervised training: We use transfer learning to train KiwiNet [17] for our *Atlapetes blancae* recognition problem. KiwiNet is a Convolutional Neural Network (CNN) based on VGG19 [36] architecture and is used for supervised training in acoustic data analysis and identifying individuals based on their calls. VGG19 was modified to improve the regularization of the latent space when used as a feature extractor [17]. KiwiNet and VGG19 differ in that KiwiNet has a convolutional layer before the fully connected layers to reduce the number of filters from 512 to 32 and a global average pooling layer to embed the call characteristics into a 32-element feature set (latent space). Moreover, the KiwiNet analyzes the input data utilizing a colormap (KRGB - Black-Red-Green-Blue) to correlate the image colors with the levels of intensity in the spectrogram. Additionally, the model applies a median equalizer after spectrogram estimation to noise-reduce the data [17]. Furthermore, the backbone of KiwiNet (VGG19) was pre-trained with the ImageNet dataset [37].

In this work, the KiwiNet [17] is trained using the Stochastic Gradient Descent (SGD) optimizer [38] with a learning rate of 0.0001 for 15 epochs on 1-minute recordings with the primary objective of classifying the input record in target class (presence of *Atlapetes blancae*) or noisy class (absence of *Atlapetes blancae*). Additionally, the spectrogram calculation parameters are configured as follows: the discrete Fourier transform utilizes 1024 sampling points, the spectrogram's window length is set to 1024, and the overlap between consecutive windows is 768. This supervised approach enhances the performance of recognizing *Atlapetes blancae* in new audio recordings.

4) Recognition: In the training stage, we trained a model for *Atlapetes blancae* recognition (KiwiNet [17]). This model is used to classify new audios of real-environment and determine the presence or absence of *Atlapetes blancae*. The preprocessing use in the training phase is not necessary for this stage. The KiwiNet is trained on 1-minute recordings (as our audio recordings). Therefore, the recordings can be directly passed to the model for classification.

Based on this methodology, our approach introduces several novel elements. First, we propose a semi-automatic method for analyzing unlabeled audio recordings, specifically targeting the detection of *Atlapetes blancae*. Unlike traditional methods, our approach combines unsupervised acoustic data extraction with supervised learning. By utilizing the segmentation and clustering techniques from the acoustic animal identification

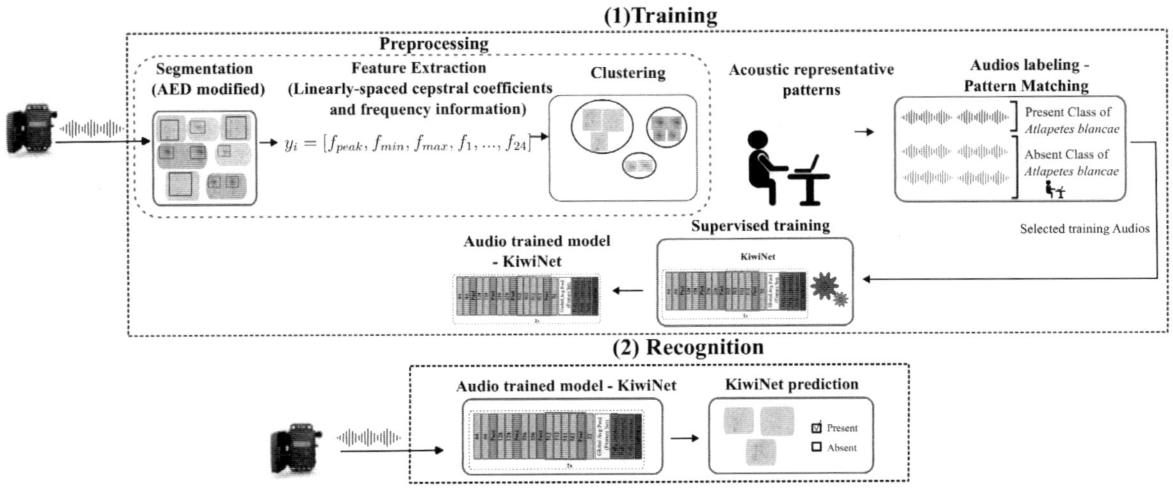

Figure 1. Proposed audio methodology schema: Spectrograms are segmented, features extracted, and clustered using acoustic animal identification. Patterns are identified and labeled to train a KiwiNet model. For recognition, the model classifies new recordings.

method [15], we identify representative vocalization patterns of *Atlapetes blancae*. These patterns are then used in conjunction with the Arbimon software's pattern-matching tool to label potential segments in the dataset, followed by a manual validation process to ensure accuracy. Furthermore, our use of KiwiNet [17], a modified VGG19 architecture, leverages transfer learning to enhance the recognition of *Atlapetes blancae*. The use of a colormap (KRGB) in KiwiNet, along with median equalization for noise reduction, ensures robust performance even in noisy environments. This integrated methodology not only improves the accuracy of *Atlapetes blancae* detection in new audio recordings but also addresses the challenge of working with unlabeled data.

B. Video analysis proposal

In the video analysis methodology, as shown in Figure 2, the first step is to extract the frames. Then, we use the Multi-layer RPCA method [19] to segment these frames and obtain a bounding box, which facilitates the cropping of the original frame and extraction of the image background. We refer to the results of the segmentation stage as cropped images. Afterward, we manually label the cropped images where the *Atlapetes blancae* is present to train the ResNet-18 architecture [20].

1) Segmentation: The Multi-Layer RPCA, proposed by [19], is utilized for camera-trap image segmentation [39] and incorporates texture and color descriptors. This approach decomposes an image into a low-rank matrix representing the background and a sparse matrix representing the foreground in background subtraction. The algorithm employed in this study involves the computation of Multi-layer RPCA, followed by a post-processing step.

During Multi-layer RPCA computation, the sparse and low-rank matrices are calculated for background subtraction. To evaluate the impact of texture descriptors on the entire image, we utilize a parameter called $\beta \in [0, 1]$. In this work, we chose $\beta = 0.6$, based on the best performance observed with our dataset. [19] tested nine algorithms to solve the RPCA problem, and among them, we select the Non-Smooth Augmented Lagrangian v1 (NSA1) algorithm [40] due to its effectiveness with our dataset [19], [39]. The post-processing step involves the application of morphological filters, as described by [19], [39].

2) Image cropping: After segmentation, a binary image is obtained with the bounding box of the segmented object. This bounding box is used to locate and crop the original frame, enabling background subtraction.

3) Image feature-based categorization: The cropped images are classified into four distinct classes: the target class (*Atlapetes blancae*) and three other classes (other birds, animals, and background). The segmentation stage enables us to isolate the moving objects in the videos, which may consist *Atlapetes blancae*, other animals, or noise. Consequently, a classification model is necessary to learn distinguishing patterns and accurately differentiate *Atlapetes blancae* from other moving animals and objects within the videos.

To improve the model's accuracy in distinguishing *Atlapetes blancae* from other bird species, we introduce an additional bird class. This inclusion enhances the model's specificity and enables more precise differentiation. The dataset is divided manually into training and test sets, comprising the target class (*Atlapetes blancae*) and three other classes (other birds, animals, and background).

4) Supervised training: ResNet-18 is a CNN architecture introduced by [20]. It belongs to the ResNet family of models, specifically designed to tackle the issue of vanishing gradients in deep neural networks. This architecture consists of a series of convolutional layers followed by residual blocks [20]. Furthermore, the architecture resizes the image with its shorter side randomly sampled in the range [256, 480] for scale

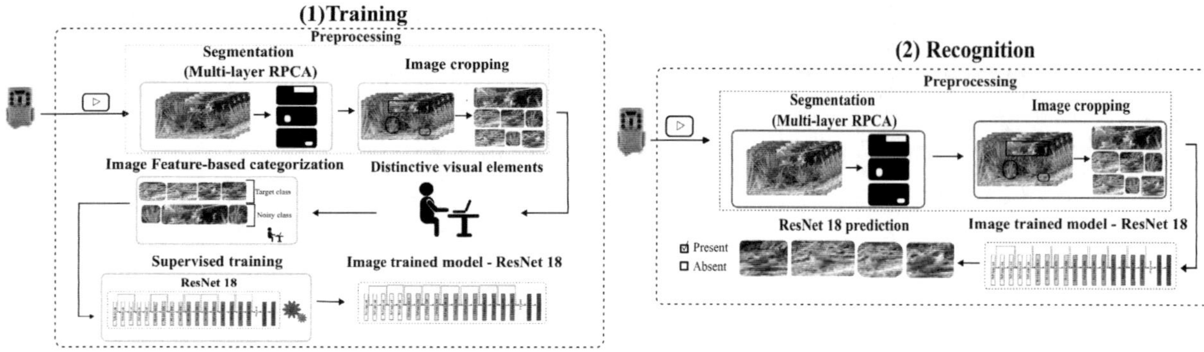

Figure 2. Proposed video methodology schema: Frames are segmented with Multi-layer RPCA, cropped, and used to train a ResNet-18 model. For recognition, new frames are similarly processed and classified by the trained model.

augmentation as part of the preprocessing of the input images. Next, a 224 x 224 crop with per-pixel mean subtraction is randomly selected from the scaled image or its flipped form horizontally [20].

The ResNet-18 architecture was employed with its original parameters and pre-trained weights from the ImageNet dataset [37]. In this work, we trained the ResNet-18 with the principal aim to classify input cropped images into four different classes: one target class (*Atlapetes blancae*) and three other classes (other birds, other animals, and background). As a result, we adjust the output size of the fully connected layer from 1000 to 4, reflecting the number of classes in our dataset. The model was trained using the SGD [38] optimizer with a learning rate of 0.0001 and a momentum of 0.9 for 15 epochs.

5) Recognition: In this stage, we apply the pre-processing step to extract cropped images and use the previously trained model to determine the presence or absence of *Atlapetes blancae*.

Based on this methodology, our approach introduces several novel elements in the field of video analysis for wildlife detection. Firstly, we implement a semi-automatic process that combines Multi-layer RPCA segmentation with manual labeling to create a robust training set. This allows for the precise extraction of frames containing *Atlapetes blancae* from complex backgrounds. Unlike traditional segmentation techniques, Multi-layer RPCA effectively decomposes frames into background and foreground components, enabling accurate isolation of the target species. Additionally, by training the ResNet-18 model on these segmented and manually labeled images, we ensure that the model learns to distinguish *Atlapetes blancae* from other birds, animals, and noise with high specificity. Our inclusion of an additional bird class further enhances the model's precision in identifying *Atlapetes blancae* amidst similar species. This comprehensive methodology not only improves detection accuracy but also addresses the challenges of working with unlabeled and complex video data, providing a significant advancement in automated wildlife monitoring.

C. Evaluation Metrics

The F-measure with macro averaging is chosen as the metric to evaluate the performance of the different models using the test data featuring N classes. Our evaluation involves a comparison of our audio methodology proposal with two software solutions, Arbimon [16] and the acoustic animal identification method [15], alongside one CNN architecture, ResNet-18 [20]. Similarly, we assess our video methodology proposal against two distinct ResNet architectures, ResNet-50 and ResNet-101 [20]. We use the F-measure as the metric of performance, which is given as follows:

First, calculate precision and recall for each $class_i$:

$$\begin{aligned} \text{precision}_i &= \frac{\text{True Positives}_i}{\text{True Positives}_i + \text{False Positives}_i}, \\ \text{recall}_i &= \frac{\text{True Positives}_i}{\text{True Positives}_i + \text{False Negatives}_i}, \end{aligned} \tag{1}$$

Then, average precision and recall across all classes:

$$\begin{aligned} \text{Precision avg} &= \frac{1}{N}\sum_{i=1}^{N} \text{precision}_i, \\ \text{Recall avg} &= \frac{1}{N}\sum_{i=1}^{N} \text{recall}_i, \end{aligned} \tag{2}$$

Finally, calculate the F-measure average:

$$\text{F-measure avg} = 2\frac{\text{Precision avg} \times \text{Recall avg}}{\text{Precision avg} + \text{Recall avg}}, \tag{3}$$

where precision (or confidence) denotes the proportion of predicted positive cases that are correctly real positives. On the other hand, recall (or sensitivity) represents the proportion of real positive cases that are correctly predicted positive [41]. Additionally, to evaluate the performance of the audio and video recognition model, we set aside 56 audio samples and 11,105 frames as test data for the audio and video recognition model.

IV. Data base

A. Study site

The study was conducted in the Yarumal and Santa Rosa de Osos municipalities on the northern highlands of Antioquia of the central Andes mountain in Colombia. Two areas were sampled from November 2021 to February 2022. These areas are Batallón BITER IV (Tactical Instruction Battalion of the Colombian National Army) and El Vergel (cattle farm); in both cases with natural areas of *Atlapetes blancae* habitat.

B. Study case

1) Audios: We installed three acoustic sensors (SM4, Wildlife Acoustics) in each of the two sampling locations (Batallón and El Vergel), where sporadic observations of *Atlapetes blancae* had been previously reported. One acoustic sensor was placed in the El Vergel location and two in the Batallón location, with a separation of 500 meters between them. We sampled recordings for two months (November - December 2021). The sensors were set to record 60-second audio clips every 15 minutes, covering sound registers from 0:00 to 24:00 UTC. We recorded the audio in uncompressed WAV format, with a sampling rate of 48 kHz and a bit rate of 768 kbps. In total, we collected 7,147 audios, out of which *Atlapetes blancae* song was present in only 11 recordings. For the training phase, we selected 124 audio samples of absences and 8 of presences, while 53 audio samples of absences and 3 of presences were reserved for testing.

2) Videos: For two months (December 2021 - February 2022), we deployed 13 camera traps (Bushnell Trophy cam), seven in the Batallón and six in the El Vergel locations. The mean distance between sample sites was 200 m. Each camera trap was placed around 50 cm above the ground, recording videos of 15 seconds in response to the activation of a passive infrared sensor. Out of the 17,159 videos that were collected, only 48 have the presence of *Atlapetes blancae*. A total of 30,759 frames, which is an individual image captured from the video sequence, were randomly selected for the training dataset, while an additional 11,105 frames were set aside for testing data.

V. RESULTS

In order to compare the audio and the video approaches, this section presents the results of both methodologies described in Section III. To assess the performance of the models, we applied the metric described in Section III-C to the test data.

A. Audio trained models

The audio recognition model (see Fig. 1, part 2-bottom), based on KiwiNet [17], analyzes each input audio to identify the specific acoustic pattern of *Atlapetes blancae*. In order to evaluate the proposed audio model results, we compared our audio model with software applications designed for recognizing multiple species classes, such as the acoustic animal identification method [15] and Arbimon software [16]. In each case, the model analyses the performance considering the presence of *Atlapetes blancae* in the whole audio and not for segments. Table I compares the F-measure average, precision average, recall average and accuracy obtained from the audio recognition models. The results reveal that the best-performing model is our audio model based on KiwiNet with a F-measure average of 0.823 and an Accuracy of 0.964. The performance of our audio recognition model is attributed to one of the primary functions of KiwiNet, which is to identify individuals based on their calls. In this study, we leverage the pre-existing knowledge of the KiwiNet architecture as a starting point to search for *Atlapetes blancae* by utilizing the acoustic patterns identified through the acoustic animal identification method. The software Arbimon has a F-measure average of 0.794 and an accuracy of 0.964, which matches the accuracy of our audio recognition model but has a lower F-measure average. Furthermore, when comparing recall average, Arbimon performs significantly worse than our model. In contrast to Arbimon software, which requires the user to specify a Region Of Interest (ROI), our audio model based on KiwiNet architecture, automatically identifies patterns by searching within its database. The acoustic animal identification method proposed in [15], used as a classifier and not like acoustic patterns identification, achieved a F-measure average of 0.743 and an accuracy of 0.929. While the accuracy shows only a slight decrease compared to our audio model, the F-measure average is significantly lower. Additionally, when comparing precision average, their method performs worse than our model. Unlike supervised models, which require labeled data to learn specific acoustic patterns of the target class, the unsupervised model is trained without labels and identifies various acoustic patterns from different species. However, due to the nature of our target species, a more tailored model for *Atlapetes blancae* recognition is required in this case.

TABLE I
COMPARING THE PERFORMANCE OF AUDIO MODELS ON TESTING DATA.

Model	F-measure avg	Precision avg	Recall avg	Accuracy
Our audio recognition model	0.823	0.823	0.823	0.964
Acoustic animal identification [15]	0.743	0.690	0.805	0.929
Arbimon [16]	0.794	0.981	0.667	0.964
ResNet-18 [20]	0.653	0.580	0.748	0.821

When using CNN architectures as classifiers in audio processing, the most common approach involves the analysis of audio spectrograms, specifically focusing on species vocalization rather than the entire audio spectrogram [9]. For this reason, we utilized the ResNet-18 architecture pre-trained on ImageNet [37]. We trained the ResNet-18 with output segments of the AED algorithm, which capture the part of the spectrogram where the animal vocalization is present. It is worth noting that this ResNet-18 is not trained with the whole spectrogram as the models before, therefore, we take into account the number of segments corresponding to each audio recording to calculate the result. The ResNet-18 achieves a F-measure average of 0.653.

The audio analysis results contribute to scientific and engineering knowledge by demonstrating the efficacy of combining unsupervised and supervised learning techniques for species-specific audio recognition. The integration of the acoustic animal identification method with KiwiNet's architecture has yielded a highly accurate model for detecting *Atlapetes blancae* vocalizations. This approach leverages pre-existing acoustic patterns and enhances them with supervised learning, significantly improving detection performance compared to traditional methods. Other experts in the field can use this methodology to develop and refine bioacoustic monitoring systems for various species, facilitating more precise and automated wildlife tracking and conservation efforts.

B. Image trained models

In the field of image analysis, there is currently no specific approach available to recognize *Atlapetes blancae*. Furthermore, pre-trained image-based animal identification systems do not include *Atlapetes blancae* in their datasets.

Initially, we attempted to train a ResNet-18 architecture using the whole image as input (frame), but the results were unsatisfactory, with a F-measure average of 0.473 and Accuracy of 0.467. This led us to realize the significance of giving a better context to the input image, which greatly improved the network's ability to recognize and learn the relevant patterns. Therefore we include a previous stage, which limits the input image of the network and facilitates the learning of distinctive patterns by CNN. Table II presents a comparison of the ResNet architecture [20] with different depths, including ResNet-18, ResNet-50, and ResNet-101. This table evaluates the classification performance of these models in detecting the presence or absence of *Atlapetes blancae* in cropped images obtained by the Multi-Layer RPCA algorithm [19]. The increase in the performance of all three ResNet architecture variations can be observed in Table II in comparison to initially ResNet-18 trained on frames. We selected the ResNet-18 architecture because it presents the best performance and we called the hold methodology as RPCA ResNet-18 model. We adjust the evaluation metric of the RPCA ResNet-18 model, taking into account the number of cropped images corresponding to each video to calculate the result. This analysis shows that the F-measure average decreases from 0.940 to 0.495.

The video analysis results enhance the understanding of effective segmentation and classification methods for species detection in camera-trap footage. By utilizing the Multi-layer RPCA method for accurate image segmentation and subsequently training a ResNet-18 model on the cropped images, the study demonstrates a novel approach to isolating and recognizing *Atlapetes blancae*. This methodology's significant improvement in detection accuracy underscores its potential application in similar ecological and wildlife monitoring projects. Researchers and engineers can adopt these techniques to improve the specificity and accuracy of automated image-based species identification systems, thus advancing the capabilities of remote sensing and conservation technologies.

TABLE II
COMPARING THE PERFORMANCE OF IMAGE MODELS ON TESTING DATA.

CNN	F-measure avg	Precision avg	Recall avg	Acc	Type of Data
RPCA ResNet-18 (ours)	0.940	0.953	0.928	0.967	Cropped images
RPCA ResNet-50 (ours)	0.937	0.954	0.921	0.966	Cropped images
RPCA ResNet-101 (ours)	0.926	0.947	0.905	0.956	Cropped images
RPCA ResNet-18 (ours)	0.495	0.512	0.882	0.889	Videos
ResNet-18 [20]	0.473	0.475	0.472	0.467	Frames

VI. CONCLUSION AND FUTURE WORK

In this paper, we present a methodology for recognizing *Atlapetes blancae*, an endemic bird species in a critically endangered state. Previous works have not included *Atlapetes blancae* in their list of recognized species. Furthermore, *Atlapetes blancae* identification with artificial intelligence algorithms is a big challenge due to this species having small data for training and less data labeled. In our proposal, we employ a novel semi-automatic methodology to acquire acoustic information about the target species and to label the audio registers. Additionally, we conduct a comparative analysis between an audio model and a video model, with our findings indicating that the audio model is the preferred choice for processing the data. However, this model represents just the initial step in the development of a sufficiently robust tool for *Atlapetes blancae*. For future work, we believe that integrating sensor information is crucial to the creation of more robust models, rather than relying on separate models for each sensor. Sensor information integration entails the utilization of data from various heterogeneous sources, often with asynchronous data streams, to extract more robust and informative features. By combining data from multiple sensors, we can enhance the accuracy and reliability of our recognition system for *Atlapetes blancae*. Furthermore, there is a pressing need to reduce the computational cost associated with image preprocessing, as this is essential for streamlining the image analysis process. Developing multi-modal algorithms will alleviate the computational burden and expedite image analysis. These advancements will significantly enhance the practicality and scalability of our methodology for large-scale monitoring and conservation efforts. It is important to note that while the analysis of multi-modal sequential data has gained significant traction in recent machine learning research, it has yet to address the specific domain of animal monitoring. As a result, further research and development are required to adapt these approaches to the challenges posed by animal monitoring.

ACKNOWLEDGMENT

This work was supported by Universidad de Antioquia - CODI and Alexander von Humboldt Institute for Research on Biological Resources [code project: 2020-33250].

REFERENCES

[1] M. Diaz-Vallejo *et al.*, "Use of acoustic monitoring to estimate occupancy of the antioquia brushfinch (atlapetes blancae), a critically endangered species, in san pedro de los milagros, antioquia," *Journal of Field Ornithology*, vol. 94, 2023.

[2] BirdLife International, *Atlapetes blancae*, The IUCN Red List of Threatened Species 2021: e.T22735460A181746724, https://dx.doi.org/10.2305/IUCN.UK.2021-3.RLTS.T22735460A181746724.en. Accessed on 2024.03.05., 2021.

[3] T. Donegan, "A new species of brush finch (emberizidae: Atlapetes) from the northern central andes of colombia," *Bulletin of the British Ornithologists' Club*, vol. 127, p. 255, 2007.

[4] R. Correa Peña, S. Chaparro-Herrera, A. Lopera-Salazar, and J. Parra, "Rediscovery of the antioquia brush finch atlapetes blancae. redescubrimiento del gorrión-montés paisa atlapetes blancae," *Cotinga*, vol. 41, pp. 101–108, 2019.

[5] R. T. Buxton, P. E. Lendrum, K. R. Crooks, and G. Wittemyer, "Pairing camera traps and acoustic recorders to monitor the ecological impact of human disturbance," *Global Ecology and conservation*, vol. 16, e00493, 2018.

[6] J. Xie, S. Zhao, X. Li, D. Ni, and J. Zhang, "Kd-cldnn: Lightweight automatic recognition model based on bird vocalization," *Applied Acoustics*, vol. 188, p. 108 550, 2022.

[7] D.-Y. Meng *et al.*, "A method for automatic identification and separation of wildlife images using ensemble learning," *Ecological Informatics*, vol. 77, p. 102 262, 2023.

[8] M. Zhong *et al.*, "Multispecies bioacoustic classification using transfer learning of deep convolutional neural networks with pseudo-labeling," *Applied Acoustics*, vol. 166, p. 107 375, 2020.

[9] A. Noumida and R. Rajan, "Multi-label bird species classification from audio recordings using attention framework," *Applied Acoustics*, vol. 197, p. 108 901, 2022.

[10] E. Dufourq, C. Batist, R. Foquet, and I. Durbach, "Passive acoustic monitoring of animal populations with transfer learning," *Ecological Informatics*, vol. 70, p. 101 688, 2022.

[11] H. Xiao, D. Liu, K. Chen, and M. Zhu, "Amresnet: An automatic recognition model of bird sounds in real environment," *Applied Acoustics*, vol. 201, p. 109 121, 2022.

[12] X. Han and J. Peng, "Bird sound classification based on ecoc-svm," *Applied Acoustics*, vol. 204, p. 109 245, 2023.

[13] H. Böhner, E. F. Kleiven, R. A. Ims, and E. M. Soininen, "A semi-automatic workflow to process images from small mammal camera traps," *Ecological Informatics*, p. 102 150, 2023.

[14] F. Simões, C. Bouveyron, and F. Precioso, "Deepwild: Wildlife identification, localisation and estimation on camera trap videos using deep learning," *Ecological Informatics*, vol. 75, p. 102 095, 2023.

[15] M. J. Guerrero, C. L. Bedoya, J. D. López, J. M. Daza, and C. Isaza, "Acoustic animal identification using unsupervised learning," *Methods in Ecology and Evolution*, vol. 14, 2023.

[16] T. M. Aide *et al.*, "Real-time bioacoustics monitoring and automated species identification," *PeerJ*, vol. 1, e103, 2013.

[17] C. Bedoya and L. Molles, "Acoustic censusing and individual identification of birds in the wild," *bioRxiv Preprint*, 2021.

[18] S. Beery *et al.*, "Efficient pipeline for automating species id in new camera trap projects," *Biodiversity Information Science and Standards*, vol. 3, 2019.

[19] J.-H. Giraldo-Zuluaga, A. Salazar, A. Gomez, and A. Diaz-Pulido, "Camera-trap images segmentation using multi-layer robust principal component analysis," *The Visual Computer*, vol. 35, pp. 335–347, 2019.

[20] K. He, X. Zhang, S. Ren, and J. Sun, "Deep residual learning for image recognition," in *2016 IEEE Conference on Computer Vision and Pattern Recognition (CVPR)*, 2016, pp. 770–778.

[21] J. D. Santamaria P, *Blancaenet: A computational tool*, https://github.com/Julian075/BlancaeNet. Accessed on 2024.06.025, 2024.

[22] K. Lisa Yang Center for Conservation Bioacoustics, *Raven Pro: Interactive Sound Analysis Software (Version 1.6.1)*, https://ravensoundsoftware.com/. Accessed on 2024.03.05., 2019.

[23] S. Kahl, C. M. Wood, M. Eibl, and H. Klinck, "Birdnet: A deep learning solution for avian diversity monitoring," *Ecological Informatics*, vol. 61, p. 101 236, 2021.

[24] Cornell Lab of Ornithology, *Merlin Bird ID*, https://merlin.allaboutbirds.org. Accessed on 2024.03.05., 2023.

[25] C. Zhang, Q. Li, H. Zhan, Y. Li, and X. Gao, "One-step progressive representation transfer learning for bird sound classification," *Applied Acoustics*, vol. 212, p. 109 614, 2023.

[26] L. Breiman, "Random forests," *Machine learning*, vol. 45, pp. 5–32, 2001.

[27] A. C. Ferreira *et al.*, "Deep learning-based methods for individual recognition in small birds," *Methods in Ecology and Evolution*, vol. 11, pp. 1072–1085, 2020.

[28] J. Guo *et al.*, "Graph knows unknowns: Reformulate zero-shot learning as sample-level graph recognition," in *Proceedings of the AAAI Conference on Artificial Intelligence*, 2023, pp. 7775–7783.

[29] M. Favorskaya and A. Pakhirka, "Animal species recognition in the wildlife based on muzzle and shape

features using joint cnn," *Procedia Computer Science*, vol. 159, pp. 933–942, 2019.

[30] C. Chalmers, P. Fergus, S. Wich, and A. C. Montanez, "Conservation ai: Live stream analysis for the detection of endangered species using convolutional neural networks and drone technology," *arXiv Preprint arXiv:1910.07360*, 2019.

[31] M. A. Tabak *et al.*, "Improving the accessibility and transferability of machine learning algorithms for identification of animals in camera trap images: Mlwic2," *Ecology and Evolution*, vol. 10, pp. 10 374–10 383, 2020.

[32] J. A. Ahumada *et al.*, "Wildlife insights: A platform to maximize the potential of camera trap and other passive sensor wildlife data for the planet," *Environmental Conservation*, vol. 47, pp. 1–6, 2020.

[33] S. Leorna and T. Brinkman, "Human vs. machine: Detecting wildlife in camera trap images," *Ecological Informatics*, vol. 72, p. 101 876, 2022.

[34] J. Xie, M. Towsey, M. Zhu, J. Zhang, and P. Roe, "An intelligent system for estimating frog community calling activity and species richness," *Ecological Indicators*, vol. 82, pp. 13–22, 2017.

[35] J. Aguilar-Martin and R. L. De Mantaras, "The process of classification and learning the meaning of linguistic descriptors of concepts," *Approximate reasoning in decision analysis*, vol. 1982, pp. 165–175, 1982.

[36] K. Simonyan and A. Zisserman, "Very deep convolutional networks for large-scale image recognition," *arXiv Preprint arXiv:1409.1556*, 2014.

[37] J. Deng *et al.*, "Imagenet: A large-scale hierarchical image database," in *2009 IEEE conference on computer vision and pattern recognition*, 2009, pp. 248–255.

[38] Y. LeCun *et al.*, "Backpropagation applied to handwritten zip code recognition," *Neural computation*, vol. 1, pp. 541–551, 1989.

[39] J.-H. Giraldo-Zuluaga, A. Salazar, A. Gomez, and A. Diaz-Pulido, "Recognition of mammal genera on camera-trap images using multi-layer robust principal component analysis and mixture neural networks," in *2017 IEEE 29th International Conference on Tools with Artificial Intelligence (ICTAI)*, 2017, pp. 53–60.

[40] N. S. Aybat, D. Goldfarb, and G. Iyengar, "Fast first-order methods for stable principal component pursuit," *arXiv preprint arXiv:1105.2126*, 2011.

[41] D. M. Powers, "Evaluation: From precision, recall and f-measure to roc, informedness, markedness and correlation," *arXiv Preprint arXiv:2010.16061*, 2020.

The Conceptual Architecture Requirements for French Digital Building Logbook

Alan Martin Redmond
CSTB
Sophia Antipolis, France
email: alan.redmond@cstb.fr

Abstract— **This article is based on Horizon Europe Project Demo-BLog were the business needs were pre-defined, and the challenges focused on defining requirements at an abstract opportunity/problem space domain level for an automated renovation advice tool. To accomplish this task, a System Definition process was undertaken to achieve the Engineering solution space domain. And to achieve the System Definition methodology the author decided to focus on first creating an Interface Control Document that consisted of a high-level overview architecture of the target system CLEA (Le Carnet d'Information du Logement par Qualitel - Digital Building Logbook) and the source system BDNB (Base de Données Nationale des Bâtiments/National Buildings Database). However, the alternative architectures presented challenges such as how to validate the requirements at this stage. The chosen tool/technique was Thales (Model-Based System Engineering) – Capella Tool and Arcadia Methodology. The article presents this approach, which included: operational analysis, system needs analysis, logical architecture and discussions reflecting the physical architecture relating to the requirement phases of need understanding and solution architecture design. The outcome of this article is The French Demonstration Preliminary Requirements and acknowledgement to the benefits of Model-Based System Engineering (MBSE): Improved Communications, Increased Ability to Manage System Complexity, Improved Product Quality, Reduced Recycled Time, Reduced Risk, Enhanced Knowledge Capture and Reuse of the Information.**

Keywords: Requirements, Stakeholder Needs, Interfaces, Architecture Analysis, System Engineering, "MBSE"

I. INTRODUCTION

"Requirements management is another pervasive mechanism that forces conversation between program managers and chief systems engineers. Effective requirements management practices help program managers and chief systems engineers align their work so that customers receive ideal solutions and desired program benefits, and value is realized for the business" [1]. ISO/IEC/IEEE 15288 is recognized by International Council on Systems Engineering (INCOSE) handbooks as a Technical Process compartmentalized into 4 sections: i) Concept Definition – comprising of Business Mission Analysis and Stakeholder Needs and Requirements Definition; ii) System Definition – referring to System Requirements Definition, System Architecture Definition, and Design Definition; iii) System Realization – implementation, integration, verification and validation; and iv) System Deployment and Use – transition, operation, maintenance and disposal. Each of these sections require recursion and collectively they are executed via iteration [2]. This article is based on Horizon Europe Project Demo-Blog where the business needs where pre-defined, and the challenges were associated to defining requirements at an abstract opportunity/problem space domain level for an automated renovation advice tool. To accomplish this task, a System Definition process was undertaken to achieve the Engineering solution space domain. The process is composed of: system requirements definition (transform the stakeholder, user-oriented view of desired capabilities into a technical view of a solution that meets the operational needs of the user) ; system architecture definition (to generate system architecture alternatives, select one or more alternatives that address stakeholder concerns and system requirements, and express this in consistent views and models) ; and design definition (to provide sufficient detailed data and information about the system and its elements to realize the solution in accordance with the system requirements and system architecture). Leveraging experience as project manager for CSTB on the Demo Blog project, to achieve the System Definition methodology, we decided to focus on epistemic modality (logic of the statements) of the design requirements by first creating an Interface Control Document (ICD) for the interoperable architecture of CLEA and the BDNB.

The rest of the paper is structured as follows. Section II introduces the concept of the Digital Building Logbook (DBL) and the French Demonstration whereas Section III analyses the development of requirements from abstract to domain solutions. Section IV presents a novel architecture of French Demonstration, which is an extraction from the actual ICD document produced for the Demo BLog project where each of the components are numerated and the interfaces are presented. In acknowledgement of the challenges associated to validating the requirements at this stage, section V explains the chosen tools/technique rationale of MBSE and the use of semantics to define the French Demonstration Requirements. This article's main contribution is the requirements for the demonstration that is currently under development.

II. THE DIGITAL BUILDING LOGBOOK

The Semantic Data Model [3] identifies a DBL as a common repository for all relevant data. Furthermore, it enables a variety of data, information, and documents to be recorded, accessed, enriched, and organized, under specific categories. It also represents a record of major events and changes over a building's lifecycle. However, most of this data stored (Indoor Air Quality (IAQ), operational energy use, smart buildings potential and life cycle emissions, building ratings, cert, and circularity) in the logbook have a more static nature, while others, such as smart meters and intelligent devices, are dynamic and need to be automatically and regularly updated.

According to [4], platforms are focused on the adoption of a microservice-based event-driven architecture. In our opinion, the process of mono-lithic architecture comprising of user interface, business logic, and data access layer has certainly evolved into microservice architecture (user interface, many separate micro services, and data bases) for the built environment. The adaption of Industry 4.0 (Internet of Things - IoT) including real-time smart meters and intelligent devices has changed the complexity of the platform architecture associated with buildings and smart cities.

A. The Demo BLog Project

The Horizon Europe project, 'Development and Demonstration of DBLs' (Demo-BLog), focuses on "the idea to collect data throughout the lifespan of a building and create a common digital data repository to ensure efficient design, construction, operation, and financing of buildings. In this context, the EU-funded Demo-BLog project will bring together five different DBLs with a total of 4.5 million registered units. It will demonstrate how DBLs facilitate transparency, trust, informed decision-making, and information sharing in the construction sector, among building owners and occupiers, as well as within financial institutions and public authorities" [5]. The project is compartmentalized into six work packages where the first three concern: Functionalities and user experience methodology (WP1); Data collection and interoperability, processing, governance (WP2); and Demonstration & Evaluation (WP3).

When reflecting on the System engineering process [2], the following elements are evident: concurrency – the parallel application of two or more processes at a given level in system hierarchy, iteration – the repeated application of and interaction between two or more processes at a given level in the system hierarchy, and recursion – the repeated application of the set of the life cycle processes, tailored as appropriate, at successive levels in the system hierarchy. As the work packages are progressing synchronously, iteration is in fact needed to accommodate the stakeholders (Energy Saving Trust - EST, and Qualitel - governance of CLEA software and DBL provider) decisions and evolving understanding to account for the architectural development.

B. *Define specifications and French Demonstration*

This article is based on WP1 subtask 1.1.3: Define specifications for the automated renovation advice tool were the parties involved is EST (UK), CSTB and QUALITEL (France) – The specifications produced for each demo will be presented according to general requirements/capabilities, behavior, architecture/structure, verification, and validation. This common approach will enable in-depth comparison of the planned scenarios between the demonstrations and encourages wider adoption of the learnings. Figure 1 captures and consolidates the operational needs from the stakeholders. It is a basic model; however, it creates the foundation of the process and starts to define what the users of the system have to accomplish; identifies entities, actors, roles, activities and concepts.

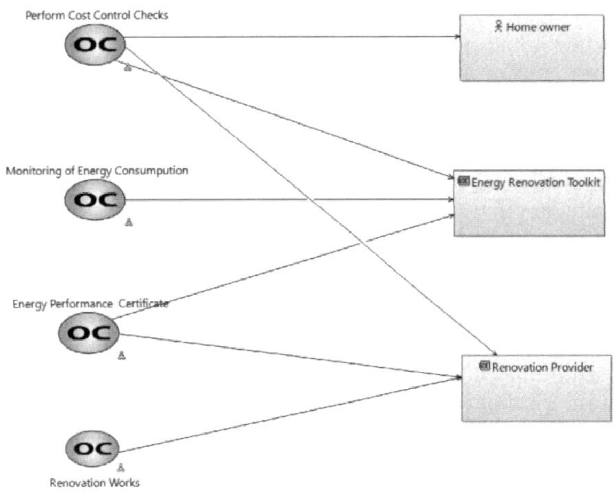

Fig. 1. Define the Stakeholder Needs and Environment for Automated Renovation Advice Tool

The French Demonstration 'Demo of user-centric automated renovation advice within CLEA DBL' concept is to exploit several new functionalities of the CLEA DBL with a stronger focus on the automatic renovation advice functionality. The main emphasis of the demonstration is to show the development and application of a renovation decision tool support within the DBL. This decision support tool will provide tailor made solutions using the building characteristics from BDNB and building owner/occupant input data. The development and application of this tool is to be demonstrated for 50 dwellings as a first step (the final target being to make it available for the 50.000 dwellings currently using CLEA). The financial and environmental benefits and the achieved energy performance certificate will be presented for these houses through CLEA. The BDNB (national repository) is governed by CSTB, and it includes:

- Open data: Project Building-ID, National benchmarks (open repositories buildings/addresses/plots) - National address base, Cadastre, BD Topo, and Official geographic code; Data from open data sources - Le diagnostic de performance énergétique/The Energy Performance Diagnosis (DPE) 2012, Agence de l'Environnement et de la Maîtrise de l'Energie/French Environment and Energy Management Agency (ADEME), Local energy data (ENEDIS), Gaz Réseau Distribution France/Gas Network Distribution France (GrDF), and Land value data (Centre d'études et d'expertise sur les risques, l'environnement, la mobilité et l'aménagement/Center for Studies and Expertise on Risks, Environment, Mobility and Planning - CEREMA);
- Closed data: Restricted access " Assigns " Under commercial conditions - Land files, Registre national d'Immatriculation des Copropriétés/National Register of Condominium Registration (RNIC) and Complete Le Répertoire des logements locatifs des bailleurs sociaux/The Directory of Rental Housing from Social Landlords (RPLS); CSTB "business" services (Restricted Under commercial conditions) - Missing Data Prediction, Simulations (DPE 2021, cometh, etc.), Decision indicators (Renovation potential, Land value, etc.) and Measurements.

III. WHY SYSTEMS ENGINEERING

[6] highlighted the costs committed to the life cycle cost against time. The image described below is derived from 1993 Defense Acquisition University (DAU):

- The cumulative percentage life cycle cost against time was presented from 0 to 100% and the time duration included: concept; design; develop, production/test; and operations through disposal.
- The diagrams graph recognized that at the concept stage where 8% of time had passed the committed cost was 70% of the project budget, design representing 15% and develop 20% showed 85% committed costs.
- While production/test resulted in 95% leaving operations through disposal at both 100% for committed costs and time.

The main evaluation from the graph identifies that to extract defects at design stage it is 3-6x (costs), and at the develop stage it is 20-100x and at Production/Test stage it is 500-1000x.

A. *Requirements*

For the Demo BLog project, the process of drafting the French Demonstration requirement was not just to comply with the projects required task but also to provide a collaboration mechanism between the two main partners involved in the French Demonstration: CSTB & Qualitel and the UK demonstration leader EST and their DBL provider Chimni.

The INCOSE guide to writing requirements [7] places the requirements and specification within two separate but adjoining spheres where sphere 1 includes – Design inputs: focusing on design inputs, preliminary logical & physical architectures, and sphere 2 – design outputs: focusing on design outputs, maturing the logical & physical architectures, design, design output specification, and realized system element. The step formation between the two spheres transits from 'Integrated Set of Needs transforming to Design Input Requirements (emphasizing the question design to "what") which then transforms to Architecture & Design (representing sphere 2). The continuation of the process leads to Design Output Specifications (representing "how" – build-to/code-to) before finally transforming to the System Element. The diagram also acknowledged that within the second phase (sphere) the design output specifications can include specifications, algorithms, for-mutations, drawings, & other design output artifacts. This point is key to the Demo Blog project as it enabled the author to explore further opportunities such as Thales MBSE Pillars (as explained in Workflow of CLEA and BDNB Interface).

B. *Develop Requirements from Abstract to Domain Solution*

[8] identified that the requirements process requires various steps: 1) understand the entity's opportunity/problem and solution spaces, 2) develop the entity's requirements domain solution, 3) develop the entity's operations domain solution, 4) develop the entity's behavioral solution, 5) develop the entity's physical domain solution, and 6) evaluate and optimize the entity's total design solution. In Wasson [9] the four domain solutions of requirements, operations, behavioral, and physical relationships are mapped to Archer's Design Process Model for integrated design solutions encompassing: data collection, analysis, synthesis, development, and communication. These four-domain solutions were aligned with the Demo BLog Task 1.1.3 specific request that the specifications produced for each demo will be presented according to general requirements/capabilities, behavior.

Furthermore, in [8] it is acknowledged that such methods require a derivation process where the mechanism involves a loop that commences with questioning 'What Outcomes' must be achieved, then 'what capabilities" are required to achieve each outcome, before referring to "under what scenarios & conditions" should each capability be achieved, and then "How Well Must" each capability be performed to accommodate scenarios/conditions. These five stages lead to identifying the performance requirement, however, to write the derived requirements statements Wasson introduces the "How" should each capability be verified to demonstrate its contribution to this requirement into the method. After one has acknowledged the "how" he suggests 'Verification Methods' and 'Valid Requirement' to achieve 'Compliance Verification' which consequently is looped back to the 'What Capability' stage before confirming a requirement. We believe this explanation of derived requirements provided the final process logic for Task 1.1.3 architecture/structure, verification, and validation.

IV. THE INTERFACE CONTROL DOCUMENT (ICD)

The concept of the ICD is to describe the relationship between the French National Building Database, called BDNB, (the source system) and the housing information booklet called CLEA (the target system). This ICD specifies the interface requirements that the participating systems must meet. It describes the concept of operations for the interface, defines the message structure and protocols that govern the interchange of data, and identifies the communication paths along which the project team expects data to flow.

For each interface, the ICD provides the following information:

- A description of the data exchange format and protocol for exchange.
- A general description of the interface.
- Assumptions where appropriate.

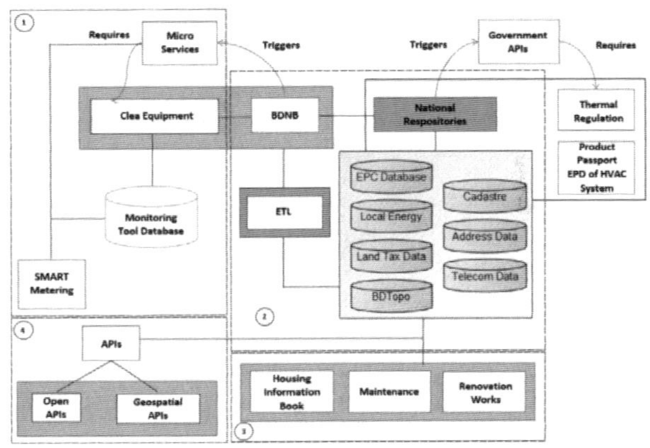

Fig. 2. Interface Control Document – French Demonstration

1) Capturing Data - The concept of microservices is embedded in the structure of Event-driven architecture. This is a type of software architecture that ingests, processes, stores, and reacts to real-time data as it's being generated, opening new capabilities in the way businesses run. The challenges associated to traditional architecture such as a time series database inefficiency with handling relational use cases or modelling, and likewise a document database structure failing to provide good analytics against those documents has increased the needs of microservices. The requirements of system design have revolved around the notion of real-time events (events drive actions and reactions, and transform between different streams, splitting, merging, and evolving). For the French Demo: Post-Occupancy Monitoring of Federated Data the event driven architecture will involve Smart Metering as an IoT device connected to CLEA equipment comprises of monitoring tools database for energy and maintenance.

2) Synchronizations of information – The French Demo pilot will provide RESTful Application Performance Interface (API) for CLEA to connect to the BDNB. As a centralized system the BDNB is openly connected to the French National Repositories including DPE (the national EPC database), Local Energy, Land value data, and INSEE - Le code officiel géographique/ The Official Geographic Code (COG). The characteristics of BDNB include 2D (+ buildings height) modeling of the territory and its infrastructures

throughout France (BD Topo) and the plan of a plot entered in a register showing the state of land ownership (Cadaster) coupled with the National Repositories will be very beneficial to The French Demo via advancing a middleware computer technology that allows massive synchronizations of information from one data source (usually a database) to another, the term associated with this middleware is called Extract-Transform-Load (ETL).

3) Energy Renovation Toolkit – The French Demo 'CLEA Equipment' will comprise of three main elements: a) Housing Information - centralization and storage of information and documents: commercial proposal, plan sketch, project, contract and descriptive notice, plan PC, A monitoring tool for regular information on progress site and alerts, photos, a booklet complete reception containing all the equipment of the house listed with its notes, etc., EPC b) Maintenance of Accommodation - information, opinions and advice maintenance, consumption monitoring energy tool, reminders for the maintenance of equipment. c) Renovation Works – details of renovation provider and certification. These external attributes will be connected to Renovation Toolkits and accessed through CLEA database.

4) APIs - REST applications are event command pattern, and they are coupled in multiple ways such as the endpoint is known (i.e., the service address); the method being called is also known (i.e., an API call) and the calls return value; they are synchronous. RESTful protocols involve the process of sending a command which will be integrated within the composition of French Demo Post-Occupancy Monitoring of Federated Data.

V. DIGITAL MODELS

[10] identified that 'System Health Management (SHM) is a reasoning process and is therefore model dependent, accuracy, completeness, and interoperability of the models are paramount. The use of automatic model abstraction, and model checking will greatly reduce the effort to certify models and the overall SHM system. And this benefit accumulates as the models are improved over the system's lifecycle.' [11] emphasized the evolution of models transition through various stages: stage 1 'document-based', stage 2 'document-centric', stage 3 'model-enhanced', stage 4 'model-centric' and, stage 5 'model-based'. The following sections identify the need for MBSE.

A. Model-based systems engineering

The ICD provided: 'Business Process Map' - the visual display of French Demonstration process from start to completion and the sequence of steps that must take place, 'Simplified Architecture' - consisting of data sources (CEREMA, INSEE, ADEME, and Cadastre et Territoires), data acquisitions (prediction services INSEE, typological prediction, INSEE requests for land values, and Digital Product Passport), 'data repositories' (PostgreSQL, ETL, PostgreGIS, and BD Topo), and data exchange (Linky ENEDiS – LINKYAPI, RESTAPI, gpkg (GeoPackage), and TCP/IP). It also included the 'System Elements' components breakdown of the French Demonstration, and 'Capabilities & Requirements' featuring System Product Structure (physical hierarchy) of the French Demonstration consisting of CLEA equipment, National repositories, CSTB (BDNB), and Communications (connectivity) and their interaction with multi-level behavioral capability operation and tasks comprising of Housing Information Pack, Maintenance of Accommodation and Renovation Works. However, the documentation of these models was static with no intelligent decision making defining the knowledge contribution of the models. In other words, there was no semantic attributes capturing the various elements of the models.

"MBSE is a methodology that focuses on creating and exploiting digital system and engineering domain models as the primary means of exchange of information, feedback, and requirements, as opposed to document-centric systems engineering. It involves the entire process of capturing, communicating, and making sure that all the digital models we use to represent a system are coordinated and maintained throughout the entire lifecycle of the system" [12]. The following section addresses how Thales MBSE pillars of language, method and tool was used to improve the performance of the models.

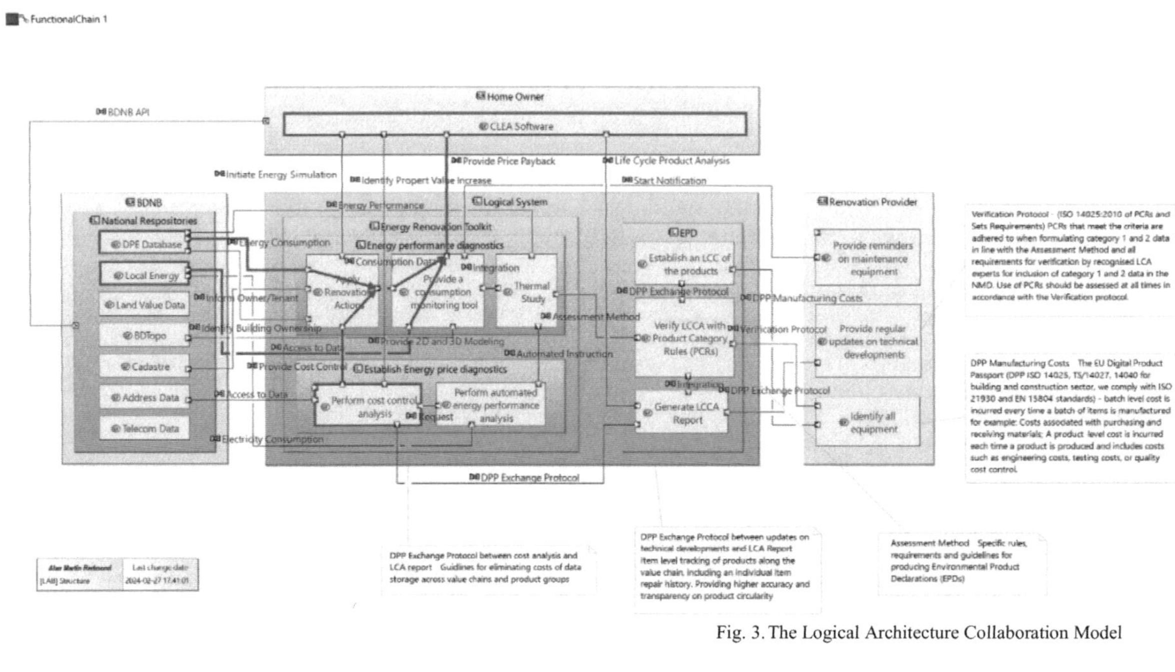

Fig. 3. The Logical Architecture Collaboration Model

These pillars changed the viewpoints of the original architecture and techniques such as capturing the exchange of information to be documented in an uncoordinated manner. And challenged the status quo of the rudimentary approach to deliver a heuristic model that captured the microservices in an agile process while also addressing the atomic design components.

B. *Workflow of CLEA and BDNB Interface*

Thales MBSE comprises of the tool 'Capella' an open source MBSE solution' purposely built to provide the notation and fitting the method 'Arcadia approach' high level concepts and viewpoints. The methodology for the Demo BLog requirements is divided into four phases where each phase requires different levels of modeling pertaining to different diagrams.

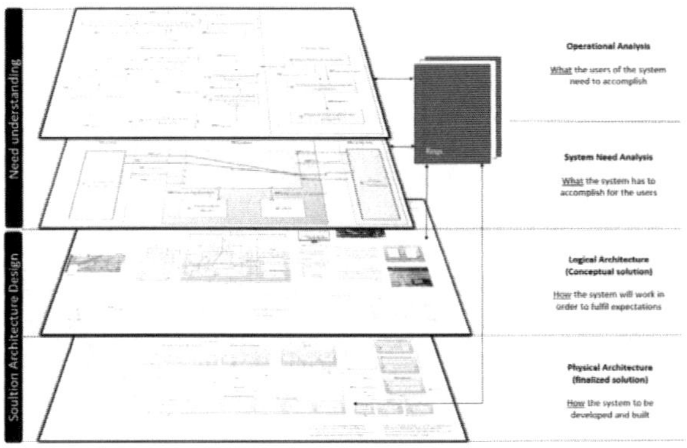

Fig. 4. MBSE – The Arcadia perspectives

Definition of the levels: the need of understanding levels comprises of: the operational analysis - what the users of the system need to accomplish, and system need analysis – what the system has to accomplish for the users, the solution architecture level include logical architecture (conceptual solution) – how the system will work in order to fulfill expectations, and physical architecture (finalized solution) – how the system is to be developed and built. Figure 3 is an illustration of the logical architecture for French Demonstration. It has been developed based on the need understanding levels and each of these levels required several diagrams such as: operational capabilities, operational analysis, architecture, entity scenarios, function data flows, functions and traceability, functional chains, states and modes, and system architecture. The next level 'solution architecture' incorporated logical functions, data flow scenarios, class diagrams, refine logical functions and assign functions to components. Figure 4 shows the various levels for the French Demonstration use of MBSE aligned to the Arcadia methodology.

C. *French Demonstrations requirements*

Data Modeling in Arcadia/Capella consists of functional exchanges from one component to the next for example in Figure 3 Logical Architectural, the Homeowner interface is connected to the National Repository component via the BDNB API. The National Repositories functions DPE (Energy Performance Certificate) database exchanges energy consumption information to function apply renovation action, and local energy function exchanges provide a consumption monitoring tool. The focus of the functional chain (highlighted in bold connecting lines) identifies the main exchanges between the data from perform cost control analysis, apply renovation actions, and provide a consumption monitoring tool. As illustrated in the diagram the provide consumption monitoring tool groups the chain of information before providing price payback data via CLEA Software. At this stage for the French Demonstration the functional chain has suggested that this path represents the main components and functional exchanges. This semantic decision is an attribute of Capella/Arcadia tool based on information accumulated from the previous layers (operational, capabilities, and system analysis).

However, as noted in 'MBSE section' the model in a holistic view captures the Housing Information Pack, Maintenance of Accommodation and Renovation Works logical functions characteristics to provide reminders on maintenance equipment, provide regular updates on technical developments, and identify all equipment.

TABLE I. FRENCH DEMO REQUIREMENTS

1.1	***Information Exchange (Files and Data)***
1.1.1	The Energy Renovation Toolkit shall provide a mechanism and interfaces for CLEA software to connect with BDNB dataset allowing a technical characterization of existing buildings. Reminder, the BDNB is the merging of national repositories (EPCs for example), data-crossing algorithms and CSTB energy simulation tool.
1.1.2	CSTB shall facilitate the exchange mechanism between the USER via CLEA Software and BDNB with secure access, reception, and registration of requests linked by BDNB RESTful APIs. The required open data databases (Building-ID, National address base, Cadastre, BD Topo, Official geographic code, DPE 2012, Local energy data) of the BDNB shall be interconnected by CSTB ETL.
1.1.3	The exchange mechanism shall also facilitate the calculation indicators of performance for energy simulations diagnostics, and access to registered EPC data.
1.1.4	The CLEA Software shall provide the Energy Renovation Toolkit with RESTful API access to LINKY ENEDIS and GAZPAR GRDF data streams. They are respectively the electricity and gas national network providers and handle real hourly energy consumption at deliver point (generally at dwelling scale).
1.1.5	The CLEA Software shall provide a mechanism and interfaces for Energy Renovation ToolKit to supply the renovation provider with access to submit the required data files for the Housing Information Book, and centralization storage of information and documents: commercial proposal, plan sketch, project, contract and descriptive notice, plan layout, and experts' advice (LCC). Typically, Automatic completion of key information exchanges shall be provided.
1.1.6	The exchange mechanism shall also facilitate exchange of data (XML files) for the integration of the thermal study and consumption monitoring tool provided by CERQUAL.
1.1.7	The CLEA Software shall provide a mechanism and interfaces for Energy Renovation ToolKit to supply the client with open access to submit the required data files for the House maintenance, and A pre-existing library of equipment to customize (regular update in depending on technical developments).
1.1.8	The exchange mechanism shall also facilitate a user-interface to retrieve data from cadaster provided by BDNB API to obtain general dwelling information. Typically, equipment modules (user guides for HVAC & devices, maintenance alerts) shall be provided.
1.2	***Information from other sources***
1.2.1	Information provided by the renovation provider on identified equipment prior to installing shall be referenced to The EU

1.1	***Information Exchange (Files and Data)***
	Digital Product Passport DPP ISO 14040 and EN 15804 standards for batch and product level costs and exchanged as part of the EPD to establish an LCA of the products.
1.2.2	Information provided by the renovation provider on regular updates on technical developments shall be verified by ISO 14025:2010 of PCRs Set requirements that adhered to formulating category 1 and 2 data in line with the assessment method of all requirements for verification by recognized LCA experts for inclusion of category 1 (in relation to EN 15804) and 2 (in relation to EN 15804/A2:2019) data in the National Environmental Database.
1.2.3	Information provided to the EPD system shall be managed by CLEA and exchange protocols for generating LCA reports and inputs to perform cost control analysis.

These functions main exchanges are between the Environmental Product Declarations (EPDs) components: Establish a Life Cycle Costing (LCA) of products, verify Life Cycle Costing Analysis (LCCA) with Product Category Rules (PCRs) and generate LCCA report. In Figure 3 the yellow boxes address the specific requirement associated with these operations for example, to provide regular updates on technical developments, this operation will require a verification LCCA with PCR. The verification protocol (ISO 14025.2010 of PCRs & sets requirements) identifies that technical developments meet the criteria of category 1 (proprietary products) and 2 (non-proprietary products) data in line with the assessment method: 'specific rules, requirements, and guidelines for producing EPDs, such information can be sourced from Product Environmental Profile (PEP) ecopassport [13] and BCG [14]. The model in Figure 3 reflects the architecture in Figure 2 where the Thales MBSE pillars of language, method and tool enriched the model to produce the French Demo Requirements as shown in Table 1. Requirement 1.1 'Information Exchange' refers to the main interactions between CLEA software and BDNB and Requirements 1.2 'Information from other sources' illustrates the assessment methods targeting EPDs for Digital Product Passports.

VI. Advancing Future Works

CSTB advancements with BDNB have already been well applied in relation to BTP-flux model where data mining, analytical techniques, and GIS tool were used to assess different datasets available at the national level to develop a common database for French buildings, BDNB [15]. The Demo BLog project will create an open API for connection to the French national repositories governed by CSTB. However, in the opinion of this article author, the future of DBL advancements will rely on graph databases/knowledge graphs and polyglot resistance (different types of data in different ways) were the Building-ID (sourced through the BDNB) is connected to a Product Catalogue (renovation products used on previous buildings) via cloud connection. This data will be sourced via Awesome Procedures (APOC) for Neo4j where the user defined procedures are written in Java, deployed into the database, and called by the Cypher. The process requires using data relationships for recommendations, such as content-based filtering to recommend items based on what previous renovation providers have used and collaborative filtering to predict products based on similarity (location, building, type) and preferences.

VII. Conclusion

This article reflects the preliminary contribution of work on French Demo Requirements undertaken by CSTB for the Horizon Europe Demo BLog project. The article acknowledges the advanced changes in platform architectures from monolithic to event-driven architecture and demonstrates the benefits of MBSE to create requirements for the adaptation of industrial 4.0 complexities associated with buildings and smart cities.

Acknowledgment

The author would like to take this opportunity to acknowledge the contribution of Mathieu THOREL (CSTB) during the Demo Blog project, and Martin Le Bourgeois (Business Developer – OBEO) and M. Lionel YAPI (Thales Group) for providing the training for the Capella Tool and Arcadia Methodology.

References

[1] Project Management Institute and INCOSE, 'Integrating Program Management and Systems Engineering, Methods, Tools, and Organizational Systems for Improving Performance', Eric S. Rebentisch, editor in Chief with foreward by L. Prusak, Published by: John Wiley & Sons, Inc., Hoboken, New Jersey, pp. 157, 2017. (Section 8.3.4 Requirements Management).

[2] INCOSE, Systems Engineering Handbook, A Guide for System Life Cycle Processes and Activities, 5th Edition, INCOSE-TP-2023-002-05, pre-pared by: International Council on Systems Engineering, 7670 opportunity Rd, Suite 220, San Diego, CA, USA 92111-2222, pp. 42-43, 2023.

[3] M. Böhms et al., 'DBL Semantic Data Model, Providing Standard Form and Meaning to Digital Building Logbook Data', DG Grow, 23. (Final), pp. 8, May 2023.

[4] R. Laigner Nunes et al., "From a Monolithic Big Data System to a Microservices Event-Driven Architecture". Conference: Euromicro Conference on Software Engineering and Advanced Applications (SEAA) At: Portorož, Slovenia, pp. 213-220, 2020. DOI:10.1109/SEAA51224.2020.00045

[5] CORDIS Résultats de la recherche de l'UE [Online]. Available from: https://cordis.europa.eu/project/id/101091749, Fact Sheet, Last update: 10 March 2023, 2024.03.15

[6] INCOSE, Systems Engineering Handbook, 'A Guide for System Life Cycle Processes and Activities', 4th Edition, INCOSE-TP-2003-002-04, 2015 pre-pared by: International Council on Systems Engineering, 7670 opportunity Rd, Suite 220, San Diego, CA, USA 92111-2222, pp. 14, 2015.

[7] M. Ryan, and L. Wheatcraft, 'Guide to Writing Requirements', INCOSE-TP-2010-006-04 | VERS/REV: 4 | 1 April 2022, prepared by: Requirements Working Group International Council on Systems Engineering 7670 Opportunity Road, Suite 220, San Diego, California 92111-2222 USA, INCOSE 2023, pp. 9, April 2022.

[8] C.S. Wasson, 'System Analysis, Design and Development, Concepts, Principles, and Practices', Published by John Wiley & Sons, Inc., Hoboken, New Jersey, Chapter 26, The SE Process Model, pp.278 and Chapter 32, Requirements Derivation, Flow Down, Allocation, And Traceability, pp. 363, 2006.

[9] C.S. Wasson, 'System Engineering, Analysis, Design, and Development', 2nd Edition, Published by John Wiley & Sons, Inc., Hoboken, New Jersey, Chapter 11, Analytical Problem-Solving and Solution Development Synthesis, pp. 251, 2016.

[10] R.M. Mackey, 'System Health Management with Aerospace Applications', edited by S.B. Johnson, T.J. Gormley, S.S. Kessler, C. D. Mott, A. Patterson-Hine, K.M. Richard and P.A. Scandura, Jr, Published by: John Wiley & Sons Ltd, The Atrium, Southern Gate, Chichester, West Sussex, PO19 8SQ, UK, 2011, Chapter 9, Accessing and Maturing Technology Readiness Levels, pp. 152, 2011.

[11] J. Holt, 'Systems Engineering Demystified: A practitioner's handbook for developing complex systems using a model-based approach'. Packt Publishing Ltd, 2021, Chapter 2, Model-Based Systems Engineering, pp 51, 2021.

[12] ANSYS BLOG, 'Model-Based Systems Engineering (MBSE) Explained'. [Online]. Available from: https://www.ansys.com/blog/model-based-systems-engineering-explained#:~:text=Model%2Dbased%20systems%20engineering%20(MBSE)%20is%20a%20methodology%20that,to%20document%2Dcentric%20systems%20engineering. 2024.05.06

[13] PEP ecopassport® PROGRAM, Product Category Rules for Electrical, Electronic and HVAC-R Products, PCR-ed3-EN-2015 04 02© 2015 P.E.P. Association, http://www.pep-ecopassport.org/index.php?eID=dumpFile&t=f&f=773&token=d99658b4286d15a36ec908161ca64e93ade0cfc2

[14] WBCSD x BCG DPP, 'The EU Digital Product Passport shapes the future of value chains: What it is and how to prepare now' [Online]. Available from: https://www.wbcsd.org/Pathways/Products-and Materials/Resources/The-EU-Digital-Product-Passport. 2024.05.06.

[15] R. Tirado, A. Aublet, S. Laurenceau, M. Thorel, M. Louërat, and G. Habert, "Component-Based Model for Building Material Stock and Waste-Flow Characterization: A case in the île-de-France Region", Sustainability 2021, 13, 13159. pp. 1-34 https://doi.org/10.3390/su132313159

Avatars and Identity in the Metaverse: Navigating the Potentials and Pitfalls of Digital Self-Representation

Myrto Dimitriou
Rome Business School
Rome, Italy
e-mail: myrto.dimitriou@gmail.com

Leonie Hallo
Adelaide Business School
The University of Adelaide, Australia
e-mail: leonie.hallo@adelaide.edu.au

Abstract— **Rapid digitization, the impact of social media and now the continuous growth of the Metaverse have met both positive and negative responses. Along with the optimism about the possibilities and efficiencies created via Artificial Intelligence (AI), there have also been concerns. Many fields are now using the Metaverse in commercial applications, leading to new ways of increasing revenues and enhancing sustainability. Central to this concept are avatars, which serve as digital embodiments of users, facilitating interactions and the representation of self within this virtual environment. This paper emphasizes the critical implications of virtual identity combined with the psychological and sociocultural dimensions of avatar selection, highlighting the complex motivations behind avatar customization. The potential for avatars to influence user behavior, facilitate escapism, and impact psychological well-being is significant, and this emphasizes the need for ethical considerations and protective measures for users navigating these virtual spaces. There is also the possibility that cultural differences may exist within choices of avatars, adding to the complexity of the field. This paper explores the potentials and pitfalls regarding the use of avatars as digital representations of people, and the impact of such developments on an individual's personal identity concept.**

Keywords-Metaverse; avatars; self-expression; identity; well-being.

I. INTRODUCTION

The term Metaverse is used to describe a collective virtual shared space in which virtual worlds, augmented reality and the Internet provide virtually enhanced physical reality for people. Virtual worlds are persistent and interconnected so that people can move seamlessly between them. This allows immersive experiences and the digital presentation of people as avatars with the ability to interact and participate within the virtual world. Decentralization of control means that the virtual world presents people with the opportunity to interact in a way which is free and self-determined. Technology, thus, presents opportunities for people to create virtual representations of themselves through a range of avatars that are generally visual icons depicting a person or user in the digital environment including video games, online communities, social media platforms and virtual worlds. Avatars are an alter ego for a person in a digital form so that users can create a unique persona within the digital space. Some avatars are highly realistic and can be customized in various ways, moving well beyond profile pictures, and allowing opportunities for interaction with other players' avatars. Thus, a person establishes their presence, which is recognizable to other users in the space. Avatars have been used in a variety of fields including helping deaf individuals with sign language [1], education [2][3], telehealth [4], and oncology [5]. Human to virtual human interaction is beginning to be studied, including the factors that influence social interaction with virtual humans [6], as well as the benefit of avatars in promoting independent living for the elderly [7]. Clearly, we are just at the beginning of the exploration of the benefits and possible downsides of this exciting technology.

Despite the promising aspects of the Metaverse, several challenges need to be addressed. The business and scientific problems related to the Metaverse encompass issues of identity, privacy, security, and the ethical implications of virtual interactions. One significant challenge is ensuring secure and private user data while providing seamless and immersive experiences. Another is the potential psychological impact of prolonged engagement with virtual environments, including issues of identity dissociation and the potential for social isolation.

The idea behind this paper is to explore the relationship between avatars and user identity within the Metaverse, examining how virtual representations influence personal expression, social connectivity, and psychological well-being. This exploration aims to understand the broader implications of Metaverse engagement on both individual and societal levels.

The research questions guiding this paper are as follows: How does the use of avatars in the Metaverse affect users' perceptions of their identity? What are the psychological and social implications of avatar use in virtual environments? How can the Metaverse be designed to enhance positive user experiences while mitigating potential negative effects?

The purpose of this paper is to provide a comprehensive analysis of the impact of avatars on user identity within the Metaverse and in the real world. By examining existing literature, this paper aims to offer insights into the opportunities and challenges associated with avatar use in virtual environments, ultimately contributing to the development of more inclusive, secure, and beneficial Metaverse experiences.

However, this approach has limitations. The rapidly evolving nature of Metaverse technologies means that literature review findings may quickly become outdated. Additionally, the subjective nature of identity and personal experience can lead to variability in how users interact with and perceive their avatars. The ethical considerations surrounding virtual interactions are complex and multifaceted, requiring ongoing discourse and regulation. Qualitative research via semi-structured interviews with relevant authorities as planned in the future will provide further important information that can elaborate other researchers' findings.

The remainder of this paper is structured as follows: Section II provides a detailed definition and context for understanding the Metaverse while Section III explores the concept of identity across various domains and its relevance within virtual environments. Section IV discusses the evolution, types, and significance of avatars in the digital realm and Section V considers how avatars influence user identity and the implications for digital interactions. Section VI examines the psychological, social, and cultural factors driving avatar selection. Section VII considers the potential benefits and risks associated with avatar use. Section VIII summarizes the key findings from the literature and their implications for future Metaverse development. Section IX discusses future work including qualitative data collection planned by the authors.

II. METAVERSE: DEFINING THE NEW IMMERSIVE WORLD

The scope of this section is to establish a comprehensive definition and understanding of the Metaverse, elucidating its multifaceted nature as a virtual environment that blends the physical and digital realms.

There are many different definitions of the Metaverse, but the following description is used in this paper: a virtual environment that blends the physical and the digital, facilitated by the convergence of Internet and Web technologies and extended reality [8]. The Metaverse represents the top-level hierarchy of persistent virtual spaces that may also integrate in real life, so that social, commercial, and personal experiences emerge through Web 3.0 technologies [9]. The Metaverse is the next stage of the Internet, and results from the evolution of a wide variety of emerging, exponential technologies maturing simultaneously, converging and enabling new interconnected relationships between the physical and the digital [10]. The Metaverse can be viewed as a shared, persistent, three-dimensional virtual realm where people interact with objects, the environment and each other through digital representations of themselves or avatars. The Metaverse enables a tactile, sensorially immersive experience that creates the feeling of being present without requiring actual presence, and it would allow us and the places and things we value to not just be on the Internet but inside it [11]. Thus, while the Metaverse is often seen as a separate virtual world, its essential promise is that it can operate as an extension of the real world, a complement to it, offering new and innovative ways for people to interact, in order to enhance and enrich many aspects of our real-world lives.

The word Metaverse is the combination of the Greek prefix "Meta" meaning "beyond" and "verse" referring to the "universe." The term Meta used as a prefix has various meanings: occurring later than or in succession to; after, situated behind or beyond, later or more highly organized or specialized form of change; transformation, more comprehensive; transcending [12]. It is important to acknowledge and be aware of cultural or linguistic differences when introducing new concepts or technologies such as the Metaverse. In the Hebrew language, the word meta has a completely different meaning, meaning "dead" or "deceased", referring to a person, animal, or any living thing that has passed away [13].

In linking to the next section, it is important to note that the semantic identity, including the words and vocabulary used to describe and navigate the Metaverse, significantly influences how users perceive and interact within this new paradigm. The terminology shapes the user experience and the overall understanding of the Metaverse, thereby impacting identity formation and self-representation within these digital spaces.

III. IDENTITY AND SELF-REPRESENTATION

The concept of identity has been studied across many domains including psychoanalysis, politics, sociology, history and psychology [14]. At its core, identity refers to the distinct characteristics, qualities, or beliefs that make an individual or group unique. It encompasses an array of elements including, but not limited to, personal self-concept, social roles, cultural affiliations, and digital personas. From a psychological perspective, identity is often seen as an internal process of self-recognition and differentiation from others, highlighting aspects, such as personal traits, values, and experiences that contribute to one's sense of self. These two different but complementary strands, internal self-verification and linkages with social structures have formed the foundation of research on identity. Identity development is viewed as a key task of adolescence [15]. The development of identity is understood to occur through two interrelated cycles: identity formation in which adolescents question their identity and explore alternatives and eventually commit to an identity; and identity maintenance where they strengthen a chosen identity and synthesize, producing a sensation of internal consistency [16], and a stable identity [17], who draws on the work of Erikson on identity crisis. Erikson's definition of identity is as follows: "Ego identity, then, in its subjective aspect, is the awareness of the fact that there is self-sameness and continuity to the ego's synthesizing methods, the style of one's individuality, and that this style coincides with the sameness and continuity of one's meaning for significant others in the immediate community." [18].

Sociologically, identity incorporates the roles and statuses individuals hold within society, reflecting the influence of social structures, relationships, and cultural norms on the formation of self, while anthropologically is deeply tied to cultural heritage, traditions, and the collective history of the group to which one belongs. Within sociology, identity is seen as both a precious asset and treasure, and a difficult problem. In this view, identity consists of a "bundle of phenomena that are... consubstantial with social experience" [19]. Identity is about permanence within rapid change, unity among diverse people under pressure. It is about what is unique and what is common, what is authentic, partly hidden and partly visible. The tension between shared identity and unique identity, and of some kind of stability during change, are at the heart of the notion of identity.

Three dimensions of identity formation: commitment, in-depth exploration, and reconsideration [20] change during the teenage years as the person matures, revealing greater in-depth exploration, decreasing reconsideration, and increasingly greater stable identity. These changes reflect the evolving ways adolescents deal with their commitments as they mature.

Identity is relevant because it fundamentally shapes how individuals perceive themselves and are perceived by others, influencing behavior, interactions, and well-being. However, mechanisms for identity formation and maintenance in digital spaces have often failed to address the complexities of real-world identities, including inadequate representation of diverse identities, insufficient privacy protections, and the potential for identity manipulation. As we transition into the Metaverse, addressing these shortcomings is critical to fostering authentic and secure digital identities.

This understanding of identity sets the stage for examining the role of avatars in the Metaverse, which are integral to self-representation and identity formation in virtual environments.

IV. AVATARS

The term "avatar" has multiple layers of meaning, evolving significantly over time, especially with advances in technology and virtual reality. At its core, the word "avatar" comes from Sanskrit "avatāra," which means "descent." In Hinduism, it refers to the incarnation or physical manifestation of a deity, especially Vishnu, on Earth. However, in the context of digital technology, Virtual Reality (VR), and the Metaverse, the meaning shifts considerably. In the realm of VR and the Metaverse, an avatar is a graphical representation of the user and serves as the digital embodiment of the user, allowing for interaction within these virtual environments. Avatars are a key element in forming a virtual identity, offering users the ability to represent themselves in ways that may or may not correspond to their real-world appearance or identity. An avatar can take the form of a three-dimensional model used in computer games, a two-dimensional icon (picture) used on Internet forums and other communities, or something in between. As technology has advanced, so has the complexity and realism of these avatars, with current VR and Metaverse avatars offering highly detailed, customizable representations of their users.

There are various types of avatars: customizable, self-representational, non-human avatars, abstract avatars, VR avatars, 2D and 3D avatars, human-like avatars, full-body/ leg-less avatars [21]. One interesting flow on of the explosion in avatars concerns its impact on fashion. The burgeoning role of avatars within digital spaces is reshaping the landscape here. As avatars become central to individual identity and expression in virtual environments, the demand for avatar customization options, particularly in terms of fashion, is experiencing a significant uptick. This trend reflects a broader shift in consumer behavior, where digital identity is increasingly seen as an extension of one's physical self, and thus, the desire to curate an avatar's appearance with various outfits and accessories mirrors real-world fashion behaviors [22] [23].

The concept of avatars in VR and the Metaverse reflects a blend of technological advancements, cultural shifts, and human desires for exploration, expression, and connectivity in virtual spaces. As VR technology continues to evolve, so too will the sophistication and capabilities of avatars, further blurring the lines between the virtual and the real. The global digital avatar market was valued at approximately USD 14.34 billion in 2022 and is projected to experience a Compound Annual Growth Rate (CAGR) of 47.1% from 2023 to 2030 [24].

People are increasingly becoming immersed in social virtual environments which provide them with the opportunity to explore aspects of their identity. This enables them to challenge established norms via exploration [25]. Technology also now exists to allow people to share past experiences using VR and relive a previous experience [26].

V. THE RELATIONSHIP BETWEEN THE AVATAR AND IDENTITY

The concept of Metaverse identity marks a significant evolution in the understanding and application of identity in the digital age. It extends the traditional notion of identity beyond its current confines, integrating it with the foundational digital aspects of the Internet. As a complex, multi-faceted construct, Metaverse identity encompasses an individual or entity's representation, data, and identification, effectively bridging the gap between the physical and virtual realms. This identity serves not only as a personal anchor in both worlds but also as a critical component underpinning privacy, security, and the facilitation of digital transactions. Metaverse identity forms the cornerstone upon which the digital economy and virtual interactions are grounded. It ensures the recognition and movement of money and objects within digital spaces, thereby enabling a seamless flow of complex interactions and transactions. As the virtual and physical worlds become increasingly intertwined, the demand for a robust, flexible identity framework becomes paramount. Such a framework is essential for fostering digital trust and authenticity, elements that are crucial for the development of enriching Metaverse experiences. This paper explores the overlaps and differentiation between the real-world identity of the person and their virtual identity, and this exposes the real problems that could arise if these two identities become coalesced in a way which is confusing for the person. Guidance to individuals about the delineation between these two separate worlds may be a useful goal for policy bodies to consider, as well as presenting constructive avenues for future academic research.

The legal and policy choices made concerning Metaverse identity today bear significant implications for the future, particularly concerning the processing of information related to children and other vulnerable groups. These decisions will shape not only the security and privacy measures necessary to protect individuals in the Metaverse but also the ethical standards governing the collection, use, and sharing of personal data. Consider a virtual classroom in the Metaverse where children use avatars to attend lessons and interact with their peers. The choices made regarding the identity and data privacy of these child avatars will have lasting implications. For instance, if avatars can be designed and customized with minimal oversight, children might create identities that expose them to cyberbullying, inappropriate content, or exploitation. In a corporate environment, if policies allow extensive tracking of employees' virtual activities without adequate privacy protections, sensitive information about employees' productivity, behavior, and even personal interactions could be exposed, leading to potential misuse or breaches of confidentiality.

It is essential to implement robust privacy settings to ensure that the users -or their guardians- have control over what information is shared about their virtual activities and interactions, using secure encryption, customizable privacy dashboards, and parental control features. Data collection and usage policies are also important by establishing clear policies ensuring compliance with regulations like Children's Online Privacy Protection Act (COPPA) [27]. Decisions should be made about acceptable customization parameters for employee avatars to maintain professionalism and prevent inappropriate or harmful representations, implementing content moderation tools, AI-based filters, and predefined customization options suitable for children. The use of AI and machine learning algorithms could be useful in order to flag suspicious activities, employ human moderators, and provide mechanisms for reporting misconduct. The development of educational programs, interactive tutorials, and awareness campaigns about online safety workplace etiquette and digital citizenship is crucial to train the new generation of users.

The development of Metaverse identity frameworks, thus, requires careful consideration of their long-term impact on society, emphasizing the need for safeguards that protect the most vulnerable while enabling the growth and evolution of digital communities. In this context, it is imperative that stakeholders across the board, from technology developers to policymakers and educators, engage in thoughtful deliberation and collaborative effort to ensure that Metaverse identities are constructed with an eye toward inclusivity, security, and ethical responsibility. The goal should be to create a digital environment where every individual's identity is respected and protected, paving the way for a future where the Metaverse serves as a space for positive, secure, and empowering experiences for all users.

One aspect of the avatar is its ability to enable people to express their personality, either actual or desired through styling and customization. The avatar is, thus, an integral part of many digital experiences. The ability to express oneself in the digital environment is provided via customization of the avatar's appearance, enabling the user to create an avatar in a desired fashion and experiment with different looks and styles. Further, users are free to create virtual personas that may be entirely different from the real-life identity. This offers the opportunity for people to explore alternative aspects of their identity. They can experiment with various personas without any constraint or judgement. In some environments, the avatar can be created from scratch enabling a unique appearance and design. Avatars can convey emotional states. They can use symbolic elements that the user finds meaningful; for example, symbols and motives. Within role-play, users can create avatars representing the personalities or traits of the characters they want to betray, increasing immersion possibilities. Because users have a high degree of control over this virtual representation, the possibilities of self-expression are significant, enabling people to explore various aspects of their personalities within the virtual world.

Wood and Szymanski explored identity issues within the use of avatars in video games as these relate to gifted adolescents [28]. They comment that the use of avatars in games can be a positive activity, enabling adolescents to explore their identity through the creation of possible selves reflecting their imagination of themselves in the future and what they might become. Similarity identification occurs when a user identifies with an avatar that they think closely resembles the real-life identity. Wishful identification occurs when the person wants to emulate the avatar in some way. Identifiability might be based upon personal characteristics, beliefs, and behaviors. These authors explored choices that the gifted students made, the limitations of their choices and the impact of various identities including race/ethnicity and gender identity. Trying on various identities was considered by these authors as a useful process of imagining possible selves in the future, assisting in the consolidation of a preferred identity.

VI. MOTIVATION FOR CHOOSING PARTICULAR AVATARS

There are many factors which can influence the choice of an avatar. One is the ability to transcend the current confines and be someone or something entirely different. Escapism can be an objective for entering the virtual world and creating an idealized representative version of oneself [29][30].

The appearance of one's avatar can influence communication and interaction in the Metaverse. One study explored three different types of avatar appearances and reported that motion-controlled avatars, and avatars with only heads and hands, still managed to produce a feeling of behavioral interdependence, although a complete avatar body with movements mapped from the user's own movements was more effective in generating a sense of co-presence [31].

The Proteus effect [32] underscores the profound influence of an avatar's appearance on the behavior of its user within virtual environments. This phenomenon, where modifications as superficial as the attire of an avatar can engender more negative behaviors [33], elucidates the complex interplay between virtual representation and real-world conduct. This dynamic suggests that the decision to adopt an appearance divergent from one's physical self can significantly impact personal behavior, influence interpersonal interactions, and potentially alter one's sense of identity. This capacity for virtual reinvention presents both opportunities and risks within the context of personal and professional development. On the one hand, it offers individuals the chance to explore facets of their identity in a manner that might be restricted in the physical world, thereby fostering a sense of empowerment and self-discovery. On the other hand, the dissonance between an individual's real-world persona and their virtual avatar can lead to complexities, particularly in professional settings where the authenticity of personal expression is valued.

Given these insights, the virtual realm -and by extension, the choices individuals make regarding their avatars- can serve as a double-edged sword in the context of professional identity and psychological wellbeing. While virtual environments offer unprecedented avenues for exploration and expression, they also necessitate a nuanced understanding of how such digital embodiments can affect real-world perceptions and interactions. This emphasizes the need for organizational policies and practices that recognize and accommodate the complexities of virtual identities, ensuring that all employees feel psychologically safe and valued for their authentic selves.

VII. Avatars: An Opportunity to Reinvent Yourself or a Tool to Access Another Reality?

It can be seen that the motivation to create avatars is driven by a complex interplay of psychological, social, and cultural factors. The decision of the avatar look selected is different if the main motivation derives from a point of identity exploration, social connection, or escapism.

Given the continuous and persistent nature of the Metaverse, avatars exist and can operate independently even when users are not actively engaged. This autonomy may foster a deeper attachment to these digital personas and introduce complex behaviors within virtual environments. The enduring presence of avatars raises significant privacy and security concerns, particularly regarding the protection of user data and the potential manipulation of avatar actions when the user is offline. Additionally, the ongoing activity of avatars blurs the lines between the virtual and physical worlds, potentially confusing the distinctions between users' real and virtual identities. This blurring can have profound psychological effects, such as excessive immersion or attachment to one's avatar, leading to issues like dissociation, depersonalization, and a detachment from one's physical self and the real world. Such conditions might cause users to become overly engrossed in their virtual lives to the detriment of their real-world responsibilities and relationships, resulting in social withdrawal and isolation. Furthermore, individuals with body image concerns might find themselves overly identifying with their idealized avatars, which could exacerbate feelings of low self-esteem in the real world. This could also affect how they regulate their emotions outside the virtual realm.

The dynamic interplay between users' perceptions of their avatars in the Metaverse and the feedback from other users forms a complex feedback loop that significantly influences self-evaluation and identity interpretation. This interaction can profoundly affect one's sense of self, potentially altering self-perception not only within virtual environments but also in the physical world. The concept hinges on the notion that embodying a different physical form in a virtual setting allows for novel experiences and forms of expression, which can in turn shape individual identity and self-perception.

Social interactions and relationships are essential for maintaining mental health, and the importance of social support for well-being is widely recognized, reflecting the consensus on the positive effects of social relationships [34]. On the other hand, the creation of an avatar opens new dimensions and possibilities, especially in the fields of education and training. Metaverse and virtual worlds provide immersive learning environments that can be tailored to individual learning styles, enhancing educational and training processes across various fields. Simulations of real-life settings and scenarios provide a more engaging and effective learning experience, extending educational possibilities to limits only bound by the imagination [35].

In the workplace, the implementation of virtual training and simulated work environments can significantly reduce training costs for organizations. Employees are able to hone skills and practice procedures without the risk of real-world harm or damage, thereby not only cutting costs but also improving safety and efficiency [36].

Avatars serve additional, vital roles, particularly for individuals navigating personal challenges. For those with low self-esteem or introverted personalities, avatars can be a tool for expressing emotions and exploring personal identity in a supportive, virtual space. Similarly, individuals with social anxiety can use these controlled environments to practice and enhance their social skills safely. This innovative use of avatars not only facilitates personal development but also offers a refuge for practicing interpersonal interactions without the intense pressures often encountered in physical settings.

VIII. Conclusion

The emergence of the Metaverse represents a significant evolution in the digital landscape, offering unprecedented opportunities for interaction, identity exploration, and immersion in virtual environments. Avatars serve not only as representations of users but as essential mediators of social, psychological, and economic activities within these spaces. This paper has highlighted the intricate relationship between avatars and user identity, revealing the depth of influence that virtual embodiments can have on personal expression, social connectivity, and psychological well-being. The dynamic interplay between virtual and physical realities, facilitated by avatars, necessitates a thoughtful consideration of the implications for privacy, security, and ethical standards within the Metaverse.

Through the power of imagination, we are able to envision and craft new realities and identities within the Metaverse, breathing life into an innovative existence that mirrors our aspirations. This process mirrors the initial steps of the "Hero's Journey" as outlined by Joseph Campbell, where the hero departs from the mundane to a realm filled with extraordinary challenges and triumphs, eventually returning with newfound wisdom and gifts for humanity [36]. In this digital odyssey, akin to that of legendary heroes, we are the central figures of our narratives. The role of critical thinking becomes pivotal as it guides us through this voyage, enabling us to navigate the complexities of this new world thoughtfully and effectively. It equips us with the tools to discern, evaluate, and assimilate the experiences we encounter, ensuring that our journey is not only transformative but also enriching.

The question then becomes: How can we leverage these insights gained from our adventures in the Metaverse to enhance the real world? How can the knowledge and experiences we acquire make our current existence more meaningful, beautiful, and worth cherishing? This pursuit of bringing back value to our real-world context is the essence of our hero's journey, challenging us to apply our learnings in ways that enrich not just our own lives but also those of others around us.

"What I think is that a good life is one hero journey after another. Over and over again, you are called to the realm of adventure, you are called to new horizons. Each time, there is the same problem: do I dare? And then if you do dare, the dangers are there, and the help also, and the fulfillment or the fiasco. There's always the possibility of a fiasco. But there's also the possibility of bliss." [37].

IX. FUTURE WORK

The emergence of the metaverse represents a significant evolution in the digital landscape, offering unprecedented opportunities for interaction, identity exploration, and immersion in virtual environments. This paper has highlighted the intricate relationship between avatars and user identity, revealing the profound influence that virtual embodiments can have on personal expression, social connectivity, and psychological well-being. Given the dynamic interplay between virtual and physical realities facilitated by avatars, there is a need for thoughtful consideration of the implications for privacy, security, and ethical standards within the Metaverse.

As part of future work, the authors intend to survey subject matter experts such as psychologists, social workers, and members of ethics bodies about how to reap the benefits of this development while minimizing the chance of damage for the individual and on a wider scale. The results of such interviews would indicate areas for close focus in better understanding of the risks involved, risks which could be overlooked in the face of the enthusiasm evoked by such beguiling developments. The interview findings may also enable the development of a set of guidelines for individuals and organizations about the optimal use of Metaverse identities and avatars. Interview insights could also be used in the future to create a model that could be useful for organizations and individuals to protect the benefits of avatar use through a checklist that might raise awareness about priorities in addressing these matters.

Future research should focus on longitudinal studies to better understand the long-term effects of avatar use on identity and psychological well-being. These studies would help reveal how continuous interaction within the Metaverse influences an individual's self-perception and mental health over time. Additionally, investigating diverse user demographics can provide insights into how different populations experience and benefit from the Metaverse, highlighting variations in engagement and impact across age, gender, cultural background, and socio-economic status.

Given the rapid pace of technological development, it is urgent to quickly gain a better understanding of how these advancements should be optimized and controlled. This paper represents a starting point, emphasizing the need for ongoing research and dialogue to navigate the complexities of identity, self-representation, and avatars in the Metaverse effectively.

REFERENCES

[1] K. Jaballah and M. Jemni, "A Review on 3D signing avatars: Benefits, uses and challenges," International Journal of Multimedia Data Engineering and Management (IJMDEM), vol. 4, no. 1, pp. 21-45, 2013.

[2] M. A. González, B. S. N. Santos, A. R. Vargas, J. Martín-Gutiérrez, and A. R. Orihuela, "Virtual worlds. Opportunities and challenges in the 21st century," Procedia Computer Science, vol. 25, pp. 330-337, 2013.

[3] B. Eschenbrenner, F. F.-H. Nah, and K. Siau, "3-D virtual worlds in education: Applications, benefits, issues, and opportunities," Journal of Database Management (JDM), vol. 19, no. 4, pp. 91-110, 2008.

[4] L. A. Baccon, E. Chiarovano, and H. G. MacDougall, "Virtual reality for teletherapy: Avatars may combine the benefits of face-to-face communication with the anonymity of online text-based communication," Cyberpsychology, Behavior, and Social Networking, vol. 22, no. 1, pp. 158-165, 2019.

[5] S. Bose et al. "A path to translation: How 3D patient tumor avatars enable next generation precision oncology," Cancer cell, vol. 40, no. 12, pp. 1448-1453, 2022.

[6] C. Kyrlitsias and D. Michael-Grigoriou, "Social interaction with agents and avatars in immersive virtual environments: A survey," Frontiers in Virtual Reality, 2, 786665, 2022.

[7] M. F. Bertoa et al. "Digital avatars: Promoting independent living for older adults," Wireless Communications and Mobile Computing, 2020, 1-11, 2020.

[8] Lee, Lik-Hang et al. "All One Needs to Know about Metaverse: A Complete Survey on Technological Singularity, Virtual Ecosystem, and Research Agenda," 10.13140/RG.2.2.11200.05124/8, 2021.

[9] C. Hackl, D. Lueth, and Di Bartolo, T. "Navigating the metaverse: A guide to limitless possibilities in a Web 3.0 world", John Wiley & Sons, 2022.

[10] L. B. Martins and S. G. Wolfe, "Metaversed: See beyond the hype", John Wiley & Sons, 2022.

[11] N. M. Bianzino, Metaverse: 5 questions shaping the next frontier of human experience, 2022 [Online]. Available from: https://www.ey.com/en_gl/digital/metaverse-5-questions-shaping-the-next-frontier-of-human-experience [retrieved: May, 2024]

[12] G. Merriam, (Ed.) Merriam-Webster. Springfield US, 2024.

[13] BBC News, Meta: Facebook's new name ridiculed by Hebrew speakers, 2021 [Online]. Available from: https://www.bbc.com/news/world-59090067 [retrieved: May, 2024]

[14] S. Stryker and P. J. Burke, "The past, present, and future of an identity theory," Social psychology quarterly, pp. 284-297, 2000.

[15] S. Branje, "Adolescent identity development in context," Current Opinion in Psychology, 45, Article 101286, Jun. 2022, https://doi.org/10.1016/j.copsyc.2021.11.006

[16] E. Crocetti, "Identity formation in adolescence: The dynamic of forming and consolidating identity commitments," Child

Development Perspectives, vol. 11, no. 2, pp. 145-150, Feb. 2017, https://doi.org/10.1111/cdep.12226

[17] A. S. Waterman, "What does it mean to engage in identity exploration and to hold identity commitments? A methodological critique of multidimensional measures for the study of identity processes," Identity: An International Journal of Theory and Research, vol. 15, no. 4, pp. 309–349, Oct. 2015, https://doi.org/10.1080/15283488.2015.1089403

[18] E. H. Erikson, Identity: Youth and crisis: WW Norton & company, 1994.

[19] F. Delmotte, "Identity, Identification, Habitus: A Process Sociology Approach," In: McCallum, D. (eds) The Palgrave Handbook of the History of Human Sciences. Palgrave Macmillan, Singapore, Aug. 2022, https://doi.org/10.1007/978-981-16-7255-2_53

[20] T. A. Klimstra, W. W. Hale Iii, Q. A. W. Raaijmakers, S. J. T. Branje, and W. H. J. Meeus, "Identity formation in adolescence: Change or stability?", Journal of Youth and Adolescence, vol. 39, no. 2, pp. 150-162, 2010, https://doi.org/10.1007/s10964-009-9401-4

[21] Meetaverse, Metaverse Avatars Unveiled: Detailed Guide to Building Your Digital Identity in 2024 [Online]. Available from: https://meetaverse.com/blog/metaverse-avatars/ [retrieved: May, 2024]

[22] M. McDowel, Shaping online avatars: Why our digital identities differ, 2021, [Online]. Available from: https://www.voguebusiness.com/technology/shaping-online-avatars-why-our-digital-identities-differ [retrieved: May, 2024]

[23] B. Ryder, Digital avatars will be fashion's next big disruptor. Is luxury ready? 2024, [Online]. Available from: https://jingdaily.com/posts/digital-avatars-will-be-fashion-s-next-big-disruptor-but-is-luxury-ready [retrieved: May, 2024]

[24] Grand View Research, Digital Avatar Market Size, Share & Trends Analysis Report By Product (Interactive Digital Avatar, Non-interactive Digital Avatar), By Category, By Industry Vertical, By Region, And Segment Forecasts, 2023 – 2030, [Online]. Available from: https://www.grandviewresearch.com/industry-analysis/digital-avatar-market-report [retrieved: May, 2024]

[25] S. Gunkel et al. "Experiencing virtual reality together: Social VR use case study," pp. 233-238. 10.1145/3210825.3213566, 2018.

[26] C. Y. Wang, M. Sakashita, U. Ehsan, J. Li, and A. S. Won, "Again, together: Socially reliving virtual reality experiences when separated," 1-12. 10.1145/3313831.3376642, 2020.

[27] Federal Trade Commission, Children's Online Privacy Protection Rule [Online]. Available from: https://www.ftc.gov/legal-library/browse/rules/childrens-online-privacy-protection-rule-coppa [retrieved: May, 2024]

[28] S. M. Wood and A. Szymanski, "The me I want you to see": The use of video game avatars to explore identity in gifted adolescents," Gifted Child Today, vol. 43, no. 2, pp. 124-134, 2020, https://doi.org/10.1177/1076217519898217

[29] R. Fraser, J. Slattery, and I. Yakovenko, "Escaping through video games: Using your avatar to find meaning in life," Computers in Human Behavior, 144, 107756, 2023.

[30] A. Kuo, R. J. Lutz, and J. L. Hiler, "Brave new World of Warcraft: A conceptual framework for active escapism," Journal of Consumer Marketing, vol. 33, pp. 498–506, 2016, https://doi.org/10.1108/JCM-04-2016-1775

[31] P. Heidicker, E. Langbehn, and F. Steinicke, "Influence of avatar appearance on presence in social VR," 2017, 10.13140/RG.2.2.15302.06720.

[32] N. Yee and J. Bailenson, "The Proteus effect: The effect of transformed self-representation on behavior," Human communication research, vol. 33, no. 3, pp. 271-290, 2007.

[33] J. Peña, J. T. Hancock, N. A. Merola, "The Priming Effects of Avatars in Virtual Settings," Communication Research XX. 36. 1-19. 10.1177/0093650209346802, 2009.

[34] S. D. Pressman, B. N. Jenkins, and J. T. Moskowitz, "Positive affect and health: what do we know and where next should we go?" Annu. Rev. Psychol. 70, pp. 627–650, 2019, doi: 10.1146/annurev-psych-010418-102955

[35] K. Hirsh-Pasek et al. A whole new world: Education meets the metaverse, 2022 [Online]. Available from: https://www.brookings.edu/articles/a-whole-new-world-education-meets-the-metaverse/ [retrieved: May, 2024]

[36] Talespin, Using Virtual Reality for Employee Training: Benefits and Challenges, 2023 [Online]. Available from: https://www.talespin.com/reading/using-virtual-reality-for-employee-training-benefits-and-challenges [retrieved: May, 2024]

[37] J. Campbell, "The hero's journey: Joseph Campbell on his life and work" vol. 7, New World Library, 2003.

Towards BIM-integrated Labour Productivity Measurement

Inventory of Current Work Processes and Identification of User Needs

Pauline Harou; Samia Ben Rajeb
BATir Department, Ecole Polytechnique de Bruxelles
Université Libre de Bruxelles (ULB)
Brussels, Belgium
e-mail: pauline.harou@ulb.be; samia.ben.rajeb@ulb.be

Abstract— **This article marks the beginning of an innovative initiative aimed at integrating construction labour productivity measurements into the 3D Building Information Model / Modeling / Management (BIM) digital model, actively involving the workforce in real-time execution data encoding. Adopting a human-centered approach, the main objective is to ensure the tool's adoption and adaptation to the specificities of the existing processes and the construction site context. To achieve this, the article seeks to understand current performance tracking practices and identify emerging user needs through in-depth analysis of their activity. The research methodology combines field immersion with semi-structured interviews involving various stakeholders of a construction company. This approach helps to define the existing workflow of performance tracking and to identify three distinct typologies of use and their related characteristics. Additionally, the article highlights several challenges related to the integration of labour productivity into the BIM model by connecting it to the 3D objects. These include the need for a comprehensive definition of performance calculation, the accuracy of digital models to extract acceptable quantities, ease of encoding by foremen and stakeholders' perceptions of benefits in a context of major subcontracted activities. Finally, the initial development hypotheses are introduced, laying the groundwork for a new approach to improving performance monitoring practices in the construction sector.**

Keywords-construction sector; BIM, labour productivity; performance monitoring; human-centred approach.

I. Introduction

Despite the advent of new technologies, there is still a serious lack of effective and consistent tools to improve productivity and reduce losses on construction sites [1]. Field actors (whether they are workers, foremen, technicians, subcontractors, project managers or site managers) still often suffer from a lack of visibility over the tasks they perform. Currently, data related to performance are largely under-exploited in guiding companies' strategies [2] toward better project management for continuous improvement [3]. Construction labour productivity is calculated differently from one project to another, and even within the same company. The methods used are prone to approximations and errors; they are either archaic through paper-based notetaking or completely disconnected from the field through tools used by users who are external to the observed tasks. Moreover, they do not leverage Building Information Model / Modeling / Management (BIM) digital models, which are now perceived as an effective support for information management and digitization in the Architecture, Engineering and Construction (AEC) sector [4].

Starting from this observation, the project in which this article is embedded aims to develop a tool enabling construction site stakeholders to integrate directly and in real-time execution data into the building's 3D BIM model. The objective is to involve the workforce in this input process and data centralization for performance monitoring by providing innovative and sector-specific tools to workers (in this case, worker team leaders or foremen). Through this direct input by the concerned stakeholder, activity analysis would be more detailed, and process optimization would be more easily quantifiable. It is therefore appropriate to adopt a human-centered approach to ensure ownership and adaptation to the specificities of the process, the site context, and the Brussels ecosystem. This article constitutes the first phase of this process and aims to address the following questions:

- What is the current process for labour productivity monitoring on construction sites?
- What are the specific needs of the stakeholders involved in this process?
- What challenges are involved in developing an innovative tool that integrates labour productivity into BIM?

To address these questions, the article is organized as follows. Section 2 offers a review on construction labour productivity and its integration with BIM. Section 3 describes the objectives and research framework and Section 4 details the methodology employed in this investigation. The obtained results are described in Section 5. The article concludes with a summary of contributions, identified limitations, and future perspectives in Section 6.

II. State of the Art

A. *Labour productivity*

It is easy to find agreement in the literature regarding the primary goal of labour productivity monitoring, which is to analyze and evaluate performance on construction sites [3][5]. However, it is much more challenging to find a common definition and real performance measuring techniques. Usually, the discussion will center on the output of a specific task based on the resources used for it [3]. The resource is mostly taken as hours of manual labour, as it constitutes the largest source of variation in site productivity. The output refers to the amount of work completed, which is measured in various units depending on the performed task (e.g., kg for steel and m^3 for concrete). Gathe and Mind [6] thus define labour productivity as an output per work hour, as in (1). It can underpin most of the other productivity-related factors [5][6][7]. Labour productivity is measured in units of work accomplished per man-hour, but there is also discussion about unit rates; man-hours per unit of work [7].

$$Labour\ productivity = \frac{Output}{Work\ Hour} \tag{1}$$

To optimize its performance, the goal of a construction company is therefore to maximize its labour productivity or to minimize its unit rates. This article seeks to explore the practice of this kind of performance measurement in the AEC sector as well as the existing tools used, with the aim of fostering continuous improvement on construction sites. In the next sections, the terms performance measurement and labour productivity will be used interchangeably.

B. Using BIM for labour productivity monitoring

Through methods and tools, BIM enables the centralization of all building data around a digital version to facilitate the sharing and efficient exploitation of data by the various project stakeholders throughout its lifecycle [8]. In order to better manage and optimize team work on construction sites, several authors propose to centralize data related to performance calculation in these BIM models, which are increasingly being utilized in large-scale projects. Cha and Kim [2] emphasize the relevance of associating performance measurement with 3D/BIM object-based technology to counter the inefficiency of conventional text-based systems. They propose a site performance measurement system that associates a 3D object with a spreadsheet. Katiyar and Kumar [9] propose a method to monitor real-time progress of prefabricated structure construction using Building Information Modeling (BIM) and Internet of Things (IoT) with sensors, to improve labour productivity factors. Matthews et al. [10] also proposed a BIM-based approach to track construction progress in real-time, using the BIM 360™ Field application to capture site data. Although these studies highlight the importance of combining performance calculation and BIM, none have yet resulted in a concrete application implemented on construction sites. Currently, no tool on the market directly integrates BIM with labour productivity calculation. Existing applications either focus on encoding execution data without connection to the digital model, or on BIM metadata without focusing on on-site performance and the underlying issues. To be closer to the needs of the sector, the following question arises: what is the best methodology to adopt in order to make it easier for these tools and apps to be implemented and tailored for the AEC sector?

C. Towards construction 4.0: adopting new technologies

Today, the construction industry is undergoing a digital revolution towards Construction 4.0. The main objectives of this transition include improving productivity, reducing environmental impact, increasing sector attractiveness, and cost control [11]. This evolution involves numerous challenges related to technology adoption, explained among others by the complexity of building projects, the diversity of actors involved, resistance to change, shortages of qualified labour, and interoperability issues between existing technologies and processes [12][13]. Among the social issues, the introduction of new technologies such as process automation or real-time monitoring of workers raises ethical concerns [14]. In addition, there is concern about the lack of skilled professionals capable of mastering the application of these technologies and the practical changes they entail [1]. To address the various challenges raised, some authors emphasize the importance of adopting a user-centered approach for implementing digital tools on construction sites [15][16]. A user-centered approach for the development of interactive tools, or human-centered design, aims to actively involve users in the design process [17][18]. This approach encourages optimization of performance and profitability, while enhancing user comfort, satisfaction levels, ease of access, and sustainability [17][18]. User-centered design is used in different fields but very few studies have been found in the construction industry. Thus, this article proposes a methodological contribution for defining and implementing such an approach for the development of innovative tools tailored to the AEC sector.

III. Objective and Scope

The previous paragraphs have highlighted the interest in developing an innovative application aimed at optimizing performance monitoring by integrating it with BIM, while exploring the effect of a human-centered methodology. This is the objective of the project in which this article is embedded. This project, named HARPO (Human-centered Application for the Resource and Productivity Optimization of buildings), is funded by the Brussels-Capital Region - Innoviris and consists of a consortium between a construction company (CIT Blaton), a start-up developing BIM technologies (Kabandy), the Belgian innovation center for the construction sector (Buildwise), and the Brussels Polytechnic School (AIA_BATir).

This article constitutes the first phase of the HARPO project and focuses on field immersion, understanding user profiles, and activity analysis. One of the fundamental principles of a human-centered approach is active user participation and a clear understanding of user needs and tasks [17][18]. In this perspective, the aim here is to thoroughly study current practices on construction sites regarding performance monitoring and to identify the different profiles involved. The objective is to understand the performance monitoring processes on-site, to identify specific issues related to these processes, and to address the challenges associated with their optimization through integration with BIM. To achieve this, we have implemented a two-stages methodology, based on a pragmatic epistemological stance carried out through action and practical problem-solving anchored in concrete situations [19][20].

IV. Methodology

Firstly, the analysis comprised a complete immersion on a construction site over a period of two months in a participatory-observational approach. This type of approach involves significant engagement from a researcher within a group, community, or organization, with active, concrete, and preponderant participation in fieldwork while aiming to accumulate knowledge through observation [21]. To maintain an objective distance and a continuous reflection, essential for implementing such an approach, a journal was completed during and after each day on the construction site [22]. Through this journal, a structure was well-defined to systematically capture the various actions taking place, the involved actors, the tools used, the site management methods implemented, etc. This immersion thus allowed for understanding the general workings of a typical construction site and the roles of actors within it. Although the preliminary immersion phase on the construction site only partially addressed the question of performance, it was fundamental for the subsequent steps. It continuously provided context for performance monitoring processes within the broader reality of the construction site, including a multitude of actors and various dynamic and complex processes.

Secondly, it was necessary to understand the specific processes related to performance monitoring. To do so, 15 semi-structured interviews were conducted with different profiles within the construction company. Initially, 3 interviews were conducted at the company's headquarters with 'office' type actors: a price study engineer, a quantity surveyor, and a financial engineer. These interviews allowed for a first interpretation of performance-related processes from the perspective of actors external to the construction site but engaged in anticipating performance before work execution, as well as in monitoring actual performance collected throughout the execution. Subsequently, 12 interviews were conducted on various types of construction sites, with 'field' type actors: 5 site managers, 3 project managers, and 4 foremen. These interviews enabled to understand labour productivity from perspectives related to on-site activity and to develop workflows specific to the construction company under study. To ensure clear interpretation of these processes, the workflows were created drawing inspiration from the Business Process Model and Notation (BPMN) method, a standardized way of modeling a business process [23]. Lastly, after the development of these specific workflows based on observation and interviews, they were compared to the sector to verify their alignment with on-site realities and project-specific requirements. The analysis of these workflows thus served to highlight current on-site needs and identify challenges in digitizing processes. Furthermore, the comparison of these workflows 1/ with future needs expressed by users and representatives of the AEC sector, and 2/ with purely technical and technological constraints regarding existing tools and their interoperability, framed the initial hypotheses necessary for the development of an application tailored to on-site usage and actor profiles.

V. Results

A. *Labour productivity monitoring process*

The general workflow for labour productivity monitoring is depicted in **Figure 1**, and was constructed and adapted progressively through the interviews and observations. It is subdivided into two 'lanes' representing two phases: the price study phase and the execution phase. It is important to clarify that terms like *performance measurement* and *labour productivity* will be used here because it is similarly used within the partner company, although it refers to *unit rates* as explained in the state of the art [5][7]. The first involvement of labour productivity measurement occurs during the preliminary phase to execution, namely the price study. This activity is carried out with the assistance of a software developed by the company itself, enabling the submission of a sales price and the tracking of site finances. Upon receiving a file from a potential client, the *price study engineer* imports the various workstations (or tasks) necessary for execution, applying quantities measured by the *quantity surveyor*. The software automatically calculates the sales price by incorporating reference budgets for each item. Behind these budgets lie those related to labour productivity, estimated based on company reference performances or the *price study engineer* expertise (e.g., 1h/m3 for pouring a concrete wall). Excel spreadsheets can be exported from the in-house software. If the submitted offer is accepted by the client, the project proceeds to the execution phase. Execution methods defined during the price study are often adjusted by the site team, leading to a redefinition of tasks and associated budgets (behind which lie the performance measures). The financial engineer adjusts the budgets on the same software, and work can then start.

After each working day, the *foreman* fills out a 'foreman report' on paper, summarizing the number of hours performed by each worker and for each type of task. These reports are transmitted to the *site manager*, who allocates the hours among a list of tasks in Excel. This item list must correspond to the budget spreadsheet item list, to compare planned and actual performances and assess the productivity of a workstation. Simultaneously, the *project manager* progressively enters executed quantities and expenses per task into the in-house company software already used during the price study phase. The software then compares the released quantities (and thus also the released hours) and

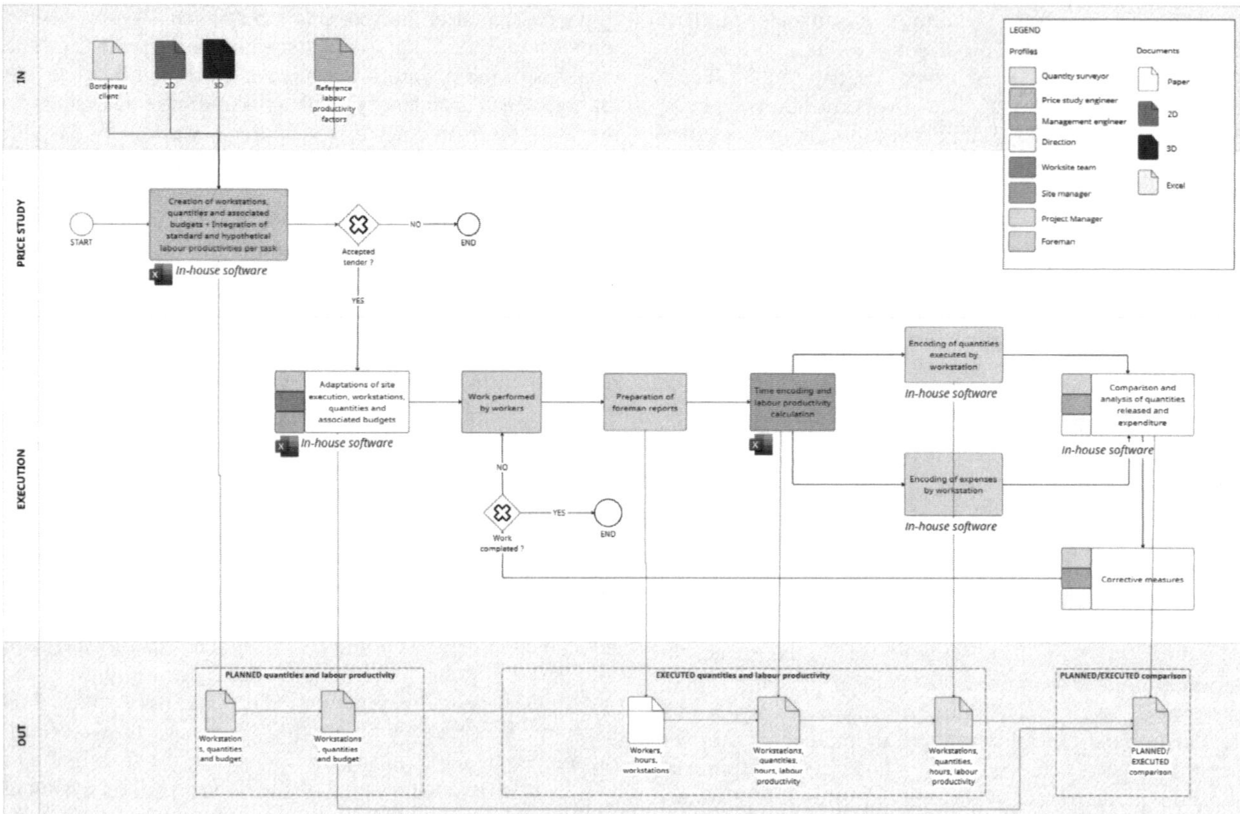

Figure 1. Labour Productivity Measurement Workflow.

expenses, enabling the *project manager* and the *financial engineer* to identify any budget deviations and their roots (which may be related to poor performance). If possible, corrective measures are then taken to reduce identified losses. The performance monitoring process by the *site manager* and budget monitoring by the *project manager* are continuous throughout the construction site progress.

Through this workflow it can be noticed that monitoring performances and assessing the productivity of items essentially involves comparing realized labour productivity with pre-planned labour productivity. The development of this workflow, combined with the multiple discourses and perceptions gathered during the 'office' and 'site' profile interviews, highlight the presence of a wide variety of uses and stakeholders in this process. More specifically, three typologies of performance assessments can be distinguished, which correspond to three different uses in short-, medium-, and long-term temporalities.

B. *From a single workflow to three typologies of workflows*

While each of the three typologies is relevant for the stakeholders involved in it, they are not all implemented in practice and present some shortcomings in their operations. This sub-section presents the three identified types along with their problematics.

The first use concerns the development of daily reports by the foreman and subsequent performance monitoring by the site manager. It can be considered from a short-term perspective as it involves real-time execution monitoring. Interviews revealed that these foremen reports are hardly ever used by site managers to monitor performances. Indeed, most works are performed by subcontractors who pay their workers per square meter, which means the site manager has no direct interest in optimizing performances since the risk of inefficiency lies with the subcontractor. Furthermore, the site manager must undertake a time-consuming task when allocating hours to a high number of items on an Excel spreadsheet that do not always correspond to the tasks listed by the foreman. Additionally, it is not always easy to find the right definition of labour productivity for a specific task and the 'hidden' tasks it should contain (e.g., preparing material before starting a work).

The second typology is manifested through budget monitoring and the identification of discrepancies between allocated hours and incurred expenses. This involves a medium-term analysis as it entails monthly meetings between the project manager and the financial engineer. Performance is not the essence of this process but is rather 'hidden' behind an analysis of budget gaps, which can sometimes be the consequence of poor performances. This process is perceived as optimal by the actors, although it is carried out on an old interface and sometimes requires the transfer of information from multiple stakeholders to the project manager. Unlike the first identified typology, this process is always achieved.

The third typology focuses on analyzing achieved performance on construction sites, in order to provide more accurate budget forecasts in a long-term perspective. Today, this feedback remains very limited, although it would optimize submission files and draw lessons from previous construction projects. Despite this perceived opportunity, several interviewed profiles emphasize the difficulty of labour productivity standardization due to the numerous factors that can influence them in a construction context that is never the same.

The analysis of these three typologies confirms the need for centralized executed data to exploit it in different ways and optimize the work of the stakeholders involved. To sum up, it would save time for the site manager and the project manager in the short and medium term and provide a performance database in the long run. The adaptability of data management is therefore central, relative to the needs of each profile, whether it concerns the specific construction site or in relation to other construction projects.

C. The challenges of BIM-integrated labour productivity

In addition to the importance of acquiring a flexible system, the analysis of the activity allowed to identify several key challenges to consider during software development.

Firstly, the very nature of performance measurement presents quite a challenge. Stakeholders struggle to define labour productivity calculation of items and its required sub-items. Interviews revealed the various possible approaches to interpreting performances, demonstrating the difficulty of standardizing them due to the lack of agreement on the tasks contained within a same item and the complexity of factors to consider on site. This is in line with the lack of a precise definitions found in the state of the art, pointing to the need for a deep investigation into the complex network of workstations on construction sites and their related labour productivities.

The second point concerns the accuracy of the 3D digital model. Since the goal is to use quantities from the BIM model and apply hours to calculate performances, it is crucial to rely on quantities representing reality in an acceptable way. However, this could be compromised by modeling errors or inaccuracies that do not faithfully reflect the reality of execution, especially at junctions between several objects.

Another point concerns the ease of digital encoding of execution data by foremen. Stakeholders emphasize the need for a straightforward tool and sufficient prior training to use it. While some worry about the possibility of mistakes due to the increasing shortage of skilled labour, others see it as a chance to empower and elevate them.

Finally, the last point concerns the predominant context of subcontracting in the construction sector. As mentioned earlier, this reality questions the future value perceived by actors studying their labour performance in a scenario where the inefficiency risks do not lie in their hands. The project partners seem to predict a future with decreasing use of subcontractors, or new forms of subcontracting with hourly wages where this problem would disappear. However, this needs to be verified and trends need to be carefully studied to make sure to align with the sector.

D. Development hypotheses

The identified existing processes and points of attention, when confronted with the first needs expressed by the users as well as the technical and technological constraints identified by the project partners, enabled to establishing initial development hypotheses. These hypotheses have been thoroughly built, discussed and revised in meetings with the partners. Some have been given priority, while others will be taken into consideration in a future iteration of the application, allowing for an initial primary focus on the essentials. They are still referred to as hypotheses to be confronted and re-questioned with end-users throughout the tests of mockups during Living Lab's.

These theories include, for instance, which profiles are best suited for which tasks based on their roles and skill sets, or what format is more appropriate and whether portability of the tool is required. Some hypotheses are more specific to the general workflow of the future application and the intervention of the 3D digital model in it. For example, two options are considered: starting from a 3D model and integrating tasks and hours, or starting from a list of tasks and integrating hours and a 3D model. The first option provides a familiar starting point for site actors but raises issues related to tasks not represented in the model. The second option offers technical simplicity but requires selecting from a large task list. A compromise is found by allowing foremen to choose from a limited task list, opening the 3D model only if this task is linked to it. To maintain track of decision-making processes, each hypothesis and its supporting evidence are purposefully documented.

VI. CONCLUSION

This article tries to comprehend the details of current performance tracking on construction sites in order to develop a digital application integrating this kind of data into the BIM digital model. The initial phase of the user-centered approach allowed to identify three current typologies for performance tracking, each benefiting different stakeholders. This has emphasized the importance of centralizing execution data for its multiple purposes and assisted in identifying the specific needs of each profile.

However, it is important to note that this study was conducted within the partner company, and further investigation among other general contractor companies is still required. Initial discussions with the Belgian construction research center already indicated that performance tracking is primarily integrated into site budget monitoring as highlighted in this article. However, it is still somewhat undefined to what extend the two other identified processes are present in the rest of the sector.

Furthermore, this article represents only the first step of a broader research endeavor. It has outlined a set of needs and specificities to consider in framing the initial hypotheses that will serve as the basis for the development of the future application. But, it does not yet offer a user-centered methodological contribution for the creation of other on-site technologies that considers factors like interoperability, appropriation and adaptability to the context.

Therefore, the next phase of the research will involve a more participatory ergonomic study involving future users in defining the front-end of the solution. This will be accomplished through the creation of mock-ups based on the hypotheses established through the methodology described in this article, then evaluated during living labs, and subsequently adapted to each identified profile and usage typology. The first use will involve testing data encoding methods by team leaders, which is a crucial aspect of the performance tracking process. To optimize this encoding and address identified challenges, considerable effort will be devoted to defining the most relevant definition of labour productivity. This process entails collecting numerous existing foremen reports and conducting an in-depth analysis of the tasks they contain.

ACKNOWLEDGEMENTS

We gratefully acknowledge de Brussels-Capital Region – Innoviris (Brussels public organization for research and innovation) for financial support under grant number ‘2023-RDIR-20d’.

REFERENCES

[1] O. Nagy, I. Papp, and R. Z. Szabó, “Construction 4.0 Organisational Level Challenges and Solutions,” *Sustainability*, vol. 13, no. 21: 12321, Jan. 2021, doi: 10.3390/su132112321.

[2] H. Cha and J. Kim, “A study on 3D/BIM-based on-site performance measurement system for building construction,” *J. of Asian Architecture and Building Eng.*, vol. 19, no. 6, pp. 574–585, Nov. 2020, doi: 10.1080/13467581.2020.1763364.

[3] P. Crawford and B. Vogl, “Measuring productivity in the construction industry,” *Building Res. & Inf.*, vol. 34, no. 3, pp. 208–219, May 2006, doi: 10.1080/09613210600590041.

[4] L. Sattler, S. Lamouri, and R. Pellerin, “Retro-BIM or the question of integration: an anachronistic review,” *SHS Web Conf.*, vol. 82, p. 02003, 2020, doi: 10.1051/shsconf/20208202003.

[5] M. Hamza, S. Shahid, M. R. Bin Hainin, and M. S. Nashwan, “Construction labour productivity: review of factors identified,” *International J. Constr. Manage.*, vol. 22, no. 3, pp. 413–425, Feb. 2022, doi: 10.1080/15623599.2019.1627503.

[6] P. R. Ghate and P. R. Minde, “Importance of Measurement of Labour Productivity in Construction,” *International J. of Res. Eng. and Technol.*, vol. 05, no. 07, pp. 413–417, Jul. 2016, doi: 10.15623/ijret.2016.0507065.

[7] D. W. Halligan, L. A. Demsetz, J. D. Brown, and C. B. Pace, “Action-Response Model and Loss of Productivity in Construction,” *J. Constr. Eng. Manage.*, vol. 120, no. 1, pp. 47–64, Mar. 1994, doi: 10.1061/(ASCE)0733-9364(1994)120:1(47).

[8] P. Poinet, “Enhancing Collaborative Practices in Architecture, Engineering and Construction through Multi-Scalar Modelling Methodologies,” PhD Thesis, Aarhus School of Architecture, Denmark, 2020.

[9] A. Katiyar and P. Kumar, “Real Time Construction Progress Monitoring of Prefabricated Structures Using Building Information Modeling and Internet of Things,” *International J. of Eng. Applied Sci. and Technol.*, vol. 7, no. 2, pp. 343-351, 2022.

[10] J. Matthews *et al.*, “Real time progress management: Re-engineering processes for cloud-based BIM in construction,” *Automation in Construction*, vol. 58, pp. 38–47, Oct. 2015, doi: 10.1016/j.autcon.2015.07.004.

[11] A. Sawhney, M. Riley, and J. Irizarry, Eds., *Construction 4.0: an innovation platform for the built environment*. London New York: Routledge, Taylor & Francis Group, 2020.

[12] S. M. E. Sepasgozar, M. Loosemore, and S. R. Davis, “Conceptualising information and equipment technology adoption in construction: A critical review of existing research,” *Eng., Construction and Architectural Management*, vol. 23, no. 2, pp. 158–176, Mar. 2016, doi: 10.1108/ECAM-05-2015-0083.

[13] J. Van Der Heijden, “Construction 4.0 in a narrow and broad sense: A systematic and comprehensive literature review,” *Building and Environment*, vol. 244, p. 110788, Oct. 2023, doi: 10.1016/j.buildenv.2023.110788.

[14] D. Calvetti, P. N. M. Magalhães, S. F. Sujan, M. C. Gonçalves, and H. J. Campos de Sousa, “Challenges of upgrading craft workforce into Construction 4.0: framework and agreements,” *Proceedings of the Institution of Civil Engineers - Management, Procurement and Law*, vol. 173, no. 4, pp. 158–165, Nov. 2020, doi: 10.1680/jmapl.20.00004.

[15] C. Cimini, A. Boffelli, A. Lagorio, M. Kalchschmidt, and R. Pinto, “How do industry 4.0 technologies influence organisational change? An empirical analysis of Italian SMEs,” vol. 32, no. 3, pp. 695–721, 2021, doi: 10.1108/JMTM-04-2019-0135.

[16] K. Noueihed and F. Hamzeh, “Envisioning a Human Centric Approach to C4.0 Technologies. Lean Construction Journal,” *Lean Construction Journal (LCJ)*, pp. 2022–156, Dec. 2022.

[17] Online Browsing Platform (OBP) “ISO 9241-210:2019(en), Ergonomics of human-system interaction — Part 210: Human-centred design for interactive systems.”. Available from: https://www.iso.org/obp/ui/en/#iso:std:77520:en [retrieved: May, 2024].

[18] M. Maguire, “Methods to support human-centred design,” *International Journal of Human-Computer Studies*, vol. 55, no. 4, pp. 587–634, Oct. 2001, doi: 10.1006/ijhc.2001.0503.

[19] D. Vallat, “Managing knowledge in a complex environment: ethical, epistemological and strategic issues,” Gestion et management, Université Jean Moulin – Lyon III, 2017.

[20] R. Lowe and L. F. Chiu, “Innovation in deep housing retrofit in the United Kingdom: The role of situated creativity in transforming practice,” *Energy Research & Social Science*, vol. 63, p. 101391, May 2020, doi: 10.1016/j.erss.2019.101391.

[21] S. Bastien, “Participatory observation or observant participation? Uses and justifications of the notion of observational participation in the social sciences,” *Recherches qualitatives*, vol. 27, no. 1, pp. 127-140, 2007, doi: 10.7202/1085359ar.

[22] A. Laszczuk and L. Garreau, “The sibyllic logbook,” *Finance Contrôle Stratégie*, no. 21–3, Art. no. 21–3, Dec. 2018, doi: 10.4000/fcs.2773.

[23] “BPMN Specification - Business Process Model and Notation.” Available from: https://www.bpmn.org/ [retrieved: May, 2024].

Database Technology Evolution III: Knowledge Graphs and Linked Data

Malcolm Crowe
Emeritus Professor, Computing Science
University of the West of Scotland
Paisley, United Kingdom
Email: Malcolm.Crowe@uws.ac.uk

Fritz Laux
Emeritus Professor, Business Computing
Reutlingen University
Reutlingen, Germany
Email: Fritz.Laux@reutlingen-university.de

Abstract— **This paper reviews the changes for database technology represented by the current development of the draft international standard ISO 39075 (Database Languages - GQL), which seeks a unified specification for property graphs and knowledge graphs. This paper examines these current developments as part of our review of the evolution of database technology, and their relation to the longer-term goal of supporting the Semantic Web using relational technology.**

Keywords— **semantic web; linked data; knowledge graphs; relational database; knowledge management; database management system; property graph; information integration.**

I. Introduction

Tim Berners-Lee originated the concept of the Semantic Web in 1999, as a way of enabling computers to analyze all the content, links and transactions between people and computers on the Web [1]. Initial approaches to this dream focused initially on the addition of semantic information to everything in all documents [2], documenting semantic information using subject-relation-object triples. Thinking of objects as nodes or vertices and triples as edges or relationships yields the concept of a knowledge graph [3][4] [5]. While some triples merely described the content in a document, those that were links to other documents proved to be more interesting to human readers, leading to the topic of linked data [6]. There are now many open data projects whose nodes are items of information on the Web with less focus today on the detail of document internals [7].

The underlying technology for managing such knowledge bases originally seemed completely different from relational databases, which processed representations in the form of tabular data while in knowledge bases the links were first-class objects. There were also differences in scale: databases dealt with the needs of individual companies, while knowledge is worldwide.

Graph database technology is more efficient than relational technology in following chains of relationships, because in relational technology such sequences imply joins of all the corresponding tables. Many graph database products are now available [8] and the business case for further development in this area is compelling, with use cases including medical research [9], fraud detection [10] and cybersecurity [11], global engineering design [12] and supply chain management [13].

Even the most radical products for processing knowledge data use data storage, and there is now a new international standard for a database language GQL [14] to include triple graphs and property graphs (the name GQL in the title of the standard is not an acronym, although some authors have been persuaded to invent a three word phrase with these initials). In the past, databases of triples (subject, predicate, object) tied to HTTP urls looked very different from databases consisting of linked sets of objects with given property values. Implementations of this new GQL standard can be expected soon.

In 2023 we reported at IARIA [15, sec III.A] on a way of implementing GQL by adding new metadata to the ISO 9075 Standard Query Language (SQL) [16], and we exemplified this in 2024 with a brief account of a Financial Benchmark for GQL [17][18]. The implementation described was relational in nature, using the property graph approach of GQL, and did not discuss knowledge graphs, cross-platform linked data, issues evident in the recent research papers referenced above, so that it makes sense to continue our story of database evolution [19][20] in this paper by introducing a very lightweight implementation of knowledge graphs and web services.

This paper is thus a practical contribution to data and systems research, through concept development in the context of a lightweight open-source proof of concept implementation [21]. It also takes up the question of semantic alignment from [22] and implements ideas for graph schema under discussion in the GQL community.

The plan of this paper is to motivate these developments in Section II, with the help of two examples from recent publications and some discussion of related implementation issues. The first example, in Figure 1, is from [23] and links two graphs, the second, in Table 1, is from [5] and illustrates the triples approach to knowledge representation. We briefly cover linking data by web services in Section III, and graph schema ideas in Section IV. Section V provides some conclusions and our plans for completing the work as an open-source research contribution.

II. Knowledge Graph Implementation

Neither example in this section fits well with relational database model, and they continue to require development of the GQL specification.

A. *The Yacht Club example*

The current edition of GQL allows "open" graphs without defined graph types and "closed" graphs where all node and edge types are predefined, but there is no mechanism for modifying such types once defined.

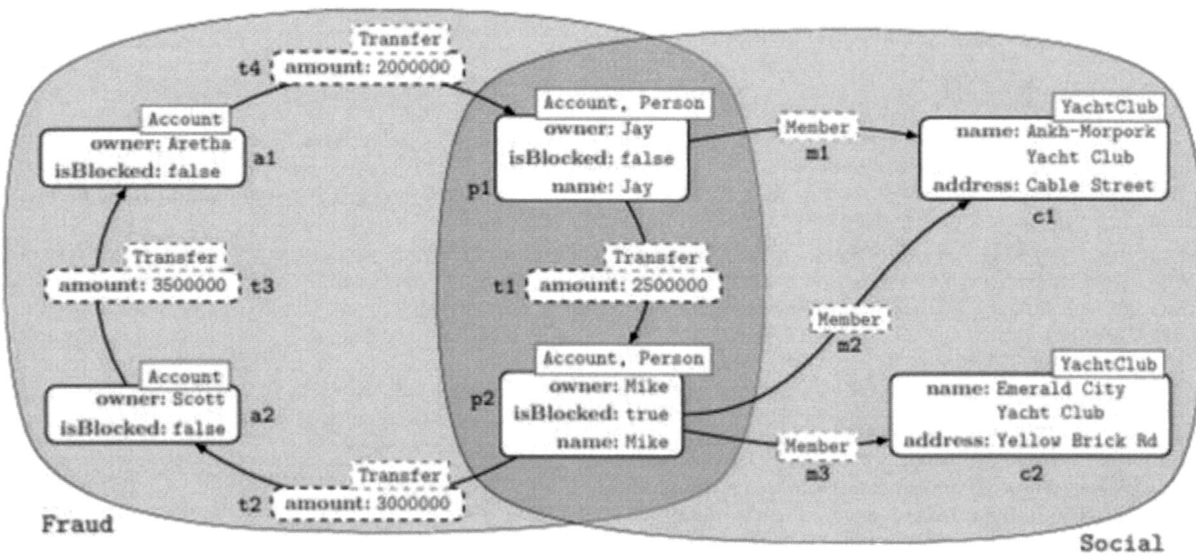

Figure 1: The Yacht Club example [23]

TABLE I: CREATING THE GRAPH OF FIGURE 1 IN GQL

```
create schema /yc;
create graph type /yc/Social {node Person {name string},
        node YachtClub {name string,address string},
        directed edge "Member" connecting (Person->YachtClub)};
create graph /yc/Fraud ANY;
insert (a2 :Account{owner:'Scott',isBlocked:false})-[:Transfer{amount:350000}]->
(:Account{owner:'Aretha',isBlocked:false})-[:Transfer{amount:2000000}]->
(p1 :Person&Account{owner:'Jay',name:'Jay',isBlocked:false})
-[:"Member"]->(:YachtClub {name:'Ankh-Morpork Yacht Club',address: 'Cable Street'})
<-[:"Member"]-(p2 :Person&Account {owner:'Mike',name:'Mike', isBlocked:true})
-[:"Member"]->(:YachtClub{name:'Emerald City Yacht Club',address:'Yellow Brick Road'}),
(p1)-[:Transfer{amount:2500000}]->(p2)-[:Transfer{amount:3000000}]->(a2);
```

However, this example is motivated by combining information from two separately developed graphs.

In Figure 1, we see two graphs called Fraud and Social, both of which contain nodes p1 and p2. In the Fraud graph, these are of type Account, while in the Social graph, they are of type Person. Nodes cannot belong to several graphs in the current GQL standard, and GQL statements can make changes to the data in at most one graph. With a little goodwill on these points, the script in Table I constructs an open graph (Fraud) and a closed graph type (Social).

Here the labels Person and Account make up p1's *label set*. GQL types have label sets (unlike its predecessors such as Neo4j). The single node p1 has properties from a node type in each graph and so belongs to both graphs, while Person&Account is a label expression, not a node type. From the relational database viewpoint, tables consist of relations of the same type, so that, if both Person and Account are row types, each corresponding table gets a row when the record for p1 is inserted.

Open graphs allow new node and edge types to be introduced on insertion, but labels such as Person and Account need to be well defined (property sets, connections) before they can be combined with others. In Table II, Transfer is defined as connecting Account nodes before it is used for Person&Account. Note that the aliases a2, p1, and p2 are local to the insert statement as is usual in SQL. Using match-insert combinations as suggested above can avoid long insert sequences.

The second example is shown in Table II.

It needs to declare somehow that <sp is a relation between edge types. This also would require changes to the current edition of the GQL standard and we return to this point in Section IV below.

TABLE II: A KNOWLEDGE GRAPH [5]

t1 = (:John :masterFrom :DauphineUni),
t2 = (:John :phdFrom :DauphineUni),
t3 = (:masterFrom $<_{sp}$:degreeFrom),
t4 = (:phdFrom $<_{sp}$:degreeFrom)

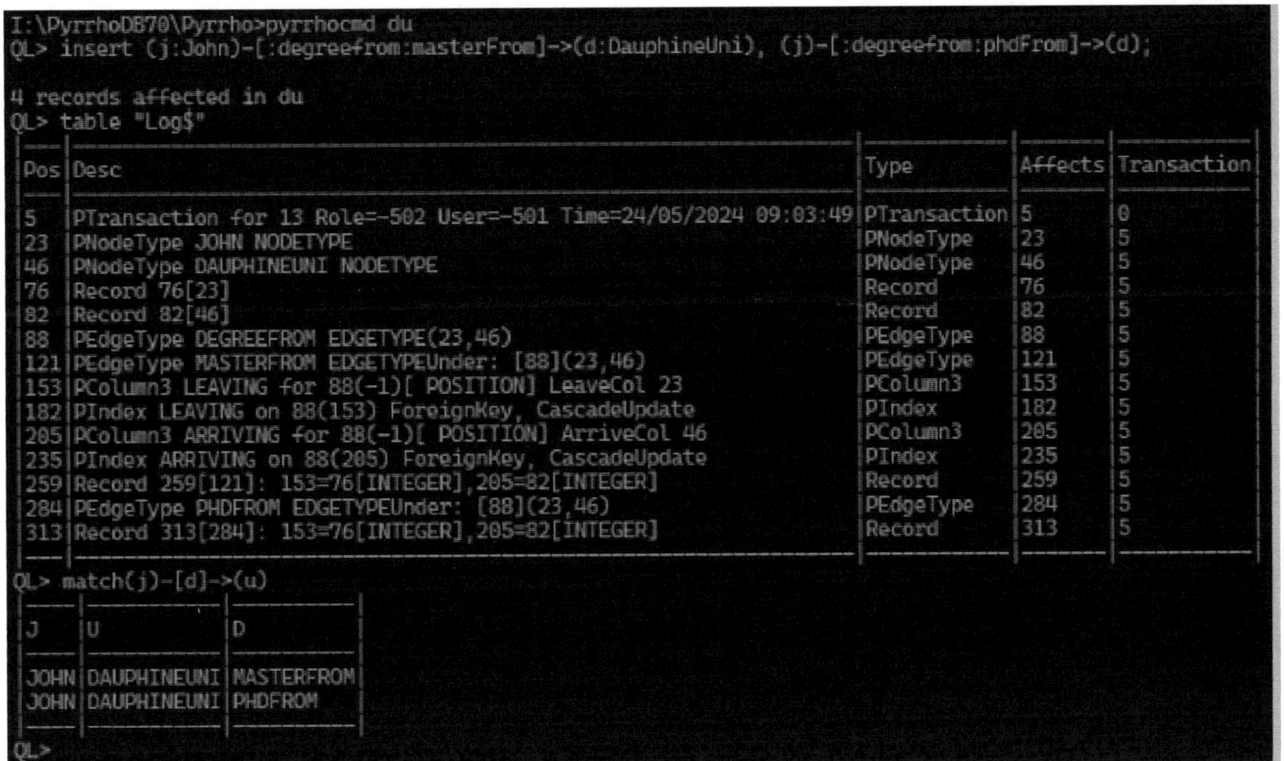

Figure 2: The transaction log and a simple Match statement for the example in Table II.

In [15, III.C] we showed that graphs based on SQL user defined types can be constructed without prior declaration of types (in GQL this is called using open graph types), so the simple database for the second example can be constructed in Pyrrho with just one statement. Starting with an empty database,

insert (j:John)-[:degreefrom:masterFrom]->
(d:DauphineUni), (j)-[:degreefrom:phdFrom]->(d);

Figure 2 shows the transaction log resulting from this statement in Pyrrho: it shows the mixture of type and data creation steps This little database occupies only 339 bytes on disk.

Match statements in GQL provide a simple way of retrieving information from a graph, by binding free variables to graph contents according to a graph pattern. A graph pattern can specify labels or properties required for the match: in this case there is no need to do so. Graph patterns can also specify alternatives and trails through the graph, and Match can have dependent statements with access to the binding results, such as selection (or RETURN) of results and aggregations, or data-modifying statements such as INSERT, DELETE, SET or REMOVE that can modify the graph and its contents.

B. An open-source prototype GQL implementation

Our sample implementation, Pyrrho [21] has the ambition not only to address both these examples together with GQL and SQL syntax. By design, the GQL specification has chosen to accommodate this sort of fusion, but there is an issue that some of SQL's reserved words are not reserved in GQL. This will mean that if a database defines some SQL reserved words to mean something else, syntax depending on these words will not be available.

As a research laboratory for database management, Pyrrho also has been evolving for over two decades, and as of May 2024 it accommodates graph objects (node and edges) and their types alongside the standard SQL apparatus, in the manner described above.

Some basic features of Pyrrho make the task of implementing GQL easier. First, in this RDBMS the database file is an append-storage transaction log so that the position of any committed database object or record does not change even if the contents are updated. Pyrrho makes this position into a pseudo-column, so that the next step in the evolution of our implementation is to use this position where primary keys would normally be used. Introducing this sort of flexibility into a relational DBMS is quite a step.

Another feature of Pyrrho is its optimistic concurrency control based on shareable data structures. These two aspects allow transactions to mix schema changes and data modification and avoid the complications involved in two-phase locking.

Pyrrho already provides triggers and type alteration. GQL's structure comes from the edge relationships, so that the current edition of GQL does not have any concept of integrity constraints such as primary keys or foreign keys. Many business applications can benefit from the additional structure provided by allowing relational constraints in a graphical database.

In this section it remains to include a brief discussion of the effect on the database model of Pyrrho [21]. Before the evolution above, the node and edge structure of graph database models used primary and foreign keys. so that columns ID, LEAVING and ARRIVING would be added to node types and edge types, and values for these would be added if they were not provided. From the viewpoint of GQL, this process is unnecessary, and now in Pyrrho the position pseudocolumn is used instead of a new ID column, but if an Id or primary key is already in a new node type it will be used instead. The metadata syntax for declaring node types and edge types includes ways of specifying which existing columns are used for such structural properties.

This leads to smaller and faster implementation of large graphs: smaller because fewer indexes need to be constructed or checked, and faster because the overhead of finding suitable values for the automatic keys is not required.

Pyrrho's client program currently requires multiline statements to be enclosed in square brackets, so that square brackets within multiline statements should not be at the ends of lines.

III. Web Services Vs Big Data

This section describes an implementation of cross-platform linking of data. Previous work [24] discussed how data distributed in different institutions could be processed without the mass import of linked data by extra-transform-load. The key idea was view mediation: a view could be defined with a url for retrieval from a remote source. Assuming that the remote source granted the necessary authorizations, selection and modification of remote data could be allowed using HTTP, and with HTTP POST the mechanism allowed a sequence of operations to be performed on the remote system in a single transaction.

GQL has no details yet on viewed graphs, but the basic idea is clear: like a viewed table, the system can retrieve and process, but does not store, the viewed contents.

A suitable syntax for supplying the url for such remote access is in GQL's USE GRAPH syntax. We can simply write USE GRAPH (url) . As before it is up to the remote system to grant access: the local system will provide its CURRENT_USER information within the HTTP header. Ordinary GQL statements follow the USE GRAPH and become the body of the HTTP POST request, and the result of the final step (e.g. MATCH or RETURN) will be returned from the remote server, along with a suitable ETag as described in [24].

IV. Graph Schema Implementation

A new suggestion for Graph Schema has arisen in discussions about GQL [25] that is very close to the suggestions for Typed Graph Schema in [21]. The idea is that for any graph G, the Graph Schema should itself have the form of a graph S so that nodes of S are node types of G, edges of S are edge types of G, the properties of object types in S are the property types of corresponding objects in G.

Schema information can then be accessed using a MATCH SCHEMA statement. The vision here is that data-modifying statements affecting S should provide a mechanism for altering the graph types of G.

For example, it could be argued that since [5] is all about the consequences of implication, the discussion of example 2 above assumed assertions t3 and t4 (see Table II) at the outset. It would be more in keeping with the context of [5] to be able to implement example 2 using the original triples as follows:

```
INSERT (:John)-[:masterFrom]->(:DauphineUni);
INSERT (:John)-[:phdFrom]->(:DauphineUni);
INSERT SCHEMA [:masterFrom=>:DegreeFrom];
INSERT SCHEMA [:phdFrom=>:DegreeFrom];
```

This respects the statement in [5] that the last two triples specify a relationship at the schema level: that :masterFrom and :phdFrom are subproperties of :degreeFrom, and we assume this is done without creating new instance nodes in the graph. In an open graph, the first statement would be allowed in GQL, with the use of unbound identifiers in the first INSERT implying the creation of nodes and edges and associated (singleton) types. The second does something similar for the unbound label :phdFrom but is at least unusual in its use of the singleton labels :John and :DauphineUni. Normally such an insertion would be specified by a statement such as

```
MATCH (j:John),(u:DauphineUni)
INSERT (j)-[:phDFrom]->(u);
```

If so, it is arguable that the third statement implies the creation of an edge type for the unbound :DegreeFrom, while the fourth inserts the implies relationship.

This represents ongoing research in discussions with the GQL community.

V. Conclusions

This short paper has provided some notes on the current developments in the new database language GQL, and their relationship with recent research papers on knowledge graphs and linked data. Our SQL implementation, Pyrrho [21] is being updated to take account of these changes, and in time will implement all of GQL. Despite this ambition, Pyrrho's executable binaries are very lightweight (less than 2 MB in total) and are very economical with disk space as indicated in section II above. Pyrrho's test suite includes simple cases that show the integration of the relational and typed graph model concepts, and benchmark tests on databases of 500MB show that the design scales well.

Research will continue in order to find the best way of implementing a full GQL implementation while offering a full SQL feature set.

REFERENCES

[1] T. Berners-Lee, J. Hendler, and O. Lassila, "The Semantic Web," Scientific American, pp. 34-43, May 2001.

[2] C. A. Lynch, "Networked information resource discovery: an overview of current issues", IEEE Journal on selected areas in communications 13.8 pp. 1505-1522, 1995.

[3] J. F. Sowa, "Conceptual graphs as a universal knowledge representation", Computers & Mathematics with Applications 23.2-5, pp. 75-93, 1992.

[4] C. Steinfield, R. Kraut, and A. Plummer, "The impact of interorganizational networks on buyer-seller relationships", Journal of computer-mediated communication 1.3 (137), 1995.

[5] K. Belhajjame and M.-Y. Mejri, "Online maintenance of evolving knowledge graphs with RDFS-based saturation and why-provenance support", Web Semantics: Science, Services and Agents on the World Wide Web 78, pp. 100796, 2023.

[6] M. Bennett, and K. Baclawski, "The role of ontologies in linked data, big data and semantic web applications", Applied Ontology 12.3-4, pp. 189-194, 2017.

[7] H. Kaindl, S. Kramer, and L. M. Afonso, "Combining structure search and content search for the World-Wide Web", Proceedings of the Ninth ACM conference on Hypertext and hypermedia: links, objects, time and space, 1998.

[8] Gartner Research, Market Guide for Graph Database Management Systems, 2022.

[9] C. Payal, K. Huang, and M. Zitnik, "Building a knowledge graph to enable precision medicine", Scientific Data 10(1), p.67, 2023.

[10] X. Mao, S. Hao, X. Zhu, and J. Li, "Financial fraud detection using the related-party transaction knowledge graph", Procedia Computer Science 199, pp. 733-740, 2022.

[11] X. Zhao, R. Jiang, H. Yue, A. Li, and Z. Peng, "A survey on cybersecurity knowledge graph construction", Computers & Security, 103524, 2023.

[12] A. Haruna, M. Yang, P. Jiang, and H. Ren, "Collaborative task of entity and relation recognition for developing a knowledge graph to support knowledge reasoning for design for additive manufacturing", Advanced Engineering Informatics 60, 102364, 2024.

[13] J. Deng, C. Chen, X. Huang, W. Chen, and L. Cheng. "Research on the construction of event logic knowledge graph of supply chain management", Advanced Engineering Informatics 56, 101921, 2023.

[14] S. Plantikow and S. Cannan, International Standards Organization, ISO/IEC 39075:2024 "Information Technology - Database Languages – GQL", 12 April 2024.

[15] M. Crowe and F. Laux, "Graph Data Models and Relational Database Technology", DBKDA 2023: The Fifteenth International Conference on Advances in Databases, Knowledge, and Data Applications, IARIA, pp. 33-37, ISSN: 2308-4332, ISBN: 978-1-68558-056-8, 2023.

[16] ISO 9075 Information technology - Database languages - SQL, International Standards Organisation, 2023.

[17] LDBCouncil.org, "The LDBC Financial Benchmark (v.0.1.0)", Arxiv preprint, 2306.15975v2 (retrieved June 2023)

[18] M. Crowe and F. Laux, "Implementing the draft Graph Query Language Standard: The Financial Benchmark", DBKDA 2024, The Sixteenth International Conference on Advances in Databases, Knowledge, and Data Applications, ISSN 2308-4332, p.7-11, 2024.

[19] M. Crowe and F. Laux, "Database Technology Evolution", IARIA International Journal on Advances in Software, vol 15 (3-4), pp. 224-234, ISSN: 1942-2628, 2022

[20] M. Crowe and F. Laux, "Database Technology Evolution II: Graph Database Language", IARIA Congress 2023, The 2023 IARIA Annual Congress on Frontiers in Science, Technology, Services, and Applications, ISBN 978-1-68558-089-6, p.215-222, 2023.

[21] M. Crowe, PyrrhoV7alpha, https://github.com/MalcolmCrowe/ShareableDataStructures

[22] F. Laux, "The Typed Graph Model - a Supermodel for Model Management and Data Integration", arXiv preprint arXiv:2110.02021, 2021

[23] N. Francis et al., "A Researcher's Digest of GQL", The 26th International Conference on Database Theory, Schloss Dagstuhl-Leibniz-Zentrum für Informatik, 2023.

[24] M. Crowe, C. Begg, F. Laux, and M. Laiho, "Data validation for big live data", DBKDA 2017, The Ninth International Conference on Advances in Database, Knowledge, and Data Applications, ISSN 2308-4332, pp 30-36, 2017.

[25] R. Angles et al., "PG-Schema: Schemas for property graphs", Proceedings of the ACM on Management of Data, 1(2), pp.1-25, 2023.

Prediction of Centroid Pixel Values in Image Triangulations Using a Graph Neural Network

Luka Lukač
Faculty of Electrical Engineering and Computer Science
University of Maribor
Maribor, Slovenia
E-mail: luka.lukac@um.si

Andrej Nerat
Faculty of Electrical Engineering and Computer Science
University of Maribor
Maribor, Slovenia
E-mail: andrej.nerat@um.si

Damjan Strnad
Faculty of Electrical Engineering and Computer Science
University of Maribor
Maribor, Slovenia
E-mail: damjan.strnad@um.si

Filip Hácha
Department of Computer Science and Engineering
University of West Bohemia
Plzeň, Czech Republic
E-mail: hachaf@kiv.zcu.cz

Borut Žalik
Faculty of Electrical Engineering and Computer Science
University of Maribor
Maribor, Slovenia
E-mail: borut.zalik@um.si

***Abstract*—Image triangulation is a simple and abstract representation of an image. Important image structures are represented with triangles that are scattered across the image in an unstructured manner. However, quite often, when dealing with an image triangulation, the user's object of interest is the original image. Various interpolation methods have been used in order to predict the original pixel values inside the triangulation simplices. Although yielding accurate results in some cases, their results can be significantly inaccurate when dealing with high-frequency details in simplices of the image triangulation, or if the triangulation simplices have a highly irregular structure. In this paper, a new interpolation method based on a graph neural network is proposed. The experimental results on the popular dataset DIV2K showed that the proposed method, in most cases, produces smaller prediction errors than the existing interpolation methods, such as Barycentric Coordinates or Inverse-Distance Weighting.**

Keywords-image processing; Delaunay triangulation; machine learning; Graph Neural Network; interpolation.

I. Introduction

Image compression methods often use prediction methods to achieve better compression ratios. Neighbouring pixels in a real-life image are usually highly correlated [1]. Therefore, the current (unknown) pixel value can be predicted fairly accurately from previously-encoded pixels in the close neighbourhood with a non-complex texture [2]. Such a prediction approach assumes that pixels are encoded in a pre-determined order, which represents a serious limitation in the case of non-structured data, such as irregularly sampled pixels. In the case of an image triangulation, the key pixels can be scattered across the raster space without a specified order, which is why conventional methods based on image convolution cannot be applied directly to predict unknown values of pixels that are not a part of the triangulation.

In another part of computer science, Geographic Information Systems (GIS), data sampling locations are usually also distributed irregularly across the observed area [3]. Quite often, the object of our interest are locations with no available data [4]. To enable performing environmental analyses at such locations, many interpolation methods have been developed in the past [5]–[8]. In terms of images, interpolation methods have been used mostly for tasks such as super-resolution [9] and steganography [10].

In contrast to many machine learning methods, Graph Neural Networks (GNNs) represent a method that operates on a graph domain instead of in the Euclidean space [11]. In the past, GNNs were used for a variety of tasks (e.g., materials science [12][13], recommendation systems [14], and natural phenomena forecasting [15]). There are applications of GNNs in the field of image processing as well, including tasks such as super-resolution [16][17], structural image classification [18], and image clustering [19]. However, despite the fact that graph representation is well-suited and used widely for the prediction of values in locations with unknown data, none of the existing methods deal with pixel values' prediction in image triangulations.

This paper presents a novel method using a GNN to perform the task of centroid pixel values' prediction in greyscale image triangulations. The remainder of the paper is structured in the following way: in Section II, the proposed prediction method is described in detail, Section III summarises and discusses the results of the experiment, while Section IV concludes the paper.

II. METHOD

The proposed method consists of three major parts:

- detection of the key pixels, where pixels are detected that carry important information about an image,
- graph construction, where the detected key pixels are transformed into a graph with the Delaunay triangulation [20]–[22] to which additional, centroid pixels' nodes are added,
- centroid pixel value predictions, where a GNN is utilised to predict the value of a centroid pixel inside the corresponding triangulation simplex.

In the continuation of this section, each part is described in detail.

A. Detection of Key Pixels

Let I be a greyscale image embedded into a raster space with x columns and y rows. In the first step of the method, the key pixels $\mathcal{P}^k = \{p_i^k\} \subseteq I$ are detected using one of the established methods for image feature detection. Key pixels can, in principle, represent various important image features. However, in our case, the most beneficial features in an image are pixels with maximum gradients (i.e., edges and corners) as they carry the most important information about the image structure. Therefore, the most suitable methods for feature selection are edge detectors and corner detectors (e.g., Scale-Invariant Feature Transform (SIFT) [23] or Features from Accelerated Segment Test (FAST) [24]). Those methods are slightly adapted in our case, enabling a user to determine the rate r of all pixels in I (with maximum gradients) that shall be considered key pixels. An example of a greyscale image and its corresponding set of detected key pixels are displayed in Figure 1.

(a)

(b)

Figure 1. Detection of the key pixels: (a) A greyscale image I [25], (b) Detected key pixels $\mathcal{P}^k$ ($r = 0.05$).

B. Graph Construction

In the next step, a graph $\mathcal{G} = (V, E)$ is constructed, where $V = \{v_i\}$ denotes its vertices, while $E = \{e_{i,j}\}$ represents its edges. Firstly, the method constructs $\mathcal{G}$ with a Delaunay triangulation of $\mathcal{P}^k$ (an example is shown in Figure 2). After that, the centroid pixels $\mathcal{P}^c = \{p_i^c\}$ of the triangulation simplices are calculated, added to the graph, and marked as vertices that shall be predicted with a GNN. Three additional, secondary edges are formed from each p_i^c to all three vertices of the simplex in which the currently observed centroid is located. Lastly, the edge weights are calculated according to (1).

$$w_{i,j} = \begin{cases} 1 & d(v_i, v_j) = 0 \\ \frac{1}{d(v_i, v_j)} & \text{otherwise} \end{cases} \quad (1)$$

where $w_{i,j}$ denotes the weight between the i-th and j-th vertices, while d represents the Euclidean distance between two vertices.

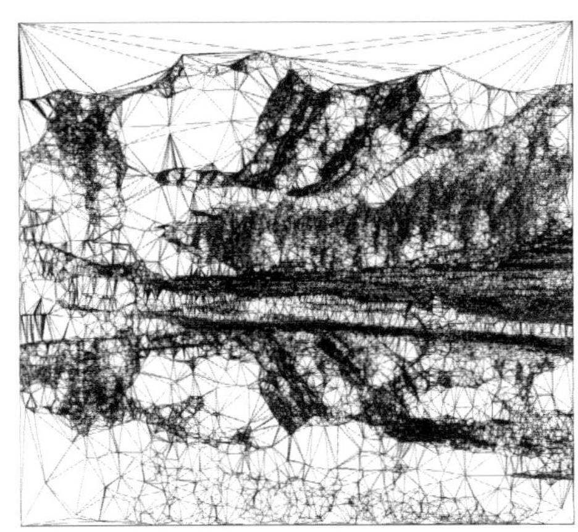

Figure 2. Delaunay triangulation of $\mathcal{P}^k$.

C. Centroid Pixel Value Predictions

After the construction of $\mathcal{G}$, a GNN is used to predict the values of $\mathcal{P}^c$. The GNN consists of two main parts: a graph convolution sequence and a linear sequence (as shown in Figure 3).

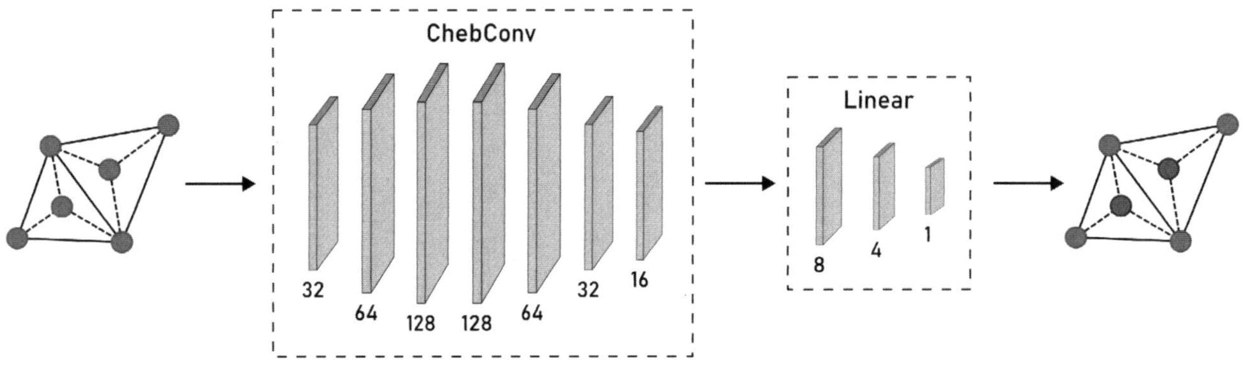

Figure 3. Design of the GNN: the embedding of the graph $\mathcal{G}$ is passed through ChebConv and Linear layers. A graph embedding, containing predictions of centroid pixel values (marked with green), represents the output of the GNN.

As an input, the GNN receives $\mathcal{G}$, that is, afterwards, passed through 7 Chebyshev graph convolutional (ChebConv) layers [26] with the value $K = 3$. Rectified Linear Unit (ReLU) activation function is applied after each layer. The number of ChebConv layers indicates that the result of the convolution is composed of vertices, which are 7 edge connections apart from the current vertex at most. The initial value of p_i^c is set to the average pixel value of its corresponding triangulation simplex. The embedding of $\mathcal{G}$ is constructed from the initial centroid pixel values of $\mathcal{P}^c$. The first ChebConv layer transforms the initial embedding into a graph representation with 32 channels, while the following ChebConv layers transform the intermediate representation into representations with 64, 128, 128, 64, 32, and 16 channels, respectively. In the second part, the values of $\mathcal{P}^c$ are predicted using 3 fully-connected layers with 8, 4, and 1 output, sequentially. The output of the final fully-connected layer (after applying the ReLU activation function) represents the graph embedding that includes the predictions of the centroid pixel values.

III. RESULTS

The results of the method are presented and briefly discussed in this section. One of the most popular image datasets, DIV2K [25], was used for the training of the GNN. Among 1,000 photos, 800 were selected for the training of the GNN, 100 for the validation, and 100 for testing purposes. The image dataset was augmented, in order to reduce the overfitting effect of the neural network. During the data augmentation, the detection of key pixels in each image was performed in a way where their rate varied from 2% to 10% of the total pixel count in an image (effectively producing 9 different key pixel sets from one image). Min-max normalisation of the pixel values and graph attributes was performed, in order to rescale the features to the interval [0,1]. The GNN was implemented with the framework PyG (PyTorch Geometric) [27] and trained on NVIDIA GeForce RTX 3080 Graphics Processing Unit (GPU).

The hyperparameters of the GNN were tuned with a random search, and are summarised in Table I. However, there were some limitations that had to be considered while tuning the hyperparameters. As DIV2K contains large images, their graph representations are very memory-demanding. Consequently, the batch size for training had to be set to 1 in order to prevent running out of memory on the GPU. Furthermore, as the training phase was significantly time-demanding due to large graph representations, the number of epochs was limited to 10. After each mini-batch, the training loss was calculated on $\mathcal{P}^c$.

TABLE I. TRAINING HYPERPARAMETERS OF THE GNN.

Number of epochs	10
Learning rate	0.001
Batch size	1
Optimisation algorithm	Adam [28]
Loss function	Mean Squared Error (MSE)

The results of the GNN were compared with two popular methods used for interpolation: Barycentric Coordinates (BC) and Inverse-Distance Weighting (IDW). Root-Mean-Square Error (RMSE) was used to evaluate the error of the predictions on the test set (within the pixel range [0,255]). The experimental results of the three methods are presented in Table II.

TABLE II. AVERAGE PREDICTION ERROR WITH DIFFERENT INTERPOLATION METHODS.

Method	RMSE
BC	22.54
IDW	23.23
GNN	**20.26**

The comparison between BC, IDW, and the GNN revealed that, on average, our method outperformed BC by 10.11% and IDW by 12.79%. The latter indicates that our method significantly improves the prediction accuracy. Furthermore, the results of the experiment showed that, among 900 test images, the GNN outperformed BC and IDW in 839 cases, meaning that our method's prediction produced the best result in 93.22% of the test samples. Graphically, the results of the tests are shown in Figure 4.

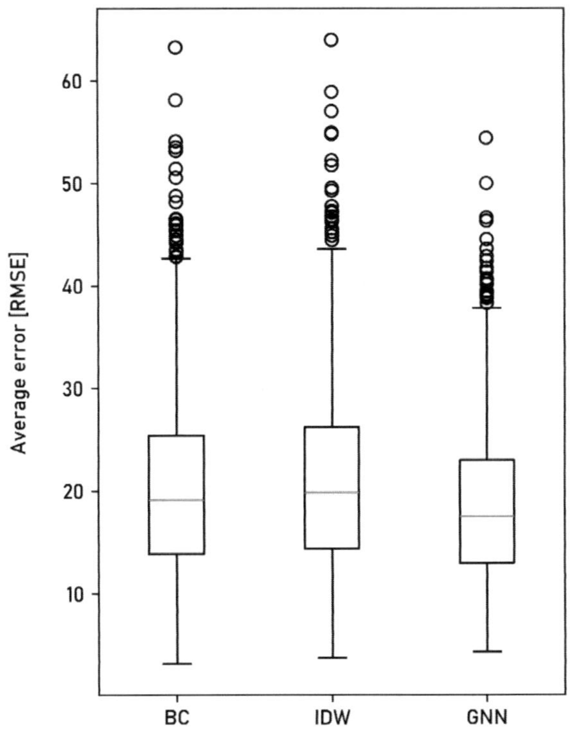

Figure 4. Average errors of the tested interpolation methods: BC, IDW, and the GNN.

The GNN-based prediction achieved the best result in terms of median error and InterQuartile Range (IQR). The upper 1.5*IQR whisker of the GNN also lies significantly lower than the BC and IDW counterparts, which indicates that the image samples with larger error are less common when predicting pixels with the GNN. The only case where both BC and IDW performed better than the GNN is the lower 1.5*IQR whisker, indicating that, in some cases, conventional interpolation methods can outperform machine learning methods.

IV. Conclusion and Future Work

A new method for the prediction of centroid pixel values in image triangulations with a GNN is introduced in this paper. The key pixels that are detected with one of the established methods for important image features extraction are used to form a graph with a Delaunay triangulation. After that, the unknown pixel values, lying at the centroids of the triangulation simplices, are predicted using the GNN. The proposed GNN was trained on a large dataset of diverse greyscale images, which enhanced its versatility and efficiency. The GNN significantly outperformed the widely used conventional interpolation methods BC and IDW.

In the future, the proposed method could be integrated into algorithms for data compression that operate on unstructured data. In that case, it would probably be beneficial to perform prediction not only for centroid pixels but also for all non-key pixels in a raster space. A hierarchical GNN architecture [29] could be used for doing that. Such task, however, could be exceedingly demanding in terms of the computation power and the prediction performance. Another way in which we could continue our work is adapting our method to spatiotemporal domains such as video.

Acknowledgment

This research was funded by Slovenian Research and Innovation Agency under Research Project J2-4458 and Research Programme P2-0041, and the Czech Science Foundation under Research Project 23-04622L.

References

[1] L. Lukač, A. Jeromel, and L. Váša, "A short overview of prediction methods for image compression," in *Proceedings of the 32nd International Electrotechnical and Computer Science Conference*, (Portorož), pp. 145–148, IEEE Slovenia, September 2023.

[2] T. Dumas, A. Roumy, and C. Guillemot, "Context-adaptive neural network-based prediction for image compression," *IEEE Transactions on Image Processing*, vol. 29, pp. 679–693, 2020.

[3] J. Li and A. D. Heap, "Spatial interpolation methods applied in the environmental sciences: A review," *Environmental Modelling & Software*, vol. 53, pp. 173–189, 2014.

[4] L. Mitas and H. Mitasova, "Spatial interpolation," *Geographical Information Systems: Principles, Techniques, Management and Applications*, vol. 1, no. 2, pp. 481–492, 1999.

[5] D. Shepard, "A two-dimensional interpolation function for irregularly-spaced data," in *Proceedings of the 1968 23rd ACM National Conference*, ACM '68, (New York, NY, USA), p. 517–524, Association for Computing Machinery, 1968.

[6] R. Sibson, "A brief description of natural neighbor interpolation," *Interpreting Multivariate Data*, pp. 21–36, 1981.

[7] B. Yang, Q. Li, and W. Shi, "Constructing multi-resolution triangulated irregular network model for visualization," *Computers & Geosciences*, vol. 31, no. 1, pp. 77–86, 2005.

[8] A. Möbius, *Der barycentrische Calcul*. Johann Ambrosius Barth, 1827.

[9] W.-C. Siu and K.-W. Hung, "Review of image interpolation and super-resolution," in *Proceedings of The 2012 Asia Pacific Signal and Information Processing Association Annual Summit and Conference*, pp. 1–10, 2012.

[10] Y.-Q. Chen, W.-J. Sun, L.-Y. Li, C.-C. Chang, and X. Wang, "An efficient general data hiding scheme based on image interpolation," *Journal of Information Security and Applications*, vol. 54, p. 102584, 2020.

[11] J. Zhou *et al.*, "Graph neural networks: A review of methods and applications," *AI Open*, vol. 1, pp. 57–81, 2020.

[12] P. Reiser *et al.*, "Graph neural networks for materials science and chemistry," *Communications Materials*, vol. 3, no. 1, p. 93, 2022.

[13] V. Fung, J. Zhang, E. Juarez, and B. G. Sumpter, "Benchmarking graph neural networks for materials chemistry," *npj Computational Materials*, vol. 7, no. 1, p. 84, 2021.

[14] X. Li, L. Sun, M. Ling, and Y. Peng, "A survey of graph neural network based recommendation in social networks," *Neurocomputing*, vol. 549, p. 126441, 2023.

[15] F.-H. Zhang and Z.-G. Shao, "ST-GRF: Spatiotemporal graph neural networks for rainfall forecasting," *Digital Signal Processing*, vol. 136, p. 103989, 2023.

[16] S. Zhou, J. Zhang, W. Zuo, and C. C. Loy, "Cross-scale internal graph neural network for image super-resolution," *Advances in Neural Information Processing Systems*, vol. 33, pp. 3499–3509, 2020.

[17] T. Tarasiewicz, J. Nalepa, and M. Kawulok, "A graph neural network for multiple-image super-resolution," in *2021 IEEE International Conference on Image Processing (ICIP)*, pp. 1824–1828, 2021.

[18] A. Quek, Z. Wang, J. Zhang, and D. Feng, "Structural image classification with graph neural networks," in *2011 International Conference on Digital Image Computing: Techniques and Applications*, pp. 416–421, 2011.

[19] Y. Xing *et al.*, "Learning hierarchical graph neural networks for image clustering," in *Proceedings of the IEEE/CVF International Conference on Computer Vision (ICCV)*, pp. 3467–3477, October 2021.

[20] B. Delaunay, "Sur la sphere vide," *Izv. Akad. Nauk SSSR, Otdelenie Matematicheskii i Estestvennyka Nauk*, vol. 7, no. 793-800, pp. 1–2, 1934.

[21] I. Kolingerová and B. Žalik, "Improvements to randomized incremental Delaunay insertion," *Computers & Graphics*, vol. 26, no. 3, pp. 477–490, 2002.

[22] B. Žalik, "An efficient sweep-line Delaunay triangulation algorithm," *Computer-Aided Design*, vol. 37, no. 10, pp. 1027–1038, 2005.

[23] D. Lowe, "Object recognition from local scale-invariant features," in *Proceedings of the Seventh IEEE International Conference on Computer Vision*, vol. 2, pp. 1150–1157 vol.2, 1999.

[24] E. Rosten and T. Drummond, "Machine learning for high-speed corner detection," in *Computer Vision – ECCV 2006* (A. Leonardis, H. Bischof, and A. Pinz, eds.), (Berlin, Heidelberg), pp. 430–443, Springer Berlin Heidelberg, 2006.

[25] E. Agustsson and R. Timofte, "NTIRE 2017 challenge on single image super-resolution: Dataset and study," in *2017 IEEE Conference on Computer Vision and Pattern Recognition Workshops (CVPRW)*, pp. 1122–1131, July 2017.

[26] M. Defferrard, X. Bresson, and P. Vandergheynst, "Convolutional neural networks on graphs with fast localized spectral filtering," *arXiv*, 2017.

[27] M. Fey and J. E. Lenssen, "Fast graph representation learning with PyTorch Geometric," in *ICLR Workshop on Representation Learning on Graphs and Manifolds*, 2019.

[28] D. P. Kingma and J. Ba, "Adam: A method for stochastic optimization," *arXiv*, 2014.

[29] S. Sobolevsky, "Hierarchical graph neural networks," *arXiv preprint arXiv:2105.03388*, 2021.

Real-time Optimization of Testbeds for Cloudified Radio Access Networks Using Artificial Intelligence

Animesh Singh
Ericsson AB
Stockholm, Sweden
animesh.singh@ericsson.com

Chen Song
Uppsala University
Uppsala, Sweden
chen.song.1637@student.uu.se

Jiecong Yang
Uppsala University
Uppsala, Sweden
jiecong.yang.2357@student.uu.se

Sahar Tahvili
Ericsson AB
Stockholm, Sweden
sahar.tahvili@ericsson.com

***Abstract*—The evolution towards cloudification in Radio Access Networks (RAN) is transforming the telecommunications industry. To validate and assess the performance of Cloudified Radio Access Networks (C-RAN) applications, deploying cloud-native infrastructures in the form of test environments, testbeds, and test infrastructures becomes imperative. However, the intricacies and expenses associated with these testbeds surpass those of traditional testing environments. Effectively utilizing the potential of cloud-native testbeds necessitates real-time decision-making on multiple criteria, including compatibility, capability, cost, capacity, and availability. This paper introduces an Artificial Intelligence-based expert system designed to automatically schedule C-RAN testbeds. The proposed expert system is designed to consider and balance various factors in real time, ensuring optimal utilization of resources and test infrastructures. Employing Artificial Intelligence (AI) based solutions optimizes scheduling decisions, adapts to dynamic environments, maximizes resource utilization, reduces operational costs, and improves turnaround times by dynamically adjusting priorities based on real-time conditions. The feasibility of the AI-based solution proposed in this paper is rigorously assessed through an empirical evaluation conducted on a Telecom use case at Ericsson AB in Sweden. The results demonstrate a remarkable 17% optimization in overall costs with the implementation of the proposed solution.**

Keywords-Software Testing; Artificial Intelligence; C-RAN; Testbed; Optimization; Reinforcement Learning

I. INTRODUCTION

The rapidly evolving telecommunication industry places a growing demand on expediting the delivery of telecommunication applications and products. Finding a balance between product quality, cost-effectiveness, and swift deployment remains a persistent challenge in large-scale industries [1] [2]. To address this, various solutions, like Cloudification, have emerged in this domain, offering the potential to maintain scalability, accessibility, and mobility for telecom products. One key concept gaining significant attention is Cloud RAN (C-RAN), which involves the utilization of cloud-based services and infrastructures for radio access networks [3]. While the C-RAN solution provides numerous advantages, it also has its challenges, including system complexity and infrastructure costs, such as those associated with developing, building, constructing, establishing, and utilizing the C-RAN infrastructure. The main differences between a traditional RAN and a C-RAN architecture lie in their respective testing environments, testbeds, and infrastructure. In a traditional RAN setting, the testing infrastructure tends to be well-established and relatively straightforward. The equipment and procedures used for testing are typically well-defined and familiar to telecom professionals. In contrast, the testing environment for C-RAN introduces a range of complexities, flexibilities, and differences. Since C-RAN relies on cloud-based solutions and virtualized network functions, a testing environment (often called a testbed) must embed various virtualized components, such as hardware, radio gateways, simulators, and software components. These components are essential for emulating the C-RAN environment accurately. In essence, a configuration serves as a comprehensive description of a test bed's capabilities and capacities, which can be presented as a unique ID. The utilization of a configuration ID proves invaluable in distinguishing and uniquely identifying various configurations within the testing environment. This systematic approach facilitates efficient management and organization of testing resources. Efficiently optimizing the utilization of C-RAN infrastructure, including testbeds, offers a host of compelling advantages that span well beyond cost reduction, scalability, performance, energy efficiency, and network reliability. Furthermore, considering the crucial aspects of on-time delivery and the diverse dimensions of C-RAN products, traditional optimization models may prove less effective. In contrast, employing the power of AI and Machine Learning (ML) techniques introduces a plethora of advantages for the dynamic optimization of C-RAN testbeds during the testing process. By aligning the availability of testbeds with the timing of requests, the system can strategically power on and off these resources. This on-demand usage minimizes overall energy consumption, promoting energy efficiency and reducing the carbon footprint of the testing infrastructure. Utilizing agile methodologies, such as different IT service management software (e.g., Jira, Azure DevOps) for testbed scheduling can help teams manage software development. However, some manual tasks like request creation, analysis, and information provision still face challenges of ambiguity, uncertainty, and time efficiency. This challenge is more pronounced in large industries, where engineers use distinct terminologies when requesting testbed bookings. For example, the testing team manually initiates a ticket in text format, navigating through predefined options to specify the testing requirements. Subsequently, test managers assess the compatibility and availability of a suitable testbed, relying heavily on domain knowledge. This manual process introduces subjectivity, risking, e.g., double bookings or delaying product delivery. As C-RAN products scale, these inefficiencies highlight the impracticality and scalability of manual processes in modern software development. Addressing these issues requires automated, streamlined approaches to enhance efficiency, accuracy, and productivity. This paper introduces, implements, and evaluates an AI-based solution for dynamically scheduling testbeds in the context of testing the C-RAN applications. The feasibility of the proposed solution is studied by an empirical evaluation that has been performed on a telecommunication use case at Ericsson AB (EAB) in Sweden. The empirical evaluation demonstrates promising results, indicating the adaptability and potential applicability of the proposed AI-based solution in larger industries. The performance of the proposed AI-based solution in this paper has also been compared with a first-come, first-served (FCFS) queuing approach. The positive outcomes suggest that the scheduling system can be effectively integrated into diverse industrial settings, showcasing its versatility and suitability for broader applications within the telecommunications domain. The organization of this paper is laid out as follows: Section II provides a background of the initial problem and also an overview of research on test environment optimization, Section III describes the proposed AI-based expert system. An industrial case study has been designed in Section IV. Section V clarifies some points of future directions of the present work and finally, Section VI concludes the paper.

II. Background and Related Work

Test optimization holds a vital role in the software development life cycle. One avenue for achieving this is through the management of the available testing resources, such as testbeds, and test environments, to ensure that the overall quality of the final product is improved while the time to market is reduced [1] [4]. Employing the traditional analytical technique that attempts to find the globally optimal solution through mathematical models can be excessively time-consuming due to the large search space. On the other hand, heuristic or meta-heuristic techniques might discover a sub-optimal solution but within a reasonable timeframe [5]. Moreover, addressing a substantial set of available data in the industry requires a solution capable of handling large-scale data within a tight deadline. The generalizability and extensibility of machine learning-based solutions have been demonstrated and validated across various industrial, real-world problems in the software testing domain [2]. The process of enhancing test activities including test planning and analysis, test design, test execution, and test evaluation, through the application of AI is referred to as test optimization. The test resource scheduling approaches can enable an optimized allocation of resources, ensuring that testbeds are actively used which reduces unnecessary energy consumption and operational costs associated with maintaining idle testbeds. Optimized resource utilization not only benefits the environment but also leads to cost savings. By dynamically managing testbeds based on demand, organizations can minimize operational expenses associated with energy consumption and maintenance. The AI and ML-based solutions prove to be a promising approach for optimization in industrial systems due to their ability to adapt and learn from interactions with dynamic environments [4]. In industrial settings, where system dynamics, constraints, and objectives may evolve, AI and ML-based models, such as reinforcement learning offer a flexible framework. This benefit lets the system learn the best ways to make decisions by trying things out, which helps it improve tasks like scheduling, managing resources, and controlling things. The adaptability of AI-based solutions makes them well-suited for handling complex, uncertain, and changing conditions in industrial systems, ultimately leading to improved efficiency, resource utilization, and overall performance. Testbeds and test resource management can be viewed as dynamic scheduling problems. In this context, AI-based solutions, particularly reinforcement learning, which is capable of handling large-scale data, can be dynamically applied in the industry to make informed decisions regarding the scheduling of testing resources. Q-learning, Genetic Algorithms (GA), and Ant Colony Optimization (ACO) are some examples of the optimization techniques used in scheduling, where each has its strengths and weaknesses. Considering dynamic changes and large data sizes utilizing AI/ML-based approaches for dynamic scheduling has received a great deal of attention. In this regard, AI/ML-based solutions (such as Q-learning) stand out due to their adaptability to dynamic environments and ease of implementation, especially when the state and action spaces are well-defined. On the contrary, while traditional optimization solutions, such as Genetic Algorithms (GA) and Ant Colony Optimization (ACO) demonstrate prowess in managing large search spaces and intricate objective functions, they often encounter challenges in dynamic environments and demand meticulous parameter tuning. These factors can hinder their effectiveness, particularly in scenarios characterized by fluctuating conditions and extensive datasets [6]. In contrast, Q-learning's adaptability positions it as an attractive choice for such dynamic environments and substantial data sizes. Its ability to learn and adjust strategies based on real-time feedback makes it well-suited to navigate unpredictable scenarios efficiently. Additionally, Q-learning's capacity to prioritize cost optimization while considering request priorities enhances its versatility in addressing various scheduling challenges. Furthermore, FCFS scheduling, although simplistic, has its merits [7]. It offers a straightforward and intuitive approach, making it easy to implement and understand. In scenarios where task priorities are relatively homogeneous or where quick task processing is essential, FCFS can provide a pragmatic solution with minimal computational overhead. However, FCFS may struggle in situations with highly variable task priorities or when resource allocation requires more sophisticated decision-making processes. While Q-learning shines in dynamic and data-intensive scheduling environments, FCFS remains a viable option in certain scenarios due to its simplicity and ease of implementation. The choice between Q-learning and FCFS, as well as other optimization algorithms, should be made based on a thorough understanding of the specific characteristics and requirements of the scheduling problem at hand. Using Reinforcement Learning algorithms helps optimize testbeds

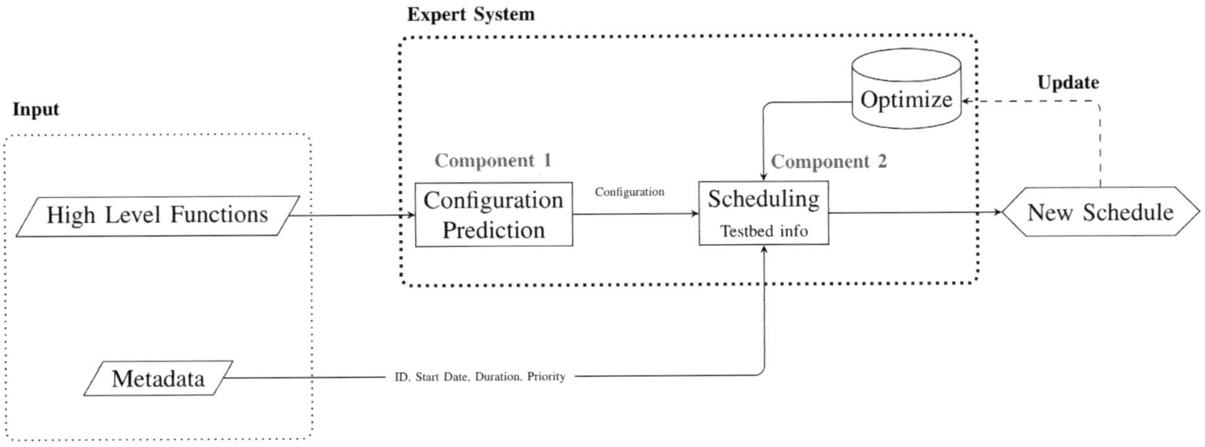

Figure 1. A holistic overview of the proposed expert system in this study.

by learning the best scheduling methods through ongoing interaction with the testing environment. This means making smarter decisions and improving testbed setups over time, using past data and changing needs. Machine Learning also plays a key role in managing test resources effectively, predicting resource needs by studying past usage, test requirements, and outside factors. This predictive analysis helps allocate resources better, making testing more efficient in industries. Reinforcement learning has been explored in previous research for solving scheduling problems. In a study by Reyna et al. [8], they presented a Q-Learning-based approach specifically addressing scheduling problems like the Job Shop Scheduling Problem (JSSP) and Flow Shop Scheduling Problem (FSSP). Another work by Martinez [9] introduced a generic multi-agent reinforcement learning approach adaptable to various scheduling scenarios. However, both studies mainly focused on JSSP, FSSP, and their multi-stage job variants. Kaur et al. [10] explore three distinct approaches within Goal Programming: the Weighted Approach, the Preemptive Approach, and the Chebyshev Approach, providing a comprehensive analysis. Additionally, the study discusses the handling of the three objectives individually as single-objective problems. The proposed optimization models are validated using a dataset from agile-based software development, and sensitivity analysis is conducted to assess the impact of the involved variables. Anand et al. [11] investigate the aspect of multi-upgradation, proposing various optimization problems that address the optimal allocation of testing resources to different versions. The solution presented in [11] comprises a set of models solved using a dynamic programming approach, complemented with numerical illustrations.

III. The Proposed Solution

The AI-based expert system proposed in this study contains two main components. Figure 1 shows a detailed representation of the expert system, emphasizing the essential elements, the necessary input, the sequential steps involved, and the expected output. The development path of the expert system introduced in this study embarks on a journey that commences with the analysis of numerous requests which are composed in semi-controlled natural language by the testing team. To analyze this textual data, various natural language processing techniques are deployed. However, even with AI assistance, the process of natural text analysis can be time-consuming and prone to errors. Through our experiences in text analysis, we arrived at a significant insight: a subset of the information provided by the testing team can be sufficient for discerning the anticipated capabilities and characteristics of a Cloud-native testbed. In light of this realization, we turned to different keyword extraction techniques to efficiently identify the essential information required for configuration prediction. This shift in approach not only streamlines the process but also reduces the potential for errors and accelerates the development of the expert system. It underscores the value of leveraging keyword extraction as a powerful tool for discerning the vital details within the textual requests, facilitating the seamless prediction of configurations for a Cloud-native testbed. The following paragraphs provide more details about the data, the embedded components, and the expected output of the proposed AI-based expert system in this study.

A. Input Data

As highlighted in Figure 1, the extracted keywords have been categorized into two primary groups: 1- High-Level C-RAN Functions and 2- Metadata. The metadata category plays a crucial role in facilitating real-time decision-making processes. Metadata refers to additional information or data that provides context or details about the main data. In the context of the proposed AI-based expert system, metadata includes details, such as request ID, timestamps, source locations, priority of each request, or other relevant contextual information. Capturing the metadata enhances the understanding and utility of the primary information, contributing significantly to the system's effectiveness in real-time decision-making for scheduling C-RAN testbeds. Meanwhile, the high-level functions category is instrumental in the automated prediction of configurations for the testbed. A testbed configuration represents the capacity and capability of a C-RAN testbed. The high-level functions, as illustrated in Figure 1, provide essential elements for configuring the C-RAN testbed. These elements, derived from the extracted keywords, include parameters, such as network topology, bandwidth, number of cells, and other key hardware (HW) and software (SW) settings. The AI-based expert system can efficiently adapt the testbed to various scenarios, optimizing its capacity and capabilities based on the provided information. This ensures a flexible and adaptive C-RAN testbed configuration tailored to specific needs and requirements.

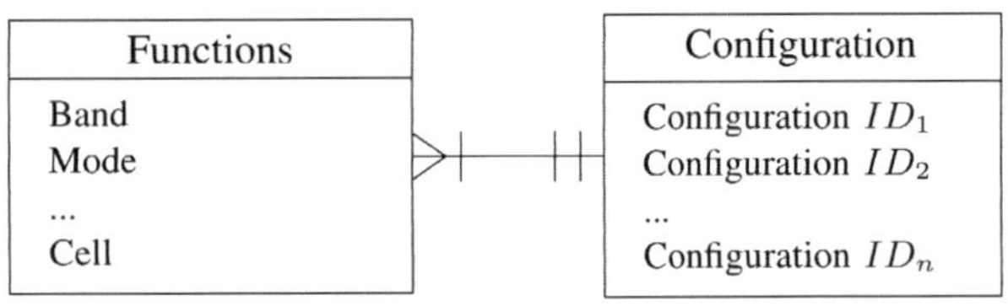

Figure 2. The Many-To-One mapping of the high-level functions using classification models for configuration prediction.

To acquire the requisite input for the proposed expert system, we have created a graphical user interface (GUI). This interface displays a spectrum of metadata choices, including Request ID, Date, Duration, and Request Priority. In essence, the proposed expert system in this study will receive input from all possible combinations of the mentioned data. Figure 2 provides a high-level overview of the prediction process for C-RAN testbed configurations using high-level functions provided by the end users. To generate a testbed configuration, it is recommended to employ multiple classification models, enabling many-to-one mapping. In a general sense, many-to-one mapping signifies a single-valued association, wherein a group of entities can be linked to a similar entity. This methodology improves the adaptability of the system by permitting the creation of diverse configurations grounded in different sets of input parameters. The many-to-one mapping is particularly useful in situations where multiple inputs correspond to a single configuration option. This flexible modeling approach significantly enhances the robustness and versatility of the C-RAN testbed configuration prediction process.

B. Component 1

As illustrated in Figure 1, the proposed expert system in this paper comprises two core AI-based components intricately linked together. As we can see in Figure 1, the output of Component 1 feeds into the second component, establishing a vital connection between these essential elements of the system's architecture. Component 1 focuses on the prediction of configurations based on the high-level function information provided by the end user. As mentioned earlier, a testbed configuration describes crucial details about a testbed's capacity, capability, and properties. In this process, employing various classification models, such as random forest and Support Vector Machine (SVM), enables the expert system to create a unique identifier describing the distinctive features of the testbed. The mentioned classifiers analyze the high-level function information and assign a specific identifier or unique ID to each configuration. This ID serves as a comprehensive representation of the testbed's distinctive characteristics. It is important to note that, even though each configuration is unique, there might be instances where multiple testbeds share the same configuration. This occurrence is due to the inherent complexity of the C-RAN environment, where different testbeds may exhibit similar features or capacities despite being distinct entities. Using classification models enhances the system's ability to efficiently categorize and identify various configurations, contributing to a more nuanced understanding of the C-RAN testbed landscape. Figure 2 offers an insightful depiction of the configuration prediction process, showcasing the innovative solution proposed in this study.

C. Component 2

Component 2 focuses on scheduling the testbed using both the metadata provided by end users and the configurations generated by Component 1. As previously mentioned, the configuration of a testbed highlights its features, and multiple testbeds may share the same features. However, even if testbeds have identical features, their costs can vary. For instance, the cost of an embedded simulator may differ across testbeds, even if the simulators have the same capacity and capability. The final cost of a testbed is influenced by various factors, including the brand of hardware, software, and suppliers involved. Considering the diversity in costs and features, optimal testbed scheduling involves factoring in the gathered metadata. The metadata, provided by end users, provides some essential details, such as the starting date, duration, and priority of each request. Integrating this metadata information with the generated configurations and the associated costs of each testbed enables the expert system to schedule testbeds more efficiently. Combining the metadata information with the generated configuration and cost of each testbed can help the expert system, to schedule the testbeds more efficiently. Considering a broad spectrum of upcoming requests from end users and a multitude of testbeds with diverse configurations and costs, reinforcement learning models are embedded into Component 2 for the real-time scheduling of the C-RAN testbed. In a reinforcement learning approach, an agent, action, state, and reward are all abstract concepts that can be differently defined to solve various problems. In a Reinforcement Learning (RL) model, agents must learn through interaction with the state by sensing and influencing it. The application of RL to the scheduling problem in this study is fitting, considering an agent capable of continuously assigning newly arrived requests for scheduling a testbed. The state, action, and reward can also be defined as the arrangement of existing requests, the assignment of a new incoming request, and the optimization objective, respectively. In this context, an RL model can be seen as an intelligent search method seeking the most optimal scheduling strategy by interacting dynamically with incoming requests.

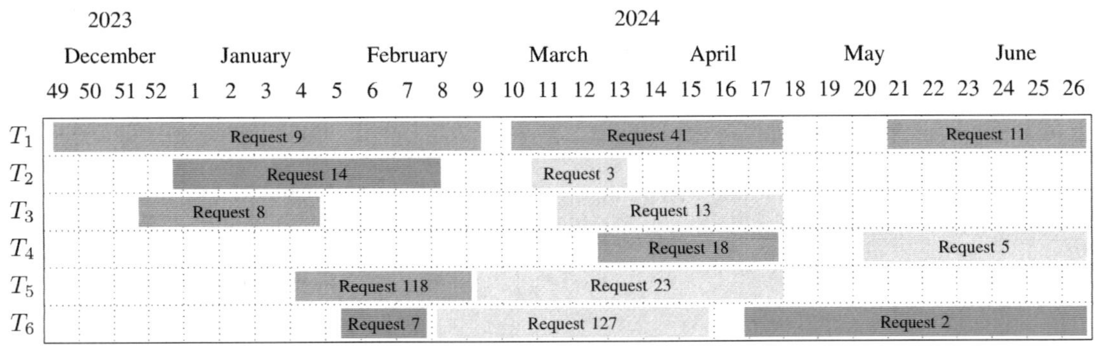

Figure 3. A holistic overview of scheduled C-RAN testbeds utilizing the proposed AI-based expert system. The Y-axis denotes the testbeds, while the X-axis depicts calendar time. Each color represents the priority of each request.

In this paper, Q-learning model has been implemented in the AI-based expert system to determine optimal scheduling for C-RAN testbeds. Q-learning is particularly well-suited for scenarios where an agent interacts with an environment, learning to make decisions that maximize cumulative rewards over time. In Q-Learning, a *Q-function* defines the computation of the expected reward of each state-action pair, and a *Q-table* is used to store the expected reward of all state-action pairs. Their concrete format and structure depend on the problem to be solved. The following list is the overall steps of Q-learning, and it describes how the Q-learning algorithm does scheduling tasks briefly.

1) Initialize the Q-table:
   a) The structure and initialization of the Q-table depend on the concrete problem.
2) Define Q-function and reward:
   a) The format of the Q-function depends on the concrete problem.
3) Learning loop for multiple episodes:
   a) **Select and perform an action to perform**: first, the agent will capture the current state, and then it will choose an action with the highest Q-value.
   b) **Measure the reward**: To learn more optimally, the rewards need to be measured and the Q-table needs to be updated dynamically by the program.
   c) **Update the Q-table**: using the measured reward, the expected reward corresponding to the selected action and current state will be updated based on Equation (1) and Equation (2).

$$TD = r + \gamma \times max(Q) - Q_{old} \quad (1)$$

where, TD is the temporal difference, γ shows discount factor, $max(Q)$ means estimated optimal future (next state) value, Q_{old} is current Q value of the given state and given action.

$$Q_{new} = Q_{old} + \alpha \times TD \quad (2)$$

where, α indicates learning rate, Q_{new} shows the new Q value in the Q-table of the given state and action.
4) Generate the most optimal scheduling decision
   a) The scheduling decision with the highest reward which has been found during the learning loop will be selected as the final decision.

D. Optimization

As depicted in Figure 1, the expert system dynamically receives new requests for scheduling and booking the testbeds. Within the optimization segment of the proposed AI-based expert system in this study, a self-defined optimization objective needs to be established. In this regard, a testbed's total cost (*Overall Cost*) is employed as the objective, calculated as Equation (3):

$$OC = i_1 \cdot makespan + i_2 \cdot \sum_{i=1}^{N} w_i \cdot p_i + i_3 \cdot \sum_{i=1}^{N} c_i \quad (3)$$

where i_1, i_2, and i_3 are weights that require manual configuration by end users, $makespan$ denotes the maximum completion time of all requests, w_i signifies the waiting time (real starting time - release time) for each request, p_i represents the priority of each request, and c_i corresponds to the cost of executing each request on its designated testbed. However, simply summing different objectives with weights can make the setting of weights challenging in practice due to their different scales [12]. Therefore, normalization is necessary to ensure that this single optimization objective yields meaningful information. To bring all three sections to similar scales, the normalized Overall Cost (OC) can be calculated, as shown in Equation (4).

$$OC_{norm} = i_1 \cdot \frac{makespan}{\overline{r} + \overline{d}} + i_2 \cdot \log \sum_{i=1}^{N} w_i \cdot p_i + i_3 \cdot \frac{\sum_{i=1}^{N} c_i}{N \cdot \overline{c}} \quad (4)$$

where $\overline{r}$ and $\overline{d}$ represent the average release time and duration of all requests, respectively, and $\bar{c}$ denotes the average utilization cost of all testbeds. The use of log in the second section is necessitated by the fact that waiting time cannot be estimated in advance. Although log cannot map the original numbers into a fixed range, it helps align the scale of the second section with the other two. Alternative functions like $sigmoid$ or other normalization methods can also be considered. It is important to note that all Overall Costs mentioned later in this study refer to this normalized form. The objective's intuition is straightforward. By minimizing OC, the generated schedule can, in general, reduce the finish time, decrease waiting times for requests with higher priority, and cut down on the cost of utilizing testbeds. The three weighting factors, set with different ratios, allow different parts to dominate the objective, leading to schedules suitable for different scenarios.

E. Expected Output

The expected output of the proposed AI-based expert system in this study is the real-time scheduling of the C-RAN testbeds. Given that each request may vary in time span and priority, the expert system must be executed upon receiving a new request. Furthermore, considering the finite number of testbeds and their distinct costs, the priority assigned to a request (as provided by the end user in the Metadata section, see Figure 1) significantly influences decision-making. Indeed, the decision to schedule a request on a particular testbed may be subject to change if the expert system receives a new request with a higher priority for the same testbed configuration. This dynamic consideration of priorities ensures that the expert system adapts to changing conditions and optimally manages the allocation of resources based on the most pressing needs. Figure 3 provides a comprehensive view of the real-time scheduling of the C-RAN testbeds using the solution presented in Figure 1. As illustrated, multiple requests are received and scheduled concurrently. The Y-axis represents the testbeds, and the X-axis depicts calendar time. Each color represents the priority of each request.

IV. Empirical Evaluation

To analyze the feasibility of the proposed AI-based expert system, we designed an industrial case study at Ericsson AB (EAB) in Sweden, by following the proposed guidelines of Runeson and Höst [13] and also Tahvili and Hatvani in [2]. A subset of the utilized database to simulate the case study can be found at the GitHub repository [14].

A. Unit of analysis and procedure

The units of analysis in this study consist of a set of available C-RAN testbeds and requests submitted by the testing team for scheduling and booking a testbed for testing a C-RAN application. The case study in this paper is conducted in several sequential steps:

- A total of 500 requests have been extracted from the internal database at EAB and are submitted to book a testbed for testing various C-RAN applications.
- Various text analysis techniques are employed to extract critical keywords, which are then presented in the Graphical User Interface (GUI) of the AI-based expert system. This guides end-users in submitting their requests to book a C-RAN testbed.
- A total of 23 unique configurations for several testbeds are analyzed, and the resulting configuration information is incorporated into the internal database of the AI-based expert system. Subsequently, 197 testbeds are identified that match these unique configurations.
- Evaluations from test managers concerning the generated configurations for each testbed and the scheduling of requests are collected and analyzed.

B. Case Study Report

As mentioned earlier, the primary objective of the proposed AI-based expert system is real-time testbed scheduling. Making accurate real-time decisions for scheduling a testbed is directly linked to the upcoming testing requests and the corresponding capacity and capability of the testbeds. Booking a testbed that fails to meet the engineering requirements of a submitted request can have a direct impact on the testing process. In essence, if the capacity, capabilities, and features of a testbed do not align with the testing requirements, the testing team will be unable to successfully execute the test cases. As mentioned before to apply Q-Learning to the problem, both the Q-table and the Q-function need to be defined. The Q-table further depends on how the state and action are defined based on the problem. In the proposed solution in this paper, the Q-table is organized around three different states that signify the state of a request: "Start", "In Process", and "Finish". Simultaneously, an integer set defines the action space: "0" denotes the "Wait" action, while the remaining values represent various test beds. Moreover, the total number of actions is limited by the number of available testbeds, plus one extra action for "Wait".

Table I. An example of a Q-table illustrating the scheduling of 5 different testbeds (TB), with states including "Start", "In Process", and "Finish".

Actions States	**Wait (0)**	**TB1 (1)**	**TB2 (2)**	**TB3 (3)**	**TB4 (4)**	**TB5 (5)**
Start (0)	0	1	0	0	0	0
In Process (1)	0	0	2	0	0	0
Finish (2)	0	0	0	0	3	0

This design results in a Q-table arrangement, where available actions are represented in columns and request states are represented in rows. Each cell in the table has a Q-value representing the expected total reward for carrying out a specific action in a particular state. The learning process is facilitated by the repeated update of these Q-values, allowing the model to intelligently allocate testbeds based on prior experiences and input from the environment. Table I provides an example of a Q-table for scheduling five different testbeds. The definition of the Q-function further depends on the definition of the reward. To minimize the overall cost (OC), the expected reward in our proposed solution is described in Equation (5).

$$r_{total\ reward} = \frac{1}{OC_{norm}} \tag{5}$$

C. Performance Evaluation

Given that the expert system introduced in this paper integrates multiple ML and AI techniques, it becomes imperative to conduct performance evaluations for each step and model independently. Similarly, assessing the performance of an RL model for real-time scheduling presents a multifaceted challenge. This process necessitates the consideration of diverse metrics that are tailored to align with the specific objectives and constraints of the scheduling problem at hand. The selection of evaluation criteria must be thoughtfully tailored to the application's unique requirements, highlighting the importance of striking a balanced approach to optimize real-time scheduling performance.

1) Component 1 Evaluation: In the experiment, the Train/Test split ratio on the dataset is set to $0.8/0.2$. Metrics, such as Precision, Recall, and F1-Score are essential for assessing multi-class classification performance as they offer a thorough understanding of the model's efficacy. Precision highlights the accuracy of positive predictions by calculating the ratio of accurately predicted instances to all instances anticipated as positive. Conversely, Recall evaluates how well the model captures all relevant cases by calculating the ratio of all real positive instances to all correctly predicted positive instances. The experimental results for the mentioned metrics on different classifiers are presented in Table II.

Table II. PERFORMANCE EVALUATION OF COMPONENT 1 USING PRECISION, RECALL, AND F1-SCORE ARE MEASURED ON MULTIPLE CLASSIFIERS.

Classification Model	Precision	Recall	F1-Score
KNN	0.92	0.91	0.91
Random Forest	0.99	0.99	0.99
Logistic Regression	0.98	0.97	0.98
SVM	0.97	0.97	0.97
Multinomial Naive Bayes	0.89	0.89	0.89

Table II, indicating that Random Forest achieved a significantly higher F1-Score compared to the other classifiers. This could be attributed to its ensemble learning approach, which combines multiple decision trees to improve classification accuracy and generalization. The inherent randomness in Random Forest helps reduce overfitting and increases robustness, which can lead to better performance, especially in complex datasets like the one being analyzed.

2) Component 2 Evaluation: The performance of the second component is evaluated using the following metrics:

- Cumulative Cost (CC): this metric measures the sum of the costs associated with all tasks or components assigned to the testbeds. The lower the CC, the more cost-effective the solution, aligning with our objective of minimizing expenses.
- Tardiness (T_i), also known as cumulative days difference, represents the difference between the actual start date and the requested start date for the tasks or components assigned to the testbeds. The lower the tardiness, the more efficient the solution, reflecting our aim for expedited project timelines.
- Cumulative Reward (CR): this metric, denoted as CR, is calculated by considering cost, priority, and days which is defined as follows:

$$CR = K \cdot \sum_{i=1}^{N}(L - p_i \cdot IC_i) - M \cdot \sum_{i=1}^{N}(T_i) - Makespan \tag{6}$$

where K, L, and M represent weights that require manual configuration by end users. N denotes the total number of requests, and T_i signifies the tardiness, calculated as the real starting time minus the requested time. Moreover, for each request, p_i denotes the priority of the request and IC_i corresponds to the cost of executing that request on its designated testbed. Makespan in 6 represents the total time required to complete a set of tasks on a given set of resources.

D. Performance comparison between Q-Learning and First Come, First Served (FCFS) scheduling approaches

As reviewed earlier in Section II, various approaches have been proposed for scheduling testbeds and environments in the state of the art. Among these methods, we have chosen to compare the performance of our proposed AI-based solution with the First Come, First Served (FCFS) scheduling approach. FCFS is widely utilized due to its simplicity and straightforward rule: it schedules the first request to arrive and allows it to run to completion. It is important to note that in certain real industrial cases, FCFS scheduling can enhance efficiency compared to more complex and advanced scheduling techniques. This is because FCFS prioritizes simplicity and immediacy, ensuring that tasks are processed in the order they are received. In scenarios where tasks have similar priorities or where quick turnaround times are critical, FCFS can provide a straightforward and effective solution. Additionally, FCFS minimizes the overhead associated with decision-making and prioritization, making it suitable for environments where resource allocation needs to be rapid and uncomplicated [7]. However, it is also crucial to acknowledge that FCFS may not always be the optimal choice, particularly in situations where task priorities vary significantly or where certain tasks require high costs. In such cases, more sophisticated scheduling algorithms, including AI-based approaches, may offer better performance by dynamically adjusting resource allocation based on various factors, such as task urgency, resource availability, and overall system optimization goals. Therefore, while FCFS remains a valuable and widely used scheduling strategy, its effectiveness ultimately depends on the specific requirements and constraints of the given scenario. As mentioned earlier, this case study involves the utilization of multiple testbeds and requests, each operating within distinct timelines. The study adheres to a set of rules extracted from EAB's industrial projects, which govern the allocation and scheduling of resources. These rules are meticulously applied to ensure the accuracy and relevance of the study's findings to real-world industrial scenarios. For the training of the Q-learning model, the following has been initialized:

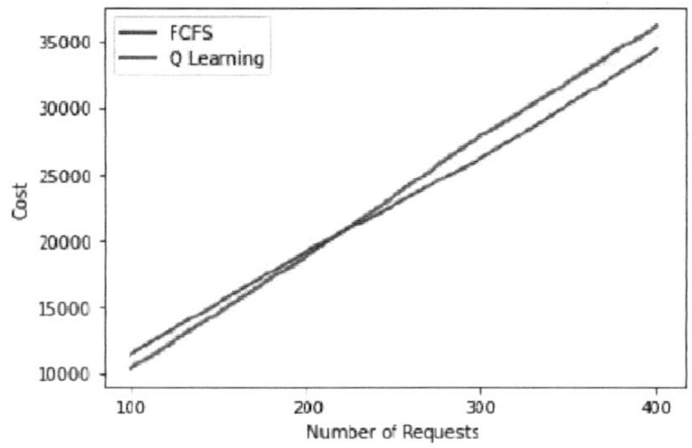

(a) Cumulative cost evaluation

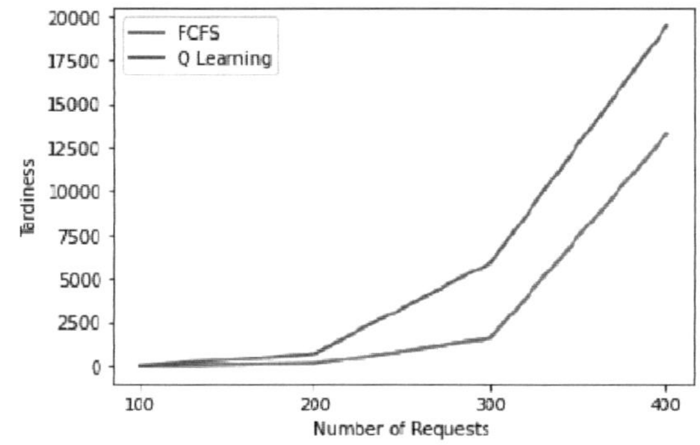

(b) Cumulative tardiness evaluation

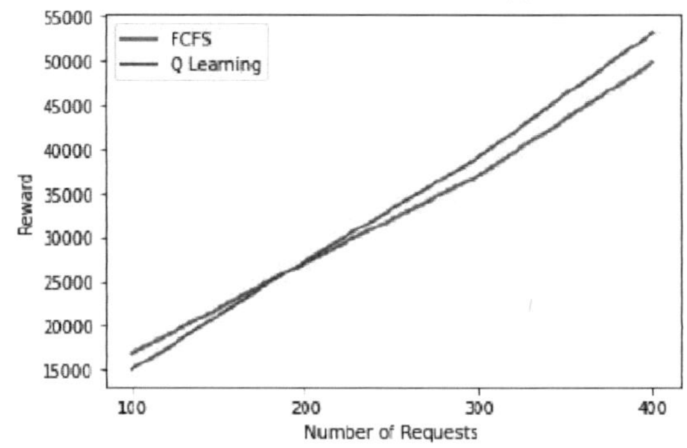

(c) Cumulative reward evaluation

Figure 4. Performance comparison of Component 2 with Q-learning and FCFS approaches, utilizing cost, tardiness, priority, and reward metrics.

1) The release timetable: each element is generated as a discrete random integer variable ranging from 0 to 20 (representing different starting weeks) with a uniform distribution.
2) The compatibility table: each element is generated as a boolean variable with a uniform distribution. Additionally, at least one testbed is compatible with each request.
3) The testbeds cost table: each element is randomly chosen from a set of real cost numbers of the testbeds provided by the industrial partner.
4) The priority table: each element is generated as a discrete random integer variable ranging from 1 to 5. The distribution decreases from 1 to 5, simulating that most requests have low priority while only a few requests have high priority.
5) The duration table: each element is generated as a discrete random integer variable ranging from 1 to 6 (representing different numbers of weeks). The distribution of 2 is higher while others are the same, simulating that the number of requests requiring two weeks is relatively higher based on our observation of real data.

Figure 4 presents a comparative performance study of the Q-learning and First-Come-First-Served (FCFS) scheduling approaches. This study delves into the metrics of cumulative cost, tardiness, priority, and reward as they relate to the number of processed requests. The results are encapsulated within three graphs, each depicting a unique aspect of performance and providing valuable insights into the effectiveness of the scheduling methods. Figure 4a demonstrates that the Q-learning method consistently surpasses FCFS in terms of cost optimization across different request volumes. This trend persists, highlighting the robustness of the Q-learning approach in reducing costs by up to 17% compared to the FCFS approach. Contrarily, Figure 4b demonstrates FCFS's strength in minimizing tardiness. It consistently exhibits high efficiency in this aspect compared to Q-learning. The Q-learning model excels in prioritizing both the cost-optimized allocation of testbeds for each request and their associated priorities. As depicted in Figure 4c, with the increase in requests, both strategies demonstrate a similar and consistent rise in rewards. Furthermore, the Q-learning approach outperforms the FCFS model, showcasing its superior performance as the workload intensifies. This convergence of reward trajectories highlights the comparable overall performance between Q-learning and FCFS, with Q-learning demonstrating its effectiveness in managing increasing request volumes. When the number of requests escalates from 100 to 400, employing the Q-learning approach leads to a significant 19% growth in the overall cumulative reward compared to the FCFS approach. In conclusion, the Q-learning algorithm offers a more economical solution despite its tendency to incur more tardiness compared to FCFS. The cumulative reward evaluation illustrates a noticeable trend of reward growth favoring Q-learning over FCFS. This trend suggests that Q-learning gradually outperforms FCFS in optimizing task allocation, showcasing its capability to achieve higher rewards as the number of requests increases. The Q-learning model used for comparison was trained over 1000 episodes with a learning rate of 0.1 and a discount factor of 0.9. This rigorous training regime underscores the reliability of the findings and the robustness of the Q-learning approach in scheduling testbeds effectively.

V. Discussion and Future Direction

The main objective of this study is to design, implement, and evaluate an AI-based expert system dedicated to scheduling C-RAN testbeds for diverse applications. In pursuit of this goal, we present the following contributions:

- Multiple Natural Language Processing (NLP) based approaches are used to extract critical keywords, enabling end users to configure and schedule a C-RAN testbed effectively. The extracted keywords are later embedded and presented in the GUI of the proposed solution in this study.
- Multiple machine learning models are employed to predict configurations for C-RAN testbeds based on end-user input.
- A Reinforcement Learning approach has been proposed for the optimal scheduling of testbeds, utilizing Q-learning to identify feasible time slots.
- These outlined phases are seamlessly integrated into a Python-based tool.

However, during conducting this study, several challenges have been faced including the lack of sufficient and balanced datasets makes the usage of oversampling necessary which may affect the model's performance in production due to overfitting [2]. Moreover, some potential threats to the validity of the obtained results in this study can be summarized as follows. Addressing these threats through sensitivity analysis, robust experimental design, and validation against real-world data can strengthen the reliability and generalizability of the results.

- Simulation assumptions: the results may be influenced by the assumptions made in the simulation environment. Assumptions regarding testbed compatibility, request priorities, and cost distributions could impact the generalizability of the findings to real-world scenarios.
- Parameter sensitivity: the performance of the algorithms could be sensitive to the choice of hyperparameters, such as learning rate, discount factor, and exploration-exploitation trade-off in the case of Q-learning. Small variations in these parameters may lead to different results and interpretations.
- Algorithm initialization: the initial state of the Q-learning algorithm, including the initialization of Q-values and exploration strategy, could impact the learning process and subsequent performance. Variations in initialization methods may yield different results.
- Environmental dynamics: the simulation environment may not fully capture the complexity and dynamics of real-world industrial scheduling scenarios. Factors, such as changing priorities, unexpected events, and resource constraints could influence the performance of the algorithms differently in practice.
- Evaluation metrics: the choice of evaluation metrics, such as cumulative cost, tardiness, and reward, may not fully capture the overall performance of the scheduling algorithms. Other important factors, such as resource utilization, scalability, and robustness, should also be considered for a comprehensive evaluation.

The future scope of this paper may involve transitioning to a multi-label categorization paradigm. In contrast to the existing method, multi-label categorization acknowledges the potential overlap or presence of distinct qualities by allowing the simultaneous examination of multiple test beds for a given set of functionalities. This transition would empower the model to identify more intricate linkages and nuances in the data, fostering a more comprehensive understanding of the underlying patterns. Expanding to multi-label categorization has the potential to unveil previously undiscovered aspects of predictive power. This is especially relevant in situations where a group of selections may concurrently belong to several testbeds. Such an extension could result in a classification model that is more resilient and adaptable, effectively handling scenarios in which examples exhibit different attributes and simultaneously belong to different categories. The enhanced model's ability to capture complex relationships within the data may lead to more accurate predictions and a deeper insight into the intricacies of the underlying system. Moreover, in this paper, our focus was on scheduling the currently existing testbed. However, the same approach can be extended to the creation of new testbeds in response to upcoming requests. In practice, testbeds can be commissioned for a limited period, leveraging the provided metadata specified in the submitted build requests. The decision on whether to retain, decommission, or update a testbed can be informed by the nature of upcoming requests. This expansion of the approach to include the creation of new testbeds allows for a more dynamic and adaptive system. The system can respond proactively to emerging requirements, optimizing resource allocation not only for the current testbeds but also for the potential introduction of new ones. This adaptability enhances the overall efficiency and responsiveness of the scheduling system, ensuring that the available resources are aligned with the evolving needs of the testing environment. Utilizing the above-mentioned approach has several advantages, particularly in terms of energy efficiency and environmental impact. The approach's adaptability to create new testbeds based on upcoming requests ensures that the testing environment can scale efficiently. This scalability is essential for accommodating growth in testing demands without compromising energy efficiency.

VI. Conclusion

Test optimization plays a crucial role in the software development life cycle, and effective scheduling of testbeds and environments stands out as a key strategy for achieving this optimization. In this paper, we have introduced, implemented, and evaluated our proposed approach and tool for scheduling C-RAN testbeds to facilitate testing across various applications. The AI-based expert system presented in this study provides a user-friendly GUI, allowing end-users to input requests in the form of high-level functions and metadata. The system comprises two main components. The first component automatically predicts and presents configurations that include the capability, capacity, and required features for testing a C-RAN application. The second component prioritizes testing requests for execution based on their metadata. Empirical evaluations conducted at Ericsson AB, combined with an analysis of results from an industrial project, confirm that the proposed AI-based system is a practical tool for scheduling testbeds effectively. Furthermore, the proposed system exhibits versatility in handling a diverse set of testing requirements and testbeds with distinct configurations. Its adaptability is evident in dynamically receiving and analyzing upcoming testing requests, providing different decisions based on the inserted requests. This adaptability ensures that the system remains responsive to changing testing needs and effectively manages the scheduling of testbeds accordingly. By optimizing the utilization of testbed resources, our approach not only improves operational efficiency but also aligns with sustainable practices. The dynamic management of testbeds, powering them on and off based on demand, contributes to energy efficiency and reduced environmental impact. This holistic approach positions our AI-based expert system as a comprehensive solution for testbed scheduling, combining user-friendliness, adaptability, and sustainability for an enhanced testing environment. In conclusion, while First Come, First Served (FCFS) offers a straightforward and easily implementable approach to scheduling, the utilization of reinforcement learning, such as Q-learning, presents significant advantages in handling dynamic environments, large datasets, and improving accuracy over time. The continuous learning capability of reinforcement learning algorithms allows for adaptability to changing conditions and optimization of resource allocation strategies. We need to consider that AI/ML-based approaches to industrial processes require an initial investment in terms of cost and effort. However, the return on investment typically outweighs these initial expenses [15] [16]. The enhanced efficiency, improved resource allocation, and ability to adapt to evolving conditions offered by reinforcement learning justify the adoption of such advanced techniques in industrial settings. Therefore, while FCFS and other traditional scheduling and optimization approaches remain viable options in certain scenarios, the recommendation is to leverage reinforcement learning algorithms for scheduling tasks in dynamic and data-intensive environments. This strategic shift towards AI/ML-based approaches promises to unlock new levels of productivity and efficiency in industrial operations, ultimately leading to substantial gains in performance and competitiveness.

Acknowledgments

This work was supported by the VINNOVA grant 2023-00244 through the D-RODS project.

References

[1] S. Tahvili, "Multi-criteria optimization of system integration testing", Ph.D. dissertation, Mälardalen University, Dec. 2018, ISBN: 978-91-7485-414-5.

[2] S. Tahvili and L. Hatvani, *Artificial Intelligence Methods for Optimization of the Software Testing Process With Practical Examples and Exercises*, Elsevier, Ed. Elsevier, Jun. 2022, ISBN: 978-0323919135.

[3] A. Younis, T. X. Tran, and D. Pompili, "Bandwidth and energy-aware resource allocation for cloud radio access networks", *IEEE Transactions on Wireless Communications*, vol. 17, no. 10, pp. 6487–6500, 2018.

[4] M. Felderer, E. P. Enoiu, and S. Tahvili, "Artificial intelligence techniques in system testing", in *Optimising the Software Development Process with Artificial Intelligence*, F. C. José Raúl Romero Inmaculada Medina-Bulo, Ed., Springer, Jun. 2023, ISBN: 978-981-19-9947-5.

[5] A. Arisha, P. Young, and M. El Baradie, "Job shop scheduling problem: An overview", in *International Conference for Flexible Automation and Intelligent Manufacturing (FAIM 01)*, 2001, pp. 682–693.

[6] N. Sariff and N. Buniyamin, "Comparative study of genetic algorithm and ant colony optimization algorithm performances for robot path planning in global static environments of different complexities", Jan. 2010, pp. 132–137.

[7] T. Aladwani, "Types of task scheduling algorithms in cloud computing environment", *Scheduling Problems-New Applications and Trends*, pp. 1–12, 2020.

[8] Y. Fonseca-Reyna, Y. Martinez, J. Cabrera, and B. Méndez-Hernández, "A reinforcement learning approach for scheduling problems", *Investigacion Operacional*, vol. 36, pp. 225–231, Jan. 2015.

[9] Y. M. Jiménez, "A generic multi-agent reinforcement learning approach for scheduling problems", *PhD, Vrije Universiteit Brussel*, vol. 128, 2012.

[10] J. Kaur, O. Singh, A. Anand, and M. Agarwal, "A goal programming approach for agile-based software development resource allocation", *Decision Analytics Journal*, vol. 6, p. 100 146, 2023, ISSN: 2772-6622.

[11] A. Anand, S. Das, O. Singh, and V. Kumar, "Resource allocation problem for multi versions of software system", in *2019 Amity International Conference on Artificial Intelligence (AICAI)*, 2019, pp. 571–576.

[12] Z. Wang, K. Tang, and X. Yao, "Multi-Objective Approaches to Optimal Testing Resource Allocation in Modular Software Systems", *IEEE Transactions on Reliability*, vol. 59, no. 3, pp. 563–575, 2010.

[13] P. Runeson and M. Höst, "Guidelines for conducting and reporting case study research in software engineering", *Empirical Softw. Engg.*, vol. 14, no. 2, pp. 131–164, Apr. 2009, ISSN: 1382-3256.

[14] A. Singh, *Real time optimization of testbeds*, https://github.com/Animesh963/Real-time-Optimization-of-Testbeds, 2024.

[15] H. Eljak *et al.*, "E-learning-based cloud computing environment: A systematic review, challenges, and opportunities", *IEEE Access*, vol. 12, pp. 7329–7355, 2024.

[16] S. Tahvili *et al.*, "Cost-benefit analysis of using dependency knowledge at integration testing", in *The 17th International Conference On Product-Focused Software Process Improvement*, Nov. 2016.

Symbolic Unfolding of Similarity-based Fuzzy Logic Programs

Ginés Moreno
Department of Computing Systems
University of Castilla-La Mancha
02071 Albacete (Spain)
Email: Gines.Moreno@uclm.es

José Antonio Riaza
Department of Computing Systems
University of Castilla-La Mancha
02071 Albacete (Spain)
Email: JoseAntonio.Riaza@uclm.es

***Abstract*—FASILL introduces "*Fuzzy Aggregators and Similarity Into a Logic Language*". In its symbolic extension, called sFASILL, some truth degrees, similarity annotations and fuzzy connectives can be left unknown, so that the user can easily figure out the impact of their possible values at execution time. In this paper, we adapt to this last setting a similarity-based, symbolic variant of unfolding rule, which is very well known in most declarative frameworks. This semantics-preserving transformation technique is based on the application of computational steps on the bodies of program rules for improving efficiency. The method has been implemented in a freely available online tool and, to the best of our knowledge, it represents the first approach for unfolding fuzzy logic programs coping with symbolic similarity relations.**

***Index Terms*—Fuzzy Logic Programming; Similarity; Symbolic Unfolding.**

I. Introduction

During the last decades, the logic language Prolog has been fuzzified by embedding similarity relations or using fuzzy connectives for dealing with truth degrees beyond $\{true, false\}$, respectively. We have recently combined both approaches in the design of FASILL [2], whose symbolic extension (inspired by our initial experiences with MALP [8]) is called sFASILL [11].

This last symbolic language is useful for *flexibly tuning* (according to users preferences) the fuzzy components of fuzzy logic programs. Although there exist other approaches which are able to *tune* fuzzy truth degrees and connectives [15][16][17], none of them manage similarity relations as the tuning technique we describe in [11] does. We have used sFASILL, and its tuning engine, for developing two real world applications in the fields of the semantic web [1] and neural networks [9].

Besides this, unfolding is a well-known and widely used semantics-preserving program transformation rule, which is able to improve programs, generating more efficient code. The unfolding transformation traditionally considered in pure logic programming consists in the replacement of a program clause C by the set of clauses obtained after applying a computation step in all its possible forms on the body of C [14][19].

In order to briefly illustrate the essence and benefits of the transformation, consider a very simple Prolog program containing a clause, say $p(X)$:-$q(X)$, and a fact, say $q(a)$, for defining two (crisp, not fuzzy) predicates, p and q. It is easy to see that both rules must be used in two computational steps for successfully executing a goal like $p(a)$. Alternatively, we can unfold the first clause by applying a computational step on its body $q(X)$ (using the fact $q(a)$) and next instantiating the head with the achieved substitution $\{X/a\}$. Then, the new unfolded rule is just the simple fact $p(a)$, which must be used in only one computational step (instead of two, as before) to solve goal $p(a)$. This very simple example reveals that all computational steps applied at unfolding time *remain compiled* on unfolded rules forever, and hence, those steps have no longer to be repeated in all subsequent executions of the transformed programs. This justifies why unfolding is able to improve the efficiency of transformed programs by accelerating their computational behaviour.

In [3][4], we successfully adapted such operation to fuzzy logic programs dealing with lattices of truth degrees and similarity relations, but this type of unfolding was not symbolic yet. On the contrary, in [10] we defined a symbolic version of the transformation but in absence of similarities. Inspired by both works, in this paper we plan to go an step beyond by fusing both approaches in the definition of a similarity-based symbolic transformation.

The structure of this paper is as follows. After summarizing, in Section II, the syntax of FASILL and sFASILL, in Section III we detail how to execute and unfold such programs. Finally, we conclude and propose future work in Section IV.

II. The FASILL Language and its Symbolic Extension

In this work, given a complete lattice L, we consider a first order language $\mathcal{L}_L$ built upon a signature Σ_L, that contains the elements of a countably infinite set of variables $\mathcal{V}$, function and predicate symbols (denoted by $\mathcal{F}$ and Π, respectively) with an associated arity—usually expressed as pairs f/n or p/n, respectively, where n represents its arity—, and the truth degree literals Σ_L^T and connectives Σ_L^C from L. Therefore, a well-formed formula in $\mathcal{L}_L$ can be either:

- A *value* $v \in \Sigma_L^T$, which will be interpreted as itself, i.e., as the truth degree $v \in L$.
- $p(t_1, \ldots, t_n)$, if $t_1, \ldots, t_n$ are terms over $\mathcal{V} \cup \mathcal{F}$ and p/n is an n-ary predicate. This formula is called *atomic* (atom, for short).
- $\varsigma(e_1, \ldots, e_n)$, if $e_1, \ldots, e_n$ are well-formed formulas and ς is an n-ary connective with truth function $[\![\varsigma]\!] : L^n \mapsto L$.

Definition 1 (Complete Lattice). A *complete lattice* is a partially ordered set $(L, \leq)$ such that every subset S of L

$\&_{\texttt{prod}}(x, y) \triangleq x * y$	$\vert_{\texttt{prod}}(x, y) \triangleq x + y - xy$	*Product logic*
$\&_{\texttt{godel}}(x, y) \triangleq \min(x, y)$	$\vert_{\texttt{godel}}(x, y) \triangleq \max(x, y)$	*Gödel logic*
$\&_{\texttt{luka}}(x, y) \triangleq \max(0, x + y - 1)$	$\vert_{\texttt{luka}}(x, y) \triangleq \min(x + y, 1)$	*Łukasiewicz logic*

Fig. 1. Conjunctions and disjunctions of three different fuzzy logics over $([0, 1], \leq)$.

has infimum and supremum elements. Then, it is a bounded lattice, i.e., it has bottom and top elements, denoted by $\bot$ and $\top$, respectively.

Example 1. In this paper, we use the lattice $([0, 1], \leq)$, where $\leq$ is the usual ordering relation on real numbers, and three sets of conjunctions/disjunctions corresponding to the fuzzy logics of Gödel, Łukasiewicz and Product (with different capabilities for modelling *pessimistic*, *optimistic* and *realistic scenarios*), defined in Figure 1. It is possible to also include other fuzzy connectives (aggregators) like the arithmetical average $@_{\texttt{aver}}(x, y) \triangleq (x + y)/2$ or the linguistic modifier $@_{\texttt{very}}(x) \triangleq x^2$.

Definition 2 (Similarity Relation)**.** Given a domain $\mathcal{U}$ and a lattice L with a fixed t-norm $\wedge$, a *similarity relation* $\mathcal{R}$ is a fuzzy binary relation on $\mathcal{U}$, that is, a fuzzy subset on $\mathcal{U} \times \mathcal{U}$ (namely, a mapping $\mathcal{R} : \mathcal{U} \times \mathcal{U} \to L$) fulfilling the following properties: reflexive $\forall x \in \mathcal{U}, \mathcal{R}(x, x) = \top$, symmetric $\forall x, y \in \mathcal{U}, \mathcal{R}(x, y) = \mathcal{R}(y, x)$, and transitive $\forall x, y, z \in \mathcal{U}, \mathcal{R}(x, z) \geq \mathcal{R}(x, y) \wedge \mathcal{R}(y, z)$.

The fuzzy logic language FASILL relies on complete lattices and similarity relations [2]. We are now ready for summarizing its *symbolic* extension where, in essence, we allow some undefined values (truth degrees) and connectives in program rules as well as in the associated similarity relation, so that these elements can be systematically computed afterwards. The symbolic extension of FASILL we initially presented in [11] is called sFASILL.

Given a complete lattice L, we consider an augmented signature $\Sigma_L^\#$ producing an augmented language $\mathcal{L}_L^\# \supseteq \mathcal{L}_L$, which may also include a number of symbolic values and symbolic connectives, which do not belong to L. Symbolic objects are usually denoted as $o^\#$ with a superscript $\#$ and, in our tool, their identifiers always start with $\#$. An $L^\#$-*expression* is now a well-formed formula of $\mathcal{L}_L^\#$, which is composed by values and connectives from L as well as by symbolic values and connectives. We let $\mathsf{exp}_L^\#$ denote the set of all $L^\#$-expressions in $\mathcal{L}_L^\#$. Given a $L^\#$-expression E, $[\![E]\!]$ refers to the new $L^\#$-expression obtained after evaluating as much as possible the connectives in E. Particularly, if E does not contain any symbolic value or connective, then $[\![E]\!] = v \in L$.

In the following, we consider *symbolic substitutions* that are mappings from symbolic values and connectives to expressions over $\Sigma_L^T \cup \Sigma_L^C$. We let $\mathsf{sym}(o^\#)$ denote the symbolic values and connectives in $o^\#$. Given a symbolic substitution Θ for $\mathsf{sym}(o^\#)$, we denote by $o^\#\Theta$ the object that results from $o^\#$ by replacing every symbolic symbol $e^\#$ by $e^\#\Theta$.

Definition 3 (Symbolic Similarity Relation)**.** Given a domain $\mathcal{U}$ and a lattice L with a fixed —possibly symbolic— t-norm $\wedge$, a *symbolic similarity relation* is a mapping $\mathcal{R}^\# : \mathcal{U} \times \mathcal{U} \to \mathsf{exp}_L^\#$ such that, for any symbolic substitution Θ for $\mathsf{sym}(\mathcal{R}^\#)$, the result of fully evaluating all L-expressions in $\mathcal{R}^\#\Theta$, say $[\![\mathcal{R}^\#\Theta]\!]$, is a similarity relation.

Definition 4 (Symbolic Rule and Symbolic Program)**.** Let L be a complete lattice. A *symbolic rule* over L is a formula $A \leftarrow \mathcal{B}$, where the following conditions hold:

- A is an atomic formula of $\mathcal{L}_L$ (the head of the rule);
- $\leftarrow$ is an implication from L or a symbolic implication;
- $\mathcal{B}$ (the body of the rule) is a symbolic goal, i.e., a well-formed formula of $\mathcal{L}_L^\#$;

A sFASILL *program* is a tuple $\mathcal{P}^\# = \langle \Pi^\#, \mathcal{R}^\#, L \rangle$ where $\Pi^\#$ is a set of symbolic rules, $\mathcal{R}^\#$ is a symbolic similarity relation between the elements of the signature Σ of $\Pi^\#$, and L is a complete lattice.

Example 2. Consider a symbolic sFASILL program $\mathcal{P}^\# = \langle \Pi^\#, \mathcal{R}^\#, L \rangle$ based on lattice $L = ([0, 1], \leq)$, where $\Pi^\#$ is the following set of symbolic rules:

$$\Pi^\# = \begin{cases} R_1: & vanguardist(rizt) \leftarrow 0.9 \\ R_2: & elegant(hydropolis) \leftarrow s_3^\# \\ R_3: & close(hydropolis, taxi) \leftarrow 0.7 \\ R_4: & good\_hotel(x) \leftarrow \\ & \quad @_{s4}^\#(elegant(x), @_{very}(close(x, metro))) \end{cases}$$

Note here that we leave unknown the level in which the hotel $hydropolis$ is more or less elegant (see the symbolic constant $s_3^\#$ in the second fact) as well as which should be the most appropriate connective for combining two features required on good hotels (see the symbolic constant $@_{s4}^\#$ in the body of the fourth rule).

The symbolic similarity relation $\mathcal{R}^\#$ on $\mathcal{U} = \{vanguardist, \quad elegant, modern, metro, taxi, bus\}$, is represented by the graph shown in Figure 2 (a matrix can be also used to represent this concept).

This symbolic similarity relation $\mathcal{R}^\#$ has been obtained after applying the closure algorithm we initially introduced in [11], which is inspired by [6][7][13] and, in essence, is an adaptation of the classical Warshall's algorithm for computing transitive closures. In this particular example, we have selected the symbolic t-norm $\&_{s2}^\#$ and the following set of similarity equations: $elegant \sim modern = s_0^\#$, $modern \sim vanguardist = 0.9$, $metro \sim bus = 0.5$ and $bus \sim taxi = s_1^\#$.

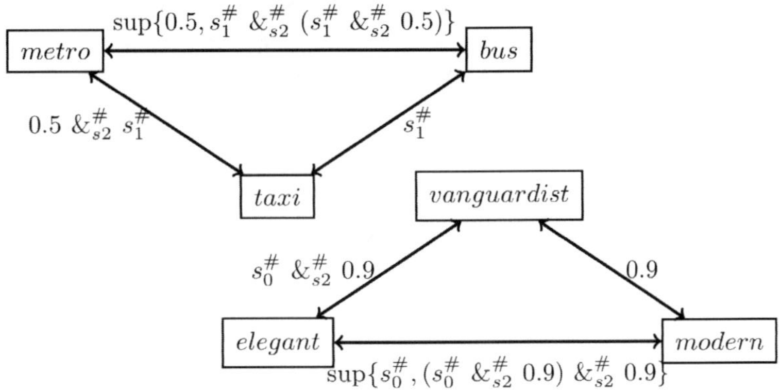

Fig. 2. Example of symbolic similarity relation $\mathcal{R}^\#$.

III. Running and Unfolding sFASILL Programs

As a logic language, sFASILL inherits the concepts of substitution, unifier and most general unifier (mgu) from pure logic programming, but extending some of them in order to cope with similarities, as Bousi∼Prolog [5] does, where the concept of most general unifier is replaced by the one of *weak most general unifier* (w.m.g.u.). One step beyond, in [11] we extended again this notion by referring to *symbolic weak most general unifiers* (s.w.m.g.u.) and a symbolic weak unification algorithm was introduced to compute them. Roughly speaking, the *symbolic weak unification algorithm* states that two *expressions* (i.e, terms or atomic formulas) $f(t_1, \ldots, t_n)$ and $g(s_1, \ldots, s_n)$ weakly unify if the root symbols f and g are close with a certain —possibly symbolic— degree (i.e. $\mathcal{R}^\#(f, g) = r \neq \bot$) and each of their arguments t_i and s_i weakly unify. Therefore, there is a symbolic weak unifier for two expressions even if the symbols at their roots are not syntactically equal ($f \not\equiv g$).

More technically, the symbolic weak unification algorithm can be seen as an reformulation/extension of the ones appearing in [18] (since now we manage arbitrary complete lattices) and [2][5] (because now we deal with symbolic similarity relations). In essence, the *symbolic weak most general unifier* of two expressions $\mathcal{E}_1$ and $\mathcal{E}_2$, say $wmgu^\#(\mathcal{E}_1, \mathcal{E}_2) = \langle \sigma, E \rangle$, is the simplest *symbolic substitution* σ of $\mathcal{E}_1$ and $\mathcal{E}_2$ together with its *symbolic unification degree* E verifying that $E = \hat{\mathcal{R}}(E_1\sigma, E_2\sigma)$.

Example 3. Given the complete lattice $L = ([0,1], \leq)$ of Example 1 and the symbolic similarity relation $\mathcal{R}^\#$ of Example 2, we can use the symbolic t-norm $\&_{s2}^\#$ for computing the following two symbolic symbolic weak most general unifiers: $wmgu^\#(modern(taxi), vanguardist(bus)) = \langle \{\}, 0.9 \ \&_{s2}^\# \ s_1^\# \rangle$ and $wmgu^\#(close\_to(X, taxi), close\_to(ritz, bus)) = \langle \{X/ritz\}, s_1^\# \rangle$

In order to describe the procedural semantics of the sFASILL language, in the following, we denote by $\mathcal{C}[A]$ a formula where A is a sub-expression (usually an atom) which occurs in the –possibly empty– context $\mathcal{C}[]$ whereas $\mathcal{C}[A/A']$ means the replacement of A by A' in the context $\mathcal{C}[]$. Moreover, $\mathcal{V}ar(s)$ denotes the set of distinct variables occurring in the syntactic object s and $\theta[\mathcal{V}ar(s)]$ refers to the substitution obtained from θ by restricting its domain to $\mathcal{V}ar(s)$. In the next definition, we always consider that A is the selected atom in a goal $\mathcal{Q}$, L is the complete lattice associated to $\Pi^\#$ and, as usual, rules are renamed apart:

Definition 5 (Computational Step). Let $\mathcal{Q}$ be a goal and σ a substitution. The pair $\langle \mathcal{Q}; \sigma \rangle$ is a *state*. Given a symbolic program $\langle \Pi^\#, \mathcal{R}^\#, L \rangle$ and a (possibly symbolic) t-norm $\wedge$ in L, a *computation* is formalized as a state transition system, whose transition relation $\leadsto$ is the smallest relation satisfying these rules:

1) *Successful step* (denoted as $\overset{\text{SS}}{\leadsto}$):

$$\frac{\langle \mathcal{Q}[A], \sigma \rangle \quad A' \leftarrow \mathcal{B} \in \Pi^\# \quad wmgu^\#(A, A') = \langle \theta, E \rangle \quad E \neq \bot}{\langle \mathcal{Q}[A/E \wedge \mathcal{B}]\theta, \sigma\theta \rangle} \text{ SS}$$

2) *Failure step* (denoted as $\overset{\text{FS}}{\leadsto}$):

$$\frac{\langle \mathcal{Q}[A], \sigma \rangle \quad \nexists A' \leftarrow \mathcal{B} \in \Pi^\# : wmgu^\#(A, A') = \langle \theta, E \rangle}{\langle \mathcal{Q}[A/\bot], \sigma \rangle} \text{ FS}$$

3) *Interpretive step* (denoted as $\overset{\text{IS}}{\leadsto}$):

$$\frac{\langle \mathcal{Q}; \sigma \rangle \text{ where } \mathcal{Q} \text{ is a } L^\#\text{-expression}}{\langle [\![\mathcal{Q}]\!]; \sigma \rangle} \text{ IS}$$

Definition 6 (Derivation and Symbolic Fuzzy Computed Answer). A *derivation* is a sequence of arbitrary length $\langle \mathcal{Q}; id \rangle \leadsto^* \langle \mathcal{Q}'; \sigma \rangle$. When $\mathcal{Q}'$ is an $L^\#$-expression that cannot be further reduced, $\langle \mathcal{Q}'; \sigma' \rangle$, where $\sigma' = \sigma[\mathcal{V}ar(\mathcal{Q})]$, is called a *symbolic fuzzy computed answer* (sfca). Also, if $\mathcal{Q}'$ is a concrete value of L, we say that $\langle \mathcal{Q}'; \sigma' \rangle$ is a *fuzzy computed answer* (fca).

The following example illustrates the operational semantics of sFASILL.

Example 4. Let $\mathcal{P}^{\#} = \langle \Pi^{\#}, \mathcal{R}^{\#}, L \rangle$ be the program from Example 2. It is possible to perform the following derivation for $\mathcal{P}^{\#}$ and goal $\mathcal{Q} = good\_hotel(x)$ obtaining the sfca $\langle \mathcal{Q}_1; \sigma_1 \rangle = \langle @^{\#}_{s4}(\&^{\#}_{s2}(\&^{\#}_{s2}(s^{\#}_0, 0.9), 0.9), 0.0); \{x/ritz\} \rangle$:

$$
\begin{array}{ll}
\langle \underline{good\_hotel(x)}, id \rangle & \overset{\text{SS}}{\leadsto}{}^{R4} \\
\langle @^{\#}_{s4}(\underline{elegant(x_1)}, @_{very}(close(x_1, metro))), \{x/x_1\} \rangle & \overset{\text{SS}}{\leadsto}{}^{R1} \\
\langle @^{\#}_{s4}(\&^{\#}_{s2}(\&^{\#}_{s2}(s^{\#}_0, 0.9), 0.9), & \\
\quad @_{very}(\underline{close(ritz, metro)})), \{x/ritz\} \rangle & \overset{\text{FS}}{\leadsto} \\
\langle @^{\#}_{s4}(\&^{\#}_{s2}(\&^{\#}_{s2}(s^{\#}_0, 0.9), 0.9), \underline{@_{very}(0.0)}), \{x/ritz\} \rangle & \overset{\text{IS}}{\leadsto} \\
\langle @^{\#}_{s4}(\&^{\#}_{s2}(\&^{\#}_{s2}(s^{\#}_0, 0.9), 0.9), 0.0), \{x/ritz\} \rangle &
\end{array}
$$

Apart from this derivation, there exists a second one ending with the alternative sfca $\langle \mathcal{Q}_2; \sigma_2 \rangle = \langle @^{\#}_{s4}(s^{\#}_3, @_{very}(\&^{\#}_{s2}(\&^{\#}_{s2}(0.5, s^{\#}_1), 0.7))); \{x/hydropolis\} \rangle$ associated to the same goal. Observe the presence of symbolic constants coming from the symbolic similarity relation, which contrast with our precedent work [8].

Now, let $\Theta = \{s^{\#}_0/0.8, s^{\#}_1/0.8, \&^{\#}_{s2}/\&_{\texttt{luka}}, s^{\#}_3/1.0, @^{\#}_{s4}/@_{\texttt{aver}}\}$ be a symbolic substitution that can be used for instantiating the previous sFASILL program in order to obtain a non-symbolic, fully executable FASILL program. This substitution can be automatically obtained by the tuning tool we described in [11] after introducing a couple of test cases (i.e., `0.4-> good_hotel(hydropolis)` and `0.6-> good_hotel(ritz)`), which represent the desired degrees for two goals accordingly to the user preferences.

Now we are ready to introduce the similarity-based symbolic unfolding transformations relying on the operational semantics described so far.

Definition 7 (Symbolic Unfolding). Let $\mathcal{P}^{\#} = \langle \Pi^{\#}, \mathcal{R}^{\#}, L \rangle$ be a sFASILL program and $R : (H \leftarrow \mathcal{B}) \in \Pi^{\#}$ be a rule (with non-empty body $\mathcal{B}$). Then, the *symbolic unfolding* of rule R in program $\mathcal{P}^{\#}$ is the new sFASILL program $\mathcal{P}'^{\#} = \langle \Pi'^{\#}, \mathcal{R}^{\#}, L \rangle$, where $\Pi'^{\#} = (\Pi^{\#} - \{R\}) \cup \{H\sigma \leftarrow \mathcal{B}' \mid \langle \mathcal{B}; id \rangle \leadsto \langle \mathcal{B}'; \sigma \rangle\}$.

Example 5. Let us built a transformation sequence where each sFASILL program in the sequence is obtained from the immediately preceding one by applying symbolic unfolding, except the initial one $\mathcal{P}^{\#}_0 = \langle \Pi^{\#}_0, \mathcal{R}^{\#}, L \rangle$, which, in our case, is the one illustrated in Example 2, that is:

$$
\Pi^{\#}_0 = \left\{
\begin{array}{ll}
R_1 : & vanguardist(rizt) \leftarrow 0.9 \\
R_2 : & elegant(hydropolis) \leftarrow s^{\#}_3 \\
R_3 : & close(hydropolis, taxi) \leftarrow 0.7 \\
R_4 : & good\_hotel(x) \leftarrow \\
 & \quad @^{\#}_{s4}(elegant(x), @_{very}(close(x, metro)))
\end{array}
\right.
$$

Program $\mathcal{P}^{\#}_1 = \langle \Pi^{\#}_1, \mathcal{R}^{\#}, L \rangle$ is obtained after unfolding rule R_4 (with selected atom $elegant(x)$) by applying a $\overset{\text{SS}}{\leadsto}$ step with rules R_1 and R_2:

$$
\Pi^{\#}_1 = \left\{
\begin{array}{ll}
R_1 : & vanguardist(rizt) \leftarrow 0.9 \\
R_2 : & elegant(hydropolis) \leftarrow s^{\#}_3 \\
R_3 : & close(hydropolis, taxi) \leftarrow 0.7 \\
R_{41} : & good\_hotel(ritz) \leftarrow @^{\#}_{s4}(\\
 & \quad \&^{\#}_{s2}(\&^{\#}_{s2}(s^{\#}_0, 0.9), 0.9), \\
 & \quad @_{very}(close(ritz, metro))) \\
R_{42} : & good\_hotel(hydropolis) \leftarrow \\
 & \quad @^{\#}_{s4}(s^{\#}_3, @_{very}(close(hydropolis, metro)))
\end{array}
\right.
$$

After unfolding rule R_{41} (with selected atom $close(ritz, metro)$) by applying a $\overset{\text{FS}}{\leadsto}$ step, we obtain program $\mathcal{P}^{\#}_2 = \langle \Pi^{\#}_2, \mathcal{R}^{\#}, L \rangle$:

$$
\Pi^{\#}_2 = \left\{
\begin{array}{ll}
R_1 : & vanguardist(rizt) \leftarrow 0.9 \\
R_2 : & elegant(hydropolis) \leftarrow s^{\#}_3 \\
R_3 : & close(hydropolis, taxi) \leftarrow 0.7 \\
R_{41F} : & good\_hotel(ritz) \leftarrow \\
 & \quad @^{\#}_{s4}(\&^{\#}_{s2}(\&^{\#}_{s2}(s^{\#}_0, 0.9), 0.9), @_{very}(0.0)) \\
R_{42} : & good\_hotel(hydropolis) \leftarrow \\
 & \quad @^{\#}_{s4}(s^{\#}_3, @_{very}(close(hydropolis, metro)))
\end{array}
\right.
$$

When unfolding rule R_{42} (with selected atom $close(hydropolis, metro)$) by applying a $\overset{\text{SS}}{\leadsto}$ step with rule R_3, we reach the program $\mathcal{P}^{\#}_3 = \langle \Pi^{\#}_3, \mathcal{R}^{\#}, L \rangle$:

$$
\Pi^{\#}_3 = \left\{
\begin{array}{ll}
R_1 : & vanguardist(rizt) \leftarrow 0.9 \\
R_2 : & elegant(hydropolis) \leftarrow s^{\#}_3 \\
R_3 : & close(hydropolis, taxi) \leftarrow 0.7 \\
R_{41F} : & good\_hotel(ritz) \leftarrow \\
 & \quad @^{\#}_{s4}(\&^{\#}_{s2}(\&^{\#}_{s2}(s^{\#}_0, 0.9), 0.9), @_{very}(0.0)) \\
R_{423} : & good\_hotel(hydropolis) \leftarrow \\
 & \quad @^{\#}_{s4}(s^{\#}_3, @_{very}(\&^{\#}_{s2}(\&^{\#}_{s2}(0.5, s^{\#}_1), 0.7)))
\end{array}
\right.
$$

Finally, by unfolding rule R_{41F} (with selected expression $@_{very}(0.0)$) after applying a $\overset{\text{IS}}{\leadsto}$ step, we obtain the final program $\mathcal{P}^{\#}_4 = \langle \Pi^{\#}_4, \mathcal{R}^{\#}, L \rangle$:

$$
\Pi^{\#}_4 = \left\{
\begin{array}{ll}
R_1 : & vanguardist(rizt) \leftarrow 0.9 \\
R_2 : & elegant(hydropolis) \leftarrow s^{\#}_3 \\
R_3 : & close(hydropolis, taxi) \leftarrow 0.7 \\
R_{41FI} : & good\_hotel(ritz) \leftarrow \\
 & \quad @^{\#}_{s4}(\&^{\#}_{s2}(\&^{\#}_{s2}(s^{\#}_0, 0.9), 0.9), 0.0) \\
R_{423} : & good\_hotel(hydropolis) \leftarrow \\
 & \quad @^{\#}_{s4}(s^{\#}_3, @_{very}(\&^{\#}_{s2}(\&^{\#}_{s2}(0.5, s^{\#}_1), 0.7)))
\end{array}
\right.
$$

In the previous example, it is easy to see that each program in the sequence produces the same set of sfca's for a given goal but reducing the length of derivations. For instance, the derivation performed w.r.t. the original program $\mathcal{P}^{\#}_0$ illustrated in Example 4, can be emulated in the final program $\mathcal{P}^{\#}_4$ with just one computational step (instead of four) as:

$$
\begin{array}{ll}
\langle good\_hotel(x); id \rangle & \overset{\text{SS}}{\leadsto}{}^{R41FI} \\
\langle @^{\#}_{s4}(\&^{\#}_{s2}(\&^{\#}_{s2}(s^{\#}_0, 0.9), 0.9), 0.0); \{x/ritz\} \rangle. &
\end{array}
$$

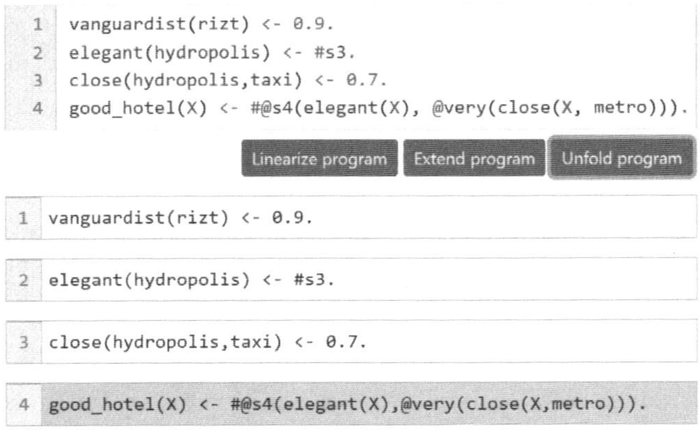

(a) Original sFASILL program before being transformed.

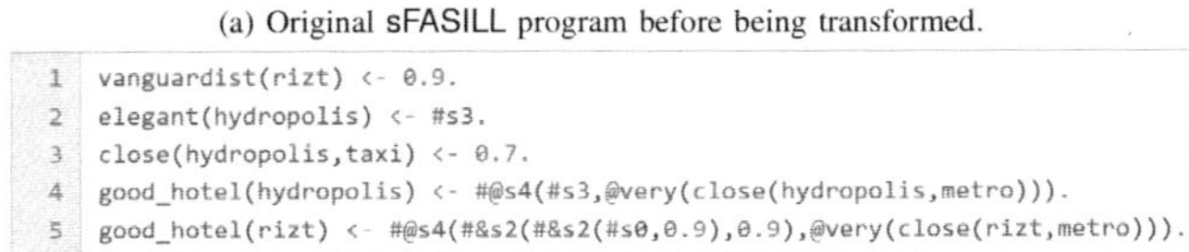

(b) sFASILL program obtained after unfolding the last program rule.

Fig. 3. The FASILL online tool unfolding a symbolic program.

However, in the symbolic case, the unfolding transformation is not always safe, as the following example reveals.

Example 6. Consider a sFASILL program $\mathcal{P} = \langle \Pi^{\#}, \mathcal{R}^{\#}, L \rangle$ whose symbolic similarity relation establishes that $\mathcal{R}^{\#}(a, b) = v^{\#}$ and $\mathcal{R}^{\#}(q, r) = 0.5$ with a fixed t-norm $\wedge = \&_{luka}$:

$$\Pi^{\#} = \left\{ \begin{array}{l} p(x) \leftarrow q(x, b) \\ r(a, a) \leftarrow 0.5 \end{array} \right. \quad \Pi'^{\#} = \left\{ \begin{array}{l} p(a) \leftarrow 0.5 \wedge 0.5 \wedge v^{\#} \\ r(a, a) \leftarrow 0.5 \end{array} \right.$$

Now, if we apply to $\mathcal{P}$ a symbolic substitution Θ which replaces $v^{\#}$ by 0.4 then, the unfolding of $\mathcal{P}\Theta = \langle \Pi^{\#}\Theta, \mathcal{R}^{\#}\Theta, L \rangle$, where $(\mathcal{R}^{\#}\Theta)(a, b) = 0.4$, produces the following set of rules:

$$(\Pi^{\#}\Theta)' = \{p(x) \leftarrow 0, \ r(a, a) \leftarrow 0.5\}$$

This program is different to the instantiated unfolded one (observe, in particular, that the head of the first rule in both programs are different):

$$\Pi'^{\#}\Theta = \{p(a) \leftarrow 0.5 \wedge 0.5 \wedge 0.4, \ r(a, a) \leftarrow 0.5\}$$

IV. Conclusion and Future Work

The symbolic extension of the FASILL language based on symbolic similarity relations we introduced in [11] has been used in this paper for developing an effective unfolding technique for sFASILL programs, which is available at [12] (see in Figure 3 two screenshots of a work session with the FASILL online tool, before and after unfolding a symbolic program). Here, we have surpassed both the similarity-based (but non-symbolic) unfolding of [3][4], thus permitting the optimization of sFASILL programs in an unified, similarity-based symbolic framework.

As ongoing work, we are nowadays developing the formal proofs that ensure the correctness of the transformation under certain safe applicability conditions.

Acknowledgment

This work has been partially supported by the EU (FEDER), the State Research Agency (AEI) of the Spanish Ministry of Science and Innovation under grant PID2019-104735RB-C42 (SAFER).

References

[1] J. M. Almendros-Jiménez, A. Becerra-Terón, G. Moreno, and J. A. Riaza, "Tuning fuzzy sparql queries," *International Journal of Approximate Reasoning*, vol. 170, pp. 109209, 2024.

[2] P. Julián, G. Moreno, and J. Penabad, "Thresholded semantic framework for a fully integrated fuzzy logic language," *J. Log. Algebr. Meth. Program.*, vol. 93, pp. 42–67, 2017.

[3] P. Julián, G. Moreno, and J. A. Riaza, "Seeking a safe and efficient similarity-based unfolding rule," *Int. J. Approx. Reason.*, vol. 163, pp. 109038, 2023.

[4] P. Julián, G. Moreno, and J. A. Riaza, "Some properties of substitutions in the framework of similarity relations," *Fuzzy Sets Syst.*, vol. 465, pp. 108510, 2023.

[5] P. Julián and C. Rubio, "A declarative semantics for bousi∼prolog," In *Proc. of 11th Int. ACM SIGPLAN Conference on Principles and Practice of Declarative Programming, PPDP'09, ACM*, pp. 149–160, 2009.

[6] P. Julián, "A procedure for the construction of a similarity relation," In *Proc. of the 12th International Conference on Information Processing and Management of Uncertainty in Knoledge-based Systems, IPMU'08, U. Málaga (ISBN 978-84-612-3061-7)*, pp. 489–496, 2008.

[7] A. Kandel and L. Yelowitz, "Fuzzy chains," *IEEE Trans. on Systems, Man, and Cybernetics*, vol. SMC-4, no. 5, pp. 472–475, 1974.

[8] G. Moreno, J. Penabad, J. A. Riaza, and G. Vidal, "Symbolic execution and thresholding for efficiently tuning fuzzy logic programs," In *Logic-Based Program Synthesis and Transformation, Proc. of the 26th International Symposium LOPSTR'16*, vol. 10184 LNCS-Springer, pp. 131–147, 2016.

[9] G. Moreno, J. Pérez, and J. A. Riaza, "Fuzzy logic programming for tuning neural networks," In *Rules and Reasoning - Proc. of the Third International Joint Conference, RuleML+RR'19*, vol. 11784 LNCS-Springer, pages 190–197, 2019.

[10] G. Moreno and J. A. Riaza, "An online tool for unfolding symbolic fuzzy logic programs," In *Advances in Computational Intelligence - Proc. of the 15th International Work-Conference on Artificial Neural Networks (Part II), IWANN'19*, vol. 11507 LNCS-Springer, pp. 475–487, 2019.

[11] G. Moreno and J. A. Riaza, "A safe and effective tuning technique for similarity-based fuzzy logic programs," In *Advances in Computational Intelligence - Proc. of the 16th International Work-Conference on Artificial Neural Networks, IWANN'21*, vol. 12861 LNCS-Springer, pp. 190–201, 2021.

[12] G. Moreno and J. A. Riaza, "FASILL: Sandbox," https://dectau.uclm.es/fasill/sandbox. *Accessed: 2024-06-24.*

[13] H. Naessens, H. De Meyer, and B. De Baets, "Algorithms for the computation of t-transitive closures," *IEEE Trans. Fuzzy Systems*, vol. 10, no. 4, pp. 541–551, 2002.

[14] A. Pettorossi and M. Proietti, "Rules and strategies for transforming functional and logic programs," *ACM Computing Surveys*, vol. 28, no. 2, pp. 360–414, 1996.

[15] L. De Raedt and A. Kimmig, "Probabilistic (logic) programming concepts," *Mach. Learn.*, vol. 100, no. 1, pp. 5–47, 2015.

[16] F. Riguzzi and T. Swift, "The PITA system: Tabling and answer subsumption for reasoning under uncertainty," *Theory Pract. Log. Program.*, vol. 11, no. 4-5, pp. 433–449, 2011.

[17] K. F. Sagonas, T. Swift, and D. S. Warren, "XSB as an efficient deductive database engine," In *Proc. of the ACM SIGMOD International Conference on Management of Data*, pp. 442–453, ACM Press, 1994.

[18] M. I. Sessa, "Approximate reasoning by similarity-based SLD resolution," *Theoretical Computer Science*, vol. 275, no. 1-2, pp. 389–426, 2002.

[19] H. Tamaki and T. Sato, "Unfold/Fold transformations of logic programs," In *Proc. of the Second International Conference on Logic Programming*, pp. 127–139, 1984.

A Comparative Study of Computational Intelligence Methods for Audio Analysis in Animal Identification within Tropical Ecosystems

Maria J. Guerrero
SISTEMIC, Engineering Faculty
Universidad de Antioquia UdeA
Calle 67 No.53-108
Medellín, Colombia
email: mariaj.guerrero@udea.edu.co

Santiago Taborda
SISTEMIC, Engineering Faculty
Universidad de Antioquia UdeA
Calle 67 No.53-108
Medellín, Colombia
email: santiago.taborda2@udea.edu.co

Juan M. Daza
GHA, Biology Institute
Universidad de Antioquia UdeA
Calle 67 No.53-108
Medellín, Colombia
email: juanm.daza@udea.edu.co

Claudia Isaza
SISTEMIC, Engineering Faculty
Universidad de Antioquia UdeA
Calle 67 No.53-108
Medellín, Colombia
email: victoria.isaza@udea.edu.co

***Abstract*—Passive Acoustic Monitoring (PAM) using computational intelligence techniques offers new avenues for biodiversity conservation, particularly in identifying and monitoring species within tropical ecosystems. While various methods exist for animal sound identification, a comprehensive understanding of their advantages and disadvantages is often lacking. This work evaluates five methods for automatically identifying species vocalizations across different taxonomic groups using an acoustic dataset from a Colombian agricultural ecosystem. We conducted a comparative analysis of supervised techniques, including Convolutional Neural Networks (CNN), Random Forest (RF), and Support Vector Machine (SVM), as well as unsupervised methods such as spectral clustering, DBSCAN, and the Learning Algorithm for Multivariate Data Analysis (LAMDA) 3pi, evaluating their species detection performance through the F1-Score metric. Our research underscores the critical role of methodological selection in achieving accurate species identification. Furthermore, this study advances the understanding of clustering interpretation, illustrating its potential beyond bioacoustic studies. It presents how unsupervised learning techniques can be valuable in scenarios characterized by limited labeled data, common in tropical ecosystems, and high uncertainty regarding the number of clusters obtained. This approach facilitates the exploration of prototype patterns, aiding species association and potentially extending to other areas requiring insight into unidentified clusters. This study offers valuable insights into selecting suitable tools for bioacoustic studies, emphasizing the need for comprehensive input preparation for model training. The findings underscore the potential of PAM and computational strategies in furthering biodiversity research and conservation efforts, effectively addressing the challenges of species identification and clustering interpretation.**

Keywords-Machine learning, Deep learning, Clustering, Bioacoustics, Soundscape, Species identification.

I. INTRODUCTION

Monitoring ecosystems and their species is crucial for understanding and conserving biodiversity [1]. Traditionally, species identification has been performed through direct observation, which faces significant challenges, such as detecting individuals in densely vegetated areas common in tropical ecosystems. Therefore, it is essential to have alternatives that support this task. Passive Acoustic Monitoring (PAM) emerges as an alternative tool that enables the identification of patterns in ecosystems using sound from different sources, such as biological organisms, geophysical phenomena, and human activities [2]. This alternative involves deploying acoustic sensors to record sounds across different areas, thereby serving as a helpful tool to detect the presence of animal species at a specific location and time, answering biological questions that help identify the conservation state of ecosystems due to external impacts [3].

The evolution of sensor technology has significantly enhanced the collection of acoustic data, allowing sampling for months at a time, recording every minute, resulting in vast volumes of acoustic recordings that must be processed and analyzed by biology and ecology experts [4], [5]. In the case of acoustic animal identification, this process, if conducted manually, demands extensive time to identify specific species' vocalizations or calls within each recording. Automatic species call detection algorithms offer a solution by employing various computational intelligence techniques to detect and classify animal vocalizations or calls from diverse taxonomic groups [6]–[11].

Generally, available methodologies encompass a series of stages, such as signal processing, in the case of machine learning methods, segmentation, and feature extraction stages, and finally, the implementation of algorithms to classify species calls. Many of these proposals are implemented in software solutions, such as Avisoft [12], Arbimon [13], and Kaleidoscope Pro [14], offering a practical application of these methodologies. On the supervised side, commonly used computational intelligence techniques include Convolutional Neural Networks (CNN) [8], [15], [16], Random Forest [17], [18], Support Vector Machine [18], [19], and Hidden Markov Models [12]. Meanwhile, in the unsupervised domain, techniques such as spectral clustering [14], LAMDA - Learning Algorithm for Multivariate Data Analysis - [10], [16], [20], and DBSCAN [21] are available.

Each technique within species identification brings its own set of characteristics and advantages, tailored to address distinct research questions ranging from species-specific, individual identification to the detection of multiple animal species. While supervised methodologies dominate the field, requiring extensive, labeled datasets for model training [22], unsupervised identification methods are necessary. These approaches, free from the constraints of prior species knowledge or labeled data, offer the potential to uncover data patterns indicative of specific species in a habitat, especially in countries with high biodiversity like Colombia, where unknown species to science still exist, making the process of obtaining large, labeled datasets difficult. However, the challenge with unsupervised techniques, such as clustering, primarily revolves around interpreting the results. Accurately associating each cluster with a particular species requires time and expert knowledge.

This work aims to analyze and compare different machine learning and deep learning methodologies, encompassing supervised and unsupervised approaches, proposed for automatically detecting calls and vocalizations of multiple animal species in soundscapes. Additionally, by leveraging the unsupervised approach proposed in [10], we performed an analysis to interpret clusters and automatically assign them to specific species. The performance of each method was assessed using a collection of audio recordings from the Colombian agricultural ecosystem. Our objective was to facilitate the selection of the most appropriate methodology tailored to the specific research problem, thereby advancing the field of bioacoustic monitoring by identifying the most effective tools for species identification in soundscapes.

The structure of this article is organized as follows: Section II outlines the data utilized, a description of the characteristics of the analyzed algorithms, and a description of clustering interpretation. Section III presents the results obtained from our analysis. Finally, conclusions and future work are drawn in Section IV.

II. Materials and Methods

A. Study site and acoustic dataset

The data used in this work were provided by Antioquia's Herpetological Group (GHA), collected via passive acoustic monitoring conducted in a rural area of the municipality of Puerto Wilches, Santander, Colombia ($7°21'52.5"N, 73°51'33.0"W$). The area of this study site is primarily dominated by oil palm plantations, accounting for 75% of the land, of varying ages. Additionally, it encompasses a diverse mixture of secondary vegetation (7.6%), forest patches (6.13%), grasslands (5.5%), and aquatic vegetation zones (3.2%). The region is dotted with several buildings and crisscrossed by a secondary road network that serves the palm oil and livestock industries.

The analyzed dataset is composed of acoustic data from the audible and ultrasonic spectrum. Audible data consists of a subset of 207 recordings from the primary collection (19,598 recordings), which were rigorously labeled by experts to make the comparison. Experts found 11 species, including six bird species, four anuran species, and one primate. This dataset was collected using a Song Meter Mini device (Wildlife Acoustics, Inc.), configured to record one minute every 10 minutes with a sampling rate of 48 kHz. The ultrasonic dataset consists of 197 recordings collected in the same location as the audible dataset using a Song Meter Mini bat device (Wildlife Acoustics, Inc.), recording 15 s every 15 min with a sampling rate of 384 kHz. In these recordings, 7 species of bats were found. Labels provided by experts were used for the training process of supervised methods and the validation of unsupervised methods.

B. Computational intelligence methods for species identification

The selection of computational intelligence methods for multi-species identification started with a detailed literature review to ascertain the most widely used and popular methodologies in the field. This preliminary phase aims to identify techniques that have been effectively implemented in both software applications and open-source code environments. Further, our analysis examined both supervised and unsupervised learning approaches, ensuring a comprehensive understanding of their application in species identification tasks. The selected approaches are described as follows:

1) Arbimon [13]: Arbimon is a free web-based platform that enhances passive acoustic monitoring with cloud storage and data analysis capabilities. It utilizes artificial intelligence algorithms, such as Random Forest for the supervised classification of animal vocalizations and includes a BETA version of a clustering tool that employs the DBSCAN algorithm for enhanced vocalization detection and categorization. The analysis in this software starts with uploading audio databases to the web platform and organizing them into playlists, which are crucial for the model's training phase. The platform facilitates audio labeling through a pattern matching tool by selecting the acoustic pattern of interest, streamlining the training of the Random Forest model with identified species presences and absences. Additionally, Arbimon is developing an unsupervised tool that includes Acoustic Event Detection (AED) and cluster analysis, using the same database for Random Forest model training. This process requires setting species-specific parameters, such as species frequency information and thresholds, to detect and classify vocalizations accurately. The importance of precise parameter configuration is crucial to achieving accurate detection and analysis outcomes. Each parameter was fine-tuned according to specific species requirements.

2) Raven Pro/Koogu [23]: This methodology integrates the widely recognized Raven Pro software, created by the Cornell Lab of Ornithology [24], known for its spectrogram visualization and manual species calls labeling tools, with the Koogu Python library, designed to train a convolutional neural network model using Raven's selection table. The process involves manually labeling species calls on the Raven platform, organizing species labels and audio recordings, as well as configuring parameters in the Convolutional Neural Network (CNN) model. In this case, a DenseNet architecture was trained, where parameterization included species-specific bandwidth information, the number of training epochs, and batch size. Upon completion of the model's training, the results can be incorporated back into Raven Pro to observe the identification of species calls. In our study, each species was trained individually, allowing for the fine-tuning of parameters to the specific requirements of each species, ensuring precise and effective species identification.

3) Kaleidoscope Pro [14]: This software requires a paid license and is designed to detect animal vocalizations in audible and ultrasound spectrum through a Hidden Markov Model (HMM) and spectral clustering. The use of this software begins with the preparation of an initial database containing audio recordings of the targeted species. This software demands the configuration of several parameters, such as frequency range, the maximum and minimum detection durations, and the maximum time interval between vocalizations, all of which were manually adjusted for each species under study. The clustering analysis option also requires setting the maximum distance to the cluster center, the Fast Fourier Transform (FFT) window size, the number of maximum states, and the maximum cluster number. In this case, after testing with different values, most parameters were maintained at their default settings; the FFT window size was adjusted according to the frequency range of interest (5.33 ms [128 @0–12 kHz, 256 @13–24 kHz, 512 @25–48 kHz, and 1024 @49–96 kHz]).

4) Unsupervised Acoustic Animal Identification [10]: This unsupervised methodology proposed by Guerrero et al. (2023) employs the LAMDA 3pi algorithm to analyze acoustic data without needing pre-defined labels in the database. The methodology simultaneously facilitates analysis across the audible spectrum and ultrasound for multiple species. It includes a segmentation stage that isolates potential acoustic events or species calls, followed by a feature extraction stage that captures relevant acoustic information from each segment. The process culminates in a fuzzy clustering stage, which groups segments based on acoustic similarity, enabling the simultaneous identification of multiple species associated with various taxonomic groups. Although this method effectively identifies vocalizations in all frequency ranges simultaneously and does not require user-defined parameters, it has difficulties with cluster interpretation. The generation of numerous clusters, while beneficial for exhaustive audio analysis, poses a significant challenge for researchers due to the number of clusters to analyze and the inherent intra-cluster variation that results from data uncertainty. This aspect can make the manual examination of each cluster labor-intensive and complex, underscoring a critical consideration in the balance between comprehensive analysis and practical feasibility.

C. Clustering interpretation

Addressing a prevalent challenge in species identification via clustering, we focus on the manual linking between clusters and species-specific vocal patterns. While this method is not constrained by the requirement for labeled data, the process of interpreting clustering results can be time-consuming for experts. We used the fuzzy clustering approach presented in [10], which decomposes the soundscape into acoustic entities named sonotypes (clusters). This method not only validates the possibility of associating sonotypes with species calls but also reveals that the aggregation of these clusters provides insights into acoustic biodiversity patterns over time. Remarkably, this biodiversity pattern aligns with those identified by alternative methods, with the distinctive advantage of enabling the breakdown of these patterns by individual species, a feature unattainable with other techniques.

To streamline the process, our study also ventured into automating the linkage of sonotypes to species by utilizing readily available public datasets or targeted species-specific recordings, aiming to minimize manual efforts in interpreting clustering outcomes.

Pursuing the methodology described in [10], we generated clusters or sonotypes and segmented calls of species detected in the study site utilizing directional recordings from preceding studies and datasets from sources such as xeno-canto [25]. We extracted pivotal time-frequency features from these segments, including minimum and maximum vocalization frequencies, bandwidth, peak frequency, and call duration. These features are also automatically extracted when generating sonotypes. The fuzzy clustering approach enables the determination of each segment's membership degree to its assigned cluster, thereby identifying the cluster's representative element, the segment with the highest degree of belonging to its cluster.

The association of sonotypes to species was then achieved by calculating the Euclidean distance between the median value of the bandwidth, maximum, and minimum frequency bands of the representative elements and the 10 segments with the highest membership values of each sonotype, alongside the same features of manually species segments. Scatter plots illustrating the minimum and maximum frequencies of both species segments and sonotypes aided in visually confirming similarities.

D. Evaluation metrics

In the performance evaluation section, the effectiveness of the algorithms for detecting species calls was assessed using confusion matrices. These matrices were constructed by comparing the original labels from the database against the predictions made by each model, providing values for True Positives (TP), True Negatives (TN), False Positives (FP), and False Negatives (FN). True Positives represent correctly identified presences, True Negatives denote correctly identified absences, False Positives indicate presences incorrectly classified as absences and False Negatives refer to absences incorrectly classified as presences.

To evaluate model accuracy, especially in cases with unbalanced datasets across different classes, the F1-Score metric is extensively used. This metric, derived from the confusion matrix for each analyzed methodology, offers a balanced measure of a model's precision and recall. The F1-Score is calculated using the following formula:

$$F1 - score = 2 \times \frac{\text{precision} \times \text{recall}}{\text{precision} + \text{recall}} \quad (1)$$

where precision is defined as the ratio of correctly predicted positive cases to the total predicted positives, indicating the accuracy of positive predictions and recall measures the ratio of actual positives accurately identified by the model, reflecting the model's ability to capture all relevant cases.

III. Results

A. Analysis of computational intelligence methods for species identification

We applied the different methods to our dataset for species identification across different frequency bands, including those within the ultrasound range. For each species, models were constructed using Arbimon in both supervised and unsupervised manners, as well as in the case of Raven Pro/Koogu and Kaleidoscope Pro, highlighting the general limitations of simultaneously identifying multiple species and species-specific parameterization. Figure 1 showcases the F1-score results achieved with each method, detailing performance across broad taxonomic groups and specific species.

The literature presents several detection proposals for ultrasound species analysis. Within this domain, Kaleidoscope Pro and the approach introduced by Guerrero et al. [10], are distinguishable in their methodologies for effectively identifying both ultrasound and audible species.

Utilizing the Random Forest algorithm, Arbimon exhibited high performance in accurately detecting mammal species and certain bird species. This level of accuracy, however, was not mirrored in the detection of anuran species, with the models notably underperforming in identifying *Leptodactylus fuscus* and *Leptodactylus fragilis*.

The advent of Arbimon's BETA tool, which adopts a cluster analysis via the DBSCAN algorithm, signaled a significant advancement in the identification capabilities for mammals and some avian species, marking an improvement over its supervised analog. Yet, it too faltered with anurans, unable to discern the calls of *Leptodactylus fuscus* and *Leptodactylus fragilis*. Achieving results with this methodology proved challenging due to clustering interpretation. There is no tool to automatically associate clusters with species labels. Additionally, the fine-tuning of detection parameters, such as duration, bandwidth, and threshold areas, became pivotal, as

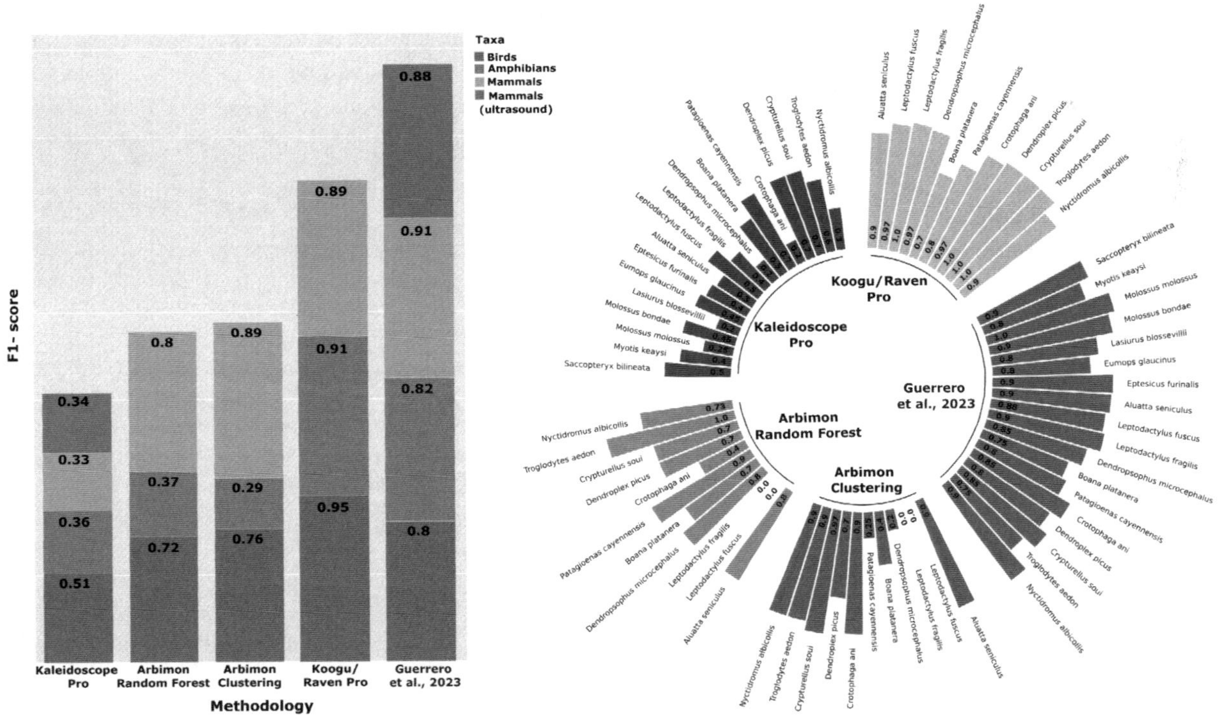

Figure 1. Comparative F1-score results for species identification methodologies. The bar graph on the left delineates the F1-score performance of different methodologies applied to various taxonomic groups. The radial chart on the right provides a detailed breakdown of the F1-scores for each species within these groups.

they significantly influenced the detector's sensitivity to the diverse vocalization characteristics inherent to each species. An improper adjustment of these parameters often resulted in either an overabundance of irrelevant acoustic events or a failure to identify critical species-specific vocal segments, which subsequently compromised the clustering process.

The methodology developed by the Cornell Lab of Ornithology seamlessly combines Raven Pro's capabilities for manual call segmentation and time-frequency feature extraction with the Python library Koogu for generating Convolutional Neural Network (CNN) models. This approach has displayed remarkable efficacy, showcasing high F1-scores across all examined taxonomic groups and most of the species cataloged, thus reinforcing CNNs' versatility and powerful pattern recognition capabilities. CNNs' ability to automatically learn and distinguish subtle differences in spectrogram patterns enables precise species identification from acoustic data.

Koogu is specifically designed to recognize labels from a Raven Pro selection table, making the initiation of the CNN model training straightforward. However, this process faced its own set of challenges, particularly when bandwidth configurations were narrowly aligned with the spectral extremities of segments identified in Raven Pro. To circumvent this constraint, a strategy involving the use of expanded bandwidths was adopted, allowing for a more generous and inclusive detection range.

The performance of Kaleidoscope Pro, in contrast, was found to be less effective than other methods. This tool tended to produce segments of prolonged duration that captured a variety of calls and classified them based on the most prominent pattern in the spectrogram. Consequently, this often led to clusters representing insect stridulations due to their high-intensity frequencies. Moreover, the presence of clusters with vocalizations from multiple species complicated the process of selecting a representative cluster for each species. While Kaleidoscope Pro provides a manual interface for cluster-to-species association, the task can be complex and prone to inaccuracies when sifting through a vast number of clusters, particularly when some contain a significant amount of noise.

Finally, the approach proposed by Guerrero et al. [10], capable of concurrently detecting species across different frequency bands, showcased F1-scores exceeding 0.75 for all taxonomic groups and species, ultrasound range included. A notable advantage of their fuzzy clustering model is calculating the membership degree of the segments to their assigned clusters. This capability enables further data processing by setting a segment membership threshold. This threshold helps to minimize the number of false positives in the final detections, thereby enhancing the accuracy of species detection. This method also allows for a graphical cluster-to-species association using the acoustic pattern and the sound of the cluster segments. However, similar to Kaleidoscope Pro, this task can be time-consuming if there are a large number of clusters.

B. Clustering interpretation

Implementing the methodology described in Section II-C, our endeavor in clustering interpretation sought to streamline the automatization of associations between species-specific vocalizations and corresponding sonotypes. Within the scope of the audible spectrum study conducted, the LAMDA 3pi algorithm generated 130 clusters, 6 of them successfully associated with 5 out of the 11 species accentuated in Section III-A. This subset of species encompasses three avian species: *Cryptorellus soi*, *Dendroplex picus*, and *Nyctidromus albicollis*, along with two anurans: *Dendropsophus microcephalus* and *Leptodactylus fuscus*. Vocalizations for these species were

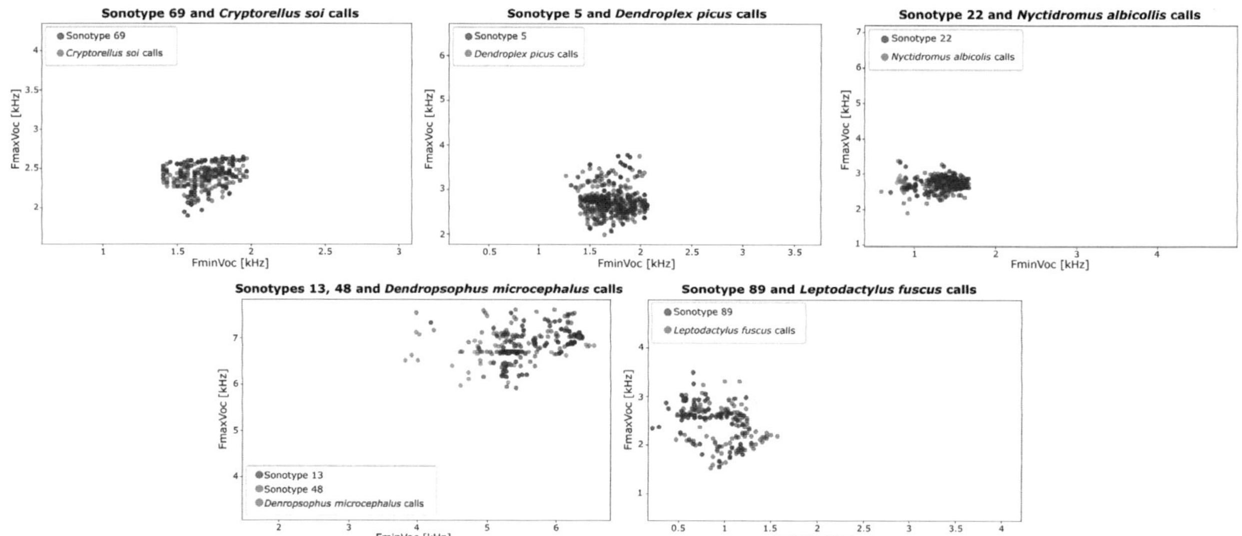

Figure 2. Clustering association results displaying the relationship between sonotypes and species-specific calls. Scatter plots show the minimum frequency (FminVoc) and maximum frequency (FmaxVoc) features for sonotypes (blue dots) and manual call segments (red dots) for select bird and anuran species.

extracted from public datasets, with avian calls being curated from xeno-canto [25] and anuran calls sourced from AmphibiaWeb [26]. This alternative provides valuable support for experts by minimizing the requirement for extensive labeled data to train models.

Figure 2 presents a visual representation of two pivotal acoustic features for the automatic association of species. Each blue and green dot in this figure represents an acoustic segment automatically generated utilizing Guerrero et al. [10] proposed framework. Conversely, the red dots depict manually extracted segments from public databases, showcasing the intersection and validation of automated clustering against recognized species-specific acoustic signatures.

In the case of anuran species *Dendropsophus microcephalus*, it was observed that more than one cluster could be associated with a single species (sonotype 13 and 48). This represents an advantage, as it allows for the description of the variability in the species' calls across multiple clusters, thereby revealing distinct vocal patterns. Such granularity in clustering could prove beneficial for future analyses, offering insights into the diverse calls produced by species.

Due to the need for more information on species present in the study location in public databases, we were able to automatically associate just 5 of 11 audible species that we know are present on the site. Labels for the other species identification were just used for cluster association validation.

IV. Conclusion and Future Work

This work provides pivotal insights for researchers seeking to select the most fitting tools for biodiversity exploration via acoustic monitoring and automatic call recognition. Our comparative study assessed the performance of various computational intelligence methods, focusing on both machine and deep learning techniques across different taxonomic groups using audio recordings from an agricultural ecosystem. Evaluating these methods with the F1-Score metric, we uncovered the critical need to adapt the choice of methodology to the specific requirements of targeted species. This adaptation is crucial, as we observed significant variances in effectiveness across birds, amphibians, and mammals, each presenting unique challenges that demand specific analytical solutions. Additionally, our findings highlight the importance of comprehensive input preparation for model training (labels, audio formats, among others) and understanding the specifications and requirements of each tool to maximize the advantages of passive acoustic monitoring and automatic detection in biodiversity studies. We also present an approach to cluster interpretation and species association using minimal data, making clustering a promising alternative for grouping patterns and labeling them without extensive expert intervention when labeled data is scarce.

Our results underscore the importance of selecting methodologies based on the specific biological question, whether it involves identifying calls from a particular species or detecting multiple species within an ecosystem. Supervised learning methods, particularly CNNs, are highly effective when sufficient labeled data is available and when the focus is on specific species identification. In contrast, unsupervised methods provide valuable alternatives in data-scarce environments, especially when the goal is to identify the biophonic components of the landscape. Furthermore, the significance of streamlining parameter configuration and adopting strategies that enhance the reproducibility of results was emphasized. For instance, leveraging Koogu to train classifiers from Raven-exported selection tables facilitates the sharing and replication of experimental data among collaborators, potentially enhancing model accuracy through retraining with Koogu-generated results, in a similar way as the methodology presented by Guerrero et al. [10].

By comparing machine learning and deep learning approaches, we pinpointed machine learning's superior capability in understanding and interpreting the features pivotal to the success of the learning model. This insight was particularly evident in our analysis with the LAMDA 3pi clustering algorithm, where features extracted from species calls, commonly utilized by experts for manual identification, aided significantly in cluster interpretation through membership degree information. This methodology not only deepens our comprehension of clustering results but also illustrates its applicability in other scientific domains facing similar challenges of undefined cluster numbers and a scarcity of labeled examples for supervised learning.

While we successfully established automatic species-to-cluster associations based on frequency attributes such as minimum and maximum frequencies, bandwidth, and peak frequency, the overlap of these features among different species poses a challenge in discrimination. To overcome this, employing additional information, such as unique signal features identifying vocalization differences within the same frequency ranges, may prove effective. This approach can significantly improve species differentiation, showing the importance of selecting and fine-tuning features critical to accurately identifying and conserving biodiversity.

Future research should focus on advancing supervised methods to reduce dependence on large amounts of labeled data by using novel computational frameworks, such as few-shot learning. Additionally, addressing the challenge of model parameter setting is crucial in practical applications. From an unsupervised perspective and related to clustering interpretation, future research should explore the clustering variability observed within species calls, where multiple clusters can be associated with a single species. This approach allows for the analysis of call patterns, their features, and the specific circumstances under which they are produced, providing a deeper understanding of species dynamics. Integrating acoustic data with other ecological datasets, such as habitat characteristics and climate data, can provide a deeper understanding of ecosystem health and dynamics, leading to more robust tools for biodiversity monitoring and conservation

Acknowledgment

This work was supported by Universidad de Antioquia - CODI and Alexander von Humboldt Institute for Research on

Biological Resources [code project:2020-33250]. Data from Puerto Wilches was funded by Universidad de Antioquia, SGI, and Ecopetrol under contract FOGR09.

REFERENCES

[1] J. Gibbs, H. Snell, and C. Causton, "Effective monitoring for adaptive wildlife management: Lessons from the galapagos islands," *Journal of Wildlife Management*, vol. 63, pp. 1055–1065, 1999. DOI: 10.2307/3802825.

[2] B. Pijanowski *et al.*, "Soundscape ecology: The science of sound in the landscape," *BioScience*, vol. 61, pp. 203–216, 2011. DOI: 10.1525/bio.2011.61.3.6.

[3] P. Wrege, E. Rowland, S. Keen, and Y. Shiu, "Acoustic monitoring for conservation in tropical forests: Examples from forest elephants," *Methods in Ecology and Evolution*, vol. 8, 2017. DOI: 10.1111/2041-210X.12730.

[4] M. Acevedo and L. Villanueva-Rivera, "Using automated digital recording systems as effective tools for the monitoring of birds and amphibians," *Wildlife Society Bulletin*, vol. 34, pp. 211–214, 2006. DOI: 10.2193/0091-7648(2006)34[211:UADRSA]2.0.CO;2.

[5] R. Gibb, E. Browning, P. Glover-Kapfer, and K. E. Jones, "Emerging opportunities and challenges for passive acoustics in ecological assessment and monitoring," *Methods in Ecology and Evolution*, vol. 2019, no. September 2018, pp. 169–185, 2018, ISSN: 2041210X. DOI: 10.1111/2041-210X.13101.

[6] D. Stowell and J. Sueur, "Ecoacoustics: Acoustic sensing for biodiversity monitoring at scale," *Remote Sensing in Ecology and Conservation*, vol. 6, pp. 217–219, 3 2020. DOI: 10.1002/rse2.174.

[7] Z. Zhao *et al.*, "How well do acoustic indices measure biodiversity? computational experiments to determine effect of sound unit shape, vocalization intensity, and frequency of vocalization occurrence on performance of acoustic indices," *Ecological Indicators*, vol. 107, 2019.

[8] J. LeBien *et al.*, "A pipeline for identification of bird and frog species in tropical soundscape recordings using a convolutional neural network," *Ecological Informatics*, vol. 59, p. 101 113, 2020. DOI: 10.1016/j.ecoinf.2020.101113.

[9] J. Xie *et al.*, "Acoustic classification of frog within-species and species-specific calls," *Applied Acoustics*, vol. 131, pp. 79–86, 2018. DOI: 10.1016/j.apacoust.2017.10.024.

[10] M. J. Guerrero, C. L. Bedoya, J. D. López, J. M. Daza, and C. Isaza, "Acoustic animal identification using unsupervised learning.," *Methods in Ecology and Evolution*, vol. 14, pp. 1500–1514, 2023. DOI: 10.1111/2041-210X.14103.

[11] Z. J. Ruff, D. B. Lesmeister, C. L. Appel, and C. M. Sullivan, "Workflow and convolutional neural network for automated identification of animal sounds," *Ecological Indicators*, vol. 124, p. 107 419, 2021. DOI: 10.1016/j.ecolind.2021.107419.

[12] Avisoft Bioacoustics, *Avisoft-saslab pro: Sound analysis and synthesis laboratory*, https://www.avisoft.com/, Accessed: 2024-05-20, 2024.

[13] T. Aide *et al.*, "Real-time bioacoustics monitoring and automated species identification," *PeerJ*, vol. 103, 2013. DOI: doi.org/10.7717/peerj.103.

[14] Wildlife Acoustics, "Kaleidoscope pro 5 user guide," *Wildlife Acoustics, Inc.: Maynard, MA, USA*, 2020.

[15] J. Xie *et al.*, "Frog calling activity detection using lightweight cnn with multi-view spectrogram: A case study on kroombit tinker frog," *Machine Learning with Applications*, vol. 7, p. 100 202, 2021. DOI: 10.1016/j.mlwa.2021.100202.

[16] C. L. Bedoya and L. E. Molles, "Acoustic censusing and individual identification of birds in the wild," *bioRxiv*, 19 2021. DOI: 10.1101/2021.10.29.466450.

[17] C. Corrada Bravo, R. Álvarez Berríos, and T. Aide, "Species-specific audio detection: A comparison of three template-based detection algorithms using random forests," *PeerJ Computer Science*, vol. 113, 2017. DOI: 10.7717/peerj-cs.113.

[18] M. Malfante, M. Dalla Mura, J. Mars, and C. Gervaise, "Automatic fish sounds classification," *Journal of the Acoustical Society of America*, vol. 139, pp. 2115–2116, 2016. DOI: 10.1121/1.4950295.

[19] N. K. Widyastuti, A. Aibinu, M. Salami, R. Akmeliawati, and A. Muthalif, "Animal sound activity detection using multi-class support vector machines," *4th international conference on mechatronics (ICOM). IEEE*, 2011. DOI: 10.1109/ICOM.2011.5937122.

[20] C. Bedoya, C. Isaza, J. M. Daza, and J. D. López, "Automatic recognition of anuran species based on syllable identification," *Ecological Informatics*, vol. 24, pp. 200–209, 2014. DOI: 10.1016/j.ecoinf.2014.08.009.

[21] F. Michaud, J. Sueur, M. Le Cesne, and S. Haupert, "Unsupervised classification to improve the quality of a bird song recording dataset," *Ecological Informatics*, vol. 74, p. 101 952, 2022. DOI: 10.1016/j.ecoinf.2022.101952.

[22] L. S. M. Sugai, T. S. F. Silva, J. W. Ribeiro, and D. Llusia, "Terrestrial passive acoustic monitoring: Review and perspectives," *BioScience*, vol. 69, pp. 5–11, 1 2019, ISSN: 15253244. DOI: 10.1093/biosci/biy147.

[23] B. Miller, S. Madhusudhana, M. Aulich, and N. Kelly, "Deep learning algorithm outperforms experienced human observer at detection of blue whale d-calls: A double-observer analysis," *Remote Sensing in Ecology and Conservation*, vol. 9, 2023. DOI: 10.1002/rse2.297.

[24] Cornell Lab of Ornithology, *Raven pro: Interactive sound analysis software (version 1.6)*, https://ravensoundsoftware.com/, Ithaca, NY: The Cornell Lab of Ornithology. Accessed: 2024-05-20, 2024.

[25] Xeno-canto Foundation, *Xeno-canto: Sharing bird sounds from around the world*, https://www.xeno-canto.org, Accessed: 2024-05-20, 2024.

[26] AmphibiaWeb, *Amphibiaweb: Information on amphibian biology and conservation*, https://amphibiaweb.org, Accessed: 2024-05-20, 2024.

Optimising Value Creation in Service System Design: Digital Twin of the Organisation for Customer Journeys

Uwe V. Riss, Wolfgang Groher
Institute for Information and Process Management
Eastern Switzerland University of Applied Sciences
St.Gallen, Switzerland
email: {uwe.riss, wolfgang.groher}@ost.ch

***Abstract*—This paper focuses on optimising value creation and co-creation in service-based, interaction-oriented applications using digital technologies like digital twins. Digital technologies play a crucial role in enhancing customer experiences, improving service quality, and streamlining processes in service systems, making it essential to systemise value creation in service systems. Previous efforts have focused on digital transformation and service design but neglected the role of human activity. This contribution addresses the utilisation of digital twins for managing digital and person-based services in traditional sectors, offering a unique perspective on optimising value creation in interaction-oriented service systems. The solution involves leveraging the Service-Oriented Activity System methodology to enhance the value of digital twins by considering their characteristics in service design and optimisation.**

***Keywords*—digital twin of the organisation; insight engine; customer journey representation; value of digital applications; service-oriented activity systems.**

I. INTRODUCTION

Digital technologies and digitalisation of processes provide opportunities for new ways of value creation. However, to fully exploit the potential of this approach, the perspective must be shifted from a company-centred view to service systems in ecosystems [1] [2]. This concerns service design that must explicitly take value creation into account [3] [4]. Service systems have been defined as value creating "configurations of people, technology, value propositions connecting internal and external service systems, and shared information." [5].

Currently, the main framework to describe the creation of value creation in service systems is Service-Dominant Logic (SDL) [6]. However, once the interaction between digital services and human actors becomes more intense, human action must be included in the consideration. In this respect, Activity Theory (AT) has proven its strength in describing tool-mediated systems of collaborating actors, which includes the interaction with technologies [7]. Recently, a synthesis of SDL and AT has been suggested that connects the strengths of both approaches to deal with systems that are characterised by close interaction of digital technologies and human actors. This synthesis, called Service-Oriented Activity Systems (SOAS), describes how service systems and human actors work together to optimize the value created in service-based applications [8].

In this paper, we will show how the SOAS framework supports service design in enhancing the value creation opportunities of digital technologies as means of human action beyond simple automation of activities and make use to the specific strengths of digital service systems. We will apply SOAS to the concept of Digital Twins of an Organisation (DTO), which is a more recent development [10]. As one possible application of DTO, this paper will examine the support of service management processes [9]. We will demonstrate this using the example of the digital twin of an organisation. Digital twins have been successfully applied in various fields [11].

For related work, we can to Meierhofer and West [12] who have shown that digital twins can serve as data providers and enablers to increase the value creation in service systems. Recently, Bart et al. [13] have presented another framework for designing value creation through digital twins, which does not go back to theories like SDL or ST and presents a rather empirically oriented framework. Wagner and Cozmiuc [14] have argued that digital twins are a suitable addition to new technologies such as extended reality. Woitsch et al. [15] have pointed out that simulation with digital twins help estimate the impact of specific decisions and, thus minimise the risk.

This paper is based on a case study in which a DTO tool is developed for a service organisation in the quality management sector. [16] The entity for which the DTO has been developed is the set of all Customer Journeys (CJ) conducted by the service recipients. The central questions to be answered by applying the SOAS framework: How can DTO enhance the value creation for the management that operates with it? How is the service system to be designed to make use of such value creation opportunities? This application is also a test for the SOAS framework how well value creation in the design of such a service system can be supported.

The paper is organised as follows. Section II describes the details of the case study on which the investigation is based. Section III summarises the central features of SOAS in terms of service and activity coordination. In Section IV, we apply the SOAS framework to the case of the DTO elaborating the 5 value dimensions described by SOAS and concretise them individually. Finally, in Section V, we discuss the findings and insights gained from applying the framework to derive indications for further use.

II. Case Study — Service Sector

The case study, to which this investigation refers, is related to a Swiss service company offering trainings and certifications. Their offerings consist in traditional offline services which are more and more complemented by digital services. Labour costs that make up more than 80% of the total costs are crucial factor, which makes digitalisation attractive, in particular if it supports the customer relationships. Since the traditional services are already largely individualised, the introduction of additional digital services leads to even more complex customer interactions. This investigation focuses on a DTO that encompasses the existing CJ associated with the company. The aim is to systematically design the digitalisation that is related to the introduction of these tools. Details can be found in [9].

A. Customer Journey

The concept of CJ refers to the processual and experiential aspects of service processes from the customers' perspective as they become manifest in the data that report the interaction with customers (e.g., emails, conversation notes). The CJ encompass various types of interactions resulting in specific customer experiences that are described as touchpoints [17].

The systematic management of CJ supports sales and quality of customer services by using information of previous interaction with customers as well as information about these customers from external sources. It aims at detecting shortcomings in the customer processes and at preparing future interactions. Main data sources are a Customer Relationship Management (CRM) system for internal information and commercial third-party databases for external information.

As we will show in the following, the straightforward approach of management only addresses the surface of customer interaction and does not take advantage of the full potential of digitalisation.

B. Digital Twin of an Organisation

Digital Twins of an Organisation (DTO) are inspired by digital twins in industrial engineering, where they support production and other processes [18]. Digital twins are virtual representations of physical objects or settings that allow for a bidirectional information flow between digital and physical constituents [19]. Digital twins stand out due to their information aggregation, real-time capabilities and visualisation that support human decision making. The core idea of DTO is the transfer of this concept to organisational settings [20].

The special challenge of DTO lies in the fact that they describe sociotechnical systems with open and often unclear boundaries. However, the complexity of today's CJ requires tools like DTO that provide a high degree of information aggregation and a comprehensible visual interface.

For the further consideration, it is important to also have a look at the DTO architecture. Generally, one distinguishes 5 layers in DTO [21]: (1) data collection, (2) data processing, (3) model-based data aggregation, (4) analytic processing, and (5) visualisation. For the current case, layer (4) and partially layer (2) have been realised by an insight engine that we present in the following. In contrast to a traditional digital twin, the data collection layer (1) does not consist of sensors, but it receives data from the company's CRM system and external sources. The complexity of data for the DTO does not consist in their mass but in their heterogeneity due to the various nature of sources and the fact that they are mainly textual.

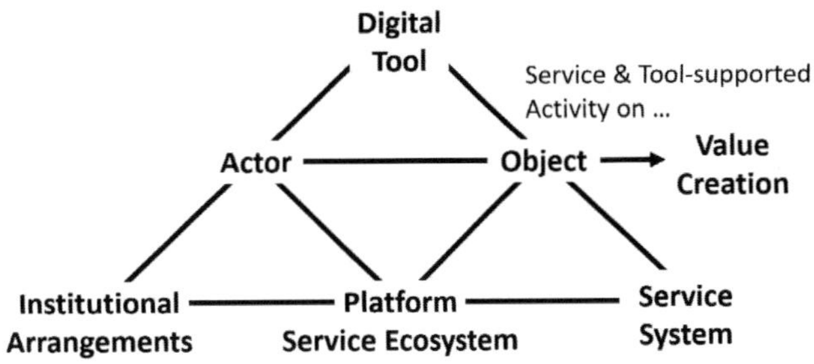

Fig. 1. Overview of the SOAS framework according to Riss et al. [8].

C. Insight Engines

We have used the insight engine of Squirro [22] for the implementation of some of the mentioned layers and tightly integrated the insight engine with the DTO. The analytic services of the insight engine support text mining und structuring. The engine is also open for using knowledge graphs and machine learning. In addition, it is used to access external data sources that are processed by its analytical services.

Through an API to the company's CRM system, it is also possible to get access to internal data. In this respect, the insight engine also implements the data processing layer. With its variety of services and processing pipelines, the insight engine is ideal for processing textual data.

III. Service-oriented Activity Systems

The SOAS framework has been developed to explore the interplay of digital services and human activities in terms of value creation when actors use specific digital tools to achieve their goals. [8] The framework describes in which way such tools interact with a service system and how the interaction with the service system creates value for the actor. The general structure of SOAS is depicted in Figure 1.

Human actions are generally related to an object upon which the actor performs the action. The object is thoroughly relevant for the actor. The interaction can also happen within an organisation for which the actor is working. Both objects and tools can interact with digital services. Central questions that the framework addresses are how the value creation for an individual actor can be increased in the service system and what this means for the service system and the digital tool.

As long as human activities and services can be clearly separated, we can treat the activity and the service system separately. In cases, in which the human action significantly interferes with the digital services, this separation does not work any longer. These cases increasingly gain relevance as the interplay of human action and digital services becomes more and more important. The growing importance becomes manifest in the increasing number of smart applications, in which human activities and digital services are tightly linked to generate value [23]. Therefore, smartness is a clear indicator for digital tools that require a joint approach.

We will use the term smart in contrast to the term *intelligent* for applications with significant user interaction, that is, not for autonomous applications. In this sense, user recommendations in online shops are smart while autonomously driving vehicles should be mainly regarded as intelligent when they use artificial intelligence to move around without a human driver. Against this background, the SOAS framework is applicable to smart application but not necessarily to intelligent applications.

To address both digital service and activity-related aspects of value creation, the SOAS framework has been derived as a synthesis from Service-Dominant Logic (SDL) [24] and Activity Theory (AT) [25]. The connection between the two perspectives is the value creation, which is attributed to the service beneficiary in SDL and to the actor in AT. SDL describes value co-creation as the result of the integration of resources provided by several services whereas in AT value creation is related to the successful accomplishment of human action [26].

At the centre of SOAS, there is the actor who uses information provided by services to achieve a specific objective. This centrally concerns decision making, which mostly depends on evaluating existing information. The target upon which the actors intend to act mostly appears to them as an object. This focal object can be any artefact or organisational component that is of interest and needs to be acted upon. Examples are production systems or organisational processes. Action on the focal object is expected to produce some value for the organisation. In the example of a production system, the action can consist in maintenance activities that prevent costly downtimes.

While tools are under the control of the organisation, services that support the action are mostly provided by external partners. These partners are organised in a service ecosystem that is related to a service system, which allows the access to individual partner services. The service must support the distribution of tasks among the available services so that more complex tasks can be performed. The service system also requires a digital platform that gives service users access to all services in the ecosystem and supports their combination. Moreover, the interaction of services is mediated by agreements about the use of service interfaces that ensure that the individual service components work together.

Finally, the handling of service systems requires human actors who control the service system and are supported by tools that are designed to fit to the respective activities. To this end, actors need tools that reduce the complexity of the available service systems. The value created depends on how well tools support the human coordination of available services.

IV. Application of the SOAS Framework

SOAS suggests 5 dimensions that contribute to the value generation by digital technologies: Dematerialisation, Objectification, Servitisation, Platformisation and Institutionalisation. They start from the user activities and enhance them by digital services to create value by integrating additional resources (e.g., services) made available in the ecosystem [27]. In the following, we contextualise these dimensions for the case study and point out the meaning for the development of the service system around the DTO. We will investigate these 5 value dimensions for the DTO used in the current case study.

A. Dematerialisation

The idea of dematerialisation (DEM) goes back to [28] and describes the separation of information from the material object that produces this information. In the current case study, the challenge consists in defining the proper material object because the object consists in the collection of CJ, an object that cannot be measured by sensors.

The major feature of a DTO is to replace sensor data by information that determines the process to be observed. This includes emails, phone notes, tasks produced in the process (in the current case mostly accessible from a CRM system) as well as information from external sources such as commercial newsfeeds or company data bases. The aggregation level is higher in this case compared to sensor data in a machine whereas the volume of data is lower. The major task consists in associating such information with the respective CJ.

The value resulting from DEM consists in bringing together various sources of information related to the CJ in real-time. This also concerns the presentation of the DTO which can be augmented by such information immediately on the actor's request. For the CJ, the open boundaries of the system represented in the DTO are important since the inclusion of external information sources provides insights that might not be comprehensible from an insight perspective only.

B. Objectification

Objectification (OBJ) refers to the fact that human comprehension and action is usually directed towards an object [29]. Whereas DEM leads to a breakdown of the object structure and a disintegration into a plethora of informational bits, OBJ aims at reuniting this information for the purpose of human sensemaking and intervention. It is not only that information is physically integration (e.g., in a large number of diagrams of a dashboard) but also logically by establishing semantic relationships between pieces of information. DT can be seen as the most obvious incarnation of OBJ and it is not surprising that the idea of DT directly follows servitisation at its heels [30].

The current DTO expresses various relationships between pieces of information. Primarily, it provides a temporal order that helps identify causes and effects. Secondly, information is organised per customer, which opens other aggregations such as for business or regional sectors. The multitude of different aggregation makes it necessary to allow for specific views of the object that still serves as common reference point of all these views.

The value that results from OBJ is to make it easier for human actors dealing with the DTO to faster comprehend features. Patterns can be identified more easily if the individual clues that make up this pattern are not too dispersed. Thus, the DTO improves the actor's comprehension of the CJ by providing a coherent object which the actor can explore through different views. This accelerates the actor's comprehension of different situations and leads to faster and less error-prone decision making.

C. Servitisation

Servitisation (SRV) describes the decomposition of a service system into interacting service modules [31]. While DEM only enhances the accessibility of information, SRV improves the processing of this information by flexibly employing a variety of services to enhances the informational content provided to the actor. Services can aggregate information according to specific rules or they can identify patterns in complex ensembles of data. Services can involve other actors, who contribute to the execution of a task by their specific expertise.

In the case study, the external information sources can be regarded information services provided by third parties. However, it is not only the raw information that is provided by the service included in an insight engine [23]. Hereby, the mass of available external data is aggregated according to the purpose of analysing the CJ. For example, this might concern questions regarding the market environment of a particular customer or group of customers.

The value of SRV in the DTO consists in making further information processing available in an instant. Services that utilise external data source enhance the information provided for the CJ. They do not only add this information to the visual DTO, but they help analyse the interaction with the customers. For example, it is possible to look for specific occasions that happened to a customer or their sectors during the CJ and can explain why customers took certain decisions reflected in the CJ.

D. Platformisation

According to Poel et al. [32], a platform is a "(re-)programmable digital infrastructure that facilitates and shapes personalised interactions" among actors and service providers, "organised through the systematic collection, algorithmic processing, monetisation, and circulation of data." Such infrastructure does not only enable services to work together but also allows actors to interact with these services. Platformisation (PLA) stands for the creation of access and interaction opportunities for service providers around a digital platform [33]. Such a platform must provide services and infrastructure to service providers that allow them to join the ecosystem. The central value of platformisation from the actors' perspective consists in the speed and variety of providing services that enable them to accomplish their tasks better. For example, this might include search facilities or analytical functionalities.

DTO can be understood as interfaces between the physical and the virtual world. In this respect, they make digital services available for acting upon the respective physical object. This allows actors to use the available services in a flexible manner. In the current case, the insight engine provides the Data Processing Layer for the DTO [9]. This reflects the crucial role of information retrieval for using the DTO. The platform character of the insight engine comes to the fore when one regards how it makes information available. Among other features, it gives access to a variety of commercial data bases, data analytics services and machine learning facilities. Moreover, it provides access to various internal information systems (e.g., the customer relationship management system). It also enables the use to large language models [34].

The connection between the DTO and platformisation is related to the platform's task to organise the access to the services. Which services are required depends on the part of the DTO that is analysed. For example, the actor examines a specific part of the CJ for those customers that belong to a specific sector. While the actor recognises an increased activity of customers in a certain period of time, it is possible to use context information provided by the DTO to search company data bases for news that might be related to the customers' activities. Thus, the specific section of the DTO implicitly helps to formulate a specific search and accelerates the search process. The platform offers the actor search tools fitting to the issue the actor is dealing with.

E. Institutionilisation

Institutionalisation (INS) refers to the process of establishing norms, rules, standards, meaning and even organisational boundaries that enable and constrain human action [35]. This concerns various issues regarding the CJ: Who gets control over which customer and other information? How is the payment of service use organised? How do service providers get access to the service systems or the platform? These questions must be clarified to ensure the viability of the service system.

For the CJ, a central issue is the access to external information sources. Regarding the technical side, such access is no problem, but the access is not free and it must be clarified how much the access to these data sources costs while using the DTO and whether the resulting value for the actor is large enough to justify these costs. A successful DTO that establishes a widely used digital platform can impose institutional pressure on service providers to deal with this platform [36].

The specific value of a DTO for the actor resulting from INS consists in the growing relevance of the DTO as a platform that allows to control the conditions under which services are made available. This can be related to the price of a service but also to its quality that might improve due to the competition between different service providers.

F. Synthesis of the Different Dimensions

The strategic perspective in developing a DTO for the CJ must keep in the focus the value of the DTO for actors working with it. The purpose of the DTO for the CJ has been seen in the possibility to path the way how customers interact with the company over various touchpoints.

In this sense, it is primarily an *analytical tool*. This purpose is supported by dematerialisation and servitisation which starts from the available CRM data, augments them by further information about customers provided by external data providers and analyses all information by means of an insight engine from another service provider. Other services can be included as they are needed.

The analytical component is further supported by the objectification made available by the DTO. Here, the objective is to go beyond the usual information presentation of digital dashboards towards a visual and semantically enriched provision of information in a comprehensible object. It is important that human actors mainly make sense of their environment through their visual and object-centred capabilities. Actors may decide which information they can additionally need for the analysis of the DTO. We must distinguish two different situations: (1) Actors want to make sure that the CJ is not disturbed and runs smoothly. The DTO should provide means to make this visible. (2) Actors might also face exceptional situations that fundamentally differ from their routines and require extraordinary analytical tools. These cases are usually unpredictable and often required non-standard analytical services.

Servitisation is the basic condition to provide such services but not sufficient to make them available in time. To support decision making, it has been shown that the object representation can be enhanced by advisory services that improve the quality of decision [36].

Here, platformisation comes into play. A digital platform can offer a variety of services that actors choose as they need them. However, a digital platform usually requires more than one service beneficiary to be economically viable. This means that the platform might be opened to other potential service providers and beneficiaries. In a first approach, customers and partners of the central service provider can be such beneficiaries; customers get a better insight of the service and access to related information, partners can better exchange information and get access to customer information. With this transition, the DTO becomes a *digital platform* for a variety of customers around the CJ.

V. Discussion of the Results

We have pursued two objectives in this study. On the one hand, we wanted to find out how the added value of DTOs can be increased through an associated service system and how services can be integrated for this purpose. To this end, we were able to show that DTOs should not only be understood as an analytical tool, but also offer further opportunities for value creation via the service system. A first version of the visualization of the CJ could be realised. From the first experiences the challenges of the implementation becomes clear.

(1) Dematerialisation: Whereas the access to external data proved to be easy (except for the costs related), the collection of internal data via the CRM system proved to be a challenge. Interaction often takes place verbally and is not always adequately recorded in the system. Data quality is another issue in this respect.

(2) Objectification: For the first, the visual representation of the customer journey gives users an idea of what is going on in the CJ. Selecting certain part of the CJ and applying specific filters, brings up new questions and provides new insights. Here, the challenge is rather that the opportunities are not yet fully understood, which needs more time.

(3) Servitization: The integration between the CRM system and the services provided by the insight engine works well but the idea to include more services required more integration efforts that comes at a cost. We expect this to become demand-driven in the future.

(4) Platformization: The idea that a platform can be used to access new services is not particularly strong because it is an approach that does not correspond to the usual procedures. This step required more conviction.

(5) Institutionalisation: Working in networks is already well established in the company. However, the transfer of this collaboration to a digital media is not a matter of course. New rules how to use the digital service system and the DTO must be established and this takes time.

(6) The interplay of the different dimensions is not yet understood as being natural. In particular, working with the visual DTO increases the need for support from digital services, which can be seen as a driver for greater coordination of dimensions. The integration of a platform could require the most rethinking of employees and management.

The second objective was to prove that the SOAS framework is a suitable instrument for the design of digital tools and associated service systems. The described results show that the SOAS framework can help tool and service designers in the development process by pointing out the interactions between human behaviour and the performance of service systems. Accordingly, optimization of value creation is not meant in a quantitative sense but must be understood qualitatively, i.e., that service designers must consider *all* dimensions and how they work together. A promising path forward might consist in a stepwise approach that start form the visual component and the employees' demands in working with it. It quickly becomes clear that more services mean faster and better decisions. In particular, AI-based services seem to be rather attractive in this respect. The demand for more services and information san then support the acceptance of a platform as common access point. This can be seen as the next step in this optimisation. The establishing of new rules and collaboration must happen in parallel to accompany this process. A decisive step consist in opening up the platform to other parties. Here, the value creation lies in the potential synergies with these new parties.

The focus for future development will be the closer integration of the visual CJ and the insight engine. This requires more experience of users working with the system to come up with information demands stimulated by the DTO. One particular interest is the combination of aspects of the DTO (via selected parts of the CJ) with AI-based natural-language inquiries that refer to the selected aspects. We see particular potential in this type of use.

ACKNOWLEDGMENT

The authors would like to acknowledge financial support from Innovation project 101.623 IP-SBM, by Innosuisse.

REFERENCES

[1] R. Adner, and R. Kapoor, "Value creation in innovation ecosystems: How the structure of technological interdependence affects firm performance in new technology generations," Strategic management journal, vol. 31 no. 3, pp. 306-333, 2010, doi: 10.1002/smj.821.

[2] R. Amit and Xu Han, "Value creation through novel resource configurations in a digitally enabled world," Strategic Entrepreneurship Journal, vol. 11 no. 3, pp. 228-242, 2017, doi:10.1002/sej.1256.

[3] S. Nambisan, K. Lyytinen, A. Majchrzak, and M. Song, "Digital innovation management," MIS quarterly, vol. 41 no. 1, pp. 223-238, 2017, doi: 10.25300/MISQ/2017/41:1.03.

[4] J. Häikiö and T. Koivumäki, "Exploring digital service innovation process through value creation," Journal of Innovation Management, vol. 4 no. 2, pp. 96-124, 2016, doi: 10.24840/2183-0606_004.002_0006.

[5] P. P. Maglio and J. Spohrer, "Fundamentals of service science," Journal of the academy of marketing science, vol. 36, pp. 18-20, 2008, doi: 10.1007/s11747-007-0058-9.

[6] R. F. Lusch and S. L. Vargo, The service-dominant logic of marketing: Premises, perspectives, possibilities, Cambridge, UK: Cambridge University Press, 2014.

[7] V. Kaptelinin and B. A. Nardi, Acting with technology: Activity theory and interaction design, Cambridge, MA: MIT press, 2009.

[8] U. V. Riss, M. Ziegler, and L. J. Smith, "Value dimensions of digital applications and services: the example of voice assistants," International Journal of Web Engineering and Technology, vol. 18 no.4, pp. 319-343, 2023, doi: 10.1504/ijwet.2023.10061112.

[9] W. Groher and U. V. Riss, "Digital Twin of the Organization for Support of Customer Journeys and Business Processe,." International Conference on Business Process Management. Cham: Springer Nature Switzerland, pp. 341–352, 2023, doi: 10.1007/978-3-031-50974-2_26.

[10] R. Parmar, A. Leiponen, and D. W. T. Llewellyn, "Building an organizational digital twin," Business Horizons, vol. 63 no.6, pp. 725-736, 2020, doi: 10.1016/j.bushor.2020.08.001.

[11] C. Semeraro, M. Lezoche, H. Panetto, anf M. Dassisti, "Digital twin paradigm: A systematic literature review," Computers in Industry, vol. 130, 2022, doi: 10.1016/j.compind.2021.103469.

[12] J. Meierhofer and S. West, "Service value creation using a digital twin," Naples Forum on Service, Service Dominant Logic, Network & Systems Theory and Service Science: Integrating Three Perspectives for a New Service Agenda, Ischia, June 2019, p. 4-7

[13] L. Barth, L. Schweiger, G. Galeno, N. Schaal, and M. Ehrat, "Value creation with digital twins: Application-oriented conceptual framework and case study," Applied Sciences, vol. 13 no. 6, 2023, doi: 10.3390/app13063511.

[14] R. Wagner and D. Cozmiuc, "Extended reality in marketing—a multiple case study on internet of things platforms," Information, vol. 13, no. 6, 2022, doi: 10.3390/info13060278.

[15] R. Woitsch, A. Sumereder, and D. Falcioni, "Model-based data integration along the product & service life cycle supported by digital twinning," Computers in Industry, vol. 140, 2022, doi: 10.1016/j.compind.2022.103648.

[16] U. V. Riss and W. Groher, "Digital Twin of the Organization – New Requirements in Business Process Management and beyond," SAP Academic Community Conference DACH Sep. 2022, pp. 209-221, doi:10.14459/2022md1685828.

[17] S. D. Clatworthy, "Service innovation through touch-points: Development of an innovation toolkit for the first stages of new service development," International Journal of Design, vol. 5 no. 2, pp. 15-28, 2011.

[18] F. Tao, H. Zhang, A. Liu, and A. Y. Nee, "Digital twin in industry: State-of-the-art," IEEE Transactions on industrial informatics, vol. 15 no. 4, pp. 2405-2415, 2019, doi: 10.1109/tii.2018.2873186.

[19] M. Grieves and J. Vickers, "Digital twin: Mitigating unpredictable, undesirable emergent behavior, complex systems," in Transdisciplinary perspectives on complex systems: New findings and approaches, F.-J. Kahlen, S. Flumerfelt, A. Alvespp, Eds., Cham, Switzerland: Springer, pp. 85-113, doi: 10.1007/978-3-319-38756-7_4

[20] F. Edrisi, D. Perez-Palacin, M. Caporuscio, and S. Giussani, "Developing and Evolving a Digital Twin of the Organization," IEEE Access, 2024, doi: 10.1109/ACCESS.2024.3381778.

[21] S. M. Bazaz, M. Lohtander, and J. Varis, "5-dimensional definition for a manufacturing digital twin," Procedia Manufacturing, vol. 38, pp. 1705-1712, doi: 10.1016/j.promfg.2020.01.107.

[22] U. V. Riss, H. Maus, S. Javid, and C. Jelinek, "Digital twins of an organization for enterprise modeling," 13th IFIP Working Conference, PoEM 2020, Nov. 2020, pp 25–40, doi: 10.1007/978-3-030-63479-7_3.

[23] D. Selz, "From electronic markets to data driven insights," Electronic Markets, vol. 30 no. 1, pp. 57–59, 2020, doi: 10.1007/s12525-019-00393-4.

[24] L. Gonçalves, L. Patrício, J. Grenha Teixeira, and N. V. Wuenderlich, "Understanding the customer experience with smart services," Journal of Service Management, vol. 31 no. 4, pp.723–744, 2020, doi: 10.1108/josm-11-2019-0349.

[25] Y. Engeström, Learning by Expanding, Helsinki: Orienta-Konsultit Oy, 1987.

[26] M. Lambek, "The value of (performative) acts," HAU: Journal of Ethnographic Theory, vol. 3 no. 2, pp. 141-160, 2013, doi: 10.14318/hau3.2.009.

[27] M. Blaschke, U. V. Riss, K. Haki, and S. Aier, "Design principles for digital value co-creation networks: A service-dominant logic perspective," Electronic Markets, vol. 29, pp. 443-472, 2019, doi:10.1007/s12525-019-00356-9.

[28] R. Normann, Reframing business: When the map changes the landscape. Chichester, UK: Wiley, 2001.

[29] B. Ewenstein and J. Whyte, "Knowledge practices in design: the role of visual representations asepistemic objects'," Organization studies, vol. 30 no.1, pp. 7-30, 2008, doi: 10.1177/0170840608083014.

[30] J. Meierhofer, S. West, M. Rapaccini, and C. Barbieri, "The digital twin as a service enabler: From the service ecosystem to the simulation model," 10th International Conference (IESS 2020), Springer, Feb. 2020, pp. 347-359, doi: 10.1007/978-3-030-38724-2_25.

[31] S. Vandermerwe and J. Rada, "Servitization of business: adding value by adding services," European management journal, vol. 6 no. 4, pp. 314-324, 1988, doi: 10.1016/0263-2373(88)90033-3.

[32] T. Poell, D. Nieborg, and J. F. T. M. Van Dijck, "Concepts of the Digital Society: Platformisation," Internet Policy Review vol. 8 no. 4, 2019, doi: 10.14763/2019.4.1425.

[33] A. Benlian, W. J. Kettinger, A. Sunyaev, and T. J. Winkler, "The transformative value of cloud computing: a decoupling, platformization, and recombination theoretical framework." Journal of management information systems, vol. 35 no. 3, pp. 719-739, 2018, doi:10.1080/07421222.2018.1481634.

[34] B. M. Ampel, C. H. Yang, J. Hu, and H. Chen, "Large Language Models for Conducting Advanced Text Analytics Information Systems Research." arXiv preprint, 2023, doi: 10.48550/arxiv.2312.17278.

[35] S. Vargo, H. Wieland, and M. Archpru Akaka, "Innovation through institutionalization: A service ecosystems perspective," Industrial Marketing Management vol. 44, pp. 63-72, 2015, doi: 10.1016/j.indmarman.2014.10.008.

[36] A. Bennich, "The digital imperative: Institutional pressures to digitalise," Technology in Society, vol. 76, 2024, doi: 10.1016/j.techsoc.2023.102436.

[37] S. West, O. Stoll, J. Meierhofer, and S. Züst, "Digital twin providing new opportunities for value co-creation through supporting decision-making," Applied Sciences, vol. 11 no. 9, 2021, doi: 10.3390/app11093750.

Identifying the Invisible: A Comprehensive Approach to Distinguishing Software Bots

Zhixiong Chen
Math & Computer Science Dept.
Mercy University
Dobbs Ferry, New York, USA
email: zxchen@mercy.edu

Deming Chen
Electrical & Computer Engineering Dept.
University of Illinois Urbana Champaign
Champaign, Illinois, USA
email: dchen@uiuc.edu

Abstract— **In the evolving digital landscape, software bots or bots have emerged as autonomous agents capable of engaging in complex interactions within computer-mediated environments. This research paper delves into the unique features and characteristics of bots, proposing a sophisticated framework for their identification and registration. These captured features are certainly different from those for human users. Central to our approach is the development of a holistic identification model that treats bots as integral components of social-technological ecosystems. By adopting a comprehensive methodology that includes the construction of portfolio artifacts, we aim to encapsulate both invariant identification characteristics and dynamic, verifiable credentials of bots. These artifacts serve not only as a means of distinction but also as a basis for ensuring security and authenticity in interactions involving them. Our work underscores the importance of a nuanced understanding of bots, advocating for a system that recognizes their potential while safeguarding against misuse. Through a meticulous analysis of bot behavior and interaction patterns, we contribute to the establishment of a more secure, transparent, and efficient digital environment where bots and human users coexist harmoniously.**

Keywords - Software Bot, Identification, Invariant, Registrar, Verifiable Credentials, Portfolio Artifacts.

I. INTRODUCTION

Bots, mingling with human users, have become an established practice in many social media applications [1]. Human users are gradually accepting bots not only as an inevitable technological development but also because they are increasingly humanized and intelligent [2][3]. Recently, Large Language Model (LLM) powered Artificial Intelligence (AI) assistants have demonstrated their capability of understanding human questions in depth and can provide comprehensible answers [4]-[6]. Furthermore, with techniques, such as downstream model fine-tuning, prompt tuning, Retrieval-Augmented Generation (RAG), and prompt engineering, these bots will become more understandable, intelligent, specialized, and eventually integrated into digital workforce. To prepare for this new reality, we need to have understanding to identify bots and to aggregate their timed verifiable credentials.

This position paper seeks to identify invariant characteristics of bots so we can use them to differentiate bots among themselves and also from human actors across a wide range of contexts. The goal is to treat a bot just like any other actor in social-technological applications, or akin to a worker in various workplaces. To achieve this accurately, we compiled a comprehensive glossary of vocabulary and special terminology specific to bot identification and provided clear definitions for each of them. This list will continue to expand as we gain a deeper understanding of the intrinsic nature of bots, their enabling technologies, and associated threat models.

The primary contribution of this paper is the definition of bot identity through various attributes. While no single attribute may uniquely identify a bot, a combination of them could do the work. We utilize similarity distances between bots for identification purposes. Additionally, we link bot invariant identity with verifiable credentials that evolve gradually, all recorded as Portfolio Artifacts (PAs). These PAs provide a holistic view on bot and would have an impact on bot development and registration.

Furthermore, we introduce 'Vital Plugins'—essential to bot functionality. These plugins function as standard APIs, enabling bots to perform a range of operations and services, including secure communications, to update Pas, and to response to requests for identification, authentication, and verification.

We employ ontology technology to ensure that PAs are well-defined within their schema, making them portable across different applications and machines. We design the format to be extendable, accommodating future developments and advancements, and scalable to meet the demands of an expanding digital workforce.

Our study emphasizes the crucial role of bot identification across a diverse range of applications, from education, social media to healthcare. This research highlights how effectively identifying bots can address challenges inherent in various sectors.

We organize our paper as follows. In Section II, we present literature review and related work. We brainstorm five mind maps in Section III. They include robots, botulation, botfession, botvaluaton, enabling technology, bot registrar, services, threat models, invariants, and applications, providing a comprehensive classification and framework. In Section IV, we detail the representation of bot identity in a standardized format using JavaScript Object Notation for Linked Data (JSON-LD). This ensures we define all key attributes clearly within its schema. In Section V, we discuss the bot registration service. It employs blockchain technology to ensure data integrity and traceability. We conclude the paper with insightful discussions on both technological solutions and legal recommendations aimed at incentivizing the registration of bots. This includes a critical analysis of potential impacts and the benefits of formalizing bot identity in digital ecosystems.

II. RELATED WORK

Recent research has significantly advanced the development of chatbots, particularly through the utilization of LLMs [6]-[11]. It is evident that LLM powered bots are becoming increasingly proficient at mimicking human conversation. However, literature searches focusing on invariant identity characteristics and dynamic, verifiable unique abilities of bots yield few results. Similarly, studies on bot threat models, including ethical considerations, are limited, with only a handful of papers mostly focused on bot detection [20]. One intriguing experiment noted that participants could only correctly identify the nature of other users—bot or human—42% of the time, even though they were aware of both bots and humans in the experiment. This indicates that there is still much to learn about identifying intrinsic bot features. Further, [13] observed that AI powered bot detectors could sanitize social media applications and enhance bot detection capabilities. IDPro's blog offered a brief list of suggestions for developing basic bot identity capabilities [7]. Additionally, a report at [22] suggests that to achieve more intuitive and adaptive learning capabilities, AI systems might benefit from a set of foundational behaviors, akin to biological CliffsNotes, which could serve as a form of inherited digital DNA.

Completely Automated Public Turing test to tell Computers and Humans Apart (CATCHA), is a type of challenge-response system used in computing to determine whether the user is human. It is a common security tool used on websites to prevent bot-based spam and automated data extraction. As AI technology evolves, CAPTCHAs have become obsolete to sophisticated bots capable of image recognition and text analysis. So, we believe such features, such as text, image, audio, math based CAPCHAs, are no longer distinguish software bots from human users.

III. INDENTIFICATIONS

We employ mind maps to brainstorm the terminology associated with bots and their interrelationships.

A. Bot

Figures 1-5 depict a bot ecosystem. In the right side of Figure 1, we list tangible side of bots, robots. We physically touch and feel them. The most advanced are 'synthetic robots' capable of reasoning, feeling, and consciousness, although they are shown only in fiction now. It is inspired by the synthetic beings featured in the TV series Humans [21]. The left side highlights distinct types of bots, collectively referred to as 'botulation'—a term we use to describe the bot population.

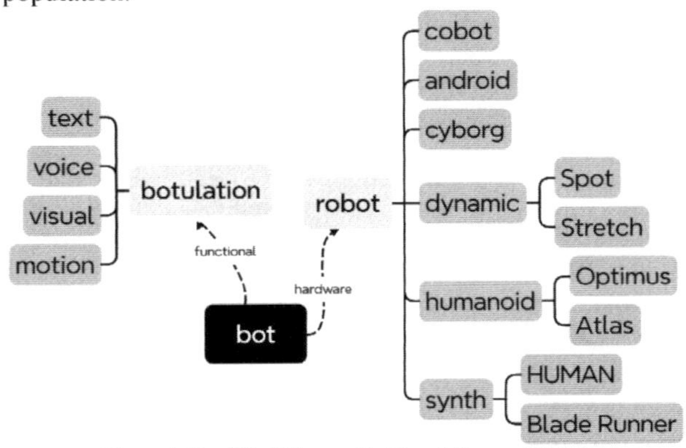

Figure 1. Bot Mind Map on Bot Population and Robot.

The right side of Figure 2 highlights the capabilities of bots within specific professional domains or sectors, which we use 'botfession,' anticipating their integration into the digital workforce. The left focuses on the metrics, tools, and techniques used to evaluate and assess bot's abilities, akin to methods used in grade school evaluations.

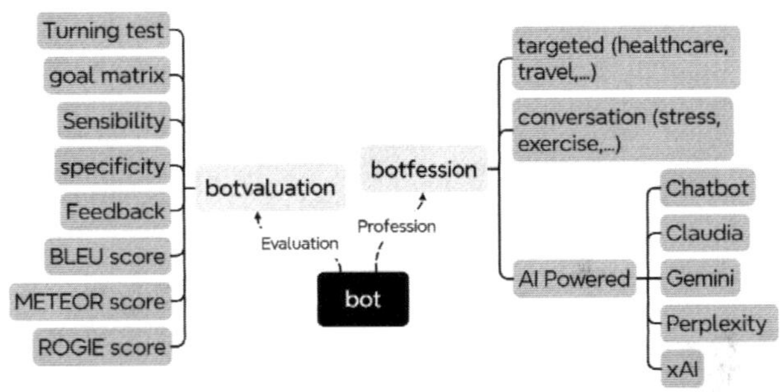

Figure 2. Bot Mind Map on Bot Profession and Evaluation.

Figure 3 delves into the enabling technologies for bots and registration authority. The left side explores the infrastructure that supports bot registration. This can be either centralized, similar to a certificate authority or a government agency, or decentralized platform, such as blockchain technology or any append-only storage. Given that our implementation utilizes blockchain, detailed insights into this technology are provided in the following sections.

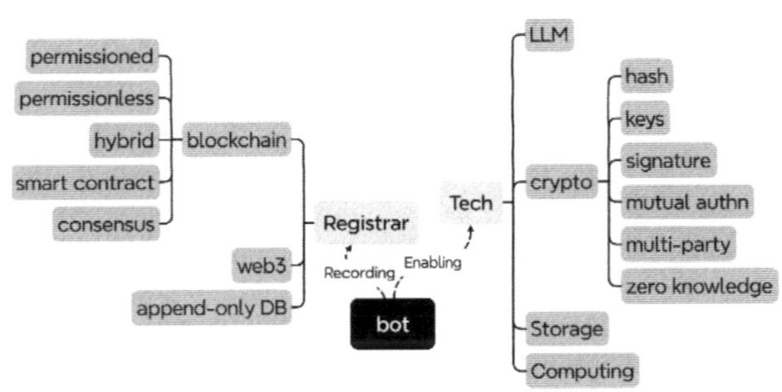

Figure 3. Bot Mind Map on Bot Enabling Technologies and Registering.

Figure 4 lists bot services and potential threat models that typically target human users. Bots are no longer considered categorically as bad actors. The right side presents a collection of operations and services essential for maintaining a bot's health. This includes bot registration, which is crucial for officially declaring a bot's existence. Updating is vital for fixing code bugs and continuous upgrades. Identification operations are crucial for verifying identity and assessing credentials, while secure communication ensures the use of secure protocols. Finally, interoperability is the key for automation of machine to machine. These operations are implemented as software plugins, which can be developed by third parties and invoked as needed. Collectively, these essential functions are referred to as 'vital plugins'.

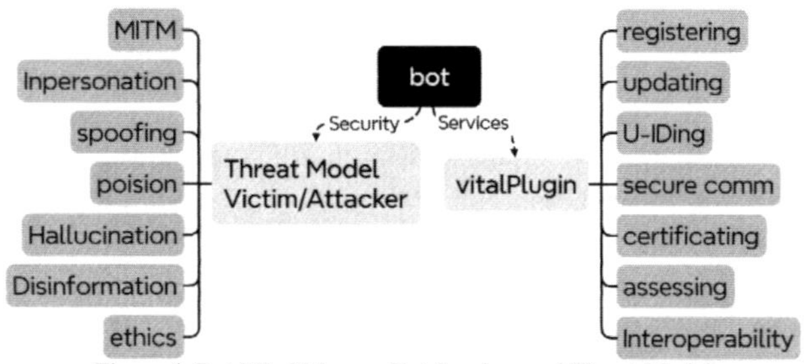

Figure 4. Bot Mind Map on Bot Services and Threat Model.

The right side of Figure 5 highlights invariants that can uniquely identify a bot from others. It is holistic that includes a variety of identifications, such as LLM models, codebase, training data (in other words, knowledge domain), configuration and portfolio. The left side lists examples bot applications.

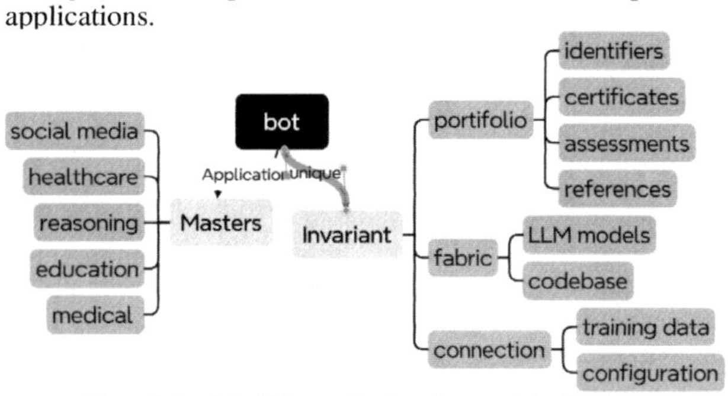

Figure 5. Bot Mind Map on Bot Invariants and Applications.

B. *Identification characteristics*

We can categorize bot identification into two types: assigned and inherited, analogous to Social Security Numbers (SSN) versus DNA. We begin by exploring the assigned features.

- UID Group

This group encompasses identities, such as given names, universal IDs, and domain professions. The Universal ID is structured as a sequence of bits separated by dots, like an IP address. Each segment represents a level of sub-grouping, allowing for specific sub-group information to be retrieved through masks.

- Crypto Group

This group includes a unique pair of public and private keys for each bot, which are essential for unique identification, secure communication, authentication, and integration. The key pair is generated using a randomized algorithm. To prevent man-in-the-middle attacks, the public key should be registered in a publicly verifiable domain, which could be managed by a trusted third party like a Certificate Authority (CA) or stored on a decentralized, immutable blockchain. An Initialization Vector (IV) may be introduced to protect against replay attacks. The private key remains secured within the bot and shall never be transmitted externally.

- Master

This group records information about the bot's owner, revealing the intended use of the bot, its service duration, and other pertinent details. It includes built-in control mechanisms to ensure that the bot adheres to the expectations set by its master. Mathematically, it reflects applications.

We now turn to the extraction of inherited features of a bot, which are indicative of its development process.

- Code Base and Configuration

This group identifies the bot's code base, incorporating elements such as a code hash or checksum, referred to as a 'tag,' to detect any unauthorized alterations. This tag is digitally stamped, ensuring code assurance and security—vital for maintaining a healthy bot ecosystem in the digital workforce. The code version maintains a log of changes and updates, reflecting the bot's evolution over time. Additionally, more granular aspects of the code base, such as the code structure, token sequences, and distributions, provide deeper insights into the bot's internal structure beyond what a tag can offer. We propose using LangChain to achieve this detailed analysis [23].

Configuration holds equal importance as it details the training processes of the bot and the operational parameters under which it was utilized. Together, the codebase and its configuration form a comprehensive bot signature.

- Credentials

Credentials consist of one or more claims made by an issuer. A verifiable credential is a tamper-evident credential whose authorship can be cryptographically verified [16][17]. This category is unique in that it not only reflects a bot's capabilities but also its achievements over time. It includes specialized skills, underlying AI architecture (e.g., rule-based, retrieval-based, deep neural network, or hybrid), performance metrics to date, and areas of continuous learning.

Bot metrics also serve as unique identifiers, derived from consistent measures, such as the bot's latency, vocabulary size, and conversational patterns, some of which are detailed in the 'Botvaluation' in Figure 2.

Additional credentials, such as licenses issued to the bot by various platforms, can further enrich this profile.

C. *Identification and Security*

- Bot Identification

Bot identification is a critical process designed to verify a bot's identity, ideally without human intervention. This process is facilitated by a software plugin, referred to as

'VitalPlugin,' embedded into the bot's code. It includes a standard API that processes identification requests among other functions. Using cryptographic tools, the plugin enables secure communication—a common practice in social media applications. We propose designing specific protocols for handshakes and identity verification, adhering to the principle of 'always ask, never assume.' This approach ensures that the bot can autonomously confirm its identity and operate securely.

- Mitigating Security Threats

To counteract potential attacks identified in the threat models of Figure 1, we employ advanced cryptographic techniques, including digital signatures, multi-layered protection, and unique challenge-response sets that only the bot can generate. Protecting the private key is paramount to prevent unauthorized access and impersonation.

- Enhancing Verification Measures

While basic identifying information can be spoofed, true verification requires additional authenticity signals.

a) Registry Systems: A centralized registry could officially list verified bot identities and credentials, making it difficult for impersonators to falsify these details.
b) Multi-factor Authentication: Bots could be required to periodically re-verify their identities through multiple authentication factors, such as keys, signatures, and one-time codes.
c) Platform Verification: Platforms on which bots operate could provide verification indicators, such as a verified checkmark, to confirm the authenticity of the bots.
d) Behavioral Analysis: Analyzing and comparing the conversational patterns and tendencies of an original bot against those of a potential impersonator can help detect deviations in interaction styles.
e) Code Analysis: Ensuring the integrity of a bot's codebase involves verifying that the actual code of an impersonator matches the identified hashes and expected programming standards.
f) Social Graph Analysis: Examining the social connections and interaction patterns of an original bot versus an impersonator can reveal significant differences, aiding in the detection of fraudulent entities.

IV. REPRESENTATION OF BOT IDENTITY

We utilize PAs to represent the identity attributes of bots [18][19]. PAs serve as fundamental components for identifying not only human beings but also bots and other applications. In this context, our focus is specifically on bots. We employ JSON-LD to outline the ontology design, which can be visualized using tools like the JSON-LD Playground. JSON-LD leverages URLs, @context, and IRIs to enhance semantics, extensibility, and interoperability. It allows for the linking of entities using IRIs instead of internal indices and supports integration with digital signatures and proofs. Proof mechanisms, such as LD Signatures, enable the signing of JSON-LD documents.

Figure 6 highlights a simple example of a translation bot, although it does not present many features defined in Section 2. Figure 7 illustrates a segment specifically for identification purposes. They represent a single type of bot. The use of ontology and JSON-LD offers significant advantages in aggregating and reasoning about data.

```
{
  "@context": {
    "schema": "https://schema.org/",
    "Bot": "schema:SoftwareApplication",
    "feature": "schema:feature"
  },
  "@type": "Chatbot",
  "name": "ZC",
  "feature": [
   {
    "@type": "feature",
    "name": "Natural language processing",
    "description": "Processes and understands natural language input"
   },
   {
    "@type": "feature",
    "name": "Speech recognition",
    "description": "Converts spoken audio to text"
   },
   {
    "@type": "feature",
    "name": "Text-to-speech",
    "description": "Converts text to human-like speech"
   },
   {
    "@type": "feature",
    "name": "Conversational intelligence",
    "description": "Dialog management, context tracking, personalization"
   }
  ]
}
```

Figure 6. Bot Representation.

```
"issuer": "https://example.edu/issuers/14",
"issuanceDate": "2023-10-15T10:20:24Z",
"proof": {
  "type": "RsaSignature2018",
  "created": "2023-10-15T10:20:54Z",
  "proofPurpose": "assertionMethod",
  "verificationMethod": "https://example.edu/issuers/keys/1",
  "jws": "xxxxx"
}
```

Figure 7. Bot Identification.

A. PA Aggregation

PAs can be organized in a hierarchical format, analogous to branches in a body of knowledge. This structure allows for the aggregation of tags like <ComputerScience ∘ ProgrammingLanguage ∘ *> to demonstrate a bot's proficiency in various programming languages within computer science, such as Python, Rust, or Go. The aggregated claims are stored and communicated using descriptive rather than numerical identifiers from the PA tags, though actual execution relies on a numerical system for efficiency.

Aggregation is particularly useful when employing existing PAs to generate specialized credentials for tasks that require specific knowledge and skills, while deemphasizing other credentials.

B. PA Reasoner

We can also derive new claims using a PA Reasoner, which infers certain credentials from existing PAs. Our colleagues at Cyber Talent Bridge [24] developed a proof of concept for this approach. They utilized a rich set of linked data vocabularies published [e.g., 25] to enhance the Cyber Talent Bridge credentials. According to the open world principle, any vocabulary can be employed to extend the data of a Cyber Talent Bridge credential, which is also encoded in JSON-LD. JSON-LD facilitates the transformation of JSON documents to and from RDF serializations, such as N-Quads based on the specified @context.

V. IMPLEMENTATIONS

Introduced and refined since 2017, the Personal Archive Service System (PASS) and its enhanced iteration, PASS+, are built around blockchain technology [18]. The core of PASS uses PAs as foundational elements to establish unique digital identifiers for subjects, focusing particularly on non-human entities. It is used as a register platform for bot identification storage.

The PASS framework consists of an integrated system of modules, applications, and libraries. These components work collaboratively to facilitate the creation, storage, retrieval, and presentation of PAs. The structure of PASS is designed to leverage the decentralized and secure nature of blockchain, ensuring that each PA remains tamper-proof and verifiable. This architecture not only enhances the reliability of digital identities but also supports a scalable system for managing digital archives across various applications.

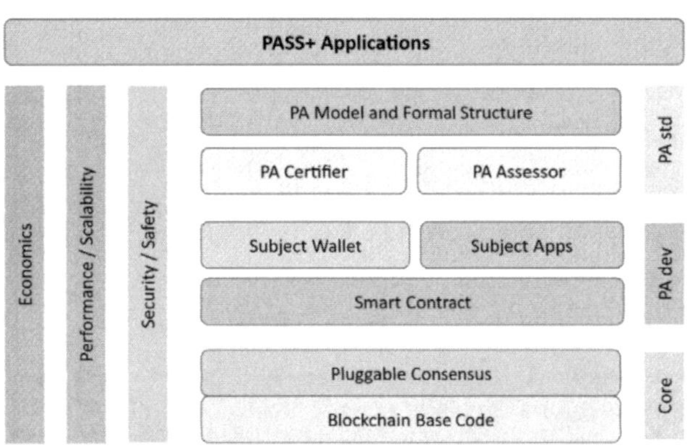

Figure 8. PASS Framework Layered Overview.

The architecture of the Personal Archive Service System (PASS) is depicted in Figure 5, showcasing a multi-layered framework. At its core, the system builds on blockchain technology, utilizing the Ethereum open-source code base along with pluggable consensus protocols. We have also implemented a permissioned blockchain using Hyperledger Fabric to meet specific security and governance requirements.

Above the core blockchain layer is the PA Standard (PA std) Layer, dedicated to the modeling and formal structure analysis of PAs. This layer ensures the systematic definition, classification, and organization of PAs. It features key modules, such as the PA Assessor and PA Certifier, which are crucial for evaluating and certifying the integrity and accuracy of PAs.

The PA Development (PA dev) Layer follows, focusing on the creation of decentralized applications. This layer includes modules for smart contracts, subject wallets, and web communication APIs that interface with other modules. The smart contract module is specifically designed for creating, storing, and retrieving PAs, ensuring that interactions with the blockchain are secure and efficient.

At the top of the architecture are the user applications that leverage PASS for various specific use scenarios, demonstrating the practical application of the system in real-world contexts.

Running parallel on the left side of the architecture are cross-layer considerations: security and safety, performance and scalability, and economic factors. These aspects are integral to the architecture, influencing every layer to ensure that the system remains robust, efficient, and economically viable.

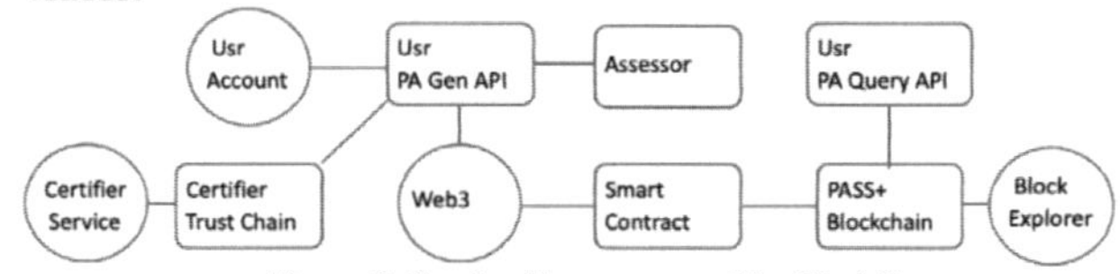

Figure 9. Service Ecosystem and Its Workflow.

Figure 9 presents an alternative view of the PASS system, specifically illustrating the workflow diagram. In this visualization, internal modules within the system are depicted as squares, while external applications or libraries are represented by circles, clearly distinguishing between PASS components and external integrations.

PASS interacts with bot applications primarily through the 'VitalPlugin', which utilizes a standard API to facilitate communication. This setup positions PASS as a decentralized registrar, a critical function in managing digital identities. We advocate that, particularly within social media platforms, this decentralized approach is preferable to traditional centralized authorities. This is due to its ability to enhance security, ensure greater privacy, and provide resilience against single points of failure.

This workflow diagram in Figure 9 not only highlights the structural and functional relationships within the PASS system but also underscores the system's adaptability and efficiency in handling real-world application demands in social media contexts.

VI. CONCLUSION AND FUTURE WORK

Registering bots and making their presence explicit in social media or any applications is challenging, particularly in environments like bot farms, which are often employed to influence public opinion. While technology has improved our ability to detect bots in social media applications—for instance, using conversational data to train bot detectors—these advancements also aid in the development of bots that can evade detection. This creates a continuous cycle of improvement in both AI-powered bots and AI-powered bot detectors, complicating efforts to fully expose all bots. A viable approach to encouraging transparency is through legislation. With advancements in technology, such as the development of sophisticated LLMs, public acceptance of bots in social interactions is increasing, potentially reducing resistance to registration. However, the challenge remains significant. Legislation could be a powerful tool to mandate the registration of all bots.

Although threat modeling is a well-established research area when the focus is on human users, it is less frequently discussed in the context of bots. We believe that results from traditional threat modeling can be adapted to address threats posed by bots, enhancing security measures and protocols.

Several critical questions remain unanswered, including who controls the Bot Registrar, who develops and standardizes the VitalPlugin, and who is responsible for auditing and approving these systems. Additionally, what types of evaluation and assessment are necessary? How do we monitor a bot that evolves over time or potentially goes rogue? What metrics should we use to assess bot performance?

This paper outlines our recent research on bot identification and security, highlighting the complexity of managing bot in digital environments. The issues discussed require further investigation and the development of robust, standardized solutions to ensure the safe integration of bots into social media and beyond.

ACKNOWLEDGMENT

We would like to extend our gratitude to the various online resources and support tools that have provided invaluable guidance and feedback throughout the drafting of this paper. Additionally, this research was conducted under an appointment to the Summer Research Team Program for the U.S. Department of Homeland Security Science & Technology Directorate, Office of University Programs. We are thankful for the opportunity and support that have significantly contributed to the development of this work.

REFERENCES

[1] Z. Chen, Z. Lu, A. Sane, and A. Bhimsain, "Trustworthy When Human and Bots Are Mingled", in Proceeding of the 7th IEEE International Conference on Cyber Security and Cloud Computing (CSCloud), pp. 76-81. 2020.

[2] S. B. Kondracki and N. J. Nikiforakis, "Uninvited Guests: Analyzing the Identity and Behavior of Certificate Transparency Bots", in Proceedings of the 31st USENIX Security Symposium, Security 2022, pp. 53-70, 2022.

[3] "The ultimate guide to machine-learning chatbots and conversational AI", https://www.ibm.com/watson-advertising/thought-leadership/machine-learning-chatbot, last accessed 5/15/2024.

[4] A. Vaswani et al., "Attention Is All You Need", v7, 2023, https://arxiv.org/abs/1706.03762, last accessed 5/15/2024.

[5] H. Touvron et al., "LLaMA: Open and Efficient Foundation Language Models", https://arxiv.org/pdf/2302.13971.pdf, 2023, last accessed 5/15/2024.

[6] W. X. Zhao et al., "A Survey of Large Language Models", https://arxiv.org/pdf/2303.18223.pdf, 2023, last accessed 5/15/2024.

[7] https://idpro.org/bot-identity/, last accessed 5/15/2024

[8] D. Banerjee, P. Singh, A. Avadhanam, and S. Srivastava, "Benchmarking LLM powered Chatbots: Methods and Metrics", https://arxiv.org/pdf/2308.04624.pdf, 2023, last accessed 5/15/2024.

[9] S. Roller et al., "Recipes for building an open-domain chatbot", in Proceedings of the 16th Conf. of the European Compt. Ling., https://aclanthology.org/2021.eacl-main.24/, last accessed 5/15/2024.

[10] Y. Li, S. Qu, J. Shen, S. Min, and Z. Yu, "Curriculum-Driven Edubot: A Framework for Developing Language Learning Chatbots Through Synthesizing Conversational Data", in CHI'24, 2024.

[11] M. A. Kuhail, N. Alturki, S. Alramlawi, and K. Alhejori, "Interacting with educational chatbots: A systematic review", Education and Information Technologies, V. 28, No 1, pp. 973–1018, 2023.

[12] Y. Bai et al., "Constitutional AI: Harmlessness from AI Feedback", https://arxiv.org/abs/2212.08073, 2022 last accessed 5/15/2024.

[13] Davis University of California, "Gunrock 2.0: A user adaptive social conversational system", in Alexa Prize SocialBot Grand Challenge 3.

[14] Amazon Science, https://www.amazon.science/alexa-prize/proceedings/gunrock-2-0-a-user-adaptive-social-conversational-system, last accessed 5/15/2024.

[15] K. C. Yang and F. Menczer, "Anatomy of an AI-powered malicious social botnet", arXiv:2307.16336, 2023, last accessed 5/15/2024.

[16] W3C, "Decentralized Identifiers (DIDs)", DID-CORE, https://www.w3.org/TR/did-core/, accessed 5/15/2024.

[17] W3C, "Verifiable Credentials Data Model v1.1", Publication VC Data Model, https://github.com/w3c/vc-data-model/, https://w3c.github.io/vc-imp-guide/, 2023, last accessed 5/15/2024.

[18] Z. Chen and Y. Zhu. "Personal Archive Service System using Blockchain technology: Case study, Promising and Challenging", in Proceeding of the 2017 IEEE International Conference on AI & Mobile Services, pp. 93-99, 2017.

[19] Y. Zhu and Z. Chen, "RealID: Building A Secure Anonymous Yet Transparent Immutable ID Service", in Proceeding of the IEEE International Conference on Intelligent Data and Security, pp. 26-28, 2017.

[20] K. Radivojevic, N. Clark and P. Brenner, "LLMs Among Us: Generative AI Participating in Digital Discourse", https://arxiv.org/abs/2402.07940, 2024, last accessed 5/15/2024.

[21] https://en.wikipedia.org/wiki/Humans_(TV_series), last accessed 5/15/2024.

[22] L. Zeldovich, "Why AI needs a genome", https://www.cshl.edu/why-ai-needs-a-genome/, 2021, accessed 5/15/2024.

[23] LangChain, https://www.langchain.com/, accessed 5/15/2024.

[24] https://cybertalentbridge.com/, last accessed 5/15/2024.

[25] https://csrc.nist.gov/pubs/sp/800/181/r1/final, last accessed 5/15/2024.

Camera Model Identification Using Audio and Visual Content from Videos

Ioannis Tsingalis
Department of Informatics
Aristotle University of Thessaloniki
Thessaloniki 54124, Greece
Email: tsingalis@csd.auth.gr

Christos Korgialas
Department of Informatics
Aristotle University of Thessaloniki
Thessaloniki 54124, Greece
Email: ckorgial@csd.auth.gr

Constantine Kotropoulos
Department of Informatics
Aristotle University of Thessaloniki
Thessaloniki 54124, Greece
Email: costas@csd.auth.gr

***Abstract*—The identification of device brands and models plays a pivotal role in the realm of multimedia forensic applications. This paper presents a framework capable of identifying devices using audio, visual content, or a fusion of them. The fusion of visual and audio content occurs later by applying two fundamental fusion rules: the product and the sum. The device identification problem is tackled as a classification one by leveraging Convolutional Neural Networks. Experimental evaluation illustrates that the proposed framework exhibits promising classification performance when independently using audio or visual content. Furthermore, although the fusion results don't consistently surpass both individual modalities, they demonstrate promising potential for enhancing classification performance. Future research could refine the fusion process to improve classification performance in both modalities consistently. Finally, a statistical significance test is performed for a more in-depth study of the classification results.**

Keywords-Camera Model Identification (CMI); Convolutional Neural Networks (CNNs); Sum and Product Fusion Rules; Statistical Testing; Multimedia Forensics.

I. Introduction

Camera Model Identification (CMI) [1] [2] emerges as an essential forensic tool, particularly in the pursuit of discerning the brand or model of a mobile phone from a recording [3] [4]. The forensic analysis delves into various multimedia elements, including audio recordings, images, and videos, to unravel the distinct characteristics and signatures of different mobile phone brands/models. By exploiting these signatures, forensic analysts can accurately determine the particular device that recorded the multimedia content, providing crucial insights into various investigations, such as identifying the perpetrators behind a felony scene.

Two prominent types of signatures employed in device identification are Photo-Response Non-Uniformity (PRNU) [5] for images and Mel-Frequency Cepstral Coefficients (MFCCs) [6] [7] [8] [9] extracted from audio recordings. PRNU analysis involves studying the unique noise patterns present in images, allowing forensic experts to identify the camera model with high precision. On the other hand, MFCCs, extracted from the audio recorded by a mobile phone speaker, serve as distinctive "fingerprints" that enable analysts to discern which mobile device is used for recording.

Both methodologies contribute substantially to the forensic toolkit, offering valuable and intricate details regarding multimedia content's recording time and place. This encompasses insights into its creation process, source, authenticity, and other pertinent characteristics.

However, the evolution of deep learning has catalyzed a notable shift in research focus, particularly emphasizing the application of Convolutional Neural Networks (CNNs) in extracting inherent patterns from multimedia content [10].

This advancement has significantly enhanced the ability to classify and identify devices by analyzing raw video frames and log-Mel spectrograms as key inputs of CNNs, as described in Section IV-A.

Consequently, this approach has expanded the scope of modalities used, going beyond traditional PRNU and MFCC analysis to incorporate a broader spectrum of features. The integration of CNNs marks a pivotal stride in the ongoing refinement of forensic techniques, offering a framework for device identification. The framework combines conditional probability densities of device identification given the audio and visual content in a late fusion manner, hoping to overcome any caveats when one of the two modalities is employed for CMI (i.e., a high noise regime in the visual content).

Motivation and Contribution. Inspired by the application of CMI in forensics, this paper introduces a framework for CMI, treating it as a classification problem. CNNs trained on either audio or visual content are employed for this purpose. Experimental findings showcase promising performance when employing either audio or visual content individually. Furthermore, late fusion integrates the decision given the audio and visual content by utilizing fundamental fusion rules, namely the product and sum rule [11]. Applying these rules for classification offers valuable insights for future research in the fusion of modalities for CMI. Given the limited existing research in this area, this work represents a significant contribution to the literature, paving the way for further exploration. The code for the proposed framework can be found at [12].

The remaining paper is organized as follows. In Section II, a survey of related works is undertaken. In Section III, the dataset is described. Section IV outlines the proposed methodology with experimental results presented and discussed in Section V. Finally, the paper is concluded in Section VII, discussing the results obtained and outlining potential methods for future research.

II. Related Work

Research on brand device identification has focused on examining camera video sequences to ensure accurate recognition. In [13], an approach to CMI from videos was presented, utilizing extended constrained convolutional layers for

TABLE I. THE 35 DEVICES FEATURED IN THE VISION DATASET.

ID	Model	ID	Model
D01	Samsung Galaxy S3 Mini	D19	Apple iPhone 6 Plus
D02	Apple iPhone 4s	D20	Apple iPad Mini
D03	Huawei P9	D21	Wiko Ridge 4G
D04	LG D2 90	D22	Samsung Galaxy Trend Plus
D05	Apple iPhone 5c	D23	Asus Zenfone 2 Laser
D06	Apple iPhone 6	D24	Xiaomi Redmi Note 3
D07	Lenovo P70 A	D25	OnePlus A3000
D08	Samsung Galaxy Tab 3	D26	Samsung Galaxy S3
D09	Apple iPhone 4	D27	Samsung Galaxy S5
D10	Apple iPhone 4s	D28	Huawei P8
D11	Samsung Galaxy S3	D29	Apple iPhone 5
D12	Sony Xperia Z1 Compact	D30	Huawei Honor 5c
D13	Apple iPad 2	D31	Samsung Galaxy S4 Mini
D14	Apple iPhone 5c	D32	OnePlus A3003
D15	Apple iPhone 6	D33	Huawei Ascend
D16	Huawei P9 Lite	D34	Apple iPhone 5
D17	Microsoft Lumia 640 LTE	D35	Samsung Galaxy Tab A
D18	Apple iPhone 5c		

extracting camera-specific noise patterns from color video frames. The approach offered robustness against compression techniques like WhatsApp and YouTube. An algorithm was proposed in [14] for the CMI of the mobile device that created a video, utilizing sensor noise and wavelet transform for identification. The experiments demonstrated its effectiveness. In [15], an algorithm addressing geometric misalignment in device brand identification was introduced, leveraging frequency domain searches for scaling and rotation parameters to efficiently align characteristic noise patterns with camera sensor traces, employing real videos from a benchmark dataset. Moreover, in [16], a CMI method was elaborated, incorporating encoding and encapsulation aspects into a joint metadata framework and employing a two-level hierarchical classification to achieve a 91% accuracy in identifying video classes among over 20,000 videos from four public datasets. In [17], a CNN named PRNU-Net, integrating a PRNU-based layer for source camera identification, was developed in response to the security challenges posed by the widespread distribution of digital videos, demonstrating competitive performance by emphasizing low-level features. Deep learning methods were applied to the identification of source camera devices from digital videos in [18], achieving record accuracies on the VISION [19] and QUFVD [20] datasets without the constraints of traditional PRNU-noise-based approaches. In [21], an approach was introduced to address the challenges of video-based source camera identification, exacerbated by compression artifacts and pixel misalignment, by leveraging a resilient global stochastic fingerprint in the low- and mid-frequency bands.

Additionally, fusion techniques were developed, employing multiple modalities further to enhance the robustness and accuracy of CMI tasks. In [22], a deep learning-based system was introduced to address the gap in video CMI effectiveness, utilizing a CNN for analyzing temporally distributed patches from video frames and employing a fusion system to consolidate forensic information. An ensemble classifier was introduced in [23] for source camera identification, leveraging fusion features to detect software-related, hardware-related, and statistical characteristics imprinted on images by digital cameras. In [24], an approach to CMI for video sequences was introduced, employing fusion techniques that leverage both audio and visual information within a multi-modal framework, demonstrating better performance over traditional mono-modal methods in tests conducted on the VISION dataset described in Section III.

III. Dataset Description and Preparation

Here, the publicly available VISION dataset [19] [25] is utilized, comprising images and videos captured across various scenes and imaging conditions. As can be observed in Table I, a total of 35 camera devices, representing 29 camera models and 11 camera brands, are encompassed within this dataset. Specifically, there are 6 camera models featuring multiple instances per model, facilitating an investigation into the performance of the proposed approach at the device level.

VISION includes 648 native videos, which remain unaltered post-capture by the camera. These native videos were disseminated via social media platforms like YouTube and WhatsApp, with corresponding versions available in the dataset. Of the 684 native videos, 644 were shared via YouTube and 622 via WhatsApp. Upon being uploaded to YouTube, videos are compressed yet retain their initial resolutions, which span from 640×480 pixels for standard definition to as high as 1920×1080 pixels. In contrast, an alteration is observed when videos are shared on WhatsApp. Regardless of their original quality, they are rescaled to a resolution of 480×848 pixels. Through this process, the original video quality is often compromised on WhatsApp videos to ensure swift sharing and reduced data usage.

Moreover, the videos obtained from each camera are classified into three distinct scenarios: flat, indoor, and outdoor. Flat videos depict scenes with relatively homogeneous content, such as skies and white walls. Indoor scenarios encompass videos captured within indoor settings, such as offices and homes. Conversely, outdoor scenarios feature videos of gardens and streets. This diversity in scene content underscores the suitability of the VISION dataset as a benchmark for assessing source camera identification.

Taking into account the VISION dataset naming conventions outlined in [19], videos captured by devices D04, D12, D17, and D22 are excluded due to issues encountered during frame extraction or audio track retrieval.

The VISION dataset is partitioned into training, testing, and validation sets to conduct a typical five-fold stratified cross-validation so that the standard deviation of accuracy is estimated. The choice of 5 folds is a compromise between an acceptable estimation of the standard deviation of accuracy and computational time. The standard deviation is reduced after fusion. This demonstrates the precision of the method.

IV. FRAMEWORK

A. Audio and Visual Content Feature Extraction

Our approach integrates audio and visual content to classify the videos within the VISION dataset. A description of the features extracted from the audio and visual content follows.

Audio content. This phase encompasses extracting audio data from each video sequence and the computation of the log-Mel spectrogram. The log-Mel representation of each extracted audio is computed using three distinct windows and hop sizes. This results in a 3-channel log-Mel spectrogram that captures various frequency details, serving as a comprehensive feature representation for the CMI task.

The log-Mel spectrograms are computed as follows. The Short-Time Fourier Transform (STFT) is performed on the audio signal, segmenting it into overlapping frames and providing a spectrogram representation of the signal's frequency content over time. Mathematically, the STFT of the input signal $x[n]$ is expressed as

$$X(m, f) = \sum_{n=-\infty}^{\infty} x[n]\, w[n-m]\, e^{-j2\pi f n}, \tag{1}$$

where $X(m, f)$ denotes the STFT at a specific time index m and frequency f, with $w[n-m]$ representing the window function applied to the signal. The outcome of the STFT is a two-dimensional representation of the signal $x[n]$, $\boldsymbol{X}$ of size $T \times F$, with T denoting the number of temporal samples (i.e., overlapping frames) and F standing for the number of frequency bins. $\boldsymbol{X}$ is referred to as the spectrogram of signal $x[n]$, having as elements the magnitude of the STFT.

Following the STFT, the frequencies are transformed onto the Mel scale to produce the Mel spectrogram. This involves converting linear frequencies to the Mel scale using the expression

$$\mathrm{Mel}(f) = 2595 \cdot \log_{10}\left(1 + \frac{f}{700}\right). \tag{2}$$

Then, a series of triangular filters based on these Mel frequencies are applied to the magnitude spectrum of the STFT. The Mel filter bank is denoted by a two-dimensional matrix $\boldsymbol{H}$ of size $F \times K$, where K is the number of triangular filters. The triangular Mel filters, each centered at a Mel frequency corresponding to a pitch p, are defined as

$$\boldsymbol{H}_p(f) = \begin{cases} \frac{f - f_{p-1}}{f_p - f_{p-1}} & \text{for } f_{p-1} \le f < f_p \\ \frac{f_{p+1} - f}{f_{p+1} - f_p} & \text{for } f_p \le f < f_{p+1} \\ 0 & \text{otherwise,} \end{cases} \tag{3}$$

where $f_p = \mathrm{Mel}^{-1}(p)$ represents the center frequency of the filter corresponding to pitch p, and f_{p-1} and f_{p+1} are the center frequencies of the immediately adjacent filters.

Finally, the Mel spectrogram is converted into a log-Mel spectrogram by applying a logarithmic transformation to its values

$$\text{Log-Mel Spectrogram} = \boldsymbol{L} = \ln(\boldsymbol{X}\boldsymbol{H} + \epsilon), \tag{4}$$

where ϵ is a small constant added to prevent zero values. This logarithmic transformation mirrors the logarithmic nature of human loudness perception, ensuring that the resulting log-Mel spectrogram closely aligns with human auditory processing.

Visual content. This stage involves extracting video frames and preprocessing them by resizing them to a predefined size of $256 \times 256 \times 3$. Here, we use the raw video frames without performing any feature extraction, such as PRNU analysis.

B. Unimodal Classification Methodology

Let us consider a scenario where a pattern needs to be assigned to one of the classes $\{\mathscr{C}_c\}_{c=1}^{C}$. Furthermore, let $\{\boldsymbol{\gamma}_m\}_{m=1}^{M}$ be the set of random variables whose instances represent data samples of the mth modality. We denote the instances of the mth modality as $\{\boldsymbol{\gamma}_m^{(n)}\}_{n=1}^{N}$.

Furthermore, let $\circ$ be the function composition. If the classification system of the mth modality is realized by a neural network of L layers, we can denote its output activation as

$$\boldsymbol{a}_m^{(n)[L]} = \left(f^{[L]}_{\boldsymbol{W}_m^{[L]}} \circ f^{[L-1]}_{\boldsymbol{W}_m^{[L-1]}} \circ \cdots f^{[1]}_{\boldsymbol{W}_m^{[1]}}\right)(\boldsymbol{\gamma}_m^{(n)}), \tag{5}$$

where $\boldsymbol{W}_m^{[l]}$ and $f^{[l]}_{\boldsymbol{W}_m^{[l]}}$ are the parameters and the activation function of the lth layer, respectively.

Consider the collection of parameters belonging to the Lth layer where each element is associated with the c'th classification node $\{\boldsymbol{w}_m^{c',[L]}\}_{c'=1}^{C}$. Also, let $\exp(\cdot)$ be the exponential function. When the output activation function $f^{[L]}$ is the softmax function, the classification probabilities of the c' classification node are given by

$$\Pr(\mathscr{C}_{c'} \mid \boldsymbol{\gamma}_m^{(n)}; \boldsymbol{w}_m^{c',[L]}) = \frac{\exp\left({\boldsymbol{w}_m^{c',[L]}}^{\top} \boldsymbol{a}_m^{(n)[L-1]}\right)}{\sum_{c=1}^{C} \exp\left({\boldsymbol{w}_m^{c,[L]}}^{\top} \boldsymbol{a}_m^{(n)[L-1]}\right)}. \tag{6}$$

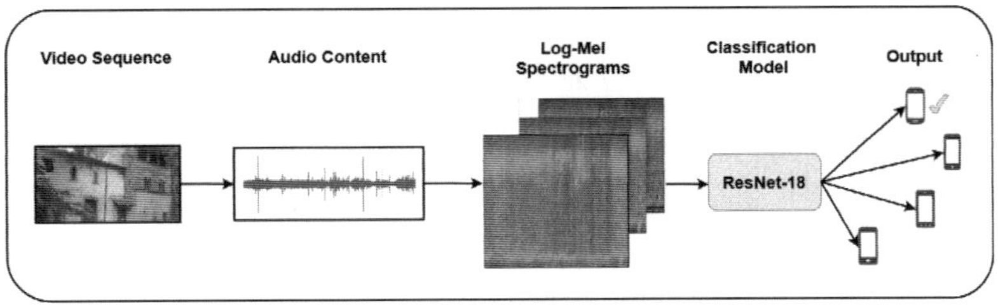

Figure 1. Flowchart depicting the CMI using only the audio content.

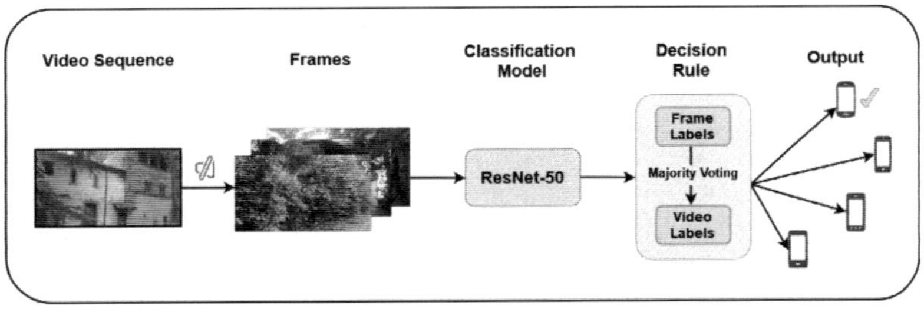

Figure 2. Flowchart depicting the CMI employing frames extracted from video sequences.

In addition, the classification probabilities of the nth sample $\boldsymbol{\gamma}_m^{(n)}$ related to the mth modality are given by

$$\boldsymbol{p}_m^{(n)[L]} = \begin{bmatrix} \Pr(\mathscr{C}_1 \mid \boldsymbol{\gamma}_m^{(n)} ; \boldsymbol{w}_m^{1,[L]}) \\ \Pr(\mathscr{C}_2 \mid \boldsymbol{\gamma}_m^{(n)} ; \boldsymbol{w}_m^{2,[L]}) \\ \vdots \\ \Pr(\mathscr{C}_C \mid \boldsymbol{\gamma}_m^{(n)} ; \boldsymbol{w}_m^{C,[L]}) \end{bmatrix} \in \mathbb{R}^C. \quad (7)$$

In the remaining analysis, for simplicity, the superscript $[L]$ is omitted. Given the samples $\{\boldsymbol{\gamma}_m^{(n)}\}_{n=1}^N$ of the mth modality, we obtain

$$\boldsymbol{P}_m = [\boldsymbol{p}_m^{(1)}, \boldsymbol{p}_m^{(2)}, \ldots, \boldsymbol{p}_m^{(N)}] \in \mathbb{R}^{C \times N}. \quad (8)$$

Loss function. Let $\boldsymbol{T} = [\boldsymbol{t}^{(1)}, \ldots, \boldsymbol{t}^{(N)}] \in \mathbb{R}^{C \times N}$ be the matrix of target variables. The (c', n) element of $\boldsymbol{T}$ is denoted by $t_{c'}^{(n)}$. The target vector $\boldsymbol{t}^{(n)}$, that corresponds to the sample $\boldsymbol{\gamma}_m^{(n)}$, adheres to the one-hot encoding scheme. In this scheme, if $\boldsymbol{\gamma}_m^{(n)}$ belongs to class $\mathscr{C}_{c'}$, the target vector $\boldsymbol{t}^{(n)}$ has zero elements except for the c'th element, which is set to one. In the proposed framework, the cross-entropy loss

$$E\left(\{\boldsymbol{\gamma}^{(n)}\}_{n=1}^N, \{\boldsymbol{W}_m^{[l]}\}_{l=1}^L\right) = -\sum_{n=1}^{N}\sum_{c'=1}^{C} t_{c'}^{(n)} \ln\, [\boldsymbol{p}_m^{(n)}]_{c'}, \quad (9)$$

is used by the mth classification system.

Unimodal Training Our objective is to identify the camera model of each video within the VISION dataset. This task is treated as a classification problem, where each class in $\{\mathscr{C}_{c=1}^C\}$ refers to the IDs in Table I, with $C = 25$. Each video is characterized by a single audio file and multiple video frames prepossessed following the guidelines in Section IV-A. The audio files are related to the audio content modality ($m = 1$), while the video frames are associated with the visual content modality ($m = 2$). Given this distinction, two separate CNNs are trained, one for each modality.

To classify the audio files into one of the classes $\{\mathscr{C}_{c=1}^{25}\}$, a `ResNet18` model [26] is utilized. The nth audio file, denoted by $\boldsymbol{\gamma}_1^{(n)}$, is assigned a vector of classification probabilities represented by $\boldsymbol{p}_1^{(n)}$. Figure 1 depicts the flow chart of the CMI using only the audio content.

Similarly, to classify the video frames into one of the classes $\{\mathscr{C}_{c=1}^{25}\}$, a `ResNet50` [26] model is utilized. The nth video file, denoted by $\boldsymbol{\gamma}_2^{(n)}$, is assigned a vector of classification probabilities represented by $\boldsymbol{p}_2^{(n)}$. As the `ResNet50` model computes a probability vector for each video frame, $\boldsymbol{p}_2^{(n)}$ is calculated as the average probability vector of all frames of the nth video. Figure 2 depicts the flow chart of the CMI using only the video content.

Unimodal Testing Procedure. The predicted classes of each sample $\{\boldsymbol{\gamma}_m^{(n)}\}_{n=1}^N$ are given by

$$\boldsymbol{c}_m = [\mathcal{C}_m^1, \mathcal{C}_m^2, \ldots, \mathcal{C}_m^N]^\top \in \mathbb{R}^N, \quad (10)$$

where

$$\mathcal{C}_m^n = \underset{c=1,\ldots,C}{\arg\max} \left[\boldsymbol{p}_m^{(n)}\right]_c, \quad (11)$$

is the predicted class of the nth sample with $\mathcal{C}_m^n \in \{\mathscr{C}_{c=1}^C\}$.

C. *Multimodal Classification Methodology*

Multi-modal deep learning has demonstrated effectiveness in previous studies [27], [28]. Here, we utilize the product and sum rule for late fusion [11]. Note that late fusion occurs subsequent to training classification models, which are utilized to generate classification probabilities for each sample. The *product rule* is given by

$$\boldsymbol{P}_{\text{prod}} = \boldsymbol{P}_1 \odot \boldsymbol{P}_2 \odot \cdots \odot \boldsymbol{P}_M \in \mathbb{R}^{C \times N}, \quad (12)$$

where $\odot$ denotes the Hadamard, element-wise, product. The *sum rule* is given by

$$\boldsymbol{P}_{\text{sum}} = \boldsymbol{P}_1 + \boldsymbol{P}_2 + \cdots + \boldsymbol{P}_M \in \mathbb{R}^{C \times N}. \quad (13)$$

Testing Procedure. After performing late fusion, the predicted class for each sample in $\{\gamma_m^{(n)}\}_{n=1}^{N}$ is determined by applying (11) to $\boldsymbol{P}_{\text{prod}}$ or $\boldsymbol{P}_{\text{sum}}$. This process yields the classification results obtained using the product or sum rule, respectively.

V. EXPERIMENTAL EVALUATION

Table II summarizes the results when the visual and the audio content are used separately. As can be seen, the mean accuracy using visual content in the Native, WhatsUp, and YouTube is 88.24%, 69.43%, and 71.77%, respectively. When audio content is used, the mean accuracy in the Native, WhatsUp, and YouTube is 93.99%, 91.11%, and 91.89%, respectively.

TABLE II. ACCURACY (%) RESULTS USING VISUAL AND AUDIO CONTENT

	Visual-ResNet-50			Audio-ResNet-18		
	Native	WhatsApp	YouTube	Native	WhatsApp	YouTube
Fold 0	88.31	67.53	77.02	96.10	93.50	91.9
Fold 1	85.70	83.11	72.97	94.80	90.90	93.24
Fold 2	89.60	63.63	77.02	90.90	88.31	95.94
Fold 3	89.47	68.42	63.51	93.42	94.73	82.43
Fold 4	88.15	64.47	78.37	94.73	88.15	95.94
Mean ± StD	88.24 ± 1.4	69.43 ± 7.07	71.77 ± 5.44	93.99 ± 1.76	91.11 ± 2.66	91.89 ± 4.98

Table III summarizes the results achieved by applying late fusion on the outcomes obtained by the classifiers related to the visual and audio content. The late fusion uses the product or sum rule described in Section IV-C. As can be seen, the mean accuracy using the product rule in the Native, WhatsUp, and YouTube is 97.64%, 92.93%, and 95.59%, respectively. When the sum rule is used, the mean accuracy in the Native, WhatsUp, and YouTube is 96.33%, 93.72%, and 93.77%, respectively.

TABLE III. ACCURACY (%) RESULTS USING THE PRODUCT AND SUM RULE

	Product Rule			Sum Rule		
	Native	WhatsApp	YouTube	Native	WhatsApp	YouTube
Fold 0	97.40	94.80	95.94	97.40	96.10	94.59
Fold 1	97.40	94.80	94.59	96.10	96.10	93.24
Fold 2	98.70	93.50	95.94	97.40	90.90	97.29
Fold 3	97.36	94.73	90.54	94.73	97.36	86.48
Fold 4	97.36	86.84	95.94	96.05	88.15	97.29
Mean ± StD	97.64 ± 0.52	92.93 ± 3.08	95.59 ± 0.52	96.33 ± 0.99	93.72 ± 3.56	93.77 ± 3.97

Comparing the results in Tables II and III, when the product rule performs the fusion, the mean accuracy in the Native, WhatsUp, and Youtube is improved by 9.4%, 23.5%, and 23.82%, respectively. When the sum rule performs the fusion, the accuracy results in the Native, WhatsUp, and YouTube are improved by 2.34%, 2.61%, and 1.88%, respectively. In summary, combining the classification probabilities obtained from visual and audio content demonstrates a promising improvement in classification performance.

Next, we study the null hypotheses:

- $H_{0,1}$: The classification performances achieved by the two fusion rules are equivalent.

TABLE IV. MCNEMAR'S p-VALUES TO EVALUATE THE NULL HYPOTHESIS $H_{0,1}$

Folds	Native	WhatsApp	YouTube
Fold 0	0.0	1.0	1.0
Fold 1	1.0	1.0	1.0
Fold 2	1.0	0.5	1.0
Fold 3	0.5	0.5	0.3
Fold 4	1.0	1.0	1.0

- $H_{0,2}$: The classification performance achieved solely with visual content is equivalent to that achieved with the product rule.
- $H_{0,3}$: The classification performance achieved solely with audio content is equivalent to that achieved with the product rule.

We have significant evidence or highly significant evidence against $H_{0,i}$, for $i = 1, 2, 3$, when the p-value falls within the range $[0.01, 0.05]$ or $[0, 0.01]$, respectively. When p-value is greater that 0.05, we have not a significant evidence against $H_{0,i}$, for $i = 1, 2, 2$. Here, p-values are computed by applying McNemar's significance test [29] [30].

TABLE V. MCNEMAR'S p-VALUES TO EVALUATE THE NULL HYPOTHESES $H_{0,2}$ AND $H_{0,3}$

	Visual-ResNet-50			Audio-ResNet-18		
	Native	WhatsApp	YouTube	Native	WhatsApp	YouTube
Fold 0	0.023	10^{-5}	0.001	1.0	1.0	0.371
Fold 1	0.007	0.026	0.001	0.617	0.248	1.0
Fold 2	0.044	10^{-5}	0.001	0.041	0.133	0.479
Fold 3	0.041	10^{-5}	10^{-5}	0.248	0.617	0.007
Fold 4	0.045	10^{-4}	0.002	0.617	1.0	0.479

Table IV summarizes the computed p-values for $H_{0,1}$. Most of the p-values exceed the predetermined significance threshold, so we lack significant evidence against $H_{0,1}$. Table V summarizes the computed p-values for $H_{0,2}$. It is evident that we have significant evidence against $H_{0,2}$. Table V summarizes also the computed p-values for $H_{0,3}$. Most of the p-values exceed the predetermined significance threshold, so we lack significant evidence against $H_{0,3}$.

VI. DISCUSSION AND FUTURE WORK

Unlike [24] which analyzes smaller segments (patches) extracted from video frames and log-mel spectrograms, our framework utilizes the entirety of these data sources for prediction. While this difference in the prediction process prevents a direct comparison, we still report the accuracy results achieved by [24] to provide a general sense of our framework potential.

The proposed framework achieves a mean accuracy of 76.31% and 92.33% when the visual and audio content is used, respectively, in Table II. The mean accuracy is computed across the categories Native, WhatsApp, and YouTube. The corresponding accuracies in [24] for the visual and audio content are 74.84% and 67.81%, respectively.

Regarding the fusion results returned by the proposed framework, the best mean accuracy across the Native, WhatsApp, and YouTube categories in Table III is $95,38\%$. The latter accuracy is achieved by the product rule. The corresponding accuracy in [24] is 95.27%.

Both unimodal and bimodal classification indicate the potential of our approach for CMI, with the product rule demonstrating better performance than the sum rule. The superior performance of the product rule can be attributed to the higher joint probabilities generated when all modalities align, as observed in the mean results presented in Table II.

Future work will focus on various key areas to further analyse our framework. The robustness of the framework can be investigated on different levels of noise. Possible overfitting issues can be analyzed by performing training with more lightweight models [31]. Other datasets that contain more recent devices, like the FloreView dataset [32], can be employed to evaluate the proposed framework.

VII. CONCLUSION

CMI holds significant importance in multimedia forensic applications. This paper introduces a framework capable of device identification using audio, visual content, or a combination of both. CNNs are employed to address the device identification problem as a classification task. Experimental evaluation demonstrates a promising classification accuracy when independently using audio or visual content. Additionally, combining audio and visual content may lead to notable enhancements in classification performance, suggesting a potential area for further research.

VIII. ACKNOWLEDGMENTS

This research was supported by the Hellenic Foundation for Research and Innovation (HFRI) under the "2nd Call for HFRI Research Projects to support Faculty Members & Researchers" (Project Number: 3888).

REFERENCES

[1] A. Berdich, B. Groza, and R. Mayrhofer, "A survey on fingerprinting technologies for smartphones based on embedded transducers," *IEEE Internet of Things Journal*, vol. 10, no. 16, pp. 14 646–14 670, 2023.

[2] C. E. Nwokeji, A. Sheikh-Akbari, A. Gorbenko, and I. Mporas, "Source camera identification techniques: A survey," *Journal of Imaging*, vol. 10, no. 2, p. 31, 2024.

[3] M. C. Stamm, M. Wu, and K. J. R. Liu, "Information forensics: An overview of the first decade," *IEEE Access*, vol. 1, pp. 167–200, 2013.

[4] A. Diwan and U. Sonkar, "Visualizing the truth: A survey of multimedia forensic analysis," *Multimedia Tools and Applications*, pp. 1–28, 2023.

[5] J. Lukas, J. Fridrich, and M. Goljan, "Digital camera identification from sensor pattern noise," *IEEE Transactions on Information Forensics and Security*, vol. 1, no. 2, pp. 205–214, 2006.

[6] S. Davis and P. Mermelstein, "Comparison of parametric representations for monosyllabic word recognition in continuously spoken sentences," *IEEE Transactions on Acoustics, Speech, and Signal Processing*, vol. 28, no. 4, pp. 357–366, 1980.

[7] C. Kotropoulos, "Source phone identification using sketches of features," *IET biometrics*, vol. 3, no. 2, pp. 75–83, 2014.

[8] C. Kotropoulos and S. Samaras, "Mobile phone identification using recorded speech signals," in *Proceedings of the 19th International Conference on Digital Signal Processing*. IEEE, 2014, pp. 586–591.

[9] D. Kritsiolis and C. Kotropoulos, "Mobile phone identification from recorded speech signals using non-speech segments and universal background model adaptation," in *Proceedings of the 13th International Conference on Pattern Recognition Applications and Methods*, 2024, pp. 793–800.

[10] L. Bondi *et al.*, "First steps toward camera model identification with convolutional neural networks," *IEEE Signal Processing Letters*, vol. 24, no. 3, pp. 259–263, 2016.

[11] J. Kittler, M. Hatef, R. P. Duin, and J. Matas, "On combining classifiers," *IEEE Transactions on Pattern Analysis and Machine Intelligence*, vol. 20, no. 3, pp. 226–239, 1998.

[12] "Camera model identification fusing audio and visual content," [retrieved: May 20, 2024]. [Online]. Available: https://github.com/iTsingalis/IARIADevIDFusion

[13] D. Timmerman, S. Bennabhaktula, E. Alegre, and G. Azzopardi, "Video camera identification from sensor pattern noise with a constrained convnet," *arXiv preprint arXiv:2012.06277*, 2020.

[14] R. R. López, A. El-Khattabi, A. L. S. Orozco, and L. J. G. Villalba, "Smartphone video source identification based on sensor pattern noise," *International Journal of Electronics and Communication Engineering*, vol. 11, no. 5, pp. 597–600, 2017.

[15] S. Mandelli *et al.*, "A modified Fourier-Mellin approach for source device identification on stabilized videos," in *Proceedings of the International Conference on Image Processing*. IEEE, 2020, pp. 1266–1270.

[16] E. Altinisik, H. T. Sencar, and D. Tabaa, "Video source characterization using encoding and encapsulation characteristics," *IEEE Transactions on Information Forensics and Security*, vol. 17, pp. 3211–3224, 2022.

[17] Y. Akbari, N. Almaadeed, S. Al-Maadeed, F. Khelifi, and A. Bouridane, "PRNU-net: A deep learning approach for source camera model identification based on videos taken with smartphone," in *Proceedings of the 26th International Conference on Pattern Recognition*. IEEE, 2022, pp. 599–605.

[18] G. S. Bennabhaktula, D. Timmerman, E. Alegre, and G. Azzopardi, "Source camera device identification from videos," *SN Computer Science*, vol. 3, no. 4, p. 316, 2022.

[19] D. Shullani, M. Fontani, M. Iuliani, O. A. Shaya, and A. Piva, "Vision: A video and image dataset for source identification," *EURASIP Journal on Information Security*, vol. 2017, pp. 1–16, 2017.

[20] Y. Akbari *et al.*, "A new forensic video database for source smartphone identification: Description and analysis," *IEEE Access*, vol. 10, pp. 20 080–20 091, 2022.

[21] N. Manisha, C.-T. Li, and K. A. Kotegar, "Source camera identification with a robust device fingerprint: Evolution from image-based to video-based approaches," *Sensors*, vol. 23, no. 17, p. 7385, 2023.

[22] B. Hosler *et al.*, "A video camera model identification system using deep learning and fusion," in *Proceedings of the IEEE International Conference on Acoustics, Speech, and Signal Processing*. IEEE, 2019, pp. 8271–8275.

[23] B. Wang, K. Zhong, and M. Li, "Ensemble classifier-based source camera identification using fusion features," *Multimedia Tools and Applications*, vol. 78, no. 7, pp. 8397–8422, 2019.

[24] D. Dal Cortivo, S. Mandelli, P. Bestagini, and S. Tubaro, "CNN-based multi-modal camera model identification on video sequences," *Journal of Imaging*, vol. 7, no. 8, p. 135, 2021.

[25] "Vision dataset," [retrieved: May 20, 2024]. [Online]. Available: https://lesc.dinfo.unifi.it/VISION/

[26] K. He, X. Zhang, S. Ren, and J. Sun, "Deep residual learning for image recognition," in *Proceedings of the IEEE Conference on Computer Vision and Pattern Recognition*, 2016, pp. 770–778.

[27] J. Ngiam *et al.*, "Multimodal deep learning," in *Proceedings of the International Conference on Machine Learning*, 2011, pp. 689–696.

[28] K. Liu, Y. Li, N. Xu, and P. Natarajan, "Learn to combine modalities in multimodal deep learning," *arXiv preprint arXiv:1805.11730*, 2018.

[29] Q. McNemar, "Note on the sampling error of the difference between correlated proportions or percentages," *Psychometrika*, vol. 12, no. 2, pp. 153–157, 1947.

[30] "McNemar's test for classifier comparisons," [retrieved: May 20, 2024]. [Online]. Available: https://rasbt.github.io/mlxtend/user_guide/evaluate/mcnemar/

[31] C.-H. Wang, K.-Y. Huang, Y. Yao, J.-C. Chen, H.-H. Shuai, and W.-H. Cheng, "Lightweight Deep Learning: An Overview," *IEEE Consumer Electronics Magazine*, 2022.

[32] D. Baracchi, D. Shullani, M. Iuliani, and A. Piva, "FloreView: An image and video dataset for forensic analysis," *IEEE Access*, 2023.

Using Security Metrics to improve Cyber-Resilience

Tobias Eggendorfer
TH Ingolstadt
Faculty of Computer Science
Ingolstadt, Germany
Email: tobias.eggendorfer@thi.de

Katja Andresen
HWR Berlin
Department of Business and Economics
Berlin, Germany
Email: katja.andresen@hwr-berlin.de

***Abstract*—Not only critical infrastructure but also everyday interaction in a society relies heavily on secure IT systems. Examples of patients dying due to hospitals unable to admit them because of a ransomware incident indicate a low level of cyber-resilience. To increase cyber-resilience, suggested measures range from anti-malware via backups and redundancy to regular security updates. While following these guidelines, there is an intensive discussion which systems provides the best security. There is no answer – yet. IT security lacks a reliable system to measure security in order to compare systems and make a qualified decision. This paper discusses current research in security metrics and why it is important to provide a security metric to improve cyber-resilience. The authors discuss the advantages, the state of the art and future research needed in order to improve cyber-resillience with security metrics.**

Keywords-Security Metrics; Quality Metrics; Software Security; Software Quality, Cyber-Security; Cyber-Resillience

I. Introduction

In March 2022, the German Federal Office for IT-Security (BSI) issued a security warning regarding the use of Kaspersky Anti-Virus. Since the company is owned by Russians, in light of the Ukraine-Russia war, this would pose a security risk [1]. This was the first warning the BSI has ever released, and it was not based on a software security issue, but on ownership of a software company. This decision meant to increase Germany's cyber-resilience was heavily discussed in and out of court [2].

The Russian war also introduced cyber-attacks by pro as well as contra Russian groups. Those included the usual ransomware incidents, but also attacking railway networks to disturb Russian troop movement [3]. In the wake of these attacks, a cyber-physical security issue in uninterruptible power supplies that could set them and connected devices on fire, was discovered [4]. Whether it was actively exploited is currently unknown, however it demonstrates that even systems meant to increase Information Technology (IT) safety could be attacked. The same holds true for IT security tools with security issues, such as attacks on firewalls [5] or anti-malware [6].

A. The need for security metrics

The vendors of both security and regular software claim their products were secure, or at least as secure as currently possible. However, there is no approved and commonly accepted method to verify this. For most cases even measurable security requirements do not exist.

Based on a broadly understood security metric, also combinations of systems could be evaluated and compared on a security scale. Applying this, IT security professionals could easily identify whether adding e.g., an anti malware solution would actually help security or even reduce security levels.

B. Cyber-Resilience through security metrics

The US government has recently been urged to stop using Microsoft products, amid fears government data could be stolen considering the still ongoing "hacking attack" on Microsoft. To the US Government their software seems to be too vulnerable, posing a too high risk on the US society. If a nations government and thus public infrastructure has such a high risk of being successfully hacked, cyber-resilience of this nation is not satisfactory. Hence, using different software could increase the national cyber-resilience [7].

Whether or not the US government is right, is uncertain - even though the authors share this impression. But rather than belief, anecdotal reports or personal experience, a security metric would support objective judgement. It would immediately enhance cyber-resilience by allow to select appropriate systems.

C. Structure of this paper

The paper is structured as follows: Section II provides a background on security issues (Section II-A), attack vectors, current cyber-security measures (Section II-B), cyber-resilience (Section II-D) and legal requirements for cyber-security (Section II-C). It concludes with how cyber-security issues are currently prevented (Section II-E), how ownership and thereby responsibility could affect cyber-resilience (Section II-G) and how security is managed outside IT (Section II-F).

Section III then discusses software quality and security metrics as well as software quality standards. Additionally it looks at formal verification as a software security measure.

We then continue in Section IV on the impact a security metric would have on cyber-resilience, and approach this from a legal and economic perspective.

Section V provides a conclusion and gives an outlook.

II. Background

To some, security incidents happen like accidents, hardly predictable and are the product of avid hackers. To others security incidents are a result of insufficient software quality assurance in the development process. We asume, strict quality management could prevent the vast majority of them, since security issues follow patterns and abuse flaws introduced during development. This also considers factors such as the legal perspective on system quality and vendor ownership.

A. *Typical attack vectors*

This dispute may not be fully resolved, however analysing typical attack vectors could provide an indication. The two most prevalent is the abuse of a security flaw in software, be it a publicly known and patched or yet unknown "zero-day", and tricking users into insecure behaviour such as running unknown programs or installing software.

1) Security relevant software issues: While for web applications the OWASP Foundation provides a regularly updated list of their perception of the ten most relevant security issues [8], there is nothing equivalent for regular software, such as operating systems or office software.

On a very high level of abstraction security issues result from the possibility to alter the program's work flow to execute commands in favour of the attacker or to ignore restrictions in accessing data. Examples include shell code injections through buffer overflows or format string vulnerabilities as well as remote shell command injections, which might even be achieved through Structured Query Language (SQL)-injections by "selecting" a series of commands into a local file that is later executed.

Some of these injections are straight forward, such as using a script language's `eval`-function with not sanitised user input, others are a lot more complex, such as the buffer overflows triggered by integer overflows in stage-fright [9].

These two examples not only differ in their exploitation complexity but also in the difficulty to discover them in the source code: While `eval` is detected with automated code review [10], stage-fright was partly due to how a C-compiler handled a type conversion between 32 and 64 bit integers when multiplying two 32-bit values: Without an explicit typecast of at least one of the two factors to 64 bit, despite the result variable being 64 bit, the compiler used a 32 bit multiplication, resulting in an integer overflow. To detect this and the resulting buffer overflow a deep understanding of the compiler and its behaviour are needed [9].

Prevention of the first is as simple as detecting it, while the latter might require more and deeper code analysis.

The complexity of security issues, both in exploiting as well as preventing them might have an impact on the overall security of software. One would assume if a system is vulnerable to simple security issues, it might have an overall lower security level than one that requires more elaborate exploits.

2) Human behaviour: Often security incidents are said to be related to user behaviour, with awareness and training proposed as a remedy [11][12][13][14][15][16]: Clicking on suspicious software or otherwise allowing attackers to install malware is often considered to be a major security issue. However if a simple, unaware user interaction breaks a system's security one might as well argue that this system has a low overall security level and is not resilient to attacks.

Current ransomware attacks serve as example: Installed by the user in reaction to a Trojan like attack, i.e., social engineering, they abuse the ability of a single mal-functioning process to escalate privileges to encrypt the disk.

3) Impact of security issues: Both the complexity to exploit security issues and the impact might vary. Scores like the Common Vulnerability Scoring System (CVSS) [17] only estimate the impact, helping a system administrator to decide on the urgency of a patch or other counter measures. However, they do neither provide a metric for the overall security of software or systems, nor does the score address context.

B. *Current counter measures*

To prevent security incidents currently system administrators are requested to install additional, potentially vulnerable software, such as malware scanners, firewalls or content filtering proxies [5][6], considered state of the art security measures. Simoultanously, users learn what to click and what not [18], including elaborate spear phishing to show users how vulnerable they are – or how well they detect threads.

This moves the perception of the reason for the security issue far away from the software quality issue, it actually is: It is often considered to a user or human factors problem.

C. *Legal requirements on software security*

EU regulations such as NIS-2 require software manufacturers to provide better security, the same holds true for concepts such as the BSI introducing a "Software Quality"-seal, based on a self-evaluation by the software manufacturers .The seal also uses a fair bit of their reputation and how fast they would provide security patches [2]. While the speed of fixing issues is a reasonable measure, neither the frequency of the need for fixes nor the severity of the flaws is not taken into account. Nor whether they could have been prevented. Even the manufacturers attitude and interaction towards external security researchers is not considered – there still are software providers threatening to sue those reporting security issues [19], while other embrace them, providing bug bounties. Some manufacturer even try to downplay reports as not security relevant, e.g., because they do not provide a proof-of-concept exploit. For the seal matters, they are better off.

The frequency of security patches might as well give a rough estimate on how efficient quality management is: In other industries, such as cars, if a manufacturer often needs to recall his cars, it immediately affects the quality perception.

Recently, the EU Cyber-Resilliance-Act (CRA) transported concepts such as a Bill of Materials (BoM), well known outside IT, to software. The Software Bill of Materials (SBoM) lists third party software, e.g., external libraries used, with the intention to identify security issues related to external software. The log4shell issue [20] is a good example for the benefits of a SBoM, since many projects relied on Log4J. The SBoM might also help to estimate the quality of software.

D. *Cyber-Resilience*

Cyber-resilience is the ability to react, respond, adapt or pro actively anticipate incidents on cyber-connected infrastructures [21][22][23][24]. It deploys cyber-security by continuously learning from incidents to adapt to new levels of robustness to fulfil business objectives. Therefore, for any organisation or government institution in an interconnected cyber-physical world increasing cyber-resilience is considered highly relevant.

Cyber-resilience prevents security incidents through system design. This might include concepts such as backup- and recovery-plans, emergency procedures, but first and foremost requires systems secure by design. This is what security metrics measure.

Software security metrics therefore would also contribute to defence capabilities, incident detection, crisis management while additionally increasing the collective resilience. They would also reduce the effects of cyber-warfare.

E. Preventing these attacks

An effective way to prevent software issues might well be to educate software developers more. Projects with high security levels such as OpenBSD use simple concepts, such as code reviews, clear coding standards, automated software testing etc. [25]. The OWASP SAMM provides a similar guidance for the software development cycle consisting of governance design, implementation and verification measures as well as defined processes if issues would arise despite all the effort put into the project so far [26]. Both aim to avoid typical programming mistakes that could lead to security issues.

These measures preventing attacks need to have an immediate impact on a security score. Currently, they are not accounted for in most software buying decisions. With a security metric, they become visible, affect procurement decission and thus impact cyber-resilience.

F. Measuring security outside IT

Measuring requires to code observations with numbers, which would then create a scale - be it a physical feature like temperature or a non-physical feature like quality [27].

Measuring security and quality of software, an intangible good, is much harder than for tangible ones. Still, some quality measurement concepts could be adapted from other areas.

In automobile industry, security as well as safety issues due to quality problems are of high relevance: They cannot easily be fixed with an update customers install, but requires to transport the vehicles to a workshop, potentially providing customers with a replacement car while the issue is fixed, and thereby generates high costs for the manufacturer. These alone may provide a relevant motivation for higher quality. A recall by national car safety associations, forcing manufacturers to fix all relevant models immediately, is also public.

Therefore car industry implements massive quality checking on items bought by external manufacturers, often with contractual penalties if requirements are not met. This concept only slowly moves over to software industry with the concept of a SBoM by both the CRA and the US Executive Order 14028. Still neither requires any of the library providers to document quality measures.

Car industry invests heavily in crash tests to analyse safety issues, the results of these tests provide a score, which in turn influences development of future cars and allows for comparison – again, regulations such as General Data Protection Regulation (GDPR) [28] and CRA slowly introduce the need for penetration tests, which is an equivalent to a crash test in providing both a security measure and input to a feedback loop affecting the development cycle. However this has not yet been widely adopted.

Those measures do not substitute quality management, they only report on the effects. By contrast, a software security metric measures quality and thereby has an immediate effect on the development process.

G. Responsibility and Ownership

A key challenge to be solved is to determine the indicators to consider as part of the metric. On an operational level the scope and impact of potential attacks appear to be based on security flaws immanent to the software. The (quality) assessment addresses critical aspects by analysing the system behaviour and identifying the effects.

The software in use is usually part of a contract system including parties such as vendors and manufacturers in charge of updates, customising and changes. The BSI warning on replacing security software of a certain vendor (see Section I was purely based on ownership issues. The manufacturer and not the software itself gave reason to alert the nation [1].

A broadened perspective on impact factors could include further indirect aspects as expressed responsibility for security and safety. A "responsibility model" might include an assessment of security compliance rules, e.g., in terms of openness and communication towards security researchers reporting potential bugs (sued or rewarded).

Hence, current challenges impose a need to discuss issues as ownership and responsibility to increase cyber-resilience. Adding company profiles along with a technical software assessment might therefore contribute to a meaningful metric.

III. Research in Software Quality and Security Metrics

Despite the importance of measurable software quality and security, currently there are no metrics available. Software quality serves as a proxy for security: Quality means the absence of flaws, each flaw could result in a security issue.

A. Software Quality measurement

Early research on software quality includes [29], proposing to identify parts of a program with a high probability for flaws – the focus was not on security issues, but on functional problems. But this research only analysed the final product without incorporating earlier unit tests into analysis. Other early researchers suffer from different understandings of software quality and security, with no common definition [30][31]. The latter introduces a complex metric with weights for several aspects of quality, however it does not provide how to compute the individual quality measures.

[32] uses a retrospective approach by measuring reported flaws in software. For a security score, this could be replicated using the Common Vulnerabilities and Exposures (CVE)-database. But neither are all issues are assigned a CVE-number

nor are all published, the score is not precise. Also some software is hardly ever scrutinised by security experts, but other under heavy analysis. Thus CVEs would only provide a rough indication rather than a precise score. Additionally the score measures past not current quality.

B. *Software Security Metrics*

Later work focused more on security metrics, such as [33], providing relevant reasons for measuring security, but no metric, since this would be too complex. in [34] the author suggests to divide complex systems into smaller components for analysis.

[35] encounters the same issue: While the authors consider security metrics as highly relevant, and provide a definition of security, they eventually consider a measured metric as far too complex. As a work-around they suggest to at provide estimation methods, which they then demonstrate outside the IT security world. Unfortunately they do not back-port the results to IT. [36] and [37] come to the same conclusion, when providing accurate computation methods to compose security scores, but are unable to provide the individual scores.

[38] defines a Software Reliabilty Metric, which differs from a security metric, in that it analyses how often software faults occur during a given time frame. The work also discusses several testing methods for this metric, either based on black box testing, which could be adapted to security metrics by a penetration test, or on a software metric, like lines of code, complexity and developer experience, or finally from analysing the software components, called "architecture based" by the respective authors. The work clearly points out that reliability issues in software are never based on wear, but always on design and usage. But overall, while the work provides good concepts, it does not deliver an usable metric, that could be modified to a software security metric.

More recently [39] as well as [40] started analysis into security metrics, however their focus is on cryptographic protocols. While still hard to apply quantifiable metrics to them, feasibility seems to be higher, since the scope is more focused. Another more accessible area for security metrics is networking [41], since it is less complex than software.

[42] suggests a metric to measure the security of web applications, thereby reducing the complexity to a subset of possible programs. However the metric is still mostly reactive, contains some data that cannot be measured like "knowledge in security". The work however indicates there is still a need for research.

Additionally there are some reactive scores, including Time to Patch or Mean Time to Remediate (MTTR), both indicating how long it took for a reported issue to be mitigated, Vulnerability Density, a measure for how many issues exists, Mean Time to Detect (MTTD), giving an idea how long an issues remains undetected. All of these however do neither measure the quality nor the security of the code, they only provide *ex-post* measure.

C. *Quality standards*

Some ISO standards relate to security and quality, such as ISO 27000 series, ISO 15408 and the derived common criteria as well as IEEE 1028. All of these define processes related to quality, but no measurable quality criteria. By that any certification does not indicate whether a software product is secure. A, e.g., ISO 27001 certified organisation would know how to cope with security issues, but there are no prevention mechanisms for flaws in the code. These however would increase security and thus affect a security metric.

D. *Formal Verification*

A mathematical approach to software quality is formal verification with, e.g., Hoare logics [43]. Clearly defined pre- and post-conditions for a command or a set of commands identify logic flaws in programs. By enhancing these conditions also issues such as off-by-one or buffer-overflow could be detected and thus be prevented [44]. However formal verification is a tedious and slow process. Current research tries to establish faster and more efficient methods and support schemes [45].

IV. Impact of a security metric

While software security metrics seem hard to achieve and will require more research, there is an immediate need for them, since they would have a multitude of effects, be them legal, economical or by improving cyber-resilience. [33] pointed some of these effects out, a list we add on in this paper.

A. *Legal effects*

With the GDPR forcing data processors to both evaluate their own IT security as well as that of sub-processors when it comes to processing personal data, a security metric would allow them to speed up this evaluation process while maintaining independence from vendor claims. While larger corporations may be able to do their security assessments from a technical perspective, smaller entrepreneurs can hardly afford the extra costs and time. Often enough they do not have the expertise either. In practice whenever security assessments in a GDPR context are performed, vendors usually require non disclosure agreements, preventing sharing the results with other interested parties, which could streamline the process at least.

As a result most data processors resort to either using software and systems they assume to be secure based on vendors' claims or, even worse, because others use these systems. Ironically those others will also point to other users. The issue is well known with data protection authorities, they therefore tend to be reluctant in punishing those confronted with the impossibility to verify claims. From a legal and a socio-technical perspective this is highly unsatisfactory, since it provides a factual bypass. It is also counter-productive to the concept of cyber-resilience as it is endorsed by the GDPR.

With a security metric in place, both data processors as well as authorities could much easier enforce the use of secure products and sanction the use of insecure, by that creating a market incentive for vendors to (finally) improve their products' security.

Critical infrastructure regulations in different legislations also enforce assessment of IT security and thus adequate levels of security. To do so, they would as well need to be able to assess any software vendors systems. This is hardly feasible, especially when it comes to closed source software. With a security metric the assessment was simplified, which would allow for more straight-forward compliance with the legal requirements. Currently, this is achieved by claiming "best practices" were used, which often means using the same product as others do, often by simply calling it an industry standard. That "standard" provides then the default security level. As many security incidents demonstrate, this self-reinforcing industry standard obviously is not up to the levels needed.

Without knowing which system is secure and which is not, critical infrastructure providers cannot invest in the most secure solution, which – by definition of critical infrastructure – has a negative effect on the cyber-resilience.

Similar legal requirements are put forward by regulations such as the CRA and NIS-2. Thus the legal system has a strong desire and need for objective software security metrics.

B. Economic effects

As shown above, Investing in software requires by law to buy a secure product, which is hard to identify. The markets lack of transparency results in non-optimal buying-decisions. Market mechanisms as set forward by the free market concept [46] [47] however require buyers to be able to make wise and educated decisions, they should neither be fooled by wrong advertising nor decide under an obvious lack of information.

In most markets for tangible goods there are quality tests and measures in place, almost everywhere in the world there are product testing organisations such as "Consumer Bonds" in the US, "Which?" In the UK or "Stiftung Warentest" in Germany. The same is available for industry grade products. This provides for well-informed buyers and their educated market decisions.

For a free market an objective security metric is therefore an important requirement. Again the car industry could provide an example: 140 years ago, when the "Benz Motorwagen" was the first car, customers did invest in this new means of transportation for various reasons, safety and reliability were not among those. In the 1960s, when Volvo introduced reinforced passenger cells and the three point security belt, as well as Mercedes started with crash testing their vehicles, customers slowly started to understand the need for safety measures and made them a requirement. Since then, wearing a seat belt has become mandatory by law in most countries, passive security has been encompassed by an easy to understand star system in the NCAP series.

As a consequence safety has influenced buyers decision since, and has become so common place that by now, it is taken as granted and customer interest has since moved to other parameters, such as eco-friendliness and usability.

C. Effects on Cyber-Resilience

In a market where purveyors of software have a strong incentive to invest in more secure systems due to customers demand, triggered by an objective software security metric, it is to be expected that cyber-resilience increases – much similar to a constantly decreasing amount of deadly traffic accidents due to increased safety there.

Compared to other industries, the current system of trusting software vendors' security promises and relying on the buying decision of others seems inferior. It undermines cyber-resilience by providing software vendors with the wrong incentive to constantly increase their customer base, potentially consider lock-in-effects in order to keep their customers and thereby hope that their installed base would keep them ahead of competitors, making their products a *de-facto* 'industry standard".

More impact is to be expected once scores for single programs could be combined to provide an overall system score rather than an individual score for just a software product. With this measure, deciding which operating system to run a word processor on becomes feasible, e.g., whether a system providing LibreOffice should run with Linux, MacOS, BSD or Windows, when security is paramount. The combined would also identify the weakest link and to mitigate the risks associated to it.

V. Conclusion and Outlook

The concept of introducing a software security metrics is not new, it has been discussed since decades – first with a focus on quality, later with an explicit focus on security. Research in that field has stalled, current research therefore has not yet provided any practical applicable results. Since not providing immediate results, funding seems to have stopped, furthering the stall.

In this paper we address the current state as well as impact factors to be discussed in the future. Our work demonstrates that there is a strong need for further research in security metrics, as we show security metrics are already required by law. We also show that security metrics would have a massive economical impact and help the software market to move to more secure software. By doing so we show that cyber-resilience would increase. We therefore strongly suggest to increase research into security metrics.

References

[1] Bundesregierung, "Aktuelle Warnung des BSI (translated: Current BSI warnings)," 2022. [Online]. Available: https://www.bundesregierung.de/breg-de/themen/sicherheit-und-verteidigung/cybersicherheitslage-kaspersky-2015970

[2] F. Deusch and T. Eggendorfer, "Update IT-Sicherheitsrecht 2021/2022 (translated: Update IT-security-law 2021/2022)," *K&R*, vol. 2022, no. 12, pp. 794–803, 2022.

[3] A. Roth, "Cyberpartisans hack belarusian railway to disrupt russian buildup," 2022. [Online]. Available: https://www.theguardian.com/world/2022/jan/25/cyberpartisans-hack-belarusian-railway-to-disrupt-russian-buildup

[4] G. Levy, Y. Sarel, B. Seri, and B. Hadad, "Tlsstorm," 2022. [Online]. Available: https://info.armis.com/rs/645-PDC-047/images/Armis-TLStorm-WP%20%281%29.pdf

[5] CISA, "Threat actors exploiting F5 BIG-IP CVE-2022-1388," 2022. [Online]. Available: https://www.cisa.gov/news-events/cybersecurity-advisories/aa22-138a

[6] NIST, "CVE-2023-24934: Microsoft defender security feature bypass vulnerability," 2023. [Online]. Available: https://nvd.nist.gov/vuln/detail/CVE-2023-24934

[7] U. D. of Homeland Security, "Cyber safety review board releases report on Microsoft Online Exchange incident from summer 2023." [Online]. Available: https://www.dhs.gov/news/2024/04/02/cyber-safety-review-board-releases-report-microsoft-online-exchange-incident-summer

[8] OWASP, "OWASP top ten," 2021. [Online]. Available: https://owasp.org/Top10/

[9] J. Drake, "Stagefright: Scary code in the heart of Android," Zimperium, 2015. [Online]. Available: https://www.blackhat.com/docs/us-15/materials/us-15-Drake-Stagefright-Scary-Code-In-The-Heart-Of-Android.pdf

[10] T. Eggendorfer, "At the source. static code analysis finds avoidable errors," *Admin Magazine*, vol. 2019, no. 53, 2019. [Online]. Available: https://www.admin-magazine.com/Archive/2019/53/Static-code-analysis-finds-avoidable-errors

[11] Verizon, "Data breach investigations report." [Online]. Available: https://www.verizon.com/business/resources/reports/dbir/

[12] R. Rohan, S. Funilkul, D. Pal, and W. Chutimaskul, "Understanding of human factors in cybersecurity: A systematic literature review," in *2021 International Conference on Computational Performance Evaluation (ComPE)*, Dec 2021, pp. 133–140.

[13] E. Metalidou, C. Marinagi, P. Trivellas, N. Eberhagen, C. Skourlas, and G. Giannakopoulos, "The human factor of information security: Unintentional damage perspective," *Procedia - Social and Behavioral Sciences*, vol. 147, pp. 424–428, 2014, 3rd International Conference on Integrated Information (IC-ININFO). [Online]. Available: https://www.sciencedirect.com/science/article/pii/S1877042814040440

[14] M. J. Dupuis, R. E. Crossler, and B. Endicott-Popovsky, "Measuring the human factor in information security and privacy," in *Proceedings of the 2016 49th Hawaii International Conference on System Sciences (HICSS)*, ser. HICSS '16. USA: IEEE Computer Society, 2016, p. 3676–3685. [Online]. Available: https://doi.org/10.1109/HICSS.2016.459

[15] J. Hielscher, U. Menges, S. Parkin, A. Kluge, and M. A. Sasse, ""employees who don't accept the time security takes are not aware enough": The CISO view of human-centred security," in *Proceedings of the 32nd USENIX Conference on Security Symposium*, ser. SEC '23. USA: USENIX Association, 2023.

[16] J. Hielscher, A. Kluge, U. Menges, and M. A. Sasse, "Taking out the trash: Why security behavior change requires intentional forgetting," in *Proceedings of the 2021 New Security Paradigms Workshop*, ser. NSPW '21. New York, NY, USA: Association for Computing Machinery, 2022, p. 108–122. [Online]. Available: https://doi.org/10.1145/3498891.3498902

[17] NIST, "Vulnerability metrics," NIST, 2022. [Online]. Available: https://nvd.nist.gov/vuln-metrics/cvss

[18] M. Bada, A. M. Sasse, and J. R. C. Nurse, "Cyber security awareness campaigns: Why do they fail to change behaviour?" *ArXiv*, vol. abs/1901.02672, 2014. [Online]. Available: https://api.semanticscholar.org/CorpusID:17775217

[19] F. Deusch and T. Eggendorfer, "Strafbarkeit von IT-Sicherheitsforschern und Pentestern (translated: Criminal liability of IT-security researchers and pentesters)," *K&R*, vol. 2023, no. 10, pp. 649–656, 10 20223.

[20] "Log4shell (cve-2021-44228, cve-2021-45046)," 2021. [Online]. Available: https://log4.sh/

[21] NIST, "cyber resiliency." [Online]. Available: https://csrc.nist.gov/glossary/term/cyber_resiliency

[22] K. Hausken, "Cyber resilience in firms, organizations and societies," *Internet of Things*, vol. 11, p. 100204, 2020. [Online]. Available: https://www.sciencedirect.com/science/article/pii/S2542660520300408

[23] I. Linkov and A. Kott, *Fundamental Concepts of Cyber Resilience: Introduction and Overview*. Cham: Springer International Publishing, 2019, pp. 1–25. [Online]. Available: https://doi.org/10.1007/978-3-319-77492-3_1

[24] F. Björck, M. Henkel, J. Stirna, and J. Zdravkovic, "Cyber resilience – fundamentals for a definition," in *New Contributions in Information Systems and Technologies*, A. Rocha, A. M. Correia, S. Costanzo, and L. P. Reis, Eds. Cham: Springer International Publishing, 2015, pp. 311–316.

[25] OpenBSD, "OpenBSD security." [Online]. Available: http://www.openbsd.org/security.html

[26] OWASP, "SAMM model overview," OWASP. [Online]. Available: https://owaspsamm.org/model/

[27] R. Böhme and F. C. Freiling, *On Metrics and Measurements*. Berlin, Heidelberg: Springer Berlin Heidelberg, 2008, pp. 7–13. [Online]. Available: https://doi.org/10.1007/978-3-540-68947-8_2

[28] F. Deusch and T. Eggendorfer, "Penetrationstest bei Auftragsverarbeitung (translated: Penetrationtesting sub-processors)," *K&R*, vol. 2018, no. 04, pp. 223–230, 2018.

[29] V. Y. Shen, T.-J. Yu, S. M. Thebaut, and L. R. Paulsen, "Identifying error-prone software an empirical study," *IEEE Trans. Softw. Eng.*, vol. 11, no. 4, p. 317–324, apr 1985. [Online]. Available: https://doi.org/10.1109/TSE.1985.232222

[30] T. Khoshgoftaar, J. Munson, G. Richardson, and B. Bhattacharya, "Predictive modeling techniques of software quality from software measures," *IEEE Transactions on Software Engineering*, vol. 18, no. 11, pp. 979–987, nov 1992.

[31] J. P. Cavano and J. A. McCall, "A framework for the measurement of software quality," in *Proceedings of the Software Quality Assurance Workshop on Functional and Performance Issues*. New York, NY, USA: Association for Computing Machinery, 1978, p. 133–139. [Online]. Available: https://doi.org/10.1145/800283.811113

[32] W. Florac, "Software quality measurement: A framework for counting problems and defects," Carnegie Mellon University, Software Engineering Institute's Digital Library, Carnegie Mellon University, Tech. Rep. CMU/SEI-92-TR-022, Sep 1992. [Online]. Available: https://insights.sei.cmu.edu/library/software-quality-measurement-a-framework-for-counting-problems-and-defects/

[33] R. Savola, "On the feasibility of utilizing security metrics in software-intensive systems," in *IJCSNS International Journal of Computer Science and Network Security*, vol. 10, no. 1, 01 2010.

[34] R. M. Savola, "Strategies for security measurement objective decomposition," in *2012 Information Security for South Africa*, 2012, pp. 1–8.

[35] C. Wang and W. A. Wulf, "Towards a framework for security measurement," in *Proceedings of the 20th NISSC*, 1997. [Online]. Available: https://api.semanticscholar.org/CorpusID:14546880

[36] S. Islam and P. Falcarin, "Measuring security requirements for software security," in *2011 IEEE 10th International Conference on Cybernetic Intelligent Systems (CIS)*, Sep. 2011, pp. 70–75.

[37] G. Hatzivasilis, I. Papaefstathiou, and C. Manifavas, "Software security, privacy, and dependability: Metrics and measurement," *IEEE Software*, vol. 33, no. 4, pp. 46–54, July 2016.

[38] I. Eusgeld, F. Fraikin, M. Rohr, F. Salfner, and U. Wappler, *Software Reliability*. Berlin, Heidelberg: Springer Berlin Heidelberg, 2008, pp. 104–125. [Online]. Available: https://doi.org/10.1007/978-3-540-68947-8_10

[39] J. Müller-Quade, L. Benz, C. F. Fruböse, C. Martin, and J. Mechler, "Quantification of security." [Online]. Available: https://crypto.iti.kit.edu/quantification-of-security.php

[40] Z. Benenson, U. Kühn, and S. Lucks, *Cryptographic Attack Metrics*. Berlin, Heidelberg: Springer Berlin Heidelberg, 2008, pp. 133–156. [Online]. Available: https://doi.org/10.1007/978-3-540-68947-8_12

[41] T. Holz, *Security Measurements and Metrics for Networks*. Berlin, Heidelberg: Springer Berlin Heidelberg, 2008, pp. 157–165. [Online]. Available: https://doi.org/10.1007/978-3-540-68947-8_13

[42] C. Binder, *Entwurf einer Metrik zur Bewertung des IT-Sicherheitsniveaus am Beispiel von Webanwendungen (translated: Design of a metric to measure the IT security level of web applications)*. Hagen: Masterthesis, FernUniversität in Hagen, February 2024.

[43] C. A. R. Hoare, "An axiomatic basis for computer programming," *Commun. ACM*, vol. 12, no. 10, p. 576–580, oct 1969. [Online]. Available: https://doi.org/10.1145/363235.363259

[44] G. Klein, J. Andronick, K. Elphinstone, G. Heiser, D. Cock, P. Derrin, D. Elkaduwe, K. Engelhardt, R. Kolanski, M. Norrish, T. Sewell, H. Tuch, and S. Winwood, "SeL4: Formal verification of an operating-system kernel," *Commun. ACM*, vol. 53, no. 6, p. 107–115, jun 2010. [Online]. Available: https://doi.org/10.1145/1743546.1743574

[45] A. für Innovation in der Cybersicherheit, "Tender on övit – ökosystem vertrauenswürdige it. beweisbare cybersicherheit (translation: Ecosystem trustworthy IT. proofable cyber-security)." [Online]. Available: https://www.cyberagentur.de/ausschreibungen/

[46] A. Smith, *An Inquiry into the Nature and Causes of the Wealth of Nations*. n/a, 1776.

[47] F. Daumann, *Die Rolle der Evolution in Hayeks Konzept freiheitssichernder Regeln (Translation: The role of evolution in Hayek's concept of freedom-securing rules*. Berlin, Boston: De Gruyter Oldenbourg, 2001, pp. 83–102. [Online]. Available: https://doi.org/10.1515/9783110506129-007

Automatic Assessment of Student Answers using Large Language Models: Decoding Didactic Concepts

Daniel Schönle
IDACUS Insitute
Furtwangen University
Furtwangen, Germany
email:schonledanielhfu@gmail.com

Christoph Reich
IDACUS Insitute
Furtwangen University
Furtwangen, Germany
email:christoph.reich@hs-furtwangen.de

Djaffar Ould Abdeslam
Institut IRIMAS
Université de Haute Alsace
Mulhouse, France
email:djafar.ould-abdeslam@uha.fr

Daniela Fiedler
Department of Science Education
University of Copenhagen
Copenhagen, Denmark
email:dfiedler@ind.ku.dk

Ute Harms
Department of Biology Education
IPN - Leibniz Institute for
Science and Mathematics Education
Kiel, Germany
email:harms@leibniz-ipn.de

Johannes Poser
Department of Biology Education
IPN - Leibniz Institute for
Science and Mathematics Education
Kiel, Germany
email:poser@leibniz-ipn.de

***Abstract*—This study evaluates machine learning for automating the evaluation of textual responses in virtual learning environments, particularly by applying advanced linguistic enhancement techniques. Techniques such as Transformer-based data augmentation, Part-of-Speech enhanced feature selection, and LinPair tokenisation were employed. The evaluation focused on classification quality and training efficiency using a synthetically created question-and-answer dataset, characterised by its limited sample size, extensive class range, and the complexity of identifying didactical elements. The findings indicate that while the Support Vector Machine (SVM) consistently outperforms the distilled version of the large language model Bidirectional Encoder Representations from Transformers (DistilBERT) in quality metrics, the integration of linguistic elements improved DistilBERT's performance significantly—achieving a 7.62% increase in F1-Score and a 17.02% rise in Hamming-Score. Despite these gains, DistilBERT recorded lower efficiency scores compared to SVM. This suggests that while SVM excels with synthetic data, Large Language Models demonstrate substantial potential in processing complex linguistic data when provided with linguistic information. These insights confirm the viability of both approaches as effective tools for automated assessment in educational settings.**

Keywords-machine learning; efficiency; linguistic; text classification; assessment.

I. Introduction

The advent of Virtual Learning Environments (VLE) marks a profound shift in educational paradigms, driven by the fusion of digital technologies and Machine Learning (ML) algorithms. This shift addresses the growing demand for educational experiences that are accessible, adaptable, and personalised to meet the needs of a diverse global learner population [1][2]. Sophisticated ML techniques enable VLEs to analyse learner data and deliver personalised content along with adaptive learning paths, significantly improving engagement and outcomes. The instrumental role of ML in fostering this adaptivity is paramount, as it dynamically refines content and pedagogical approaches based on learner interactions, optimising the educational pathway [3].

The typical interaction between teacher and student during the learning process is illustrated in Figure 1. When answering textual diagnostic questions, students provide open-text responses. The automation of diagnostic responses can be effectively integrated by analysing these open-text responses based on both the content of the student's response and the underlying didactic principles embedded within it. This integration facilitates a more nuanced understanding of student understanding and learning needs. This study evaluates the use of ML, especially Large Language Models (LLM), to automate the evaluation of text in VLEs. This research highlights the usefulness of advanced configurations in real-world educational settings by comparing established state-of-the-art methods with innovative techniques, such as LLM-based data augmentation, LLM-based text classification, Part-of-Speech enrichment (POS-Enrichment), *LinPair* Tokenization [4], and *UnImportant-Part-of-Speech* (UIP) feature selection [5]. Challenges related to the training dataset include small sample sizes, often reflecting data scarcity, the use of artificially created curated datasets, and the complexity of accurately identifying nuanced labels. Method setups are evaluated based on quality by F1-Score [6] and Hamming Loss [7]. A particular focus was on the integration of *LinPair*-Tokenization, *UIP* feature selection, and a quality-focused evaluation of efficiency via the *COmpact Efficiency* (CO) score [8]. This approach is novel in this domain.

The *Teacher questions and student answers for the SCRBio in the context of evolution* (QASCRBio) dataset [9], integral to the FiSK-Research-Project within the domain of didactic science, forms the foundation of this research. It includes questions, student responses, and corresponding assessment results as specific didactical diagnostic aspects. These elements are used for text classification to identify didactic attributes within student answers, which can be used for automated formative feedback or as assistive information for educators. The study presents a reliable setup for the automated assessment of

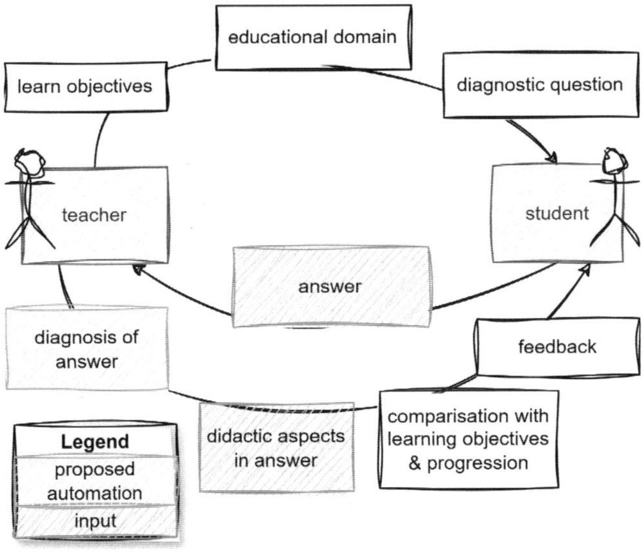

Figure 1. Context of Automatisation.

students' responses that can be used and is of value in real-life educational scenarios.

A. Didactic Background

In education, assessment tasks are crucial for improving the learning and teaching process. Constructing questions, underpinned by sound educational theory and practice, is a fundamental mechanism for diagnosing student understanding, revealing misconceptions and encouraging more profound engagement with the subject matter. Figure 2 provides an overview of the assessment and feedback process. Diagnostic questions are designed to reveal the basis of students' responses, highlighting correct and incorrect thinking patterns. They are particularly adept at identifying misconceptions by using distractors that target known misconceptions, providing insights into students' conceptual understanding [10]. Basic characteristics and theoretical frameworks of practical assessment questions have been established, drawing on the seminal contributions of scholars such as Popham (1995) [11], Brookhart (2017) [10], Black and Dylan (1998) [12].

B. Structure

This paper is organised into six sections. (i) Introduction; (ii) Related work, reviewing relevant e-learning and assessment literature; (iii) Automated didactic assessment, providing definitions, research questions, a description of the methodology and limitations of the work; (iv) Experiment, elaborating on the approach including the data set, implementation and evaluation; (v) Discussion, offering insights and implications of the findings; and (vi) Conclusion, reflecting on the broader implications and suggesting avenues for further research.

II. Related Work

This section provides an overview of the application of ML in VLEs. First, a summary of existing research on ML applications in VLEs is presented, positioning this research within the broader landscape of technological interventions. The focus then shifts to examining approaches that emphasise educational assessment automation, highlighting the progressive integration of ML to streamline and improve assessment processes. Finally, the discussion extends to the study of simulated learning environments.

A. Machine Learning in Virtual Learning Environments

The integration of ML into VLEs has been increasingly recognised for its potential to tailor education to individual learning needs, a concept referred to as precision education. Luan and Tsai systematically reviewed 40 empirical studies, revealing a focus on predicting student performance and dropout rates within online or blended learning settings, particularly among students in Science, Technology, Engineering and Mathematics (STEM) fields [1]. Dogan et al. conducted a systematic review on the use of Artificial Intelligence (AI) in online learning and distance education, noting a significant increase in research, with substantial contributions from China, India, and the United States. Their analysis identified three dominant clusters of research themes, underscoring the versatility of AI in enhancing online teaching, learning processes, and personalisation [13].

B. Automated educational assessment

In their comprehensive survey, Das et al. examine the burgeoning field of automatic question generation and answer assessment, pivotal for enhancing learning through internet-based platforms [14]. The study aggregates and critiques a decade's worth of research, elucidating the state-of-the-art techniques that automate the creation and evaluation of questions across textual, pictorial learning resources. The survey underscores the growing integration of such methodologies in intelligent education systems, reflecting on their potential to transform self-paced learning by identifying learning gaps effectively. This synthesis of past and current methodologies provides a critical baseline for future explorations in automated educational assessments.

The systematic review by González-Calatayud et al. [15] delves into the use of artificial intelligence in student assessments, analysing data from over 450 papers to discern the impact and implications of AI on educational practices. The review reveals a marked focus on formative assessment and grading, albeit with a noted deficiency in pedagogical integration within the AI applications reviewed. Highlighting the need for educational models that synergise with technological advancements, this work calls for enhanced teacher training and research that bridges the gap between AI capabilities and pedagogical needs, ensuring that AI supports rather than supplants the educational process.

INCEpTION, a novel annotation platform detailed by Klie et al., integrates ML to support and enhance the annotation

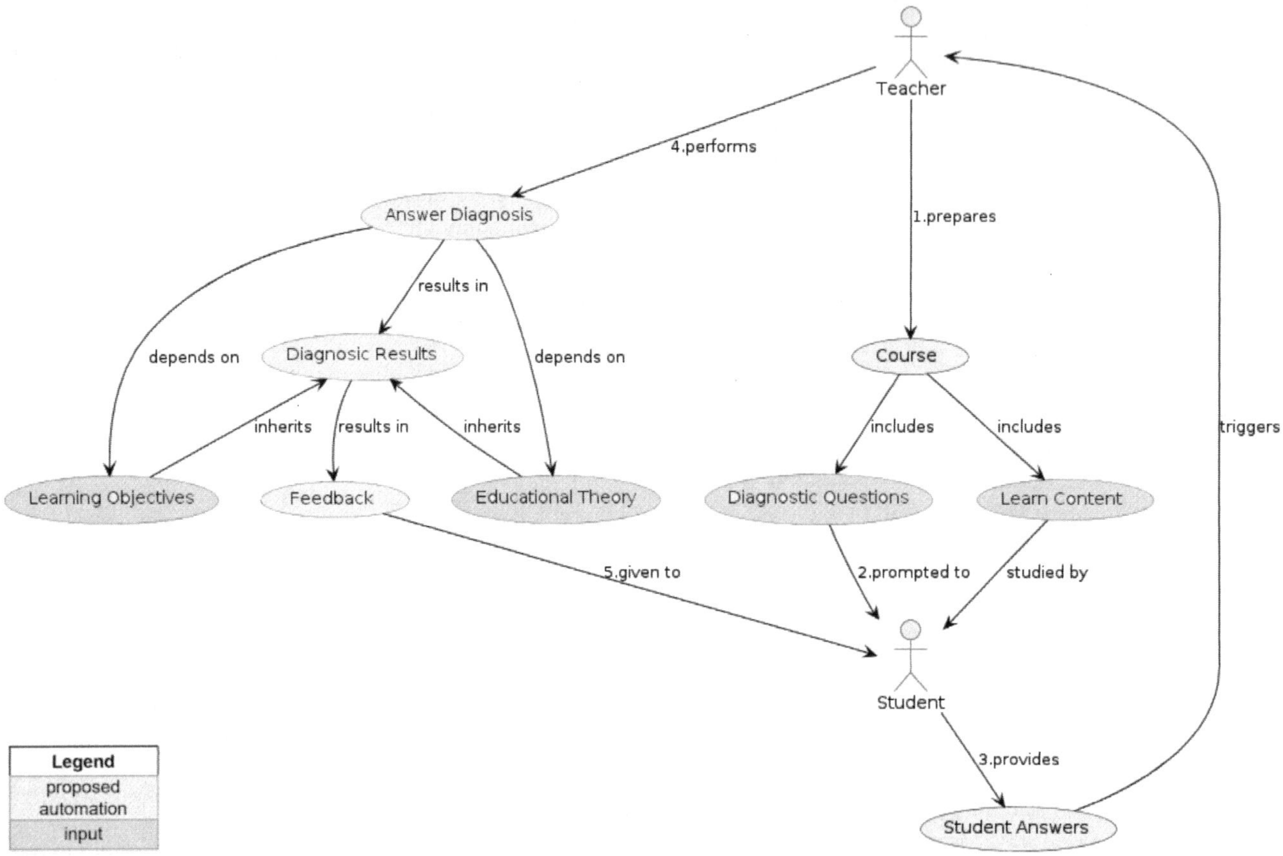

Figure 2. Use Case of Assessment and Feedback.

process. Tailored for semantic tasks like concept linking and semantic frame annotation, INCEpTION addresses the complex demands of creating high-quality annotated corpora by incorporating active learning and entity linking. This platform is designed to be adaptable across various fields, demonstrating its utility in collecting and managing domain-specific knowledge through an interactive, machine-assisted environment. This innovation represents a significant step forward in the semantic annotation domain, offering robust support for researchers and annotators alike [16].

Hartmann et al. compare ten text classification methods to understand their efficacy in analysing social media content for marketing applications. Their empirical study identifies Naive Bayes (NB) [17] and Random Forest [18] as superior in aligning with human intuition over traditional methods like Support Vector Machine (SVM) [19] and lexicon-based approaches. By demonstrating the relative performance of these methods across varied datasets, this research provides valuable insights into the optimisation of text classification in marketing, suggesting a pivot towards more dynamic and statistically robust methods [20]. Das et al. presented a survey of automatic question generation and assessment strategies from textual and pictorial learning resources, emphasising the importance of assessment systems in identifying learning gaps [14]. Furthermore, González-Calatayud, Prendes-Espinosa, and Roig-Vila analysed the application of AI in student assessment, revealing a prevalent focus on formative evaluation and the necessity for pedagogical grounding in AI applications [15].

C. Simulated Learning Environments

In the field of simulated learning environments, incorporating digital technologies offers novel ways to improve pre-service biology teachers' pedagogical skills, particularly in diagnostic competence. Fiedler et al. explored this through a classroom simulation integrated with a chatbot designed to enhance teachers' ability to accurately assess students' understanding of evolutionary processes - a crucial skill given the scarcity of practical teaching opportunities in university settings [21]. Their research showed that while participants were able to diagnose clear, naive, or scientific explanations, they struggled with mixed model explanations and identifying specific misconceptions, highlighting the need for targeted feedback to refine diagnostic strategies.

Adelana et al. [22] explored pre-service biology teachers' attitudes and intentions towards using AI-based intelligent tutoring systems for teaching genetics, a subject known for its teaching challenges. Through the Theory of Planned Behaviour lens, their study highlighted the influence of perceived usefulness and subjective norms on these teachers' behavioural intentions while noting the non-significant impact of perceived behavioural control on such intentions. Furthermore, the research highlighted gendered nuances in subjective norms, particularly among female pre-service teachers, while revealing consistent attitudes across other dimensions. This research not only highlights the importance of social norms and attitudes in adopting AI technologies in education but also points to broader implications for integrating AI in the promotion of effective teaching strategies in science. The classroom simulation *Simulated Classroom Biology* (SCRBio) [23] demonstrates the validation of action-oriented pedagogical content knowledge of pre-service biology teachers, focusing specifically on evolution education.

Rogers et al. [24] explore the educational potential of Virtual Reality (VR) technologies in STEM education through the operation of a virtual CNC milling machine. Their study evaluates the usability and pedagogical effectiveness of immersive VR environments, providing evidence from usability studies that highlight the benefits of such technologies in enhancing hands-on learning without physical constraints. The findings suggest that VR can significantly enhance the educational experience by providing intuitive and engaging ways to learn complex machine operations, marking a significant step forward in the integration of immersive technologies in education.

III. Automatic assessment

Automatic assessment in e-learning aims to accurately assess learner responses using computational methods, thereby increasing the scalability and efficiency of educational systems. This is achieved by integrating ML algorithms that automate the assessment process, thereby reducing the burden on instructors and providing timely feedback to learners.

Information Sources:

1) Learner input: Primary data includes textual responses, quiz results and interactive logs that capture learner interactions within the e-learning environment.
2) Instructional materials: Secondary sources include the instructional content against which learner responses are assessed, including guidelines for correct answers and grading rubrics.
3) Historical data: Archived assessments and their results contribute to the training of ML models, enabling them to learn from past instructional scenarios.

Techniques:

1) Text classification: Used to classify open-ended responses into predefined response categories or to identify thematic consistencies within learner submissions.
2) Natural Language Processing (NLP): Uses linguistic analysis to understand and assess the quality of text responses, focusing on grammar, relevance and content accuracy.
3) ML algorithms: Applies techniques such as supervised learning to recognise patterns in responses and unsupervised learning to discover underlying patterns in unstructured data.
4) Feedback generation: Algorithms generate automated feedback based on assessment results tailored to individual learner needs and performance, supporting personalised learning pathways.

A. Research Questions

This study investigates automatic assessment in eLearning frameworks where free text input needs to be evaluated. The expected training data consists of textual responses accompanied by diagnosed labels of corresponding assessment results.

RQ1 Which machine learning methods offer the best performance and efficiency for automated assessment? This question focuses on selecting pre-processing, tokenisation, and classification approaches that enable automated assessment of responses to learning content.

RQ2 What are the indicators of quality and efficiency in automated assessment? This question aims to select benchmarks for measuring the quality and efficiency of automated assessment processes.

RQ3 What factors significantly influence the performance of automated assessment? This question examines the factors that are crucial in determining the performance of automated assessment tools. These factors include algorithmic, data attributes, and contextual variables.

This research aims to examine the challenges and opportunities related to the automatic assessment of e-learning data. It is assumed that progress in ML could significantly contribute to the evolution of digital education.

B. Methodology

This research proposes and evaluates new technologies for automated assessment through empirical validation. The methodology involves preparing the dataset, applying ML algorithms and critically analysing the results to validate the effectiveness of these technologies. A publicly available dataset that represents the real-world conditions in which the technology will be used is selected. The design and conduct of the experiment is documented and justified. Systematic evaluation allows for a detailed comparison with traditional methods, highlighting potential accuracy, efficiency and scalability improvements in educational assessment.

C. Limitations

This study focuses on scenarios that require the evaluation of free text input. The validation of the methods used is empirical and depends on the parameters of the experiment. To mitigate this dependency, a real-world dataset is selected, accompanied by a variety of methods for pre-processing, tokenisation and classification. The behaviour of the appliance may differ in response to alternative use cases or datasets, depending on the specific requirements, the text and the quality of the labels. Furthermore, performance and efficiency results

TABLE I
QASCRBIO DATASET EXCERPT

QG^1 German	QL^1 Labels	Q^2 English	Q_W Word-List Word	Q_L Lemmatized Lem	$Q_{LP}{}^3$ Token+POS-Tag LemPair	$Q_{WP}{}^3$ Token+POS-Tag WordPair	$Q_{WP-Us}{}^4$ UIP Feature Selection Us Us
Die Natur bewirkte die Veränderung beim Seepferdchen	F1	Nature brought about the change in the seahorse	'Nature', 'brought', 'about', 'the', 'change', 'in', 'the', 'seahorse'	'nature', 'bring', 'about', 'the', 'change', 'in', 'the', 'seahorse'	'nature_NN-nsubj', 'bring_VBD', 'about_RP', 'the_DT', 'change_NN-dobj', 'in_IN', 'the_DT', 'seahorse_NN-pobj'	'Nature_NN-nsubj', 'brought_VBD', 'about_RP', 'the_DT', 'change_NN-dobj', 'in_IN', 'the_DT', 'seahorse_NN-pobj'	'Nature_NN-nsubj', 'brought_VBD', 'about_RP', 'change_NN-dobj', 'in_IN', 'seahorse_NN-pobj'

Sample Excerpt of QASCRBio dataset along with the results of the pre-processing variants.
[1] QASCRBio dataset [9], [2] Deepl-Translator [25], [3] UIP feature selection [5], [4] LinPairTokenization [4]

TABLE II
QASCRBIO DATASET LABELS

Principle			Threshold			Misconception		
P1_Variability	P2_Inheritance	P3_Selection	T1_Chance	T2_Probability	T3_Time	F1_Anthropomorphic	F2_Teleological	F3_Usage

QASCRBio dataset [9]: Multilabel-Dataset: single label or multiple labels per sample

may be influenced by the host setup. This study does not extend to the subsequent application of assessment results, such as feedback determination or generation, nor does it explore integration with learner models for predicting student profiles.

IV. EXPERIMENT

The use of automated assessment in educational settings requires the execution of several software engineering steps. First, a text classification system is designed to facilitate the assessment process. Next, a relevant data set is carefully curated. The implementation phase involves setting up an automated system to accurately process and classify student responses. The culmination of this process is the systematic evaluation, where the effectiveness and accuracy of the automated assessment are rigorously tested to ensure its reliability and pedagogical utility. This methodological approach ensures a robust framework for integrating automated assessment tools into educational contexts, improving student assessment's efficiency and accuracy.

A. Classification Procedure

The design of the classification procedure is targeted at the presentation and evaluation of automatic evaluation using innovative techniques (Figure 3). This includes an extensive pre-processing phase that integrates state-of-the-art methods to optimise the input data for subsequent classification. The key pre-processing steps are (i) selective feature selection, which focuses on removing text segments that are not considered essential for the classification objectives, and (ii) information enrichment strategies, which enhance the dataset by incorporating Part-Of-Speech (POS) tags to provide syntactic context. The classification process uses sophisticated tokenisation techniques designed to minimise data loss. This is followed by the application of selected classification algorithms that categorise the text according to the pre-trained labels. The overall approach ensures a robust framework for tackling complex text classification challenges in diverse applications.

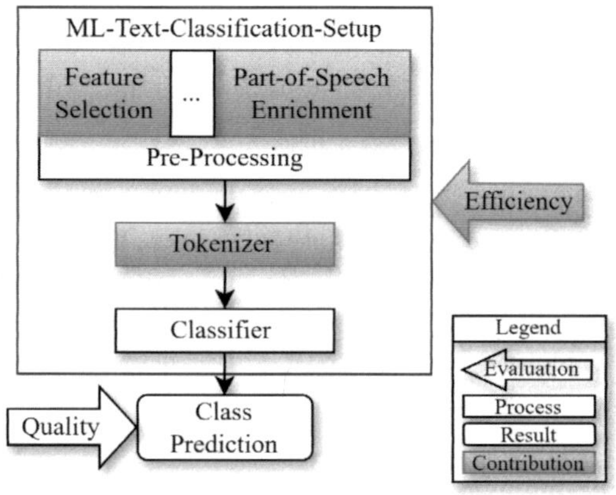

Figure 3. Text Classification Setup Overview.

B. Dataset

This study investigated the automation of the didactic diagnosis process for German university student responses using the QASCRBio dataset. A diagnostic question was used to assess the students' learning outcomes (Table I). The results are not suitable for grading but for providing formative feedback. The diagnostic aspects are divided into nine labels, reflecting the analytical challenges of sentiment analysis. These aspects are grouped into three categories (Table II). The main engineering objective was to classify the texts into one or more classes, overcoming the challenges posed by a dataset limited to 540 samples, a multi-classification problem and the complicated detection complexity of the labels. The dataset

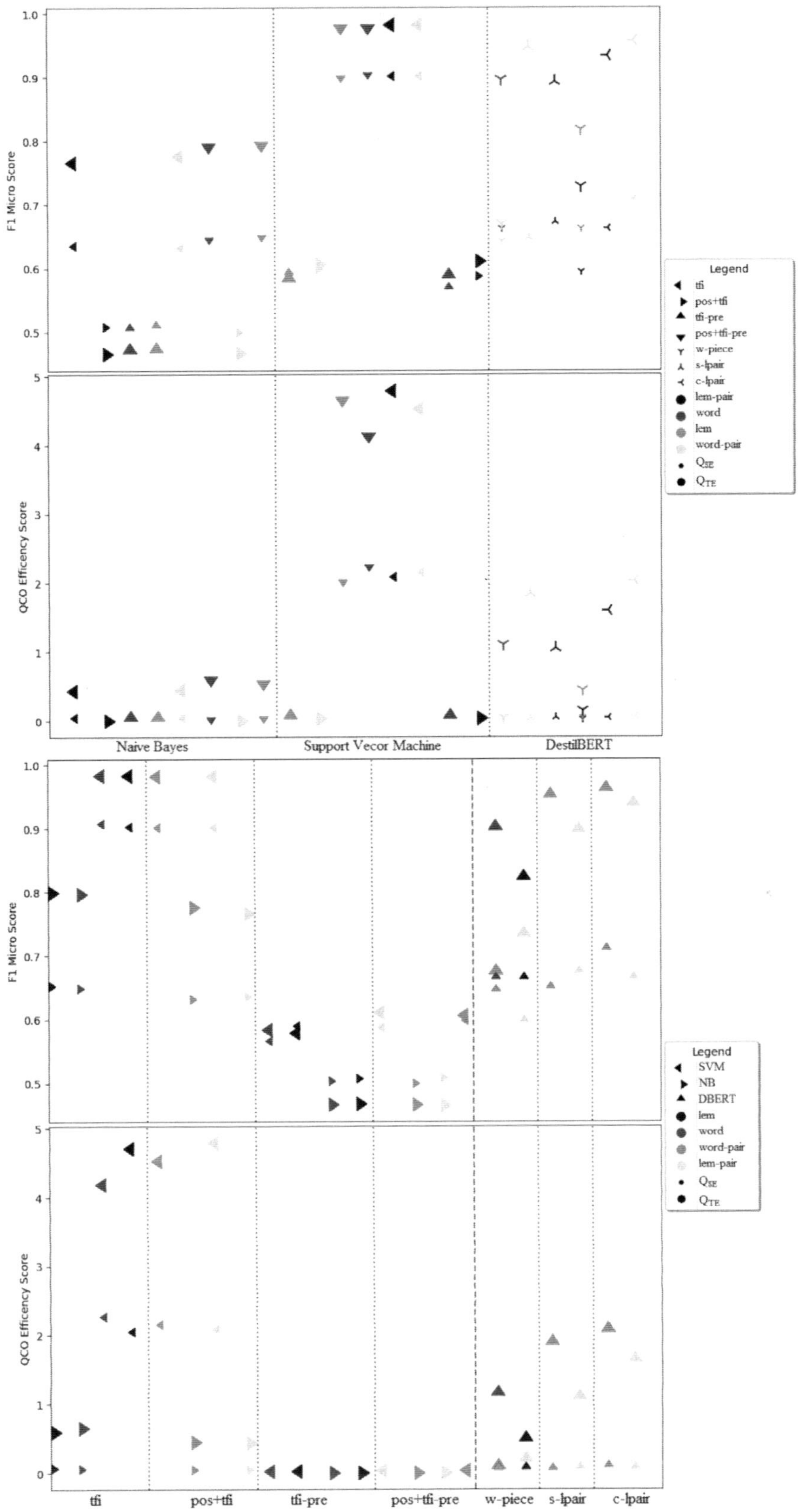

Figure 4. Quality and Efficiency of Classifiers and Tokenizers.

TABLE III
UNIMPORTANT PART-OF-SPEECH LISTS

Origin	UIP-List	POS-Tags	Description
UIP for NB	U_N	UH;NNPS	Interjection;Proper Nouns, Plural
UIP for SVM	U_S	WP;JJS;RP;CC;WRB;EX; MD;PRP;WDT;IN;TO; POS;JJ;VBP;JJR;NNS	Wh-pronoun; Superl. Adjective; Particle; Coord. Conjunction; Wh-adverb; Exist. There; Modal; Pers. Pronoun; Wh-determiner; Prep. Conjunction; To; Poss. Ending; Adjective; Verb, Sing. Present; Comp. Adjective; Plural Noun
Linguistic Set 1	U_X	DT	Determiner
Linguistic Set 2	U_Y	DT;IN;CC	Determiner; Preposition or Subordinating Conjunction; Coordinating Conjunction

used for research was created by specialists in the didactic field who synthetically generated and annotated the texts.

TABLE IV
TOKENIZERS

Tokenizer	Abbrev.	Elements	Method
WordPiece[26]	w-piece	tokens	Split into subtokens
SmartLinPair[4]	s-slpair	pairs of token and POS-tag	Split into subtokens, use POS-tag on OOV
CompleteLinPair[4]	c-lpair	pairs of token and POS-tag	Split into subpairs

TABLE V
DEFINITION OF DIMENSIONS

Dimension	Measurements & Scores	Weight
Quality	(F1MacroScore + F1MicroScore + Hamming) / 3	6
Work	FLOPS [count] / DatasetSize [kB]	1
Space	AverageRSS [MB] * DurationTime [s]	1
Duration	DurationTime [s]	1

TABLE VI
HOST-SETUP

No.	Type	CPU-Model	Clock	Threads	RAM
1	Virtualised	AMD EPYC 7742	2,2 GHz	16	32 GB

OS: Linux Ubuntu 22, Language: Python3.10,
Libraries: Scikit-learn [27], DistilBERT [28], torch [29], pandas [30].

C. Implementation

Data augmentation was performed to overcome the size limitations of the dataset (RQ3) using Transformer-based text translation methods: DeeplTranslator [25], a combination of DeeplTranslator and DeeplWrite, and Google Translator [31]. Two datasets were created: QASCRBio-SingleEnglish (QASCRBioSE) with the Google Translator, consisting of 432 training and 108 test samples; and QASCRBio-TripleEnglish (QASCRBioTE) with all three translations, consisting of 1296 training and 324 test samples after removing duplicates.

The pre-processing included lemmatising, POS-tagging, and feature selection, resulting in seven text variants: original text, lemmatised text - and both texts with added POS information (Table I). For feature selection, UIP [5] was used to select tokens based on their importance in English and specific classifiers. In addition to the two available UIP lists for NB and SVM, two standard sets (x, y) were used (Table III). The tokenisation methods selected were Term Frequency–Inverse Document Frequency (TF-IDF) [32], WordPiece [26], and the CompleteLinPair and SmartLinPair tokenisation techniques from the LinPair framework [4] (Table IV). The classifiers were chosen to compare the fast models SVM and NB with the more sophisticated Large Language Model, DistilBert (DBERT) [28].

D. Evaluation

In response to RQ2, F1-Micro, F1-Macro, and the Hamming score were used to evaluate the quality of class prediction. The Quality-Focused Compact Efficiency Metric (QCO) from the Compact Efficiency Metrics Framework [8] was used to assess computational efficiency. QCO provides a score to compare the training effectiveness of the model and the operational efficiency as defined by the metric configuration. Training effectiveness was captured based on the measurements of the efficiency dimensions in Table V. QCO was calculated as defined by Equation (1). The impact of the UIP feature selection was evaluated by comparing the quality of the classification results and by measuring the data size savings. The computation of the implementation was performed on a system whose specifications are documented in Table VI, thus ensuring the reproducibility and reliability of the results. This comprehensive setup included two datasets, up to 3 feature selection methods, five tokenisation methods, and three classifiers mentioned above.

V. DISCUSSION

The analysis of the results, shown in Figure 4, provides valuable insights into candidate outcomes regarding research questions RQ1 and RQ3. Figure 4 consists of four plots, the top two displaying the results for each classification method and the bottom two illustrating the results associated with each tokeniser method. Regarding classification accuracy, SVM and DBERT exceeded the threshold of a 0.9 F1 Micro Score. The top-performing SVM configurations used either TF-IDF (tf) or TF-IDF with pre-processing (tfpre) and showed similar performance levels across various pre-processing methods. Notably, SVM did not show significant improvement when using POS-optimised TF-IDF tokenisers or incorporating POS tags, indicating a degree of robustness to pre-processing variations.

$$QCO(M) = \frac{((\frac{F1MAC+F1MIC+HUM}{3})^6)}{(\log_{47,5B} FLOPS/DS[kB] + \log_{3,5K} RSS[MB] * log_{3,7T} D[s] + \log_{3,7T} D[s]} * 10 \quad (1)$$

where HUM = Humming Sc., $FLOPS$ = Float. Point OP, DS = Dataset-S., RSS = Resident Set S., D = Duration

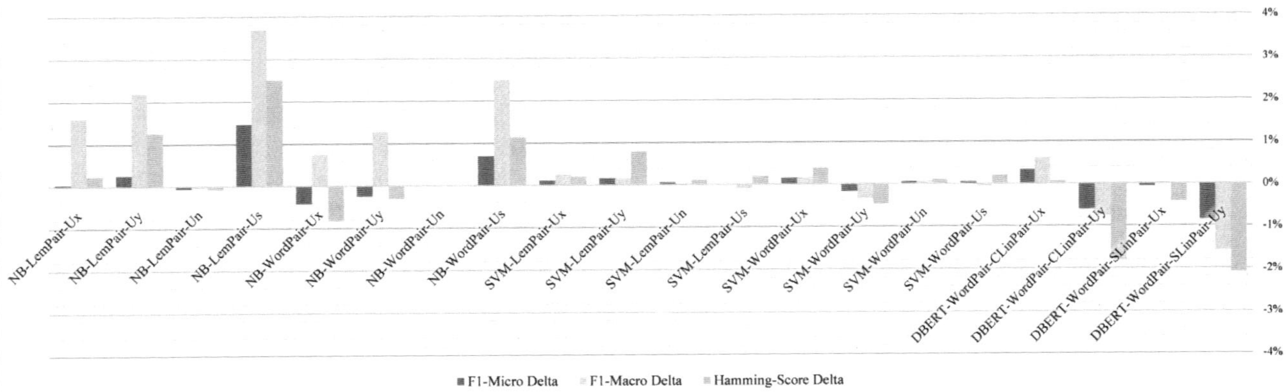

Figure 5. UIP-Effects: Relative Quality Gain against baseline without UIP feature selection.

DBERT significantly improved by data augmentation, particularly with outcomes related to the $WordPair$ pre-processing method. This indicates that performance has been enhanced in most cases by including POS information, but performance has decreased in a few cases. The LinPair-Tokenizers SmartLinPair and CompleteLinPair consistently outperformed the WordPiece Tokenizer when comparing tokenisation strategies across the board. This disparity is accentuated when taking into account the size of the dataset and the pre-processing technique. Regarding efficiency, SVM proved to be the superior option when using the QASCRBioTE dataset due to its fast processing times, low memory requirements, and high classification accuracy. DBERT exhibited its most effective results with $WordPair$ pre-processing, significantly enhancing its efficiency by applying LinPair tokenisers.

The results show significant differences between the setups regarding quality (F1 Score) and efficiency (QCO-Efficieny) as seen in Figure 4. Surprisingly, the SVM outperformed the standard DBERT model in terms of quality and efficiency. DBERT setups with innovative improvements in pre-processing, feature selection, and tokenisation achieve similar quality to SVM. POS enrichment, POS-based filtering, and LinPair tokenisation lead to quality improvements with production-ready results. SVM and DBERT benefited from Transformer-based data augmentation (Deepl-Translation), while the quality of NB deteriorated with augmentation. POS enhancement improved the results of DBERT but degraded those of SVM and NB.

LinPair is currently only available for subset-based techniques, such as DBERT. It significantly improves quality by up to 12% (Figure 6) while increasing efficiency (Figure 4). Therefore, the quality improvement compensates for the additional computation required for LinPair. This highlights the potential of customised tokenisation strategies in enhancing the effectiveness of ML models in automatic student response evaluation.

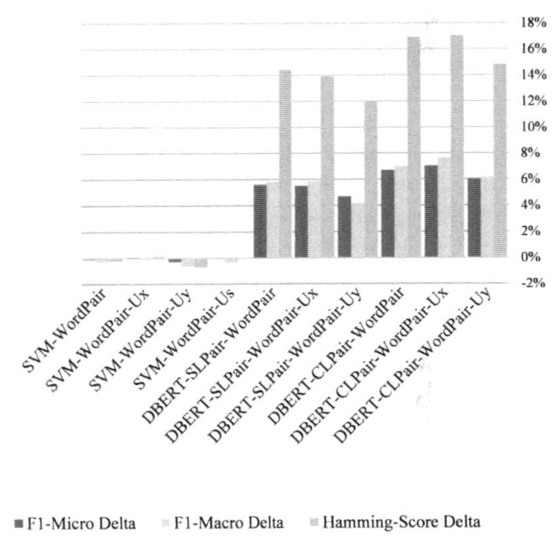

Figure 6. Overall Effects: Relative Quality Gain against baseline without POS usage.

The UIP feature selection's evaluation demonstrated mixed outcomes, as depicted in Figure 5. Notably, NB exhibited gains, enhancing the F1-Macro Score by up to 3.7%. Conversely, SVM showed no discernible benefits from UIP feature selection, while DBERT registered only marginal improvements when employing the minimal UIP-Set Ux with Complete LinPair. Given that DBERT is trained on complete sentences to capitalise on contextual relationships, the elimination of parts of sentences through feature selection might adversely impact its performance.

	Word	Lem	LemPair	WordPair	WordPairUn	WordPairUs	WordPairUx	WordPairUy	LemPairUn	LemPairUs	LemPairUx	LemPairUy
Word	0	-8	61	58	58	29	41	23	61	32	44	26
Lem	8	0	74	71	71	40	53	33	74	43	56	36
LemPair	-38	-43	0	-2	-2	-20	-12	-23	0	-18	-11	-22
WordPair	-37	-42	2	0	0	-18	-11	-22	2	-16	-9	-20
WordPairUn	-37	-42	2	0	0	-18	-11	-22	2	-16	-9	-20
WordPairUs	-23	-28	25	22	22	0	9	-4	25	2	11	-2
WordPairUx	-29	-34	14	12	12	-8	0	-13	14	-6	2	-11
WordPairUy	-19	-25	30	28	28	5	14	0	30	7	17	2
LemPairUn	-38	-43	0	-2	-2	-20	-12	-23	0	-18	-11	-22
LemPairUs	-24	-30	22	20	20	-2	7	-7	22	0	9	-5
LemPairUx	-30	-36	12	10	10	-10	-2	-14	12	-8	0	-12
LemPairUy	-21	-27	28	25	25	2	12	-2	28	5	14	0

Figure 7. UIP Effects on Dataset Size.

To explore potential side effects correlating with these outcomes (RQ2), variations in dataset size induced by preprocessing techniques, such as POS enrichment and feature selection, were analysed. The heatmap in Figure 7 illustrates the relative changes in dataset size, tracing the trajectory from initial word counts to lemmatised forms and subsequent modifications through POS-Enrichment and UIP feature selection. The transformations between comparable and successive processing stages are particularly telling, which align with the aggregate findings presented in Figures 4 and 6.

DBERT's response to different text processing methods was marked. The WordPair configuration yielded the most substantial quality increase by 58%, attributed to the inclusion of POS tags. All feature selection techniques generally resulted in reduced data sizes. Noteworthy are two specific combinations: WordSVM, which decreased the size of WordPair by 18% while maintaining classification performance—evidenced by SVM-WordPair-Us in Figure 5; and WordPairUx, which lessened the size by 11% and had only a slight impact on DBERT performance when using tokens by SmartLinPair (DBERT-WordPair-SLPair-Ux). NB presented intriguing results with the LemSVM configuration, which diminished the size of LemPair by 12% and led to an improvement in F1-Macro Score by 3.7% (NB-LemPair-Us in Figure 6) for the pared-down dataset.

VI. Conclusion and Future Work

The implementation of transformer models trained on large datasets typically improves ML performance in a variety of tasks. This research has shown that tuning the model with specialised data generally improves text classification performance. However, in the context of the QASCRBio dataset, all optimisation strategies failed to improve the performance of DBERT beyond that of SVM. This study attempted to maximise the utility of the data by exploiting latent linguistic information, such as Part-of-Speech, which inevitably increased the computational requirements and improved the classification quality of DBERT.

Despite these efforts, LLM setups were consistently outperformed by statistical methods, such as SVM, in terms of quality and efficiency. The synthetic nature of the QASCR-Bio dataset, with carefully crafted texts and perfectly balanced classes, may inherently favour statistical approaches. In contrast, LLMs are adept at processing texts of varying orthographic quality and skewed information levels, such as tweets, possibly due to their training in different text types.

This research has opened up new avenues for exploration. While the selected LLM has proven its efficacy in analysing well-structured student responses, its application to naturally written responses presents a promising area for future research. The QASCRBio dataset, which primarily evaluates the biological and didactic elements within students' responses, may not fully capture the complexity of real student submissions. These submissions often contain spelling and grammatical errors, as well as extraneous information, such as emotional expressions, which could provide valuable insights for a comprehensive assessment.

This research highlights the need for advanced methods capable of interpreting such complexities within student responses. For example, the use of Part-of-Speech information has demonstrated potential benefits for automated assessment, suggesting that deeper linguistic analysis could provide significant benefits. Further studies should explore the refinement of LLM capabilities to handle better the nuanced and diverse nature of authentic student responses, thereby increasing the effectiveness and applicability of machine learning in educational assessment.

Acknowledgments

This research was funded by the Federal Ministry of Education and Research of Germany in the framework of FiSK (Project-Number 16DHB4005).

References

[1] H. Luan and C.-C. Tsai, "A review of using machine learning approaches for precision education," *Educational Technology & Society*, vol. 24, no. 1, pp. 250–266, 2021.

[2] W. Villegas-Ch, M. Román-Cañizares, and X. Palacios-Pacheco, "Improvement of an online education model with the integration of machine learning and data analysis in an LMS," *Applied Sciences*, vol. 10, no. 15, p. 5371, 2020.

[3] H. A. El-Sabagh, "Adaptive e-learning environment based on learning styles and its impact on development students' engagement," *International Journal of Educational Technology in Higher Education*, vol. 18, no. 1, p. 53, 2021.

[4] D. Schönle, C. Reich, and D. Ould-Abdeslam, "Linguistic-Aware WordPiece Tokenization: Semantic Enrichment and OOV Mitigation," in *6th International Conference on Natural Language Processing (ICNLP 2024)*, 2024, p. tba. Forthcoming.

[5] D. Schönle, C. Reich, and D. O. Abdeslam, "Linguistic driven feature selection for text classification as stop word replacement," *Journal of Advances in Information Technology*, vol. 14, no. 4, pp. 796–802, 2023.

[6] J. Makhoul, F. Kubala, R. Schwartz, R. Weischedel, *et al.*, "Performance measures for information extraction," in *Proceedings of DARPA broadcast news workshop*, Herndon, VA, 1999, pp. 249–252.

[7] R. W. Hamming, "Error detecting and error correcting codes," *The Bell system technical journal*, vol. 29, no. 2, pp. 147–160, 1950.

[8] D. Schönle, C. Reich, and D. Ould-Abdeslam, "Streamlining AI: Techniques for Efficient Machine Learning Model Selection," *The International Journal on Advances in Intelligent Systems*, vol. 17, no. 12, p. tba. 2024, forthcoming.

[9] D. Fiedler, J. Poser, and U. Harms, *Teacher questions and student answers for the SCRBio in the context of evolution*, 2024.

[10] S. M. Brookhart, *How to give effective feedback to your students*. Ascd, 2017.

[11] W. J. Popham, *Classroom assessment*. Allyn and Bacon Boston, 1995.

[12] P. Black and D. Wiliam, "Assessment and classroom learning," *Assessment in Education: principles, policy & practice*, vol. 5, no. 1, pp. 7–74, 1998.

[13] M. E. Dogan, T. Goru Dogan, and A. Bozkurt, "The use of artificial intelligence (AI) in online learning and distance education processes: A systematic review of empirical studies," *Applied Sciences*, vol. 13, no. 5, p. 3056, 2023.

[14] B. Das, M. Majumder, S. Phadikar, and A. A. Sekh, "Automatic question generation and answer assessment: a survey," *Research and Practice in Technology Enhanced Learning*, vol. 16, no. 1, p. 5, 2021.

[15] V. González-Calatayud, P. Prendes-Espinosa, and R. Roig-Vila, "Artificial intelligence for student assessment: A systematic review," *Applied Sciences*, vol. 11, no. 12, p. 5467, 2021.

[16] J.-C. Klie, M. Bugert, B. Boullosa, R. E. de Castilho, and I. Gurevych, "The inception platform: Machine-assisted and knowledge-oriented interactive annotation," in *Proceedings of the 27th international conference on computational linguistics: system demonstrations*, 2018, pp. 5–9.

[17] I. Kononenko, "Comparison of inductive and naive bayesian learning approaches to automatic knowledge acquisition," *Current trends in knowledge acquisition*, vol. 8, p. 190, 1990.

[18] T. K. Ho, "Random decision forests," in *Proceedings of 3rd international conference on document analysis and recognition*, IEEE, vol. 1, 1995, pp. 278–282.

[19] C. Cortes and V. Vapnik, "Support-vector networks," *Machine learning*, vol. 20, no. 3, pp. 273–297, 1995.

[20] J. Hartmann, J. Huppertz, C. Schamp, and M. Heitmann, "Comparing automated text classification methods," *International Journal of Research in Marketing*, vol. 36, no. 1, pp. 20–38, 2019.

[21] D. Fiedler, D. Schönle, C. Reich, and U. Harms, "When practical situations are rare: Improving pre-service biology teachers' diagnostic competency in a classroom simulation with chatbot," *Herausforderung Zukunft*, p. 294, 2023.

[22] O. P. Adelana, M. A. Ayanwale, and I. T. Sanusi, "Exploring pre-service biology teachers' intention to teach genetics using an AI intelligent tutoring-based system," *Cogent Education*, vol. 11, no. 1, p. 2 310 976, 2024.

[23] J. Fischer, N. Machts, T. Bruckermann, J. Möller, and U. Harms, "The Simulated Classroom Biology—A simulated classroom environment for capturing the action-oriented professional knowledge of pre-service teachers about evolution," *Journal of Computer Assisted Learning*, vol. 38, no. 6, pp. 1765–1778, 2022.

[24] C. Rogers, H. El-Mounaryi, T. Wasfy, and J. Satterwhite, "Assessment of STEM e-learning in an immersive virtual reality (VR) environment," *Computers in Education Journal*, vol. 8, p. 15 724, Oct. 2017.

[25] DeepL SE, *How does DeepL work?* 2024. [Online]. Available: www.deepl.com/en/blog/how-does-deepl-work (visited on 05/29/2024).

[26] J. Devlin, M.-W. Chang, K. Lee, and K. Toutanova, "Bert: Pre-training of deep bidirectional transformers for language understanding," *arXiv preprint arXiv:1810.04805*, 2018.

[27] F. Pedregosa *et al.*, "Scikit-learn: Machine Learning in Python," *Journal of Machine Learning Research*, vol. 12, pp. 2825–2830, 2011.

[28] V. Sanh, L. Debut, J. Chaumond, and T. Wolf, "DistilBERT, a distilled version of BERT: smaller, faster, cheaper and lighter," *arXiv preprint arXiv:1910.01108*, 2019.

[29] R. Collobert, K. Kavukcuoglu, and C. Farabet, "Torch7: A Matlab-like Environment for Machine Learning," in *BigLearn, NIPS Workshop*, 2011.

[30] W. McKinney, "Data Structures for Statistical Computing in Python," in *Proceedings of the 9th Python in Science Conference*, Stéfan van der Walt and Jarrod Millman, Eds., 2010, pp. 56–61.

[31] La Vivien, *Google Translate Architecture illustrated*, 2022. [Online]. Available: https://www.lavivienpost.com/google-translate-and-transformer-model/ (visited on 05/29/2024).

[32] K. Sparck Jones, "A statistical interpretation of term specificity and its application in retrieval," *Journal of documentation*, vol. 28, no. 1, pp. 11–21, 1972.

Surface Defect Detection System for AI Vision-Based Press Formed Products

Dong Hyun Kim, Seung Ho Lee, and Jong Deok Kim*
Department of Computer Science and Engineering
Pusan National University
Pusan, South Korea
e-mail: {dhkim1106, issyong, kimjd}@pusan.ac.kr

Abstract— **The appearance of a product is the first thing consumers evaluate for defects, making surface inspection crucial. Among these exterior products, surface inspection of press-formed products is still done manually by visual inspection, prompting exploration of solutions for surface inspection automation through machine learning systems to adapt to various on-site changes. For machine learning-based surface defect detection models, there is often insufficient defect data for training, and a small amount of defect data makes it difficult to improve the learning performance. Particularly, as manufacturing processes stabilize, defect occurrences decrease, making it time-consuming to collect desired defect training data. This paper proposes a method for training models for defect detection by using only normal product data to train the defect detection model. It identifies defects on the product surface by generating defect data from normal data input, calculating the difference between normal data through restoration, and identifying defects on the product surface through connection and separation.**

Keywords-AI; Surface Detection; Press Formed Product; Anomaly detection.

I. INTRODUCTION

With the advent of the Fourth Industrial Revolution, the manufacturing industry is hastening its transition to smart factories, which integrate Information and Communications Technology (ICT) into traditional manufacturing processes. In this process, technologies for process automation and quality inspection automation are rapidly growing. However, surface defect inspection of products in press processing processes still relies on visual inspection by workers, who directly examine defects or damages on the product surface with their eyes. Such visual inspections are influenced by factors, such as ambient lighting, worker fatigue, and inspection proficiency. In particular, in high-speed press lines, due to short cycle times and mass production systems, there is a high probability of mass consecutive defects if surface defects occur. In such cases, it is crucial to prevent foreign matter ingress in mold areas and to rapidly detect surface defects to prevent mass consecutive defects. If undetected defective products are delivered to customers, a full inspection for product defects must be conducted, leading to increased costs.

This study proposes a method for acquiring surface anomaly data of products using stainless steel, which exhibits intense light reflection, and suggests a surface anomaly detection method for press processed products based on unsupervised learning using normal data for cases where anomaly data is insufficient. Through this, we aim to confirm the potential for replacing conventional visual inspections, quantifying surface inspections, and contributing to productivity and quality enhancement through continuous defect prevention.

This study aims to answer the following research questions:

1. How can machine learning models be effectively trained for surface defect detection with limited defect data?
2. What the are potential limitations of using only normal product data for defect detection?

This paper focuses on a subset of open issues, including the scarcity of defect data in stable manufacturing processes and the time-consuming nature of collecting sufficient defect data for model training. Potential limitations of our approach include the accuracy of defect generation from normal data and the reliability of defect identification in varying on-site conditions.

The structure of the paper is as follows: In Section 2, we discuss related work and the background of surface defect detection. Section 3 outlines the design and implementation of our proposed method. Section 4 presents the results and analysis. In Section 5, we conclude with lessons learned and future work directions.

II. RELATED WORK

This section reviews the existing literature and methods related to surface defect detection in manufacturing processes. It covers the target products and production processes, the type of defects encountered, and the current methods used for surface inspection. Additionally, it discusses unsupervised learning based on normal images for anomaly detection, highlighting recent advancements and methodologies.

A. Target Products and Production Processes, and Types of Defects

The Decor Frame, as shown in Figure 1, is attached inside the drum of a washing machine to act as a filter membrane, filtering out laundry residues. It is a product produced through press processing, using stainless steel material. The manufacturing process consists of two stages: after material input, the first stage involves drawing, trimming, and piercing processes using a 200-ton servo press, while the second stage involves bending the joints using a 150-ton servo press. Subsequently, after inspection, the products are packaged. During the inspection process, surface defect inspection is conducted by workers through visual inspection. Figure 2 depicts the raw materials and products by process.

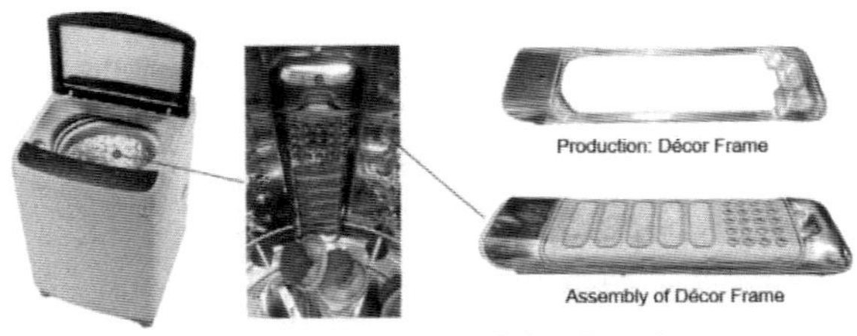

Figure 1. Target product (Décor Frame).

Figure 2. Raw material and products by process.

In the manufacturing process, various types of defects occur in each process. In the first process, defects, such as burrs, necking, sleeves, and fractures occur, while in the second process, chip and hook defects occur. The monthly average defect rate is 2.86%, with process defects accounting for 2.65%. Among them, chip defects on the product surface account for 1.89% of the process defect rate, representing 71%. This indicates a very high frequency of chip defects. These chip defects occur when foreign substances in the air or vinyl and chips generated during cutting in the first process adhere to the molds of the first or second process. Among these, the defect types to be detected through surface inspection are necking, sleeves, fractures, and chips. Figure 3 illustrates the types of defects by process and the types of defects targeted for surface inspection [1]-[2].

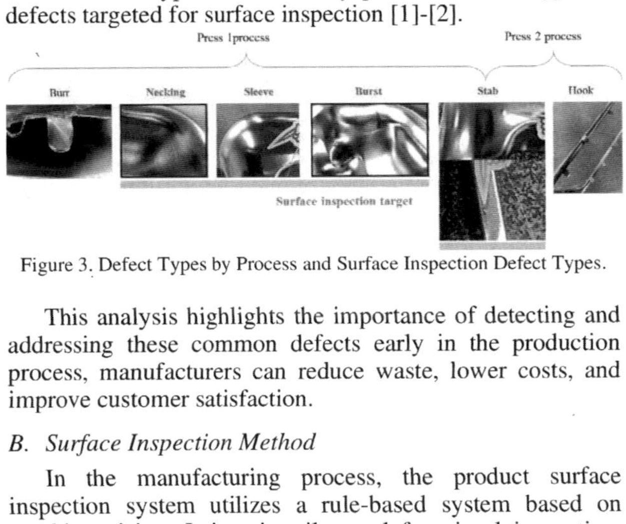

Figure 3. Defect Types by Process and Surface Inspection Defect Types.

This analysis highlights the importance of detecting and addressing these common defects early in the production process, manufacturers can reduce waste, lower costs, and improve customer satisfaction.

B. Surface Inspection Method

In the manufacturing process, the product surface inspection system utilizes a rule-based system based on machine vision. It is primarily used for visual inspection, defect detection, part position determination and measurement, product identification, alignment, tracking, and also for detecting surface defects. The advantage of this rule-based technology is its ability to quickly confirm and make decisions based on given rules. However, it can be considered rigid as it is programmed to only do what is specified by the rules. There are limitations in accommodating the diverse problems of the manufacturing field that constantly change since the rules are not self-added, changed, or updated [3].

In contrast, a Machine Learning System aims to emulate human-like behavior by learning new rules autonomously and discarding outdated ones, rather than relying on fixed rules. While rule-based systems can easily be applied in controlled environments, such as manufacturing lines, many undefined tasks occur in real work environments. To address the practical problems of these dynamically changing manufacturing environments, transitioning to machine learning should be considered. In particular, Deep Learning plays an increasingly significant role as it can intelligently predict and make decisions through image recognition [4]-[7].

C. Unsupervised Learning Based on Normal Image

Unsupervised learning based on normal data is used when collecting defective training data is difficult or labeling of training data is challenging. Among them, there is DRÆM, which particularly deals with pixel-level anomaly detection as an image anomaly detection method. This method is based on reconstruction and segmentation, consisting of anomaly generation through perturbed noise, and is structured by combining a reconstruction network and a discriminative network [8]-[10]. As shown in Figure 4, the structure and steps of reconstruction-based anomaly detection are detailed.

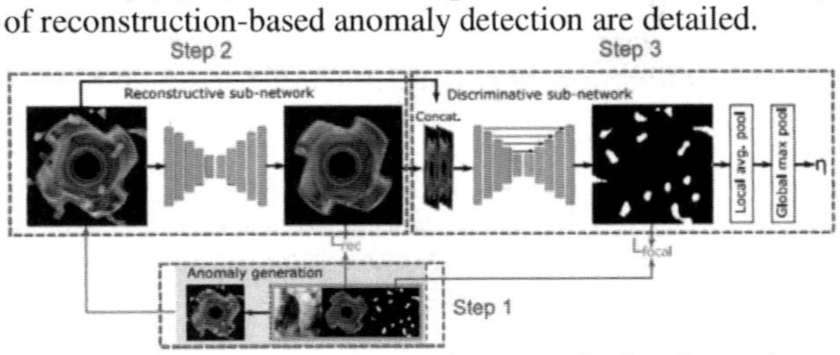

Figure 4. The structure and steps of reconstruction-based anomaly detection.

Examining the structure, in the first step, instead of using defective images as training data, defective images are generated using a Perlin noise generator (as illustrated in Figure 4). The Perlin noise generator creates anomaly shapes, which are combined with various shapes of different original images, and then synthesized with normal original images to generate defective images.

In the second step, the generated defective images are passed through the reconstructive sub-network to train them to be restored to the original images with defects removed. Here, the reconstruction loss, which is the difference between the original images and the restored images with defects removed through the reconstructive sub-network, is calculated to evaluate how closely the original images have been restored during the reconstruction training.

In the third step, the generated defective images through Perlin noise and the restored images through the reconstructive sub-network are combined (Concatenated) and passed through the discriminative sub-network to separate the anomaly mask images of the anomaly shapes. In other words, segmentation learning is performed with the goal of obtaining the anomaly mask images corresponding to the anomaly shapes applied to the original images. The segmented anomaly mask images are then compared to the noise area images generated by the Perlin noise generator through focal loss calculation to assess the performance of the discriminative network. Figure 5 depicts the entire process of the reconstruction-based anomaly detection methodology [11]-[16].

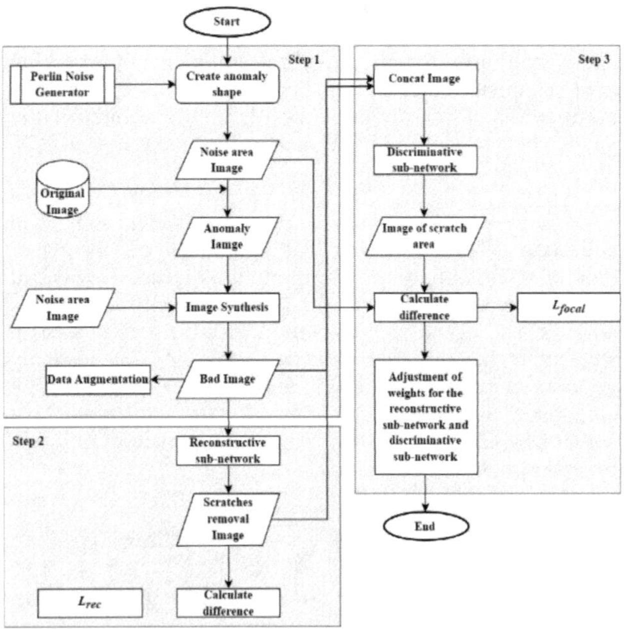

Figure 5. The entire process of reconstruction-based anomaly detection methodology.

This reconstruction-based anomaly detection method shows promise for detecting subtle anomalies in images, making it a valuable tool for improving quality control in manufacturing processes.

III. DESIGN AND IMPLEMENTATION

This section describes the methodology and implementation steps taken to develop the surface defect detection system. It includes the setup of the environment for collecting learning data, the configuration of machine vision components, and the application of unsupervised learning techniques based on normal images. Each subsection provides detailed explanations of the processes involved, including data collection, anomaly generation, and network training for effective surface defect detection.

A. Collect Learning Data

We have set up the environment to acquire product images for training. We configured the image capture conditions through lighting, including cameras and lenses, to ensure that the defective areas of surface defective products are distinguishable in the captured product images. Machine vision comprises cameras, lenses, lighting, and a controller/system package. However, in this paper, we used dome & coaxial type lighting. By processing the acquired images with contrast enhancement, we were able to measure surface attribute information, such as inclination, roughness, and reflectivity, enabling us to obtain images capable of discriminating surface defects, such as chips, scratches, and stains. The changes in surface properties due to lighting are illustrated in Figure 6.

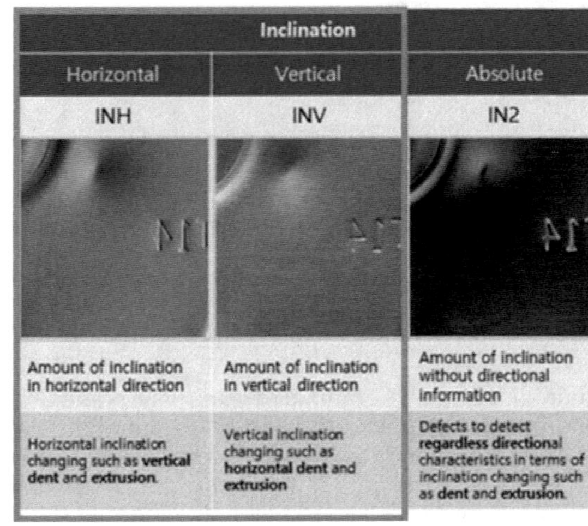

Figure 6. Changes in surface properties due to lighting.

In this paper, it was decided to collect attribute images of vertical and horizontal surfaces according to the inclination of illumination. To collect a total of four images per product, two images per product part, we set up an image data collection environment in the manufacturing site.

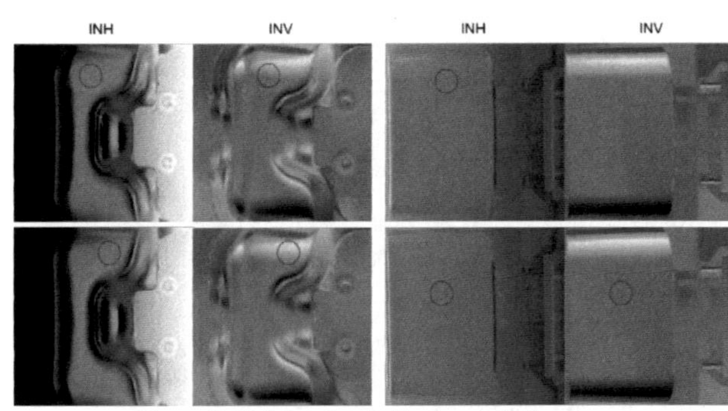

Figure 7. Training data indicating defective areas.

As the tilt of the illumination changes, the results of capturing product images show that surface defects, such as indentation are more clearly distinguished in either the INH (lighting directions in horizontal) or INV (vertical part when light is horizontally or vertically projected. Figure 7 represents the defects in the images.

B. Unsupervised learing based on normal images

Unsupervised learning based on normal images utilizes the reconstruction-based anomaly detection methodology. It generates defective images from normal images and trains these generated defective images separately using a reconstructive sub-network and a discriminative sub-network. The reconstructive sub-network is trained to pass the defective images, which are synthesized with noise, through to obtain the original images. Meanwhile, the discriminative sub-network is trained to detect the noisy regions. The configuration diagram of the reconstruction-based anomaly detection system is shown in Figure 8.

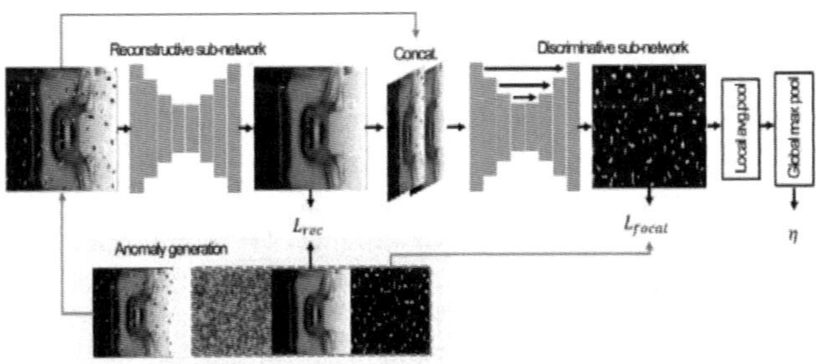

Figure 8. The configuration diagram of the reconstruction-based anomaly detection system.

The sequence of the unsupervised learning process consists of three steps: anomaly data generation, reconstructive network calculation, and discriminative network calculation. This process involves training based on normal product data in the initial state when sufficient defective product data is not available.

Anomaly generation involves inserting noise to generate defective product images. First, when a normal product image is input, Perlin noise, which has the same size as the normal product image, is generated. The Perlin noise image undergoes binarization based on a threshold to create a noise area image. Here, the noise area image is created such that if the value of a pixel in the Perlin noise image exceeds the threshold (0.5), it is set to 1; otherwise, it is set to 0. Multiple noise data are added to the noise area image, and then combined with the normal product image. The parts of the noise area image that are set to 1 represent noise data, while those set to 0 represent the normal product image, resulting in the generation of synthesized defective product images.

The reconstructive sub-network restores defective product images to normal product images. Defective product images synthesized during anomaly generation are passed through the reconstructive sub-network, which outputs defect-removed images of the same size as the defective product images. These defect-removed images remove the defective parts from the synthesized defective product images, restoring them to normal product images. The difference (L_{rec}) between the defect-removed images and the original normal product images is calculated. A smaller difference indicates that the reconstructive sub-network has effectively removed defects, producing defect-removed images similar to the original normal product images.

The discriminative sub-network extracts defective areas by comparing the difference between the synthesized defective product images and the defect-removed images. In the anomaly generation process, the synthesized defective product images and the defect-removed images are combined (concat) and inputted into the discriminative sub-network, producing defect area images of the same size as the product images. These defect area images calculate the difference (L_{focal}) with the noise area images. A smaller difference indicates that the discriminative sub-network can identify the difference between the defective product images and the defect-removed images, thereby extracting defective areas. A sample implementation image of the discriminative sub-network is shown in Figure 9.

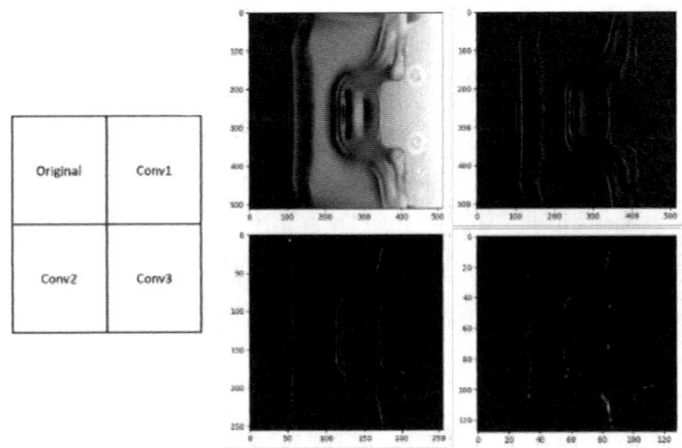

Figure 9. Sample implementation image of the discriminative sub-network.

The differences calculated in both networks, L_{rec} and L_{focal}, respectively modify the weights of the reconstructive network and the discriminative network. Figure 10 illustrates the process of unsupervised learning based on normal data.

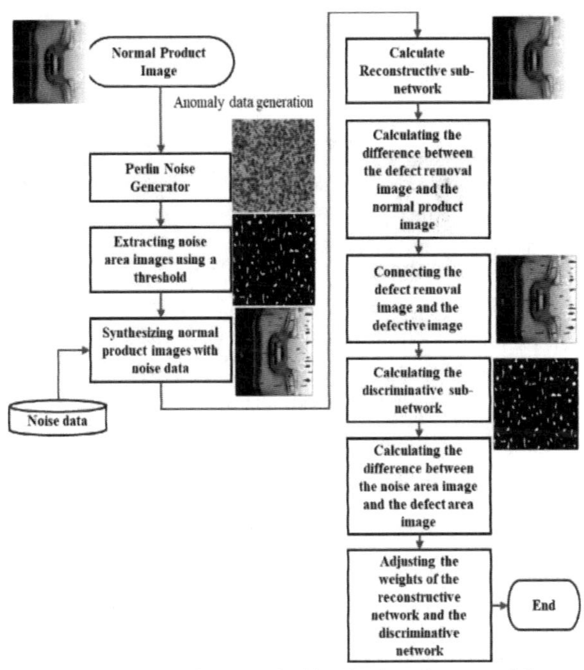

Figure 10. The process of unsupervised learning based on normal data.

IV. PERFORMANCE ANALYSIS

Performance evaluation of the learning model can be done by directly inspecting the data due to the small number of defective images and classifying the cases. Judging product defects means segmenting the scratch areas in the result images of the discriminative network. We will describe normal detection cases and false detection cases and analyze the results.

A. *Good segmentation case*

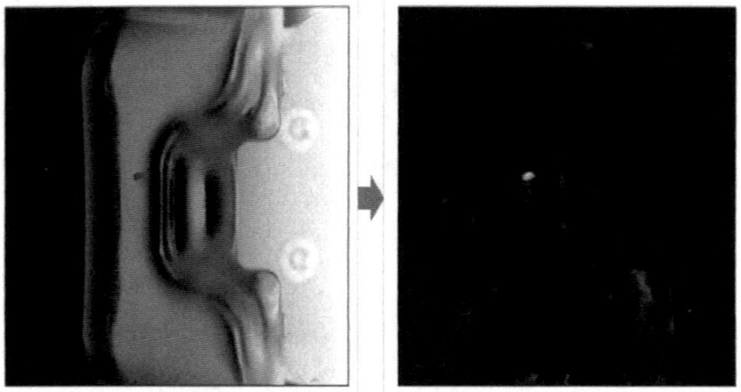

Figure 11. Good segmentation case.

Figure 11 depicts a good segmentation case. The left side of Figure 11 shows the original surface image of the defective data, with the defect indicated by a black spot in the center of the image. The right side of Figure 11 shows the result image after passing through the discriminative network, where only the defective area of the product is segmented in white. However, the result image is not entirely black in the areas excluding the defective region. This indicates that the reconstruction network did not properly restore the image in areas with curvature when generating the scratch-removed image.

B. *Bad sementation case*

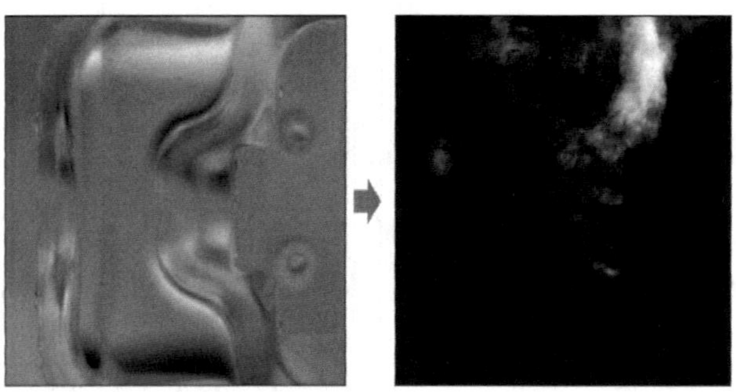

Figure 12. Bad segmentation case.

Figure 12 represents a case where the defective area of the original image and the curved surface area are not well distinguished. In Figure 12, the curved portion at the top is not properly restored. The presence of a large white area indicating differences in the curved portion suggests that there is significant disparity between the scratch-removed image and the original image in the curved area. In other words, the reconstruction network fails to generate the scratch-removed image accurately. This phenomenon particularly occurs frequently in vertical inspections at the top portion, speculated to be due to less color variation compared to horizontal inspections.

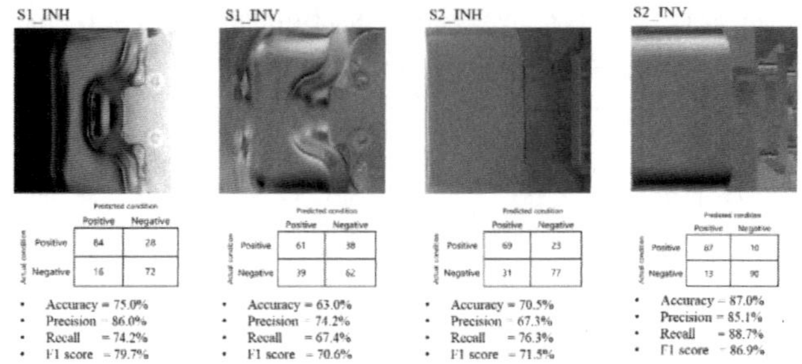

Figure 13. Result of performance evaluation (Accuracy, Precision, Recall, F1-score).

The number of image data used for the final performance evaluation is 200 for each of the top (S1) and bottom (S2) regions, with lighting directions in horizontal (INH) and vertical (INV) inspection methods. Figure 13 illustrates the performance evaluation for each image. In the top region (S1), an accuracy of 75% for INH and 63% for INV was observed, while in the bottom region (S2), an accuracy of 70.5% for INH and 87% for INV was achieved. The accuracy, precision, recall, and F1-score for the learning results are as shown in Figure 13.

V. CONCLUSION AND FUTURE WORK

The press processing process is a method of transforming metal materials in the form of coils or plates into desired products using presses and molds. With the proliferation of smart factories, the press processing process has actively utilized Information and Communication Technology (ICT) not only to monitor abnormal conditions of equipment through facilities and various sensors but also to enhance productivity. Moreover, activities aimed at automating the surface defect detection of appearance products for quality improvement have consistently taken place. It is predicted that surface defect detection technology through computer vision and machine learning will rapidly advance in the future.

This paper proposed and validated a surface defect detection method for press-processed products using stainless steel materials with intense light reflection. The method utilized unsupervised learning based on normal data to detect surface defects in products with insufficient abnormal data. The performance of the model was evaluated using accuracy, precision, recall, and F1-score metrics based on a confusion matrix, achieving a meaningful level of performance.

Throughout the study, several lessons were learned, including the effectiveness of the unsupervised learning approach using normal data, particularly in environments with insufficient defect data. However, challenges, such as the variability in lighting conditions and the difficulty in generating realistic defect images from normal data were encountered. The reconstruction network occasionally failed to accurately restore images in areas with high curvature, leading to false positives.

Future work will focus on addressing these limitations by enhancing the defect generation process to create more realistic defect images that better represent actual defect conditions, potentially using advanced noise generation techniques and integrating domain knowledge about common defect patterns. Additionally, improving the robustness of the detection model under varying lighting conditions through adaptive lighting systems or image normalization techniques will be prioritized. Exploring the integration of additional sensor data, such as thermal or ultrasonic sensors, could provide more comprehensive defect detection capabilities. Furthermore, expanding the dataset to include a wider variety of defect types and conditions will help to further validate and improve the model's performance, making the defect detection system more reliable and applicable in diverse industrial settings.

ACKNOWLEDGMENT.

This research was supported by Basic Science Research Program through the National Research Foundation of Korea (NRF) funded by the Ministry of Education (No.2020R1IA3065947) and by Korea Institute for Advancement of Technology (KIAT) grant funded by the Korea Government (MOTIE) (P0017006, HRD Program for Industrial Innovation).

REFERENCES

[1] J. Villalba-Diez, W. Wellbrock, D. Schmidt, R. Gevers, J. Ordieres-Meré, and M. Buchwitz, "Deep learning for industrial computer vision quality control in the printing industry 4.0," Sensors, vol. 19, no. 18, 2019.

[2] D. Weimer, B. Scholz-Reiter, and M. Shpitalni, "Design of deep convolutional neural network architectures for automated feature extraction in industrial inspection," CIRP Annals - Manufacturing Technology, vol. 65, no. 1, pp. 417–420, 2016.

[3] Y. Liau and K. Ryu, "Framework of Automated Inspection System for Real-time Injection Molding," in Proceedings of the 2017 Journal of Academic Conference of the Korean Society of Business Administration and Sciences, Yeosu, Korea, Apr. 26-29, 2017.

[4] B. Liu, S. Wu, and S. Zou, "Automatic detection technology of surface defects on plastic products based on machine vision," in Proceedings of the 2010 International Conference on Mechanic Automation and Control Engineering (MACE2010), Wuhan, China, Jun. 26-28, 2010.

[5] T. Czimmermann, G. Ciuti, M. Milazzo, M. Chiurazzi, S. Roccella, and C. M. Oddo, "Visual-Based Defect Detection and Classification Approaches for Industrial Applications—A Survey," Sensors, vol. 20, no. 5, 1459, 2020.

[6] B. Scholz-Reiter, D. Weimer, and H. Thamer, "Automated surface inspection of cold-formed micro-parts," CIRP Annals – Manufacturing Technology, vol. 61, no. 1, pp. 531–534, 2012.

[7] A. Kumar, "Computer-Vision-Based Fabric Defect Detection: A Survey," IEEE Transactions on Industrial Electronics, vol. 55, no. 1, pp. 348–363, 2008.

[8] A. Voulodimos, N. Doulamis, A. Doulamis, and E. Protopapadakis, "Deep Learning for Computer Vision: A Brief Review," Computational Intelligence and Neuroscience, vol. 2018, Article ID 7068349, 2018.

[9] Injection molding defects and how to prevent them, Available online: https://www.intouch-quality.com/blog/injection-molding-defects-and-how-to-prevent (retrieved: Oct. 22, 2021).

[10] P. Tatzer, C. Wögerer, T. Panner, and G. Nittmann, "Tampon Inspection Unit – Automation and Image Processing Application in an Industrial Production Process," IFAC Proceedings, vol. 37, no. 14, pp. 395–400, 2004.

[11] X. Xie, "A review of recent advances in surface defect detection using texture analysis techniques," Electron. Lett. Comput. Vis. Image Anal., vol. 7, pp. 1–22, 2008.

[12] G. Wen, Z. Gao, Q. Cai, Y. Wang, and S. Mei, "A Novel Method Based on Deep Convolutional Neural Networks for Wafer Semiconductor Surface Defect Inspection," IEEE Transactions on Instrumentation and Measurement, vol. 69, no. 12, pp. 9668–9680, 2020.

[13] J. Scharcanski, "Stochastic Texture Analysis for Measuring Sheet Formation Variability in the Industry," IEEE Transactions on Instrumentation and Measurement, vol. 55, no. 5, pp. 1778–1785, 2006.

[14] D. Schneider and D. Merhof, "Blind weave detection for woven fabrics," Pattern Analysis and Applications, vol. 18, no. 3, pp. 725–737, 2015.

[15] T. M. A. Basile, L. Caponetti, G. Castellano, and G. Sforza, "A texture-based image processing approach for the description of human oocyte cytoplasm," IEEE Transactions on Instrumentation and Measurement, vol. 59, no. 10, pp. 2591–2601, 2010.

[16] Y. LeCun, B. Boxer, J. S. Denker, D. Henderson, R. E. Howard, W. Hubbard, and L. D. Jackel, "Backpropagation Applied to Handwritten Zip Code Recognition," Neural Computation, vol. 1, pp. 541–551, 1989.

Bus Indoor Situation Monitoring System Based on Congestion Model Using Lightweight Platform

Dong Hyun Kim, Yun Seob Kim, and Jong Deok Kim*
Department of Computer Science and Engineering
Pusan National University
Busan, South Korea
e-mail: {dhkim1106, giet278, kimjd}@pusan.ac.kr

Abstract— **The utilization of data is becoming increasingly prevalent across various domains including public services, security, transportation, marketing, and more, leading to a growing interest in data utilization. Especially in the case of public buses, which are heavily used by many people, the importance of congestion is increasingly recognized due to its direct correlation with safety and the potential for numerous associated problems. The bus indoor situation monitoring system aims to predict bus interior congestion and ensure passenger safety through the use of Internet of Things (IoT) and artificial intelligence technology. This paper designs and implements a bus indoor situation monitoring system based on artificial intelligence to predict congestion inside the bus, demonstrating its practicality.**

Keywords-AI; Congestion model; Indoor situation monitoring; Lightweight platform.

I. INTRODUCTION

The utilization of data is expanding into various fields such as public services, security, transportation, and marketing, and there is a growing interest in data utilization. This paper collects and utilizes data related to public transportation among various application domains.

This paper focuses on collecting data and designing systems for buses, which have a broad range of applications in public transportation. The system identifies passenger movement direction, travel duration, and peak usage hours through cameras installed on the bus. Due to the ongoing occurrence of various forms of incidents inside buses, there has been an increasing demand for camera installations. By using cameras to understand the situation inside the bus, it is possible to design various application systems. Therefore, the data available from both inside and outside the bus includes factors such as the number of passengers inside the bus, congestion level, and occurrence of incidents. Based on this data, public agencies can utilize it in fields, such as tourism and security, while bus users can benefit from smooth bus travel by understanding the number of passengers inside the bus by time slots. Then, bus administrators can utilize incident and accident monitoring for accident prevention.

This paper aims to predict congestion using passenger count via cameras installed inside the bus, employing a lightweight platform. In Section 2, we will discuss the models used for object detection, the algorithms employed for tracking, and the protocols used for multimedia stream transmission in the 'Related Work' section. Section 3 will describe the actual development structure and implementation details. In Section 4, we will explain the performance evaluation, and in Section 5, we will present the conclusions and future work.

II. RELATED WORK

The bus indoor situation monitoring system based on a congestion model using a lightweight platform utilizes YOLO, DeepSORT, Real Time Streaming Protocol (RTSP), HTTP Live Streaming (HLS), and Message Queuing Telemetry Transport (MQTT) technologies as component technologies.

A. YOLO (You Only Look Once)

YOLO was introduced at the Computer Vision and Pattern Recognition (CVPR) conference in 2016 [1]. This technology enables real-time object detection and overcomes the drawbacks of traditional CNN-based methods, providing high-accuracy object detection even at high speeds. YOLO uses a 1-stage detection method that processes both localization and classification of objects in a single step.

The inference process of YOLO can be broadly divided into two parts. Firstly, through Bounding Box Regression, it infers the location information of objects. In Figure 1, this involves generating two bounding boxes for each grid cell and calculating the class scores for those boxes. In Figure 2, these class scores indicate how well a specific class fits within the bounding box and the probability of that object appearing. Secondly, in the Classification stage, it classifies the bounding boxes based on the class scores. Boxes with scores lower than a certain threshold are excluded, and after applying the Non-Maximum Suppression (NMS) algorithm to remove overlapping boxes, the boxes are classified into the class with the highest score [2].

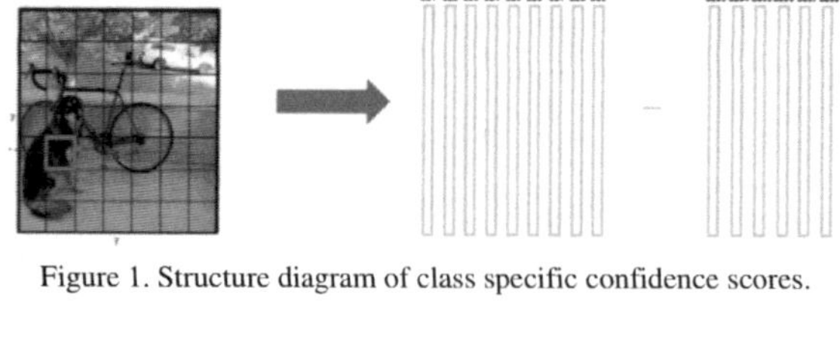

Figure 1. Structure diagram of class specific confidence scores.

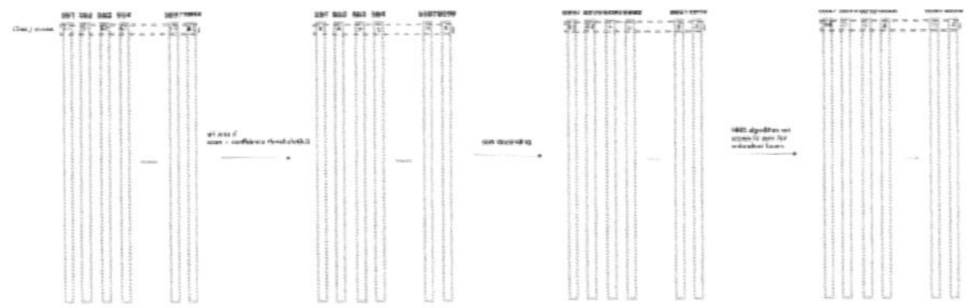

Figure 2. Concept diagram of classification stage.

B. Deep Simple Online and Realtime Protocol (DeepSORT)

DeepSORT goes beyond simple object detection by assigning IDs to each object, enabling them to be distinguished from one another and allowing for more precise operations than just basic object detection by utilizing movement path tracking data. Simple Online and Realtime Tracking (SORT) is one of the technologies used for object tracking in this process [3].

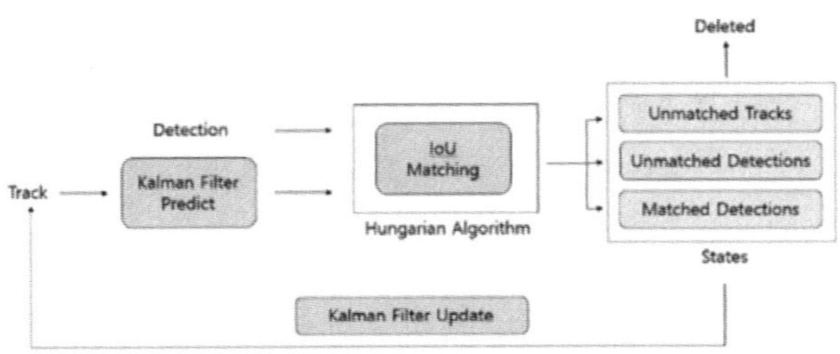

Figure 3. Concept diagram of SORT.

The object tracking algorithm SORT is structured in the order depicted in Figure 3. It involves predicting the position of objects being continuously tracked from the previous frame to the next frame. The predicted values are then compared with the objects detected by YOLO in the current frame to find the optimal match among the currently detected objects. In Figure 4, the 3-state configuration diagram of SORT is explained. Depending on the processing result, it is categorized into three states: matched, new detection, or deleted. If matched or newly detected, the information of the tracked object is updated or created with new values; otherwise, it is deleted.

However, SORT exhibits poor performance when encountering occlusion where objects overlap, re-entry when objects leave and re-enter the frame, and appearance changes due to noise. To address this issue, DeepSORT has been proposed.

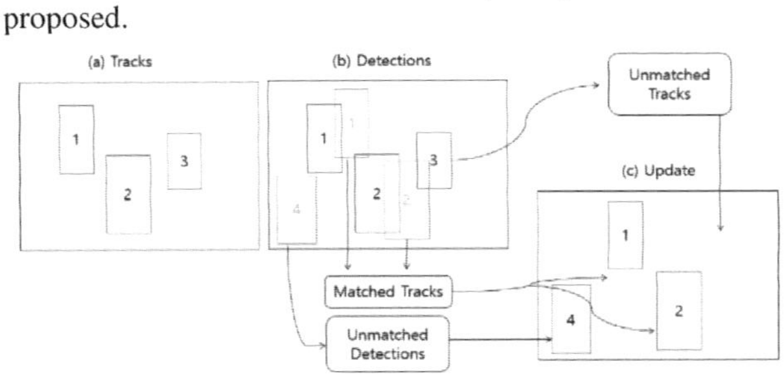

Figure 4. 3-State configuration diagram of SORT.

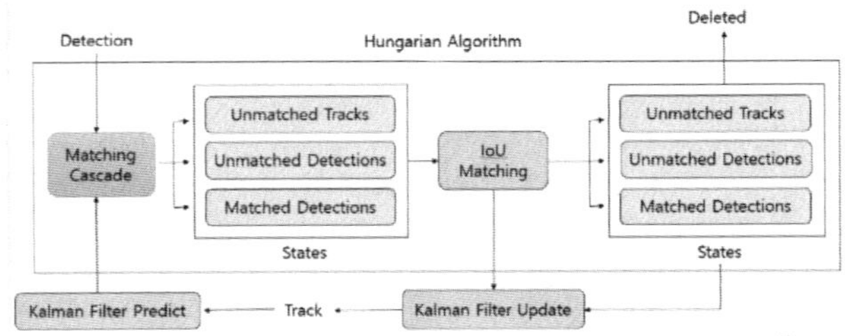

Figure 5. Concept diagram of DeepSORT.

To enhance the performance of SORT, DeepSORT improves the data association process. Figure 5 illustrates the data association process in DeepSORT, where Matching Cascade is introduced. Matching Cascade enhances accuracy by incorporating appearance and distance information of objects into the tracking process. Ultimately, DeepSORT is utilized to achieve higher accuracy compared to SORT and reduce the occurrence of multiple detections of the same object [4].

C. Real Time Streaming Protocol (RTSP)

RTSP is a control protocol designed to control streaming servers. It serves the purpose of control rather than transmitting media data.

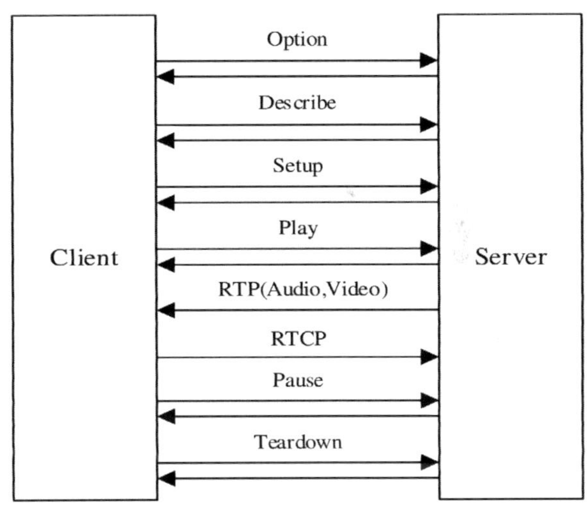

Figure 6. Streaming control process of RTSP.

Figure 6 depicts the overall process of the streaming control protocol, where OPTIONS retrieves available commands. DESCRIBE requests media information from the server, while SETUP retrieves information on how it should be transmitted. Subsequently, PLAY initiates media playback. This allows RTP and RTCP to transmit actual media data and quality control data. Additionally, PAUSE can temporarily halt streaming, and TEARDOWN terminates all sessions [5].

D. *HTTP Live Streaming (HLS)*

HLS is an Apple protocol for video streaming introduced in 2009, used for delivering media content over the internet. In Figure 7, the operation process of HLS is depicted. This involves encapsulating streaming data into MPEG-2 Transport Stream, segmenting it, and then transmitting it. The Stream Segmenter divides the MPEG-2 Transport Stream into segments based on a set time interval and generates an m3u8 file containing metadata about the segments. Subsequently, the client uses HTTP to request the ts files and metadata from the server for streaming [5].

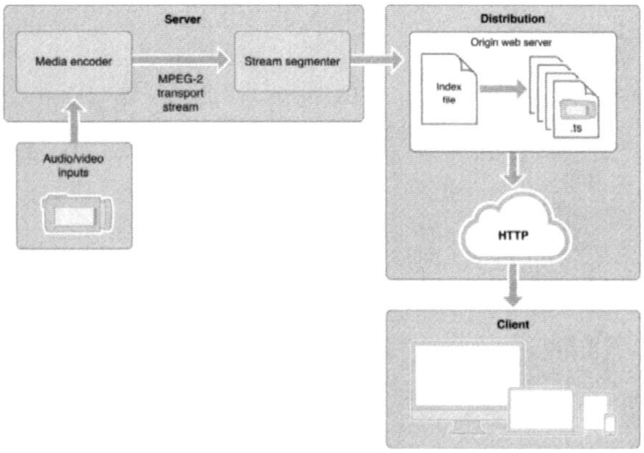

Figure 7. Operation structure of HLS.

E. *Message Queue Telemetry Transport (MQTT)*

MQTT is a lightweight messaging protocol based on the Publish-Subscribe model, developed in 1999 for exchanging messages between IoT devices and systems. It is widely used due to its suitability for devices with limited resources, such as those found in IoT. MQTT was chosen for use inside the bus because it can be advantageously utilized in limited bandwidth and low-power environments

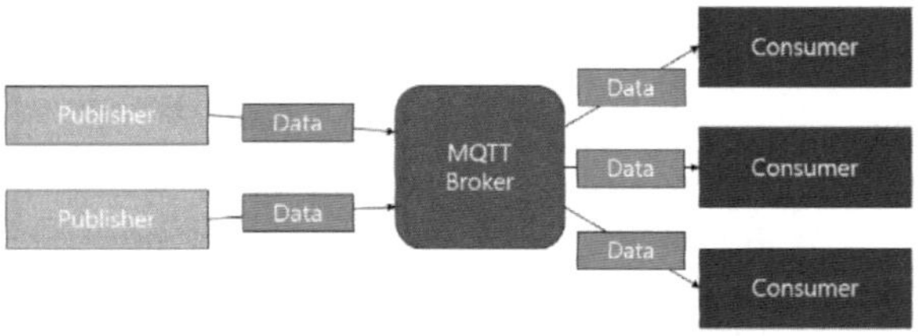

Figure 8. Operation structure of MQTT.

In Figure 8, MQTT operates on a Publish/Subscribe model, where devices publish to specific topics and other devices communicate by subscribing to desired topics. Devices can subscribe to one or more topics, which are organized hierarchically as sub-topics. Additionally, devices can choose the Quality of Service (QoS) level to determine the reliability of message delivery. QoS 0 indicates 'At most once' delivery, meaning messages are simply transmitted through the topic. QoS 1 indicates 'At least once' delivery, where the subscribing client may receive the message at least once, and if it's uncertain whether the message was received, it will be resent a predetermined number of times. Lastly, QoS 2 indicates 'Exactly once' delivery, providing maximum reliability by applying strict handshaking to ensure the message is delivered exactly once [6][7].

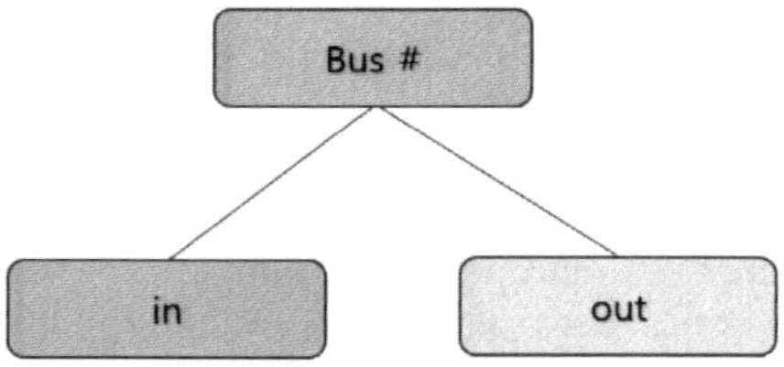

Figure 9. Hierarchical structure of topic.

In Figure 9, the MQTT protocol was utilized to efficiently communicate on the lightweight platform, Jetson [8]. Topics were structured as /{bus#}/in and /{bus#}/out to publish the boarding and alighting passenger counts for each bus. Additionally, to enhance reliability while considering duplicates, the QoS level was set to 1, as data is published only when the passenger count changes, rather than periodically.

III. DESIGN AND IMPLEMENTATION

The system proposed in this paper was initially designed assuming a single bus. However, as the research progressed, multiple bus scenarios were assumed to increase the applicability by implementing them as closely as possible to real-world situations. In Figure 10, the overall system configuration is depicted. As a result, the use of Jetson and communication with Jetson became inevitable. Video processing within each bus was conducted through Jetson, while data storage and transmission were handled using Amazon Web Services (AWS) IoT and S3.

Previously, in traditional web development, the front-end and back-end frameworks were separated. However, as the data to be transmitted was not extensive and complex UI/UX was not necessary for directly providing data to users, the system's architecture was changed to implement the front-end within Django.

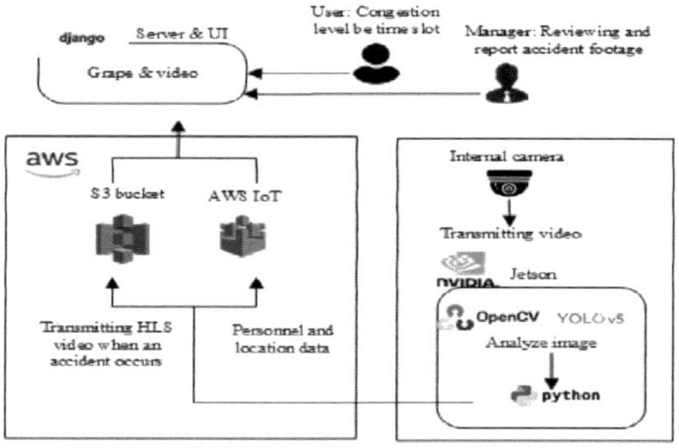

Figure 10. The overall system configuration.

A. Congestion measurement model

The bus congestion measurement model is given by (1), where the bus congestion is denoted by R_C, the number of seats by N_S, the number of handrails by N_H, and the number of passengers by P_N.

$$R_C = \frac{P_N}{N_S + N_H} \times 100 \tag{1}$$

The bus interior footage predominantly captures boarding and alighting activities, as well as the central area of the bus, making it difficult to ascertain the number of seats and handrails. Therefore, the denominator of the model was set to 110% of the seating capacity. For example, for Hyundai Elec City buses in Korea, this would correspond to 54 passengers.

The congestion level of the bus is defined into four categories: 'Spacious,' 'Normal,' 'Crowded,' and 'Very Crowded,' based on the real-time number of passengers on board. The index for these four categories is shown in Table I. While individuals may perceive congestion differently, the levels were established based on general situations.

TABLE I. BUS CONGESTION STATUE INDEX

Spacious	Normal	Crowded	Very Crowded
50% or less	50 ~ 70%	70 ~ 100%	Over 100%

The percentage criteria were calculated based on the bus with the highest number of seats. For 'Spacious,' it refers to before all seats are occupied; 'Normal' indicates roughly half of the standing capacity being occupied, and beyond that, it is divided into 'Crowded' when the seating capacity is filled, and 'Very Crowded' when it exceeds the seating capacity.

B. People counting

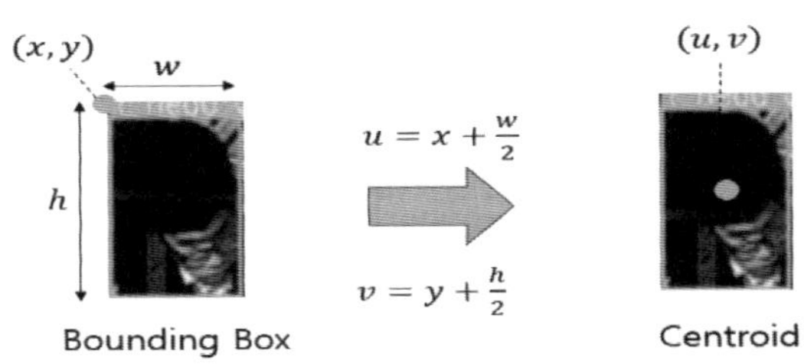

Figure 11. Concept of counting people using bounding box.

To determine the number of passengers inside the bus, we utilized the information from the Bounding Boxes (BBox) of the objects. As shown in Figure 11, objects inherently possess the coordinates of the top-left corner. We adjusted the position of these coordinates to the center of the BBox, and based on whether the baseline passed through the center of the head, we calculated the number of passengers.

Based on the information being tracked, we determined changes in the number of passengers in the current frame compared to the previous frame, depending on whether the objects crossed the baseline. As illustrated in Figure 12, the change in the number of passengers before and after crossing the baseline can be observed.

To definitively identify individuals boarding the bus after climbing the stairs and exclude those outside, we positioned the baseline at the end of the staircase where it meets the bus structure. Consequently, passengers who have fully boarded the bus are counted, while individuals outside remain undetected as they are obstructed by the structure and cannot pass through the baseline. Furthermore, to avoid duplicate counting, a unique ID is assigned during tracking, ensuring that objects previously processed are not counted again if they cross the baseline.

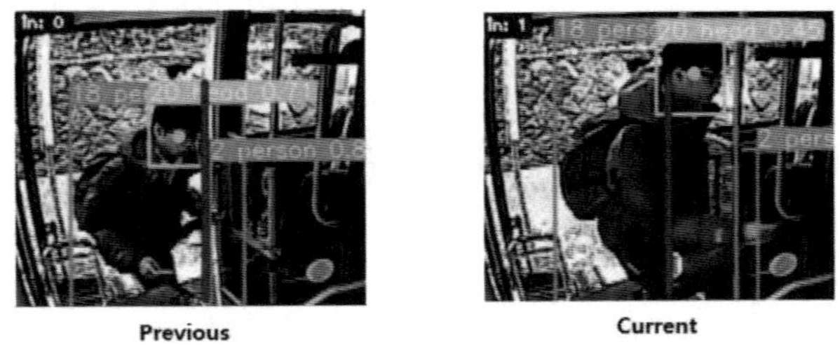

Figure 12. Before and after passengers cross the baseline.

C. Communication between Jetson and the cloud.

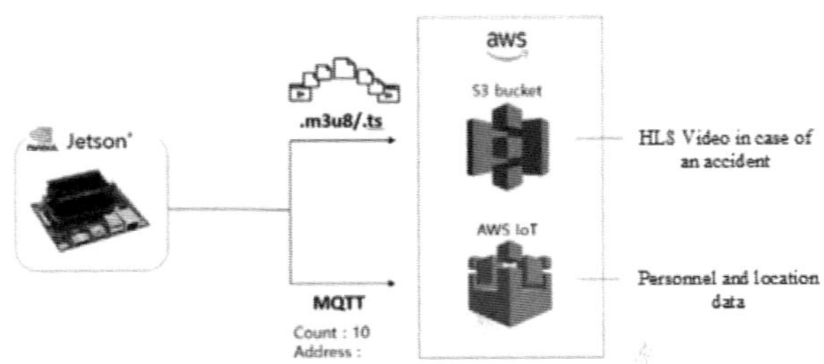

Figure 13. Operation process of Jetson.

In Figure 13, operation process of Jetson is depicted. Developed by NVIDIA, Jetson is an AI computing platform designed for Graphic Processing Unit (GPU)-accelerated parallel processing. Installing Jetson on each bus enables real-time analysis of incoming footage, extracting necessary information, and communicating with AWS IoT and S3. In Figure 14, the operation process of AWS IoT is depicted. This allows for alleviating the burden of transmitting large video data itself and accessing AWS IoT and S3 from clients to utilize congestion graphs and accident footage.

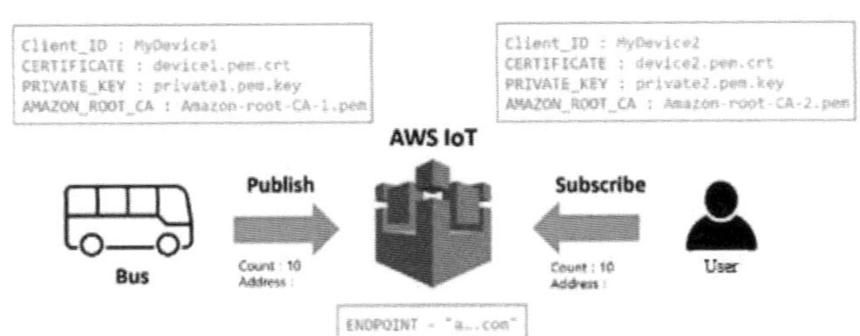

Figure 14. The operation process of AWS IoT.

Devices used within public transportation and by users communicate with respective brokers. The central broker in Figure 15 acts as a system that coordinates messages between buses and user clients, handling tasks such as message reception and filtering, identifying clients subscribing to each message, and message transmission. Additionally, it can be observed that each device accesses the broker with different certificates.

IV. PERFORMANCE ANALYZE

Figure 15. Jetson connection screen.

In Figure 15, the screen displayed when Jetson is running is shown, allowing real-time monitoring of the number of passengers boarding and alighting inside the bus.

Figure 16. Human recognition result.

Figure 16 shows the video being processed for object detection inside the Jetson. Object detection is performed based on the received video, and the counts for boarding and alighting individuals are tallied separately. Figure 16 depicts the result of detecting human objects.

TABLE II. THE ACCURACY OF PEOPLE DETECTION

	Bus number 1	Bus number 2	Bus number 3	Bus number 4	accuracy (%)
Get on	9/14	8/11	5/8	11/14	70.21
Get off	0/0	4/5	13/15	16/19	84.62

After testing with several videos, the accuracy of passenger detection is as shown in Table II. While there is a certain percentage difference between manual counting and counting using YOLOv5, it maintains an accuracy of over 70%. With improvements in video quality and additional data collection and training, it is expected to achieve even more accurate results.

TABLE III. THE ACCURACY OF PEOPLE DETECTION

	Bus number 1	Bus number 2	Bus number 3	Bus number 4	accuracy (%)
Get on	9/14	8/11	5/8	11/14	70.21
Get off	0/0	4/5	13/15	16/19	84.62

V. CONCLUSION AND FUTURE WORK

Various application services developed using data are actively underway. Especially in the transportation sector such as buses, diverse application services are being developed, making our lives more convenient.

The bus indoor environment monitoring system based on a lightweight platform and congestion model utilizes vision-based artificial intelligence technology to predict the congestion level inside the bus. In this paper, video data was collected and stored by installing cameras inside the bus. To calculate congestion levels, vision technology was used to estimate passenger counts during boarding and alighting. Passenger counting utilized vision technologies such as YOLOv5 and OpenCV, and data was transmitted using technologies like RTSP, HLS, and MQTT, assuming various bus scenarios. Leveraging these technological components, we designed a congestion model-based bus indoor environment monitoring system using a lightweight platform and validated its practicality using Jetson, considering its application in real buses. In future work, we will focus on enhancing system accuracy and efficiency through several technical improvements. We plan to integrate advanced AI models such as YOLOv7 and EfficientDet for more precise passenger counting and congestion prediction. Additionally, we will adopt more powerful edge computing devices like the NVIDIA Jetson Xavier to reduce latency and improve real-time processing. Incorporating IoT sensors for monitoring environmental factors such as temperature, humidity, and CO2 levels will provide a more comprehensive solution.

ACKNOWLEDGMENT

This research was supported by the Basic Science Research Program through the National Research Foundation of Korea (NRF) funded by the Ministry of Education (No. 2020R1I1A3065947) and by a Korea Institute for Advancement of Technology (KIAT) grant funded by the Korea Government (MOTIE) (P0017006, HRD Program for Industrial Innovation).

REFERENCES

[1] J. Redmon, S. Divvala, R. Girshick, and A. Farhadi, You only look once: Unified, real-time object detection. In Proceedings of the IEEE conference on computer vision and pattern recognition, pp. 779-788, 2016.

[2] J. Terven, and D. Cordova-Esparza, D. (2023). A comprehensive review of YOLO: From YOLOv1 to YOLOv8 and beyond. arXiv preprint arXiv:2304.00501.

[3] A. Bewley, Z. Ge, L. Ott, F. Ramos, and B. Upcroft, "Simple online and realtime tracking" IEEE International Conference on Image Processing (ICIP), Phoenix, AZ, USA, pp. 3464-3468, Sep. 2016. https://doi.org/10.1109/ICIP.2016.7533003.

[4] N. Wojke, A. Bewley, and D. Paulus, "Simple online and realtime tracking with a deep association metric", IEEE International Conference on Image Processing (ICIP), Beijing, China, pp. 3645-3649, Sep. 2017. https://doi.org/10.1109/ICIP.2017.8296962.

[5] R. Pantos and W. May, "HTTP Live Streaming," IETF RFC 8216, Aug. 2017. [Online] Available: https://www.ietf.org/rfc/rfc8216.tx.

[6] P. Julio, "MQTT Performance Analysis with OMNeT++," M.S. thesis, IBM Zurich Research Laboratory, Institut Eurecom, Sep. 2005.

[7] The MQTT protocol, http://www.mqtt.org/, last access June 2024.

[8] M. I. Uddin, M. S. Alamgir, M. M. Rahman, M. S. Bhuiyan, and M. A. Moral, "AI traffic control system based on deepstream and IoT using NVIDIA Jetson nano", In 2021 2nd International Conference on Robotics, Electrical and Signal Processing Techniques (ICREST), pp. 115-119, IEEE, 2021.

Prediction of Residential Building Energy Star Score: A Case Study of New York City

Fan Zhang
Computer Science Department
Tuskegee University
Tuskegee, USA
e-mail: vfun.zhang@gmail.com

Baiyun Chen*
Computer Science Department
Tuskegee University
Tuskegee, USA
e-mail: bchen@tuskegee.edu

Fan Wu
Computer Science Department
Tuskegee University
Tuskegee, USA
e-mail: fwu@tuskegee.edu

Ling Bai
School of Engineering
The University of British Columbia
Kelowna, Canada
e-mail: ling.bai@ubc.ca

***Abstract*—Over the past few years, machine learning algorithms have garnered widespread attention in predicting the Energy Star Score of residential buildings. Traditional forecasting models, relying on software and statistical methods, failed to deliver accurate predictions owing to the intricacies of factors, non-linear relationships, and the noise of the data utilized in prediction. In this paper, we propose to use machine learning algorithms to enhance the performance of the Energy Star Score of residential buildings, due to their capability to capture the complex relationships between various kinds of features. We carefully choose the essential features to construct a regression model capable of accurately predicting the score through feature engineering and selection procedures. Additionally, we unveil the significant factors by ranking the importance of various features. Furthermore, we compare the performances of different machine learning algorithms in prediction and identify the optimal model, Gradient Boosting Regressor (GBR), as the best forecaster of Energy Star Scores for residential buildings in New York City. GBR outperforms all other methods, exhibiting the lowest Mean Absolute Error (MAE) of 0.89 and Sum of Squared Errors (SSE) of 6199.90, as well as R^2 of 0.9967 and adjusted R^2 of 0.9966. The variances for all the metrics in the GBR model are also minimized. Our study results not only enhance the prediction performance of energy scores but also provide valuable insights for decision-makers involved in retrofitting or constructing similar residential buildings with energy-saving considerations.**

Keywords-Machine learning, Regression, Data analysis, Model evaluation.

I. INTRODUCTION

As economic and social development has progressed, the consumption of energy and water resources by human behaviors have increased by an order of magnitude, leading to a rise in annual carbon dioxide emissions and a severe reduction of water resources [1]. This trend has significant implications for the sustainable development of human society. Buildings account for approximately 40% of the global energy consumption and this percentage will continue to grow in the coming decades [2]. Notably, residential buildings are responsible for almost 70% of the energy consumption of the sector, mainly due to the usage for cooking and heating [3]. Fortunately, it illustrates a great potential to enhance the energy efficiency of residential buildings by analyzing the retrofit options or adjusting human activities in energy consumption. Hence, it is necessary to estimate the Energy Star Score of residential buildings, which is designed to assess the energy efficiency of buildings or appliances by the U.S. Environmental Protection Agency (EPA) and the U.S. Department of Energy (DOE) [4].

The primary challenge lies in accurately predicting residential building energy consumption, which directly influences the Energy Star Score. A lot of efforts from academia, industry, and governments have originated multiple methods or tools for the estimation of residential buildings energy consumption. The Building Energy Software Tools Directory [5] provides comprehensive information on building software tools for evaluating energy efficiency and sustainability in buildings. It also shows that efforts can be derived for different components to minimize energy consumption. With the widespread application of machine learning techniques, a growing number of researchers have recently proposed to introduce machine learning algorithms in predicting residential building energy consumption. In [6], Allard et al. compare the traditional calculation methods for energy performance analysis in Nordic countries, highly depending on the definition of energy performance in various countries. In [7], a neural network is trained for modeling and estimating the hourly energy consumption for a typical residential building in Athens. In [8], Kialashaki and Reisel employ both artificial neural networks and regression models to model the energy demand in the residential sector of the United States, forecasting energy demand in the residential sector until 2030. In [9], Swan and Ugursal provide a review of the multiple techniques used for modeling residential sector energy consumption, where regression and neural networks are utilized to identify the impactors of end-use energy consumption. Although these researches concentrate on distinct areas, they all offer a basis for forecasting residential energy consumption.

This paper focuses on urban residential areas due to the high population density and energy consumption in metropolitan areas. Five representative regression models are used to forecast the Energy Star Score of residential buildings employing the

*: Baiyun Chen (bchen@tuskegee.edu) is the corresponding author.

disclosed energy and water consumption data from New York City, and the performances of various approaches are compared. Furthermore, by evaluating the significance of various features, this study identifies factors that significantly affect energy consumption, offering guidance for future home design or retrofit as well as human activities in heating and cooking to support the attempts to reduce emissions and conserve energy.

The structure of the paper is as follows. Section II briefly introduces the five conventional regression methods utilized in this work. Section III depicts the modeling procedure and results for the residential building energy consumption data in New York, presenting and discussing the findings. We conclude with Section V.

II. METHODS

Regression approaches, one of the most popular types of machine learning algorithms, demonstrate superior predictability with promising results in various domains, including energy consumption [10], bankruptcy prediction[11], air pollution [12], epidemiology [13], and some other applications. This study introduces 5 typical regression methods, including k-Nearest Neighbor Regression [14], Linear Regression [15], Random Forest Regression [16], Support Vector Regression [17], and Gradient Boosting Regression [18] to predict the Energy Star Score of residential buildings and investigates the prediction results using four metrics, i.e., MAE, SSE, R^2, Adjusted R^2 [19]. The coefficient of determination, R^2, measures the proportion of the variance in the dependent variable that is predictable from the independent variables. Adjusted R^2 is a modified version of R^2 that adjusts for the number of predictors in the model.

Mathematically, given a training dataset D with features X and target values Y, and a new data point $\boldsymbol{x}$ for which we want to predict the target value $\hat{y}$, we briefly introduce the five regression models and calculate $\hat{y}$ in each regression model accordingly.

A. k-Nearest Neighbor Regression

kNN regression, or k-Nearest Neighbors regression, is a non-parametric regression technique used for estimating the value of a continuous target variable. In kNN regression, the predicted value for a given data point is determined by averaging the target values of its k nearest neighbors [14]. Hence,

$$\hat{y} = \frac{1}{k}\sum_{i=1}^{k} y_i, \tag{1}$$

where y_i are the target values of the k nearest neighbors of $\boldsymbol{x}$. The nearest neighbors are typically determined based on a distance metric, such as Euclidean distance.

B. Linear Regression

Linear regression is a linear approach to model the relationship between a dependent variable y and one or more independent variables $\boldsymbol{x}$ [15]. The predict value $\hat{y}$ is calculated using (2):

$$\hat{y} = \beta_0 + \beta_1 x_1 + \beta_2 x_2 + \ldots + \beta_n x_n, \tag{2}$$

where β_0, β_1, β_2, ..., β_n are the estimated parameters for the linear regression model and x_1, x_2, ..., x_n are the values of the independent variables for the new data point.

C. Random Forest Regression

Random Forest Regression is an ensemble learning method that combines multiple decision trees to make predictions. Each tree in the forest independently predicts the target variable, and the final prediction is the average value of all the predictions from individual trees [16]. $\hat{y}$ is predicted by (3):

$$\hat{y} = \frac{1}{N}\sum_{i=1}^{N} f_i(\boldsymbol{x}), \tag{3}$$

where $f_i(\boldsymbol{x})$ is the prediction of the ith decision tree for the new data point $\boldsymbol{x}$ and N is the total number of decision trees in the Random Forest.

D. Support Vector Regression

Support Vector Regression uses support vector machines to search for the best-fitting hyperplane to predict the target variable. It aims to minimize margin violations while ensuring that deviations from the predicted values (the errors) are within a predefined margin [17]. $\hat{y}$ is predicted by (4):

$$\hat{y} = \mathbf{w}^T \cdot \boldsymbol{x} + b, \tag{4}$$

where $\mathbf{w}$ is the weight vector and b is the bias term.

E. Gradient Boosting Regression

Gradient Boosting Regression also builds a sequence of decision trees. The difference lies in that each tree corrects the errors made by the previous ones. It minimizes the loss function by adding trees sequentially in a greedy manner [18]. $\hat{y}$ is predicted by (5):

$$\hat{y} = \sum_{i=1}^{N} \gamma_i f_i(\boldsymbol{x}) \tag{5}$$

where γ_i is the learning rate that controls the contribution for each learner,$f_i(\boldsymbol{x})$ is the prediction of the ith decision tree for the new data point $\boldsymbol{x}$ and N is the total number of decision trees in the Gradient Boosting model.

F. Performance Metrics

Four commonly used performance metrics are employed in this work. They are Mean Absolute Error (MAE), Sum of Squared Errors (SSE), Coefficient of Determination (R-squared, R^2), and Adjusted R^2. MAE measures the average absolute difference between the predicted values and the actual values; SSE measures the total squared difference between the predicted values and the actual values; R^2 can be interpreted as the percentage of the variance in the dependent variable that is explained by the independent variables; Adjusted R^2 provides a more accurate assessment, which penalizes the addition of unnecessary variables to the regression model [20].

$$\text{MAE} = \frac{1}{n}\sum_{i=1}^{n} |y_i - \hat{y}_i| \tag{6}$$

$$\text{SSE} = \sum_{i=1}^{n} (y_i - \hat{y}_i)^2 \tag{7}$$

$$R^2 = 1 - \frac{\sum_{i=1}^{n} (y_i - \hat{y}_i)^2}{\sum_{i=1}^{n} (y_i - \bar{y})^2} \tag{8}$$

$$\text{Adjusted } R^2 = 1 - \frac{(1 - R^2) \cdot (n - 1)}{n - k - 1} \tag{9}$$

These performance measures aid in evaluating the quality of fit and accuracy of regression models, facilitating the comparison and assessment of various models and their capacity for prediction.

III. CASE STUDY

Data used for the regression prediction corresponds to the energy and water data disclosed for Local Law 84 of the New York City in the calendar year 2021 [21]. It encompasses a diverse range of building types, including schools, banks, hospitals, factories, multifamily residences, and various other structures. To focus on the residential buildings energy consumption, we utilize the subset of the multifamily energy and water data. Excluding the rows containing the missing values and outliers, we extract 7888 tuples from the entire 22479 rows.

The original dataset comprises 249 columns, with the Energy Star Score column serving as the target variable for prediction. The score quantifies the property's performance relative to similar ones, rated on a scale of 1 to 100, where 1 denotes the poorest-performing buildings, and 100 indicates the best-performing ones. The remaining columns are considered as variables constituting the potential features in the regression model. A comprehensive explanation for each column can be found in the data dictionary [21].

A. *Feature Statistics*

Prior to constructing the predictive model for residential energy consumption, it is imperative to thoroughly explore the features within the original dataset. As it is known, each feature holds varying degrees of importance, with the Energy Star Score column being the most crucial, as it serves as the target variable for prediction. Therefore, we first use a histogram to represent the distributions of this target variable, as shown in Figure 1.

From Figure 1, we can see that the distribution of the Energy Star Score does not conform to either a uniform or a normal distribution. Instead, it exhibits high frequency at both ends with a relatively lower and uneven distribution in the middle. Due to its non-uniform and non-normal distribution, traditional statistical methods are inappropriate for modeling the score distribution. Instead, regression prediction emerges as a feasible solution.

Next, we need to screen out the more important variables to the target variable for modeling from the 248 features, a step commonly known as feature selection. This process stands as one of the pivotal stages in the entire machine learning workflow. The efficacy of a machine learning model heavily

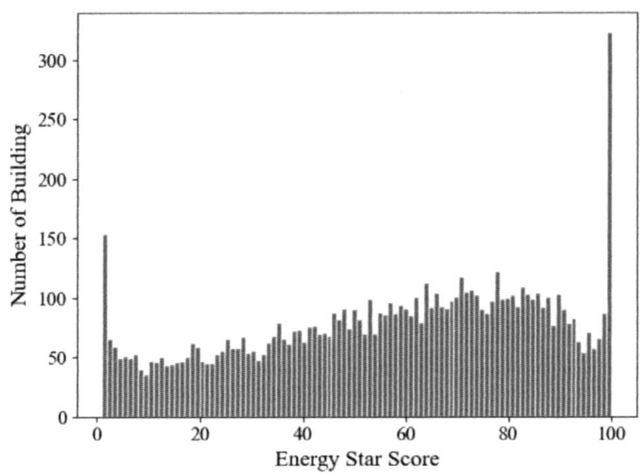

Figure 1. Distribution of energy star score.

relies on the predictive capability of the selected features. Even a simple linear model can showcase commendable performance if these features exhibit strong predictability. Conversely, the modeling process should exclude features with weaker predictive power. Their inclusion would not only increase model complexity but also compromise prediction accuracy.

In this study, we initially employ a non-parametric statistical technique, Kernel Density Estimation (KDE), to assess the effect of various variables on the distribution of the target variable. Variables demonstrating substantial fluctuations in the distribution of energy scores across different values are deemed significant, whereas those exhibiting minimal variation are deemed inconsequential. For example, we explore the impact of districts on the distribution of the Energy Star Score, as illustrated in Figure 2. We first categorize the datasets into different groups based on their different districts, then we employ the Gaussian Kernel function to smooth the probability density estimation of different groups.

From Figure 2, it can be found that the different groups show similar Energy Star Score distribution, implying that it lacks sufficient discriminative power to distinguish the target variable. Hence, this feature is not suggested to be maintained in the modeling process.

Subsequently, we conduct correlation analysis to detect multicollinearity in two or more independent variables that are highly correlated with each other, possibly resulting in instability and inflated standard errors in regression models. By identifying and removing highly correlated variables, we can mitigate multicollinearity and improve the stability and interpretability of the model.

Figure 3 demonstrates the correlation analysis result of "Site EUI" and "Weather Normalized Site EUI" in the scatter diagram. EUI is the Energy Use Intensity, which measures the ratio of actual energy consumption of a building or site to its area. The correlation coefficient between the two features is

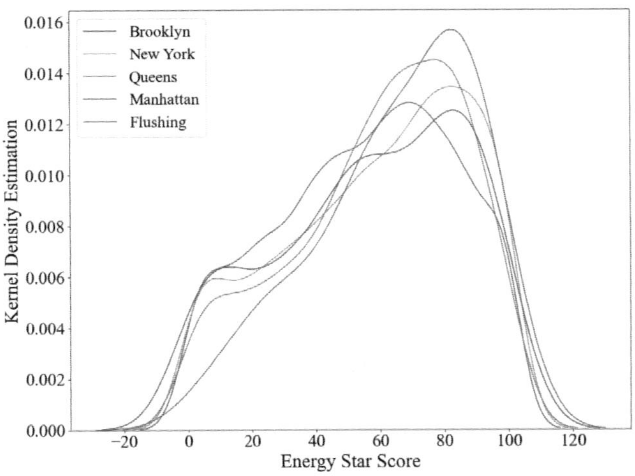

Figure 2. Distribution of energy star score in different districts.

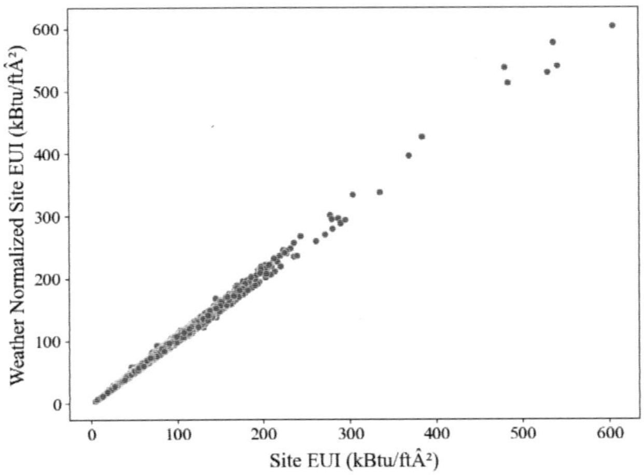

Figure 3. Distribution of correlation between "Site EUI (kBtu/ft²)" and "Weather Normalized Site EUI (kBtu/ft²)".

up to 0.9969, indicating an extremely strong positive linear relationship between them. After checking the data dictionary, we find that "Site EUI" refers to the site energy use divided by the property square foot; the "Weather Normalized Site EUI" refers to the energy use one property would have consumed during 30-year average weather conditions. Since the "Weather Normalized Site EUI" is calculated based on the "Site EUI", there is no doubt that there is such a high correlation between these two features. In this case, only one of the features needs to be retained in the later modeling process. To enhance the interpretability of the model, we opt for keeping the "Site EUI" feature.

B. Feature Selection and Feature Engineering

Due to data measurement and collection challenges, numerous features in the original dataset contain missing or unavailable data. After removing these features and those exhibiting highly correlated features, we identified a total of 11 numeric features to construct the regression model. The selected features exhibit correlations of less than 0.7 between each other, as depicted in Figure 4.

During the feature selection stage, we also engage in feature engineering. Feature engineering entails the extraction or creation of new features from raw data, often involving the transformation of certain raw variables. This may include applying natural logarithm transformations to non-normally distributed data or encoding categorical variables with one-hot codes to facilitate their inclusion in model training.

First, we apply the logarithms to the numeric features and add them to the original data. As we all know, most original data are not normally distributed. If we include this kind of data in the model directly, it might arise bias due to the skewed distribution of data. In Figure 4, the features starting with "log_" are the ones transformed by the logarithm functions.

Secondly, we utilize one-hot encoding to transform the categorical variables into numerical representations. One-hot encoding is a widely used technique for handling categorical variables. In this study, we apply one-hot encoding to the "district" feature. However, as illustrated in Figure 2, this feature demonstrates limited predictive power. Therefore, we exclude it from the regression model construction.

The last step in data preprocessing involves applying Min-Max normalization to the numerical features. Scaling these features to a comparable range helps mitigate bias toward features with larger scales, thereby fostering more accurate predictions and enhancing stability.

C. Test Bench

Our primary objective is to determine the model which best predicts the Energy Star Score of residential buildings. To achieve this goal, we split the dataset into two parts, 70% for training and 30% for testing. We enumerate a combination of different parameters and perform a 4-folds cross-validation to optimize each training model. The training model with the best performance under certain configuration will be used for the testing dataset. The entire experiment is repeated five times, and the average score and standard deviation are reported as the final results. Here, we list the parameters used for each model in the optimization process in Python 3.8.5:

- k-Nearest Neighbor Regression:
  - n_neighbors: [5, 10, 15, 20],
  - weights: ['uniform', 'distance'],
  - algorithm: ['auto', 'ball_tree', 'kd_tree', 'brute'],
  - leaf_size: [30, 40, 50]
- Random Forest Regression:
  - n_estimators: [100, 500, 900, 1100, 1500],
  - max_depth: [None, 2, 5, 10, 15],
  - min_samples_leaf: [1, 2, 4, 6, 8],
  - min_samples_split: [2, 4, 6, 10],
  - max_features: ['sqrt', None, 1]
- Support Vector Regression:
  - C: [0.1, 1, 10, 100],

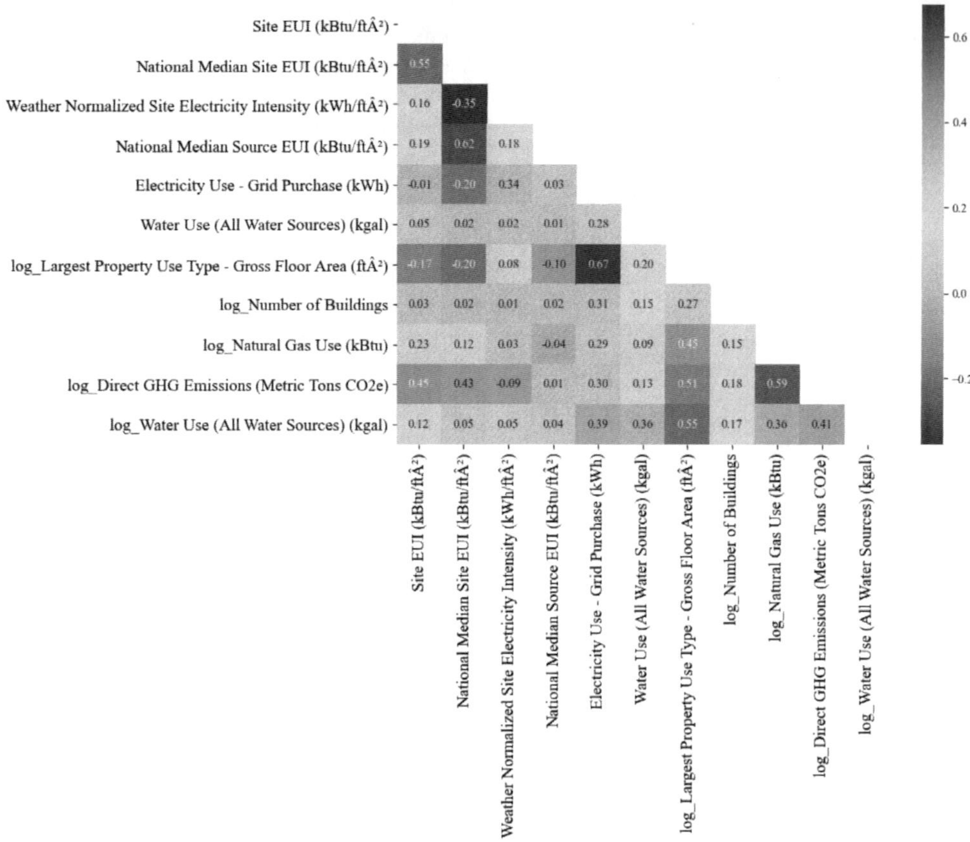

Figure 4. Correlation matrix of selected features.

TABLE I
SUMMARY OF RESULTS OF THE CASE STUDY.

Regressor	MAE	R^2	Adjusted R^2	SSE
GradientBoosting	**0.89±0.08**	**0.9967±0.0004**	**0.9966±0.0004**	**6199.90±806.99**
RandomForest	2.49±2.07	0.9739±0.0276	0.9722±0.0282	48549.10±51378.32
SVR	6.73±1.82	0.8320±0.0354	0.8288±0.0360	312705.89±68675.44
Kneighbors	12.05±0.70	0.6718±0.0281	0.6655±0.0284	609722.05±52117.79
Linear	9.28±0.16	0.7469±0.0287	0.7420±0.0292	470894.70±58898.11

  - kernel: ['linear', 'poly', 'rbf', 'sigmoid'],
  - gamma: ['scale', 'auto']
- Gradient Boosting Regression:
  - loss: ['squared_error', 'absolute_error', 'huber'],
  - n_estimators: [100, 500, 900, 1100, 1500],
  - max_depth: [None, 2, 5, 10, 15],
  - min_samples_leaf: [1, 2, 4, 6, 8],
  - min_samples_split: [2, 4, 6, 10],
  - max_features: ['sqrt', None, 1]

Note that, there are no hyperparameters in Linear Regression, since its model parameters are determined directly by minimizing the least squares loss function. All machine learning models were implemented using Python with the Scikit-learn library, and the development environment was PyCharm Community Edition. Scikit-learn is a widely-used, open-source machine learning library that provides simple and efficient tools for data mining and data analysis. Detailed documentation and source code can be found on the official website [22].

D. Results

The prediction results of the Energy Star Score of residential buildings in New York City are reported in Table I. Gradient Boosting Regression (GBR) outperforms all other methods, exhibiting the lowest Mean Absolute Error (MAE) of 0.89 and Sum of Squared Errors (SSE) of 6199.90, as well as the values

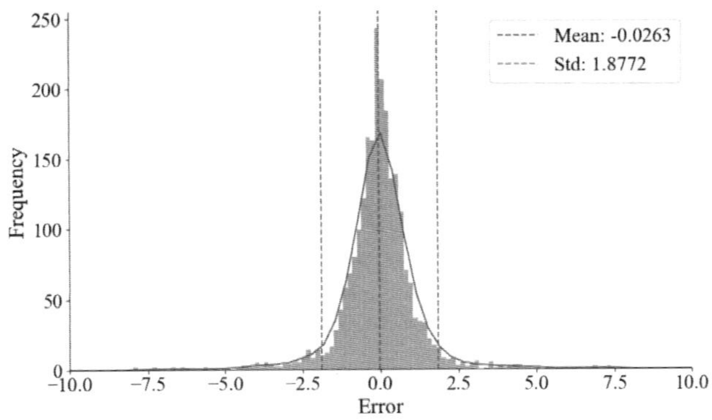

Figure 5. Distribution of residuals.

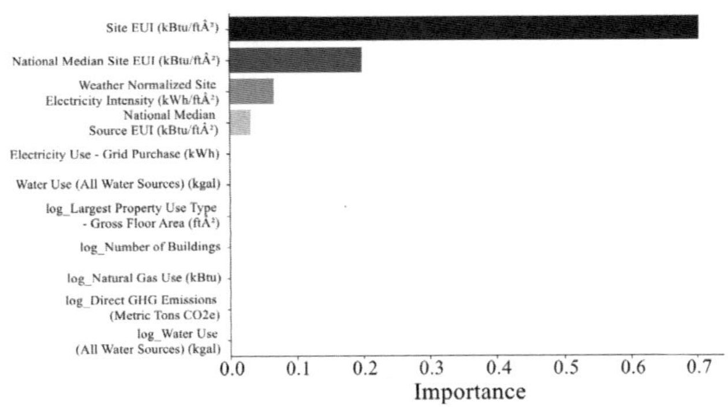

Figure 6. Distribution of importance ranking for the selected features.

closest to 1 for both R^2 of 0.9967 and adjusted R^2 of 0.9966. Besides, the variances for all the metrics in the GBR model are minimized. The promising outcome in Table I also shows the potential to exploit machine learning techniques to predict the Energy Star Score for residential buildings in urban areas. These results empower decision-makers to pinpoint necessary updates for retrofitting or constructing similar buildings, particularly for reducing energy consumption. Random Forest regression also exhibits a notable prediction performance regarding the MAE, R^2, and adjusted R^2 metrics. However, the remaining three models demonstrate weaker predictability across all metrics, indicating their limited applicability to this dataset.

Given that the GBR model yielded the best performance, it obtains a mean error of 0.0467 and a standard deviation of 1.8396. The corresponding residual histogram of predicting the Energy Star Score closely aligns with a normal distribution, as shown in Figure 5. It indicates that the residuals are distributed with a narrow dispersion around the mean, implying that the model's predictions are unbiased and reliable.

Taking a closer look at the GBR model, we focused our analysis on the features with the greatest impact on predicting the Energy Star Score. Figure 6 illustrates the rank of importance values for each numeric feature. "Site EUI" has the highest importance value of 0.703892849, suggesting that it has the most significant impact on the predicted score. "National Median Site EUI" follows with an importance value of 0.215082687, indicating that it also plays a notable role in the predictions, albeit to a lesser extent than "Site EUI". "Weather Normalized Site Electricity Intensity" and "National Median Source EUI" have importance values of 0.052931567 and 0.027565661, respectively. While these features contribute to the model's predictions, their impact is comparatively smaller compared to the previous two features.

The importance values below 0.01 for the remaining features suggest that they have minimal influence on the model's predictions and can be considered less critical in explaining the variability in the Energy Star Score.

IV. CONCLUSION AND FUTURE WORK

Regression methods, one of the most used machine learning techniques, are used to analyze and model the Energy Star Score of residential buildings in New York City. The result shows that the Gradient Boosting Regression model exceeds all other methods, achieving the best prediction with the minimum errors and variances. These findings have important ramifications for modeling and analysis of predicting energy use trends in the future. The regression model can also be broadened to forecast energy ratings for many other buildings, such as business, medical, and educational buildings. Furthermore, accurately predicting building energy scores will aid decision-makers in retrofitting or constructing similar buildings, which is crucial for reducing energy consumption and carbon emissions, and promoting sustainable development. In the future, we will further investigate real-time residential energy emissions and conduct detailed research on the distribution of residential energy usage to guide users in energy conservation and emission reduction efforts.

ACKNOWLEDGMENTS

The work is partially supported by the National Science Foundation under NSF Awards Nos. 2234911, 2209637, 2100134. Any opinions, findings, or recommendations, expressed in this material are those of the authors and do not necessarily reflect the views of the National Science Foundation.

REFERENCES

[1] J. Syvitski *et al.*, "Extraordinary human energy consumption and resultant geological impacts beginning around 1950 ce initiated the proposed anthropocene epoch", *Communications Earth & Environment*, vol. 1, no. 1, p. 32, 2020.

[2] P. Nejat, F. Jomehzadeh, M. M. Taheri, M. Gohari, and M. Z. A. Majid, "A global review of energy consumption, co2 emissions and policy in the residential sector (with an overview of the top ten co2 emitting countries)", *Renewable and sustainable energy reviews*, vol. 43, pp. 843–862, 2015.

[3] M. Santamouris and K. Vasilakopoulou, "Present and future energy consumption of buildings: Challenges and opportunities towards decarbonisation", *e-Prime-Advances in Electrical Engineering, Electronics and Energy*, vol. 1, p. 100002, 2021.

[4] T. W. Hicks and B. Von Neida, "US national energy performance rating system and energy star building certification program", in *Proceedings of the 2004 Improving Energy Efficiency of Commercial Buildings Conference*, 2004, pp. 1–9.

[5] D. B. Crawley, "Building energy tools directory", *Proceedings of Building Simulation'97*, vol. 1, pp. 63–64, 1997.

[6] I. Allard, T. Olofsson, and O. A. Hassan, "Methods for energy analysis of residential buildings in nordic countries", *Renewable and Sustainable Energy Reviews*, vol. 22, pp. 306–318, 2013.

[7] G. Mihalakakou, M. Santamouris, and A. Tsangrassoulis, "On the energy consumption in residential buildings", *Energy and buildings*, vol. 34, no. 7, pp. 727–736, 2002.

[8] A. Kialashaki and J. R. Reisel, "Modeling of the energy demand of the residential sector in the united states using regression models and artificial neural networks", *Applied Energy*, vol. 108, pp. 271–280, 2013.

[9] L. G. Swan and V. I. Ugursal, "Modeling of end-use energy consumption in the residential sector: A review of modeling techniques", *Renewable and sustainable energy reviews*, vol. 13, no. 8, pp. 1819–1835, 2009.

[10] N. Fumo and M. R. Biswas, "Regression analysis for prediction of residential energy consumption", *Renewable and sustainable energy reviews*, vol. 47, pp. 332–343, 2015.

[11] E. K. Laitinen and T. Laitinen, "Bankruptcy prediction: Application of the taylor's expansion in logistic regression", *International review of financial analysis*, vol. 9, no. 4, pp. 327–349, 2000.

[12] D. J. Briggs *et al.*, "A regression-based method for mapping traffic-related air pollution: Application and testing in four contrasting urban environments", *Science of the Total Environment*, vol. 253, no. 1-3, pp. 151–167, 2000.

[13] E. Suárez, C. M. Pérez, R. Rivera, and M. N. Martínez, *Applications of regression models in epidemiology*. John Wiley & Sons, 2017.

[14] N. S. Altman, "An introduction to kernel and nearest-neighbor nonparametric regression", *The American Statistician*, vol. 46, no. 3, pp. 175–185, 1992.

[15] J. Groß, *Linear regression*. Springer Science & Business Media, 2003, vol. 175.

[16] M. R. Segal, "Machine learning benchmarks and random forest regression", *UCSF: Center for Bioinformatics and Molecular Biostatistics*, 2004.

[17] H. Drucker, C. J. Burges, L. Kaufman, A. Smola, and V. Vapnik, "Support vector regression machines", *Advances in neural information processing systems*, vol. 9, pp. 155–161, 1996.

[18] N. Duffy and D. Helmbold, "Boosting methods for regression", *Machine Learning*, vol. 47, pp. 153–200, 2002.

[19] V. Plevris, G. Solorzano, N. P. Bakas, and M. E. A. Ben Seghier, "Investigation of performance metrics in regression analysis and machine learning-based prediction models", in *8th European Congress on Computational Methods in Applied Sciences and Engineering (ECCOMAS Congress 2022)*, European Community on Computational Methods in Applied Sciences, 2022, pp. 1–25.

[20] A. V. Tatachar, "Comparative assessment of regression models based on model evaluation metrics", *International Research Journal of Engineering and Technology (IRJET)*, vol. 8, no. 09, pp. 2395–0056, 2021.

[21] *Energy and Water Data Disclosure for Local Law 84 2022 (Data for Calendar Year 2021)*, https://data.cityofnewyork.us/Environment/Energy-and-Water-Data-Disclosure-for-Local-Law-84-/7x5e-2fxh, [Online; retrieved: May,2024].

[22] *Scikit-learn*, https://scikit-learn.org, Accessed: June 22, 2024.

Security and IoT Applications of the Cryptosystem TinyJambu

Amparo Fúster-Sabater
Inst. of Physical and Information Technologies (ITEFI)
Consejo Superior Investigaciones Científicas (CSIC)
144, Serrano, 28006, Madrid, Spain
e-mail: amparo.fuster@csic.es

María Eugenia Pazo-Robles
Inst. of Physical and Information Technologies (ITEFI)
Consejo Superior Investigaciones Científicas (CSIC)
144, Serrano, 28006, Madrid, Spain
e-mail: eugepazorobles@gmail.com

Abstract—**The cryptosystem TinyJambu is one of the ten finalists in the Lightweight Cryptography Standardization Project launched by the National Institute of Standards and Technology (NIST). In this work, we analyze the TinyJambu security from two different points of view: a) improving the best differential attack found in the literature and b) studying the randomness of its generated sequences. Possible applications of this cryptosystem in Internet of Things (IoT) environments are also considered.**

Keywords-lightweight cryptography; TinyJambu; IoT; stream cipher; randomness.

I. INTRODUCTION

In August 2018, NIST initiated a process to standardize lightweight cryptography algorithms to be deployed in constrained environments [1]. The cryptosystem TinyJambu [2] was one of the ten finalists, as well as the fastest among all the candidates submitted to this call.

Nowadays, IoT technology is being deployed to connect distinct devices of daily use. All these connections need security, i.e. cryptographic algorithms. Stream ciphers provide us with the best examples of cryptosystems to be applied in lightweight environments, e.g. IoT. In this work, we analyze TinyJambu as a stream cipher with particular attention to: (1) the best cryptanalytical attack found in the literature, and (2) a randomness study of the keystream sequences generated by the cryptosystem. After this analysis, it can be stated that TinyJambu might be used in different IoT applications, as those enumerated in Section III. The rest of the paper is structured as follows. In Section II, we discuss the security of TinyJambu. Section III presents some applications of TinyJambu in IoT scenarios. Conclusions and future work end the work in Section IV.

II. SECURITY ANALYSIS OF TINYJAMBU

TinyJambu is an Authentication and Encryption with Associated Data (AEAD) scheme with three different key sizes: 128, 192 and 256 bits. This cryptosystem is based on a keyed-permutation that provides both authentication and encryption. It uses a secret key permutation P_n in the form of Non-Linear Feedback Shift Register (NLFSR), made up of a 128-bit register and a feedback function, see Figure 1. The secret permutation is denoted by P_n where n represents the number of rounds, i.e. NLFSR shifts. In the original design - see [2] page 8, the introduction of the Nonce (message number) and Associated Data performs the permutation P_n with $n = 384$ rounds.

Next, we introduce several features concerning the cryptanalytical attacks found in the literature (specifically forgery attacks) against the cryptosystem TinyJambu.

A. *Generalities of a Forgery Attack against TinyJambu*

We denote by S_i and T_i $(i = 0,1,\ldots,127)$ the binary contents for two slightly different initial states of TinyJambu. Thus, the initial differential is defined as:

$$\Delta S_i = S_i + T_i \quad (i = 0,1,\ldots, 127), \qquad (1)$$

where the symbols "+" and "." represent the XOR and AND logic operations, respectively. After n rounds, both states have shifted according to the keyed permutation P_n. As the only nonlinear component per round in TinyJambu is the NAND logic operation (see Figure 1), then the differential of such an operation can be a good measure of how the differences propagate along n rounds. Since the NAND operation is the complementation of the AND operation, we can easily replace the NAND gate by an AND gate (omitting the 1) without affecting the result of this differential analysis and consider the differential $\Delta(S_{70+j} \,.\, S_{85+j}) = (S_{70+j} \,.\, S_{85+j}) + (T_{70+j} \,.\, T_{85+j})$ $(j = 0,1,\ldots, n)$ as the propagation measure. Finally, we define an *active AND gate* as a differential of value:

$$\Delta(S_{70+j} \,.\, S_{85+j}) = 1, \qquad (2)$$

for any j in the range $(j = 0,1,\ldots, n)$, as they propagate the actual differences that allow this cryptanalytical technique. In brief, we try to find differential trails that, after n rounds (in practice $n = 384$), minimize the number X of active AND gates, as a trail with score X can be satisfied with probability $p = 2^{-X}$. As long as the probability $p \geq 2^{-64}$, it allows one to launch an attack that breaks the 64-bit security claimed by the cryptosystem designers in [2]. This differential attack is called a forgery attack as we introduce a false Nonce that forces a particular initial differential, which in turn will allow us to obtain a number of differential trails with the minimum score X.

B. *Successive Security Evaluations of TinyJambu*

The first security evaluation of TinyJambu was performed by its own designers in [2]. In fact, they computed a forgery attack probability of value $p = 2^{-80}$, which was far away from the 64-bit security. Consequently, they stated the immunity of TinyJambu regarding this kind of differential attack. Later, a new security evaluation with 384 rounds was reported in [3] where the authors introduced a method of finding differential trails by means of Mixed Integer Linear Programming. In fact, they introduced the concept of *correlated AND gate* as a correlation between successive active AND gates, see [3]. Indeed, if $(\Delta S_{70+j}, \Delta S_{85+j}, \Delta S_{100+j}) = (1,0,1)$ and $S_{85+j} = 1$, then $\Delta(S_{70+j} \cdot S_{85+j})$ and $\Delta(S_{85+j} \cdot S_{100+j})$ are jointly active AND gates, that is active gates separated by 15 rounds (the distance between the inputs to the NAND gate). As they count both correlated gates as a single active gate, they reduce the number X of active gates through n rounds and the success probability $p = 2^{-X}$ is consequently incremented. In this way, they found a differential trail with probability $p = 2^{-74}$, as well as other trails with higher probabilities - see the numerical values computed by Saha *et al.* [3] in Table 1. Later, summing up the number of trails multiplied by their corresponding probabilities, they computed a global differential probability of value $p = 2^{-70.68}$.

C. *Our Contribution to the Security of TinyJambu*

Making use of the correlated AND gate model developed in [3], we have searched for differential trails with a number of active AND gates satisfying $X < 74$ along $n = 384$ rounds. In order to accomplish this task, we have used Gurobi Optimizer [4], several programs written in Python language (Python 3.11 64-bits) and a desktop PC with a 13th Gen Intel® Core™ with 3.00 GHz, RAM 128GB with 24 cores and Microsoft Windows 11 Pro operating system. Proceeding in this way, we have ranged in a long interval of solutions provided by Gurobi and have found several differential trails with $X = 71$ active gates (84 actives gates and 13 correlated gates) - see the numerical values computed in Table 1 for the epigraph "This work" with X in the interval [71, …, 75]. Notice that, in our case, the number of trails is greater than the number computed in [3], as well as the number of active AND gates is lower than that of [3]. Combining both effects, we compute a global differential probability of value

$$p = 2^{-65.948}. \tag{3}$$

In a more powerful computational scenario (we have just used a desktop PC), we could derive an even better differential probability to, in turn, break the claimed 64-bit security of the cryptosystem with 384 rounds.

D. *Randomness Analysis of Keystream Sequences*

TinyJambu is a stream cipher cryptosystem. Therefore, a randomness analysis of the keystream sequences generated by it must be performed. The length of our sequences is 2^{23} bits. We have used three kinds of tests: graphical tests, the Diehard battery of tests (see Figure 2) and the family of statistical tests Federal Information Processing Standards 140-2 (FIPS 140-2) developed by NIST. In our experiments, all the analyzed sequences pass satisfactorily the previous tests.

III. APPLICATIONS OF TINYJAMBU IN IOT SCENARIOS

As we have seen, TinyJambu with 384 rounds exhibits some security flaws. Consequently, the designers suggest to increase the number of rounds up to 640 in the Nonce introduction. Clearly, with 640 rounds, the number X of active gates increases and the success probability of a forgery attack will be dramatically reduced.

On the other hand, due to the lightness of the components, TinyJambu unifies in a single algorithm speed and simplicity, what means very low energy consumption, as well as less hardware involved. In spite of the security issue found for 348 rounds, TinyJambu is a very fast and ductile algorithm that allows easily to increase the number of rounds up to 640, with the corresponding increment in the security level. It is important to notice that many IoT sensors are not managed nor are equipped with security mechanisms. It is in these situations where the use of TinyJambu with 640 rounds is recommended. As examples of TinyJambu applications (see Figure 3) we can enumerate, among others:

- Any sort of wearable devices (fitness tracker, smartwatches, wearable blood pressure measuring devices, etc);
- Environmental sensors: humidity, temperature, smart agriculture (good environmental conditions);
- Smart cities (air quality, parking planification);
- Industry 4.0 (automation of industrial processes);
- Tracking for truck fleets; etc.

In general, TinyJambu can be used in any kind of application where the security levels were not very demanding. Nevertheless, the use of TinyJambu for critical infrastructures is not recommended.

IV. CONCLUSIONS

Although TinyJambu with 384 rounds exhibits clearly security flaws, the updated version with 640 rounds seems to be immune to differential attacks, in particular forgery attacks. This is the reason why this new version of TinyJambu in conjunction with good performances (good relationship throughput/area, speed in encryption/decryption process and low energy consumption) allow one to recommend this cryptosystem for its deployment in IoT applications with no high security.

The study of the relationship between the number of rounds and the minimum number of active AND gates, as well as the possible implementation of TinyJambu in the frame of the Message Queuing Telemetry Transport (MQTT) protocol (designed for connections among devices with resource constraints or limited bandwidth, such as in IoT) are some of our priorities for a near future work.

TABLE I. COMPARISON BETWEEN RESULTS

Saha et al.							
Probability	2^{-74}	2^{-75}	2^{-76}	2^{-77}	2^{-78}	2^{-79}	2^{-80}
#Trails	1	5	9	14	20	24	30
This work							
Probability	2^{-71}	2^{-72}	2^{-73}	2^{-74}	2^{-75}	2^{-76}	2^{-77}
#Trails	9	24	27	28	18	14	22

ACKNOWLEDGMENT

This work is part of the R+D+i grant P2QProMeTe (PID 2020-112586RB-I00) funded by MCIU/AEI/10.13039/501100011033. It is also funded by University of Málaga (Spain) through network "BIOMED-SEC", reference D5-2022-04.

REFERENCES

[1] National Institute of Standards and Technology (NIST). *Lightweight Cryptography (LWC) Standardization Project,* 2019. Available from: https://csrc.nist.gov/projects/lightweight-cryptography [retrieved: May, 2024]

[2] H. Wu and T. Huang, "TinyJAMBU: A Family of Lightweight Authenticated Encryption Algorithms, " The NIST Lightweight Cryptography (LWC) Standardization Project, 2020. Available from: https://csrc.nist.gov/CSRC/media/Projects/lightweight-cryptography/documents/round-2/spec-doc-rnd2/TinyJAMBU-spec-round2.pdf [retrived: May, 2024]

[3] D. Saha, Y. Sasaki, D. Shi, F. Sibleyras, S. Sun, and Y. Zhang, "On the Security Margin of TinyJAMBU with Refined Differential and Linear Cryptanalysis, " IACR Trans. on Symmetric Cryptology, vol. 3, pp. 152-174, March 2020, doi:10.13154/tosc.v2020.i3.152-174

[4] Gurobi Optimizer. https://www.gurobi.com/academia/academic-program-and-licenses/ [retrived: May, 2024]

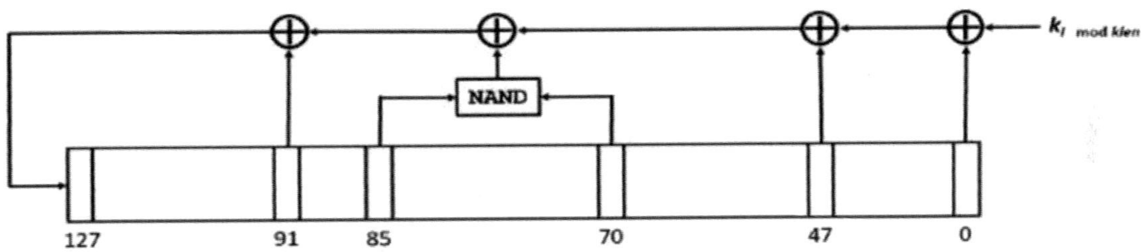

Figure 1. General scheme of the cryptosystem TinyJambu.

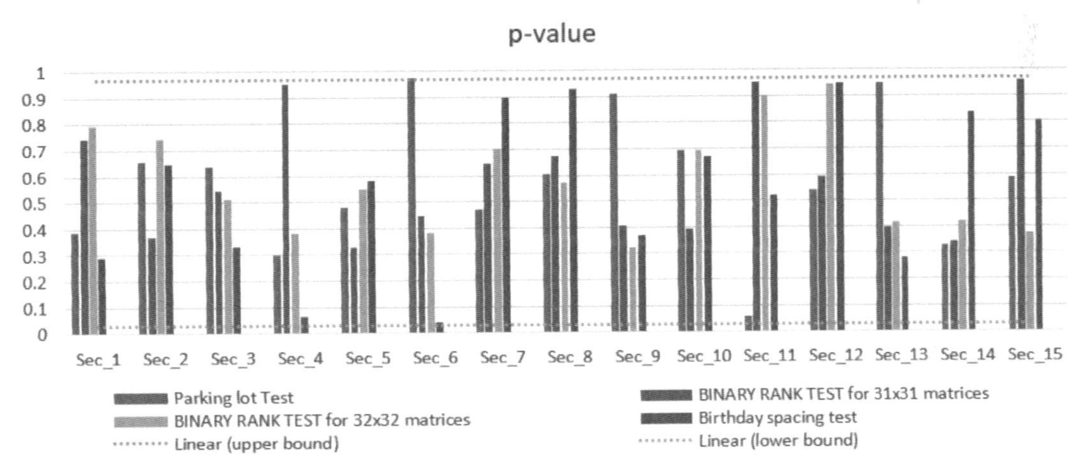

Figure 2. Results of four DIEHARD tests applied to 15 TinyJambu sequences (sequence_1 - sequence_15).

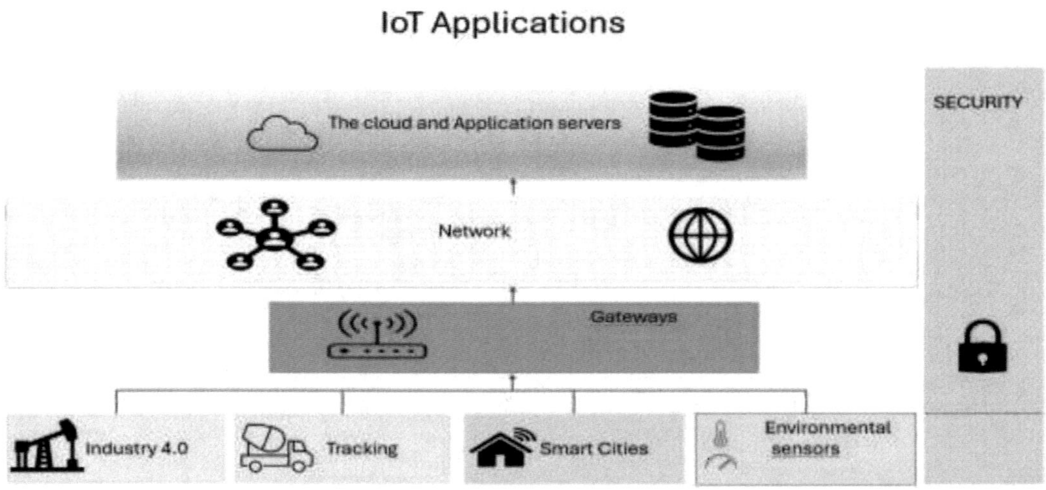

Figure 3. IoT applications.

Exploring Cooperative Positioning and Dynamic Base Stations for Potential Vehicular Positioning Accuracy Improvement: A Comprehensive Approach

Tânia Guedes*, Fabricio Botelho*, Ivo Silva†, Helder Silva†, Cristiano Pendão†‡
*Bosch, Braga, Portugal
†Centro Algoritmi University of Minho, Guimarães, Portugal
‡Department of Engineering, University of Trás-os-Montes and Alto Douro, Vila Real, Portugal
email: {tania.guedes, fabricio.botelho}@pt.bosch.com, hdsilva@dei.uminho.pt, {ivo, cpendao}@dsi.uminho.pt

***Abstract*—Cooperative positioning has appeared as a promising strategy to improve the accuracy of vehicle positioning systems, particularly in urban environments where traditional static base stations are used. This paper proposes an approach for selecting vehicles to serve as dynamic reference stations to improve positioning using Artificial Intelligence, which enables the reduction of costs associated with correction services. By leveraging the presence of nearby vehicles, our method aims to improve the precision of positioning in challenging environments like urban canyons. To achieve this goal, we utilize simulation data to create a comprehensive dataset, capturing various environmental conditions and vehicle dynamics. We then employ machine learning techniques to use this dataset and identify optimal vehicles that can serve as reference stations for improving the positioning accuracy of other vehicles in real-time. By continuously learning and adapting to changing conditions, our approach offers a flexible and robust solution for cooperative positioning in dynamic urban settings.**

***Keywords*-Cooperative Positioning; Machine Learning; Localization; GNSS.**

I. INTRODUCTION

The navigation systems are an essential component of intelligent vehicles and are being used in Advanced Driver Assistance Systems (ADAS) applications [1]. In current era of developing autonomous systems, the combination of Cooperative Positioning (CP) and Machine Learning (ML) methodologies represents an excellent pathway towards attaining accurate vehicle positioning.

CP is identified as a potentially effective approach to enhance the precision of location estimation. In contrast to conventional positioning systems that depend exclusively on data from individual sensors, CP utilize the combined capabilities of numerous sensors to create a cooperative scenario where information from various sources is effortlessly merged and integrated [2].

Improving the position accuracy for each vehicle in a non-cooperative environment can be achieved using static base stations serving as references. Assuming these stations are positioned within the same area as the Global Positioning System (GPS) receiver, it can be assumed they are affected by the same error sources, considering similar atmospheric conditions. However, this may not bring benefits in terms of infrastructure cost and implementation, as it requires a large number of scattered static reference stations, for example, in a city [3]. Additionally, independent positioning using low-cost GPS receivers may result in low positioning accuracy, in some scenarios in the order of tens of meters, which is unacceptable for vehicles requiring high accuracy in their position while in motion. However, vehicles that rely just on dynamic reference stations, especially if they use only egocentric positioning, can not achieve high precision in positioning. The advantage of relative positioning lies in the use of distance measurements obtained through Global Navigation Satellite System (GNSS) signals, which offer higher precision. The purpose of CP is to mitigate errors associated with multipath and Non-Line-Of-Sight (NLOS). Thus, vehicles in the same area can contribute with measurements to enhance positioning, reducing the reliance on a large number of static reference base stations. Furthermore, it may enable even a vehicle using a low cost GPS system to increase the accuracy in the estimated position through measurements from others [4].

Assigning responsibility to vehicles to be used or viewed as dynamic reference stations requires consideration of several aspects to facilitate decision-making. Factors such as the vehicle's operating area, susceptibility to multipath effects, relevance of measurement errors (e.g., pseudorange errors), and shared data with other vehicles (e.g., common satellites) must be taken into account [5]. This is important as it enables the subsequent application of error correction services algorithms, such as differential positioning or Real-Time Kinematic (RTK) [6]. However, obtaining real-time errors for decision-making regarding whether a vehicle can be considered a reference station is challenging. Therefore, the use of simulators can facilitate the validation of this concept and the creation of a dataset incorporating measurements obtained by a receiver. This dataset can serve as a training basis for Artificial Intelligence (AI) algorithms to develop a model capable of assessing, in real-time, the likelihood of a vehicle being considered a dynamic reference station on a scale from 0 to 1, without the need to directly examine factors such as pseudorange errors.

Creating datasets to address the mentioned challenge can be difficult using real-world technology. To establish the CP topic, it is necessary to utilize multiple vehicles with reference systems that can serve as ground truth. However, these systems are often expensive, such as the iTrace [7], which can cost thousands. Therefore, switching to simulators enables the translation of real-world scenarios into a simulation environment, facilitating the acquisition of data in a convenient manner. The software utilized for data generation in this work includes the Car Learning to Act (CARLA) [8] and GPSsoft

Satellite Navigation toolbox from MATLAB [9].

This paper contributes to improve individual positioning for vehicles in challenging scenarios, such as urban canyons, by exploring GNSS, other signals from infrastructure and vehicles in cooperation.

The paper is organized as follows. Section 2 describes fundamental knowledge regarding GNSS, CP, and ML, explicitly discussing their features. Sections 3 and 4 describes the metodology regarding the pipeline implemented to reach the results, which are described in Section 5. Finally, the respective conclusions and the work plan for the future are presented in Section 6.

II. FUNDAMENTALS

A. Cooperative Positioning

Intelligent Transport Systems (ITS) have potential to address challenges that still exist today, such as road accidents or incidents. The CP is part of these ITS because improving the individual positioning of each vehicle, it makes it possible to share this information with vehicle control system for decision making purposes [10].

CP methods rely on the exchange of position data between multiple stationary or mobile nodes to improve the accuracy of positioning [11]. Several traditional CP systems have been created with the intention of improving the precision of GPS positioning. Nonetheless, for these systems to work autonomously the GPS signal coverage must be adequate. Furthermore, CP methods have directed their attention towards enhancing positioning in regions with limited signal visibility. As a result, it was decided to utilize multi source sensor fusion to mitigate the limitations of each individual source. In regions characterized by suboptimal GPS accuracy, the utilization of Inertial Measurement Unit (IMU) sensor, Radio Detection And Ranging (Radar) or Light Detection and Ranging (LiDAR) data may facilitate a more precise car position [12].

Nevertheless, CP is not devoid of challenges and limitations. One significant challenge lies in ensuring seamless communication between vehicles, particularly in scenarios with high traffic or intermittent network connectivity. Additionally, the effectiveness of CP may be hindered by factors such as obstructions, signal interference, and varying environmental conditions, which can impact the reliability of positional data exchange [13].

B. Factors contributing to GNSS errors

Pseudoranges are utilized to determine positions on the Earth's surface, necessitating a minimum of four satellites for calculation. A fourth satellite is required to adjust for receiver clock errors [15]. Pseudorange, considered a pseudo-distance between the satellite and the receiver, is obtained through the "time of flight" of radio signals. Measurement values for pseudo-range can be affected by various error sources during signal transmission from the satellite to the receiver. Minor timing errors can result in several meters of deviation in the measured pseudo-range. For instance, an error of ten nanoseconds in satellite time measurement introduces three meters of error in the pseudorange measurement. Several sources of GNSS errors are:

- Ionospheric and tropospheric errors
- Satellite clock errors
- Receiver clock errors
- Ephemeris data errors
- Receiver noise
- Multipath error
- Dilution of Precision (DOP)

Multipath errors represent the most common source of GNSS error [14]. They arise from interference and the reception of satellite signals beyond direct line of sight. Multipath is a phenomenon of propagation of radio signals. The reception of multipath signals occurs when there is more than one replica of the signal reaching the receiver, for example, the line-of-sight signal plus a reflected copy. The reception of only a reflected signal is known as NLOS, which is more problematic than multipath. Figure 1 shows how the buildings can cause distortion in data transmitted by a satellite.

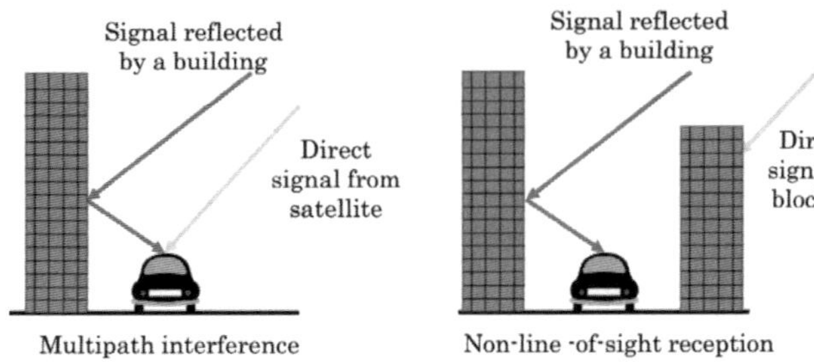

Figure 1. Multipath interference and NLOS reception situation [30].

C. Correction Services

In the preceding subsection, we explored various sources of error that can impact GNSS positioning accuracy. Mitigating these errors is essential for improving performance, achieved through corrections applied to raw GNSS observations.

In literature, two primary approaches to error handling are identified: Observation Space Representation (OSR) and State Space Representation (SSR) [16]. OSR-based systems utilize GNSS observations (pseudo-range and/or carrier-phase) from a reference station, optionally incorporating corrections from a network of Continuously Operating Reference Stations (CORS). Errors in OSR are typically aggregated as a single sum, varying in accuracy depending on available measurements and infrastructure [17]. In contrast, SSR-based systems adopt a distinct strategy for error management. Here, physical errors affecting GNSS observations are decorrelated, modeled, and represented flexibly. SSR enables users to correct their positions using observations from a single receiver and network corrections.

Actually, several correction services are available for both OSR and SSR approaches. Notable OSR services include Differential GNSS (DGNSS), Real-Time Kinematic (RTK), and Network-RTK. For SSR, available services include Satellite-

Based Augmentation Systems (SBAS), Precise Point Positioning (PPP), and International GNSS Service (IGS) products.

The primary function of reference stations is to enhance positioning. These stations are commonly positioned at well-known reference points, elevated locations with minimal signal obstruction, or high vantage points. In this paper, like in [3] we propose the concept of dynamic reference stations, where receivers installed on certain vehicles can serve as references for others needing to enhance their positioning accuracy. By sharing raw measurements, such as pseudoranges in an OSR-based approach like Differential GNSS (DGNSS), it becomes feasible to improve positioning accuracy. This is because errors associated with atmospheric conditions are consistent within the same geographical area, and additionally, errors associated with satellite orbits and clocks are cancelled. These methods are advantageous when used with phase measurements, which have higher precision than using only pseudoranges.

D. Machine Learning

A comprehensive overview on ML applications using GNSS data may be found in [18]. These investigations highlight the use of machine learning in GNSS. The three most common algorithms used are neural networks, decision trees, and Support Vector Machines (SVM). We decided use three different approaches for this study: Long Short-Term Memory (LSTM), Convolutional Neural Networks (CNN), and Random Forest (RF).

1) LSTM: Neural Networks are part of a larger category that includes Recurrent Neural Networks (RNNs). RNNs are specialized for dealing with sequential or time series data and their distinguishing feature is the ability to retain memory from previous inputs to influence current inputs as well as outputs.

For addressing the issue of vanishing gradients and managing long-term dependencies effectively, LSTM was introduced. Cells in the hidden layers of LSTM networks have three gates, an input gate, an output gate and a forget gate. These gates open or close based on input and the last hidden state encouraging selective retention or deletion of information respectively by an LSTM. LSTMs have been proven effective in capturing long-term dependencies as shown by [19] [20] and [21] among others due to this selectiveness in retaining information over a long period of time.

2) CNN: CNNs are known as Convnets and are specialized in analyzing visual data by detecting and recognizing patterns through convolutions. They can be adapted to process various signal data types although originally used for image analysis [22].

Every layer of a CNN is an improvement over the one before it and finds intricate designs. The process begins with convolution operations that use filters to detect desired features in the inputs [23].

CNN architecture usually include three kinds of layers: convolutional, pooling and fully connected [24]. Convolution layers are responsible for most computations as they traverse the input images using filters to detect features. After convolution layers, there are pooling layers which decrease spatial dimensions while retaining important information.

3) Random Forest: The RF algorithms are a versatile ensemble learning method applicable in both classification and regression. It holds the view that by aggregating the forecasts of many decision trees created while training, more accurate and consistent results can be observed than with any single tree alone [25].

During Training, RF builds an ensemble of decision trees. A random selection from the features plus a fraction of the training data are used to construct each decision tree. In a decision-tree framework, which is binary comprising nodes and branches, each internal node represents a value derived as a result of applying a feature whereas class labels or numeric values are contained in leaf nodes signifying classification or regression respectively. This will help mitigate overfitting problems and improve generalization.

As for RF voting system classification uses it to sum its predictions while averaging works for regression at the end of every training process for individual decision trees. For classification purposes, this is seen as majority voting rule in which if there is an odd number of votes within class labels then they should be considered during final outcome determination. However, ties imply no preference toward any label but only balanced outcome distribution between involved classes. Although this is the mean squared error criterion, the mean predictor outperforms individual regressors as it provides a more stable prediction [26].

III. Metodology: Creating the Dataset and Input Data

The simulated data is obtained from the CARLA simulator in conjunction with Matlab's SatNav Toolbox framework. Figure 2 illustrates the organization of data from the simulator side. CARLA is responsible for simulating the environment and vehicles' motion, thus allowing to generate reference data (exact position of the vehicles) with other sensors, such as the IMU and odometer (travelled distance). CARLA also has a GNSS virtual sensor that can be configured to output latitude, longitude and altitude whose configurable parameters are the sensor bias and standard deviation. Since the CARLA's GNSS sensor model does not account for error sources such as thermal noise, multipath, atmospheric delays, we used the the SatNav Toolbox for Matlab instead. This tool takes into account the error sources, mentioned previously, to generate raw GNSS measurements (pseudoranges and carrier phases). In order to represent the same 3D space in SatNav and CARLA the satellites' positions generated by SatNav had to be converted from SatNav's coordinate system to CARLA's coordinate system, such that they correspond to the same position in both simulators.

A 20 minute simulation was run to generate synthetic data from 6 vehicles moving in Town03 from the CARLA simulator. Data was generated at a sample rate of 20 Hz. The following data were obtained: vehicle's true position; vehicle's received pseudoranges and carrier phases; ground

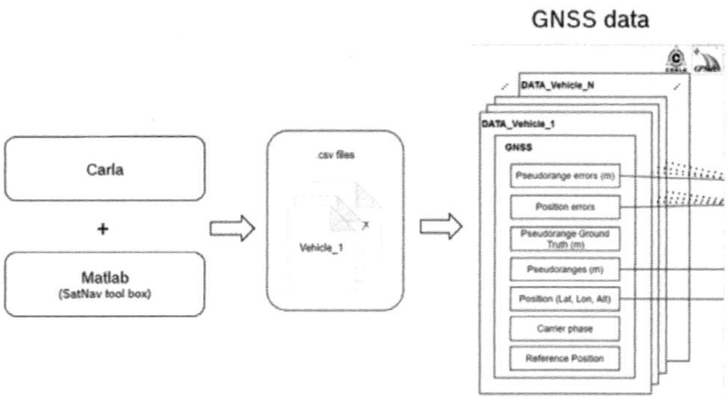

Figure 2. Organization of GNSS data.

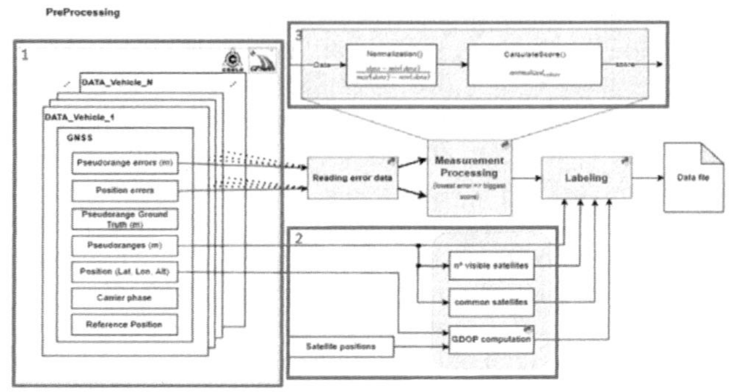

Figure 3. Data Pre-processing architecture, 1-Initial data, 2-selected features, 3-normalization and score calculation.

truth pseudoranges (for the GPS constellation, 24 satellites) for each vehicle; and satellites' positions. Other sensors' data were also generated for vehicles, e.g., IMU and odometer, but were not used for the purpose of this paper.

Figure 3 is a schematic which represents the steps that were taken to get to the dataset. To make it clear how we handled the data, we added red boxes 1, 2, and 3. First, the dataset's features were chosen, and they can be seen in box number 2. These are the pseudoranges, number of visible satellites, the number of common satellites and the Geometric Dilution Of Precision (GDOP).

A module called "Reading error data" was added to the labelling process to read data related to pseudorange and position errors. The MinMaxScaler method, Equation 1, is used to normalise the error values in Box 3. GDOP could be used, but since most of the vehicles are in the same area, the geometry of the satellites is almost the same, so it wasn't thought to be very useful. Instead, it was decided to add it as a feature and not use it during the labelling process. After normalisation, the inverse of the value that was found is used as a score, and it is saved in the dataset file with the other features. The Signal to Noise Ratio (SNR) could be used if possible. But its simulation complexity indicates that it needs to be handled carefully and cannot be obtained directly. Besides that, SNR is not generated by SatNav toolbox.

$$\text{normalizedValue} = \frac{X - X_{\text{min}}}{X_{\text{max}} - X_{\text{min}}} \quad (1)$$

The score is a number between 0 and 1 which indicates how well the vehicle is positioned and can be used as a dynamic reference station. The value should be close to 1 if the vehicle is to be used as a reference and vice-versa. Equation 2 is used to compute the score.

$$\text{Score} = 1 - \sum (\text{normPseudorangeEr} \times 0.5 + \text{normPositionEr} \times 0.5) \quad (2)$$

The developed labeling algorithm starts reading the csv files that contains all information regarding GNSS and vehicle data. The data is divided into two parts: error data (pseudo range errors, position errors) and features (n° of visible satellites, common satellites between vehicles, GDOP). All error values are normalized and a score for each vehicle can be obtained. The final step is related to dataset format where a group of features corresponds to a score value.

Table I presents a data distribution that demonstrates the amount of data associated with scores. It is clear that there is a difference between the lowest and highest scores. This could present a challenge for the final results as the dataset is not completely balanced. It can be said that a model's performance and reliability get better when the output provides a high score.

TABLE I
DATASET DISTRIBUTION, COUNTING THE NUMBER OF DATA RELATED TO SCORES.

Label(target)	Count
score <0.6	12847
$0.6 \geq$ score < 0.8	62508
score >0.8	68603

IV. MODEL TRAINING: EXPLORING LSTM, CNN AND RF

The dataset from the previous phase was trained using LSTM, CNN and RF algorithms. The dataset is not directly applicable to an AI model. Both data and neural network models must be prepared. Python and PyTorch framework library were utilised to create the models. Missing values are difficult to handle because they can affect the final result. The 24 satellites in the GPS constellation are included in created dataset, but they are not all visible at once. Missing values were replaced by -1 in order to solve the issue. The dataset had been divided using 60%, 20% and 20% of the data for the training, validation and test phases, respectively. This type of division is frequently applied to training data and is essential to prevent overfitting or even imbalanced data related issues in the future.

A. LSTM

LSTM algorithm requires a diferent data organization. Once, this algorithm is based on series data it's necessary to organize the entire dataset in samples. Each sample contains a certain number of time steps which represents a sequence of data. This characteristic allows to identify not only vehicles that can be utilized as dynamic stations, but also detect an environment scenario like entering or leaving urban canyons or other challenging environments. This can provide a more complex solution to the challenge that this paper is trying to solve.

Considering 6 timesteps per sample, a total of 3427 samples were obtained. The data shape array is represented by: (number of samples, timesteps, number of features, number of vehicles) and numerically by: (3427, 6, 4, 6). However, LSTM does not support 4D arrays as input. To handle this problem, it was necessary to reshape the array to 3D throught multiplying the number of features by number of vehicles resulting in a shape array of (3427, 6, 24).

In model implementation, it was decided to create two simple models. The difference between them is related to the number of internal layers, and the idea is to check the results considering the model complexity.

Model 1 is initialized with an LSTM layer, two linear layers and a Retified Linear Unit (ReLU) activation function. The LSTM layer takes as input the size of the input data and the size of the hidden layer. The first linear layer transforms the output of the LSTM layer to an intermediate output and the second linear layer transforms this intermediate output to the final output size. ReLU activation function introduces non linearity into the model [27].

During forward propagation the model initializes two tensors with zeros, representing the initial hidden state and cell state of the LSTM layer. These tensors are moved to the GPU for faster computation. The model's output is six values, which represents the score for each vehicle.

The model is trained using the Adam optimizer with a learning rate of 0.001. The training process is set to run for 1000 epochs and the batch size is set to 32. The size of the hidden layer is set to 50.

B. CNN and Random Forest

We implemented a CNN as a regression model to predict the score (target). The CNN model was chosen to prove the effectiveness in capturing spatial patterns in data, which was expected to be beneficial for our purpose. We tried to use different configurations of the model by changing the number of convolutional layers. The idea of this was to investigate how the complexity of the model affects the performance. A more complex model with more layers can potentially learn more patterns in the data, but it also runs the risk of overfitting to the training data. On the other hand, a simple model might not capture all the relevant patterns, but it is less likely to take overfitting.

The model was trained using the Adam optimizer with a learning rate of 0.001. The Mean Squared Error (MSE) was utilized in loss function during training, which measures the average squared difference between the predicted and actual values.

Regarding our Random Forest Regressor, we initialized it with 100. Following the training phase, we used the trained model to predict scores for our test data.

V. RESULTS AND ANALYSES

This section provides the results obtained using different AI models. The performance of these models was assessed through the training phases described in the previous section. The algorithms were trained under the following computational conditions:

- **Processor:** AMD Ryzen Threadripper PRO 5995WX 64-Cores
- **GPU:** NVIDIA RTX 4090

Processor capabilities like parallel processing, memory and cache efficiency accelerates the training tasks. Utilizing PyTorch enhances performance, underscoring the importance of processor choice in efficient tensor processing.

The results are presented using metrics commonly utilized in regression problems [28], such as MSE and R square (R2). Some plots are presented to compare the output of the model with the respective true value. These plots were obtained through test dataset.

From the perspective of the main topic associated with this paper, we are evaluating how well we can develop a model that allows us to assign a score to each vehicle in a given area in real-time. This score will determine whether or not the vehicle can be seen as a dynamic reference station to help another vehicle improve its position.

A. LSTM

As previously mentioned, two models were developed. The features utilized in these models are represented as follows: the number of visible satellites is denoted as f1, the common satellites as f2, the pseudoranges as f3 and the GDOP as f4.

TABLE II
LSTM RESULTS

Model ID	Features	Parameters	MSE	R2 Score
LSTM1.1	f1	12488	0.0002	0.9615
LSTM1.2	f1, f2, f3, f4	12488	0.0109	0.9011
LSTM2.1	f1	17078	0.0037	0.9120
LSTM2.2	f1, f3	17078	0.0021	0.9610

Table II presents the performance of two models. Among the models evaluated, the first model, LSTM1.1, exhibits the lowest MSE and the highest R2 Score. This suggests that LSTM1.1 outperforms the other models. The feature "number of visible satellites," employed in this model, appears to be more effective in predicting the target variable compared to the additional features utilized in other models. LSTM1.1 compared to LSTM2.1, only uses a single internal LSTM layer. This could indicate that, given the data at hand, simpler models may yield better results.

B. CNN

Table III presents different models changing the number of convolutional layers: model c1 has two layers, model c2 has three layers, model c3 has 4 layers and model c4 has 10 convolutional layers.

TABLE III
CNN RESULTS

Model	Features	MSE	R2 Score
c1	f1, f2, f3, f4	0.000557	0.984
c2	f1, f2, f3, f4	0.000397	0.988
c3	f1, f2, f3, f4	0.000351	0.989
c4	f1, f2, f3, f4	0.000272	0.992

The features utilized remained consistent across all tests. The results obtained were generally good, however, the model c4 achieved the highest results. This model, in comparison to the others, incorporates a higher number of convolutional layers.

The superior performance of model c4 may suggest that the additional convolutional layers helped the model to better learn from the data and make more accurate predictions.

C. Random Forest

TABLE IV
RANDOM FOREST MODEL PERFORMANCE METRICS

Model	Features	Parameters	MSE	R2 Score
RF1	f1, f4	4515040	0.0017	0.9730
RF2	f1, f3, f4	20731525	0.0001	0.9993
RF3	f1, f2, f3, f4	19715917	0.0001	0.9992
RF4	f2, f3, f4	19716091	0.0001	0.9992
RF5	f1, f2, f3	19716415	0.0001	0.9992
RF6	f1, f3, f4	19859980	0.0001	0.9956

Table IV demonstrates that the Random Forest algorithm achieved satisfactory results. Given its ease of implementation and speed in producing results, it can be considered a viable option for this dataset. The performance of the Random Forest model across all evaluation metrics strongly suggests it as a good algorithm to use with GNSS data.

D. Model results vs Groundtruth

Figure 4 presents the outcomes for the three distinct algorithms utilized: LSTM, CNN, and Random Forest. The vertical axis represents predicted values, while the horizontal axis corresponds to ground truth values. These results are derived from 20% of the total dataset, previously designated as the test dataset.

Most values fit what would be expected, with notable performance observed in the results generated by the Random Forest algorithm. However, the LSTM achieved some anomalous results regarding certain score values. This may be attributed to the dataset nature and its application in time series based algorithm.

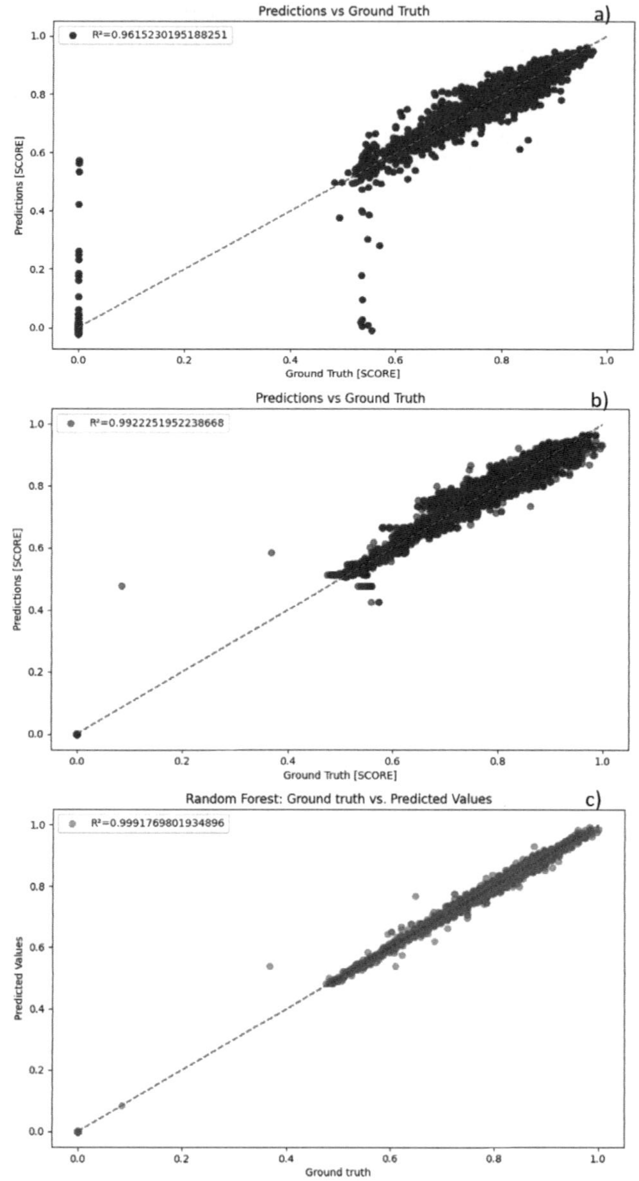

Figure 4. Inference results. a) LSTM, b) CNN regressor, c) Random Forest.

VI. CONCLUSION AND FUTURE WORK

The main focus of this work is to determine possible vehicles to be dynamic reference station and as well as to improve an estimated position with precision using AI algorithms such as LSTM, CNN and RF.

The algorithms utilized have demonstrated the potential to achive promising results using GNSS data. However, this approach still has some limitations and there is space to improve the methodology. The main limitations are related to dataset requirements for AI model applications, because using incomplete data to train algorithms can result in inaccurate results. GNSS data and missing data for non visible satellites presents a significant challenge to be addressed. Additionally, the number of vehicles may change over time.

Solutions to these challenges are related to obtaining more data using a longer simutation, acquiring data for all 24 satellites and alternative algorithms capable of handling varying input data sizes. These algorithms could be transformers and Graph Convolutional Networks (GCNs) [29].

The labeling method applied in this study was a direct

approach considering only evaluation of the provided data. However, it is intended that in the future an alternative labeling method will be implemented, that may involve, for example, the application of a method based on GNSS error corrections. By leveraging data from simulations, it is possible to compare the performance of error correction methods against the available ground truth and create a dataset where labeling is obtained using a similar scoring idea, but inversely reflecting the positioning error after applying GNSS corrections. This proposed approach, although more complex, aims to enhance the robustness of the labeling process.

ACKNOWLEDGMENT

This work is supported by: European Structural and Investment Funds in the FEDER component, through the Operational Competitiveness and Internationalization Programme (COMPETE 2020) [Project nº 179491; Funding Reference: SIFN-01-9999-FN-179491].

REFERENCES

[1] F. de Ponte Müller, E. M. Diaz, and I. Rashdan, "Cooperative positioning and radar sensor fusion for relative localization of vehicles," in 2016 IEEE Intelligent Vehicles Symposium (IV), Gothenburg, Sweden, pp. 1060-1065, 2016. https://doi.org/10.1109/IVS.2016.7535520.

[2] J. Gabela et al., "Experimental Evaluation of a UWB-Based Cooperative Positioning System for Pedestrians in GNSS-Denied Environment," Sensors, vol. 19, no. 23, pp. 5274, Nov. 2019. https://doi.org/10.3390/s19235274.

[3] M. Rohani, D. Gingras, and D. Gruyer, "A Novel Approach for Improved Vehicular Positioning Using Cooperative Map Matching and Dynamic Base Station DGPS Concept," IEEE Transactions on Intelligent Transportation Systems, vol. 17, no. 1, pp. 230-239, Jan. 2016. https://doi.org/10.1109/TITS.2015.2465141.

[4] H. J. Kim, Y. H. Kim, J. H. Lee, S. J. Park, B. S. Ko, and J. W. Song, "Improving the Accuracy of Vehicle Position in an Urban Environment Using the Outlier Mitigation Algorithm Based on GNSS Multi-Position Clustering," Remote Sens., vol. 15, pp. 3791, 2023. https://doi.org/10.3390/rs15153791.

[5] N. Zhou, W. Chen, C. Li, L. Du, D. Zhang, and M. Zhang, "An Application-Oriented Method Based on Cooperative Map Matching for Improving Vehicular Positioning Accuracy," Electronics, vol. 11, pp. 3258, 2022. https://doi.org/10.3390/electronics11193258.

[6] X. Li, J. Huang, and X. Li, "Review of PPP–RTK: achievements, challenges, and opportunities," Satell Navig 3, 28, 2022, Accessed: May. 28, 2024. https://doi.org/10.1186/s43020-022-00089-9.

[7] "Systems and Solutions for Inertial Navigation, Stabilization, Guidance and Control, Made in Germany," Accessed: May. 28, 2024. Available: https://www.imar-navigation.de/.

[8] "CARLA Simulator," Accessed: May. 28, 2024. Available: https://carla.org/.

[9] "MathWorks, Navigation Toolbox - MATLAB, 2024," Accessed: May. 28, 2024. Available: https://www.mathworks.com/products/navigation.html.

[10] E. C. M. Adrian, S. L. Chandra, S. C. M. Etienne, E. C. M. Christian, and S. P. Kulwant, "Intelligent transport systems in multimodal logistics: A case of role and contribution through wireless vehicular networks in a sea port location," International Journal of Production Economics, vol. 137, no. 1, pp. 165-175, 2012, Accessed: May. 28, 2024. https://doi.org/10.1016/j.ijpe.2011.11.006.

[11] J. Yao, A. T. Balaei, M. Hassan, N. Alam and A. G. Dempster, "Improving Cooperative Positioning for Vehicular Networks," IEEE Transactions on Vehicular Technology, vol. 60, pp. 2810-2823, 2011, Accessed: May. 28, 2024. https://doi.org/10.1109/TVT.2011.2158616.

[12] D.J. Yeong, G. Velasco-Hernandez, J. Barry, and J. Walsh, "Sensor and Sensor Fusion Technology in Autonomous Vehicles: A Review," Sensors, vol. 21, pp. 2140, 2021, Accessed: May. 28, 2024. https://doi.org/10.3390/s21062140.

[13] R. Shrestha, S.Y. Nam, R. Bajracharya, and S. Kim, "Evolution of V2X Communication and Integration of Blockchain for Security Enhancements," Electronics, vol. 9, pp. 1338, 2020, Accessed: May. 28, 2024. https://doi.org/10.3390/electronics9091338.

[14] Q. Zhang, L. Zhang, A. Sun, X. Meng, D. Zhao, and C. Hancock, "GNSS Carrier-Phase Multipath Modeling and Correction: A Review and Prospect of Data Processing Methods," Remote Sens., vol. 16, pp. 189, 2024, Accessed: May. 28, 2024. https://doi.org/10.3390/rs16010189

[15] E. Kaplan and C. Hegarty, *Understanding GPS/GNSS: Principles and Applications, Third Edition*, 2017, Accessed: May. 28, 2024.

[16] Y. Zhu, G. Feng, B. Qiu, and X. Zheng, "State Space Representation (SSR) for Real-Time PPP-RTK," in 2018 International Conference on Manipulation, Automation and Robotics at Small Scales (MARSS), 2018, pp. 1-5. DOI: 10.1109/MARSS.2018.8481158.

[17] "SSR Vs. OSR - Geo++ — GNSS technology," Accessed: May. 28, 2024. Available: https://www.geopp.de/.

[18] A. Siemuri, K. Selvan, H. Kuusniemi, P. Valisuo, and M. S. Elmusrati, "A Systematic Review of Machine Learning Techniques for GNSS Use Cases," IEEE Transactions on Aerospace and Electronic Systems, vol. 58, no. 6, pp. 5043-5077, Dec. 2022. https://doi.org/10.1109/TAES.2022.3219366.

[19] "How to apply LSTM using PyTorch," Accessed: May. 28, 2024. Available: https://cnvrg.io/pytorch-lstm/.

[20] "MathWorks, Navigation Toolbox - MATLAB, 2024," Accessed: May. 28, 2024. Available: https://de.mathworks.com/discovery/lstm.html.

[21] "exploring-potential-long short-term-memory-lstm-networks-pandey," Accessed: May. 28, 2024. Available: https://www.linkedin.com/pulse/exploring-potential-longshort-term-memory-lstm-networks-pandey.

[22] B. Yildiz et al., "CNN based sensor fusion method for real-time autonomous robotics systems," Electrical Electronics Engineering, Karamanoglu Mehmetbey University, Karaman, Turkey, Electrical Electronics Engineering, Konya Technical University, Konya, Turkey, R&D Robotics Software Engineer at Elfatek Elektronik Ltd. Şti., Konya, Turkey, Robotic Automation Control Laboratory (RAC-LAB), Konya Technical University, Konya, Turkey, 2022, Accessed: May. 28, 2024.

[23] L. Alzubaidi et al., "Review of deep learning: concepts, CNN architectures, challenges, applications, future directions," J Big Data, vol. 8, pp. 53, 2021, Accessed: May. 28, 2024. https://doi.org/10.1186/s40537-021-00444-8.

[24] X. Zhao, L. Wang, Y. Zhang, X. Han, M. Deveci, and M. Parmar, "A review of convolutional neural networks in computer vision," Artif. Intell. Rev., vol. 57, no. 4, pp. 99, Accessed: May. 28, 2024. https://doi.org/10.1007/s10462-024-10721-6.

[25] A. Loe, S. Murray, and Z. Wu, "Random Forest for Dynamic Risk Prediction of Recurrent Events: A Pseudo-Observation Approach," arXiv, Accessed: May. 28, 2024. https://ar5iv.org/abs/2312.00770.

[26] H. Zhang, D. Nettleton, and Z. Zhu, "Regression-Enhanced Random Forests," *arXiv*, vol. 19, pp. 1-26, Accessed: May. 28, 2024. https://arxiv.org/abs/1904.10416.

[27] J. Ansel et al., "PyTorch 2: Faster Machine Learning Through Dynamic Python Bytecode Transformation and Graph Compilation," *Proceedings of the 29th ACM International Conference on Architectural Support for Programming Languages and Operating Systems (ASPLOS)*, Accessed: May. 28, 2024. https://www.jokeren.tech/publication/jason-2024-pytorch/.

[28] "3 Best metrics to evaluate Regression Model? — by Songhao Wu — Towards Data Science," Accessed: May. 28, 2024. Available: https://towardsdatascience.com/.

[29] A. Mohanty and G. Gao, "Learning GNSS Positioning Corrections for Smartphones Using Graph Convolution Neural Networks," Navigation: Journal of the Institute of Navigation, vol. 70, no. 4, pp. e622, 2023. https://doi.org/10.33012/navi.622.

[30] Y. Gu, L. -T. Hsu and S. Kamijo, "GNSS/Onboard Inertial Sensor Integration With the Aid of 3-D Building Map for Lane-Level Vehicle Self-Localization in Urban Canyon," Accessed: Jun. 25, 2024. Available: https://ieeexplore.ieee.org/document/7314948.

A Comparative Analysis of CPU and GPU-Based Cloud Platforms for CNN Binary Classification

Taieba Tasnim
Department of Computer Science
Tuskegee University
Tuskegee, Alabama, U.S.A.
Email: ttasnim6386@tuskegee.edu

Mohammad Rahman
Department of Computer Science
Tuskegee University
Tuskegee, Alabama, U.S.A.
Email: mrahman@tuskegee.edu

Fan Wu
Department of Computer Science
Tuskegee University
Tuskegee, Alabama, U.S.A.
Email: fwu@tuskegee.edu

Abstract—**This study explores how Convolutional Neural Network (CNN) model performs in binary classification tasks, particularly on a cloud platform configured with Central Processing Unit (CPU) and Graphics Processing Unit (GPU) resources. We conducted simulations of the CNN model for binary classification with different parameters to compare the CPU and GPU performances. We analyzed evaluation matrices, emphasizing both binary classification accuracy and training time. This analysis aims to facilitate the selection of a computational platform by considering both budgetary constraints and specific requirements.**

Keywords- CNN; CPU; GPU; Cloud.

I. INTRODUCTION

Convolutional Neural Networks (CNNs) have become the workhorse for image recognition tasks. Their power lies in extracting relevant features from images using pooling layers. This allows the network to make accurate predictions. To achieve this, CNNs are trained on extensive datasets, where they learn to identify features and classify images through backpropagation. This automated training is guided by human decisions in configuring network architecture and parameters, ensuring that the CNN can accurately predict new image labels once trained.

An essential step in effectively utilizing CNNs is verifying their performance on different computing platforms, including CPUs and GPUs. Evaluating performance across these platforms ensures reliability, cost-effectiveness, and adaptability. This process involves understanding each hardware type's strengths and weaknesses, optimizing resource usage, ensuring compatibility, and guiding hardware-specific improvements. It also identifies current limitations and explores new technologies, shaping the future of computer development. A comprehensive evaluation considers metrics beyond processing time, including throughput, latency, memory consumption, and energy efficiency. Standardized benchmark suites like DeepBench, MLPerf, and TensorFlow Benchmark facilitate this process across different setups [1].

This work evaluates CPUs and GPUs for CNNs, emphasizing hardware selection's impact on performance, focusing on binary classification tasks within cloud-based environments. CPUs excel at sequential tasks and offer high clock speeds, making them suitable for smaller tasks and natural language processing on resource-limited devices. Conversely, GPUs' parallel architecture optimizes them for larger, complex CNNs, excelling in high-throughput, low-latency tasks ideal for image recognition. This study extends beyond traditional performance metrics to analyze cloud environments' performance, efficiency, and reproducibility. It addresses challenges such as resource variability and provides insights into how hardware selection impacts the performance and cost-efficiency of cloud-based machine learning. Cloud computing supports this by allowing scalable solutions across diverse CPU and GPU configurations, enhancing CNN deployments' flexibility and potential.

In this research, our main contributions are outlined as follows:

- We provide a detailed empirical analysis comparing the performance of CNN binary classification tasks on CPU and GPU platforms in a cloud environment, highlighting the differences in training efficiency and execution speed.
- Our study offers insights into the computational resource utilization of CNNs, identifying how different parameter settings of batch size and epoch impact the performance of CPU and GPU hardware platforms in binary classification tasks.
- We demonstrate the trade-off between training duration and the performance capabilities of both CPU and GPU hardware.

The paper is structured as follows: Section II covers the literature review, Section III outlines the methodology, including data sourcing, experimental setup, and training environment. Section IV discusses evaluation metrics, Section V analyzes the experimental findings, and Section VI concludes with a summary and future research suggestions.

II. LITERATURE REVIEW

CNNs are pivotal in deep learning, excelling in various applications. This review highlights that GPUs, with their parallel processing capabilities, outperform CPUs by 2 to 24 times in CNN tasks due to CPUs' sequential processing limitations [2]. Several recent studies confirm that GPUs outperform CPUs in CNN tasks, particularly for extensive datasets, due to their superior parallel processing capabilities [3] [4] [5]. However, selecting hardware involves more than speed; power efficiency and cost are also critical factors.

Süzen et al. [6] noted the importance of these considerations. Oh et al. revealed that, in embedded systems, CPUs achieved 65% of a PC's GPU performance while consuming only 2.6% of the power, making CPUs effective for resource-limited tasks [7]. To enhance efficiency, optimizing CNN models through techniques like pruning and quantization can reduce computational complexity. Blott et al. explored these methods, showing they are adaptable across hardware and improve performance [8]. Existing research also investigates benchmarking the performance of CPUs and GPUs for other machine learning tasks, such as Long Short-Term Memory (LSTM) networks, providing a broader understanding of hardware capabilities across different neural network architectures [9]. Machine learning predicts CNN execution time, power, and memory usage, especially on GPUs. Bouzidi et al. presented a model to aid researchers in hardware selection, further illustrating the practical applications of these predictive insights [10].

III. Methodology

A. CNN Architecture Overview

In this study, we explored the architecture of a CNN as a fundamental framework for image classification tasks, as shown in Figure 1 [11]. This illustration outlines the CNN's evolution, starting with the input layer, followed by consecutive convolution and pooling layers for feature extraction, and culminating with a series of fully connected layers that lead to the final classification output. Such an architecture is adept at recognizing and interpreting the intricate patterns in our dataset, consisting of high-quality images of dogs and cats.

B. Data Acquisition

This research leveraged data from two primary sources: Kaggle and Google, renowned for their comprehensive datasets, including the well-known dog and cat datasets. Kaggle provided a dataset that consists primarily of high-quality images of dogs and cats, complete with detailed metadata and labels. This dataset is particularly useful for studies involving CNNs due to its focus on these animals.

Additionally, we utilized Google to assemble a distinct dataset encompassing a variety of dog and cat breeds. This diverse collection was pivotal in training our machine-learning models. We also curated multiple datasets from these sources to evaluate the machine learning algorithms' performance effectively.

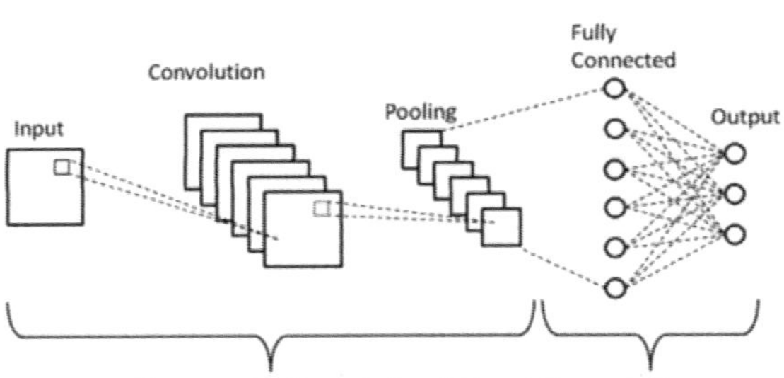

Figure 1. Diagram of a Convolutional Neural Network Structure.

C. Tools and Training Environment

For the experiment setup, we leveraged Google Colab, a Jupyter notebook environment, to train our CNN model [12]. This environment offers excellent support from Keras, allowing for network implementation and training on Google Cloud's GPUs and CPUs [13] [14]. Google Colab enables simultaneous multi-CPU and GPU usage and offers high training speeds, allowing network pruning without losing prediction accuracy. We trained the CNN model on CPU and GPU, benefiting from Colab's easy switching between runtime environments. We trained the same CNN model on both CPU and GPU, enhancing GPU performance with minor code adjustments while keeping the model's structure unchanged. Google Colab's dynamic resource allocation can cause inconsistent performance. Hardware specs and software versions, like TensorFlow or PyTorch, may also vary [1]. To ensure reproducibility, we ran several experiments to reduce resource limits and make the results more reliable.

D. Hardware and Software Integration

Google Colab provides a convenient way to import data from Google Drive. We uploaded our dataset to Google Drive and mounted it on the Colab environment. After completing CPU training, we transitioned to GPU. We improved tensor operations for parallel processing, managed memory better, adjusted GPU settings for efficiency, and changed precision settings for faster and more accurate results (Figure 2) [11]. Once adjustments were made, we resumed GPU training and monitored epoch and batch durations. Despite longer setup times due to model compilation, the enhancements significantly reduced GPU training times compared to CPU, proving the effectiveness of our optimizations.

IV. Evaluation Metrics

In this study, we employed several evaluation metrics to assess our model's performance on unseen data, particularly in classification tasks. This section briefly describes these metrics, which are paramount for ensuring the practical utility of any binary classification model. The True Positive Rate (TPR) is central to this evaluation.

$$\text{True Positive Rate (TPR)} = \frac{\text{TP}}{\text{TP+FN}} \quad (1)$$

Here TP (True Positives) is the number of correctly predicted positive instances, and FN (False Negatives) is the

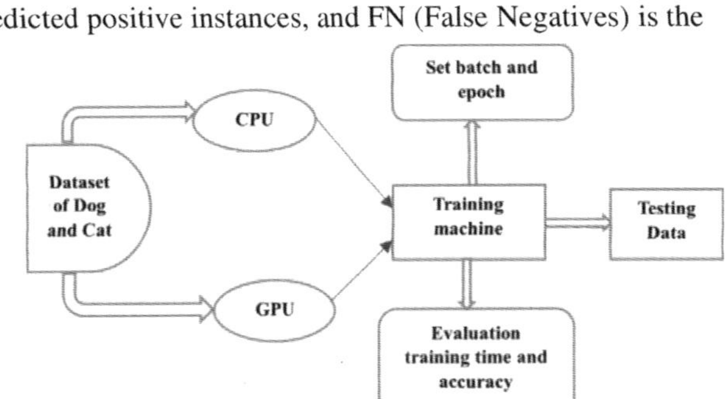

Figure 2. Comparative Analysis of CPU and GPU System Architectures.

number of positive cases incorrectly predicted as negative.

TPR quantifies the proportion of correctly identified positive instances. This metric is particularly crucial in scenarios where class imbalances exist, offering insights into the model's ability to discriminate between classes accurately. Training times were monitored to evaluate model efficiency across different hardware setups, highlighting trade-offs between accuracy and speed.

V. RESULT AND DISCUSSION

To evaluate the performance of GPU and CPU, we embarked on an experiment where the initial step involved training a model using an 8000-image dataset of dogs and cats. Employing various batch sizes (16, 32, 64, and 128) and epochs (1, 2, 3, 4, and 5), we meticulously observed the execution time, noting changes as we adjusted these parameters. An epoch in this context refers to a complete pass through the entire dataset by the learning algorithm. This setup paved the way for a comparative analysis, using a smaller, 1000-image dataset to test the machines.

Building on this groundwork, Figure 3 presents a bar graph comparing True Positive Rates (TPR) for CPU and GPU across five epochs. The TPR fluctuates with each epoch, peaking at the fifth where the GPU slightly outperforms the CPU. However, the difference in TPR performance between CPU and GPU is often negligible, indicating that both platforms can achieve similar accuracy.

The trend of improvement in correctly identifying positive instances is due to effective model learning, fine-tuning, and enhanced feature extraction with each epoch, with GPUs offering a performance edge due to their superior parallel processing capabilities.

Transitioning from TPR to training durations, Figure 4 compares the time taken by CPU and GPU across five epochs with a fixed batch size of 128. The CPU's training times notably increase at the fourth epoch before tapering off, while the GPU shows consistent time expenditure. The GPU generally outperforms the CPU, with nearly equal performance at the third epoch.

Further dissecting the performance dynamics, Figure 5 compares TPR between CPUs and GPUs at varying batch sizes during the fourth epoch. Surprisingly, the CPU outperforms the GPU at a batch size 64 due to its efficiency in managing moderately parallel tasks. This highlights the CPU's strength in handling tasks more effectively than the GPU, where operational overhead can detract from performance. As the batch size increases to 128, the GPU excels by handling larger volumes of parallel operations, delivering peak performance, and surpassing the CPU, showcasing its optimal design for high throughput computing.

The narrative of efficiency continues in Figure 6, which delineates the training durations for CPU and GPU across different batch sizes during the fourth epoch. An interesting trend is observed: while the CPU training time slightly increases at the smallest batch size, it stabilizes as batch sizes escalate, only to surge dramatically at the largest batch size of 128. Conversely, the GPU shows a steady decrease in training time, maintaining its efficiency edge across all tested batch sizes.

Culminating our analysis, Figure 7 introduces a scatter plot showing the relationship between training time and TPR for models trained on CPUs and GPUs. The graph reveals a trend: training time increases with improved accuracy, then plateaus. It shows that GPUs consistently achieve similar TPRs in shorter training times than CPUs, highlighting their superior efficiency.

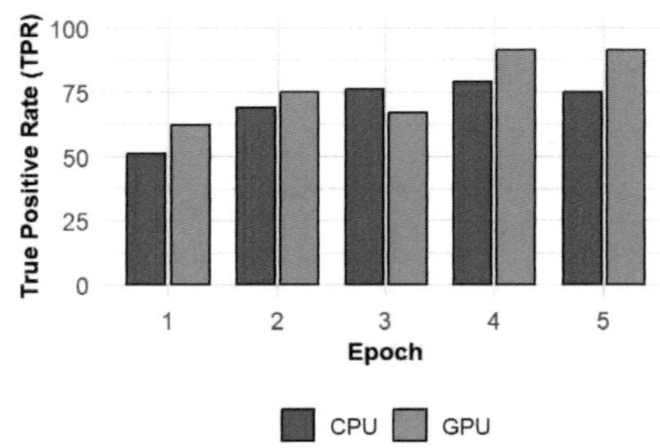

Figure 3. TPR by Epoch for CPU vs. GPU at Batch Size 128.

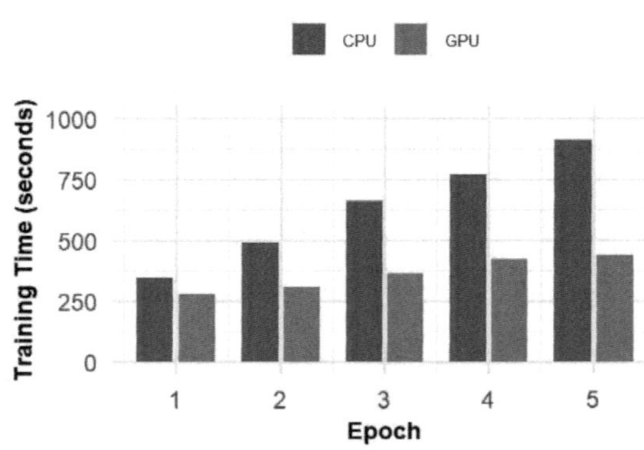

Figure 4. Training Time vs. Epoch for CPU and GPU at Batch sizes 128.

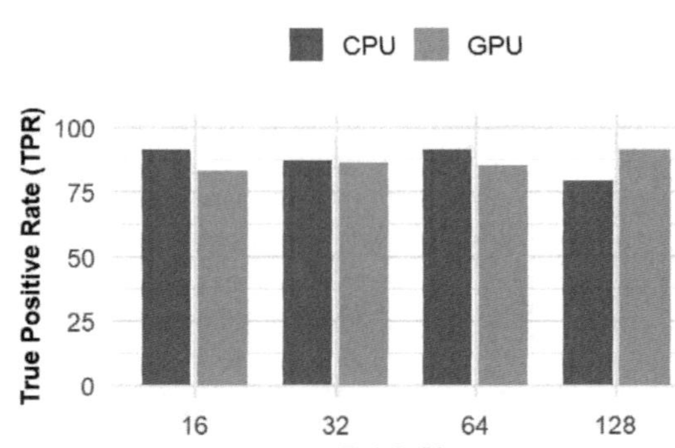

Figure 5. TPR Comparison by Batch Size for CPU and GPU at Epoch 4.

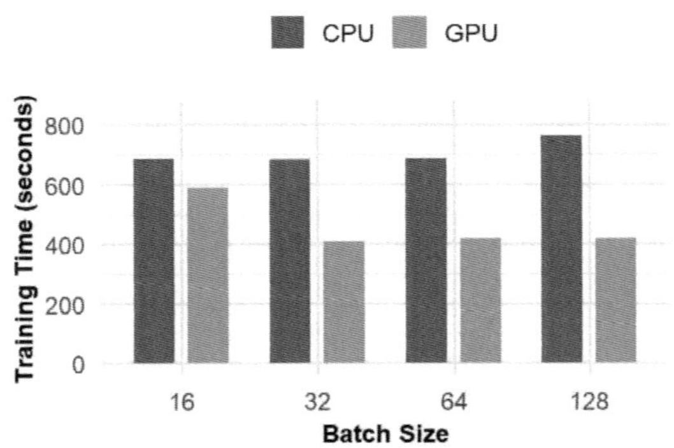

Figure 6. Training Time vs. Batch Size for CPU and GPU at Epoch 4.

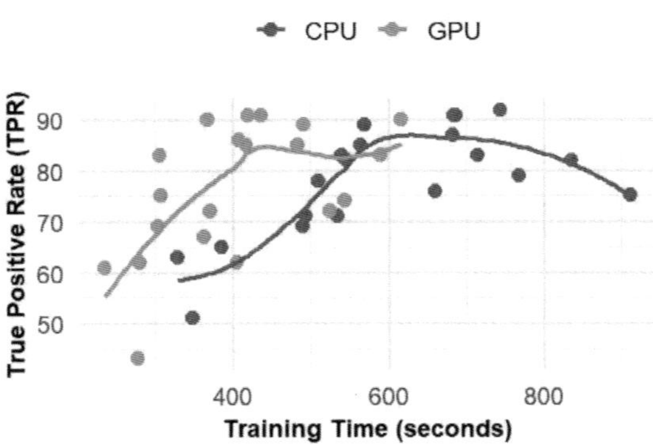

Figure 7. TPR vs. Training Time for CPU and GPU.

VI. CONCLUSION

Our investigation into the performance dynamics of GPUs and CPUs for CNN applications yielded insightful findings. Utilizing a dataset comprising 8,000 images of dogs and cats for training and an additional 1,000 for testing, we methodically analyzed the impact of various batch sizes and epochs on the system's performance. Empirical data showed GPUs consistently outperformed CPUs in training efficiency and speed, achieving higher or comparable TPRs. GPUs excelled with larger batch sizes, demonstrating superior performance for extensive CNN tasks, offering significant speed and accuracy advantages over CPUs.

Future research should include more hardware models, like NVIDIA's Tesla and RTX series, to better understand CPU and GPU performance differences. This will help select optimal hardware for CNN tasks and enhance our findings with cost and performance analysis.

ACKNOWLEDGMENT

The work is partially supported by the National Science Foundation (NSF) under NSF Awards #2019561, #2234911, #2209637, and #2100134. The opinions, findings, and recommendations in this material are those of the authors and do not necessarily reflect the views of the National Science Foundation.

REFERENCES

[1] S. Verma *et al.*, "Demystifying the MLPerf Training Benchmark Suite," in *2020 IEEE International Symposium on Performance Analysis of Systems and Software (ISPASS)*, 2020, pp. 24-33.

[2] D. Strigl, K. Kofler, and S. Podlipnig, "Performance and Scalability of GPU-Based Convolutional Neural Networks," in *2010 18th Euromicro Conference on Parallel, Distributed and Network-based Processing*, 2010, pp. 317-324.

[3] E. Buber and B. Diri, "Performance Analysis and CPU vs GPU Comparison for Deep Learning," in *2018 6th International Conference on Control Engineering & Information Technology (CEIT)*, 2018, pp. 1-6.

[4] E. Cengil, A. Çinar, and Z. Güler, "A GPU-based convolutional neural network approach for image classification," in *2017 International Artificial Intelligence and Data Processing Symposium (IDAP)*, 2017, pp. 1-6.

[5] M. U. Yaseen, A. Anjum, O. Rana, and R. Hill, "Cloud-based scalable object detection and classification in video streams," *Future Generation Computer Systems,* vol. 80, pp. 286-298, 2018/03/01/ 2018.

[6] A. A. Süzen, B. Duman, and B. Şen, "Benchmark Analysis of Jetson TX2, Jetson Nano and Raspberry PI using Deep-CNN," in *2020 International Congress on Human-Computer Interaction, Optimization and Robotic Applications (HORA)*, 2020, pp. 1-5.

[7] S. Oh, M. Kim, D. Kim, M. Jeong, and M. Lee, "Investigation on performance and energy efficiency of CNN-based object detection on embedded device," in *2017 4th International Conference on Computer Applications and Information Processing Technology (CAIPT)*, 2017, pp. 1-4.

[8] M. Blott *et al.*, "Evaluation of Optimized CNNs on FPGA and non-FPGA based Accelerators using a Novel Benchmarking Approach," *Proceedings of the 2020 ACM/SIGDA International Symposium on Field-Programmable Gate Arrays,* pp. 317-317, 2020.

[9] A. Saha, M. Rahman, and F. Wu, "Evaluating LSTM Time Series Prediction Performance on Benchmark CPUs and GPUs in Cloud Environments," 2024, pp. 321-322.

[10] H. Bouzidi, H. Ouarnoughi, S. Niar, and A. A. E. Cadi, "Performance Modeling of Computer Vision-based CNN on Edge GPUs," *ACM Transactions on Embedded Computing Systems,* vol. 21, no. 5, pp. 1-33, 2022.

[11] V. H. Phung and E. J. Rhee, "A deep learning approach for classification of cloud image patches on small datasets," *Journal of information and communication convergence engineering,* vol. 16, no. 3, pp. 173-178, 2018.

[12] *Google Colaboratory (2024). https://colab.research.google.com. Last Accessed 10 Mar 2024.*

[13] *Keras (2024). https://keras.io. Last Accessed 10 Mar 2024.*

[14] V. Sharma, G. K. Gupta, and M. Gupta, "Performance Benchmarking of GPU and TPU on Google Colaboratory for Convolutional Neural Network," in *Applications of Artificial Intelligence in Engineering*, Singapore, 2021, pp. 639-646: Springer Singapore.

K-Area: An Efficient Approach to Approximate the Spatial Boundaries of Mobility Data with k-Anonymity

Maël Gassmann
Bern University of Applied Sciences
Biel/Bienne, Switzerland
email: mael.gassmann@bfh.ch

Annett Laube
Bern University of Applied Sciences
Biel/Bienne, Switzerland
email: annett.laube@bfh.ch

Dominic Baumann
Bern University of Applied Sciences
Biel/Bienne, Switzerland
email: dominic.baumann@bfh.ch

***Abstract*—Mobility datasets, being by nature potent in utility and complexity, are hard to work with when privacy has to be preserved. Existing solutions to balance utility and privacy are very specific to certain use case or dataset types, and usually strive to provide an absolute privacy while disregarding computational efficiency. K-area is an efficient method that uses geometric operations to calculate the boundaries of movement profiles that guarantee a certain degree of anonymity and exclude areas where privacy is at risk. It is applicable to most types of mobility datasets, as it only requires a set of Global Positioning System (GPS) points tagged to an identifier. K-area provides the largest areas of the dataset, which all validate a geometric k-anonymity condition. By already providing a level of indistinguishability, these areas are the perfect starting point for many applications.**

Keywords-Mobility Data; Privacy; Indistinguishability

I. INTRODUCTION

Mobility data is very complex and can reveal sensitive information about its Data Collectors (DC). Anonymization is therefore a must, and many different methods were developed. Most of them are quite expensive and need to be customized to the intended application [1]. However, a fast and flexible mechanism is often needed to assess the anonymity of a dataset and exclude the parts where anonymity cannot be guaranteed.

Once the k-areas are calculated, they can be applied on the raw dataset to only consider data points inside their bounds.

Many use cases are envisioned, this is just a small list:

- Set a k-anonymity condition and run the algorithm periodically while collecting data.
- Generate heat-maps to visualize the readiness of a dataset and where data could be lacking.
- To be used as a pre-processing step before running computational expensive algorithms.

A mobility dataset is finite, hence, it always has clear spatio-temporal bounds; the first and last records define the temporal bounds, while the minimal spacial bounds is represented by a shape, which contains all the GPS points.

The k-area algorithm understands this and, by being aware to whom each point belongs, will strive to – roughly, but effectively – further reduce the size of the spacial bounds by cutting out distinguishable data points.

Depending on how the shape of the area is generated (e.g., a convex area), all distinguishable GPS points might not find themselves outside the bounding shape. But even if the k-area algorithm might not necessarily remove all distinguishable points, due to the nature of the shape, most outliers will be at the edge of its bounds. Thus, ensuring that the biggest portion of outlying points is cut out, and therefore greatly improve the computation efficiency of hypothetical further analyses.

The paper is structured as follows: Section II describes pertinent related works; Section III defines the concept of k-areas; finally, the work is concluded in Section IV.

II. STATE OF THE ART

There are already privacy enhancing methods that all have various effects, and all focus on anonymizing a specific aspect of data through different means [2]. Such privacy enhancing methods are described below.

a) Mitigation: Such methods are trying to mitigate the privacy risks with heuristics without theoretical or provable guarantees. Examples are swapping, obfuscation, spacial cloaking or segmentation.

b) Indistinguishability: Here, anonymity is measured in terms of how distinguishable is every DC inside the dataset. From the metric, one can reduce the risk of breaching the privacy of DCs by filtering out singularities [3]. The k-area is part of this set of methods.

c) Uninformativeness: Predominantly measured through differential privacy, uninformativeness is providing privacy warranties by assessing how much information each individual data buyer posses.

III. CONCEPT

If a convex hull can represent the spacial bound of an entire dataset, it can also represent subsets of it. The heart of the concept of k-area is to calculate the spacial bounds of the GPS points of each data collector, and from their superposition, to extract the areas that at least k bounds intersect.

A. Mobility Dataset Definition

A mobility dataset can be structured in many different ways. One common point between all such structures is that they will contain GPS points, and each will be tagged to a data collector identifier. Only finite datasets are considered.

a) Data Collector: A data collector u has a subset of GPS points of the dataset that are all tagged with the same DC identifier.

b) GPS Point: A GPS point can have many attributes. The only ones pertinent to the algorithm are its latitude, longitude and DC identifier.

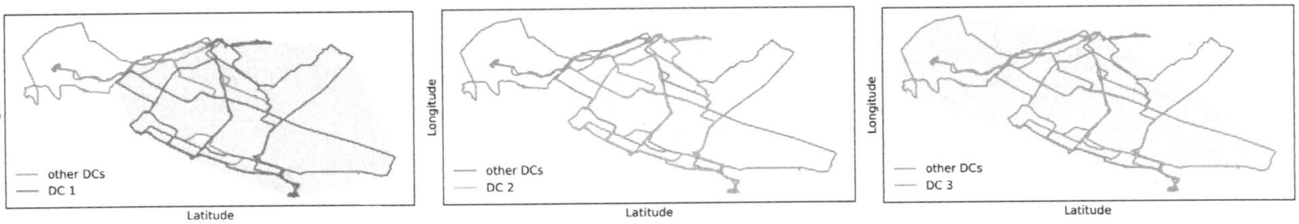

Figure 1. GPS traces of multiple DCs with their convex bounding polygons.

B. Polygon

The root of the concept is that the recorded GPS points of a DC u can be enclosed in a minimal polygon p_u. A minimal polygon can be, for instance, the smallest convex shape that contains all the DC GPS points (see examples for 3 DCs in Figure 1). It is not believed that there is an optimal minimal polygon type that fits perfectly each DC subset, a concave polygon or other types of shape might fit more complex cases, potentially at the cost of a less efficient algorithm. Further researches will focus on this subject. The inside of the intersection between two minimal polygons is following a k-anonymity of 2. To calculate the areas that follow a k-anonymity of 3, a third minimal polygon has to be intersected with the other two. Thus, if the algorithm was requested to yield the largest valid surfaces for these three DCs with a k-anonymity condition of 3, it will return their intersecting polygons.

C. K-Area

A k-area A_k is computed geometrically from all polygons p_u of P present in the data set (see illustrations in Figure 2). A k-area A_k is the union of the intersections between k polygons:

$$A_k = \bigcup (p_{i1} \cap p_{i2} \cap \cdots \cap p_{ik})$$
$$\text{for all } p_{i1}, p_{i2}, \ldots, p_{ik} \in P$$
$$\text{with } i_1 \neq i_2 \neq \ldots \neq i_k \text{ and } k \geq 2$$

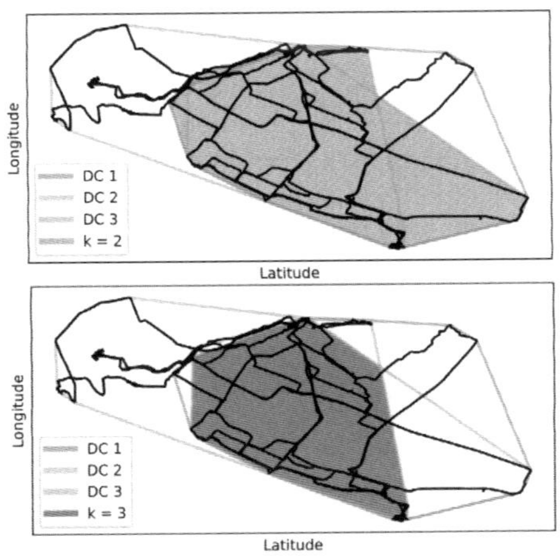

Figure 2. Three bounding polygons and the k2 and k3 areas.

D. Algorithm

To obtain an algorithm with polynomial runtime, polygon sets are used.

function K-AREA(P, k)
  $A \leftarrow$ array of size k with each entry as an empty set of polygons
  for all $p_u \in P$ **do**
    for $i \leftarrow k$ to 1 **do**
      if $i > 1$ **then**
        $A[i] \leftarrow A[i] \cup (p_u \cap A[i-1])$
      else
        $A[i] \leftarrow A[i] \cup p_u$ ▷ $i = 1$
      end if
    end for
  end for
  return A
end function

The function was successfully implemented in PostgreSQL with PostGIS extension using spacial data types.

IV. Conclusion

K-areas allow an approximation of the spatial boundaries of mobility data with a certain degree of indistinguishability. Based on geometric operations with polynomial order that can be implemented efficiently, the algorithm can significantly reduce the bounds of a dataset while ensuring relative k-anonymity. Further researches will focus on improving the results by using different types of shapes generated from GPS points while keeping the time complexity as low as possible.

V. Acknowledgment

K-area was developed in the innovation project "101.272 IP-SBM: Posmo Ethical Data Market" supported by Innosuisse.

References

[1] A. Kapp and H. Mihaljevic, "Reconsidering utility: unveiling the limitations of synthetic mobility data generation algorithms in real-life scenarios," in *Proceedings of the 31st ACM International Conference on Advances in Geographic Information Systems*, ser. SIGSPATIAL '23. New York, NY, USA: Association for Computing Machinery, 2023, pp. 1—12, [retrieved: 05, 2024]. [Online]. Available: https://doi.org/10.1145/3589132.3625661

[2] M. Fiore *et al.*, "Privacy of trajectory micro-data : a survey," *CoRR*, vol. abs/1903.12211, 2019, [retrieved: 05, 2024]. [Online]. Available: http://arxiv.org/abs/1903.12211

[3] L. Sweeney, "k-anonymity: a model for protecting privacy," *Int. J. Uncertain. Fuzziness Knowl.-Based Syst.*, vol. 10, no. 5, pp. 557—570, oct 2002, [retrieved: 05, 2024]. [Online]. Available: https://doi.org/10.1142/S0218488502001648